Machiavelli's Politics

Catherine H. Zuckert

THE UNIVERSITY OF CHICAGO PRESS
CHICAGO AND LONDON

The University of Chicago Press, Chicago 60637
The University of Chicago Press, Ltd., London

For more information, contact the University of Chicago Press, 1427 E. 60th St., Chicago, IL 60637.
Published 2017
Printed in the United States of America

26 25 24 23 22 21 20 19 18 17 1 2 3 4 5

ISBN-13: 978-0-226-43480-3 (cloth)
ISBN-13: 978-0-226-43494-0 (e-book)
DOI: 10.7208/chicago/9780226434940.001.0001

Library of Congress Cataloging-in-Publication Data
Names: Zuckert, Catherine H., 1942– author.
Title: Machiavelli's politics / Catherine H. Zuckert.
Description: Chicago ; London :
The University of Chicago Press, 2017.
Identifiers: LCCN 2016033961 |
ISBN 9780226434803 (cloth : alk. paper) |
ISBN 9780226434940 (e-book)
Subjects: LCSH: Machiavelli, Niccolò, 1469–1527—
Criticism and interpretation. | Political science.
Classification: LCC JC143.M4 Z935 2016 | DDC 320.1—dc23 LC
record available at https://lccn.loc.gov/2016033961

♾ This paper meets the requirements of
ANSI/NISO Z39.48-1992 (Permanence of Paper).

Contents

Acknowledgments

I would like to thank the University of Notre Dame for supporting my research on this book and the Institute for Scholarship in the College of Arts and Letters for supporting its publication. I am also grateful to the National Endowment for the Humanities, the Earhart Foundation, and the Social Philosophy and Policy Center for granting me fellowships that enabled me to work full-time on this project.

Parts of this book were published earlier as journal articles or a book chapter, and are reprinted here with permission of the publishers. Parts of chapter 1 appeared in "Machiavelli and the End of Nobility," *Social Research* 81, no. 1 (2014): 85–106, and "Machiavelli's Revolution in Thought," *Machiavelli's Legacy*, ed. Timothy Fuller (Philadelphia: University of Pennsylvania Press, 2016), 54–69. An earlier and much shorter version of chapter 2 was published as "Machiavelli's Democratic Republic," *History of Political Thought* 35, no. 2 (2014): 262–94. Chapter 6 contains a slightly revised version of "*The Life of Castruccio Castracani:* Machiavelli as Literary Artist, Historian, Teacher and Philosopher," *History of Political Thought* 31, no. 4 (Winter 2010): 577–603.

I would also like to thank the many students who helped me think about Machiavelli's politics in four graduate seminars. Their questions provoked me to delve ever deeper into his texts. I am also grateful to my friends Vickie B. Sullivan, who read an early version of part of the argument of chapter 1, and David Schaefer, who read a great deal of the manuscript, for their thoughtful responses. The two anonymous readers for the University of Chicago Press also raised some important questions and suggested ways in which the manuscript could be improved, as did the copyeditor,

Susan Tarcov. John Tryneski and Rodney Powell also provided crucial assistance in the long road from submission to publication.

Finally, I wish to recognize the assistance, both supportive and critical, of my husband, Michael. He was not easily persuaded that my reading of Machiavelli was correct, but from the beginning he encouraged me to develop and refine it.

Abbreviations

AW	*Art of War* (*Dell'arte della guerra*)
CC	*The Life of Castruccio Castracani* (*La vita di Castruccio Castracani*)
D	*Discourses on Livy* (*Discorsi sopra la prima Deca di Tito Livio*)
FH	*Florentine Histories* (*Istorie fiorentine*)
P	*The Prince* (*Il Principe*)
TM	Leo Strauss, *Thoughts on Machiavelli*

I have cited *The Prince* by chapter, the *Discourses* and *Florentine Histories* by book and chapter, the *Art of War* by book, and the comedies by act and scene, because these are standard in the many editions and translations of Machiavelli's works. I have used the Italian edition of *Tutte le Opere di Machiavelli*, ed. Guido Mazzoni and Mario Casella (Florence: G. Barbèra, 1929), except for *La vita di Castruccio Castracani*, for which I used the critical edition by Riekie Brakkee (Naples: Pubblicato da Liguori, 1984); citations are to pages in this edition. I have quoted the following English translations: *The Prince*, trans. Harvey C. Mansfield, 2nd ed. (Chicago: University of Chicago Press, 1998); *Discourses on Livy*, trans. Harvey C. Mansfield and Nathan Tarcov (Chicago: University of Chicago Press, 1996); *Mandragola*, trans. Mera J. Flaumenhaft (Prospect Heights, IL: Waveland Press, 1981); *Art of War*, trans. Christopher Lynch (Chicago: University of Chicago Press, 2003); *Clizia*, trans. Daniel T. Gallagher (Prospect Heights, IL: Waveland Press, 1996); *Florentine Histories*, trans. Laura E. Banfield and Harvey C. Mansfield Jr. (Princeton: Princeton University Press, 1988). Translations from the *Life of Castruccio Castracani* are my own.

INTRODUCTION
Reading Machiavelli

Machiavelli is popularly known—for obvious reasons—as a proponent of "Machiavellian politics." Certain aspects of his work support his dubious reputation and the implied opprobrium. He is often listed along with Thucydides and Hobbes as a classical "realist," who presents a "realistic" view of politics, because he takes such a dim view of human nature. Neither Thucydides nor Hobbes openly and explicitly advises a prince that he must murder the bloodline of the ruler he supplants if he wishes to maintain his conquest, however. Nor do they advocate "cruelty well-used." Especially in his *Prince*, Machiavelli appears to advocate the necessity of using force and fraud in politics with much more glee than the other "realists."

Serious students of Machiavelli's writings have nevertheless come to hold very different views of his works. The sixteenth-century English playwright Christopher Marlowe is usually included among those who popularized the view of Machiavelli as a "teacher of evil." Yet by beginning *The Jew of Malta* with a prologue delivered by a character named Machevill who declares that he "count[s] religion but a childish toy, and hold[s] there is no sin but ignorance," Marlowe also suggests that Machiavelli was a Socratic philosopher. Seventeenth-century political theorists such as Baruch Spinoza, James Harrington, and Algernon Sidney insisted that Machiavelli was a republican political thinker.[1] In the eighteenth century, Montesquieu famously declared

1. On the "reception" of Machiavelli, see Victoria Kahn, *Machiavellian Rhetoric* (Princeton: Princeton University Press, 1994), and Otfried Höffe, "Zur Machiavellis Wirkung," in *Niccolò Machiavelli "Der Fürst,"* ed. Höffe (Berlin: Akademie Verlag, 2012), 179–99.

that "one has begun to be cured of Machiavellianism," but he and Rousseau incorporated many features of Machiavelli's republic in their own proposals.[2] In the early nineteenth century Fichte and Hegel declared that Machiavelli's ideas about unifying Italy should serve as a model for Germany; and Marxist commentators such as Louis Althusser and Antonio Gramsci have continued to see him as the herald of a new form of popular nationalism.[3] In the early twentieth century Friedrich Meinecke argued that Machiavelli was an advocate of "reason of state" or "power politics"; and Benedetto Croce praised him for having declared the autonomy of politics from morality.[4] Michael Oakeshott went further by declaring Machiavelli's *Prince* to be a technical handbook exemplifying the evils of "rationalism in politics"; and Jacques Maritain expressed the hope that the end of World War II would mark "the end of Machiavellianism."[5] But in contrast to the enduring popular view of Machiavelli as a "Machiavellian" teacher of tyrants, most scholars in the late twentieth and now twenty-first centuries have understood Machiavelli to be a more benign republican, if not a kind of democrat.[6]

2. Montesquieu, *The Spirit of the Laws*, trans. Anne M. Cohler, Basia Carolyn Miller, and Harold Samuel Stone (Cambridge: Cambridge University Press, 1989), 4.21; 389.

3. J. G. Fichte, *Über Machiavelli als Schriftsteller und Stellen aus seinen Schriften*, in *Werke*, vol. 11, ed. I. H. Fichte (Berlin: Walter de Gruyter, 1971); G. W. F. Hegel, "The German Constitution," in *Hegel's Political Writings*, trans. T. M. Knox (Oxford: Clarendon Press, 1964), 143–242; Louis Althusser, *Machiavelli and Us*, trans. Gregory Elliot (London: Verso, 1999); Antonio Gramsci, "The Modern Prince," *Selections from the Prison Notebooks*, ed. and trans. Quintin Hoare and Geoffrey Nowell Smith (London: Lawrence & Wishart, 1971), pt. 2, chap. 1, 125–43.

4. Friedrich Meinecke, *Machiavellianism: The Doctrine of Raison d'etat and Its Place in Modern History*, trans. Douglas Scott (New York: Praeger, 1957); Benedetto Croce, *Elementi di politica* (Bari: Laterza, 1925), 60.

5. Michael Oakeshott, "Rationalism in Politics," *Rationalism and Politics* (Indianapolis: Liberty Fund, 1991), and Jacques Maritain, "The End of Machiavellianism," *Review of Politics* 4, no. 1 (1942): 1–33.

6. For representative selections of such views, see Gisela Bock, Quentin Skinner, and Maurizio Viroli, eds., *Machiavelli and Republicanism* (Cambridge: Cambridge University Press, 1990), and John M. Najemy, ed., *The Cambridge Companion to Machiavelli* (Cambridge: Cambridge University Press, 2010). Leo Strauss would not be included among such scholars by commentators who fail to read beyond the first chapter of *Thoughts on Machiavelli* (Chicago: University of Chicago Press, 1958) in which Strauss expresses some sympathy for the simple and old-fashioned view of Machiavelli as a "teacher of evil," but explicitly recognizes that it is inadequate. (E.g., Quentin Skinner, *Machiavelli: A Very Short Introduction* [Oxford: Oxford University Press, 1981], 99, and Barbara Spackman, "Machiavelli and Maxims," *Yale French Studies*, no. 77, *Reading the Archive: On Texts and Institutions* [New Haven: Yale University Press, 1990], 137.) Yet Strauss recognizes that "as a matter of principle he [Machiavelli] preferred, in his capacity as analyst of society, republics to monarchies" (*TM*, 20). Going even further, Strauss observes that "Machiavelli was the first philosopher who questioned in the name of the multitude or of democracy the aristocratic prejudice or the aristocratic premise which informed classical philosophy. He preferred the more democratic Roman polity to the less democratic Spartan polity. He expressed the opinion that the purpose of the people is more honest, or more just, than the purpose of the great" (127). Strauss points out, moreover, that "Machiavelli's

The plethora of scholarly interpretations of the import of Machiavelli's work suggests that each is partial, emphasizing one aspect of his work at the expense of others. In the following study I strive to present a fuller, more comprehensive view.

At present there appear to be three major approaches to reading and understanding his work. The first is contextual or historical; the second is rhetorical, literary, and ironic; the third is theoretical—scientific, philosophical, or political-theoretical. Each of these kinds of interpretation has characteristic advantages—and limitations.

Contextual or historical readings of Machiavelli begin from the undeniable fact that he presents himself in all of his major prose writings as an author who is seeking a position as a political advisor. He thus writes at a certain time and place and addresses the concerns of specific individuals. What he claims to offer his addressees, on the basis of his own practical political experience as well as his extensive reading and study of the ancient histories, is specific political advice about what they should do in their own immediate circumstances. David Wootton, for example, argues that the subject matter and advice contained in *The Prince* are, in fact, better suited to the position and circumstances of Giuliano de' Medici, to whom Machiavelli first proposed to present his book, than they are to Lorenzo, to whom he dedicated his little treatise after Giuliano died.[7] In *Between Friends*

---

emphatic attack on 'all writers' is directed, not against the traditional condemnation of tyranny but against the traditional contempt for the multitude." And this observation "may incline us to believe that [Machiavelli] was the philosopher who originated the democratic tradition" (293–94). Strauss goes on, however, to emphasize the division of labor Machiavelli suggests in *D* 1.58, where he observes that "if princes are superior to peoples in ordering laws, forming civil lives, and ordering new statutes and order, people are so much superior in maintain things ordered that . . . they attain the glory," and suggests that democratic theory proper begins with Spinoza and Rousseau. But, he concludes, "Machiavelli's book on principalities and his book on republics are both republican" (282). "By radically depreciating the pretensions to 'virtue' of the nobility, and simultaneously making the people 'honest,'" Pierre Manent, *An Intellectual History of Liberalism*, trans. Rebecca Balinski (Princeton: Princeton University Press, 1995), suggests that "Machiavelli becomes the first *democratic* thinker" (16). More recently, Miguel Vatter, *Between Form and Event: Machiavelli's Theory of Political Freedom* (Dordrecht: Kluwer, 2000), and John McCormick, *Machiavellian Democracy* (Cambridge: Cambridge University Press, 2011), have argued that Machiavelli shows the benefits of democratic political action. Vatter argues that the periodic outbursts of popular fury in riots he characterizes as "events" give rise to historical change by destroying old forms and orders, whereas McCormick emphasizes the "ferocious populism" with which Machiavelli encourages the people to resist oppression by the "*grandi*." Arguing, in effect, against McCormick's attempt to show that Machiavelli did not champion a Madison-like republican form of politics, Alissa M. Ardito, *Machiavelli and the Modern State* (New York: Cambridge University Press, 2015), contends that Machiavelli precedes James Madison as a proponent of an extended territorial republic.

7. David Wootton, introduction to Niccolò Machiavelli, *The Prince* (Indianapolis: Hackett, 1995), viii–xxiii. As Wooton indicates (xxxix n20), this argument was made earlier by Cecil H.

John Najemy contends that Machiavelli's famous analysis of the opposition between *fortuna* and *virtù* is designed primarily, if not exclusively, to counteract the belief of his good friend Francesco Vettori that human beings do not have control over their own existence.[8] Similarly, Claude Lefort maintains that Machiavelli's *Discourses on the First Ten Books of Titus Livy's History* should be read as somewhat covertly showing the young Florentines to whom it is dedicated what they should do to reform their republic.[9]

The problem with simply historical readings of Machiavelli's works is that they deprive his works of any interest except as historical documents.[10] Yet Machiavelli suggests in the dedications to his two most comprehensive works that he is conveying knowledge of broader and more enduring interest. He does not restrict his reflections merely to the needs of particular individuals or of Florence or even of Italy as a whole. On the contrary, he offers advice to the king of France and the Holy Roman Emperor of Germany as well as to his fellow countrymen; and he uses examples from Asia, both ancient and modern, to support his arguments. Moreover, in emphasizing the development of new and larger monarchies in France and Spain, he points toward the emergence of a new international order in Europe.[11]

Because they emphasize the character of the audience Machiavelli was presumably trying to reach and persuade, contextual readings tend to become rhetorical readings as well. However, those rhetorical readings that emphasize the continuity between Machiavelli and his predecessors fly in

---

Clough (in "Machiavelli's Political Assumptions and Objectives," *Bulletin of the John Rylands Library* 53, no. 1 [1970]: 43–57). But in contrast to Wootton, Clough concludes that "quite apart from its composition for an *ad hoc* problem, Machiavelli wanted his *Prince* to be considered as a blueprint for any new prince with a new princedom, and as such it remains a part of his scheme of social science" (74).

8. John M. Najemy, *Between Friends* (Princeton: Princeton University Press, 1993).

9. Claude Lefort, *Le travail de l'oeuvre Machiavel* (Paris: Gallimard, 1972), 467–690 (*Machiavelli in the Making*, trans. Michael B. Smith [Evanston, IL: Northwestern University Press, 2012], 220–426).

10. Skinner thus modified his reading of Machiavelli greatly when he began to argue that Machiavelli represented a "third way," an understanding of liberty as "non-domination," that not only lay between Isaiah Berlin's two concepts of freedom as either negative or positive, but was also tenable in our time. Quentin Skinner, "The Republican Ideal of Political Liberty," in Bock, Skinner, and Viroli, eds., *Machiavelli and Republicanism*, 293–309. On the changes in Skinner's thought, see Paul Rahe, "Situating Machiavelli," in *Renaissance Civic Humanism*, ed. James Hankins (Cambridge: Cambridge University Press, 2000), 270–308.

11. Ardito, *Machiavelli and the Modern State*, 172–82, argues not only that Machiavelli saw that the Italian city-states could no longer be defended from invasions by the armies of the national monarchies emerging in France and Spain and sought to show his contemporaries how a republic could be instituted and maintained over an extended territory. She also shows that Machiavelli predicted the development of entities like the modern nation-state before the fact along the lines Charles Tilly and other historians have shown that such states actually did emerge, after the fact, on the basis of their military power.

the face of his own clear declarations in *P* 15 and *D* 1.58 that he has departed from the writings of all previous authors. By presenting Machiavelli as writing in a "civic humanist" or even "classical" tradition, commentators such as Quentin Skinner and Erica Benner diminish, if they do not simply deny, the explicitly innovative character of his work.[12] But commentators such as Claude Lefort and Maurizio Viroli, who argue that Machiavelli was actually trying to rouse his contemporaries to take revolutionary political action, face another difficulty.[13] There is evidence in Machiavelli's texts that he does not think that his immediate addressees will understand his arguments or be able actually to undertake the glorious enterprises he puts before them. At the beginning of *P* 6, for example, Machiavelli indicates that the most he expects from Lorenzo is to be able to imitate great men of the past; he does not expect him to be able to become the founder of a new republic or principality. And in the *Art of War* Machiavelli shows that the young Florentines to whom he dedicated his *Discourses on Livy* do not know the only art he says a prince should study and practice (*P* 14). It becomes difficult, therefore, to understand why he says that his two young friends deserve to be princes—except that they would honor and employ him, if they could. They do not know nor are they apt to learn what they would need to know in order to become effective rulers (or to stage a successful revolution in Florence).[14]

12. Strangely enough, Quentin Skinner, *Machiavelli* (New York: Hill and Wang, 1981), and Erica Benner, *The Prince: A New Reading* (New York: Oxford University Press, 2013), both recognize the dramatic change Machiavelli made in the meaning of virtue, especially in *The Prince*, when he argued that virtue was and should be conceived as what led to political success rather than as a set of characteristics that were, as both Aristotle and Cicero had maintained, good in themselves. Skinner nevertheless emphasizes the continuity between Machiavelli's writings and those of the "classical humanists," and Erica Benner, *Machiavelli's Ethics* (Princeton: Princeton University Press, 2009), goes so far as to argue that Machiavelli not merely drew on ancient political philosophers but was an ethical Socratic.

13. Maurizio Viroli, *Redeeming "The Prince"* (Princeton: Princeton University Press, 2014), contends that in concluding *The Prince* with a passionate call for the liberation and unification of Italy, Machiavelli purposefully downplayed the difficulties (which, according to Strauss, *TM*, 61–84, showed that the proposal was not really serious) because Machiavelli wanted to convince his readers to undertake such a project.

14. Explicitly "deconstructive" readings such as those of Steven M. Fallon, "Hunting the Fox: Equivocation and Authorial Duplicity in *The Prince*," *PMLA* (*Publications of the Modern Language Association*) 107 (1992): 1181–95, and Thomas Greene, "The End of Discourse in Machiavelli's *Prince*," in *Literary Theory/Renaissance Texts*, ed. Patricia Parker and David Quint (Baltimore: Johns Hopkins University Press, 1986), 63–44, go even further. If, as they argue, Machiavelli's text undermines itself, it has no "teaching" or lessons that political actors could use or follow. Such readings contradict Machiavelli's explicit statements concerning his desire to convey something of use that would have an effect.

If Machiavelli did not think that his immediate addressees would understand what he had written, then why did he write? And for whom?

In the preface to the second book of his *Discourses* Machiavelli complains that the "malignity of fortune" forces him to hope that young people in the future will take the path he has indicated to its completion. He did not publish the *Discourses* during his lifetime, but he explicitly addresses future readers.

As Leo Strauss contends, Machiavelli sought to attract young readers in particular by means of his exaggerations and understatements.[15] He is a notoriously playful, ironic author, who not only seeks to shock the sensibilities of his readers by arguing, for example, that "cruelty" can be "well-used."[16] He also tries to entertain them, especially in his comedies. Yet he claims that those comedies have a "useful lesson" lying underneath.[17]

Machiavelli had good reason not to present his most revolutionary thoughts too openly. He had been one of the few officials of the Florentine republic the Medici dismissed when they regained control, because they did not trust him. After they found his name on a list of conspirators, they imprisoned and tortured him. The irony with which Machiavelli describes his own lowly station compared with that of the dedicatees of *The Prince* and *Discourses* is particularly heavy. As he states in the prologue to *Mandragola*, a comedy in which everything said can be dismissed as a joke, "the author . . . doesn't stand in awe of anyone, even though he might play the servant to one who can wear a better coat than he can" (11). He himself was not wealthy or from an aristocratic background, but he had to appeal to those who were in order to convince them of the soundness of his advice and to act on it. He understood that the advisor who counsels a prince well will never receive full credit for the wisdom of his advice.[18] He was thus prepared to let those who understand the implications of the "path" he laid out in his *Discourses* receive the glory associated with founding a new republic. He also counseled a prince who wanted to found a new regime to which everyone would consent that he should follow the example of Lucius Junius Brutus and use old names in describing offices

15. *TM*, 127.

16. Friedrich Nietzsche, *Beyond Good and Evil*, aph. 28. On Machiavelli's "irony," see also Kahn, *Machiavellian Rhetoric*, 39–44; Fallon, "Hunting the Fox"; Greene, "End of Discourse in Machiavelli's *Prince*"; Benner, *Prince*.

17. *A Dialogue on Language*, in *The Literary Works of Machiavelli*, trans. J. R. Hale (London: Oxford University Press, 1961), 188.

18. As he states explicitly in *D* 3.35.

with new powers (*D* 1.25). He himself thus used traditional terms such as 'virtue,' 'prudence,' 'mercy,' even 'justice,' giving them new meaning while playing on the old.[19] And in his *Discourses* he advocated a new, more democratic form of republic in the guise of an imitation of ancient Rome.

If Machiavelli did not think his immediate addressees would understand him, should we not forget about those addressees and their specific historical circumstances and look for Machiavelli's general arguments about what works in politics and what does not? This thought has led to more theoretical, scientific, or philosophical readings of his works.

Few scholars today accept the description of Machiavelli as the first political scientist—as Oakeshott claimed when he identified Machiavelli's *Prince* as a manual or technical handbook of rules that could be applied by any reader with the requisite authority, or as Benedetto Croce claimed when he found Machiavelli to be an early "positivist" insofar as he distinguished facts from values.[20] (There is, however, a large popular literature applying Machiavellian rules to show how a person can succeed in business or other forms of contemporary leadership.)[21]

A better reason to support the characterization of Machiavelli as the first modern political "scientist" lies in his claim to know only worldly things. Worldly things are sensible and transient. Machiavelli claims, in effect, not to know of any transcendent, eternally unchanging, and purely intelligible forms of being such as the Platonic ideas. Indeed, he suggests that no mortal human being could know any such things. Nor does he found his political analysis on a claim to know anything divine or supernatural. Because he insists that everything in the world of men is always in motion, he sees that political actors have to deal with changing circumstances. His political analysis

19. The most notorious example of this double use is Machiavelli's statement about Agathocles in *P* 8: "One cannot call it virtue to kill one's citizens, betray one's friends, to be without faith, without mercy, without religion." Yet "if one considers the virtue of Agathocles . . . one does not see why he has to be judged inferior to any most excellent captain" (35).

20. August Buck, *Erträge der Forschung* (Darmstadt: Wissenschaftliche Buchgesellschaft, 1985), is an exception. He concludes that Machiavelli was the first political scientist and explicitly concludes, following Croce, that Machiavelli established the autonomy of politics.

21. For example, A. Jay, *Management and Machiavelli* (London, 1967); R. Buskirk, *Modern Management and Machiavelli* (Boston: Cahners, 1974); Stuart Crainer, "Pioneers and Prophets—Nicolo [*sic*] Machiavelli," *Financial Times* (London, December 19, 1994); A. McAlpine, *The New Machiavelli: The Art of Politics in Business* (Hoboken, NJ: Wiley, 1997); Michael Ledeen, *Machiavelli and Modern Leadership* (New York: Truman Talley Books, 2002); Nicholas Antongiavanni, *The Suit: A Machiavellian Approach to Men's Style* (New York: Harper Collins, 2006); Virginia Heffernan, "Advice Squad," *New York Times*, July 20, 2008, http://www.nytimes.com/2008/07/20/books/review/Heffernan-t.html?pagewanted=all; H. Rubin, *Machiavelli für Frauen* (Frankfurt am Main: Fischer, 2008); Karen McCreadie, Tim Phillips, and Steve Shipside, *Strategy Power Plays* (Oxford: Infinite Ideas, 2009).

does not, therefore, culminate in the formulation of "laws" or "rules" of human behavior. When he does specify such "rules," he also points out that their application must vary as conditions change and that one "rule" may conflict with another (*P* 3). In *P* 21 he thus declares: "Nor should any state ever believe that it can always adopt safe courses; on the contrary, it should think that it has to take them all as doubtful. For in the order of things it is found that one never seeks to avoid one inconvenience without running into another; but prudence consists in knowing how to recognize the qualities of inconveniences, and in picking the less bad as good" (91). Machiavelli's writings do not culminate or consist, therefore, in a set of rules or "laws" that can be applied by anyone everywhere at all times.

Machiavelli does look for repetitions or regularities in the motions of things. At the beginning of his *Discourses* he thus observes that the heaven, sun, elements, and men have not "varied in their motion, order and power from what they were in antiquity" (*D* 1.Pref.; 6). The motions with which Machiavelli is chiefly concerned, however, are the passions that move men. Because all human beings naturally desire more than they can acquire or achieve, he observes, they always live in competition and conflict with one another. Their relations are, therefore, always contingent and changing. They form cities to protect themselves from the aggression of others; but once they form political associations, they not only try to seize the goods of others. Their cities also divide internally between the *grandi*, who seek to command and oppress the people, and the *populi*, who do not want to be commanded and oppressed. According to Machiavelli, there are three possible outcomes of this conflict: principality, license, or liberty. Because he clearly prefers liberty, his analysis is not "value-free" political science.

Nor is Machiavelli primarily a historian, recording and analyzing what happened in the past. Although Machiavelli maintains that everything in the world is continually coming into being and perishing, he also explicitly declares that he is innovating (*P* 15 and *D* 1.58). Miguel Vatter suggests that Machiavelli's ability to innovate arises from his turn away from ancient philosophy with its search for eternal truths or forms to history, which is always changing if it is not simply progressive.[22] In both *The Prince* and *Discourses*

22. Vatter, *Between Form and Event*, 1–26. Although I agree with Vatter that Machiavelli, in effect, denies that there is a natural or divinely mandated hierarchy of goods or goals, that he does not think that political order is natural, but that it has to be intentionally constructed, and that he does not accept a cyclical view of history, I think that Vatter goes too far when he denies that Machiavelli has an "essentialist" (i.e., enduring) understanding of human nature and suggests that Machiavelli thinks that human beings are free to construct whatever institutions they desire.

Machiavelli does insist on using historical examples to show that what he is recommending is possible, because what has been done by human beings before should be possible for human beings to do again, if the conditions or circumstances are right. His use of historical examples thus appears to be primarily rhetorical or persuasive. He does generalize, as shown in many of the chapter titles of the *Discourses*, but as noted above, he also regularly points out exceptions to the rule. Because he uses historical examples to illustrate his points rather than to demonstrate that any particular proposition applies to all places or circumstances in all times, he does not always describe the historical incidents or individuals to which he refers with complete precision or accuracy. In *P* 2, for example, he conflates two dukes of Ferrara (because they, after all, held the same title and office). Likewise, in the *Discourses* his descriptions of Roman institutions are not altogether precise, because he does not always distinguish the ways in which they operated in the early republic from the late. The innovations Machiavelli claims to make do not appear, therefore, to come simply or even primarily from his turn away from philosophy to history.

Machiavelli could be called a political scientist, Strauss suggests, because he sought and claimed to have discovered knowledge (the literal meaning of 'science') of politics. But Strauss argues, in opposition to almost all other commentators who regard Machiavelli primarily as a political thinker, that his work is more accurately described as philosophy. Indeed, Strauss argues, Machiavelli was the first philosopher who not merely challenged but sought to destroy the Christian-Platonic tradition that maintained that the contemplative life was the highest and best form of human existence. And as such, Machiavelli was the founder of modernity.[23]

Strauss is famous for maintaining that we need to try to understand a past thinker as he understood himself. But Machiavelli could not possibly have understood himself to be the founder of modernity; that insight is possible only in hindsight.[24] Francis Bacon famously acknowledged his debt to Machiavelli for describing what men do rather than what they ought to do, and criticizing the imaginary commonwealths proposed by previous

23. Harvey Mansfield, "Machiavelli's Enterprise," *New Criterion* (October 2013): 3–11, presents a clear and concise account of this argument. Denis Collin, *Comprendre Machiavel* (Paris: Armand Colin, 2008), observes that Machiavelli did not pretend to be a philosopher, but a man of action. However, Colin contends, in practice Machiavelli is the first philosopher of the modern epoch, as important as badly understood and decried.

24. As Manent, *Intellectual History of Liberalism*, observes, "Only a complete account of the development of modern thought and politics after Machiavelli could justify crediting him with a founding role" (12).

philosophers; but Machiavelli did not have a modern scientific understanding of nature.[25] As Steven Smith has observed, Strauss indicates the character of his analysis by entitling his book "Thoughts on Machiavelli" rather than, say, "Machiavelli's Political Thought." There is, moreover, a suggestive parallel between his *Thoughts on Machiavelli* and Machiavelli's *Discourses on Livy*.[26] In his *Discourses*, Strauss argues, Machiavelli does not explicate Livy's thought or write a commentary on it. He uses Livy's text as a means of offering an indirect critique of biblical religion and Livy as a character who delivers speeches or arguments that Machiavelli does not make in his own name. Did Strauss use Machiavelli as a character to deliver his own critique of biblical morality?[27] Thoughts are more secret than discourses.

In his *Discourses on Livy*, Machiavelli claims to have discovered "new modes and orders." But, Strauss argues, those new modes and orders are not political, as they would appear to be on the surface, so much as philosophical. In his account of "Machiavelli's teaching" Strauss thus highlights Machiavelli's critique of religion and his critique of morality. The first is not original, according to Strauss; Machiavelli's arguments for the political utility of religion are essentially the same as those offered by the *falasifa* or "Averroists." But, Strauss reminds his readers, the founder of the "Averroist" tradition was Alfarabi, and according to Strauss, Alfarabi was a kind of Platonist.[28] Like Plato and Xenophon's Socrates, Strauss points out, Machiavelli emphasized the importance of studying the human things. Unlike Plato and Xenophon, however, Machiavelli linked his understanding of human beings and their needs to an "Epicurean" understanding of the world in terms of matter in motion. But unlike Epicurus, Machiavelli tried to find and construct the best form of human society.[29]

25. Francis Bacon, *The Advancement of Learning* (Auckland, NZ: Floating Press, 2010 [1605]), 2.21.9. See Waller R. Newell, *Tyranny: A New Interpretation* (Cambridge: Cambridge University Press, 2013), 458n9, for the difference between Machiavelli and Bacon.

26. Steven B. Smith, "Leo Strauss: The Outlines of a Life," *Cambridge Companion to Leo Strauss* (New York: Cambridge University Press, 2009), 37.

27. In "Die Erneuerung der Philosophie und die Herausforderung der Offenbarungsreligion zur Intention von Leo Strauss' *Thoughts on Machiavelli*," in *Politische Philosophie und die Herausforderung der Offenbarungsreligion* (Munich: C. H. Beck, 2013), 39–148, Heinrich Meier presents a detailed argument to show that this is exactly what Strauss did, employing all the devices of the "art of writing" which he argues that Machiavelli used.

28. Leo Strauss, *Persecution and the Art of Writing* (Chicago: University of Chicago Press, 1952), 10–18. To say that Machiavelli was an "Averroist" or follower of Alfarabi is to maintain that he argued that religion was necessary to support political order and morality and that philosophers should, therefore, hide their lack of faith.

29. Leo Strauss, "Machiavelli and Classical Literature," *Review of National Literature*, no. 1 (1970): 10. Unlike "Averroist" philosophers, Machiavelli did not think that there was an eternal intelligible

A reader might have expected Strauss to present Machiavelli's critique of morality like his critique of religion in terms of its potential political utility. In teaching a prince to be able not to be good and to use that knowledge according to necessity, Machiavelli claims to be conveying "the effectual truth" of things (*P* 15). Strauss maintains, however, that "Machiavelli does not bring to light a single political phenomenon of any fundamental importance which was not fully known to the classics." Machiavelli's only true innovation is to be found in his critique of morality; and that critique constitutes an unwarranted and ultimately pernicious constriction of our understanding of the possibilities of human existence.

> The classics understood the moral-political phenomena in the light of man's highest virtue or perfection, the life of the philosopher or the contemplative life. The superiority of peace to war or of leisure to business is a reflection of the superiority of thinking to doing or making. . . . Machiavelli's philosophizing on the other hand remains on the whole within the limits set by the city . . . . Accepting the ends of the *demos* as beyond appeal, he seeks for the best means conducive to those ends. (*TM*, 295–96)

Strauss understands Machiavelli to be a philosopher, because he did not accept any authority but reason and was willing to reason or inquire about all things. But with Machiavelli, Strauss argues, the meaning of philosophy began to change. Instead of an unbridgeable conflict between philosophy and the ends of the city or the desires of the vast majority of its people, Machiavelli "achieves the decisive turn toward that notion of philosophy according to which its purpose is to relieve man's estate or to increase man's power or to guide man toward the rational society, the bond and the end of which is enlightened self-interest or the comfortable self-preservation of each of its members" (*TM*, 296). Machiavelli intended to benefit human beings, Strauss acknowledges; however, the long-run effect of his writings has been to deprive people living in late modernity of an understanding of true human excellence.

Was Machiavelli a philosopher, as Strauss maintains, or a "political theorist" concerned more, if not exclusively, about the "human things"?[30]

---

order. However, because he thought that fear of god or gods was an extremely useful instrument for acquiring and maintaining popular support for political order, Machiavelli unlike Epicurus did not try to convince his readers that gods had no reason to concern themselves about human affairs and would not, therefore, reward good behavior or punish bad.

30. Among those who have denied that Machiavelli was a philosopher are Isaiah Berlin, "The Originality of Machiavelli," *Against the Current: Essays in the History of Ideas* (New York: Viking,

Commentators who call themselves "political theorists" (as opposed to "political philosophers") celebrate rather than bemoan Machiavelli's containing his thought within the limits of the city. Following Hannah Arendt, these commentators argue that the true character and understanding of politics were lost when Plato convinced his students to turn away from the "cave" and the examination of the opinions debated there to search for transcendent, eternal truths.[31] Unlike the contextual or rhetorical commentators, these scholars do not emphasize the historical or the philosophical so much as the engaged, as opposed to "objective," character of both Machiavelli's "theoretical" enterprise and their own.[32] The best known of these scholars, Sheldon Wolin, contends that in his *Prince* Machiavelli shows that a certain amount of violence is necessary in order to establish order. But that violence or "cruelty" must be "well-used," all at once and not persistently, lest it arouse opposition and hatred. Once order is established, Wolin concludes, Machiavelli shows in his *Discourses* how republican institutions can and should be established and maintained. No further violence is needed.[33]

As both Strauss and Harvey Mansfield emphasize, however, at the beginning of the third book of his *Discourses* Machiavelli clearly insists that a republic must repeatedly be brought back to its beginnings by means of a spectacular "execution" to remind both ambitious politicians and the people at large why they should fear disobeying the law. And, Mansfield argues, the need for the use of force and "princely" leadership persists in modern republics, although scholars who emphasize the continuity of the "republican tradition" from Aristotle and Cicero to the founding of the American republic do not seem to see it.

Although he generally follows Strauss in his detailed commentary on the *Discourses*, in another book, *Taming the Prince*, Mansfield, in contrast to Strauss,

---

1980), 36; Ernst Cassirer, *The Myth of the State* (New Haven: Yale University Press, 1946), 135; Felix Gilbert, *Machiavelli and Guicciardini: Politics and History in Sixteenth Century Florence* (Princeton: Princeton University Press, 1965), 193; Christian Bec, preface, *Machiavel Oeuvres* (Paris: Éditions Robert Laffont, 1996), iii; Roberto Ridolfi, *The Life of Niccolò Machiavelli*, trans. Cecil Grayson (Chicago: University of Chicago Press, 1963), 13, 107, 252.

31. Hannah Arendt, *The Human Condition* (Chicago: University of Chicago Press, 1958), 20–21; "Philosophy and Politics," *Social Research* 57, no. 1 (1990): 73–103.

32. Sheldon S. Wolin, "Political Theory as a Vocation," *American Political Science Review* 63, no. 4 (1969): 1062–82.

33. Sheldon S. Wolin, *Politics and Vision*, 2nd ed. (Princeton: Princeton University Press, 2004), 175–213.

emphasizes the importance of one of Machiavelli's political innovations: his discovery of the need for a unitary executive. Mansfield uses this discovery to show, in opposition particularly to J. G. A. Pocock, that Machiavelli was not merely trying to preserve an Aristotelian notion of deliberative or classical "republican" politics.[34] In *The Prince* Machiavelli clearly announced that he was articulating a new understanding of human *virtù* (or excellence); and in the *Discourses* he showed how such an understanding of *virtù* provided the basis of a new, "hard-nosed" form of republican politics.

In the following studies of Machiavelli's major prose works, I have tried to incorporate the advantages of all three of these major approaches while avoiding their difficulties or limitations. Like the historians, I take seriously Machiavelli's repeated indications, especially in the dedications of his works, that he is seeking a job from a specific set of people. Such a self-presentation is fully in line with the view Machiavelli frequently announces of human beings in general, that they are self-regarding or, as we would say, self-interested. In other words, Machiavelli shows himself acting according to the principles he articulates. His presentation of himself as a job seeker also means that to make a persuasive case for himself he had to demonstrate his ability to give viable practical advice. The best way to promote one's own self-interest, he repeatedly argues, is to show other people how they can best satisfy their own desires or ambitions. That means he thought that the conquest of Italy, for which he calls at the conclusion of *The Prince* and promises to the individual who learns the art explained in the *Art of War*, was both possible and desirable. Likewise, it means that in the *Discourses* Machiavelli is gradually showing the young Florentine aristocrats to whom he dedicates the work how they could realize their own ambitions to imitate if not improve upon the Romans, by establishing a new and better form of republic on the basis of knowledge, not merely by means of trial and error as had their predecessors. Finally, in his *Florentine Histories* Machiavelli praises the Medici, who commissioned him to write it, for the prudence they displayed in acquiring a virtual monopoly on political power in Florence. But he also subtly undercuts that praise by showing that the Medici were able to acquire that power partly as a result of mistakes made by their predecessors and that they were able to maintain it only because the other four powers in Italy had equally weak foreign policies. He concludes, moreover, that the

34. J. G. A. Pocock, *The Machiavellian Moment* (Princeton: Princeton University Press, 1975), 156–218.

French invasion of 1494 showed that the policies pursued by previous Florentine governments, including those of the Medici princes, could no longer successfully be continued.

Machiavelli's relation to his audience in his comedies is, of course, a bit different from his relation to the individuals he addresses most immediately in his explicitly political writings. In his comedies Machiavelli presents himself initially as a kind of "fool" who seeks to make his audience laugh, especially at him; but he also insists that comedies are intended to benefit as well as to entertain. By means of the presentation of the priest Timoteo in *Mandragola*, Machiavelli suggests that the Church might play a more positive role in the organization of human life here and now if it restricted itself to sanctifying marriage and legitimizing the progeny so generated rather than engaging in political activity directly. More generally, he shows the way in which human beings can realize their strongest desires by means of a clever arrangement, if and only if they maintain the appearance of conventional morality. And in *Clizia* he indicates the reasons why he thinks that human life should not be organized according to the objects of human love, as both Plato and Augustine argued, because those objects are often, if not always, "fantastical" and attempts to achieve them destructive.

Like some of the commentators who emphasize the rhetorical character of Machiavelli's texts, I argue not only that he addresses specific individuals or audiences but also that he provides evidence that he does not think that his particular addressees will understand or be able and willing to take his advice. In other words, his works have a distinctly ironical cast. This point has often been made about *The Prince*; it is the basis of the reading of *The Prince* as satire, famously suggested by Jean-Jacques Rousseau and reintroduced more recently by Mary Dietz.[35] The ironical character of Machiavelli's addressing the arguments contained in his *Discourses* to Cosimo Rucellai and Zanobi Buondelmonti has not been recognized by previous commentators, because they have not read the dedication in light of what Machiavelli shows about these young Florentine aristocrats in his *Art of War.* But commentators who do not read the arguments of the *Discourses* as addressed to these young men and their ambitions tend to miss the way in which Machiavelli gradually leads them from desiring merely to imitate the grandeur of Rome to wishing to found a new and better form of republic, in which all citizens would be eligible to be elected to the highest

35. Mary Dietz, "Trapping the Prince: Machiavelli and the Politics of Deception," *American Political Science Review* 80, no. 3 (1986): 777–99.

offices and individuals suspected of trying to overthrow the republic would be subject to trials in front of large popular juries. Concluding simply that Machiavelli is an admirer of Roman imperialism, they miss the new confederal form of republican foreign policy Machiavelli recommends in the second book of his *Discourses* (as well as his implicit foresight into the balance of power politics that would develop among the European nations). Such commentators also miss the way in which Machiavelli gradually attempts to wean his young ambitious readers from a desire for glory by urging them to take more account of their own personal safety.[36] But the fact that Machiavelli did not expect the specific individuals he addresses to take his advice does not mean that his advice is bad or intentionally misleading. There is considerable evidence that he thought that the small city-states in Italy were no longer defensible and that they needed to be united—if not simply by conquest, then in the form of a federation.

Machiavelli's indications that he does not think that his immediate addressees will understand or act on the basis of his recommendations do mean that he was writing for a broader future audience. But two questions immediately arise: What more generally was he trying to teach his future readers? And why did he insist upon addressing particular individuals in their specific circumstances as well as using specific historical examples?

Machiavelli does not write as a "political philosopher," as that term is usually understood. He does not present his thought in the form of deductions from first principles or axioms the way Hobbes does in the *Leviathan*. He shies away from abstract generalizations and turns to history.[37] But he does not adhere to the ancient notion of cycles, nor does he trace a generally progressive path or development.[38] Nor does he offer a great many historical examples as data or evidence from which he derives a general theory. As noted above, his use of historical examples is partly rhetorical.

36. I disagree, therefore, with Markus Fischer, *Well-Ordered License: On the Unity of Machiavelli's Thought* (Lanham, MD: Lexington Books, 2000), who maintains that Machiavelli "elevated glory or greatness to the highest good" (86).

37. Christian Bec, *Machiavel* (Paris: Ballard, 1985), observes that he engages in "raisonnement qui, n'étant pas philosophique, ne s'élabore jamais en un système cohérent d'explication globale du monde" (127). And Otfried Höffe, "Provisorische Amoral (Kapitel 18–19)," in Höffe, *Niccolò Machiavelli "Der Fürst,"* suggests that "Machiavellis Principe gehört jedenfalls seinem genus litterarum nach zum politischen Denker, aber nicht zur politischen Philosophie, sondern weit mehr zu einer generelle Ratschläge, nicht universal Regeln suchenden politischen Rhetorik" (108). Höffe, "Zur Machiavellis Wirkung," also notes, "von Ideenhistorikern und Politikwissenschaftlern wird Machiavelli in aller Welt viel studiert, für Philosophen dagegen ist er kein Thema mehr" (195).

38. In *D* 1.2 and *FH* 5.1 he describes the cycle of generation and decay in regimes only to declare immediately thereafter that it does not hold.

In *P* 6 he observes that most people do not believe that anything they have not seen or experienced is possible. As he states in *D* 1.Pref., he reminds his readers of what people have done in the past in order to persuade them that human beings can still perform such great deeds. Machiavelli also uses historical examples and suggests "remedies" for particular problems at specific times and places because in a world in which everything is always in motion, political decisions always apply to particular circumstances, which necessarily change. The knowledge he claims to have acquired from his reading of ancient histories as well as his own practical experience in politics would not be of any use to political actors if it did not help them make such decisions. However, if they are to be useful, his analyses and recommendations cannot be restricted to the specific individuals and their immediate circumstances (because these hold only for a moment).

Machiavelli's writings nevertheless have a philosophical basis and character. As Strauss and Paul Rahe both point out, Machiavelli's political recommendations are associated with an "Epicurean" view of nature as a whole in which everything is always in motion, either coming into being or passing away.[39] But Machiavelli does not remain a mere observer who quietly contemplates the natural order. In fact, he does not look at human motions and emotions on the basis of that understanding of nature so much as he adopts that understanding of nature as a result of his reading and experience of human actions and opinions.[40] Like Socrates, he could be said to have been seeking self-knowledge in seeking knowledge of "the human things." In *D* 1.39 he declares:

> Whoever considers present and ancient things easily knows that in all cities and in all peoples there are the same desires and the same humors, and there always have been. So it is an easy thing for whoever examines past things diligently to foresee future things in every republic and to take the remedies for them that were used by the ancients, *or, if they do not find any that were used, to think up new ones through the similarity of accidents.* But because these

39. Paul A. Rahe, "In the Shadow of Lucretius: The Epicurean Foundations of Machiavelli's Political Thought," *History of Political Thought* 28, no. 1 (2006): 30–55.

40. Although Pierre Manent agrees that Machiavelli "ne construit pas de système. Ce qu'il dit paraît aussi peu abstrait que la vie même" (*Enquête sur la démocratie: études de philosophie politique* [Paris: Gallimard, 2007], 267), he observes that Strauss and Lefort, using completely opposed modes of interpretation, both conclude that Machiavelli was a philosopher. Whereas Strauss points to Socrates as the model of a philosopher who concerned himself primarily with the human things and to the Epicurean foundations of Machiavelli's conception of nature, Lefort, *Le travail de l'oeuvre Machiavel*, 425 (Smith trans., 180), derives a new ontology from Machiavelli's account of the conflict between the two humors.

> considerations are neglected or not understood by whoever reads, or, if they are understood, they are not known to whoever governs, it follows that there are always the same scandals in every time. (84)

Machiavelli does not think that it is possible to change human nature, especially the passions that prompt human beings to act as they do. However, he suggests, it is possible to channel or direct those passions so that they have better, more desirable, and less destructive results than they had in the past. He does not, therefore, want his readers simply to imitate or repeat past actions. He urges them, when needed, to devise better "remedies."

Machiavelli himself explicitly claims to be innovating. He famously states that he is differing from all previous writers in two places and in two respects. In *P* 15 he announces that he is not presenting an imaginary republic or principality based on a teaching of how human beings ought to behave. Instead he will be teaching his "princely" readers to be able not to be good and how to use or not use that knowledge according to necessity. He then proceeds to redefine the virtues not as characteristics or activities that are good in themselves, but as those qualities or deeds that enable a ruler to maintain his state. And he argues that the best way for a leader to retain control is for him to show that his government serves to protect the lives, families, and properties of his fellow citizens or subjects.[41]

Machiavelli's debunking of both traditional aristocratic and Christian virtues in *The Prince* establishes a necessary condition for his proposing a new, more democratic form of republic in his *Discourses.* In *D* 1.58 Machiavelli again famously announces that he is disagreeing with all previous authors in arguing that the people are both wiser and more stable than princes. In *Thoughts on Machiavelli* Strauss contends that Machiavelli does not actually mean what he says here, because he shows that people cannot rule themselves; they need "princes" or leaders (*TM*, 129–32). Machiavelli does show that the people cannot rule themselves.[42] Most people simply want to be left

41. If a leader is put in power by an army, he may have to allow that army to oppress the people. However, Machiavelli uses the example of Hiero of Syracuse to suggest (*P* 6, 13, 19) that it would be better, once he is in power, for the leader to see that the army which elevated him is eliminated.

42. In *D* 1.44 he declares that "a multitude without a head is useless." And in *D* 1.57 he explains, "There is nothing more formidable than an unshackled multitude without a head, [but] . . . there is nothing weaker; for even though it has arms in hand, it is easy to put it down. . . . When the spirits of men are cooled a little and each sees he has to return to his home, they begin to doubt themselves and to think of their safety, either by taking flight or by coming to accord" (115). These declarations would appear to contradict the contention by both Vatter, *Between Form and Event*, and McCormick, *Machiavellian Democracy*, that the people are the "creative" force in history.

alone to pursue their private endeavors. Only a few want to rule, and Machiavelli addresses his books to these few. However, by arguing that the people should be able to elect the individuals who rule them (for short terms and with rotation in office) and that those accused of attempting to overthrow the republic should be tried in public in front of large popular juries, who determine their innocence or guilt, I argue, Machiavelli suggests that the people can best determine whether the government has actually secured their lives, liberties, families, and property. This is the sense in which they are wiser. Without popular consent, Machiavelli sees, no state has a firm foundation. That is the sense in which a government based on the people is more stable than that of a single prince.

Because he treats the *Discourses* primarily in terms of Machiavelli's "spiritual war" against Christianity, Strauss does not pay much attention to the new form of republic Machiavelli introduces there. He does not emphasize the need for competitive elections or rotation in office that Machiavelli draws from the Roman experience (or the fact that, according to Machiavelli, one of the two main causes of the fall of the Roman republic was the prolongation of commands). Mansfield brings out the importance of Machiavelli's introduction of the executive power; but neither he nor Strauss points out that the regular "executions" Machiavelli states are necessary to preserve a republic all take the form of public trials. They are not examples of the use of "extraordinary" force, if "extraordinary" means extralegal (as it often does). As Machiavelli argues in *D* 1.7, large public trials are ways in which the people can "vent their humors," their anger or resentment against those who rule and claim to be better than the ruled, and so preserve the rule of law instead of allowing a civil war between the two "humors" to develop.[43] According to Machiavelli, "all the laws that are made in favor of freedom arise from the disunion" of the two humors, that of the great and that of the people (*D* 1.4, 1.16). In both *The Prince* and *Discourses* Machiavelli seeks to teach his readers how to design laws and institutions like the French *parlement* (a court) that guide the two humors so that each can check the excesses of the other.

However, those commentators who present Machiavelli as part of a "republican tradition" that represents a third understanding of human liberty

---

At most Machiavelli recognizes the potentially destructive power of popular uprisings, which can create "opportunities," as he calls them, for fundamental institutional innovations. But it requires a far-sighted leader to propose the innovations and to force the people to defend them when the new orders are opposed, as they will be, by those who were in control before. See *P* 6 and *D* 1.9.

43. As Fischer, *Well-Ordered License*, 20, also points out.

as "non-domination" (in contrast to the negative and positive concepts of liberty distinguished by Isaiah Berlin) overestimate the effect of law per se in inculcating "civic virtue" in naturally selfish human beings—at least as Machiavelli sees it.[44] In *P* 12 he famously states that "the principal foundations . . . [of] all states . . . are good laws and good arms." And "because there cannot be good laws where there are not good arms, and where there are good arms there must be good laws," he leaves out the reasoning about laws and speaks only of arms. In other words, laws are not good unless they are enforced. But, he emphasizes in the third book of his *Discourses*, arms are not good unless they are organized (*D* 3.30–31). Human beings can be trained to be good and reliable soldiers, but he does not argue, as Pocock does, that military training in itself makes an individual or a people virtuous.[45] Machiavelli writes of "corrupt" or "non-corrupt," not virtuous or vicious peoples. *Virtù* is a quality of an individual leader. And, he emphasizes, laws that work well so long as the people are not corrupt cease to work when they become corrupt (*D* 1.18). According to Machiavelli, it was the threat of a foreign invasion that kept the Roman people noncorrupt until the end of the Punic war. Laws and institutional innovations such as the censorship were not sufficient to check the growing corruption. Rome needed a leader such as Fabius Rullianus who understood how to reorder the population so that they would continue to elect virtuous leaders. Since the strength of the humors varies under different circumstances over time, republics need leaders who understand the need regularly to readjust the balance between them and are able to design institutional "remedies" to do just that.

Religion is one of the means by which "the great" (princes or nobles) maintain control of the people (*P* 18, *D* 1.11–15). But in both his *Discourses* and *Florentine Histories* Machiavelli is very critical of the effects the Church has had in Italy. Its prelates set bad examples of vicious rather than virtuous behavior. Because the Church has no arms of its own, moreover, it is forced to bring foreign armies into Italy in pursuing its own political goals. However, as he indicates with the example of the Swiss, the Christian religion is and can be compatible with republican politics and an effective military (*D* 1.12). Likewise, he shows how Ferdinand used the Christian religion to justify his war against the Moors and to raise money from both

44. E.g., Skinner, "Republican Ideal of Political Liberty," 293–309, and Philip Pettit, *Republicanism* (Oxford: Oxford University Press, 1997), 4–50.

45. Pocock, *Machiavellian Moment*, 200–203.

the people and the Church to support the development of the army with which he was able to unify Spain (*P* 21). As the rise of the national monarchies in both Spain and France indicates, Christian beliefs in themselves do not prevent the emergence of strong principalities. Machiavelli objects to the political role the Church has played in Italy by keeping its principalities and republics divided and so weak. At two points in the *Discourses* he states that the Christian beliefs of his contemporaries have made them weak by making them unwilling to employ some of the harsh methods of conquest and control used by the ancients (*D* 2.2, 3.27). But in the first case he suggests that the weakness derives "from the cowardice of the men who have interpreted our religion according to idleness and not according to virtue. For if they considered how it permits us the exaltation and defense of the fatherland, they would see that it wishes us to love and honor it and to prepare ourselves to be such that we can defend it" (132). And in *D* 2.5 Machiavelli suggests that Christianity may be dying of its own accord (although it may also last for another 1,500 years). In sum, in *The Prince*, *Discourses*, and *Florentine Histories* Machiavelli reminds his readers how Christian princes and even popes have successfully organized and led armies. That is, he shows that modern political leaders can and did use the Christian beliefs of their people not merely to maintain but to extend their dominion. Machiavelli's treatment of Christianity specifically, as well as of religion more generally, thus appears to be a part of his attempt to introduce a new and better understanding and practice of politics more than an attempt to obliterate such beliefs altogether.

Machiavelli emphasizes the importance of politics because he sees that our desires naturally put human beings into competition and thus into conflict with one another. Human beings form political associations in order to protect their own lives, liberty, and property. But once political societies are formed, the opposed desires of those who wish to rule and those who do not wish to be ruled threaten to tear them apart in civil wars that most often result in the imposition of a tyranny. Politics is crucial—and this is the most important lesson Machiavelli continues to convey to his readers—because human beings cannot achieve anything great or barely even survive in the absence of political order. It is absolutely imperative, therefore, that we learn how such orders are best established and maintained.

Strauss's critique of Machiavelli is not simply or primarily that he sought to destroy Christianity, using its own methods of "propaganda" over time to persuade his readers to adopt a new and better understanding of human life on earth. In the end Strauss faults Machiavelli for not recognizing and conveying the superiority of the philosophical way of life as Plato did in his dialogues. Machiavelli criticizes Christianity for having "glorified humble and contemplative more than active men" (*D* 2.2; 131). Twice in the *Discourses* he suggests that it might be best to withdraw from political activity altogether, because it requires human beings to act in nasty, destructive, and deceptive ways (*D* 1.26 and 3.2). But he insists that such a withdrawal is impossible. For "whoever does . . . , if he is a man notable for his quality, lives in continual danger." (Machiavelli does not, although he could, point to the death of Socrates as an example.) "Nor is it enough to say [like Epicurus]: 'I do not care for anything; I do not desire either honors or useful things; I wish to live quietly and without quarrel!' For these excuses are heard and not accepted; nor can men who have quality choose to abstain even when they choose it truly and without any ambition, because it is not believed of them; so if they wish to abstain, they are not allowed by others to abstain" (*D* 3.2; 213–14).

Machiavelli's political philosophy is, therefore, explicitly practical and engaged rather than merely theoretical or contemplative. He seeks to teach his readers how to act effectively so that his writings will have an effect as well. The effect he seeks is not, however, of the kind the "political theorists" who write in order to affect contemporary politics and policies wish to have. The effect he seeks is, first and foremost, on the broader understanding of politics his readers have and use; it is not limited nor is it intended to be limited to his immediate audience and circumstances. The major challenge Machiavelli poses to ancient political philosophy consists in his claim that writers need to show how their works improve the lives of ordinary people. By showing the ambitious how to organize the lives of their people so that they live more safely and prosperously, the philosopher not only secures himself from persecution but also benefits others.

In the following studies of Machiavelli's major works I have attempted to show how the moral revolution he effects in *The Prince* lays the foundation for the new form of democratic republic he proposes in the *Discourses*. Not believing that ambitious politicians would serve the public interest or common good out of the goodness of their own hearts, he sought to persuade them that the best way of achieving their own ambitions was to secure the lives, families, and properties of their subjects or fellow citizens. In the *Discourses* he then describes the kinds of laws and institutions that enable both "the great" (or those who wish to be so) and the people to attain as much as possible of what they desire. Because human beings act primarily on the basis of their passions, Machiavelli attempts to show his readers what those passions are and how they can be guided to have productive rather than destructive results. Since those same passions lead human beings to work against the laws and institutions that restrain them, Machiavelli also counsels future leaders that they must constantly be on the lookout for new problems and devise new remedies for them.

Although Machiavelli claims in his dedications to *The Prince* and the *Discourses*, and only in the dedications to these two works, that they contain everything that he knows, he continued to write.[46] In the second half of this study, I thus examine Machiavelli's later works in approximately the order in which they were written to see the way in which he develops certain aspects of his thought that were slighted if not altogether ignored in his more comprehensive works. In *Mandragola* Machiavelli shows his audience how the analysis of the passions underlying political life applies to private life. In the *Art of War*, Machiavelli explains more concretely how and to what extent he thinks the ancient principles of organization he advocated in both *The Prince* and *Discourses* should be applied in modern circumstances. In his *Life of Castruccio Castracani* he then indicates that mastery of the art of war will not suffice to make a petty tyrant into a great founder. It is necessary to master the arts of peace as well. Religion is the most important of those arts, but by quoting the sayings of the cynic philosophers, Castruccio demonstrated a complete lack of respect for the moral and religious beliefs of his people. In his comedy *Clizia*, Machiavelli illustrates what sorts of appearances of conventional morality need to be maintained and why devotion to transcendent, ill-defined, and thus illusory "fantasies" is destructive. Finally, in his *Florentine Histories*, Machiavelli shows in more or less explicit contrast to Rome why the partisan divisions in Florence produced a vacillation between tyranny and license. His fellow citizens never secured liberty for themselves because no one knew how to design a set of laws that would do so. He tried to teach them, but no one listened—or understood.

Machiavelli is widely acknowledged to have been a great literary artist, and I treat each of his works as an artistically designed whole. In his prose works I attempt to show how the argument that unifies the work is directed to the particular concerns of the individual or individuals to whom Machiavelli dedicates the work. But I also seek to bring out the irony with which

46. Strauss, *TM*, 17–20, was the first to make this observation. He uses it particularly to argue that Machiavelli's not including the soul or afterlife in either of these works indicates that he did not claim to know anything about them. However, when Strauss discusses Machiavelli's philosophy, especially in relation to Socrates, he refers to *The Life of Castruccio Castracani*. *TM*, 223–25.

Machiavelli treats both the dedicatees and his own advice to them in order to show that he is addressing a more general lesson to a broader audience. As with his treatment of Livy in the *Discourses*, so in *Mandragola*, the *Life of Castruccio Castracani*, and *Clizia*, I identify and analyze the significance of the changes Machiavelli makes to his sources in order to bring out the novel interpretation he is presenting.[47]

In contrast to the critics who fault Machiavelli for making contradictory statements and thus failing to adhere steadily to any one position, I seek to show that Machiavelli's works form a coherent whole—both individually and as a corpus. In his prose works he argues dialectically, first taking up one position, then examining the criticism or alternative to that position, then coming to a provisional conclusion, and then subjecting that conclusion to further examination. In his fictional works he presents sets of characters acting on the basis of different understandings of what is important and what works, then shows which characters succeed or fail and indicates the reasons why. In all cases he depicts human beings acting on the basis of their strongest passions, their fears and their hopes. By showing that some of these fears and hopes are illusory, he warns his readers against them. In all cases, he shows that human beings will live and prosper only if there is a person or "prince" able to design "orders" that organize and direct their efforts to achieve the means of satisfying their various desires so that they do not come into open and violent conflict, as they inevitably will if left merely to follow their natural inclinations. Since no individual lives forever, Machiavelli recognizes, the knowledge of how to create and maintain such orders in changing circumstances is the most valuable gift one human being can present to another. The reward for acquiring and spreading such knowledge is not glory, because an author who understands the transitory character of everything in the world knows that there is no such thing as "eternal" glory. The human race itself belongs to the transitory forms of

47. In writing the *Florentine Histories*, Machiavelli followed the practices of the time by not doing original research so much as drawing on previous chronicles and histories. Some scholars have pointed out the differences between Machiavelli's histories and those of the two scholars he mentions at the beginning (e.g., James Hankins, "Rhetoric, History, and Ideology: The Civic Panegyrics of Leonardo Bruni," and Harvey C. Mansfield, "Bruni and Machiavelli on Civic Humanism," in *Renaissance Civic Humanism: Reappraisals and Reflections*, ed. James Hankins [Cambridge: Cambridge University Press, 2000], 143–78, 223–46, as well as Michelle Tolman Clarke, "Machiavelli and the Imagined Rome of Renaissance Humanism," *History of Political Thought* 36, no. 3 [2015]: 452–70). These histories were generally celebrations of the civic achievements of the republic of Florence, whereas Machiavelli's are not. Nor are his "histories" merely chronicles of events as were some of his sources. No one has identified all—or even most—of the specific pieces he took or did not take from the works of Villani, Biondo, and other chroniclers; and I have not been able to do so.

existence in this world. Glory is, moreover, a matter of public opinion, and the public tends to valorize extraordinary acts of what appears to be self-denial more than more ordinary deeds that actually contribute to the welfare of the community. Machiavelli was willing to appear less than he was, to present himself in the guise of a man seeking a job rather than someone with princely knowledge, in order to create conditions under which not only he but also others could live, think, and write more freely.

No one who reads Machiavelli can deny that he emphasizes politics more than philosophy, religion, or literary form (although these are all relevant aspects of his work). In the following study I have therefore sought to emphasize, first and foremost, what Machiavelli sought to teach his readers about politics, not merely in his immediate context, but most importantly in order to improve human life in the future.

Biographical Background

Because Machiavelli presents almost all of his writings in the context of his attempt to regain public employment from the Medici, it is useful to know something about the facts of his life. He claims to be writing, at least in part, out of his own economic need. In the dedications to *The Prince* and *Discourses* he also states that the knowledge he wishes to convey arises from his own practical political experience. It is thus useful to learn something about his experience as a secretary to the Florentine republic before he was dismissed by the Medici in our efforts to understand his later writings.

He was born on May 3, 1469, into a minor branch of a venerable old Florentine family. His father, Bernardo di Niccolò di Buoninsegna, had a law degree, but he does not seem to have earned much from his profession, and the revenue from their land in the Val di Pesa barely sufficed to support a wife and four children. Bernardo could not afford to hire an illustrious tutor for his sons, Niccolò and Totto, but he did see that they learned Latin, grammar, arithmetic, and composition. He loved books and owned copies of Macrobius, Priscian, Donato Acciaiuoli on the *Ethics* of Aristotle, and the *Decades of History from the Deterioration of the Roman Empire* of Biondo, as well as Livy's *History of Rome*. (Bernardo agreed to prepare an index that took him nine months to complete in order to obtain the last.) Niccolò thus had an opportunity to read and study these works, as well as Cicero's *Philippics*, *De officiis*, and *De oratore*, the *Ethics* of Aristotle, the *Cosmography* of Ptolemy, a Pliny in translation, Justin, Biondo's *Italia illustrata*, and the

Bible, which his father is known to have borrowed.[48] It is not clear how Machiavelli acquired the classical humanist education Florentine public officials at that time were expected to have. According to the *Maxims* of the fifteenth-century historian Paolo Giovio, Machiavelli received the best part of his classical training from Marcello Adriani, when he was a professor at the university of Florence. After Adriani was appointed first chancellor of the Florentine republic in 1498, Machiavelli was chosen to be secretary to the second chancery where he "also ranked as one of the six secretaries to the first chancellor, and in this capacity he was shortly assigned the further task of serving the Ten of War."[49]

As a young man Machiavelli witnessed the rise and fall of a series of different governments in Florence. The year he was born Piero de' Medici died and rule of Florence passed into the hands of his sons, Giuliano and Lorenzo. Florence was a "republic" in name and law, but the city had been ruled effectively, if not tyrannically, by a member of the Medici family ever since Cosimo was brought back from exile in triumph in 1434.[50] One of Cosimo's grandsons, Giuliano, was murdered as a result of the Pazzi conspiracy in 1478, but Lorenzo "the Magnificent" followed the example set by his grandfather and became a great lord and patron of the arts. Lorenzo died in 1492. Two years later his son Piero lost control of Florence after he ceded fortresses to the French rather than resisting their invasion of Italy. Machiavelli thus saw the stationing and quartering of the French troops in Florentine homes before they marched south and devastated large parts of Italy. He also observed the rise and fall of the Dominican friar Girolamo Savonarola.

After he returned to Florence in 1487, Savonarola began preaching to larger and larger crowds, castigating the Florentines for their luxurious, sinful mode of life and urging them to repent. In a sermon he gave during Advent in 1492 he predicted that a new Cyrus would come from beyond the mountains. Serving as the "sword of God" to punish Florence, he would not and could not be opposed. In 1494 both the friar and his flock thought his prediction had come true when French troops led by Charles VIII invaded Italy and met no serious resistance.

48. Ridolfi, *Life*, 257–58.

49. Skinner, *Machiavelli*, 7.

50. Machiavelli describes Cosimo's return as a triumph in his *Florentine Histories* 4.33. He wrote the *Histories*, in which he traces the rise and, effective but not actual, fall of the Medici, on commission from Cardinal Giulio de' Medici before he became Pope Clement VII.

Savonarola led the Florentine delegation that successfully negotiated an agreement with the French not to sack but only to occupy Florence, and not to reinstate the Medici but to establish the most democratic form of government Florence had ever had. Savonarola himself never had an official role in the government of the "Great Council" of three thousand members who appointed all magistrates (choosing from a list of names drawn by lot), passed or rejected laws proposed by the Signoria (the traditional ruling body of the commune), and elected a smaller council of Eighty, who advised the Signoria and appointed ambassadors. Savonarola was nevertheless responsible for the design of this government and exercised great influence on it.[51] But that influence did not protect him from prosecution by the clergy, whose anger had been aroused by the friar's fiery denunciations of the corruption of the Roman Church. After he disobeyed the pope's order in 1495 that he cease preaching, on May 15, 1498, the Signoria authorized the interrogation and torture of Savonarola in the presence of the papal envoy and general of the Dominican order. A week later, Savonarola was hanged, burned, and his ashes thrown into the Arno, so that they could not be collected and venerated as relics.

The rise and fall of Savonarola affected Machiavelli in two different ways. First, his observations of these tumultuous years in Florence gave rise to some of the conclusions he recorded later about political life more generally. In his *Discourses*, for example, he takes the friar's ability to arouse popular sentiment and gather political support by passionately appealing to people's religious hopes and fears and interpreting natural phenomena as signs of the divine will to show that such appeals can be made successfully in modern as well as ancient times.[52] But he also suggests that the friar

51. See Girolamo Savonarola, *Trattato sul governo della città di Firenze* (Rome: Editori Riunti, 1999); reproduces "Prediche sopra Aggeo e Trattato del reggimento della città di Firenze," ed. Luigi Firpo, *Edizione Nazionale delle Opere di Girolamo Savonarola* (Rome: Belardetti, 1965); www.liberliber.it. A quick comparison with Niccolò Machiavelli, "A Discourse on Remodeling the Government of Florence," *Machiavelli: The Chief Works and Others*, trans. Allan Gilbert (Durham, NC: Duke University Press, 1958), 1: 101–16, shows that the republican government Machiavelli urged the Medici to establish in 1520 would have represented a return to the Savonarolan model in many respects.

52. In *D* 1.11, Machiavelli observes that the people of Florence, who do not appear to have been either ignorant or coarse, were persuaded by "Friar Girolamo Savonarola that he spoke with God." Machiavelli does not take a stand on whether it was true or not, "because one should speak with reverence of such a man." He does observe "that an infinite number believed him without having seen anything extraordinary to make them believe him," even though in 1.56 he reminds his readers of "how much had been foretold by Friar Girolamo Savonarola before the coming of King Charles VIII of France into Italy." Machiavelli rather clearly indicated what he thought about the truth of Savonarola's claims, however, in a letter he wrote to Ricciardo Becchi, the Florentine ambassador to the Holy See on March 9, 1498. In this letter Machiavelli first summarizes two sermons

contributed to his own downfall by not paying sufficient attention to his own reputation. His influence depended not on his office or powers but on the perception of his "learning, prudence, and virtue." Having successfully advocated the passage of a law establishing an appeal to the people by criminals condemned to die in state cases, he did not support five citizens who sought to make such an appeal shortly after the law was passed and thereby undermined his own standing with the people. Indeed, Machiavelli comments, Savonarola's failure even to criticize the officials who had not enforced the law made people think either that the law he had championed was not wise or that he condoned a partisan enforcement of it (*D* 1.45). As a result, the friar lost much of his popular support. Savonarola was not able, moreover, to communicate his own understanding of what was necessary to his followers and subordinates. In *The Prince* Machiavelli famously cites Savonarola as an example of an "unarmed prophet" who necessarily failed because he was unarmed. But, Machiavelli explains in *D* 3.30, the problem was not that Savonarola did not understand the need to use force, as had Moses, "to kill infinite men." Savonarola did not have the authority to use that force; he was only an advisor behind the scenes and not an officer of the republic, and "he was not understood well by those who followed him" who did have such authority. Machiavelli does not explicitly say what prevented Savonarola's followers from understanding him. His description of the character of Savonarola's influence on his fellow citizens suggests, however, that some of the friar's inability to communicate his own understanding of what was politically necessary might be traced to the figurative mode of speech he used in his sermons, in which he attributed everything to God. And the lack of clarity in his indirect mode of speaking was reinforced by

that Savonarola, fearing that the newly elected Signoria would not support or defend him against the pope, gave after he had withdrawn from preaching in the city at San Reparata and begun speaking "boldly" at his home church in San Marco. Taking as his text a passage from Exodus, "but the more they oppressed them, the more they were multiplied," Savonarola first argued that "when it comes to action, prudence is right-reason," and right-reason might counsel one to go into hiding, as he had. He then sought to encourage his followers by promising that through suffering good people grow in both spirit and number. He finally provided a bridge to his sermon the next day, by saying that the dissension in Florence might cause a tyrant to rise up among them, but that this tyrant would eventually be driven out of Italy. The next morning he returned to Exodus where it says that Moses slew an Egyptian, and reported that "God had told him that there was someone in Florence who sought to make himself a tyrant [and] . . . to excommunicate the friar." But after he heard that the Signoria had written to the pope on his behalf, Savonarola dropped all such talk of tyrants in Florence and tried to set the people against the pontiff. "Thus," Machiavelli concluded, "in my judgment, he acts in accordance with the times and colors his lies accordingly." *Machiavelli and His Friends: Their Personal Correspondence*, trans. and ed. James B. Atkinson and David Sices (DeKalb: Northern Illinois University Press, 1996), 9–10.

Savonarola's unwillingness if not inability as a representative and spokesman for the "prince of peace" to take direct part in government or enforce the laws. His followers could not perceive the thoughts that lay hidden in the friar's public speeches and deeds, and the friar either did not choose or was not able to communicate his understanding of the need to use force to eliminate the opposition in private.

The second way in which Savonarola's rise and fall affected Machiavelli was that the diminished influence of the friar's followers after his execution led almost immediately to Machiavelli's election to public office.[53] As chief of the Second Chancery and secretary to the Ten of Liberty and Peace, a commission that oversaw Florentine military matters and foreign affairs, Machiavelli was sent to negotiate with such notable figures as Caterina Sforza Riario (1499), King Louis XII of France and the cardinal of Rouen (1500), and Cesare Borgia (1502). These missions, as well as his later visits with Pope Julius II (1506) and at the court of the Emperor Maximilian (1507–8), provided material for his later reflections.[54]

After Piero Soderini was named gonfalonier for life in 1502 (and the Florentine constitution then came, in effect, to duplicate the constitution of Venice with this addition of a lifelong executive like the doge), Machiavelli became one of Soderini's most trusted advisors and representatives. As he shows at the conclusion of his *First Decennial*, an epic poem in which he details the suffering of Italy in the decade following the French invasion in 1494, and the only work he published while in office, Machiavelli had become convinced that the political divisions that made Italy vulnerable to foreign invasion would never be overcome until Florence rearmed itself. With the support of Piero's brother, Cardinal Francesco Soderini, Machiavelli thus pressed the gonfalonier to reestablish the militia Florence had lacked for more than two hundred years. The proposal aroused much opposition, especially from Soderini's aristocratic opponents, who accused him of wanting to become a tyrant (by obtaining a bodyguard). The cardinal advised Machiavelli to begin recruiting and training in the countryside, where an armed force would pose a less direct threat to citizens in power. After the mercenaries the Florentines hired in an attempt to retake Pisa were ignominiously defeated, in 1506 the Council created the *nove ufficiali dell' ordinanza e milizia fiorentina* (the nine officers of the Florentine ordinance and militia). Machiavelli was made secretary and threw himself

53. Ridolfi, *Life*, 15, reports that Machiavelli was elected five days after the execution.
54. See *D* 3.6, *FH* 7.22, 8.34; *P* 3 and 7; *P* 25 and *D* 1.27, 3.9, 3.44; *D* 2.11, 2.19.

wholeheartedly into the effort of recruiting and training a native Florentine army. On June 8, 1509, fifteen years of war ended with a Florentine victory over Pisa, thanks to Machiavelli and his battalions. Machiavelli then received authorization from the Ten to raise a detachment of light horse to supplement his infantry, but he did not have time or receive adequate support to recruit and train an army capable of defending Florence from the Holy League (founded in 1511 by Pope Julius II in alliance with the Venetians, Spanish, English, Swiss, and the Holy Roman Emperor against Louis XII of France). Although France defeated the Holy League at the Battle of Ravenna in 1512, the French commander, Gaston de Foix, was killed, and King Louis ordered his troops to withdraw. Florence was left alone to face the Spanish troops that had been defeated at Ravenna. Because they lacked supplies, the Spanish commander tried twice to negotiate a settlement with Soderini, but he and the Council refused their terms. Soderini asked Machiavelli to do something to restrain the Spanish, but with the body of Florentine troops kept at home to defend the city, Machiavelli and his ill-trained troops were not able to withstand the Spanish at Prato.[55] Hearing that four thousand men had been slaughtered there, the Florentines capitulated to Spanish demands that they dismiss Soderini and allow the Medici to return as private citizens. Within two months the Medici had again made themselves masters of Florence, sent Soderini into exile, and dismissed Machiavelli from office.[56]

Machiavelli was ordered to remain within the dominions of Florence for a year and to pay a surety of one thousand florins (supplied by his friend Francesco Vettori and his relatives Filippo and Giovanni Machiavelli), but forbidden from entering the Palazzo Vecchio (the locus of the Signoria and his former office) for a year. He was nevertheless called back within a month to testify, when his successor decided to investigate Machiavelli's management of the huge funds collected to pay the militia, but after a thorough investigation no malfeasance was discovered. Shortly thereafter, however, Machiavelli was implicated in a conspiracy against the Medici, when his name was found on a list of probable sympathizers, drawn up by Pietro Paolo Boscoli. Machiavelli was imprisoned and tortured but did not confess

55. See C. C. Bayley, *War and Society in Renaissance Florence* (Toronto: University of Toronto Press, 1961), 276–84, and Mikael Hörnqvist, "*Perché non si usa allegare i Romani*: Machiavelli and the Florentine Militia of 1507," *Renaissance Quarterly* 55 (2002): 148–91.

56. Machiavelli dispassionately summarizes the events leading to the downfall of the republic and the reinstitution of the rule of the Medici in his Letter to a Noblewoman after September 16, 1512, *Machiavelli and His Friends*, 214–17.

to any crime. He was freed in the celebration of Cardinal Giuliano de' Medici's election as Pope Leo X on March 11 or 12, 1513, and left Florence to live in the country house his father had left him.

Machiavelli was one of the few officials of the old republic who were dismissed when the Medici took over, and he began imploring Francesco Vettori to use his influence to help him regain a position almost as soon as he retired to Sant' Andrea.[57] Trying to retain their personal ties while distancing himself politically, Vettori invited Machiavelli to visit him in Rome and promised to do whatever he could when the time was ripe. When nothing happened and Machiavelli renewed his requests for assistance, Vettori responded in a letter of November 23, 1513, by describing the way in which he had been forced by a combination of expense and lack of success to withdraw from most political exchanges in Rome. Oppressed by the expenses of his position as ambassador, which exceeded his salary, he had stopped giving dinner parties and returned the silver plate people had loaned to him in the hope that he would speak to the pope on their behalf. With probable reference to Machiavelli's own petitions, Vettori said that he had done what they wished without any effect, so he had determined to rid himself of this chore and not to annoy or burden anyone else.[58]

To document the boredom and powerlessness of his current situation, Vettori then described his daily routine. Rising at ten, after breakfast he would go every other morning to the palace, where he would say twenty words to the pope, ten to Cardinal de' Medici, and six to Giuliano the Magnificent or, if he were not available, to Piero Ardinghelli, and finally to any ambassadors who happened to be present. Afterward Vettori would return home for lunch with his household, walk through the church and the garden, and, if the weather were fine, take a short horseback ride outside of Rome. At nightfall he would come home and read some of the many histories he had acquired, especially of Rome. Referring back, it would seem, to Machiavelli's enthusiastic response to his first invitation to join him in Rome, Vettori concluded that this was the life he was urging Machiavelli

57. Machiavelli and Vettori had become friends in 1508 when they served together as representatives of Florence in Germany at the court of Emperor Maximilian. The party of aristocrats who opposed Piero Soderini had initially pressured him to send a "well-born" young man instead of his loyal servant, but Soderini found that he could not rely on Vettori's reports and sent Machiavelli to join him. The conditions were not propitious, but Vettori and Machiavelli became not merely cooperative colleagues, but friends.

58. Francesco Vettori to Niccolò Machiavelli, Rome, November 23, 1513, in *Machiavelli and His Friends,* 260–62.

to share—a private life of seeing the sights and coming back home to joke, laugh, and read.

This letter from Vettori prompted Machiavelli's famous response on December 10, 1513, in which he replied to Vettori's description of his day with one of his own. The close parallels between the two suggest that we should not take Machiavelli's description of his life too literally. Our knowledge of "Machiavelli" is to a considerable extent a product of his own presentation of himself in his letters and writings. The differences between the two men's descriptions of their days nevertheless bring out the vast distance between a pedestrian and an uncommonly acute mind.

Machiavelli's account of his work outside before daybreak, followed by an interlude of reading love poetry, conversations on the road with passersby from which he learned about the various tastes and fancies of men, a meager lunch at home, raucous games and squabbles with artisans and laborers all afternoon at the inn, culminating in his four hours of study at the "ancient courts of ancient men," is designed not merely to rebuke Vettori for complaining about his reduced economic circumstances and lack of influence. It is also supposed to remind Vettori of how much more Machiavelli has suffered (and so, presumably, to arouse his sympathy).[59] Whereas Vettori had withdrawn into private life not only in order to reduce his expenses, but also in order to avoid pleas for help that he had found he could not give, Machiavelli had been forced out of office and thus to go without any salary whatsoever. He concludes his letter by observing that he cannot remain as he is for a long time "without becoming despised because of poverty."[60]

But even in conditions of economic stringency, we see, Machiavelli sought to experience life to the fullest, from the basest necessities to the highest thoughts. Like primitive men, he began his day with hunting. He did not capture many thrushes (which would have provided little food, in any case), and when they gave out, he had to find not merely another "pastime," but another form of economic support.[61] Still arising with the sun (in

59. See Giulio Ferroni, "Le 'cose vane' nelle *Lettere* di Machiavelli," *La Rassegna della letteratura italiana* 76 (1972): 231–32.

60. Machiavelli to Vettori, *P* 111.

61. Machiavelli does not state the connection explicitly, but his account of his thrush hunting could be seen as an oblique reference to the suffering he endured in prison and the failure of a former plea to Giuliano for help. In addition to two sonnets he wrote about his suffering in prison, Machiavelli dedicated a third to Giuliano which began, "I'm sending you, Giuliano, if I might, several thrushes—a small gift, I guess, but good to make Your Lordship think a bit of your poor Machiavello in distress." *Lust and Liberty: The Poems of Machiavelli*, trans. Joseph Tusiani (New

contrast to Vettori's breakfast at ten), Machiavelli found that his attempt to sell wood cut on his land involved him in arguments both with the woodcutters he employed and with former friends who tried to cheat him out of any profit he might have made from selling his wood. In his personal life as well as in his more theoretical writings, Machiavelli thus saw that human relations are fundamentally self-regarding and competitive. His economic endeavors appeared to be as fruitless as Vettori's conversations with other politicians at the Vatican. So following the model set by Vettori in his letter, Machiavelli says that he withdrew to find refreshment. He stopped at a spring to read love poetry—Dante or Petrarch, or one of the "minor poets" like Ovid—and in reading about their amorous passions, he remembered

---

York: Ivan Obolensky, 1963), 46. In a learned and provocative reading of the letter of December 10, 1513, Najemy suggests that the comparison Machiavelli draws between himself bearing the bundle of cages on his back and Geta, the servant of Amphitryon carrying his master's books on his back, reveals Machiavelli's sense of his own plight. *Geta e Birria* was an early fifteenth-century verse novella that was a remake of a twelfth-century neo-Latin comedy, *Geta*, by Vitale de Blois, which was in turn adapted from Plautus's *Amphitruo*. Machiavelli could assume that Vettori would know the story; there were at least four printed editions in his lifetime. In the novella Geta accompanies his master Amphitryon to Athens to learn philosophy. After experiencing much hardship for the sake of their studies, Amphitryon decides to return. His wife Almena sends their second servant, Birria, to meet her husband and Geta at the port; but seeing Geta trudging home loaded with books, Birria hides in a cave. The first parallel Najemy finds between Machiavelli and Geta is thus that both have books that they want to unload on a friend who ducks. (However, in the letter Machiavelli expresses uncertainty about whether he should give his book to Vettori or present it to Giuliano himself. He has reason to doubt that Vettori will press his case; so far he has not.) The second parallel Najemy finds between Machiavelli and Geta is that both have endured considerable hardship to acquire an *arte* and *scienza* that both believe will make all their suffering worthwhile by transforming and immortalizing them, but they cannot persuade or even gain the respectful attention of a former colleague. Pretending not to see that Birria has tried to hide in order to avoid helping him, Geta stands outside the cave and brags about the knowledge he has acquired. He emphasizes the hardship, the hunger and pain he has suffered in order to learn philosophy, but he concludes that what he has acquired now makes him happy, because his name will be spread throughout the world. Once a person has learned something, he further observes, that knowledge can never be taken away. Geta does not succeed in persuading Birria to come out and help him, however, until he throws a stone into the cave. Najemy does not recognize that the similarities between Machiavelli and Geta end there. Machiavelli is not in a position to force Vettori to show his hand. Moreover, in the novella Geta disavows the knowledge he thought he had acquired, after he comes to doubt his own identity as a result of his confrontation with a divine copy of himself at his former home. Najemy does not go so far as to claim that Machiavelli doubted the value of the knowledge he had acquired. He does suggest that "his self-comparison to Geta announces that the letter of 10 December was to be a parable of his year of 'exile' and of what he now fears might be a disappointing 'return' home with *The Prince* in hand" (*Between Friends*, 230). The problem with reading the entire letter in terms of this early comparison is that the comparison occurs in the section on thrush hunting, an activity Machiavelli explicitly says that he has had to give up. He had to try to find other means of economic support and entertainment, and he is taking a new tack in appealing to Giuliano with a new kind of gift. Rather than asking for mercy, Machiavelli is offering instruction and assistance in ruling. He is not approaching either Vettori or Giuliano merely as a suppliant.

his own. Unlike Vettori, Machiavelli did not have a courtesan living close by. He had to substitute intellectual recollection and enjoyment, therefore, for immediate physical pleasure. The delight Machiavelli took in his thoughts—whether they were memories or appreciations of the beautiful words—might have been greater than the pleasure he would have experienced in an actual but fleeting erotic encounter, but this intellectual delight was also transitory. So, again following the model set by Vettori, Machiavelli took a walk—not in a garden, however, but along a public road to the inn, where he spoke to the other people passing by, asked them for "news of their countries, learned various things, [including] the varying tastes and diverse characters of men." Like Vettori, Machiavelli also lunched at home—but in implicit contrast to his wealthier friend, he ate the foods his poor villa and small patrimony permitted. But instead of taking another solitary walk or ride like Vettori, Machiavelli went back to the inn, where he passed the afternoon playing games and arguing with the artisans there. He has more democratic tastes and sympathies than his aristocratic friend. And, he reports, the disputes and insults hurled among these ruffians served to shake the mold from his brain and allowed him vociferously to protest the malignity of his fate. Having thus overcome both his indolence and his resentment, Machiavelli was prepared, when evening came, to return home. There he took off his "everyday dress, full of mud and dirt," and donned "royal clothes" before he entered his study and went into "the ancient courts of ancient men, where, received lovingly by them," he ate "the only food . . . for which he was born." Vettori, too, wrote that he read histories in the evening, especially of Rome. But he did not suggest that he entered into a dialogue with the authors of, or characters to be found in, these histories. Where Vettori appeared to move, rather passively and certainly ineffectively, from one activity to another, Machiavelli emphatically learned from all the activities he undertook, whether they involved necessary work or leisure, and took his place in the company of base or highly intelligent and cultured human beings. Machiavelli seems to claim, indeed, that he encompassed the depth and breadth of possible human experience in a single day. The only thing lacking—but it appears to be the crucial thing for Machiavelli—was participation in public life.[62]

62. In his subsequent correspondence with Vettori, Machiavelli admits that the other thing lacking was immediate amorous passion. As later in *Clizia*, so in his earlier letters, Machiavelli occasionally presents himself in the role of a "fool for love." Najemy does not believe that Machiavelli actually fell in love with an unnamed and only very generically described woman, who, Machiavelli tells Vettori in a letter of August 3, 1514, led him (like his visits to the courts of ancient

Even though we cannot take it as a literal or factual description of Machiavelli's life in exile, scholars have rightly emphasized the importance of his letter of December 10, 1513, for two reasons. First, in this letter Machiavelli presents himself as a man of thought more than of action, more clearly perhaps than he does anywhere else. The books he reads are "the only food which is mine, and for which I was born." Regarding himself as an equal of the great men of old, he converses with them without shame, i.e., without restraint or a sense of his own inferiority; and they not only receive him "lovingly" but also "in their humanity" answer the questions he puts to them about the reason for their actions. Machiavelli finds not merely consolation but happiness in these conversations. "For four hours at a time," he feels no boredom, forgets all trouble, and does not fear poverty or death. As in his dedications to both *The Prince* and the *Discourses*, Machiavelli shows not merely that he regards knowledge of the deeds of great men as the most valuable possession a man can have; his suggestion that he found conversing with the great men of old to be the utmost satisfaction in life is very like what Socrates claimed for his own peculiar mode of existence, if in a more historical and bookish form.[63] Unlike Socrates, however, Machiavelli insists that the "fruits" of his conversations need to be manifested in practice.

The second reason Machiavelli's letter of December 10, 1513, is so important is that in it he makes it clear that he is not writing simply or solely to relieve his own poverty, although that creates a certain kind of necessity. More specifically, in this letter Machiavelli tells Vettori that in the months since he left prison he has composed a small treatise entitled *De principatibus* (Of principalities) in which he has investigated not merely "what a principality is," but "of what kinds they are, how they are acquired, how

---

men) to "set aside the memory of all [his] afflictions." Responding to Vettori's evident failure to act on his behalf and his friend's attempt to divert their correspondence from politics to affairs with women, in that letter Machiavelli claims to have left behind "the thoughts of great and serious things," because "neither reading about ancient things nor discussing modern ones gives me pleasure anymore" (*Between Friends*, 290–92). Yet four months later Machiavelli responded with alacrity to Vettori's request that he write out his thoughts on the foreign policy the pope ought to adopt, so that Vettori could show Machiavelli's letter to the pope. Najemy also argues, *Between Friends*, 295–309, that Vettori's request for Machiavelli's judgment and Machiavelli's advice were both quite misguided in light of (a) Machiavelli's persistent advocacy of a pro-French policy, (b) the fact that Leo had already allied himself with the Spanish king by the time Vettori wrote Machiavelli, and (c) that only two years had passed since Spanish troops had forced the pro-French Florentine republic to allow the Medici to return.

63. Cf. *Apology* 38a. See also Haig Patapan, *Machiavelli in Love* (Lanham, MD: Lexington Books, 2006), 143–46, for a discussion of the similarities and differences between Machiavelli and Socrates.

they are maintained, [and] why they are lost."[64] As he indicates in the dedication he later wrote to Lorenzo, Machiavelli informs Vettori that the treatise contains the fruits of his fifteen years of study of "the art of the state" in practice as well as in books.

The reason Machiavelli gives for his having written down "the capital I have made from the conversation" he has had with ancient authors is not, first or initially, that he thinks that he can capitalize on the knowledge he has obtained by using it to obtain a political position. It is, rather, "because Dante says that what has been learned does not become knowledge unless it is retained." In other words, Machiavelli wrote down his thoughts, first, to organize and secure them as knowledge for himself. He thought, second, but only second, about the book's possible use—by the Medici and to obtain a position with them for himself.

In his previous correspondence with Vettori Machiavelli did not mention the fact that he was writing a book. He tells Vettori about it only after he has completed a draft and shown that draft to another mutual friend, Filippo Casavecchia.[65] He is now debating with himself and others about whether he should present it to Giuliano, and if so, whether he should present it himself or ask Vettori to present it on Machiavelli's behalf. He worries that if he gives the treatise to Giuliano, "his Magnificence" will not read it, and that Giuliano's "right hand man" Ardinghelli will claim authorship and thus take credit for his work.

Machiavelli nevertheless feels driven to make his work public (although not strictly speaking to publish it) by a twofold "necessity." The first form of the necessity is economic. Because he is consuming himself (and his resources), he worries about making himself contemptible through poverty. Machiavelli is driven not by poverty per se, we see, but by his fear of contempt or, correspondingly, concern about his own standing and reputation. (He stated earlier in this very same letter that his study of ancient works made him forget his poverty; and he assured Vettori earlier in their

64. Machiavelli to Vettori, *P* 110.

65. In *Between Friends* Najemy contends that the *Prince* is directed first and foremost to Vettori's insistence that fortune rules human affairs, the view Machiavelli explicitly addresses in chapter 25 of the work we now know as *The Prince*. (Many readers have understood Machiavelli's little treatise as concerning primarily the opposition he draws between *fortuna* and *virtù*. Pocock, *Machiavellian Moment*; Skinner, *Machiavelli*; and Benner, *Prince* are a few of the most notable recent examples.) Yet in his letter of December 10, 1513, Machiavelli appears to have thought that Vettori was more valuable as a possible messenger than as an intellectual interlocutor or even as an editor. He certainly does not suggest that Vettori voiced the question that inspired him to write.

correspondence that he had been born poor and was inured to it.)[66] If Machiavelli wanted to have his worth recognized by others, he had to make his wisdom public. Since the knowledge he claimed to possess concerns affairs of state, it could not remain purely theoretical; its utility had to be demonstrated in practice. The second "necessity" that Machiavelli says drives him to present his work to Giuliano is thus his "desire to have these Medici lords begin to make use of [him]." Since the Medici controlled both Rome and Florence, and Machiavelli was a Florentine, he had little choice but to seek public employment from them.

Vettori sensibly asked Machiavelli to send him the manuscript to read, but he did not respond in any way to the sections Machiavelli sent. So Machiavelli began investigating different ways of communicating with the Medici princes. What his letter of December 10, 1513, makes clear is that he was never simply or solely seeking employment. As he stated in the dedications to all his prose works, he thought that he had important knowledge to convey. In seeking employment with the Medici he was not merely trying to find a more adequate source of economic support for himself and his family. He knew that they distrusted him, but he thought that he could benefit them and the people of Florence, if not all of Italy (and perhaps even Europe), by teaching them (as well as his other readers) how to become better rulers. In his own writings (and the rationales he provided for them) he thus exemplified some of the central tenets of his political philosophy. As individuals, human beings are weak. We need to acquire both goods and associates in order to survive. This natural, necessity-based desire to acquire puts human beings into competition with one another. As a result, some human beings get together to form political communities in order to protect themselves from the aggression of others. Once those political communities are formed, however, some members wish to command and oppress the others who do not wish to be commanded or oppressed. Most often, the conflict between these two "humors" results in either tyranny or license; but, Machiavelli argues, the conflict can produce benefits for both, *if* those who wish to command learn that the best way for them to maintain their authority is to secure the lives, families, and properties of the others.

66. Responding to Vettori's initial invitation to visit him in Rome, Machiavelli assured his friend that "if these new masters of ours see fit not to leave me lying on the ground, I shall be happy and believe that I shall act in such a way that they too will have reason to be proud of me. And if they should not, I shall get on as I did when I came here: I was born in poverty and at an early age learned how to scrimp rather than to thrive" (letter of March 18, 1513, *Machiavelli and His Friends*, 222).

Indeed, these "princes" will acquire more for themselves as well as for their people if they establish institutions and laws that not merely encourage their subjects to procreate and produce by securing the fruits of their labor, but give everyone an incentive to work for the benefit of the public by making everyone eligible for the highest offices on the basis of merit rather than heredity or wealth. A man like Machiavelli, born into modest, if not humble circumstances, would have fared better in the democratic republic he sought to persuade his readers to found than in the oligarchical republic he was forced by circumstances to try to improve. As he saw it, his self-interest and the public interest were perfectly consistent.[67]

67. In "'The Discourses,' and Machiavelli's Last Days," *Machiavelli Researches* 9, no. 1 (1967): 79–107, Cecil H. Clough states that "one of the weaknesses of the Renaissance tracts and treatises on politics, especially the Florentine ones, is that the authors could not detach themselves from the political scene. The solution that each one presents often tended to further the personal and family interest of its author" (87). Although he explicitly wrote about his need to acquire employment, I am arguing that Machiavelli had a much broader and more magnificent understanding of his "self-interest." He aspired to reform the way in which people thought about politics and thus their practice. In doing so, he could and would benefit them much more than he would benefit himself. Consistent with his principles, he presented himself as acting for his own benefit and thus dissimulated the grandeur of his own ambition in order to obtain the cooperation of others.

PART I

Machiavelli's Comprehensive Treatises

1

Machiavelli's New Approach to the Study and Practice of Politics

THE PRINCE

Few works of political philosophy have been so often or so variously read as Machiavelli's *Prince.* Failing to discern the underlying argument that ties together the apparently disparate topics he takes up, many commentators have emphasized the importance of one aspect or part.[1] By bringing out the argument that culminates in Machiavelli's passionate call for the Medici prince and pope to free Italy from the barbarians, I show that in *The Prince* Machiavelli presents an entirely new approach to the study and practice of politics.

The Dedication: Teaching or Testing Lorenzo

All the remaining manuscript copies of *De principatibus* have the dedication to "the magnificent Lorenzo de' Medici" attached. We do not know whether Machiavelli ever actually presented a copy of his little book to Lorenzo.[2] But whether Machiavelli actually presented his little book to the

1. Opposing this tendency, Strauss, *TM*, 55–64, gives a brief account of the organization of the treatise. Ardito, *Machiavelli and the Modern State*, 39, suggests that the work has a "basic structure," which differs a bit from the order of the argument traced by Strauss, but she chooses to concentrate on a set of chapters related to her theme.

2. William J. Connell, "Dating *The Prince:* Beginnings and Endings," *Review of Politics* 75, no. 4 (2013): 497–514, thinks that he can date the final version of *The Prince* and a meeting between Machiavelli and Lorenzo on the basis of three recently found documents from July 3, 1515. These documents show that Machiavelli made a very disadvantageous agreement to lease the castle at Montespertoli to Prior Battista and his two sons at no cost beyond two pounds of white wax in exchange for the assignment of the ill-paying benefice of the church at Sant' Andrea in Percussina to his brother Totto. Connell argues that Machiavelli would not have agreed to the exchange if

prince or not, he apparently wanted it to be read as if he were giving it to a Medici prince for the purpose of gaining employment.

At the beginning of the letter of dedication, Machiavelli emphasizes the unusual character of his gift. "It is customary . . . for those who desire to acquire favor with a Prince to come to meet him with things that they care most about in their own possessions or with things that they see please him most" (3). But Machiavelli clearly is not giving Lorenzo what he has seen please the prince. (Hence the anecdote about Lorenzo's liking the dogs he was given by another man much more than the book.) Machiavelli is giving Lorenzo what in his own possessions *he* cares most about; rather than trying to please the prince, Machiavelli is acting on the basis of his own understanding of what is important. And that is "the knowledge of the actions of great men, learned by me from long experience with modern things and a continuous reading of ancient ones" (3).

---

he and his brother had not felt themselves to be in dire economic straits. Machiavelli's letters to his nephew Giovanni Vernacci in August and November show that by that time he despaired of receiving any help beyond what his family and friends could offer. "Earlier in 1515, on 31 January Niccolò had been ecstatic about what seemed a likely appointment with Giuliano de' Medici [to whom Machiavelli had originally planned to dedicate *De principatibus*, according to his famous letter to Vettori of December 10, 1513], thanks to some assistance from Francesco Vettori's brother Paolo" (504). No one knows whether Machiavelli knew of the February 14, 1515, letter from Piero Ardinghelli to Giuliano de' Medici forwarding instructions from Cardinal Giulio de' Medici not to employ Machiavelli. (The relevant part of his letter is quoted in *Machiavelli and His Friends*, 529.) Connell thinks that the fact that Machiavelli dedicated his little treatise to Lorenzo indicates that he somehow found out that he could no longer hope for any assistance from Giuliano. Although Connell generally accepts Gennaro Sasso and Giorgio Inglese's contention that *The Prince* is "a tightly unified and coherent work completed in its entirety by the summer of 1514" (508), he notes that there is evidence of Machiavelli's making a few minor revisions later. As Robert Black, "Notes on the Date and Genesis of Machiavelli's *De principatibus*," in *Europa e Italia: Studi in onore di Giorgio Chittolini* (Florence: Firenze University Press, 2011), 33–34, points out, the last date explicitly referred to in *The Prince* is the death of Louis XII that occurred the night of December 31, 1514, and January 1, 1515. And as Carlo Dionisotti, "Machiavelleria ultima," *Rivista storica italiana*, no. 107 (1995): 22–23, argues, if Machiavelli had mentioned the decisive French victory at Marignano of September 12–13, 1515, his concluding exhortation to liberate Italy from the barbarians would have appeared ridiculous. Connell credits the anecdote related by Riccardo Riccardi in the late sixteenth century that Machiavelli presented his treatise to the young prince (who preferred the gift of two braces of greyhounds from another), and suggests that the most likely time for such a presentation to have occurred was after Lorenzo's return to Florence, in the company of Francesco Vettori, on May 15, 1515. Machiavelli's hopes of employment by the Medici having then been disappointed, he fell back in July on the meager resources left him by his family and friends. Doubting the authenticity of the anecdote, written down sixty-five years after the event, with no contemporary corroboration and echoing suggestions made in the dedication itself, other scholars think that Machiavelli probably changed the dedication after Giuliano's death on March 17, 1516. The anecdote was first published in Edoardo Alvisi, ed., *Lettere familiari* (Florence: Sansoni, 1883), xiv, and is translated from the Italian and reprinted in William J. Connell, *"The Prince" by Niccolò Machiavelli with Related Documents* (Boston: Bedford/St. Martin's, 2005), 142.

Machiavelli demonstrates that knowledge not by cravenly trying to please the prince, but by recognizing the demands on a prince's time and attention: he has reduced his thoughts and examinations of the deeds of great men to one small volume so that the prince will be able to peruse it in a short time.[3] In one of his several clearly ironical (dissimulating) protestations in this letter, Machiavelli "judges this work undeserving" of the prince's attention, but appeals to his "humanity." That "humanity" first appears to consist in Lorenzo's accepting the book out of a kind of charity or pity, because he understands that Machiavelli's gift of his knowledge is the greatest gift the poor ex-magistrate is able to present. However, Machiavelli goes on to state that Lorenzo could receive "no greater gift" than "the capacity to be able to understand in a very short time all that I learned in many years with so many hardships and dangers" (4). Machiavelli thus claims, in effect, to know what Lorenzo does not yet but needs to understand in order to be an effective ruler. Rather than a form of generosity, the prince's "humanity" appears to consist in a willingness to concede his own ignorance by learning from another. Having made this very bold claim in the guise of a suppliant, Machiavelli again emphasizes the unusual form of his gift and the fact that he has not ornamented it as is customary: he does not want it to be honored or to please for anything but the variety of the "matter" and gravity of the subject.[4]

Machiavelli recognizes that he may seem presumptuous in claiming to know the business of a prince better than the prince himself, but to excuse himself he offers a metaphor: Just as those who sketch landscapes have to place themselves below the mountains to consider the nature of the mountains, i.e., to see the way they tower over and above, and to place themselves on the mountains, conversely, to consider the nature of the plains, i.e., how much flatter, broader, lower, but more fertile they are, so "to know well the nature of peoples one needs to be prince" (to look down from on high), and "to know well the nature of princes one needs to be of the people" (to look up). What, we might ask, are the people able to see about a prince from below that he is not able to see so clearly about himself? The answer would seem to be, the quality of his deeds as prince. Is he ruling well and

3. As we observed earlier, however, in his December 10, 1513, letter to Vettori Machiavelli suggested that he had written down his thoughts for his own sake, because, as Dante observed, understanding without retention does not constitute knowledge. In other words, the little treatise was not written first or foremost for the sake of the prince.

4. Like Benner, *Prince*, I think that Machiavelli's text is ironic. However, I do not locate that irony primarily in "coded words." Nor do I think that Machiavelli consistently undermines the apparent meaning of his text—particularly with regard to the need to use not merely arms, but "cruelty" upon occasion, and the exemplary status of the to be sure somewhat myth-shrouded founders.

so benefiting the people, or is he failing to keep order and actively oppressing them? The people are in a position to know the effects of a prince's rule better than he.[5] What the prince sees about the nature of the people from his high position is that they are fearful and that they will, therefore, obey his commands (if and when those commands are backed by force). In *P* 18 Machiavelli observes that people do not see a prince well from their lowly station and can, therefore, easily be deceived by what he says are the reasons for his actions, although they cannot be so easily deceived about the effects of his acts. Machiavelli indicates in this brief introductory dedication, however, that he is able to see things from both perspectives. He is a member of the people who knows what a prince needs to learn.[6]

Observers see things differently from different positions, but Machiavelli makes clear in the last paragraph of his dedication that the position from which they view others (i.e., whether they are a prince or a member of the populace) is a matter not of nature or of desert, but of fortune (which, of course, includes the accident of birth into a given family). Even though his book is short, Machiavelli suggests that Lorenzo will have to read it diligently if he is to "arrive at the greatness" that Machiavelli desires for him and "that fortune and your other qualities promise." The contents of Machiavelli's little treatise are not so easily understood or quickly mastered as he first suggested; Lorenzo will probably need help. Machiavelli concludes by observing that if Lorenzo looks down from the summit of his height to these low places, he will learn how undeservedly Machiavelli endures a great and continuous malignity of fortune. That malignity of fortune, to which Machiavelli refers repeatedly in his letters, is his exclusion from public office. It consists not merely in his poverty and the contempt that poverty will bring him, but in his lack of opportunity to demonstrate the utility of the knowledge he claims to possess by advising someone who has the power to put it into practice.

In the last chapter of *The Prince* Machiavelli explicitly states that the "greatness" he desires for Lorenzo is for Lorenzo to become conqueror and

5. Althusser, *Machiavelli and Us*, observes that "Machiavelli does not hesitate to declare that 'one needs to be . . . a man of the people to understand properly the character of rulers'—hence, not to be a ruler. This means not only that rulers are incapable of knowing themselves, but that *there can be no knowledge of rulers except from the viewpoint of the people*" (24). But, Althusser adds, although "Machiavelli adopts the viewpoint of the people" and "the Prince who is assigned the mission of unifying the Italian nation must become a *popular Prince*, he is not himself the *people*. . . . [T]here is an irreducible duality" (26).

6. *TM*, 77; Kahn, *Machiavellian Rhetoric*, 20.

thus savior of Italy by freeing her from domination by "the barbarians."[7] Machiavelli explains that Lorenzo has an opportunity to become the redeemer of his nation not only because her people, now suffering from the depredations of foreign powers, will follow a leader who promises to liberate them, but also because he has the good fortune of being a member of the family that also controls the Church. Even more and better than Ferdinand of Spain (*P* 21), Lorenzo will thus be able not only to fund his wars of "liberation" with the help of the pope but also to justify or cloak his conquests in the name of religion. The "other qualities" that added to the promise of Lorenzo's greatness probably included his military tastes and ambitions.[8] By 1515 he had become the virtual ruler of Florence; he was elected captain general in May. His uncle Giuliano, to whom Machiavelli initially planned to present his treatise, died on March 17, 1516, but Lorenzo continued to show his ambition to rule. He was made duke of Urbino through papal investiture in October 1516. However, as early as February–March 1514, Machiavelli had written to Vettori:

> everyone is beginning to recognize in [Lorenzo] the beloved memory of his grandfather because His Magnificence is diligent in his work, generous and agreeable during an audience, deliberate and serious in his replies. His way of conversing is . . . [such] that people attribute no pride to it; nor does he mingle too familiarly so that he generates too low a reputation for

7. Ardito, *Machiavelli and the Modern State*, 29, also notes this connection. There has been a great deal of scholarly controversy about the status of *P* 26. Contrary to commentators (e.g., Hans Baron, "The *Principe* and the puzzle of the date of chapter 26," *Journal of Medieval and Renaissance Studies* 21, no. 1 [Spring 1991]: 83–102), who argue that the last chapter must have been a later addition, because its fervid patriotism is so different from the cold analysis of the preceding twenty-five chapters, I thus see the conclusion of *The Prince* forecast in the dedication. In his edition of *Il Principe e Discorsi sopra la prima deca di Tito Livio*, Sergio Bertelli suggests that chapter 26 was added along with the dedication to Lorenzo between September 1515 and September 1516. Because Machiavelli explicitly refers in chapter 26 to three of the four founders he treats in chapter 6, M. Martelli, "Da Poliziano a Machiavelli. Sull-epigramma 'dell-Occasione' e sull'occasione," *Interpres* 2 (1979): 230–54, argues that both chapters were added in a second edition in 1518. In different ways and for different reasons both these commentators thus admit that chapter 26 is integrated into the text we have. Strauss, *TM*, 21, argues that the last chapter is the "natural conclusion of the book." Because it is presented as a specific piece of advice to Lorenzo, however, "it is silent about the difficulties in the way." Claiming to disagree with Strauss, but seeming to underline his point, Maurizio Viroli, *Redeeming "The Prince": The Meaning of Machiavelli's Masterpiece* (Princeton: Princeton University Press, 2014), contends "that the 'Exhortation' *is* a fine piece of political rhetoric that ends an oration whose purpose is to impel action. . . . To motivate a new prince to be a redeemer, Machiavelli must depict the whole enterprise as not only possible but also easy" (5).

8. In this respect Lorenzo was more to Machiavelli's taste than his uncle Giuliano, who preferred staying at court in Rome to going into the field or the fray of politics. See Ridolfi, *Life*, 163–64.

> himself. . . . In sum, he makes himself both loved and revered rather than feared. . . . In his palace there is great magnificence and liberality, yet he does not stray from decent living. So that in all his activities . . . nobody is aware of anything offensive or reprehensible.[9]

Machiavelli might merely have been trying to seek favor with a Medici by praising him to a mutual friend and potential go-between. The "qualities" for which Machiavelli praises Lorenzo in this letter are not exactly those he recommends in *The Prince*. They might be close enough, however, to indicate an inclination on Lorenzo's part to want to act and be perceived as a "prince" and so a willingness to learn how to do so effectively from Machiavelli.

If, as Machiavelli argues in chapter 22, "there are three kinds of brains: one that understands by itself, another that discerns what others understand, the third that understands neither by itself nor through others," in giving Lorenzo *The Prince*, Machiavelli was presenting him with a test.[10] If Lorenzo recognized good counsel when he received it, he would prove himself to be prudent. If he did not perceive the wisdom of Machiavelli's advice and offer him a position, Lorenzo would show that he was not able to understand things either on his own or with the help of others.[11]

I. The Classification of Principalities—and the Foundations of Political Order

In *Discourses* 1.25 Machiavelli observes, "if someone who desires to reform a state in a city wishes it to be accepted and capable of being maintained to the satisfaction of everyone, he is under the necessity of retaining at least the shadow of its ancient modes so that it may not appear to the peoples to have changed its order even if in fact the new orders are altogether alien to the past ones" (60). And in presenting his educational treatise for a prince, Machiavelli seems to have retained bits of the outer appearance of the existing genre (as, for example, in Erasmus's *The Education of a Christian*

9. *Machiavelli and His Friends*, 283.

10. Even if Machiavelli did not actually present his little work to Lorenzo, the friends to whom he showed the manuscript could still admire his bold presumption in telling the prince what he should do.

11. Peter Schröder, "Die Kunst der Staatserhaltung (Widmung und Kapitel 1–3)," in Höffe, *Niccolò Machiavelli "Der Fürst,"* 19–21, also notes both the irony of Machiavelli's dedication and the way in which it points to the conclusion of *The Prince* in chapter 26.

Prince): Latin chapter titles and an initial dry, almost scholastic classification of types.[12]

Despite its classical cover, however, Machiavelli's classification was, in fact, revolutionary, beginning with the very first sentence: "All states, all dominions that have held and do hold empire over men have been and are either republics or principalities" (5). Whereas previous authors had categorized governments or regimes according to the number of rulers, whether they ruled for the sake of the community as a whole or their own advantage, and whether or not the government was restrained by law, Machiavelli began by dividing "states" or "dominions" simply according to the number of rulers, into republics or principalities.[13] Commentators like Benedetto Croce have taken this first division to show that Machiavelli was the first "value-free" political scientist, because he did not categorize governments as good or bad, just or unjust. However, since Machiavelli goes on to make a great many "value judgments" in *The Prince*, his analysis cannot accurately be described as value-free. Machiavelli drops the traditional distinction between governments that serve the common good and those that serve the good of the ruler(s), because he observes that human beings never act simply or solely for the sake of others. The differences among governments cannot, therefore, be attributed to differences in motive or purpose on the part of the rulers. Individuals may sacrifice their lives or their fortunes for the sake of others, but in doing so they are seeking another kind of compensation—honor or glory. Rulers may—indeed, Machiavelli will argue that they should—seek to benefit their people. But he suggests that

12. Introducing *"The Prince" by Niccolò Machiavelli with Related Documents*, Connell notes, "the initial part of the dedication appears to be modeled on the opening of a speech by Isocrates, *To Nicocles*, 1–2" (39n). But, as Robert Hariman, "Composing Modernity in Machiavelli's *Prince*," *Journal of the History of Ideas* 50, no. 1 (January 1989): 3–29, argues, not only in the dedication, but also in the treatise as a whole, Machiavelli explicitly reverses the rhetorician's valuation of speeches over deeds. Allan H. Gilbert, *Machiavelli's* Prince *and Its Forerunners:* The Prince *as a Typical Book* de Regimine Principum (Durham, NC: Duke University Press, 1938), details the common characteristics of such books and the way *The Prince* shares them; Felix Gilbert, "The Humanist Concept of the Prince and *The Prince* of Machiavelli," *Journal of Modern History* 11 (1939): 449–83, highlights the differences. So does Viroli, *Redeeming "The Prince,"* 9–10. As Quentin Skinner, *Foundations of Modern Political Thought* (Cambridge: Cambridge University Press, 1978), 1: 113–38, points out, the revolutionary meaning of Machiavelli's treatise is to be found in his direct attack on the humanist and Christian tenet that a prince, if he wishes to preserve his state and attain perennial glory, must at all times exemplify the Aristotelian virtues of justice, magnanimity, courage, prudence, and moderation as well as the Christian virtues of mercy, charity, and honesty.

13. E.g., Plato, *Statesman* 291d–303c; Aristotle, *Politics* 1279a23–1279b10; Polybius, VI. That Machiavelli knew about the traditional categorization is evident from *Discourses* 1.2. Although the account of the cycle of regimes there is often attributed to Machiavelli himself, he explicitly attributes it to "some who have written on republics."

rulers will most reliably do so if they think that defending their people and contributing to their greater prosperity will keep them in power, if not make them revered.

Machiavelli's refusal to classify governments as just or unjust does not explain why he reduces the classification apparently on the basis of number to only two types of command rather than the traditional three (one, few, or many). Does the "republican" Machiavelli not see a fundamental difference between the rule of a few in aristocracies or oligarchies and the rule of the majority or many in democracies? In chapter 9 he says that the desires of the many are more decent (*onesto*) than those of the great. But, as we have already seen, Machiavelli does not distinguish governments on the basis of their decency or desire to dominate (which would be versions of just and unjust).[14] In *The Prince* Machiavelli gradually shows not only that it is in the interest of the "prince" to seek the support of the people, but also that the people are never safe and secure without an effective leader or "prince."[15] As his explicit denomination of leaders of republics as "princes" in both the *Discourses* and his *Florentine Histories* indicates, Machiavelli thinks that all peoples need leaders to establish and maintain "law and order."[16] The fun-

14. Nor does he distinguish between regimes on the basis of whether they are law-abiding or not, because, as he famously observes in *P* 12, where there are not good arms, there are not good laws. There will not be laws at all, in fact, because laws have to be enforced. In chapter 10 Machiavelli thus suggests that the measure of strength of a prince is whether he can field an army to defend his city or not.

15. As Strauss notes, the meaning of "prince" is ambiguous. It "may mean a non-tyrannical monarch, or any monarch, or any man or body of men in a ruling position including the leading men in a republic" (*TM*, 47). Wootton, introduction to Niccolò Machiavelli, *The Prince*, observes that "by *principe* Machiavelli never means a king's son. His term usually means 'rule' . . . , and a *principato* is any system of government where power is concentrated in the hands of one man (e.g., monarchy, tyranny). But Machiavelli sometimes uses the word to mean 'leader,' so the general of an army can be *un principe*, as can an elected official in a republic; and he also occasionally calls the Medici, who held no official position in Florence, but for long periods of time effectively controlled its policies, 'princes,' meaning 'de facto rulers'" (xxviii).

16. E.g., *Discourses* 1.20, 1.52; *FH* 4.1. There was a precedent for such usage. Leo Paul de Alvarez, *The Machiavellian Enterprise: A Commentary on "The Prince"* (DeKalb: Northern Illinois University Press, 1999), suggests that the title of *De principatibus* was intended to remind readers "of the Roman principate. Augustus Caesar refused the title of dictator, which Julius Caesar had adopted, preferring instead the title of *princeps*, with its strong republican associations. The *princeps senatus* was a title designating the senior member of the senate, whose name appeared first in the roll of members. . . . The significance of the title is that Augustus wished to preserve republican form. What he established was not a *dominatio* but a *principatus*, hence a principate" (9). Just as Augustus cloaked his transformation of the republic into an empire by using an old title, so Machiavelli cloaked the revolutionary character of the new education he is providing to "princes" with his Latin title and chapter headings. Augustus did not fool many, if any, observers, however; nor, we suppose, did Machiavelli think that he would. He is a playful author. The fusion

damental question or characteristic that distinguishes "principalities" from "republics" thus proves not to be whether the first have "princes" and the second do not, but whether or not potential "princes" have to compete with each other for popular support.[17]

Having drawn the basic distinction between principalities and republics, Machiavelli proceeds to discuss the six types of principalities he lists in *P* 1.[18] The "types" are distinguished primarily by the way in which they are acquired and secondarily by the characteristics of the peoples acquired—specifically, whether the people in question is accustomed to living under a prince or under its own laws in a republic—because these characteristics make any given territory more or less difficult to acquire and retain. The first distinction between hereditary principalities "in which the bloodline of their lord has been their prince for a long time" (5) and new principalities might appear to be temporal, simply between the old and the new, or between established (and hence presumably legitimate) and "upstart" (hence questionable) governments. For Machiavelli, however, heredity is a mode of acquisition.[19] His typology embodies the general principle he announces in chapter 3: "Truly it is a very natural and ordinary thing to desire

---

or confusion of titles does nevertheless point to greater closeness between the two types of governments than might first appear.

17. In *D* 1.20, Machiavelli observes that "through the mode of electing [a republic] has not only two in succession but infinite most virtuous princes who are successors to one another" (54). And in *D* 1.52, Machiavelli says of the opponents of Cosimo de' Medici that "if those citizens who vied with him had taken his style of favoring the people, they would have come without tumult and without violence to take out of his hands those arms of which he most availed himself" (52). In contrast to his discussion of all other modes of acquiring rule in his book devoted explicitly to "principalities" (because he has discussed "republics" at length on another occasion), Machiavelli does not give particular examples in the chapter devoted to "civil principalities" in which princes acquire power through the favor of their fellow citizens. If he had, it would have become clear that he was talking about "republics" rather than "principalities"—or, more generally, that at this point, the distinction between the two kinds of regimes breaks down.

18. He will not reason about republics, he explains at the beginning of chapter 2, because he has discussed them at length on another occasion. Most scholars take this to be a reference to the *Discourses* and conclude that Machiavelli must have begun writing them at approximately the same time he did the *Prince*. However, as Benner, *Prince*, 23, notes, Machiavelli does discuss republics, at least in passing, in subsequent chapters, beginning in *P* 3. Wootton, introduction to Niccolò Machiavelli, *The Prince*, tendentiously maintains that the discussion refers to "the one that took place as he dangled at the end of a rope in the city jail. What were his interrogators interested in, if not his attitude to republics, and his commitment to the republican cause?" One might answer that rhetorical question by responding that their immediate concern was whether there was a conspiracy to unseat the Medici, and if so, who was taking part and how they planned to proceed.

19. As Machiavelli says explicitly about Cesare Borgia in *P* 7, who one's father is is ultimately a matter of chance or fortune. That the son of any given father or "line" should inherit the position is, however, a matter of custom or law.

to acquire, and always, when men do it who can, they will be praised or not blamed; but when they cannot and wish to do it anyway, here lies the error and the blame" (14–15). Recognizing that princes will be praised as such only if they retain what they have acquired, in the discussion of the types of principalities that follows Machiavelli combines considerations of how they are acquired with considerations of the relative ease or difficulty of maintaining rule once attained.

Not all ways of acquiring rule are equally onerous. Indeed, it is so easy for a person who is born first in line to inherit that Machiavelli does not even comment on the way hereditary principalities are acquired other than to describe the basis: the blood (or bloodline) of the prince. Instead he emphasizes that "the difficulties in maintaining them are much less than in new states, because it is enough only not to depart from the order of his ancestors, and then to temporize in the face of accidents" (6). An heir to an established line has less reason to "offend," i.e., to injure, his subjects by seizing their property or lives than a new prince, who has to seize and then maintain his rule. So, Machiavelli reasons, "if extraordinary vices do not make him hated, it is reasonable that he will have the good will of his own [subjects]" (7). As we see in *Discourses* 1.2, Machiavelli knew that previous writers had emphasized the way in which hereditary leaders tended to become corrupt, hated, and eventually overthrown. He might well have thought the tendency of those who are born princes to succumb to the temptation of believing that they can do whatever they please and so arouse the hatred of their subjects to be ordinary. He merely observes that a hereditary prince will have little difficulty maintaining his rule if he employs "ordinary industry." So long as "the antiquity and continuity of his dominion extinguishes the memories of revolutions and the reasons for them," he will be deprived of rule only by "an extraordinary and excessive force" (7). Machiavelli thus recasts what was traditionally considered to be a matter of morality or corruption as a question of the prince's diligence and his subjects' memories.

Because people accept what they see around them as "natural" if they have no memory that things used to be different, Machiavelli starts with a consideration of the established, hereditary, or "natural" prince. But he soon begins to take up the reasons for change (and thus the difficulties of both acquiring and maintaining rule) in chapter 3. He observes that the reasons for change become evident in a new principality, but he moves to a consideration of wholly new principalities only in stages. By first considering the "mixed principalities" that result from the acquisition of a new territory by an established prince, he reminds his readers that whatever its current character, all rule has its basis in acquisition.

A prince's control of his new dominion is uncertain as a result of "a natural difficulty that exists in all new principalities. This is that men willingly change their lords in the belief that they fare better" (7–8). In the guise merely of distinguishing the various types of principalities, Machiavelli thus reminds his readers that human beings are not naturally satisfied with their current condition and are inclined, as a result of their perpetual dissatisfaction, to seek change. But, he contends, such men are deceived in the belief that they will improve their condition by changing masters (or rebelling). The reason is "another natural and ordinary necessity that requires that one must always offend those over whom he becomes a new prince, both with men-at-arms and with the infinite other injuries that a new acquisition brings in its wake" (8). A new prince will have as enemies all those he displaced in occupying that principality, and he cannot maintain as friends those who helped put him there, because he will not be able to satisfy them in the way they hoped.

The most obvious form of the necessity that a prince will harm the people of a province he seizes is that he has to use force to take it. The prince or people who have been in charge will not willingly cede their power to him. In order to maintain his rule, Machiavelli thus insists, a new prince has to eliminate the bloodline of the old.[20] If he does not, some of them will almost surely conspire to unseat him. But if the states that are added to the old state of the acquiring prince are "of the same province and the same language," Machiavelli assures his reader, "they may be held with great ease, especially when they are not used to living in freedom" (9). The new prince should simply eliminate the bloodline of the old rulers and, Machiavelli now adds, not alter the laws or taxes. In that case, his new subjects will hardly notice the change in government.[21] Nor will they be given new reasons to rebel. Contrary to Machiavelli's initial statement, it does not

20. Nathan Tarcov, "Machiavelli and the Foundations of Modernity: A Reading of Chapter 3 of *The Prince*," *Educating the Prince*, ed. Mark Blitz and William Kristol (Lanham, MD: Rowman & Littlefield, 2000), points out: "Machiavelli neither mentions an obligation not to murder innocent children (as he did with the obligation not to use strong medicines against one's friends) nor explains why it should not be regarded as a difficulty" (32). Presumably a prince, driven by "necessity," has no moral qualms, and his victims are few and weak.

21. As Benner, *Prince*, 37, observes, this is a very important addition. Machiavelli's restatement of what is required to take and hold a province with the same customs and language here is a prime example of the way in which he often exaggerates (or simplifies) in a first statement to catch the eye of a reader, but then qualifies that first statement in important ways later.

require "infinite other injuries" to take over a state, *if* one keeps everything the same except for the person occupying the highest office.[22] People do not care so much about who is in charge as about the effects of that person's rule on their own lives.

Machiavelli forthrightly admits that it requires "great fortune and great industry" to acquire and maintain rule in places with different languages, customs, and orders. The first thing Machiavelli suggests a new prince should do under such circumstances is to go and live in his new province, "as the Turk has done in Greece" (10). If a prince is living on site, he can spot problems as they arise rather than having to wait for reports from others. Moreover, his subjects will believe that they can appeal to him to control his own officers, and those who would offend against him and his laws will be more afraid of being apprehended. But, Machiavelli urges, if a prince cannot go to live there himself, he should send colonies rather than try to occupy the province he has annexed with an army.[23] Colonists support themselves, whereas the prince has to pay and supply his armies; and he will have to offend fewer of the current inhabitants of a province (and so make them enemies) by seizing their land for his colonists to occupy.[24]

Since a prince can lose control of a province to an external power as well as to internal rebels, Machiavelli also advises the new prince to make himself leader and defender of the weaker powers in the neighborhood, partly as a way of discouraging them from inviting another power, greater than his, in to defend them.[25] Because Machiavelli earlier said that he was not going to reason about republics, a reader might be surprised to see that he uses the Roman republic as the example of the imperial policies he advocates. Machiavelli began his classification of states or empires by asserting that there were only two kinds—principalities and republics. States and empires, he now suggests, both experience the same needs and have the

22. As Harvey C. Mansfield, *Machiavelli's Virtue* (Chicago: University of Chicago Press, 1996), 289, points out, Machiavelli treats the "state" as the possession of a prince, not an impersonal entity as in later modern political thought.

23. Indeed, as Benner, *Prince*, 39, notes, he states that colonies are a "better" (*migliore*) remedy.

24. In contrast to the Medici policy of using their wealth to hire foreign soldiers and erect magnificent public displays, early in *The Prince* Machiavelli begins to urge the prince to take account of economic as well as strictly military and political considerations by minimizing his expenses.

25. Machiavelli delivered this advice to Louis in person, according to his letter to "The Ten of Liberty and Peace," from Tours, November, 21, 1500, *The Historical, Political, and Diplomatic Writings of Niccolo Machiavelli*, trans. Christian E. Detmold (Boston: Houghton, Mifflin, 1891), 3: 133.

same requirements for controlling their subject populations. Because the new acquisition was, until it was acquired, a foreign power, in a "mixed principality" domestic and foreign policy coincide.

Machiavelli contrasts the success the Roman republic had in annexing Greece with King Louis XII's failure to conquer and occupy northern Italy. A reader might again be surprised to see Machiavelli, in effect, telling a foreign prince what to do in order to seize and occupy Italy. However, at the conclusion of *The Prince*, Machiavelli calls upon Lorenzo to do precisely what he has argued the foreign prince should have done. In this chapter, we might understand Machiavelli to be showing his chief purported reader what he needs to do in order to realize the greatness Machiavelli desires for him.[26]

Louis failed to seize and occupy Italy, Machiavelli first says, because he committed five errors: he eliminated rather than befriended the small powers; he enhanced the power of a neighbor (Pope Alexander VI or the Church); he brought in another foreign power (Spain in order to take Naples); he did not come to live there in person; and he did not send colonies. But Machiavelli then adds that the mistake that forced Louis to withdraw from Italy entirely was his destroying Venice, the last remaining check on the other great powers' ambitions in Lombardy.[27] Machiavelli characteristically does not fault the French king for having turned against the allies who first invited him to come into Italy; he also recognizes that the first two "errors" for which he blames Louis resulted from the king's abiding by a promise he had made to the pope. He refers his reader to *P* 18 where he argues that a prince can always find reasons to excuse himself from abiding by a promise. According to Machiavelli, it seems, a prince should not fear divine retribution for breaking an oath—at least, if he wants to retain his position as prince. (In *P* 18 he explicitly argues that a prince must always appear, but only appear, to be religious.)

26. *TM*, 65–67.

27. Tarcov, "Machiavelli and the Foundations of Modernity," points out that Machiavelli thus blames Louis for having followed one of his "rules," i.e., to weaken rather than strengthen other powers in the neighborhood. He also excuses the Venetians for inviting another power into Lombardy (against his rule) by noting that it is natural to desire to acquire. *Pace* commentators like Michael Oakeshott, *Rationalism in Politics and Other Essays* (Indianapolis, IN: Liberty Fund Press, 1991), 6–42, who take Machiavelli to be presenting a technical manual containing the "rules of ruling," Tarcov comments: "Readers see that one cannot simply follow Machiavelli's 'rules'—they are literally made to be broken. He gives his readers practice in breaking his own rules to prepare them for breaking other rules when necessary. The prudence Machiavelli praises is not the following of rules, even his own" (37).

Machiavelli concludes his discussion of "mixed principalities" by reporting that after the cardinal of Rouen told him that the Italians did not understand war, he told the cardinal that "the French did not understand the state, because if they understood, they would not have let the Church come to such greatness" (16). In reporting this exchange, Machiavelli points to a difference between the ancient Roman republic he has used as a model of correct policy and the modern European prince to whom he is purportedly writing. Unlike the Roman republic, modern European princes have to deal with an independent power that claims a right to determine what is according to divine will and what is not. And as we are reminded by Louis's promise to lend the pope troops in exchange for the pope's granting the king a divorce, such determinations reached the basis or purported grounds of the legitimacy of the European monarchs.[28] No one can legally inherit a principality from a father to whom his mother is not legally wed. Two big questions thus arise: If Lorenzo or any other modern European prince is to follow the example of the Romans in expanding his empire in Italy, will he have to destroy the independence of the Vatican by going to live in Rome "in person" the way the Turk went to live in Greece? And if he does, will he have to impose the kind of absolute domination on his current subjects that the Turk exercises over his, so that he will not have to fear that his former subjects will revolt or conspire with a foreign power in his absence?[29]

Machiavelli takes up the example set by "the Turk" in the next chapter, where readers learn that the types of principalities differ not only in the way that they are acquired but also in the character of the people over whom rule is acquired. These differences are not matters of climate or economic enterprise, language, or culture, moreover; they are results of the previous form of government.

In his initial discussion of the ways in which a prince could acquire and maintain a "mixed principality," Machiavelli suggested that it would be

28. Tarcov, "Machiavelli and the Foundations of Modernity," points out that marriages constituted the basis of the "easy" incorporation of Burgundy, Brittany, Gascony, and Normandy into France. In striking contrast to the practices of his time, Machiavelli never suggests, in this chapter or elsewhere, that a prince should try to extend his realm by marriage, because he did not think that the promises of princes or divine punishment for the breaking of oaths provided a firm basis of acquisition. See *P* 18 and *D* 1.12–14.

29. In his *Florentine Histories* 1.9, Machiavelli traces the fall of the Roman Empire in the west to Diocletian's decision to move the seat of the empire from Rome to the east. Machiavelli was well aware of the reasons the pope had once moved the seat of the Church from Rome to Avignon as well as the divisions within the Church between popes and "antipopes" associated with this move. Machiavelli traces the political divisions within Italy that he is urging Lorenzo to overcome to the Church, not only in his *Florentine Histories* (written a decade later) but also in his *Discourses* 1.12.

easy to maintain control of a people who spoke the same language and shared the same customs. But in chapter 4 he withdraws that suggestion. The example he gave in chapter 3 of such an easy annexation was that of Burgundy, Brittany, Gascony, and Normandy by the French king. Purportedly to explain "why the kingdom of Darius which Alexander seized did not rebel from his successors after Alexander's death," in chapter 4 Machiavelli points out that "principalities of which memory remains have been governed in two diverse modes: either by one prince, and all the others servants . . . ; or by a prince and by barons who hold that rank not by favor of the lord but by antiquity of bloodline" (16–17). Examples of the two kinds of government are those of the Turk and the king of France. And "whoever considers the one and the other of these states will find difficulty in acquiring the state of the Turk, but should it be conquered, great ease in holding it. So inversely, you will find in some respects more ease in seizing the Kingdom of France, but great difficulty in holding it" (17–18).

The reason the "kingdom" of the Turk is difficult to seize but easy to keep once seized is that he has made everyone else his slave. Fearful for their lives if they disobey, the emperor's slaves are difficult to corrupt, and even if they are convinced to betray him, they cannot bring any other people with them.[30] One thus has to overcome the Turk with one's own forces in an open battle, rather than relying on the defection of some of his supporters. But if a prince defeats the Turk in an open battle, his servants will become the servants of the conqueror, because they are accustomed to following orders, not to ruling themselves.

In kingdoms ruled like France, where there are barons who have their own state and subjects, not as a grant from the king but on the basis of their own bloodline, there will always be some malcontent anxious to obtain the help of an external power in revolting. Such kingdoms are, therefore, easy to enter, but difficult to maintain. It is not sufficient to eliminate the bloodline of the prince, because the barons retain their independent forces and loyal subjects. And it is impossible to content or to eliminate all of them.

What is true of the independent barons is even more true of states that "are accustomed to live with their own laws and in liberty" (20). In chapter 5 Machiavelli explains that there are three ways of dealing with such cities: The first is to destroy them. The second is to go there in person to live. The third, which initially seems preferable, is to "let them live by their laws, taking

30. We here learn the reason that the Turk could safely leave his own country and go in person to live in the new as well as the reason the king of a province such as France could not do so.

tribute from them and creating within them an oligarchical state which keeps them friendly. For, since this state has been created by that prince, it knows that it cannot exist without his friendship and power, and it has to do everything to maintain him. And a city used to living free may be held more easily by means of its own citizens than in any other mode, if one wants to preserve it" (20). However, Machiavelli reminds his readers (again using republics as examples of "princely" foreign policy), the Spartans eventually lost Athens by using the third way. The Romans also tried to rule Greece in this manner, but found that "there is no secure mode to possess . . . a city accustomed to living in freedom" except to destroy it, because it always has a reason to rebel in "the name of liberty and its own ancient orders, which are never forgotten either through length of time or because of benefits received . . . unless the inhabitants are broken up or dispersed" (21).[31]

By the time readers come to the end of Machiavelli's discussion of "mixed principalities" (since the discussions of the relative ease of acquiring and then retaining possession of provinces ruled by different kinds of princes and republics constitute a subsection of that general discussion), they have thus acquired a great many fundamental lessons about the nature of political activity. First and foremost, Machiavelli has reminded them that human beings do not accept the government of others gladly or freely, certainly not if they have experienced freedom. In other words, government does not arise naturally or spontaneously. It rests, and presumably always will, ultimately on the ability of some to force others to obey. But not merely can human beings be forced to obey; they even can be brought to believe that the reigning government is natural, if and so long as they are not reminded of the causes of innovation. That cause, Machiavelli states in his description of "mixed principalities," is the natural desire to acquire. For if all human beings desire to acquire more than they currently have, they will obviously come into conflict with one another. This conflict may be most evident in the case of states, which fight wars to conquer others. But it

31. In chapter 4 of *Machiavelli and Empire* (Cambridge: Cambridge University Press, 2004), "To Destroy Them or to Live There," 113–31, Mikael Hörnqvist gives an expansive historical explanation of Machiavelli's one-sentence statement suggesting that the analysis he provides in this chapter could fruitfully be applied to the difficulties Florence experienced in holding Pisa. Although Florence had ruled Pisa for almost 100 years, the latter republic took the opportunity afforded by the French invasion in 1494 to rebel. During his time in the chancery Machiavelli was intimately involved in the politics and policies surrounding Florence's rule of the cities subject to it. He argued for, trained, and then led the militia that enabled Florence to retake Pisa in 1509. Machiavelli recognized that it was not politic to remind a Medici prince too much of his service to the republic.

is also the reason, Machiavelli shows in later chapters, that individuals need governments to secure their lives and property from others in their vicinity.

Both because government is not natural but has to be imposed, and because human beings tend to believe that what they see around them is natural and necessary and thus doubt that anything else is possible, Machiavelli declares in chapter 6 that "the greatest examples" of princes are those who found their states de novo. He does not expect Lorenzo or any other reader in a civilized time and place literally to reenact such a founding. It is not an accident that all his examples of such new princes are from a very distant, if not, strictly speaking, "mythical" past. Precisely because, as Machiavelli observed at the conclusion of chapter 2, men tend to forget the causes of innovation once order has been established, he has to remind his reader of how much virtue it requires, not merely to rise from a private position to become a prince (since that can also occur by mere fortune or chance), but to found a new nation. He names Moses, Cyrus, Romulus, and Theseus as the greatest examples. Recognizing that Moses might appear to be an exception, because he was directed by God, Machiavelli nevertheless points out that if one considers "Cyrus, and the others who have acquired or founded kingdoms: you will find . . . their particular actions and orders . . . no different from those of Moses" (22–23). In other words, Machiavelli is going to give a completely secular account of the origins of principalities, even though he knows (and explicitly recognizes in other works) that the founders he is about to celebrate claimed to have divine guidance, if not birth.[32]

Machiavelli insists that these founders did not get "anything from fortune other than opportunity, which gave them the matter enabling them to introduce any form they pleased" (23).[33] The "opportunity" or "matter"

32. Machiavelli begins his account of *The Life of Castruccio Castracani* by observing that "the greater part of those who have achieved outstanding things in this world . . . have been of humble birth . . . or else have suffered to an unusual degree from the travails of Fortune; all of them, indeed, have been exposed to wild beasts, or had such humble fathers that, feeling ashamed of them, they have made themselves out to be sons of Jupiter or some other god" (3). The examples to which he points in the birth story he fabricates for Castruccio are Moses (who was said to be found in the bulrushes) and Cyrus (who was said to have been raised by a dog). In *Discourses* 1.10, he reminds his readers that in founding Roman religion Numa claimed to have been instructed by a nymph.

33. If one were going to quibble, one might object that Cyrus and Theseus were both recognized to be sons of the previous ruler and so could claim a certain kind of good fortune. Machiavelli would no doubt respond that both had to seize rule with force from other claimants who opposed them. The same is true for Romulus (who had to seize power from his brother Remus as well as the king of Alba) and for Moses (who was opposed by both his adopted father the Pharaoh and his brother Aaron). Machiavelli is bringing out the common "necessities," while admitting the existence of differences in circumstances that prevent any individual from completely imitating

consists in an enslaved, discontented, or dispersed people.[34] Such people are willing to follow a self-proclaimed leader who promises to free or otherwise improve their condition, precisely because they are enslaved, discontented, or dispersed. Machiavelli's famed founders thus all appear in the guise of liberators.

The virtue of the founder is demonstrated by his ability to overcome the two different kinds of opposition he inevitably faces in attempting to establish a new order. First, there are the people who benefited from the old order and so oppose the introduction of a new. Second, those discontented with the current order who thus initially follow the new leader tend to fall away, partly from fear of the opposition, "who have the laws on their side." (Machiavelli thus acknowledges in passing that where there are enough human beings to reorganize, there must have been some previous form of organization. No one entirely begins from scratch; one has to destroy in order to build. And from the point of view of the old order, these "innovators" are criminals.) The followers of the introducer of new modes and orders also tend to fade away in the face of opposition, because of "the incredulity of men, who do not truly believe in new things unless they come to have a firm experience of them" (23–24). The founder of a new order thus has to use force not only to put down and replace those who benefit from the existing order but also to keep his own supporters in line.[35]

---

the deeds of any other. As all these examples show, Machiavelli does not follow Aristotle in thinking that political associations develop naturally (smoothly or peacefully) out of families. On the contrary, he emphasizes in *D* 3.2–5, political ambition often overcomes family affection and ties.

34. Machiavelli's use of the terms 'form' and 'matter' is intended, of course, to remind readers of the Aristotelian/Scholastic distinction that he is turning on its head by suggesting that human beings (hitherto thought to be members of a natural species) are merely "matter" to be formed not by God but by an earthly prince or series of princes. One can see here the "seed" of Martin Heidegger's discovery of the "truth of technology," i.e., that everything is potentially merely "standing reserve" to be formed or transformed at will. If, as Machiavelli insisted, "the prince acts in a world in which there are 'no prefigured meanings, no implicit teleology'" (as Sheldon Wolin, *Politics and Vision* [Boston: Little, Brown, 1960], 224, maintains), then all order is the product of human action rather than an a priori object of human cognition, as Kahn, *Machiavellian Rhetoric*, 18, suggests.

35. A dramatic example of Moses' use of force against former supporters can be seen in the way he (with God's help) put down the rebellion of Korah, Numbers 16:1–41. In *Discourses* 3.30 Machiavelli observes that Moses had to kill thousands. Benner, *Prince*, 82, misconstrues the meaning of this passage when she takes Machiavelli to be claiming simply and literally that human beings can be forced to believe. Machiavelli is writing specifically about the new prince's initial followers and what he must do when they or their "belief" wavers. If and when they question his authority, he must use force to make them act as if they believe in his new order, i.e., obey him, or destroy them.

Because the founders of new regimes have to use force against both the opposition and their own adherents, Machiavelli famously concludes that "all the armed prophets were victorious and the unarmed ones were ruined" (24). He points to Girolamo Savonarola as an example of the fate of an unarmed prophet and cites Hiero of Syracuse as a lesser example of the success of a private man who became a prince "in everything but name" by means of arms. Hiero appears, indeed, to constitute an ancient example of the use of the strategies for which Machiavelli will praise Cesare Borgia in chapter 7: "Hiero eliminated the old military and organized a new one; he left old friendships and made new ones; and when he had friendships and soldiers that were his own, he could build any building on top of such a foundation" (25). Machiavelli does not explicitly observe that the "new princes" he has described would be difficult to distinguish from tyrants like Agathocles, whom he takes up in a later chapter as an example of a prince who attained his principality through crimes. He simply concludes that having acquired rule with great difficulty, those who become princes by means solely of their own virtue maintain control easily. Indeed, he goes so far as to say that they will "begin to be held in veneration, having eliminated those who had envied them" (24). To discover how and why a bringer of new modes and orders becomes revered (as opposed to merely feared), and thus a founder rather than a criminal, we have to turn to the following chapters.[36]

Apparently proceeding in terms of the binary divisions he sketched in chapter 1, Machiavelli turns in chapter 7 to consider "new principalities that are acquired with the arms and fortune of others" (25). By contrasting them with "principalities that are acquired by one's own arms and by virtue," he connects virtue to having "one's own arms." He has argued that a new prince has to use force in order to acquire rule by means solely of his own virtue. But the greatest examples of such new princes were legendary founders whose deeds are known, to the extent to which they are known, only in fables; and Machiavelli admitted that Lorenzo could not follow their example. He urged his primary reader simply to aim high so that he could accomplish something more ordinary.[37]

36. Benner, *Prince*, 84–85, takes Hiero to be Machiavelli's true exemplar, because he was elected to office and did not seize control by force. However, Hiero did not establish a long-lasting empire or republic, nor did he come to be revered.

37. As both Eugene Garver, *Machiavelli and the History of Prudence* (Madison: University of Wisconsin Press, 1987), and Kahn, *Machiavellian Rhetoric*, point out, Machiavelli appeals to the classical notion of learning by imitating exemplary characters commonly used in earlier "humanist" Renaissance writings in order to subvert it. It is impossible to found or originate a new order by imitating the past.

The two contemporary examples Machiavelli now brings forth of men who became princes through virtue, on the one hand, and fortune, on the other, are neither so distant nor so impossible to imitate. Like the ancients, Francesco Sforza came to power by means of his own arms. This mercenary captain had been promised something like a hereditary succession to the dukedom of Milan in the form of a marriage to the daughter of the reigning duke. But Sforza actually acquired control of the city only after the citizens rebelled against the duke and invited the mercenary captain to take over the city (even though he had betrayed them earlier), because they needed someone with an army to defend them. As a result of his prudent planning, Sforza and his army "happened" to be in the neighborhood.[38] According to Machiavelli, Cesare Borgia first acquired a principality in the Romagna by fortune, because he was the illegitimate son of the pope.

In relating how Alexander disturbed the existing orders in Romagna so that his son could become prince, Machiavelli shows that one does not need to wait for an "opportunity" to found a new principality. In other words, even the "opportunity" a new prince needs can be intentionally created—by means of an external invasion or internally undermining the existing government. The Venetians made Alexander's task easier by inviting the French to invade Italy; and Alexander obtained French troops for Cesare to use in conquering the Romagna in exchange for granting the king his divorce.

Although Cesare acquired his principality by means of good fortune and the arms of others, Machiavelli uses his example to show that it is possible, even in modern times and thus for Lorenzo (who might also be said to have acquired his rule by means of his family relation to a pope), to lay one's foundations after the fact. If a new prince is not a general of his own army like Sforza, he will, like Cesare Borgia, have to use "the arms of others" in order to seize power. But once he does, like a new prince in a "mixed principality," he will have to worry about the loyalty of his "friends." Having used French arms to acquire the Romagna and hired Orsini mercenaries to beat down the Colonna, Cesare saw that the Orsini gave him only lukewarm support in his attack on Bologna and that he was ordered by the French king to desist in his attack on Urbino. Deciding that it was no longer prudent to depend upon the arms of others, Cesare first bribed the adherents of both

38. For the details of Francesco Sforza's acquisition of Milan see *FH* 5.13, 5.17, 5.19, 6.2, 6.12, 6.17–24. In praising Sforza in contrast to Cesare Borgia, Benner, *Prince*, 94–97, neglects to mention that Sforza acquired his dukedom with his mercenary army or that he and his son perpetuated the tyrannical rule of Milan.

the Orsini and the Colonna families with large allowances and government posts and brought them into his party. Then he eliminated the heads of the opposition by means of deceit.[39] Machiavelli does not explain how Cesare convinced these heads to meet him unarmed at Sinigaglia, where he had them seized and murdered. However, in the next chapter he tells his readers about the way the mercenary captain who had arms with him at Sinigaglia, but was persuaded to leave them behind, had gathered together the heads of the leading families in Fermo for a banquet where he had his soldiers murder them. Although Oliverotto praised the greatness of Pope Alexander and Cesare Borgia, he apparently did not suspect that they would be willing to use the very same tactics he had used against his own family in order to eliminate the opposition. As Machiavelli explicitly concludes with regard to Cesare Borgia, so he shows in the case of Oliverotto da Fermo, his ambitious, cutthroat contemporaries do not recognize their own desires

39. Machiavelli's account of the career of Cesare Borgia here is both briefer and much more positive than his earlier recitation of the sufferings of Italy from a Florentine perspective in his *First Decennial*. There he explains that after Duke Valentino conquered Imola and Forli with French troops, Milan recalled Duke Ludovico and the king of France recalled his troops to attack Milan, "leaving the Pope and his son in a plight" (*Lust and Liberty: The Poems of Machiavelli*, trans. Joseph Tusiana [New York: Ivan Obolensky, 1963], 161). After defeating Ludovico, the French army came into Tuscany purportedly to help Florence capture Pisa, but withdrew in defeat, for which they blamed Florence. Taking advantage of the enmity between Florence and its sometime French protector, Duke Valentino took Faenza and brought Romagna into disorder again. After attacking the Bentivogli in Bologna, he came into Tuscany and camped in Florentine territory. France joined with Spain in attacking Naples, and while Florence sought protection from the French, the duke seized Urbino. King Louis then called the duke to account. But having exonerated himself with the king, and once again enjoying French protection, the duke came back to Romagna and planned another war against Messer Giovanni Bentivogli in Bologna. He was forestalled by the Orsini and Vitelli whom, as Machiavelli also reports in *The Prince*, he nevertheless snared and killed by deceit. Fearing both the duke and his enemies, the Florentines sent Machiavelli on a mission to him. Both in the letters he sent back to the Signori (October 9 and November 13, 1502), detailing the duke's forces, and in his later "Description of the Method Used by Duke Valentino in Killing Vietellozzo Vitelli, Oliverotto da Fermo, and Others," trans. Allan Gilbert, *Machiavelli: The Chief Works and Others* (Durham, NC: Duke University Press, 1965), 1: 163–69, Machiavelli shows just how tenuous and dangerous the duke's position was, and how foolish the lords were to accept the titles and provinces he gave back to them as evidence of his own lack of ambition and goodwill toward them. They came to meet him without arms and thus succumbed, necessarily, to his. Viroli, *Redeeming "The Prince,"* 72–75, suggests that the difference between Machiavelli's earlier observations as a diplomat and what he writes in *The Prince* shows that he was intentionally creating a political myth to inspire action. Benner, *Prince*, 104–10, argues that the difference between Machiavelli's initial critical accounts of the duke's deeds and his praise of the same means that the latter is not genuine; his readers would know better. John M. Najemy, "Machiavelli and Cesare Borgia: A Reconsideration of Chapter 7 of *The Prince*," *Review of Politics* 75, no. 4 (2013): 539–56, shows that Cesare did not, in fact, do what Machiavelli claims and that Machiavelli knew that Cesare had not—although he had bragged that he would. However, like Viroli, Najemy sees that Machiavelli altered the historical record in order to recommend the deeds he attributes (unhistorically) to Cesare.

and a willingness to adopt underhanded and bloody methods of satisfying them in other equally ambitious and unprincipled would-be princes.

Before he turns to consider those, like Oliverotto, who have attained a principality through crime, Machiavelli pauses to explain how, after he seized the Romagna, Cesare "judged it necessary to give it good government" (29). In other words, Machiavelli shows that laying firm foundations does not merely entail organizing one's own (or loyal) armed forces and eliminating the opposition from other armed lords. A new prince also has to benefit the people of his new province by establishing "law and order," so securing their lives and livelihoods. Finding the Romagna "commanded by impotent lords, readier to despoil their subjects than to correct them," and the province thus "full of robberies, quarrels, and every other kind of insolence," Cesare gave a cruel and ready man full power to reduce it to peace and unity. However, once Remirro de Orco had apprehended (killed, imprisoned, and/or tortured) those insolent enough to commit the robberies and murders and, with his reputation for cruelty, had frightened others from following their examples, "the duke judged that such excessive authority was not necessary, because he feared that it might become hateful." So, in place of his fearsome executioner, "he set up a civil court in the middle of the province, with a most excellent president, where each city had its advocate."[40] And "to show that if any cruelty had been committed, it had not come from him but from the harsh nature of his minister," he had Remirro's body cut in two pieces and placed "in the piazza at Cesena with a piece of wood and bloody knife beside him" (29–30). Cesare thus not only satisfied the people's desire to avenge themselves on the immediate source of their fear and oppression (see *D* 1.16) but also "stupefied" them. The man they thought stood behind his terrible agent had not merely freed them from the domination of this hateful man; he had also brought them peace and civil government.

Cesare might well, therefore, have come to be revered as a founder, *if* he had been able to maintain himself. Because his father, Alexander (who had provided him with funds and men-at-arms), died less than five years after Cesare began to acquire his principality, however, the foundations of his rule were not yet firm. He had eliminated the bloodlines of the lords he had supplanted, won over the gentlemen in Rome, and gained influence on the College of Cardinals, but he had not acquired enough of an empire

40. Many commentators skip over this crucial step in Machiavelli's account of Cesare's founding of "good government" in the Romagna. Ardito, *Machiavelli and the Modern State*, 53, does not.

to enable him to resist an attack without support from the pope. If Cesare could not control the selection of Alexander's successor, Machiavelli argues, he should have made sure that no cardinal who had been injured by him or who had reason to fear him was appointed. Because all the candidates except the Spaniards and the French cardinal of Rouen had reason to fear or hate him, Cesare should have made sure that either a Spaniard or Rouen was elected. He did not; he allowed San Piero ad Vincula, whom he had offended, to become Julius II. (Because he thought that Julius would benefit him in return for a bribe after he was elected pope, Cesare was seized, imprisoned, and finally sent off to die fighting in Spain.) Machiavelli does not describe the results of Cesare's misjudgment. He simply warns his readers, "whoever believes that among great personages new benefits will make old injuries be forgotten deceives himself" (33). Attributing the beneficial effects of a prince's rule to an intention on his part to serve them, especially if he professes such, Machiavelli has suggested, the people may in time forget the causes of change after a principality has been firmly established. But ambitious princes do not forget or forgive old injuries—even if they are purportedly Christians. Nor, Machiavelli suggests, should they. The power Cesare had acquired in the Romagna, among the warring factions in Rome, and in the College of Cardinals made him a threat to the new pope, who, understanding how he had to lay the foundations of his own principality after he was elevated by fortune, sought to eliminate the bloodline of the previous prince. Like Oliverotto, Cesare failed to understand that other new princes would act against their competitors the way he had acted against his. As Machiavelli suggested in his dedication to Lorenzo, princes see the character of the people. In particular, princes see that the people can be coerced and deceived. But being men of action rather than reflection, "princes" tend not to understand their own natures. One has to look at a prince from the perspective of the people, i.e., as a potential oppressor, to apprehend the nature of a prince. A willingness to act ruthlessly will not suffice to enable a prince to acquire or maintain rule; he needs to understand what his competitors want and will do to achieve what they desire so that he can forestall their satisfaction at his expense.

Having first suggested that Cesare Borgia provides a model for a man like Lorenzo, who has become a prince largely as a result of his family connections, of the way in which he can lay firmer foundations for his rule after he first acquires it, but then admitted that Cesare failed not simply because of bad luck but because of bad judgment, Machiavelli somewhat surprisingly proceeds to discuss four additional categories or types of principalities he did not mention in his initial classification. All four "types" or chapters concern ways in which a prince may or may not be able to maintain his rule better than Cesare did. All can also be read as covert critiques of the Medici.

Machiavelli first observes that there are two additional ways in which a private man may become a prince that cannot be attributed, strictly speaking, entirely to his *virtù* or to his fortune. These are by means of crime or through the favor of one's fellow citizens. In chapter 8 he gives two examples of the former, one ancient and one modern, "for anyone who needs to imitate them" (34).

Machiavelli points out that both Agathocles the Sicilian and Oliverotto da Fermo rose through the ranks of their respective armies on the basis of their demonstrated merit as soldiers. They could both be said, therefore, to have demonstrated a certain kind of *virtù*. Having become the highest-ranking member of their armed forces, they both decided to seize control of their cities. Whereas Cesare openly seized control of the Romagna with French troops, as if he were a foreign prince, and then sought to eliminate the bloodlines of the lords there, Agathocles and Oliverotto proceeded more covertly and expeditiously. Having arranged for gatherings of the leading men in their respective cities, they both had soldiers waiting in hiding to slaughter these local dignitaries on the spot and so eliminated all sources of internal opposition to their rule at one stroke. Machiavelli does not point out that both "criminals" were overthrowing republics; he simply mentions in passing that Agathocles assembled the people and the senate of Syracuse and that Oliverotto arranged the murder of the maternal uncle who had raised him along with the most prominent men of Fermo "with the help of some citizens to whom serving him was more dear than the liberty of their fatherland" (36).[41] The two points Machiavelli emphasizes are, first, that the cruelties a private man who wants to found a new principality must necessarily commit in seizing control should be done all at once and, second, that this cruelty should be aimed at eliminating possible sources of opposition. These "criminals" had their own arms (or armies) and did what a man who becomes a prince on the basis of his own virtue rather than mere good luck must do in founding a new order. But, Machiavelli also suggests, they and their deeds cannot simply be called virtuous, because having seized

41. Nor, Strauss, *TM*, 26, points out, does Machiavelli mention Agathocles' pitiable end.

control, they did not cease using cruel means (as Cesare had with Remirro) and begin to use merely the threat of renewed cruelty in order to establish and maintain a legal order that benefitted their subjects.[42] As a result, these "criminals" never received the glory bestowed upon a great founder.[43]

In chapter 9 Machiavelli thus emphasizes the need for a prince, once in power, to seek popular support. Indeed, he observes that "one who becomes prince against the people with the support of the great must before everything else seek to win the people to himself, which should be easy for him when he takes up their protection. And since men who receive good from someone from whom they believed they would receive evil are more obliged to their benefactor, the people immediately wish him well more than if he had been brought to the principality through their support" (40). Machiavelli thus appears to be continuing to show his reader (Lorenzo or another) how he could succeed better than Cesare did in becoming a truly great, well-regarded, and secure prince.

Machiavelli does not name any examples of princes who came into power with the support of their fellow citizens, perhaps because, as he admitted in introducing this type of principality in chapter 8, "it might be reasoned about more extensively where republics are treated" (34).[44] But as in chapter 3 where he used the Roman republic as the model of the policy a prince ought to follow, Machiavelli again shows that the general principles of politics he is announcing in his very short little book apply to republics as well as to principalities. He takes this occasion, in fact, to announce one of his most fundamental observations or principles: "In every city two diverse

42. Strauss, *TM*, 47, observes that "Machiavelli says of the criminal Agathocles, in two consecutive sentences, first that he lacked virtue and then that he possessed virtue; in the first case 'virtue' means moral virtue in the widest sense which includes religion, and in the second case it means cleverness and courage combined." However, he also observes that "there is an intermediate meaning according to which 'virtue' designates political virtue or the sum of qualities required for rendering service to political society or for effective patriotism. Even in accordance with this intermediate meaning, inhuman cruelty could be a virtue [as Machiavelli argues in the case of Hannibal, *P* 17] and ambition a vice. In many cases it is impossible to say which kind of virtue is meant." In the case of Agathocles, however, it seems clear that he possessed some but not all of the qualities that constitute *virtù* in the full Machiavellian sense.

43. See Victoria Kahn, "Revisiting Agathocles," *Review of Politics* 75, no. 4 (2013): 557–72.

44. In chapters 8–11 Machiavelli could thus be said to be treating the ways in which republics are both overthrown and founded. Machiavelli does not make clear, as he does in *D* 1.9–21, that the successful founding of a republic (for which a prince like Romulus acquires posthumous glory) takes more than one generation and thus more than one prince. Nor does he point out, as he does in *D* 1.40, that a prince elevated by the people who uses the opportunity to destroy the nobility who previously oppressed them with the blessing of the people will surely become a tyrant.

humors are found," because "the people desire neither to be commanded nor oppressed by the great, and the great desire to command and oppress the people" (39).[45] Because these two "humors" (*umori*) are obviously opposed, and neither can be satisfied except at the expense of the other, two things follow. First, there will always be conflict at the heart of every city. Machiavelli has already indicated that government has to be imposed on human beings by means of force; now he very clearly states the reason: no one wants to be commanded or oppressed by another. That does not mean, however, that some do not want to command and oppress the rest. Machiavelli's characterization of the fundamental division means, second, that it exists primarily with respect to rule rather than wealth or economic class. As he observes in *D* 2.10, those who have arms or force can seize the wealth of those who do not.

Depending on the relative strength of these two "appetites" (*appetiti*), as Machiavelli also dubs them, there are three possible results: principality or liberty or license.[46] In a book purportedly devoted to an examination of principalities, he does not explain why he now suggests three possible outcomes of the fundamental struggle within every city rather than two, i.e., either a principality or a republic. He provides the reasoning on the basis of which he comes to this conclusion, however, in his *Florentine Histories*:

> Cities . . . frequently change their governments and their states not between liberty and servitude, as many believe, but between servitude and license. For only the name of freedom is extolled by the ministers of license, who are the men of the people, and by the ministers of servitude, who are the nobles, neither of them desiring to be subject either to the laws or to men. True, when it happens (and it happens rarely) that by the good fortune of a city there rises in it a wise, good, and powerful citizen by whom laws are ordered by which these humors of the nobles and men of the people are quieted or restrained so that they cannot do evil, then that city can be called free and that state be judged stable and firm: for a city based on good laws and good orders has no necessity, as have others, for the virtue of a single man to maintain it. (4.1)

45. Machiavelli describes the same fundamental division within all republics in *D* 1.4 and *FH* 4.1.

46. Like Viroli, *Redeeming "The Prince,"* 81, I thus see Machiavelli's "realism" to be based on an analysis of human passions, and not on medieval medicine, which did speak of various "humors" (e.g., bilious) or cosmology, as Anthony Parel contends in *The Machiavellian Cosmos* (New Haven: Yale University Press, 1992) and "Farewell to Fortune," *Review of Politics* 75, no. 4 (2013): 587–604.

Delineating the ways in which a single man can acquire and maintain his state in *The Prince*, Machiavelli observes merely that a principality is caused either by the people or by the great, when either of the humors sees that it cannot resist the other without making someone a prince to defend it. Machiavelli does not attribute the rise of such a prince to his virtue, because he does not seize power himself. He is elevated by his fellow citizens in what "one could call a civil principality." Since his fellow citizens have presumably chosen him to defend them for some reason, his elevation does not appear to be a matter of pure chance or "fortune." Machiavelli thus attributes it to a "fortunate astuteness" (*astuzia fortunate*) that leads such a man to see what needs to be done to protect his supporters from his opponents.

However such a "prince" comes into power, Machiavelli strongly urges him not to rely on "the great" to support him, if he wants to maintain himself. There are two reasons why he should seek the support of the people instead. First, the great will always see themselves as the prince's equals and demand ever more offices and goods as the price of their support. Attempts to satisfy them will, therefore, necessarily fail and, in failing, add to the prince's enemies. It is possible, however, to satisfy the people, "for the end of the people is more decent [*onesto*] than that of the great, since the great want to oppress and the people want not to be oppressed" (39).[47] The second reason why it is better to seek the support of the people than of the great is even more radical and points to another of Machiavelli's fundamental political principles. A prince will never be able to secure himself against a hostile people, because they are many whereas the great are few. As Machiavelli observed in the cases of Agathocles and Oliverotto, the great can be destroyed, but a prince will have no one to rule if he murders all or most of his people. A prince needs subordinates to help him rule, "but he can well do without the same great persons, since he can make and unmake them every day" (40), by giving them lands and offices or, conversely, taking those same lands and offices away along with their lives. The "great" are not different from the many by nature; they are not better or more ambitious or more grasping in themselves. "Greatness" is a matter of position. Those raised to office have more power and goods; and having more power and goods, they no longer feel as liable as those who are subject to

47. In *D* 1.16 Machiavelli qualifies this judgment by observing that a prince cannot satisfy a people's desire not to be ruled or commanded at all. He can, however, satisfy their desire to revenge themselves upon their previous oppressors, i.e., the great, and garner their support by protecting them from those both within and without the city who would deprive them of their lives, liberties, and property.

the government to oppression by others. Instead, they begin to desire to acquire more by oppressing others.[48] And because the "great" always want more, they will always be competitors and potential enemies of the prince, unless they and their positions remain entirely dependent on him.[49]

Although a prince should seek the support of the people, Machiavelli concludes, he should not rely on them to liberate or protect him from his enemies (the way he needs to protect the people from theirs). A prince may need a people, but his necessity will not be theirs unless he finds a way to persuade them that they need the state and his government.

Machiavelli suggests two ways a prince can convince his people that they need him and his government in the next chapter when he inquires "in what mode the forces of all principalities should be measured" (42). A prince can organize and lead an army to defend a city from attack; or if he is not able to field an army, he can construct fortifications and provide sufficient food and work to maintain the people for a year under siege (in which case it becomes too expensive for another power to attack him and his city).[50] In sum, Machiavelli suggests, if a prince provides for both the defense and the welfare of his people, he will reign secure.

It is not obvious, however, why a discussion of the forces a prince has at his disposal belongs in a discussion of the types of principalities, i.e., why

48. Readers tempted to object that "greatness" might be a matter of nature rather than simply position should remember that Machiavelli is describing two "humors" or dispositions of groups that arise in cities (and do not therefore simply exist by nature). In *P* 25 he recognizes that individual human beings have different dispositions and talents by nature although these are shaped by their experience. But, as Manent, *Enquête sur la démocratie*, observes, "rien dans la compréhension machiavélienne de la nature humaine ne permet de fonder une telle différence naturelle entre les hommes" (316).

49. As Machiavelli states in the title of *Discourses* 1.46, "Men Ascend from One Ambition to Another; First One Seeks Not to Be Offended, and Then One Offends Others." McCormick, *Machiavellian Democracy*, 23–25, characterizes the difference between the *grandi* and the *popolo* as one of "opposing natures," even though he maintains that the *grandi* are characterized especially by their desire for wealth, which Machiavelli states in *P* 3 is natural to human beings generally. According to Machiavelli, the difference between the two humors is fundamentally political. It is not natural, because the two humors differ with regard to control of the city or state, and cities are not natural entities, according to Machiavelli. He does not call the humors "natures," even though each has a distinctive character or "nature" in that sense; and he states explicitly that the *grandi* can be made and unmade (by giving or taking away offices and wealth). As Miguel Vatter, *Machiavelli's "The Prince"* (London: Bloomsbury, 2013), sees, "For him, people and nobles do not designate natural kinds; instead, whoever speaks and acts out of a desire to dominate assumes the standpoint of the nobility, and whoever speaks and acts out of a desire for non-domination assumes the standpoint of the people. One and the same individual may therefore occupy these different standpoints at different moments" (63).

50. Those who criticize Machiavelli for not having taken sufficient account of changes in military technology, particularly the introduction of artillery, should note that he includes artillery here among the necessary defensive precautions a prince unable to field an army should take.

chapter 10 comes where it does. But the distinction Machiavelli draws here between princes who have enough men or money to field an army adequate to defend them and those who are compelled of necessity to take refuge behind walls does point to a kind of principality Machiavelli has not yet taken up. As he observes in *D* 2.19, some of the cities of Germany, officially under the emperor, were principalities; and these princes were effectively free to do as they wished, partly because they were able to defend themselves with walls and supplies so that they could withstand both frontal attacks and long sieges, even though they did not have sufficient numbers to field an army, and partly because the emperor was weak. Unlike the princes Machiavelli will write about in chapter 20, these princes built fortresses not to defend themselves against their people, but to defend their people against foreigners. They did not disarm their people, but rather trained them militarily so that they could repel direct attacks. And because they sought to benefit the people in obvious ways rather than oppressing them with taxes or other burdens, these princes did not make themselves hated.

Machiavelli concludes his consideration of the different types of principalities with what appears to be a limiting case—a principality that can be acquired by either virtue or fortune and maintained without either, "for they are sustained by orders that have grown old with religion, which have been so powerful and of such a kind that they keep their princes in the state however they proceed and live. These alone have states, and do not defend them; they have subjects, and do not govern them; and the states, though undefended, are not taken from them; the subjects, though ungoverned, do not care, and they neither think of becoming estranged from such princes nor can they." Underlining the general conclusion a reader should draw from this discussion, Machiavelli baldly states, "only these principalities are secure and happy" (45). This conclusion is revealing not so much about the character of "ecclesiastical principalities," however, as about all others. No other principality, including a hereditary principality that appears to be well-established, is really secure. Nor, therefore, can its prince be happy. Rather than trusting or enjoying the company of his fellows, Machiavelli has shown, a prince has to be constantly on the lookout for possible competitors or opponents. He can never relax or be at peace without endangering the continuity of his reign.[51]

Since these ecclesiastical principalities "subsist by superior causes to

51. Machiavelli's prince thus resembles the tyrant Socrates describes in *Republic* 9. 571a–580a.

which the human mind does not reach," Machiavelli says that he will not reason about them. He thus calls his reader's attention to the fact that he will not treat anything that is not intelligible to the unassisted human mind. He can, however, explain how "the Church has come to such greatness in temporal affairs despite the fact that, before Alexander, the Italian powers . . . held her in low esteem in temporal affairs" (45).

In chapter 12 Machiavelli explains that the withdrawal of the emperor from Italy created the "opportunity" (or lack of order) that made it possible for the Church to acquire its temporal power.[52] Alexander VI may have intended to help his illegitimate son by granting him control of the French troops the pope had obtained from Louis to conquer the Romagna, but, Machiavelli points out, in the end Duke Valentino's conquests redounded (one might say "providentially," although Machiavelli does not) to the greatness of the Church. Pope Julius found the Church in control of Romagna and the factions of the Orsini and Colonna in Rome, which had previously kept the power of the Church in Rome within bounds, destroyed. And Julius not only extended the armed conquests along with "a mode of accumulating money never used before Alexander"; he also forestalled the emergence of new divisions or competitors in Rome by refusing to appoint members of either the Orsini or the Colonna families as cardinals. "If others made [the Church] great with arms," Machiavelli concludes, "one may hope that His Holiness Pope Leo with his goodness and infinite other virtues, can make it very great and venerable" (47).[53]

52. In distinguishing the temporal greatness or power of the human-all-too-human Roman Church from the "orders that have grown old with religion and of such a kind that they keep their princes in the state however they proceed and live," Machiavelli might appear to be following Augustine, who had distinguished the "city of man," which keeps order among human beings on earth, from the "city of God," which exists on earth before and while its members wait to ascend to heaven, but for the sake of their salvation there and not their safety here. The distinction had traditionally been characterized and maintained in Europe as that between the "sword," the physical power used to keep order on earth, and the "scepter" wielded by the "vicar of Christ," who leads his flock to their salvation on the basis of a "divine law" that is not known to the unassisted human mind, but depends upon revelation. That distinction had been institutionalized, although never perfectly or without controversy, in the relation between the head of the Holy Roman Empire and the head of the Holy Roman Church.

53. Despite Machiavelli's suggestion about Alexander VI's innovation, the sale of indulgences Luther was soon to protest had existed for some time. However, Greg Steinmetz, *The Richest Man Who Ever Lived: The Life and Times of Jacob Fugger* (New York: Simon and Schuster, 2015), reports, Pope Leo X extended and exaggerated it. He charged the equivalent of $4.8 million in today's money in 1514 to Albrecht of Hohenzollern, whose family ruled much of Germany, to make him archbishop of Mainz. Albrecht borrowed the money from a banker, Jacob Fugger. And to repay the loan, Albrecht's men arranged with Leo to sell indulgences, supposedly to be used to restore St. Peter's. These indulgences were sold by itinerant peddlers who carried Bibles and told worship-

The lessons Machiavelli draws from his seemingly dry and static classification of the types of principalities thus point directly to his passionate concluding call in chapter 26 for Leo and his nephew to seize Italy and free it from the "barbarians." Just as Alexander unintentionally used his illegitimate son Duke Valentino, so Machiavelli suggests, Leo should intentionally use his legitimate nephew as his instrument. The pope had already made Lorenzo commander of his troops at the battle of Marignano (1515). He could and, Machiavelli will argue, should now lead them in the conquest and "liberation" of Italy as a whole.

II. Advice to the Prince

A. The Lessons from the Ancients: The Importance of Relying upon One's Own Arms

Having completed his typology of principalities, in chapters 12–14 Machiavelli turns to examine in more detail the means he has already shown a prince must employ in order to found and maintain his state. Emphasizing the fundamental role of force both in establishing and in maintaining political order, Machiavelli infamously begins by observing that "the principal foundations" of all states "are good laws and good arms. And because there cannot be good laws where there are not good arms, and where there are good arms there must be good laws, I shall leave out the reasoning on laws and shall speak of arms" (48).

Machiavelli explains that "the arms with which a prince defends his state are either his own or mercenary or auxiliary or mixed" (48). And on the basis of an analysis of the economic and political incentives, he argues that mercenary and auxiliary arms are either useless or dangerous.

Mercenary soldiers are not apt to be any good, because the stipend is not great enough to make them willing to die for it. They will, therefore, promise to fight so long as they do not actually need to do so. Italian mercenaries have sought to minimize their costs further by relying on cavalry rather than using infantry so that they have fewer men to feed. They have reduced the risks they face in war by not killing each other in battle, but

---

ers that the indulgences would cancel every sin. The sellers used a "progressive fee schedule," according to which royalty paid twenty-five florins, laborers only one. Leo and Fugger split the proceeds. Anyone who knew anything about the way in which the former Giovanni Lorenzo de' Medici lived would know that Machiavelli's concluding hope that "with his goodness and infinite other virtues" Leo would make the papacy great and venerable was ironic.

taking prisoners without asking ransom. They also refuse to attack towns at night or to fight in winter. However, should a mercenary captain prove to be an effective commander, he immediately becomes a threat to the prince or citizens who have hired him and his men, precisely because the mercenaries are armed, whereas their employers are not.[54]

"A prince should," therefore, "go in person, and himself perform the office of captain." Acknowledging that republics (about which he was supposedly not going to speak) have to send one of their citizens to lead their troops, Machiavelli observes that if the captain does "not turn out to be a worthy man, [the republic] must change him; and if he is, it must check him with laws so that he does not step out of bounds" (49–50).[55]

Good arms do not necessarily make good laws; good laws are necessary to make arms good—at least for a republic.[56] Machiavelli's initial claim was a deliberate overstatement, which he quickly if quietly retracts. What is essential is to employ "one's own arms" and not those of others. The main difference between ancient republics like Rome and Sparta and modern Italian republics like Florence and Venice is that the former armed their own citizens, who defended their freedom, whereas the latter use mercenaries, who threaten the freedom as well as the empire of the cities that employ them.[57]

If mercenaries are so bad, the question obviously arises, why have Italians employed them? The answer Machiavelli gives is ignorance and inexperience, two factors he proposes to correct by writing *The Prince.* When the Italians began to repel the empire, he reminds his readers, the citizens of many Italian cities took up arms against their nobles with support from the pope, who wished to increase his temporal power and reputation. Because neither the citizens nor the priests had knowledge of arms, they began to hire foreigners. Although Machiavelli does not explicitly point it out, the

54. Machiavelli supplies historical examples that support his general reasoning here in *FH* 5–6.

55. Nathan Tarcov, "Arms and Politics in Machiavelli's *Prince*," *Entre Kant et Kosovo* (Paris: Presses de Sciences Po, 2003), points out that "this . . . is the only time in the *Prince* that Machiavelli explicitly considers an issue from the perspective of republics" (117). However, "the examples Machiavelli gives in Chapter XII are all of republics: Rome, Sparta, the Swiss, the Carthaginians, the Thebans, and the Milanese (during the brief republican period between the Visconti and Sforzas)" (117n2).

56. Nathan Tarcov, "Law and Innovation in Machiavelli's *Prince*," in *Enlightening Revolutions*, ed. Svetozar Minkov (Lanham, MD: Lexington Books, 2006), 77–90, observes that "good laws thus turn out after all to be the foundation or at least the safeguard of good arms in a republic" (78).

57. Machiavelli reminds his readers that mixtures like the use of citizen captains of mercenary armies by the Carthaginians or a foreign captain for a citizen army in Thebes resulted in their defeat and destruction, respectively, by Rome and Philip of Macedon.

Medici in Florence and Rome were prime examples of citizens and priests who had employed mercenary armies rather than arm their own fellow citizens or subjects.

Mercenary arms tend not to be good or reliable troops, but, Machiavelli shows when he turns to auxiliaries, the goodness or badness of arms does not depend simply on the quality of the arms themselves. It is fundamentally a matter of control. Having discovered how unreliable mercenaries are, Italian princes like Pope Julius II who sought the assistance of troops mustered and controlled by other nations left their own fates in the hands of these auxiliaries. Unlike mercenaries, auxiliary troops may be good in themselves, but they are more dangerous precisely for that reason. If they lose, so do the princes who use them; but if they win, they are apt to follow their own interests or leaders rather than the interests of the prince to whom they were loaned. Both the pope and the Florentines have escaped the dire consequences of using auxiliaries only by good luck.

"A wise prince, therefore, has always avoided these arms and turned to his own" (55). In presenting four examples of the benefits and means of turning to one's own arms, Machiavelli indicates that by "arms" he means more than armies or troops, because the examples he gives refer to strategy, that is, the intelligent employment and control of both force and fraud rather than, literally, armies and weapons. Once again he emphasizes how Cesare Borgia increased his reputation by using and then jettisoning first his French auxiliaries and, second, the Orsini mercenaries, before turning to his own arms. Machiavelli then reminds his readers of how Cesare treated the heads of those mercenaries by praising Hiero of Syracuse for arranging to have his mercenary army cut into pieces when he could no longer use them. (Hiero's treatment of these mercenaries thus represents another example of "cruelty well-used," analogous to Cesare's using cruel means [Remirro] to bring "good government" to the Romagna and then seeing to it that those means were destroyed in order to separate himself from them in public.) By changing the story of David's refusal of Saul's arms so that David uses his own sling and knife instead of the biblical stones and his faith in God, Machiavelli also signals that his insistence that a prince should rely on his own "arms" means that a prince should not rely on divine or other forces beyond human control.[58] Finally, in praising King Charles VII

58. Cf. 1 Samuel 17: 38–40, 17: 50–51. Connell, *"The Prince" by Niccolò Machiavelli with Related Documents*, suggests that "M's mistake must have been prompted by familiarity with Andrea del Verrocchio's statue *David* . . . who holds a small sword that might easily be assumed to be David's

for liberating France from England by seeing the necessity of arming himself with his own arms, Machiavelli indicates more concretely how he thinks a prince can obtain and employ the support of his people. He should recruit and train them as men-at-arms or infantry (in contrast to the less popular and less numerous cavalry employed by the Italian mercenaries) and so make them "his own." Machiavelli claims, indeed, that France would have been invincible if Louis XI had not replaced native infantry with Swiss. He admits that a mixture is better than using mercenaries or auxiliaries, but he insists that it is less good than relying entirely on one's own arms. He would presumably make a similar judgment about relying entirely on one's own arms—or wit—as opposed to relying on a combination of divine favor or good luck with one's own resources. Only the last are fully under a captain's control.

Machiavelli concludes the chapter by emphasizing that a prince without his own arms is wholly dependent upon fortune. Those "arms" include one's fellow citizens, subjects, or "creatures," that is, the human beings whose liberty, security, and prosperity depend on the perpetuation of the government they serve. To understand how those arms should be ordered, he directs his reader to "the four examples above." He seems to mean Cesare, Hiero, David, and Charles, but he might also be referring to the four founders—Moses, Cyrus, Theseus, and Romulus. It doesn't matter, because the basic point is the same: a prince who wants to found and maintain his rule securely must rely on his own virtue, which includes understanding the need to organize and use his own forces to keep his own supporters in line as well as to eliminate his competitors.

In light of the emphasis Machiavelli has put on the importance of arming oneself, a reader is not surprised to see him conclude the section of the book devoted to defense by announcing that "a prince should have no other object, nor any thought, nor take anything else as his art but that of war and its orders and discipline; for that is the only art which is of concern to one who commands" (58). The reason is simple: those who are armed control those who are not.

---

rather than Goliath's. For many years M passed this statue . . . on the way to work in the chancery" (83n7). It seems unlikely, however, that so careful a writer would forget the original, very well known story, just because he had viewed what is also a very effeminate depiction of its hero, in urging his readers to depend upon their own arms. We now admire the Renaissance generally, and Florence in particular, for its art. Machiavelli had other concerns, as shown by the paucity of references to the art of Renaissance Italy in his works.

Like the definition of one's own "arms," however, the exercise of the art of war that Machiavelli recommends turns out to have a much broader range and content than his reader might initially expect. According to Machiavelli, a prince needs to practice it even more in peace than in war (in order to be prepared for the latter, when his fortune changes), and he must practice in two modes, one with deeds and the other with his mind. The "deeds" include not merely keeping his armies well ordered and exercised, so inuring their bodies as well as his own to physical hardships. These "deeds" also entail a kind of mental training or education. By going on hunts in a variety of locations, a prince should learn the nature of sites. He should seek to discover first how to defend his own country, and from reflecting on how to deploy his own troops and defeat those of an enemy in a variety of terrains close to home, he will learn how to deploy them successfully abroad. He should also teach his subordinates by constantly asking them as they ride out together on hunts how they would defend themselves or attack an enemy in the place where they currently find themselves, examining their opinions and reasoning with them so that they will learn what to do in his absence.[59]

In addition to these "bodily" exercises, however, Machiavelli also recommends exercise of the mind. This exercise turns out to consist in doing something quite similar to what Machiavelli did in order to write *The Prince.* He thus implicitly brings his own enterprise and its importance more to the fore. By reading the histories and considering the actions of excellent men, especially how they conducted themselves in war, a prince should seek to discover the causes of their victories and losses, so that he can avoid the latter and imitate the former.

Above all, Machiavelli concludes, a prince "should do as some excellent man has done in the past who found someone to imitate who has been praised and glorified" (60). The examples of excellent men Machiavelli now names are different, however, from the "greatest examples" of the founders of entirely new principalities he urged Lorenzo to imitate earlier so that he would reach his target by aiming higher than he expected to land. Alexander, Caesar, and Scipio are described not as founders but as imitators. Moreover,

59. Benner, *Machiavelli's Ethics*, takes Machiavelli's discussion of hunting as a metaphor for education as "evidence of his affinities with Socratic ethics and political philosophy" (124) without noticing that the texts she cites from both Xenophon and Plato are non-Socratic (Xenophon's *Education of Cyrus* and Plato's *Laws*). Machiavelli clearly and explicitly embraces Xenophon's depiction of Cyrus as an exemplary *political* man; but, as Strauss, *TM*, 291, notes, Machiavelli hardly mentions Socrates (Xenophon's other "hero") or Plato.

the individuals they imitated were in at least two cases—Achilles and Xenophon's Cyrus—more literary creations than actual historical figures. And they were remembered, glorified, and praised, not for the lasting effects of their accomplishments, but as great warriors who made extensive foreign conquests, not for having initiated a new order.[60] One wonders, indeed, whether Achilles, Alexander, Caesar, Cyrus, and Scipio have been remembered for what they achieved as much as for what they destroyed. Readers are led to suspect that the imitation of a great general is not Machiavelli's last word about the necessary content of a prince's education.[61]

B. Machiavelli's New Teaching: How a Prince Ought to Treat His Subjects and Friends

By listing only ancient, pre-Christian examples of famous generals who mastered the art of war by imitating another, Machiavelli suggests that the ancients understood how to wage war against enemies. When he turns to the question of how a prince should treat his subjects and friends, however, Machiavelli explicitly finds all previous "orders" lacking. He proposes, therefore, to do something new and different. He thus claims, in effect, to be founding a new "order." This new order concerns not the means of acquiring power, which Machiavelli has shown that the ancients understood, so much as the means of maintaining it.

Seeking to determine how human beings ought to live rather than describing what they actually do, Machiavelli observes, many previous writers

60. The empire Xenophon's Cyrus wins is reported to have broken up quickly after he died, as, Machiavelli reminded his readers in chapter 4, did Alexander's empire; and Caesar is castigated for having brought the Roman republic to an end. The founding of the empire is usually attributed to his adopted heir, Augustus. For excellent studies of the relation between Xenophon's and Machiavelli's presentations and uses of Cyrus as an example of political excellence, see Waller R. Newell, "Machiavelli and Xenophon on Princely Rule: A Double-Edged Encounter," *Journal of Politics* 50, no. 1 (1988): 108–30, and *Tyranny: A New Interpretation*, 186–270; Paul J. Rasmussen, *Excellence Unleashed: Machiavelli's Critique of Xenophon and the Moral Foundation of Politics* (Lanham, MD: Lexington Books, 2007).

61. And the "imperialism" emphasized by both Mark Hulliung, *Citizen Machiavelli* (Princeton: Princeton University Press, 1983), and Hörnqvist, *Machiavelli and Empire*, would appear to be a phase or part but not the whole of either the education of the prince or of Machiavelli's own political thought. By including at least two literary examples, Machiavelli does emphasize the influence "writers" have had on the formation as well as the subsequent fame of great individual political leaders, aka "princes." Benner, *Prince*, 174–75, also raises questions about the exemplary status of individuals whose faults Machiavelli points out at other places in the text. Her further suggestion—it's not clear that she thinks that it is Machiavelli's—that Hiero and Philopoemen might be better models for contemporary Italians seems, however, to be a little far-fetched. As she admits, they were much less celebrated by previous writers.

"have imagined republics and principalities that have never been seen or known to exist in truth." (Plato's *Republic*, Aristotle's regime "to be prayed for," and Aquinas's *De regimine principum* are often taken to be prime examples.) However, Machiavelli points out, human beings do not live the way these writers have said they should. Desiring to "write something useful to whoever understands it," he thus proposes "to go directly to the effectual truth." That truth is that, living among so many people who are not good, a prince who attempts to make a profession of good in all regards will come to ruin. So if a prince "wants *to maintain himself*," he needs "to learn to be able not to be good, and to use this and not use it according to necessity" (61, emphasis added).

To learn to be able not to be good and to use that knowledge is not simply to learn to be bad. In contrast to traditional educational treatises like Aristotle's *Nicomachean Ethics* or Cicero's *De officiis*, which dealt with the ways in which an individual's character should be formed as a whole, "the effectual truth" Machiavelli proposes to teach is instrumental. A prince who needs to learn to be able to be bad is not entirely or habitually bad; it sounds, on the contrary, as if he is primarily good. He is a person who needs to learn to be able to do what are usually considered to be bad acts—when necessary.[62] He thus also needs to learn what is necessary, why, and when. By proposing to teach something useful to those who understand, Machiavelli suggests that not everyone will.

Like Aristotle, Machiavelli initially treats characterizations of people as "good" or "bad" as matters of praise and blame. But where Aristotle proceeds to seek the true virtue in a mean between two extremes, Machiavelli lists the qualities reputed to be "virtuous" or "vicious" in terms of opposites: liberal or mean, generous or rapacious, cruel or merciful, a breaker of faith or faithful, effeminate and pusillanimous or fierce and spirited, lascivious or chaste, honest or astute, hard or easy, grave or light, religious or unbelieving, and so on. When virtues are thought to be simply in opposition to vices, there can be no middle position. Machiavelli contends, moreover, that it is impossible for a prince to possess all the qualities thought to be good. The *virtù* he recommends thus represents a mixture of good and bad. The good qualities in his list of opposites appear to include a mixture

62. In *D* 1.18 Machiavelli describes the same problem as follows: "Because the reordering of a city for a political way of life presupposes a good man, and becoming prince of a republic by violence presupposes a bad man, one will find that it very rarely happens that someone good wishes to become prince by bad ways, even though his end be good, and that someone wicked, having become prince, wishes to work well" (51).

of classical virtues like liberality and Christian virtues like charity and faith; but neither the opposites nor Machiavelli's originality arises simply from the mixture.[63] The difficulty of making a good choice appears initially to be that a prince who does what is necessary to maintain his state will necessarily incur the infamy associated with some vices. Insofar as "virtue" and "vice" are merely matters of praise and blame or reputation, Machiavelli observes, a "prudent" prince will "avoid the infamy of those vices that would take his state from him," but not "care about incurring the infamy of those vices without which it is difficult to save one's state." He concludes, however, by observing that "if one considers everything well, one will find something appears to be virtue, which if pursued would be one's ruin, and something else appears to be vice, which if pursued results in one's security and well-being" (62). In other words, *virtù* is not merely a matter of opinion or reputation; it can be apparent or real. The difficulty, as Machiavelli somewhat circuitously presents it here, is that people have not understood what is truly virtuous and vicious. He will, therefore, present a new substantive teaching.[64]

1. Machiavelli's Redefinition of Virtue and Vice

In chapters 16–19 of *The Prince* Machiavelli specifies which of the opposed characteristics in the list above traditionally thought to be good should be avoided by a truly virtuous prince and which reputed "vices" he should accept if he wants to maintain his state. The first supposed virtue Machiavelli treats is liberality.[65]

63. *Pace* Isaiah Berlin, who finds "The Originality of Machiavelli," *Against the Current: Essays in the History of Ideas* (New York: Penguin, 1980), 232–325, in this (untenable) combination. Medieval political philosophers had also advocated a mixture of Christian and ancient elements. What is "original" in Machiavelli is, therefore, not the mixture, but the particular combination chosen on the basis of a new concern not with the character of the prince himself as an individual, but with the effects of his rule.

64. Clifford Orwin, "Machiavelli's Unchristian Charity," *American Political Science Review* 72, no. 4 (December 1978): 1217–28, provides a detailed textual exegesis in support of this conclusion.

65. Machiavelli begins by observing that liberality, "if it is used virtuously and as it should be used, may not be recognized," referring, it would seem, to the Christian proposition that the left hand should not know what the right hand is doing, i.e., that an individual should not seek recognition for his or her philanthropy. He also skips over the first two virtues Aristotle treats in the *Nicomachean Ethics*, courage and moderation. He has already suggested that a prince needs to be courageous by insisting that he needs to lead his own troops into war. As he indicates in chapter 17, the definition of "virtue" he proposes here could be understood to constitute a certain kind of moderation; it certainly requires that the prince exercise self-control over any tendency he might feel to be rapacious, lascivious, pusillanimous, or irresolute. Machiavelli does not ask the prince to moderate his passions, however; instead he recommends that the prince calculate the best means of satisfying his passions for the longest possible period of time. Courage and moderation (as well

Generosity has traditionally been praised as a virtue. Machiavelli objects, however, that a prince who attempts to acquire a name for his liberality by generously rewarding his friends and putting on lavish displays will necessarily deplete his own resources; and once he has depleted his own resources, he will have to burden his subjects with new taxes and so arouse their hatred.[66] As a result, he will lose the support of many, and having become poor, be contemned by all. It is better, therefore, for a prince to accept a reputation for being stingy or mean in the short run, so that he can conserve his own resources to defend himself from whoever makes war on him without burdening his people. In the long run, Machiavelli concludes, such a prince is truly liberal to "all those from whom he does not take, who are infinite" and mean "with all those to whom he does not give, who are few" (63).

Machiavelli acknowledges that the three historical figures he just told the prince to imitate—Alexander, Caesar, and Cyrus—were not liberal in his sense. In seeking to acquire power, Machiavelli admits, princes like Julius II and victorious generals like these ancients could be liberal in the traditional sense, because they gave their supporters goods seized from others. However, he warns, once these princes came to power, they would not be able to continue giving away the goods of peoples who had become their subjects without arousing their hatred.[67]

Machiavelli's discussion of whether a prince should be merciful or cruel, loved or feared follows the same pattern. Not only does he reverse traditional notions of good and bad, but he also advises the prince to secure the advantages of many rather than favoring an aristocratic few. Cesare Borgia again provides a notable example. Cesare was reputed to be cruel, but in

---

as the "prudence" of the prince who chooses to incur the infamy of vices necessary to maintain his state) thus become instrumental means of achieving the prince's goals rather than chosen, as in Aristotle (*Nicomachean Ethics* 4.1120a23–28), because they are noble in and of themselves.

66. This advice might be seen to be directed particularly to Lorenzo, whose palace Machiavelli noted in his letter to Vettori of February–March 1514 was full of "great magnificence and liberality." It definitely constitutes a criticism of the practices of past Medici princes. In *FH* 7–8 Machiavelli argues that Cosimo became, in effect, prince of the Florentine republic by means of his liberality, but that his grandson Lorenzo the Magnificent was not as successful in commerce and had to use public funds to continue building magnificent edifices and pay mercenary armies, so that the people began to complain about paying more taxes.

67. Hörnqvist, *Machiavelli and Empire*, 166–88, notes both the dialectical complexity of Machiavelli's discussion of liberality and the exception of the conquering generals, but he does not take account of the limitation Machiavelli puts on the exception. Instead he argues that the discussion as a whole is intended to serve as a justification for a Florentine imperial policy. Hörnqvist nevertheless recognizes the ultimately republican thrust of Machiavelli's insistence on the importance of the prince's seeking to maintain popular support and avoiding hatred.

using cruelty to punish a few criminals and so bringing peace and faith to the Romagna, "he was much more merciful than the Florentine people, who so as to escape a name for cruelty, allowed Pistoia to be destroyed" (65). Because he has to use force to establish order, Machiavelli reiterates, a new prince cannot avoid acquiring a reputation for cruelty. Machiavelli first urges such a prince "not to make himself feared, and to proceed in a temperate mode with prudence and humanity so that too much confidence does not make him incautious and too much diffidence does not render him intolerable."[68] But Machiavelli almost immediately reverses himself. Admitting that it would be best for a prince to be both feared and loved, as a new prince might be if he established order where there was none, Machiavelli nevertheless observes that since it is difficult to be both loved and feared, it is safer for a prince to be feared. Human beings will promise much out of "love" so long as they are not asked actually to do it; but when pressed to do what they have promised, they refuse and revolt. A prince who founds himself entirely on their words will be lost, because "love is held by a chain of obligation, which, because men are wicked, is broken at every opportunity for their own utility, but fear is held by a dread of punishment that never forsakes you" (66–67).[69]

Machiavelli brings his arguments concerning the true or effective virtues of "liberality" and "mercy" together by warning the prince that although he should make sure that he continues to be feared, he should not make himself hated. And he will not be hated if he abstains from taking the property or the women of his citizens and subjects. Indeed, Machiavelli shockingly observes, a man will more quickly forget the death of his father (who would have had to die sometime) than the loss of his patrimony. Once again Machiavelli urges the prince to exercise what could be called self-control, lest he be perceived to be rapacious and thus become hated. In making this recommendation, however, Machiavelli does not appeal to a prince's desire to be reputed to be good or virtuous. He appeals to the self-interest of the prince qua prince by arguing that a prince will maintain his power if and only if he leaves the property of his subjects alone.

68. Machiavelli thus seems rather playfully to be equating temperance, prudence, and humanity with what he earlier dubbed "cruelty well-used."

69. Machiavelli explicitly says that "friendships that are acquired at a price and not with greatness and nobility of spirit are bought" (66). That is, he admits that not all men or friendships are false. His argument is that a person in power cannot rely on the nobility of his "friends," because human beings are fundamentally fearful.

As in the case of liberality, so in the case of cruelty and mercy, Machiavelli admits that famous ancient generals constitute exceptions. He observes that Hannibal could not have controlled his large army, composed of greatly different men, who had to fight in a strange land, unless he had used "inhuman cruelty," and that Scipio would have undermined the discipline and success of the Roman army if the bad effect of his "mercy" had not been undone by the Senate. Machiavelli does not point out that, in contrast to the three generals who founded empires, whom he mentioned as exceptions to his advice concerning liberality, Hannibal and Scipio both served republics—and that both represented threats to the perpetuation of the governments they served. Had Hannibal succeeded in conquering Rome, he might well have been tempted to use his mercenary troops against Carthage in order to seize power for himself. Machiavelli does not relate the details of the incident in which Scipio displayed his "mercy," but if readers look it up in Livy (29.8–9), they will find that Scipio failed to punish an officer, i.e., another aristocrat, who had destroyed a conquered people. By failing not only to discipline a disobedient officer but also to avenge the people he oppressed, Scipio fostered potential rebellions both in the Roman army and in their subjects. Thinking about Machiavelli's two apparent exceptions, a reader comes to see that republics have to control both the cruelty and the leniency of their generals if they do not want to see their government and laws overthrown. They must, in other words, rule their generals the way a prince must rule himself if he wants to remain in power. In both cases, readers also see that Machiavelli is criticizing previous writers—in the case of Hannibal for not recognizing the cause of the success they praise, and in the case of Scipio for having tried to teach him "how not to err" (or be virtuous in himself) rather than "how to correct errors" in his subordinates and so, like Machiavelli, how to rule them effectively.

Machiavelli's virtuous prince will avoid arousing the hatred of his people, but he is not simply their friend. On the contrary, Machiavelli argues in *P* 18, a prince has to deceive both his allies and his people.

Turning to the question of how a prince should keep faith, Machiavelli insists that princes cannot rely solely on force (or the fear its use can arouse). "There are two kinds of combat," he observes, "one with laws, the other with force. The first is proper to man, the second to beasts; but because the first is often not enough, one must have recourse to the second." This lesson was taught "covertly to princes by ancient writers, who wrote that Achilles, and many other ancient princes, were given to Chiron the centaur to be raised." For "to have as teacher a half-beast, half-man means nothing other than that a prince needs to know how to use both natures" (69). The failure to recognize and deal with the bestial parts of human beings thus appears to be particularly modern or, in Machiavelli's context, Christian.

Of the methods of fighting characteristic of the beast, Machiavelli recommends that a prince should imitate those of the fox and the lion, "because the lion does not defend itself from snares and the fox does not defend itself from wolves."[70] But, he further observes, "those who stay with the lion [i.e., merely with brute force] do not understand this." As Machiavelli has already indicated, acquiring and maintaining rule is not simply a matter of mustering physical force; it requires strategic intelligence. That intelligence includes knowing that "a prudent lord . . . cannot observe faith, nor should he, when such observance turns against him, and the causes that made him promise have been eliminated" (69). Precisely because circumstances are always changing, an "astute" prince can always find a reason not to keep his word.

In insisting on the need to use fraud as well as force, Machiavelli might appear to be equating keeping "faith" with "honesty" or abiding by one's promises. He builds on the association of "faith" with religion, however, first, by justifying his advice with an ironical inversion of the "golden rule" and, second, by naming the pope as one of the "infinite modern examples" of a prince's never lacking legitimate causes to color his failure to keep faith. "If all men were good," Machiavelli admits, "this teaching would not be good; but because they are wicked and do not observe faith with you, you also do not have to observe it with them" (69). Although Machiavelli

70. Although Machiavelli does not explicitly cite Cicero, several scholars point out that he took much of the vocabulary and organization of his argument about the virtues from Cicero. See Leslie J. Walker, trans., Niccolò Machiavelli, *The Discourses* (London: 1975), 2, table 13, 277–79; Marcia Colish, "Cicero's *De Officiis* and Machiavelli's *Prince*," *Sixteenth Century Journal* 9, no. 4 (Winter 1978): 84–85; J. J. Barlow, "The Fox and the Lion: Machiavelli Replies to Cicero," *History of Political Thought* 20 (1999): 627–45; and Michelle Zerba, "The Frauds of Humanism: Cicero, Machiavelli, and the Rhetoric of Imposture," *Rhetorica* 22, no. 3 (2004): 215–40. Cicero not merely distinguished between the ways of fighting characteristic of men and beasts, but also divided the "bestial" into that of "the lion and the fox" (*De officiis* 1.31.41). He also asked whether it is better to rule through love or fear (*De officiis* 2.7.23), as well as whether and how a ruler should be liberal, and advised him not to seize the property of others (*De officiis* 1.14–1.16.52, 2.15.252–2.18.64). However, as Barlow points out in contrast to Colish, Cicero's conclusions were almost diametrically opposed to Machiavelli's. Whereas Machiavelli insists on the need for a prince to know how to fight as a beast, in both ways, and praises Severus in *P* 19 for doing so, Cicero urges his son not to use such bestial ways unless absolutely necessary in order to achieve the common good and characterizes the deception of "the fox" as even more contemptible than the brute force of the lion. Because, as Colish, 81–83, shows, Cicero's work was well-known at the time, Machiavelli's readers would have understood the implicit inversion of Cicero's arguments.

first observed that ancient writers recognized the need to fight both like men and like beasts, and so suggested that moderns might not, the connection he draws between "faith" and "religion" should remind his reader that it would be strange for Christians, who presumably believe in the doctrine of original sin, not to recognize the need to deal with the bestial aspects of human nature. And, in fact, he observes that Christian princes know very well not only "how to use the fox," but also "how to color this nature, and to be a great pretender and dissembler." Pope Alexander VI represents an example par excellence of a prince who "never did anything, nor ever thought of anything, but how to deceive men, and he always found a subject to whom he could do it." Other princes and people tended to believe the pope, especially when he swore by the God he was supposed to represent on earth. Machiavelli merely observes that "there never was a man with greater efficacy in asserting a thing, and in affirming it with greater oaths, who observed it less" (70).

Ancient princes may have been better generals, but, Machiavelli suggests, modern princes are better dissemblers. Having urged modern readers to study the art of war, as it was practiced by the ancients, Machiavelli now advises them to combine this art with the modern art of dissimulation, which he associates particularly with Christianity. Unlike the Roman emperors Machiavelli discusses in *P* 19, Christian princes could not hope to be proclaimed gods after their death and worshiped by their people as such. They claimed, instead, to be serving God or the people; and when things did not go as desired, they could attribute undesirable results to the "will" of an unfathomable "God." Rather than accepting blame for the suffering of their people, these princes tried to succor and comfort them in their misery. Machiavelli saw that the most astute of these modern princes knew that it is necessary "to appear merciful, faithful, humane, honest, and religious," but that "a prince, and especially a new prince, cannot observe all those things for which men are held good, since he is often under a necessity, to maintain his state, of acting against faith, against charity, against humanity, against religion" (70).

Machiavelli insists that a prince should take great care not to say anything that is not "merciful, faithful, humane, honest, and religious," especially religious. Most people judge by appearances. When the effects of the prince's actions correspond to his explanations of his purposes and motives, people will believe that he has done what he has done for the reasons he gives. "In the actions of all men, and especially of princes, where there is no court to appeal to, one looks to the end. So," Machiavelli concludes, "let a prince win and maintain his state: the means will always be judged honorable, and will be praised by everyone" (71). This famous observation has often been inaccurately abbreviated as simply saying that the end justifies the means. In fact, Machiavelli points to one specific end, acquiring and maintaining the state. This "end" justifies the means, moreover, particularly in the eyes of the people. If a state is led by a prince who secures the lives, family, and property of his subjects, his people will believe that the prince is doing what he says he is doing—mercifully, faithfully, humanely, and honestly—for the sake of God and his people. As Machiavelli repeatedly reminds his readers, however, in fact princes act for the sake of acquiring and maintaining their own power and fame.[71] (This is what the few who can "touch" him, i.e., feel what moves him in his "heart of hearts," know that most do not.) In *P* 9 Machiavelli attributed the rise of a private citizen to become prince of his fatherland with the support of his fellow citizens to a "fortunate astuteness" (without pointing out there, as he does in *P* 15 and 18, that astuteness or cleverness is the opposite of honesty).[72]

2. How to Avoid Hatred, Conspiracies, or Rebellions

Having specified the qualities for which a prince should seek to be reputed, in *P* 19 Machiavelli turns summarily to stating what a prince should not do if he is not to become hated and contemned. In discussing "liberality," Machiavelli already argued that a prince should not despoil his people of their property or honor if he wants to avoid hatred and contempt. So long as the prince does not despoil his people, Machiavelli now adds, they will be content and the prince will have to contend only with the ambitions of the few.

Princes should have two fears, according to Machiavelli: (1) internal from their subjects, and (2) external from powers who would attack them and seize control. But, he suggests, a prince who maintains the support of his people by arming them will secure himself from both.

71. *Pace* Benner, *Prince*, 283–84, who argues that "the obligations that help make a state strong are produced by people's reasoned judgements about the quality of a leader's action, *never* by deception or manipulation," Vatter, *Machiavelli's "The Prince,"* observes that "the exercise of a monopoly of violence, even if wielded on behalf of the people against those who engage in domination, cannot but project a 'bad,' domineering image of the state that fails to reassure its subjects. Therefore, Machiavelli argues that the modern state or civil prince must follow the path of simulation and dissimulation (see Chapter 18) in order to construct for itself an appearance of 'goodness' that stands a chance of satisfying its subjects" (66).

72. As Machiavelli states in the title of *D* 2.13: "One Comes from Base to Great Fortune More through Fraud Than through Force."

Machiavelli has already emphasized the importance of a prince's organizing his own arms to defend his state (and his people) from foreign aggressors. Now he explains that a prince who maintains popular support also secures himself from internal conspirators. Those who seek to kill or overthrow a prince always hope that the people will rally around them. But if the people are content with their prince, a would-be assassin has to fear the reaction not only of the prince's bodyguards but also of the law, his friends, the state apparatus, and the people.[73]

Although Machiavelli says that the ambitions of the few can be checked in many ways, he singles out two that happen to correspond to the two ways of fighting he pointed out in the previous chapter: one with laws like a human being, the other with force and fraud like a beast. As is characteristic of the second half of *The Prince*, the example he gives of the best way to fight, with laws, is modern whereas the example of how to fight like a beast with force and fraud is ancient.

In order to avoid conspiracies, Machiavelli observes, "well-ordered states and wise princes have thought out with all diligence how not to make the great desperate and how to satisfy the people and keep them content." The example of a well-ordered and -governed kingdom he proposes is modern France, where there are "infinite good institutions on which the liberty and security of the king depend. The first of these is the parlement" (74).[74] By enabling the people to try and judge nobles, Machiavelli explains, the French

73. As Strauss, *TM*, 26, points out, in presenting Nabis as an example, Machiavelli undercuts his claim that a popular prince will be able to withstand any challenge, because, as Mansfield notes, *Prince*, 72n3, Nabis was, in fact, killed by a conspiracy. Because he is writing to a prince, who could become the target of a conspiracy, Machiavelli does not describe the ways in which conspirators can overcome the difficulties in *The Prince*, as he does in *Discourses* 3.6. In the *Discourses* Machiavelli is writing to citizens of a republic who deserve to be princes, and would have to overthrow the existing regime, i.e., become conspirators, in order to do so.

74. Cary J. Nederman and Tatiana V. Gòmez, "Between Republic and Monarchy? Liberty, Security, and the Kingdom of France in Machiavelli," *Midwest Studies in Philosophy* 26 (2002): 83, point out that "many major contributions to Machiavelli scholarship in English have largely overlooked his remarks about the governance of France." They list Hannah Fenichel Pitkin, *Fortune Is a Woman: Gender and Politics in the Thought of Niccolò Machiavelli* (Chicago: University of Chicago Press, 1999); Mansfield, *Machiavelli's Virtue*; Skinner, *Machiavelli*; Maurizio Viroli, *Machiavelli* (Oxford: Oxford University Press, 1998); and Fischer, *Well-Ordered License*, as examples (83n4), and note that Hulliung, *Citizen Machiavelli*, 85, explicitly denies the importance of Machiavelli's comments on the "well-ordered kingdom" of France (84n5). But Wootton, introduction to Niccolò Machiavelli, *The Prince*, observes that "orderly government provides what Machiavelli sometimes calls *il vivere civile* or *il vivere politico*. Kings can provide this; indeed, Machiavelli repeatedly praises France, where royal despotism and aristocratic tyranny are kept within the law by the *parlements*" (xxxi). Establishing good institutions is a necessary but not sufficient condition for "good government," according to Machiavelli. As he shows in *P* 3, the French parlement did not prevent King Louis from adopting a seriously flawed foreign policy.

parlement beats down the ambition and insolence of the great and thus secures both the generality of the people, who fear the great, and the king, who sees the great as his competitors, without his having to take the blame. In *P* 9 Machiavelli observed that there were three possible outcomes of the conflict between the two basic "humors"—principality, liberty, and license. Here in *P* 19 we see that both the "liberty and security of the king" and the security of the people depend upon the institution of a court that enables the people to check the great.[75]

Machiavelli's praise of the "one who ordered that kingdom" is worth quoting in full:

> Knowing the ambition of the powerful and their insolence, and judging it necessary for them to have a bit in their mouths to correct them, and on the other side, knowing the hatred of the generality of people against the great, which is founded in its fear, and wanting to secure them, [he] intended this not to be the particular concern of the king, so as to take from him the blame he would have from the great when he favored the popular side, and from the popular side when he favored the great; and so he constituted a third judge to be the one who would beat down the great and favor the lesser side without blame for the king. (75)

As in the case of Cesare's use of Remirro de Orco to bring "good government" to the Romagna, followed by his instituting a "civil court" and publicly disowning and destroying the cruel means of establishing order by policing the marauding "great," so Machiavelli concludes here that "princes should have anything blameable administered by others, favors by themselves" (75). Princes should, therefore, honor the great (while making sure that others check their ambitions), and not make themselves hated by the generality of the people by seizing their property or women or allowing their "nobles" to do so.

Machiavelli recognizes that a reader might object to his insistence on the need for a prince to obtain and maintain the support of his people, without driving the great to desperation, on the basis of the succession of Roman

75. Hans Baron, "Machiavelli the Republican Citizen," *The Crisis of the Early Italian Renaissance* (Princeton: Princeton University Press, 1966), 116–17, takes the fact that in *Discourses* 3.1 Machiavelli praises the French *parlamenti* for securing the people by enforcing the law against both nobles and princes, whereas in *The Prince* he praises it as a means of securing the king, as evidence of the entirely different character or spirit of the two works. But Hörnqvist, *Machiavelli and Empire*, 225, points out that Machiavelli is presenting the same institution of a mixed or constitutional government in the two works from the two different perspectives of their immediate addressees.

emperors from Marcus "the philosopher" to Maximinus. And in light of the fates of these emperors, Machiavelli modifies his advice in two respects. First and foremost, he points out that these emperors had to contend not only with "the ambition of the great and the *insolence* of the people" (76, italics mine), but also with the cruelty and avarice of their soldiers. He thus admits, in passing, that the people can threaten the state of the prince as well as can the great.[76] Men-at-arms pose a more immediate threat, however, than unarmed subjects. Because most of these emperors were "new men" and the armed soldiers were stronger than the unarmed people, these emperors had to allow their soldiers to oppress the people if they did not want the army to overthrow them.

Of the modest, humane lovers of justice among these emperors, Machiavelli observes, only Marcus lived and died honorably. "Because he succeeded to the empire by hereditary right" and "was attended with many virtues that made him venerable," he was able to keep both the soldiers and the people within bounds. Machiavelli does not say what Marcus's "virtues" were, but by referring to Marcus as "the philosopher," he suggests that the emperor's virtues included his Stoical teachings and practices.[77] Machiavelli does remind his readers that, despite his own contemplative "exercises," Marcus did not succeed in educating his son to become equally virtuous; on the contrary, Commodus became one of the emperors hated for his cruelty and rapacity. Since Commodus succeeded by hereditary right from Marcus, Machiavelli also lets his readers see, although he does not explicitly say, that it was the virtues which made him venerable rather than his hereditary right that enabled Marcus to control both his soldiers and the people.[78] Although Machiavelli wrote in *P* 2 that a hereditary prince need use only "ordinary industry" to maintain himself, he now reminds

76. Cf. *D* 1.37, where Machiavelli explains that the people can become as ambitious, greedy, and oppressive as the "great," if and when the people acquire enough power.

77. Machiavelli does not remind his readers that Marcus wrote his *Meditations* while he was serving as general of the Roman army in Germany, where he and his men killed thousands, or that Marcus countenanced, if he did not promote, the persecution of Christians in Rome.

78. In *The Prince*, addressed to a "prince" of Florence who acquired rule on the basis of his family ties or "heredity," Machiavelli does not point out that Marcus was adopted. Writing to republican sympathizers in *D* 1.10, Machiavelli uses a longer line of emperors, including Marcus, to show that only those who were adopted succeeded, and thus that hereditary succession is bad, a judgment he shares with previous writers who saw the corruption of hereditary successors as the reason for the degenerative cycle of regimes (*D* 1.2). Machiavelli radicalizes that insight into the inadequacy of family ties as a basis for government in *D* 3.3–4, however, by arguing that maintaining a republic requires the killing of "the sons of Brutus," and reminding his readers that daughters will see their fathers murdered for the sake of acquiring rule.

his readers (including Lorenzo) that where there is a standing professional army, there is always "an extraordinary and excessive force" ready to overthrow him.[79]

Machiavelli uses the examples of the other two modest and humane imperial lovers of justice to show that "hatred is acquired through good deeds as well as bad ones." Not merely must a prince make sure that others fear the consequences of disobeying his commands; he must also recognize that laws and courts will not suffice to preserve him and his state. Pertinax was created emperor against the will of the soldiers, who, accustomed to living in license under his predecessor, Commodus, hated Pertinax for trying to make them return to decency. They also contemned him, because he was old (and thus presumably physically weak). The soldiers likewise hated and contemned Alexander, who did not allow anyone to be executed without a trial in his fourteen years as emperor but was "held to be effeminate and a man who let himself be governed by his mother" (77). As a result, they conspired against him and killed him.

As the example of Alexander shows, fighting like a man with laws does not suffice to check a corrupt people or army. A prince must, therefore, also know how to fight like a beast. Both forms of knowledge prove to be quite rare, however. Just as Marcus was the only humane emperor who did not succumb to a conspiracy, so, Machiavelli points out, Septimius Severus was the only cruel and rapacious emperor who did not suffer a wretched end. Because they acted so bestially and basely, all the others aroused the hatred of the people and became contemned by their soldiers, who then conspired to kill them.

Severus constitutes the most famous example of the successful combination of the fox and the lion, which, Machiavelli emphasizes, is particularly relevant to a new prince (like Lorenzo). Although Severus burdened the people, he was able to rule happily by maintaining the soldiers as his friends. He did so by keeping his army constantly in motion, undertaking a series of surprise attacks on his competitors, always under the cover of righting a wrong. The cruelty that satisfied his soldiers might have led the people to hate him, but his repeated successes made him feared and revered by everyone.[80]

79. As in *P* 12–14, so in the *Art of War* Machiavelli thus argues that a prince must muster and train an army of his own subjects.

80. Machiavelli reminds his readers that Severus began his career by leading his army from Slavonia to Rome, purportedly to avenge the death of Pertinax; but once in Rome, he and his army frightened the Senate into killing Julianus and declaring Severus emperor. Recognizing that the gen-

Severus was no more successful than Marcus, however, in passing on his own virtue to his son Antonius (Caracalla), who, by killing so many Romans and all of Alexandria, became hateful to the entire world. Although the empire he gained and maintained was much larger, Severus's success does not appear to be much different, in principle, from Agathocles' acquisition and maintenance of his rule in Syracuse (by "crime") for the duration of his life.[81] None of the bestial emperors Machiavelli mentions seems to have been as "astute" as Hiero, also of Syracuse, who, seeing that the mercenary arms he had used to acquire power had become a threat to him, arranged to have them destroyed in the next battle.[82]

A reader might wonder, indeed, why Machiavelli introduced the possible objection based on the line of Roman emperors when he concludes that "princes of our own times . . . have less difficulty satisfying their soldiers" (perhaps because modern mercenaries demand much less than the Roman armies for doing less), so that modern princes ought to be more concerned about satisfying their people. Machiavelli notes an exception, however, and the exception indicates the point of what might otherwise appear to be an unnecessary digression. Two modern rulers are not in a position to favor their people more than the soldiers. Because both the Turk and the sultan are surrounded by and thus in the hands of their soldiers, these princes must please the army rather than their people. And, Machiavelli observes, the state of the sultan is unlike all other principalities except the Christian pontificate. The similarity Machiavelli explicitly points out is that neither the sultanate nor the papacy can be called either a hereditary or a new principality, because in both cases the order is old, but the holders of the supreme office are elected by those who have authority to do so. The implication, however, is that neither the sultan nor the pope can establish or

erals of the Roman armies in the East and the West both also harbored imperial ambitions, Severus acted like a fox by sending a message to Albinus telling the general that, with the Senate's approval, Severus wished to share the title with him. In the meantime the lion-like Severus marched against Pescennius Niger in Asia, defeated his army, and killed him. Returning to Rome, Severus then complained to the Senate that Albinus had treacherously tried to kill him, so that it was necessary for Severus to go and punish the traitor by defeating his army in France and killing him.

81. Both Garver, *Machiavelli and the History of Prudence*, and Kahn, *Machiavellian Rhetoric*, thus go too far when they argue that Machiavelli collapses the two ways of fighting that he first distinguishes as human and bestial into the two different "bestial" modes of the fox and the lion, because fox-like deception is particularly human. The human model of the "fox and the lion," Severus, represents only half of what is necessary to gain *and maintain* rule. Impressed by Machiavelli's insistence on the need for "cruelty," these commentators do not notice Machiavelli's emphasis on the importance of laws, especially courts.

82. Another fact that Machiavelli does not mention is that the Roman armies that elevated and unseated the emperors he names included a great many mercenaries.

maintain a stable secular government. Unlike Marcus, they do not rule by hereditary right or share his Stoic virtues. Nor can they follow Machiavelli's advice to the leader of a "civic principality" and seek to gain the support of the people after they are elected by a few "grandi," because they are unarmed captives of their armed guards. Like the Roman emperors after Marcus, these "ecclesiastical" princes must either appear to be contemptibly weak or join their soldiers in oppressing others (as the Turk did in Greece). As Machiavelli reminds his readers, a head of the Church like Alexander VI might have proved to be a dissembler par excellence, but he does not have the force of a lion reliably in his own hands. Nor was he any more able than Marcus and Severus to establish a succession by hereditary right. Alexander wanted to help his illegitimate son acquire a principality, but Cesare's military gains accrued to the Church, not to the Borgia family. Alexander's successor, Julius II, led his own armies into battle, but as pope he could no more establish a hereditary succession than could his predecessor. As pope, he could not have a son as his legitimate heir. He was, moreover, elected late in life and thus had a short term of office. And he depended upon foreign—mercenary or auxiliary—troops. Only an armed secular prince can effectively combine the bestial virtues of Severus in founding a new principality, and then imitate the actions of Marcus "to conserve a state that is already established and firm" (82). Machiavelli's three examples suggest that a prince elected by the representatives of a universal religion will find it particularly difficult to do so, because those who elect and fight to maintain them are not necessarily their subjects or "creatures."[83] And their "faith" is not enough to secure their loyalty.

Machiavelli's apparent "digression" at the end of *P* 19 should alert an attentive reader to its possible application to the situation of his presumed reader. As commander of the pope's troops, Machiavelli intimates, Lorenzo was in a position to hold his uncle the pope hostage. He might also determine the cardinals' choice of his uncle's successor the way Augustus and his successors controlled the Roman Senate—not by using force directly, but by reminding them that he commanded the army.[84]

83. The guards who surrounded the Turk were young men taken from their homes (often Christian) in their youth and then raised and educated as Muslims in his palace in Constantinople. They thus lacked the desire to defend their own families and property that Machiavelli has suggested a prince should enlist in making his fellow citizens, subjects, or dependents into his own "arms." Popes had the ability to name cardinals, but since the pope changed so frequently, the college could and would contain cardinals he did not raise to that office.

84. If so, Lorenzo would not have to kill his uncle the pope in order to seize control of Italy, as argued by John T. Scott and Vickie B. Sullivan, "Patricide and the Plot of *The Prince*: Cesare Borgia

3. Tactics, Distinction, and Advice

Confounding the commentators who read *The Prince* as a "technical manual" laying out general maxims for ruling, Machiavelli begins *P* 20 by observing that princes have tried to hold their states securely in diametrically opposed ways: "Some . . . have disarmed their subjects so as to hold their states securely; some others have kept their subject towns divided; some have nourished enmities against themselves; some others have turned to gaining to themselves those who had been suspect to them at the beginning of their states; some have built fortresses; some have knocked them down and destroyed them" (83). And he concludes that he cannot say what measures or tactics would be best without examining the particular circumstances.

In considering the matter broadly, Machiavelli nevertheless highlights the general principles that inform his previous discussion of the ways in which princes can acquire and maintain states—and thus what should truly be considered to be virtuous and vicious. First, he reiterates, a new prince must arm his subjects. When he shows that he trusts and so honors them, their arms become his arms, to be used against those who were in power previously as well as anyone else who resists him and his rule. If an established prince is acquiring a new territory, however, he must disarm his new subjects; and he should also do whatever he can gradually to render the partisans who helped him enter soft and effeminate. Since, as Machiavelli pointed out in *P* 3, the prince will never be able to satisfy his partisans' desires for ever greater wealth and power, they will eventually become his enemies. As Machiavelli has made clear in his discussion of the virtues in *P* 16–19, a prince cannot successfully acquire and maintain his state merely by benefiting his adherents in order to gain and retain their love, because to benefit his followers either he will have to burden his subjects with taxes and thus arouse their hatred or he will have to lead an army on ever more distant campaigns to seize the goods of others. As the Roman emperors learned to their dismay, this army becomes a threat not only to a prince's people, but also to him.

Machiavelli argues, second, that a prince should not attempt to acquire and maintain rule by "dividing and conquering"—at home or abroad.

---

and Machiavelli's Italy," *American Political Science Review* 88 (1994): 887–900, and Joseph M. Parent, "Machiavelli's Missing Romulus and the Murderous Intent of *The Prince*," *History of Political Thought* 26, no. 4 (Winter 2005): 625–45. See John Najemy, *A History of Florence, 1200–1575* (Oxford: Blackwell, 2006), 426–34.

Machiavelli has insisted that in every city there is conflict between the two humors, which need to be balanced against each other; and he has presented Severus, who deceived one ally long enough to conquer another, as a model of the necessary combination of the fox and the lion. But Machiavelli does not accept the traditional wisdom of the Florentine elders who say that it is necessary to hold Pistoia with factions and Pisa with fortresses. On the contrary, he points out that "when an enemy approaches, of necessity divided cities are immediately lost, because the weaker party always joins the external forces" (84).

Third, Machiavelli has argued that a new prince should understand that he will not be able to satisfy the ambitions of the dissatisfied individuals who helped him acquire power; he should, therefore, look for support in the people who were content under the former government. But now he adds that these include individuals like Machiavelli himself "who at the beginning of their states were held to be suspect" and "who are of such quality that to maintain themselves they need somewhere to lean." Because they "need to cancel out with deeds the sinister opinion" the prince has of them, such individuals will serve him all the more faithfully (85). Those willing to accept the rule of a prince who does not oppress them and so arouse their hatred also include the generality of the people. Although it has been the custom of princes to build fortresses to hold their states more securely in the face of potential opposition from their own people as well as external aggressors, Machiavelli urges, "the best fortress is not to be hated by the people" (87).

Machiavelli underlines the largely negative redefinition of the virtues he has given by concluding that he will "praise whoever makes fortresses, and whoever does not make" them, because their utility depends on the circumstances, but he will "blame anyone who, trusting in fortresses, thinks little of being hated by the people" (87). Praise follows success, which is sometimes a product of chance; a prince is justly blamed, however, for not understanding his own situation and necessities. The first and foremost of those necessities, Machiavelli has shown in his redefinition of the virtues, is not to become hated by the people and thus encourage conspiracies. A prince needs to use enough force to establish order and enforce the law, but he should not further oppress or tax his people to benefit his allies or soldiers—unless he is constrained to do so by his army. In the following chapter Machiavelli suggests a way in which a prince can earn distinction not by conquering and betraying others, i.e., "fighting like a beast," but by benefiting his subjects. Human beings seek to be virtuous, because they want to be praised. Having redefined the virtues as the means of acquiring and maintaining rule, he thus reconsiders and redefines the deeds and characteristics for which princes gain distinction. These turn out to be of two rather different kinds.

The first way Machiavelli suggests that a prince can gain distinction is by undertaking great enterprises and giving rare examples of himself. From a weak king, he notes, Ferdinand of Aragon has become "by fame and glory the first king of the Christians." By attacking the Muslims at Granada in the south of Spain, Ferdinand was able to divert the barons of Castile in the north from planning other campaigns on their own, while he built up his own army and consequent reputation unnoticed by the barons. Because it was a religious war, he could obtain funds to support it from both the Church and his people. "Ever making use of religion, he also resorted to an act of pious cruelty by chasing the Marranos from his kingdom and despoiling them." He then "attacked Africa under this same cloak" (88) and expanded his campaign into Italy (Naples) and France, so that he always kept his subjects wondering and never gave anyone time to work quietly against him.

Waging war under a religious cover with the financial support of the Church in order to unite his country and expand its empire, Ferdinand would appear to represent an especially suitable contemporary model for Lorenzo, the nephew of the pope. Yet Machiavelli does not call Ferdinand's "pious cruelty," "cruelty well-used." Although Machiavelli has argued that a prince cannot keep faith (and so, presumably, should not be held to promises to allow converts to remain and hold property within his Christian country, if circumstances require that he seize their goods), Machiavelli says of Ferdinand's exiling and expropriating the Marranos that "this example could not be more wretched or more rare" (88). (Readers should recall that Machiavelli observed that a prince will always be able to find reasons to seize the goods of his subjects, but that he should not do so; seeing Ferdinand banish the converts and then seize their property, his other Christian subjects might worry that they and their property would be next.)[85] When

85. Machiavelli made his less than stellar evaluation of Ferdinand more explicit in an exchange of letters with Francesco Vettori in April 1513. In his letter of April 29, Machiavelli characterized the king of Spain as "more cunning and fortunate than wise." And he explained, "This king has risen to these heights from a low and poor fortune; he has always had new states and equivocal subjects to contend with. One method for holding on to new territories and for either stabilizing equivocal minds or keeping them hanging and irresolute is to arouse great expectations of oneself,

he goes on to cite Bernabò of Milan as a case of a prince's having given "rare examples of himself concerning internal government," moreover, Machiavelli explicitly observes that a prince can win a kind of distinction or renown for doing something extraordinarily evil as well as something good. Bernabò seized power with two of his brothers and subsequently cooperated in the poisoning of one of them. Bernabò had been largely responsible for the consolidation of the state of Milan; but he was excommunicated three times, imprisoned, and perhaps killed by his brother's son Gian Galeazzo. (Contemporary readers might think of Adolf Hitler or Josef Stalin as even more egregious examples of "princes" who achieved a certain kind of distinction as a result of their extraordinarily evil deeds.) Without giving any details and concluding simply that "a prince ought to contrive [*ingegnare*], above all, in each of his actions, to give himself the fame of a great man and of excellent ingenuity [*ingegno*]" (89), Machiavelli makes his reader wonder whether this is really the kind of "distinction" or "esteem" a prince wants, if his extraordinary cruelty does not, like "cruelty well-used," enable him to maintain his control of the state.

Following the example of the perfidious Bernabò, Machiavelli's further observation that "a prince is also esteemed when he is a true friend and true enemy" appears to be ironical. The argument he gives to show that a prince should never remain neutral circles back on itself. Machiavelli suggests that a weaker state that refuses to ally with the victor in an upcoming struggle will be prey to whoever wins, and that the weaker state retains a claim to just treatment, refuge, and future assistance by the defeated party if and only if it allies with the vanished state before the conflict. However, Machiavelli has already argued that obligations of "love" and in "words" are not to be relied upon. And here he emphasizes that "a prince must beware never to associate with someone more powerful than himself so as to attack others, except when necessity presses. . . . For when you win, you are left his prisoner" (90). An alliance with a state that is apt to lose in a conflict with a stronger one appears to benefit a prince only when he himself has enough power to determine the outcome or has a chance of doing so in the future.

always keeping men's minds busy with trying to figure out the aim of one's decision and one's new ventures. This king has recognized the need for this and has employed it to advantage; hence his attacks in Africa, the partition of the kingdom [of Naples], and all his other various campaigns. He has not tried to foresee the outcome: for his aim is not so much this, that, or the other victory, as to win prestige among his various peoples and to keep them hanging with his multifarious activities" (*Machiavelli and His Friends*, 232, 235).

The point of Machiavelli's insistence on the necessity of taking sides does not appear to be the benefits or virtue of loyalty—or the superior nobility of declaring adherence to one side or another rather than remaining weakly neutral. He has already argued that a prince cannot always "keep faith." Machiavelli's point is, rather, that "no state should ever believe that it can always make safe choice," because "in the order of things, one never tries to avoid one inconvenience without incurring another one. Prudence consists in knowing how to recognize the qualities of the inconveniences and choosing the less bad as if it were good" (91).[86] Indecision is never good—or even possible.[87] A decision not to take sides or to do nothing is nevertheless a decision that will have consequences.

Machiavelli never retracts his insistence on the importance of a prince's raising and leading his own army in order to defend both himself and his subjects. But, he now suggests, there is a domestic alternative to conquest as a means of acquiring wealth.

> A prince must also show himself to be a lover of the virtues by giving hospitality to virtuous men, and he must honor those who are excellent in an art. Next, he must encourage his citizens to be able quietly to practice their trades, in commerce, in agriculture and in every other human occupation, so that one man is not afraid to improve his properties for fear they will be taken from him, and another is not afraid to open a business for fear of taxes. But he must prepare rewards for whoever wants to do these things, and for whoever thinks to increase his city or his state in whatever way. (91)[88]

86. Even though Machiavelli does not include prudence among the qualities people think are good or the virtues for which they are praised, he refers throughout *The Prince* to what a "prudent" prince would or would not do (*P* 3, 7, 9, 15, 16, 18, 21–25). Machiavelli does not include "prudence" among the virtues, because (as both Garver, *Machiavelli and the History of Prudence*, and Kahn, *Machiavellian Rhetoric*, point out), unlike Aristotle, he does not define prudence as a steady disposition that leads one to do what is "right" or just under the particular circumstances. He defines prudence, rather, as knowing what will be effective in acquiring and maintaining rule under any particular set of circumstances. According to both Garver and Kahn, "prudence" so understood comes very close to defining *virtù* and is constituted almost if not entirely by rhetoric (understanding the use of force to be a kind of persuasion). Both Garver and Kahn also argue that Machiavelli seeks to teach "prudence" through his own dialogical way of arguing rather than the imitation of ancient or modern examples per se.

87. Hörnqvist, *Machiavelli and Empire*, 97–102, shows how Machiavelli's critique of neutrality could be applied not only to traditional canons of Florentine foreign policy but also to Florence's vacillation between allying with the French and the Holy League in the period just before the fall of the republic in 1512.

88. In *D* 2.2 Machiavelli attributes such economic benefits, including an increase in population, particularly to a free regime. Writing to a prince, in *The Prince* he cannot promise, as he does in his description of the free regime in *D* 2.2, that a man can hope that his sons may become princes. In *The Prince* Machiavelli suggests that the "liberty" of both the people and the prince is a

Instead of organizing and leading an army to seize the goods of others that will eventually become a threat to him and his people, a prince should reward the ingenuity and efforts of his people. He should not merely secure their lives and property; he should also publicly reward those who do most and "keep the people occupied with festivals and spectacles," not by descending to fight with the gladiators himself like Commodus, but by offering himself "as an example of humanity and munificence, while maintaining his dignity" (91).[89]

A prince will be able to maintain his dignity, as well as a reputation for his intelligence, Machiavelli finally adds, only if he is able to choose good advisors. No one can know everything; it is, therefore, necessary to consult. But, he suggests, there is an unfailing way of determining whether a prince can trust an advisor or not: when a prince sees that an advisor thinks more of himself and his own interests than of those of the prince, he should not be trusted. Machiavelli has demonstrated his own credentials in this respect in *The Prince* by presenting all his knowledge from the perspective of the needs of the prince.[90] Machiavelli now adds that if a prince wants to keep his minister good, he should honor and reward him. For his own sake as well as for his advisor, the prince should also be selective in the advice he receives. He should not allow anyone to approach him without his permission, and he should take advice from only a few trusted counselors. He has to make up his own mind, however, and once he does, he should stick to the decision he has made. He should not, like the Emperor Maximilian, constantly change his mind and policy on the basis of his most recent advice. This is another version of the destructive indecision Machiavelli criticized in princes who want to stay neutral or avoid making any decision at all until they are certain. Such evident indecisiveness destroys a prince's reputation, if it does not lose him his state.

---

product of a balance (or "conflict") between the humors that produces the rule of law, enforced by a court. Emphasizing the conjunction between the interest of the prince and the desires of the people allows Machiavelli to speak about "justice," even though he does not describe it as a virtue.

89. Machiavelli's suggestion here might be seen as praise for the policies of previous Medici rulers, especially Cosimo and Lorenzo the Magnificent, who employed many workers in building kingly palaces for themselves as well as decorating churches and honoring both artists and scholars. As Machiavelli shows in *FH* 7–8, the Medici acquired a great popular following by means of their liberality. However, it is not so clear that their fellow citizens or subjects felt secure from taxes (which were necessary to pay for both mercenary soldiers and Lorenzo's private building projects). In *D* 2.2 Machiavelli argues that citizens feel secure in their property and thus produce and procreate more in republics than under princes, because everything done in a principality is done for the sake of the prince and does not contribute to the general prosperity.

90. *TM*, 21–29.

III. Fortune and the Future

After having laid out the general principles of his understanding of the necessities of politics, as well as indicating the basis of that understanding in an analysis of both recent and historical events, in the last three chapters of *The Prince* Machiavelli applies these principles to his and Lorenzo's specific situation in Italy. He promises that if a new prince (presumably Lorenzo) applies what Machiavelli has written above "prudently," his state will almost immediately look ancient and established. "He will have the double glory of having made the beginning of a new principality, of having adorned it and consolidated it with good laws, good arms, and good examples, just as he has a double shame who, having been born prince, has lost it through his lack of prudence" (96).

Those lords in Italy who have lost their states, like the king of Naples, the duke of Milan, and others, had a common defect as to arms. Apparently oblivious to the difficulties Machiavelli pointed out in *P* 12–14, these princes thought they could rely on mercenaries or auxiliaries; they did not muster, train, and deploy their own subjects and so gain their own arms.[91] They also had a hostile people or, like Cesare, "did not know how to secure themselves against the great." It is necessary, but not sufficient, Machiavelli emphasizes, for a prince not to arouse the hatred of his people. As he pointed out in *P* 9 and 17, a prince should not rely on the people (or "love") to save him from the machinations of his competitors. However friendly, an unarmed people cannot withstand an armed attack. A prince must first muster and train his own arms and then establish institutions that will protect him from possible future attacks, internal as well as external.

Machiavelli recognizes "that many have held and hold the opinion that worldly things are so governed by fortune and by God, that men cannot correct them with their prudence."[92] He does not claim that human beings can control or entirely determine their own fates. "It might be true that fortune is arbiter of half of our actions," but, he judges, "she leaves the other half, or close to it, for us to govern, so that our free will not be eliminated" (98).

91. Machiavelli puts an even more dismissive description of the behavior of Italian princes into the mouth of Fabrizio Colonna in *AW* 7.229–238.

92. As Najemy, *Between Friends*, documents in considerable detail, Machiavelli's friend and correspondent Francesco Vettori explicitly held such views. Although in some of his letters, Machiavelli attempted to persuade Vettori to take a more optimistic view of the possibilities of human action, there is no reason to think, as Najemy argues, that this argument was directed primarily if not solely at Vettori. Here at the beginning of chapter 25 of *The Prince* Machiavelli explicitly addresses a view held by "many" in the past as well as now.

Fortune is like one of those violent rivers that, when angry, flood the plain and ruin everything built on it, if no one with foresight has erected dikes and dug canals to divert the water; she "demonstrates her power where virtue has not instituted an order to resist her and turns her impetus where she knows that dams and dikes have not been made to contain her" (98–99).

If we look back to Machiavelli's description of the human condition, the forces that ebb and flow with more or less positive results appear to be the passions, especially an almost universal fear of death and the unending desire to acquire to which that fear gives rise.[93] Unchecked and undirected, these passions have destructive consequences, for states as well as for individuals. As Machiavelli has argued, particularly in his discussion of the true character of virtue, human passions cannot be eradicated or directly controlled by law, much less by moral suasion. They can, however, be directed and checked by a prince who knows both how to fight like a man, by establishing institutions like the French parlement that enable the people to check the great, and how to fight like a beast, by using force to put down rebels and aggressors and fraud to deceive both his competitors and his people. By contrasting the "dikes" erected by virtuous leaders in Germany, Spain, and France with the absence of such in Italy, Machiavelli suggests that the relevant "techniques" might include building walled fortresses with a year's worth of stored supplies used to protect the people (as in the free German cities), claiming to fight wars for religious purposes and thus obtaining funds from both the people and the Church (like Ferdinand of Aragon), or training an infantry and establishing a court (like the kings in France).

It is impossible to say generally what a prince ought to do to protect his people and maintain his state under all possible circumstances, because circumstances or "the times" change. Under some conditions, it is better to be cautious; under other conditions, it is better to be impetuous. Once again, Machiavelli reminds his reader, he is not providing him with a "manual" or rule book to be mechanically applied everywhere or at all times.

As we saw in the first half of *The Prince*, Machiavelli's political science rests on his observation of some fundamental forces or passions that move all human beings. If these passions are not recognized for what they are, and checked or redirected, they produce unending conflict. He has suggested that this conflict can be managed, however, by a virtuous prince who knows how to channel it to produce beneficial results for both himself and

93. In *D* 2.29, Machiavelli explicitly argues that "Fortune Blinds the Spirits of Men When It Does Not Wish Them to Oppose Its Plans" by arousing their passions.

his people.[94] But now, Machiavelli acknowledges, no individual can ever be prudent enough to adapt his behavior to all possible circumstances. Although human beings generally are characterized by certain fundamental passions, the intensity and direction of these passions vary from individual to individual, depending not only on birth but also on that individual's formative experience or "conditioning." Like human nature generally, individual human beings are malleable only within certain limits. Once trained or formed, their characters cannot be changed.[95] That is the reason Machiavelli did not write a traditional book on the education of a prince. No education of a single individual will enable that individual to see and do what is necessary under all circumstances. Instead of trying to educate a few people to rule wisely and virtuously, Machiavelli thus tries to show his readers what can and cannot be done with the human "matter" at hand by establishing and maintaining certain kinds of institutions.

In a treatise purportedly addressed to a new prince, Machiavelli does not suggest, as he does in *D* 1.20 and 3.9, that republics are able to solve the problem of succession and to adapt to changes in the "times" or circumstances better than principalities, because republics can elect leaders who possess the necessary characteristics (and unelect those who do not). Nor does he have to acknowledge that even in republics, people do not always choose the best leaders. In *The Prince* he has already stated unequivocally that in politics no decision or method is ever entirely safe or certain; there are always "inconveniences."

Toward the end of chapter 25, Machiavelli thus turns to what has worked most recently in Italy and what the best policy for a young prince generally tends to be. The current Medici Pope Leo's immediate predecessor, Julius II, "proceeded impetuously in all his affairs, and he found the times and affairs so much in conformity with his mode of proceeding that he always achieved a happy end" (100).[96] But pointing to the problem Cesare had experienced with his father's support and a potential problem for Lorenzo to the extent to which he depends upon Pope Leo, Machiavelli also observes that "the brevity of his life did not allow [Julius] to feel the contrary." However, "if times had come when he had needed to proceed with caution, his

94. See Hillary Zmora, "Love of Country and Love of Party: Patriotism and Human Nature in Machiavelli," *History of Political Thought* 25, no. 3 (Autumn 2004): 433–34, for a similar analysis.

95. Machiavelli makes the same argument in *D* 3.9.

96. Readers should note that Machiavelli attributes the pope's successes not to divine will or providence, but rather to the fortunate match between his native temperament or habits and the character of "the times."

ruin would have followed: he would never have deviated from those modes to which nature inclined him" (101). Nevertheless, although "fortune varies and men remain obstinate in their modes," Machiavelli famously concludes, "it is better to be impetuous than cautious, because fortune is a woman; and it is necessary, if one wants to hold her down, to beat her and strike her down. And one sees that she lets herself be won more by the impetuous than by those who proceed coldly. And so always, like a woman, she is the friend of the young" (101).[97]

Machiavelli thus concludes his treatise with a passionate exhortation to the young Florentine prince to take advantage of the "opportunity" fortune has provided him, "to seize Italy and to free her from the barbarians." Explicitly echoing the analysis of the four great founders he gave in chapter 6, Machiavelli assures Lorenzo that "there is matter to give opportunity to someone prudent and virtuous to introduce a form that would bring honor to him and good to the community of men there" (102). No one would have been able to see the virtue of Moses, the greatness of Cyrus, or the excellence of Theseus, if their peoples had not been, respectively, enslaved, oppressed by their neighbors, and dispersed.[98] The Italians now suffer from all these disabilities, "and although up to now a glimmer has shone in some-

97. On the basis of his saying that "fortune is a woman" and that "it is necessary . . . to beat her and strike her down" (as well as his emphasis on war, conflict, and gaining control), some feminist readers have declared Machiavelli to be a misogynist. Most famously, in *Fortune Is a Woman*, Hannah Fenichel Pitkin argues that Machiavelli's works contain three distinct but interwoven and mutually contradictory understandings of masculinity, which reflect his own ambivalent sexual orientation. See also Susan Moller Okin, "The Roots of Realpolitik," *Women's Review of Books* 2 (January 1985): 15–16, and Wendy Brown, *Manhood and Politics: A Feminist Reading in Political Theory* (Totowa, NJ: Rowman & Littlefield, 1988). Arlene Saxonhouse, *Women in the History of Political Thought: Ancient Greece to Machiavelli* (New York: Praeger, 1985), chap. 7, contests the misogynist reading by emphasizing the malleability of human nature, including sexual orientations and behavior, according to Machiavelli. And Michelle Tolman Clarke, "On the Woman Question in Machiavelli," *Review of Politics* 67, no. 2 (Spring 2005): 227–55, points out the large number of female political actors Machiavelli cites. In "'Fortune Is a Woman'—But So Is Prudence," in *Finding a New Feminism*, ed. Pamela Jensen (Lanham, MD: Rowman & Littlefield, 1996), 23–37, I emphasize the exemplary prudence exemplified by Sofronia's rule of her household (including a character named Nicomaco) in *Clizia*. When we look simply at *The Prince*, it is difficult to take Machiavelli's concluding statement altogether seriously or literally in the context, as it follows his comparison of fortune to a river that needs to be guided by dikes and ditches built in advance (by a prudent, if not cautious prince, who would certainly not be acting impetuously). Benner, *Prince*, xlvi, makes a similar observation.

98. Several commentators have observed that Machiavelli omits Romulus, the founder whom a new unifier and liberator of Italy would seem most likely to imitate. His example would point to the need for Lorenzo to kill his uncle (the pope) as well as his brother(s)—the cardinals—in order to consolidate his power, so Machiavelli pointed to it only indirectly, by omitting Romulus where a reader would most expect to see him. *TM*, 69; Scott and Sullivan, "Patricide"; Parent, "Machiavelli's Missing Romulus."

one who could judge that he had been ordered by God for her redemption, yet later it was seen that in the highest course of his actions, he was repulsed by fortune" (102). Machiavelli might appear to be referring to himself. However, he continues: the Italians are nevertheless ready to follow anyone ready to lead, and there is no one in whom they can "hope more than in your illustrious house, which with its fortune and virtue, supported by God and by the Church of which it is now prince, can put itself at the head of this redemption" (102–3).[99]

For centuries, commentators have asked how seriously Machiavelli made this final, passionate proposal. Did he really believe that Lorenzo could become the conqueror and liberator of all Italy?

On the one hand, Machiavelli insists that although the four founders were "rare and marvelous," they were nevertheless men, "and each of them had less opportunity than the present." It would therefore be possible for the Medici to duplicate their greatness, *if* the Medici princes keep their "aim on the orders" Machiavelli has put forth. He repeats: it will be "necessary before all other things, as the true foundation of every undertaking, to provide [themselves] with [their] own arms" (104), and these arms, composed of their subjects and fellow Italians, will become better if they see themselves commanded by their own prince. This is the way Machiavelli insisted any prince needs to acquire and maintain his rule in the first half of *The Prince.* As Machiavelli made clear in his discussion of Agathocles, however, merely seizing and keeping control of one's homeland for the duration of one's life is not sufficient to bring a prince glory. It is necessary to do something more in order to become honored and revered. In discussing the qualities for which a prince should truly be praised and blamed, Machiavelli argued that he should not be liberal or lavish (as Leo was known to be, and Alexander VI and Julius II had been in decorating the Vatican) and that he should seek not to be loved but to be feared and not hated. He will be feared if he arms his own subjects to fight in their own as well as in his defense, and he will avoid arousing their hatred if he makes sure that the

99. This sentence, emphasizing the importance of the Medici control of the Church, would seem to undermine the contention of Miguel Vatter, "Machiavelli and the Republican Conception of Providence," *Review of Politics* 75, no. 4 (2013): 605–24, *pace* Maurizio Viroli, *Machiavelli's God* (Princeton: Princeton University Press, 2010), 61. Instead of writing in a *Christian* republican tradition, Vatter argues, in chapter 26 Machiavelli is appealing to the medieval Arabic and Jewish political conception of God's working to establish a republic through a philosopher-prophet-king. Acknowledging that Moses is Machiavelli's chief example, in his discussion of "The Prince as a Redeemer," in *Redeeming "The Prince,"* 23–65, Viroli does not locate him or Machiavelli's conception in an explicitly Christian tradition.

persons, families, and properties of his subjects are secure from oppressive taxes and criminal violence.

Since men can be and have been trained to be soldiers in Italy before, Machiavelli concludes, the reason that no previous prince has been able to seize control and liberate Italy from foreign invasions is not so much "the matter" as "the fact that her ancient orders were not good, and that there has not been anyone who has known how to find new ones" (103). The problem in Italy has been not so much the "limbs" as the "weakness at the head." Since "head" (*capo*) can refer both to the leader or captain and to the mind or intellect, Machiavelli is suggesting that Italian princes have lacked the intelligence or knowledge he has been claiming to supply, from his letter of dedication onward. *If* Lorenzo and Leo follow his advice, they can seize and free Italy. Like Cesare Borgia, they may have to begin by using mercenary and auxiliary troops to conquer contiguous territories. Like the Roman republic, they will have to deceive the current lords or governments of the territories they propose to "liberate" by claiming to make them allies while ultimately eliminating the bloodlines of any established leaders. But the Medici will eventually have to muster and train their own "arms," including, Machiavelli now adds, an infantry able to resist cavalry as well as other, similarly trained and armed men. (Machiavelli provides the specifics in his later treatise the *Art of War.*) Most important of all, they will also have to establish new laws and orders, most particularly civil courts to guarantee the security of their people. By not merely assuring their people that their persons and property will be protected, but positively fostering domestic prosperity, these new "heads" can also free themselves from becoming dangerously dependent upon their own armies and ever more distant imperial conquests.[100]

100. The advice Machiavelli has offered in the preceding pages of *The Prince* thus seems to be both too specific and too general to be characterized, as by Viroli, *Redeeming "The Prince,"* 5, as merely an "oration" designed to provoke immediate political action or, simply, as a "political myth." Labeling Machiavelli's concluding call for action a "myth" would appear to give support to the argument put forward by Mary Dietz, "Trapping the Prince: Machiavelli and the Politics of Deception," *American Political Science Review* 80, no. 3 (1986): 777–99. Instead of providing the Medici with advice about how to succeed in acquiring and maintaining their power, Dietz argues, Machiavelli was trying to destroy them by persuading them to undertake disastrous policies. But as Viroli, *Redeeming "The Prince,"* 12–14, following Hannah Arendt, *On Revolution* (New York: Viking, 1963), 197, points out, Machiavelli saw (correctly) that the advent of nation-states in northern Europe meant that the Italian city-states were no longer tenable. As Strauss, *TM*, 89, observes, the confederacy Machiavelli recommends in *D* 2.4 represents an alternative way of achieving the Italian unity and defensive capacity he calls for in *P* 26.

On the other hand, from the very beginning Machiavelli has raised doubts about whether he believes that Lorenzo would or could follow the advice he was about to give. In his letter of dedication to Lorenzo Machiavelli refers to "the greatness that fortune and your other qualities promise"; and in his concluding exhortation, Machiavelli bases his hopes for Italy's "redemption" not on Lorenzo's abilities or promise as an individual, but on his "illustrious house, with its fortune and virtue, supported by God and by the Church" (102).

At the end of *The Prince* Machiavelli might appear to be urging Leo to undertake a project that was, in fact, already well under way—the consolidation of the Medici's fortune in Italy.[101] Shortly after his election as pope early in 1513, Leo had begun distributing power to his nephew Lorenzo II (who became governor of Florence in August), his first cousin Giulio (who was made archbishop of Florence in May and became cardinal in September), and his brother Giuliano (who was made a patrician of Rome and captain of the ecclesiastical military forces). There was, moreover, rumor of a project to make Giuliano "prince" of part of northern Italy.[102] Machiavelli thus had reason to think that the Medici lords might listen to advice showing them how to seize control of Italy as a whole.

The problem with the pope's projected consolidation of his family's power from Machiavelli's point of view was that such openly self-serving power grabs would inevitably arouse the opposition of other lords as well as the peoples of the cities involved. Merely seizing power in a few places would not attract the surge of popular support Machiavelli predicted would arise for a redeemer of Italy. In the concluding chapter of *The Prince* Machiavelli was thus trying to convince the Medici, pope and prince, to define their ambitions more nobly and more grandly—in order to have a better chance of succeeding. He understood that they would be seeking to satisfy their own natural desires to acquire and would have to use both force and fraud in order to do so. But, as he had insisted in *P* 18, they should present all their actions in public as "all mercy, all faith, all honesty, all humanity, all religion" (70).[103] Machiavelli concludes his treatise by quoting Petrarch: "Virtue will take up arms against fury, and make the battle short, because

101. See Najemy, *History of Florence*, 426–34.

102. In his January 31, 1515, letter to Francesco Vettori Machiavelli reports that Paolo Vettori told him that "His Lordship [the pope] promised to appoint [Giuliano] governor of one of those cities over which he is currently taking control," and that he heard a rumor "that His Magnificence is to become lord of Parma, Piacenza, Modena, and Reggio" (*Machiavelli and His Friends*, 312–13).

103. See Lefort, *Le travail de l'oeuvre Machiavel*, 447–49 (Smith trans., 201–3).

the ancient valor in Italian hearts is not yet dead" (105; "Italia mia," lines 93–96).[104] He thus gives his advice a less Christian and more classical flavor and, at the same time, obscures the difference between the notion of virtue he has put forward in *The Prince* and that of the "classical humanists."

The emphasis Machiavelli has put on the necessity of a prince's mustering and training his own arms would have made his advice particularly difficult for the Medici to follow. Members of that house had not been averse to seeking popular support. That was the way in which Cosimo had first established and then consolidated his family's control of Florence.[105] Like other Florentine *ottimati*, however, the Medici had resisted the formation of a civic militia. They feared both that armed workers and peasants would revolt and that a successful captain would seize control of the city from them.[106] The Medici had, therefore, consistently employed mercenaries. According to Machiavelli, Lorenzo's fortune depended crucially, moreover, on having his uncle as pope. Julius II had led his own troops into battle, but he had not mustered and trained his own subjects or citizens. Nor was it likely that any pope as pope could do so. So long as the "prince" of Italy depended upon the support of the pope, whether financial or moral, there would be a divided leadership. According to Machiavelli, it was the priests' inexperience or lack of training in arms as well as the pope's interference in the domestic policies of other Italian cities that had kept Italy divided and weak.[107]

Did Machiavelli really believe that Leo and Lorenzo could be persuaded to depart from settled family policy? Machiavelli's own observations about the way in which individual human beings become set in their ways, as a result of both their natural dispositions and their past experience, argue against his having had much hope of convincing the Medici to change their inherited inclinations and policies.[108] It is certainly difficult to believe that Machiavelli believed his own claim that in Italy "extraordinary things

104. In Petrarch's poem, Hörnqvist points out, "these lines refer to an inner battle raging within the soul of the Italian people, a struggle seen as analogous to the civil war that at the time was tearing the country apart. They are directly related to the final verses of the poem, where the despairing poet, addressing the 'magnanimous few who love the good,' famously exclaims: 'Peace, peace, peace.' Wrenched from their original context, however, they come in *The Prince* to convey a completely different message" (*Machiavelli and Empire*, 157).

105. See *D* 1.52; *FH* 4.26–30, 7.1–6; Mark Jurdjevic, *A Great and Wretched City: Promise and Failure in Machiavelli's Florentine Political Thought* (Cambridge, MA: Harvard University Press, 2014).

106. See *AW* 1.153–57.

107. See *P* 12; *D* 1.12; *FH* 1.9. For this reason, Scott and Sullivan, "Patricide," and Parent, "Machiavelli's Missing Romulus," argue that the liberator of Italy would have to kill the pope.

108. See *P* 25; *D* 3.9, 21–23.

without example" have occurred, "brought about by God: the sea has opened; a cloud has escorted you along the way; the stone has poured forth water; here manna has rained" (103). Most readers would recognize that these were the same miracles that had reputedly accompanied Moses' rise to power among the Hebrews.[109]

Lorenzo was a military man, so he might have been tempted to lead a grand campaign to free Italy from her foreign oppressors. But if *P* 26 was a part of Machiavelli's original treatise, it was addressed to Giuliano, and Giuliano was known to prefer living at the papal court in Rome to living or ruling or leading an army in the provinces (of Italy!).[110] And if *P* 26 was added after 1515, as some commentators believe, Machiavelli would have known that Lorenzo had already proved unwilling to follow his first piece of advice to a new prince, to go and live in the province he had just acquired.[111] By that time Lorenzo had shown that, like his uncle, he preferred life at the papal court to residing in Florence, where Lorenzo had been named captain general. In December 1514 Leo had explicitly solicited Machiavelli's advice through Vettori about what he should do in the face of the French initiative against Milan, but the pope had then proved unwilling to follow it. Yet that advice was based on arguments similar to those Machiavelli gives in *The Prince* about the dangers of allying with a stronger power or remaining neutral.[112]

In sum, there are reasons, both textual and contextual, to conclude that Machiavelli did not think the Medici princes would take up his final plea. They did not have enough foresight, daring, or imagination. *P* 26 thus stands at least as much as a rebuke to the reigning princes in Italy as it does as a passionate plea to them to take the appropriate action.

We do not know whether Machiavelli actually presented *The Prince* to Lorenzo, but we do know that he gave copies to his friends and that they appear to have shared their copies with others. Machiavelli explicitly refers to *The Prince* in the *Discourses* he wrote and presented to his friends a few years later, so he must have thought that they either had copies themselves or had access to one. And the fact that Agostino Nifo plagiarized much of

109. See *TM*, 72.

110. Cecil H. Clough, *Machiavelli Researches* (Naples: Istituto Universitario Orientale, 1967), 52, insists upon this point.

111. See note 7 above.

112. See correspondence between Vettori and Machiavelli in December 1514, *Machiavelli and His Friends*, 295–309. That advice (in *P* 21) would also have revealed the problem with Lorenzo's decision to keep the pope's troops out of the battle of Marignano in the hopes of later subduing a victor weakened by the battle.

The Prince in 1523 suggests that many more of his contemporaries had an opportunity to read (and even copy!) Machiavelli's "little treatise," which soon made its way into northern Europe as well.[113]

The Prince attracted readers even before it was published, because in the guise of advice to a petty Italian prince, Machiavelli had presented an entirely new way of looking at politics.[114] He had not merely reduced the traditional six types of regimes to two, distinguished solely by the number of rulers, but also differentiated the types of principalities according to the ways in which they were acquired and the difficulties involved in maintaining them. He thus described the different kinds of rule from the point of view of someone who wanted to acquire and maintain it, rather than in terms of justice, service to the common good, or foundation in divine right. Jettisoning both the ancient concern with the education of virtuous rulers and the Christian concern with securing the salvation of both princes and peoples, Machiavelli counseled princes—both actual and potential—to learn how to organize and arm their followers. He urged them to pretend always to be religious but to do what was necessary to retain control after they had acquired it.[115]

Machiavelli made the revolutionary character of his teaching explicit when he urged princes not to act in ways traditionally thought to be virtuous—to be generous to one's friends, for example, or to be merciful to the downtrodden, in order to obtain their love. A prince should, on the contrary, seek to minimize the costs of government borne by his people and make sure that everyone—noble or ignoble—fears the consequences of disobeying his laws and orders. Observing that characterizations of virtue and vice are matters of praise and blame, and that fame, glory, and reputation are also merely matters of opinion, Machiavelli suggested that the "effective" truths in politics do not concern the character of the ruler or the basis of his claim to rule so much as the results of his rule on the lives of his people. The people (or later writers who would report their opinions) ultimately determine whether a leader is honored or reviled. Princes who wish to maintain their rule most securely should not continue to use the displays of force (or

113. Victoria Kahn, "Machiavelli's Afterlife and Reputation to the Eighteenth Century," in Najemy, *Cambridge Companion to Machiavelli*, 241.

114. For all their differences, both Strauss and Skinner treat Machiavelli as a "founder" of "modernity."

115. "Through his silences even more than his words," Althusser observes, "Machiavelli condemns definitively not only the *edifying* religious, moral or aesthetic discourses of the court humanists . . . ; not only the revolutionary sermons of a Savonarola; but also the entire tradition of Christian theology and all the political theories of antiquity" (*Machiavelli and Us*, 7–8).

"cruelty") by which they may have acquired their position, if they did not ascend to office through heredity or election. A prudent leader would seek to persuade his people, both in speech and in deed, that his government acts to secure the lives and property of its citizens or subjects, so that the people would, in turn, act either under arms or in court to oppose those who would overthrow him.

In *The Prince* Machiavelli announces the change he is advocating in the moral standards used to evaluate leaders and their governments more clearly than the basis of those evaluations in popular opinion and sentiments. He does not urge princes to serve their peoples, because he does not think that any human beings act on the basis of anything but their perceptions of their own needs or goods. He tries to persuade princes that they will retain rule most effectively by convincing their people that this prince governs in their interest, and he reminds his princely readers that their words will be most persuasive if they are backed up by deeds. Concentrating on the bestial means—force and fraud—every prince must use in order to produce results that seem to be in the common interest (because they satisfy the most powerful though different desires of both the people and their prince), Machiavelli only hints at the kinds of laws and institutions needed to maintain those results.[116]

Addressing two young Florentine aristocrats, who merely "deserve to be" princes and thus have more leisure to listen than a sitting monarch, in his *Discourses on Livy* Machiavelli describes these institutions at greater length and in much greater detail. He also makes the popular as opposed to the traditionally aristocratic character of the republican government he is advocating more explicit.

116. Rousseau's suggestion in the *Social Contract* 3.6 that *The Prince* is, despite appearances to the contrary, a book for republicans, because it reveals princes' vices to the people and thus incites antimonarchical sentiments, presupposes a degree of popular "enlightenment" that did not exist at Machiavelli's time. He wrote all his works explicitly for politically ambitious individuals who either were or hoped to become political leaders.

2

Machiavelli's New Republic

DISCOURSES ON LIVY

In *The Prince* Machiavelli purports to be telling a Florentine prince what he needs to do not merely to acquire but also to extend and maintain his power, both in general and in his specific circumstances. In his *Discourses on Livy* Machiavelli then proposes to teach two other young Florentines, who "deserve to be" princes, what they would need to know to become founders of "new modes and orders."

Dedication and Relation to *The Prince*

Recognizing that "if someone who desires or who wishes to reform a state in a city wishes it to be accepted and capable of being maintained to the satisfaction of everyone, he is under the necessity of retaining at least the shadow of its ancient modes . . . , even if in fact the new orders are altogether alien to the past ones" (*D* 1.25), Machiavelli presents his new "modes and orders" merely as an "imitation" of the Romans. As he observed in *P* 6, most people cannot even imagine the possibility of doing something that has not been done in the past. Those who do not have the ability to found something entirely new should aim at following the example of someone greater. His Florentine readers were more apt to believe that they would be able to duplicate the achievements of their Roman ancestors than that they themselves would be able to do something entirely unprecedented. (As in *The Prince*, so in the *Discourses* the suggestion that he is asking his readers merely to imitate others also enables Machiavelli to understate the difficulties they would encounter, if they actually tried to act on the basis of his advice.)

Machiavelli nevertheless seeks to arouse his young readers' ambitions at the beginning of his *Discourses* by stating explicitly that he is showing them the path on which only "a short road will remain for another to bring it to the destined place" (*D* 1.Pref.). He thus promises them, in effect, that they will receive the "credit" or fame for achieving what he has merely sketched.

Machiavelli's "Greetings" to His Two Young Friends

Machiavelli addresses his *Discourses on Livy* to two young friends, Cosimo Rucellai and Zanobi Buondelmonti. From the *Art of War* we learn that Cosimo was the grandson of Bernardo Rucellai, a close advisor of Lorenzo the Magnificent, who had broken with Lorenzo's son Piero. Bernardo had been a patron of the arts and student of philosophy, but Cosimo reports that his grandfather did not think that people now could imitate the Romans. Zanobi is also said to have taken part in the conversation that took place in the Rucellai family gardens; and in introducing the participants, Machiavelli praises Cosimo for his dedication to the good of his fatherland but suggests that Zanobi was more spirited (*AW* 1.1, 4.3). Because Machiavelli subsequently dedicated his *Life of Castruccio Castracani* to Zanobi and Luigi Alamanni, the youngest participant in the conversation related in the *Art of War*, and both of these young Florentines took part in a failed conspiracy against the life of Cardinal Giulio de' Medici in 1522, some scholars have speculated that Machiavelli incited them to take this action.[1] What we know from the *Art of War* is that the two young men to whom Machiavelli dedicated the *Discourses* were wealthy young Florentine aristocrats who spent many of their leisure hours discussing ways in which the government of their city, if not Italy as a whole, could be improved, and whether or not it was possible for them to imitate the example of their glorious Roman predecessors.[2]

In the *Art of War* Machiavelli purports to be recalling a conversation at which he was present in 1516. Scholars thus suggest that his dedicating

1. Maurizio Viroli, *Niccolò's Smile: A Biography of Machiavelli*, trans. Antony Shugaar (New York: Hill and Wang, 2000), 220. Having been tortured in 1512 after his name was found on a list of possible conspirators against the Medici, Machiavelli would surely not state such an intention clearly. In *D* 3.6 he warns conspirators against putting anything into writing that they cannot deny.

2. As Hörnqvist, *Machiavelli and Empire*, 38–75, notes, Florentines had for centuries identified themselves and their civic aims, maintaining liberty at home and expanding their empire abroad, particularly with the Romans.

the *Discourses* to his friends from the Orti Oricellari means that he began writing the *Discourses* sometime before that conversation is supposed to have occurred, probably in 1515; and they conclude with more certainty that the work was completed by 1519, when Cosimo died.[3] If this dating is correct, Machiavelli began writing the *Discourses* a mere two years after he completed his first draft of *The Prince.* It seems unlikely that he would have changed his mind fundamentally about the conclusions he had drawn from his own experience and much study of the character of political life in such a short time. He does not announce such a change, although he proclaims ways in which he differs from former "writers" in both of his major works.[4] Differences between these two works would thus appear to reflect the differences in perspective Machiavelli explicitly adopts in writing to his purported addressees. Writing as a potential advisor to the prince, he presents his arguments in an extremely concise form entirely

3. Felix Gilbert, "The Composition and Structure of Machiavelli's *Discorsi*," *Journal of the History of Ideas* 14, no. 1 (1953): 136–56; Hans Baron, "The *Principe* and the Puzzle of the Date of the *Discorsi*," *Bibliothèque d'Humanisme et Renaissance* 18 (1956): 411–26. Clough, " 'The Discourses,' and Machiavelli's Last Days," 87–88, observes that there is a tradition that "Machiavelli 'lectured upon the subject of *The Discourses*' in the Rucellai Gardens of Florence. This, however, has developed from a misunderstanding of the source, Nerli, who merely says that the assembly in the Rucellai Gardens exercised itself particularly in the reading of histories, . . . and at the instance of the participants Machiavelli wrote his work." Most commentators think that Machiavelli wrote the *Discourses* between 1513 and 1519, because all the references to contemporary events "can be dated to 1517 at the latest" and Cosimo died in 1519. Clough argues that "there is no certainty that the dedication letter itself must have been written when Rucellai was alive, and it was not uncommon for the dedication letter to be written before the work it was to accompany was finished. . . . When both Blado and Giunta independently printed the work in 1531, the dedication . . . was placed at the end of the Third book, that is, at the end of the entire work" (91). Clough suggests that the only portion of *The Discourses* in Machiavelli's hand that we now possess, a preface to the first book, which has been assumed to be a rejected draft written in 1519, may have been intended to replace the dedication and letter in a planned edition of his entire works in 1527. He takes the difference in content and order of the chapters between the *Discourses* upon which Francesco Guicciardini wrote his *Considerations,* using the manuscript in Machiavelli's hand in Cardinal Ridolfi's library, and the version first printed by Antonio Blado in 1531 and dedicated to Giovanni Gaddi, to indicate that Gaddi may have assumed the role of Machiavelli's literary executor. And in that capacity Gaddi may not merely have edited the manuscript but reordered the chapters, according to his own understanding of Machiavelli's intention. Since Machiavelli continued to revise the text until his death in 1527, Clough concludes, "it is not likely that we can ever reconstruct with confidence Machiavelli's text as it existed before his revision of 1527, or even as it was at the time of his death. . . . [So] we cannot argue too closely from the text" (104). Designed to explain away the problems or, as he dubs them, "deficiencies" of the text, Clough's reasoning with regard to the ongoing revisions appears to be extremely speculative.

4. As William J. Connell, "Machiavelli on Growth as an End," in *Historians and Ideologues: Essays in Honor of Donald R. Kelley*, ed. Anthony T. Grafton and J. H. M. Salmon (Rochester, NY: University of Rochester Press, 2001), 259–77, observes: "Students of Machiavelli's style and imagery, and even more importantly of his anthropology and ethics, have confirmed time and again a fundamental consistency in the outlook of the Florentine secretary's major works" (260).

from the point of view of the interests of the prince. As an instructor of public-spirited young Florentine "aristocrats," politically ambitious but skeptical about their ability to imitate the Romans, he proceeds in a more leisurely fashion, paying more attention to theory as well as to history, and appealing to the common, rather than simply to the prince's, good.[5]

Because Machiavelli explicitly addresses young, politically ambitious Florentines in both *The Prince* and the *Discourses*, readers should not be surprised to find a certain number of parallels between the two dedications. In both cases the undersecretary from an old, but not very distinguished family emphasizes his poverty in explaining the character of the gift he is presenting. In both cases he explicitly claims that there is nothing greater or of more value that he could deliver than "the knowledge of the actions of great men, learned by [him] from long experience with modern things and a continuous reading of ancient ones," as he states in *The Prince*, or "as much as I know and have learned through a long practice and a continual reading in worldly things," as he says in the *Discourses*.[6] And after emphasizing the "poverty" of his gift, in both dedications Machiavelli goes on to suggest not merely that he possesses knowledge that his readers need, but that they may not be able to understand or acquire the wisdom he possesses. He is their actual superior even though he is conventionally thought to be their inferior.

In his dedications to both of his explicitly comprehensive works, Machiavelli also stresses the unconventional character of the gift he is presenting. In *The Prince* that unconventionality is located in the character of the gift, the knowledge he prizes above all other things as opposed to an expensive, showy present designed to please the prince; but in the *Discourses* the unconventionality is associated with the recipients and Machiavelli's intentions in presenting it. Rather than follow "the common usage of those who . . . are accustomed always to address their works to some prince and, blinded by ambition and avarice, praise him for all virtuous qualities when they should blame him for every part worthy of reproach" (which Machiavelli did in *The Prince* only to the extent to which he expressed his

5. In *D* 2.2 Machiavelli argues that *the* difference between a principality and a republic is that in the former all actions of the government serve to benefit the ruler whereas in the latter everything is undertaken for the good of the community (with the possible exception of a few individuals).

6. Strauss, *TM*, 17, points out that Machiavelli explicitly claims to convey all that he knows in the dedications to these two works and only these works. In the dedication to the *Discourses*, Machiavelli explicitly restricts his knowledge to "worldly things"; but, Strauss suggests, what an author says about "worldly" things almost necessarily implies something about what he thinks about things beyond.

"extreme desire that [Lorenzo] arrive at the greatness that fortune and [his] other good qualities promise," and did not blame him for anything explicitly), in the *Discourses* Machiavelli explains that he is writing not to "those who are princes but those who for their infinite good parts deserve to be" (3). In proposing, in effect, an exchange of his knowledge for a job from Lorenzo, Machiavelli appeared to write primarily out of his own need. But in addressing the *Discourses* to his young friends, Machiavelli says that he "does not know which of us has to be less obligated to the other: whether I to you, who have forced me to write what I would never have written for myself; or you to me, if in writing I have not satisfied you" (3). In other words, he claims to have written not out of his own need, but in an attempt to satisfy an expressed desire or need of theirs. Machiavelli does not specify the "infinite good parts" that make these young men "deserve to be" princes.[7] However, when he explains that he has chosen to address "not those who could load me with ranks, honors, and riches but those who, though unable, would wish to do so," because "men wishing to judge rightly have to esteem those who are liberal, not those who can be; and likewise those who know, not those who can govern a kingdom," it looks as if the "infinite good parts" of his friends consist primarily in their desire to load him with riches and honors in exchange for the wisdom they wish to receive from him, and that it is he, who claims in his dedications to both works to possess the knowledge that would enable him (in contrast to his conventionally regarded "superiors") to govern a kingdom, who deserves to be a prince.[8]

In *D* 1.10 Machiavelli observes that the men who have been most praised have been founders of religions, next those who have instituted republics or kingdoms, third generals who have expanded their kingdom or fatherland, and only fourth "literary men," who are of many types. However, he concludes his dedication by reminding his readers that "writers" determine the reputation of princes by praising or blaming them.[9] The exam-

7. "Infinite" would appear to be praising, but it also literally means indeterminate.

8. Cf. *TM*, 82–83; Mansfield, *Machiavelli's Virtue*, 125; Vickie B. Sullivan, *Machiavelli's Three Romes* (DeKalb: Northern Illinois University Press, 1996), 172–73.

9. *Pace* Viroli, *Machiavelli's God*, 154, it is not true that Machiavelli places "the founders of religions above the founders of states in *his* hierarchy of excellent men, and singles out first and foremost in the ranks of detestable men those who undermine and dissipate religions" (emphasis added). On the contrary, Machiavelli states that the founders of religions have been most praised (by others), and he lists the destroyers of religion, along with squanderers of kingdoms and republics, and enemies of the virtues, of letters, and of every other art that brings utility and honor to the human race, as (equally) among the infamous and detestable. Russell Price, "The Theme

ples he gives of such praise and blame seem to be designed, moreover, to arouse the ambitions of his young readers to found a new and better political order in place of the old. These examples also emphasize the importance of knowing how to use the resources one has, as opposed to merely possessing the wealth and arms generally (and conventionally) associated with rule. "Writers praise Hiero the Syracusan when he was a private individual more than Perseus the Macedonian when he was king," Machiavelli observes, "for Hiero lacked nothing other than the principality to be a prince while the other had no part of a king other than the kingdom" (4). One of the unnamed "writers" appears to be Polybius, who emphasized Hiero's virtues as both a private individual and a ruler.[10] The other unnamed writer seems to be Plutarch, who in his "Life of Aemilius Paulus" reports that Perseus squandered the armed men and money his father had accumulated to free the Macedonians from the Romans, because he did not want to part with his treasure (and, as a result, lost it all along with his

of Gloria in Machiavelli," *Renaissance Quarterly* 30, no. 4 (1977): 595, notes that in "A Discourse on Remodeling the Government of Florence" Machiavelli wrote, "I believe that the greatest honour (*onore*) that men can receive is that which is freely given to them by their country (*patria*), and the greatest good (*bene*) that one can achieve, and the most pleasing to God, is that done for one's country. Next to this, no man is so exalted (*esalto*) as much for any action as those who have with laws and institutions reformed republics and kingdoms; after the gods, these are the most praised (*laudati*)." He does not say anything about those who found or reform religions.

10. Like Polybius, in *P* 6 Machiavelli praises Hiero for having "such virtue, even in private fortune, . . . 'that he lacked nothing of being a king except a kingdom'" (25). However, Machiavelli does not credit Hiero, as Polybius does, for having "made himself king of Syracuse unaided, without killing, exiling, or injuring a single citizen." On the contrary, in *P* 13 Machiavelli emphasizes the way in which Hiero arranged for the mercenary troops he had used to seize control of the city to be slaughtered in a later battle. Nor does Machiavelli praise Hiero, as does Polybius, for "during a reign of fifty-four years [having] kept his country at peace and his own power undisturbed by plots, . . . clear of that envy which is wont to wait on superiority" or for his virtue as an individual. "Although he lived constantly in the midst of affluence, luxury, and most lavish expenditure," according to Polybius, Hiero "survived till over ninety, and retained all his faculties, as well as keeping every part of his body sound, which seems to me to testify in no slight measure, indeed very strongly, to his having led a temperate life" (*The Histories of Polybius*, Loeb ed. [Cambridge, MA: Harvard University Press], 3.8.1–5). Machiavelli would have attributed Hiero's longevity both as a person and as a ruler to his knowledge of the princely "art of war." In his *History of Rome* Titus Livy does not describe Hiero as a private individual or his rise to power. But, as Machiavelli knew, Livy did emphasize Hiero's wisdom, first in advising the Romans to attack Carthage and thus draw Hannibal back home (which Scipio Africanus, youngest son of Aemilius Paulus, eventually did and so defeated the Carthaginians, but not until Varro had lost the battle of Cannae and endangered the existence of Rome itself). Livy also reports that the Romans merely accepted the gold and troops Hiero brought his Roman allies, but did not heed his wise advice (22.7); and that Hiero was not able to realize his desire to leave Syracuse a free regime (24.4–5). Whereas Polybius (7.8.9) reports that his son Gelo did nothing but obey Hiero for his entire fifty years, Livy says (23.30) that only his good fortune enabled Hiero to forestall the rebellion of his son, and (24.5) that Hiero was not able to prevent his daughters from making his kingship hereditary or educate his grandson to become a virtuous prince.

nation and his family). Insofar as they illustrate the deleterious effects of hereditary succession, both stories also point to the advantages of republican election. Machiavelli could be less reticent about the former in a work dedicated to young men who only deserved to be princes than he had been in a work dedicated to a prince who had risen to that status because of his family connections. Even so, Machiavelli could not be entirely open about his attack on hereditary "aristocracy" or his critique of traditional notions of political virtue at the beginning of a book explicitly written for young men whose wealth, leisure, and humanist education were all results of their families' wealth and status.[11]

Preface to Book 1: The Discovery of New Modes and Orders in the Guise of an Imitation of the Romans

In the preface to the first book, which seems also to serve as a preface to the entire work, Machiavelli begins by stressing the difficulties he confronts in proposing "new modes and orders." Explaining the resistance a new prince or "prophet" would have to overcome in *P* 6, Machiavelli emphasized the inability of his followers to believe that things could really be different. A "prophet" would have to be armed in order to succeed, because he would have to force his adherents to obey his commands after they had lost their initial enthusiasm for change in the face of armed opposition. But here Machiavelli attributes the danger confronted by an unarmed "discoverer" to the "envious nature of men," and he tries to counter that envy, first, by emphasizing his "natural desire . . . to work, without any respect, for . . . the common benefit." He claims to have taken "a path as yet untrodden by anyone" but not in search of recognition for himself. He admits that he may be rewarded by "those who consider humanely the end," but he humbly professes his possible lack of talent and knowledge (as he did in

11. John P. McCormick, "Tempering the Grandi's Appetite to Oppress: The Dedication and Intention of Machiavelli's *Discourses*," in *Politics and the Passions, 1500–1850*, ed. Victoria Kahn, Neil Saccamano, and Daniela Coli (Princeton: Princeton University Press, 2006), 27, suggests that in urging them to imitate Rome Machiavelli tried to appeal to his young oligarchical readers' desire for empire and wealth as a way of persuading them to accept more popular institutions. He does not appear to recognize the difficulties Cosimo and Zanobi would face in realizing their own political ambitions so long as the Medici controlled the Florentine government. In other words, they had reasons to foster political change as well as conquest and wealth. In placing the letter of dedication at the end rather than at the beginning of the *Discourses*, the first printers helped conceal the contemporary and potentially revolutionary implications of the argument.

his dedication), promising merely that he "will at least show the path to someone who with more virtue . . . will be able to fulfill his intention" (5).

Machiavelli almost immediately conceals the novelty of his discoveries in the second (or possibly the first) paragraph of his preface, however, by urging his contemporaries to imitate the ancients, not merely in the fine arts or civil law or medicine, but in politics.[12] Despite his claim in *P* 26 that "in Italy matter is not lacking for introducing every form; here there is great virtue in the limbs, if it were not lacking in the heads," at the beginning of his *Discourses* Machiavelli complains that "no sign of that ancient virtue remains with us" (5). He nevertheless continues to locate the reason for the absence of any sign of ancient virtue in his contemporaries' "heads" when he observes that the cause is "not so much the weakness into which the present religion has led the world" (although in *D* 2.2 Machiavelli argues that this is a real factor) or "the evil that an ambitious idleness has done to many Christian provinces and cities" (that he emphasizes in *D* 2.2 and 3.1), but "not having a true knowledge of the histories." Although an "infinite number" of his contemporaries take pleasure in reading ancient histories,[13] they do not believe that it is possible to imitate the deeds of ancient kings, republics, legislators, or generals—"as if heaven, sun, elements, men had varied in motion, order and power from what they were in antiquity." According to Machiavelli's knowledge of worldly things, nature remains the same.[14] Ignoring the Christian revelation that announces God's acting in time and so altering the course of history, he proposes to show his readers "the utility for which one should seek knowledge of histories," by writing on "all those books of Titus Livy that

12. As Mansfield and Tarcov note, *Discourses* 1.Pref., n. 5, the first paragraph of the proemium does not appear in the first two editions of the *Discourses*, but can be found in polished form in Machiavelli's hand, in the only surviving autograph fragment of the *Discourses*. If Machiavelli had, in fact, decided that emphasizing the novelty of his "discovery" at the beginning of the work was too dangerous, and so deleted the paragraph, he would have acted on the belief explicitly expressed there and more indirectly echoed in the published paragraphs that follow. Here he emphasizes the necessity of reading ancient histories in general, and that of Livy in particular, in a new way, drawing from modern as well as ancient political experience, in order to make this knowledge useful and to carry a difficult enterprise along far enough so that others could complete it. If, as Clough, "'The Discourses,' and Machiavelli's Last Days," argues, the handwritten preface was intended to be a substitute for the letter of dedication and existing preface, it points to the broader future audience Machiavelli hoped to address.

13. It thus begins to look as if Machiavelli uses "infinite" not only ironically with exaggeration, but also literally to mean undefined.

14. The attempt by Vatter, *Between Form and Event*, 30, to distinguish the view Machiavelli expresses here from the ancient cyclical view of nature is unpersuasive, partly because Vatter ignores Machiavelli's reference to the difference between an ancient or pagan view and Christianity immediately before his emphasis on the continuity of nature.

have not been intercepted by the malignity of the times." He will bring out whatever he judges "necessary for their greater understanding, according to [his] knowledge of ancient and modern things" (6).[15] Machiavelli's utilizing of his knowledge of things both ancient and modern accords with his suggestion that nature does not fundamentally change. But the "utility" of the knowledge he proposes to draw out of his reading of Livy on the basis of his knowledge of things both ancient and modern cannot simply be the same as the knowledge the ancient historian intended to communicate to his readers (if only because Livy did not possess knowledge of what is distinctively modern). Even in explicitly advocating merely an imitation of the ancients, Machiavelli indicates he is doing something new.

The Organization of the *Discourses*

Because the things done by the Romans, and celebrated by Livy, proceeded from either public or private counsel, inside or outside the city, Machiavelli devotes the first book of his discourses to those things occurring inside as a result of public counsel. He implies (and later states) that the second book concerns things occurring outside as a result of public counsel. The third book does not have a preface, but readers can infer from the general schema that it treats things done both inside and outside the city on the basis of private counsel.[16]

Although Machiavelli makes the broad organization of the *Discourses* into these three parts explicit, readers have found it difficult to determine the internal organization of each of the three parts or his line of argument in the work as a whole.[17] Sometimes the *Discourses* follow the order of Livy's narrative, but often they do not. Nor is the connection between one chapter and the next always obvious. Observing that the *Discourses*

15. By discoursing on an explicitly incomplete history, Machiavelli indicates his understanding that our knowledge of the past is incomplete, as he explicitly argues in the preface to book 2. Machiavelli shows that we learn from the histories, not by accepting the word of ancient authors like Plutarch on authority, but by observing regularities of human behavior in both modern and ancient times and then seeking the reasons or causes of the observed effects.

16. *TM*, 97. However, at *TM*, 103, Strauss notes that Machiavelli's statement of the contents at the beginning of book 3 does not actually mention counsel, but only "private benefits." Book 3 would thus appear to concern the reasons or causes the individuals whose deeds benefited the Roman republic did what they did.

17. E.g., Skinner, *Machiavelli*, 56–57; Michael Sherberg, "The Problematics of Reading in Machiavelli's *Discourses*," *Modern Philology* 89, no. 2 (1991): 175–95; Ardito, *Machiavelli and the Modern State*, 78.

are explicitly related only to the first ten books of Livy's history, but that like Livy's history as a whole, Machiavelli's work has 142 chapters and so presumably covers the whole, Strauss contends that "Machiavelli's use and nonuse of Livy is the key to the understanding of the work."[18] Livy was much more widely read and better known by educated readers in Machiavelli's time than now. Nevertheless, it is difficult to believe that Machiavelli expected his readers to follow the intricate way in which he according to Strauss used (and changed) Livy's history not merely to convey his own understanding of politics in the spaces created between the two texts, but to present a covert critique of the Bible by questioning the authority of Livy. There is no evidence, in fact, that anyone before Strauss read Machiavelli this way—brilliant as his reading is.[19] As this account of the beginning

18. Leo Strauss, "Niccolò Machiavelli," in *History of Political Philosophy*, ed. Leo Strauss and Joseph Cropsey, 3rd ed. (Chicago: University of Chicago Press, 1987), 305. Clough, " 'The Discourses,' and Machiavelli's Last Days," observes that Machiavelli's statement that he is writing on the first ten books of Livy has led some commentators to believe that he was writing a commentary. "One consequence of this conviction has been an attempt on the part of Professor Felix Gilbert to provide a table of concordance between Machiavelli's *Discourses* and Livy [in "Review: The Composition and Structure of the *Discorsi*," *Journal of the History of Ideas* 14, no. 1 (January 1953): 142–43]. . . . This table, though, is particularly misleading, since, in Whitfield's words, 'Machiavelli did not always chastely quote one Livy passage to a chapter as the table shows him doing' " (81–82, quoting J. H. Whitfield, *Discourses on Machiavelli* [Cambridge: W. Heffer & Sons, 1969], 183). In fact, as Whitfield shows, Machiavelli often refers to several places or incidents in Livy in a single chapter. Clough suggests that "a table showing all Machiavelli's references to Livy, and to other authorities, would be of inestimable value" (82). But having given a more complicated account of Machiavelli's references to Livy, Strauss concludes, "the common way of studying the relation of the *Discourses* to Livy is defective because it disregards that Machiavellian use of Livy which reveals itself only through the suppression of Livian stories. This was the reason why, in considering the relation between Machiavelli's plan and the Livian order, we limited ourselves so strictly to the references to Livy as distinguished from the mere use of Livian passages: whether Machiavelli refers or does not refer to Livy in a given place can easily be seen, and the collection of his references to Livy is a finite piece of work; but to achieve clarity about his use of Livy is an infinite task: its completion would require complete understanding of every sentence of the *Discourses* and of Livy" (*TM*, 104). Strauss either follows Machiavelli in using "infinite" ironically or admits that his own reading is partial.

19. In "Die Erneuerung der Philosophie," Meier writes, "Tatsächlich läßt er sich in *Thoughts on Machiavelli* auf das Denken von Machiavelli ein, wie keiner, der vor ihm über Machiavelli schrieb, sich auf dessen Denken einließ" (42). Meier attributes the singularity of Strauss's reading to his treatment of Machiavelli as a philosopher. But acknowledged philosophers such as Spinoza and Hobbes clearly read Machiavelli and took him seriously. They do not appear to have thought that Machiavelli was using Livy as a substitute for the Bible, however, or indicating his meaning through his use of numbers. Strauss emphasizes the importance of the number 26: there are 26 chapters in *The Prince*, he points out, and Machiavelli utters his greatest blasphemy in *D* 1.26. Meier notes that in his article "Niccolò Machiavelli" in *History of Political Philosophy*, Strauss points out that "twenty-six is the numerical value of the sacred name of God in Hebrew. . . . But did Machiavelli know of this? I do not know" (27). More generally, Meier argues that "what Strauss said about Alfarabi holds for the author of *Thoughts on Machiavelli*: He exploits the specific immunity of the commentator or the historian in order to express in an historical work what he thinks about a

of the *Discourses* indicates, I have learned a great deal from Strauss. In light of the evidence that Machiavelli hoped to have an effect on his immediate audience as well as possible later readers, and that his primary concern was not a critique of Christianity so much as an improved understanding and practice of politics, however, in the following account I have tried to show that Machiavelli's *Discourses* constitute a coherent argument about the difficulties of establishing and maintaining a free way of life by means of a republican form of government.[20] In book 1 he gradually discloses the general principles upon which the domestic order of such a government should be founded. In book 2 he then outlines a foreign policy that would preserve such a government with a particular eye to the situation of Florence. Finally, in book 3 he indicates very indirectly, because he knew from personal experience how dangerous it could be to make such recommendations, the sorts of things his young Florentine readers would need to do as private individuals in order to bring the new republican orders he is advocating into existence—and to maintain them.[21]

---

serious matter" (69). That matter is biblical religion and the way its central command for obedience to God rests on faith and thus is fundamentally inimical to philosophy.

20. In doing so, somewhat ironically, I am heeding Strauss's admonition in *Persecution and the Art of Writing* (Chicago: University of Chicago Press, 1952): "Reading between the lines is strictly prohibited in all cases where it would be less exact than not doing so. Only such reading between the lines as starts from an exact consideration of the explicit statements of the author is legitimate. The context in which a statement occurs, and the literary character of the whole work as well as its plan, must be perfectly understood before an interpretation of the statement can reasonably claim to be adequate or even correct. One is not entitled to delete a passage, nor to emend its text, before one has fully considered all reasonable possibilities of understanding the passage as it stands—one of these possibilities being that the passage may be ironic" (30). I am arguing that Machiavelli was not merely an artful but an ironic writer. He was addressing more than one audience—not only his immediate but also future readers—and he had reasons to be less than perfectly open about the revolutionary character of his praise of the Roman republic and its institutions. I do not deny that he was critical not merely of the Church but of the effects of Christian teachings more generally (as in *D* 3.1). However, I am arguing that these criticisms were for the sake of introducing a better political order that would benefit most people (including rare individuals like Machiavelli himself), not for the sake, first and foremost, of protecting such freethinking and innovative individuals from persecution. Like Meier, I think that Strauss was trying to revive philosophy. Machiavelli, however, was trying to improve politics. For Machiavelli, religion (including Christianity) is and ought to be a political tool. Like Strauss I seek to show that Machiavelli develops his argument dialectically; he does not merely formulate generalizations and present historical examples as evidence to back them up.

21. Lefort, *Le travail de l'oeuvre Machiavel*, 584–690 (Smith trans., 328–425), shows how Machiavelli's argument in book 3 can be specifically related to, and understood as a critique of, the Florentine politics that led to the demise of the republic (and Machiavelli's own ouster from office) in 1512. Lefort admits that Machiavelli's argument has a broader meaning and resonance, but he insists (and I agree) that it is necessary to see the immediate relevance and references in order to get to that broader meaning.

Because the order of Machiavelli's "discourses" is so difficult to extract from the welter of historical details and observations, I begin the account of each book with an outline of the argument as I understand it.

Outline of Book 1: How to Design and Maintain the Domestic Institutions of a Free Republic

A. The Beginnings of Cities and Rome as Exemplar (*D* 1.1)

B. Why the Roman Republic Is Exemplary (*D* 1.2–6)

   1. The Case for Sparta—the Traditional Exemplar (*D* 1.2–3)
   2. The Case for Rome—the New Exemplar (*D* 1.4–6)
      a. The Desirability of "Tumults" (D *1.4)*
      b. Why the People Should Be Trusted More Than the Great (D *1.5)*
      c. Why Republics Have to Expand (D *1.6)*
   3. Lessons Derived from the Development of the Roman Republic (*D* 1.7–27)
      a. How to Prevent "Tumults" from Becoming Civil Wars (D *1.7–8)*
      b. How to Found, Maintain, and Reorder a Republic (D *1.9–27)*
         1) The Necessity of a Single Founder (*D* 1.9)
         2) Why a Founder Should Act for the Common Good (*D* 1.10)
         3) Religion as a Means of Maintaining a Republican Order (*D* 1.11–15)
         4) The Limits of Religion and the Problem of Corruption (*D* 1.16–20)
            a) Elections as a Remedy for the Problems of Hereditary Succession (*D* 1.19–20)
            b) The Difficulty of Preventing or Remedying Corruption (*D* 1.16–18)
            c) The Need to Arm and Train the People instead of Relying on the Few Best (*D* 1.21–24)
            d) Why Gradual Reform Is Better Than Revolution and Redistribution (*D* 1.25–27)

C. Machiavelli's New Politics of Suspicion and Competition (*D* 1.28–33)

D. Successful and Unsuccessful Roman Reorderings (*D* 1.34–45)

   1. The Advantages of the Dictatorship (*D* 1.34)
   2. The Necessity of Maintaining Rotation in Office (*D* 1.35–36)
   3. Why Republics Cannot Be Reordered Effectively by Redistributing Property (*D* 1.37)

4. Why Previous Efforts to Reorder Republics Have Generally Failed (*D* 1.38–39)
5. What Is to Be Learned from the Fall of the Decemvirs (*D* 1.40–45)

E. The Lessons Machiavelli Derives from Roman History about the Best Internal Order of a Republic (*D* 1.46–60)

1. The Ever-Escalating Ambition of Men Cannot Entirely Be Restrained by Competitive Elections (*D* 1.46–48)
2. The Need for Reforms and Popular Trials to Supplement Competitive Elections (*D* 1.49)
3. No One Should Be Able to Bring Government to a Standstill (*D* 1.50)
4. The "Great" Must Demonstrate Their Willingness to Sacrifice for the Common Good in Order to Be Elected (*D* 1.51)
5. The Education of "Aristocrats" Will Not Curb Their Ambition (*D* 1.52)
6. Why Popular Government Is Best (*D* 1.53–60)
   - *a. The People Are Not Always Wise (*D *1.53–54)*
   - *b. Nor Are the People Entirely Good (*D *1.55)*
   - *c. Claims to Divinely Inspired Knowledge Are Not Necessary (*D *1.56)*
   - *d. The Power of the Multitude Is Transitory and Thus Limited (*D *1.57)*
   - *e. Nevertheless, the People Are Wiser and More Stable Than Princes (*D *1.58)*
   - *f. Popular Governments Keep Faith Better Than Princes (*D *1.59)*
   - *g. Popular Government Gives Everyone an Incentive to Work for the Benefit of All (*D *1.60)*

Book 1: How to Design and Maintain the Domestic Institutions of a Free Republic

A. The Beginnings of Cities and Rome as Exemplar (*D* 1.1)

To establish Rome as the exemplary city, Machiavelli looks back at the beginnings of cities in general; and in doing so, he dismisses several alternative accounts, either silently by omission or in passing. For example, although Machiavelli's purported source, Livy, expresses some skepticism about the truth of the stories about the founding of Rome, he nevertheless weaves them into a continuous narrative, incorporating the claims about the divine guidance and noble blood of the founders. Machiavelli's presentation of the beginnings is much less chronological and more schematic; and he does not mention much less credit any claims about divine guidance or interference.[22] As he merely suggested in *The Prince*, here he states explicitly that human beings form political associations or "cities" first in order to defend themselves and, second, to increase their wealth and dominion. In opposition to Aristotle and the Christian tradition that incorporated his philosophy, Machiavelli does not think that human beings are drawn together by natural attraction or affection.[23] It does not matter, therefore, whether the people of a city originate in a single tribe or gather together from disparate places. What is important is that their domestic orders enable them not merely to defend themselves but to conquer others. From the very first paragraph of the first part of his *Discourses* Machiavelli thus indicates that it is the close relation between their domestic orders and foreign conquests that makes the Romans exemplary.

According to Machiavelli, "all cities are built either by men native to the place . . . or by foreigners." In the first case people who were living dispersed gather together, either on their own or directed by one of them having greater authority, to defend themselves. He cites Venice as an example of the former and Athens as an example of the latter. "The second case is that of a city built by foreign races, whether free men or those depending on others, who are sent out as colonies either by a republic or by a prince to relieve their lands of inhabitants or to secure a newly acquired country . . . without expense." Having recommended such a policy to a prince who acquired a new territory in *P* 3, Machiavelli observes here that the Roman people built many such cities throughout their empire. But, he adds, "because such cities do not have a free origin, it rarely happens that they make great strides and can be numbered among the heads of kingdoms" (8). Whether one accepts the story of its founding by Sulla's soldiers or by the inhabitants of Fiesole descending from their mountains to the plain during the peace established by Octavian, Florence was built as a colony. Setting up the contrast between his own city and its great Roman predecessor that runs throughout the *Discourses*, although often only implicitly, Machiavelli notes that the modern republic without free origins has proved to be weaker.[24] As he states explicitly with regard to Rome later

22. Mansfield, "Necessity in the Beginning of Cities," in *Machiavelli's Virtue*, 66.

23. *Pace* Pocock, *Machiavellian Moment*, 75–76, who claims that Machiavelli writes in an Aristotelian tradition. We see here that Machiavelli does not perpetuate an Aristotelian understanding of politics in this very fundamental respect.

24. He describes the weakness to which Florence's origins as a colony gave rise more fully in *FH* 2.

in the chapter, Machiavelli does not think that the specific (quasi-mythical) accounts of the foundings of cities are as important (or reliable) as the general reasons and causes for the differences among them that he derives from his knowledge of things both ancient and modern.

Machiavelli somewhat ironically says that peoples have free origins when they "are *constrained* by disease, hunger, or war to abandon their ancestral country and to seek for themselves a new seat" (emphasis added), presumably because these peoples are not, like colonists, subject to an external political authority. These peoples may either inhabit cities they find in the countries they acquire, as did Moses (according to Machiavelli), or build anew, as did Aeneas.[25] In either case, Machiavelli adds, the virtue of the builder will be shown in his choice of the site and the laws he orders. It might seem better for the "builder" to choose a sterile site in which circumstances would force people to work of their own accord in order to survive (as they were constrained by natural or man-made disasters to emigrate "freely"), rather than to command them to do so directly with laws, "if men were content to live off their own and did not wish to command others." However, he has already observed, people form cities because they perceive the need to defend themselves from those who wish not merely to seize their goods, but also to oppress them. So, Machiavelli concludes, it is necessary to choose the most fertile places, where the city can expand so as to be able to defend itself, and to counteract the idleness to which the fertility of the place might give rise by ordering laws that impose a necessity to exercise on those who have to be soldiers. As a result of this exercise, they will become better soldiers than those who live in countries that are naturally harsh and sterile.[26]

Machiavelli does not explicitly apply the standards he has just articulated to the two "builders" he named. Judged by such standards, however, Moses was not a virtuous "builder." He not merely failed to reach the

25. Readers ought to observe that both examples, in fact, involved wars of conquest, and that Machiavelli characterizes them as examples of wars fought by necessity rather than by choice in *D* 2.8. In the Bible Moses famously did not reach or inhabit "the land of milk and honey," and, as Machiavelli will remind his readers in *D* 2.3, the city Aeneas founded was conquered and absorbed by the city founded by Romulus. As Machiavelli indicates at the end of this chapter and argues in more detail in *D* 9–20, a city is not founded "in a day" or by one man alone, because he needs successors to maintain and extend what he started.

26. In the *Art of War* Fabrizio thus instructs Cosimo and Zanobi that in mustering an army they should rely more on training than on the natural spirit of some (*AW* 1.121–24) and that in deploying or camping they should rely more on discipline and organization than on the natural advantages of certain sites the way the Greeks did (*AW* 6.12–18).

promised land; he relied on their experience in the sterile Sinai desert to make his people tough enough to seize Canaan, and did not give them laws that made them good enough soldiers to defend themselves in the future.[27] Machiavelli observes that it does not matter whether one takes Aeneas or Romulus as the progenitor of Rome, because in either case the Romans had a free beginning. He thus discounts the importance both of his own initial distinction between cities settled by natives and those settled by foreigners (and thus similar tribal, ethnic, or racial origins), and of the noble blood as well as the divine guidance attributed to the founders of a city with "a free beginning, without depending on anyone" (including, it seems, any god).

According to Machiavelli, it was the "many necessities the laws made by Romulus, Numa, and the others imposed" that prevented "the fertility of the site, the advantages of the sea, the frequent victories, and the greatness of its empire" from corrupting Rome "for many centuries." These laws kept Rome "full of as much virtue as has ever adorned any other city or republic" (9). He thus turns to analyzing the "necessities" imposed by these laws.

B. Why the Roman Republic Is Exemplary (*D* 1.2–6)

Having argued in *D* 1.1 that a city's laws are more important than its location or the composition of the population in establishing and maintaining its freedom, Machiavelli turns in *D* 1.2 to review and contest previous accounts of the best legislation or legislator. Emphasizing the importance of the beginnings of cities, Machiavelli initially classifies republics according to their foundings: best, if they acquired all their laws and institutions all at once, as Sparta did from Lycurgus; second best, if they acquired them over time, through chance and in response to "accidents," as did Rome; or worst, if they never succeeded in acquiring a firm basis for maintaining their freedom. "That republic *can be called* happy," Machiavelli comments, "whose lot is to get one man so prudent that he gives it laws ordered so that it can live securely under them without needing to correct them" (10,

27. The same might be said about Theseus who gathered together people who had sought refuge in the unsettled because barren land of Attica (Thucydides 1.2) and Cyrus, whose soldiers were tough because they had been shepherds, according to Plato, *Laws* 3.694a–695a, and whose empire did not last beyond his own life, according to Xenophon, *The Education of Cyrus* 8.7.2. The successes of these founders depended too much on the circumstances and not enough on the laws they established. In *D* 1.1 Machiavelli thus points to the reasons he takes the founding of Rome, in particular, to be exemplary.

emphasis added). Having lasted for eight hundred years without corruption or any dangerous tumult, Sparta appears to represent a much better example of a free republic than Rome, which became perfect only as a result of a series of accidents.[28]

Cities can "never re-order themselves without danger," Machiavelli explains, "because enough men never agree to a new law that looks to a new order in a city unless they are shown by a necessity that they need to do it" (10–11). And, he indicates by pointing to the contemporary relevance of the discussion, that necessity consists in the danger of foreign conquest. Florence was reordered as a result of the "accident" in Arezzo in '02 (a rebellion against Florentine rule that led the republic to appoint Machiavelli's patron, Piero Soderini, gonfalonier for life), and disordered by the "accident" in Prato in '12 (the defeat of the Florentine militia by the Spanish army, which led to the overthrow of the republic and the return of the Medici). As in his account of the beginnings of cities, so in discussing their internal order, Machiavelli points to the close connection he sees between the internal ordering of a city and the requirements of its external defense.

I. The Case for Sparta—the Traditional Exemplar (*D* I.2–3)

To show that Rome is a more exemplary republic than Sparta Machiavelli has to examine and criticize the arguments raised on behalf of Sparta. The first such argument is based on the traditional division of regimes, according to the number of rulers, into monarchies, aristocracies, and democracies, and a purported cycle that occurs as a result of the degeneration of each good form into its opposite. Although we know from the first chapter of *The Prince* that Machiavelli does not accept the traditional tripartite division of regimes, many commentators have taken his summary account of the cycle to represent his own understanding.[29] However, after summarizing the argument for the cycle, taken largely from Polybius, but adapted slightly to reflect his own understanding, Machiavelli distances

28. In *D* 1.9 Machiavelli recognizes that Sparta did not, in fact, last without corruption or serious tumult. *D* 1.2 is thus an opening, provisional statement.

29. One of those commentators, Wolfgang Kersting, *Niccolò Machiavelli* (Munich: C. H. Beck, 1988), 62–73, observes that Machiavelli's understanding of the cycles, unlike that of ancient philosophers, is not based on a conception of a cosmological order; it is rather based on his understanding of human passions, both the need for political order and the limits of that order those passions impose.

himself sharply from it.[30] No republic would last long enough to go through the full cycle, he protests, because "a republic always lacking in counsel and forces becomes subject to a neighboring state that is ordered better than it." He dismisses all six of the "pure" forms of government as "pestiferous," the three good ones, because of their brief life, along with the bad into which the good tend to degenerate. "Those who prudently order laws, having recognized this defect, avoid each of these modes by itself" and "chose one that shared in all, judging it firmer and more stable" (13), because in a city where there is simultaneously a principality, aristocracy, and popular government, each part guards the other. Machiavelli thus agrees with previous writers and legislators like Lycurgus that a mixed

30. Gennaro Sasso, *Studi su Machiavelli* (Naples: Morano, 1967), chaps. 4 and 5, details the similarities and differences between Polybius and Machiavelli. One of the most important differences, pointed out by Harvey C. Mansfield, *Machiavelli's New Modes and Orders: A Study of the "Discourses on Livy"* (Ithaca: Cornell University Press, 1979), 35, is that Polybius attributes the cycle to nature, whereas Machiavelli attributes it to chance. In *D* 1.1 Machiavelli argues that the effects of "nature" or natural "accidents" can be duplicated, overcome, and improved upon by means of law; and if that is the case, the corruption that seems to occur regularly and thus "naturally" in each of the three basic regimes does not happen necessarily. The corruption occurs because legislators either do not know or do not choose to enact the laws necessary to forestall it. "Since inhabitants were sparse in the beginning of the world," Machiavelli explains, "they lived dispersed for a time like beasts" (instead of "together like beasts," as Polybius wrote, and Mansfield, *Machiavelli's New Modes and Orders*, 36, notes). When population increased and people gathered together to defend themselves, they first made the one who was most robust and courageous the captain and obeyed him. But they soon discovered that ordering a city involves more than a strong defense. It was necessary also to pass laws. Whereas Polybius emphasized the role of reason in the development of an understanding and institutions of justice, Michael Zuckert argues in an unpublished paper "Rome: Machiavelli's New Constitutionalism," Machiavelli emphasizes the root of this "knowledge" in empathy, the sympathy onlookers have for the pain of a beneficiary who is not repaid. Their calculations of their own self-interest under similar circumstances led such sympathetic onlookers to see the need for mechanisms to enforce contracts. And their discovery of the need for laws and punishments for those who disobeyed them led people to select not the most hardy, but one more prudent and just to be their prince. (See also Sullivan, *Machiavelli's Three Romes*, 89–95.) As soon as rule became hereditary, however, the monarchy began to degenerate. The prince began to be hated and, because he was hated, to fear his opponents and thus to try to destroy them. Plots and conspiracies against the tyrant arose in response to his violence, not among the weak, but among the more generous and great spirited. Following the example of the powerful, the multitude took up arms and obeyed the aristocrats as their liberators after the prince was eliminated. Because they had come to hate the name of a sole ruler, these aristocrats constituted a government of themselves, which began by following the laws and acting for the common utility rather than its own advantage. But when their sons came into office, not having experienced the ill effects of tyranny, they became avaricious and ambitious. Someone quickly rose up to eliminate them with the help of the multitude; and they, remembering the evils of princely as well as of oligarchic rule, instituted a popular state, which lasted for a time, but eventually became so licentious that no one could count on the protection of the law. "So, constrained by necessity, or by the suggestion of some good man, or to escape such license," the writers who traced such a cycle concluded, the people "returned anew to the principality" (13).

regime is better than any of the simple or "pure" kinds, but he does not endorse it for quite the same reasons. Whereas they praised the superior justice and stability of such mixed regimes, he characteristically relates the goodness (or badness) of the internal order to a government's capacity (or not) to defend itself from external aggression.

Constructed as a mixed regime from the beginning, Sparta still appears to be the exemplary republic. Machiavelli contrasts the longevity of the balance of the monarchical, aristocratic, and popular elements Lycurgus established with the instability and brief life of the Athenian laws ordered by Solon, who incorporated only a popular element. Like Sparta, Rome ultimately incorporated all three elements, but Machiavelli admits that it took some time and several changes of government to achieve the perfect mixture. It was first necessary to overthrow the tyrannical kings to establish a true mixture of aristocracy with a monarchical element (in the two consuls elected from the senate to lead the armies). The Roman people did not learn that they had to demand protection against the nobles, however, until the death of the last Tarquin made the nobles lose their fear that the plebs would not take their side in a renewed dispute and they began to treat the plebs inhumanely. After much contention between the plebs and the nobility, they created tribunes with so much eminence and reputation that they could not merely serve as intermediaries between the plebs and the Senate, but counter the insolence of the nobles.

2. The Case for Rome—the New Exemplar (*D* I.4–6)

The general lessons Machiavelli draws from the development of Rome explain why he ultimately considers Rome to be a "perfect republic," even though it did not have a legislator who provided it with a mixed regime from the very beginning. His extremely selective, if not simply inaccurate use of historical examples to document that superiority shows, moreover, that he is recommending Rome not as its history was depicted by Livy, but as a model he has derived from that history on the basis of his own knowledge of things both ancient and modern.[31]

31. J. Patrick Coby, *Machiavelli's Romans* (Lanham, MD: Rowman & Littlefield, 1999), documents many ways in which Machiavelli departs from Roman history, but he nevertheless concludes that Machiavelli is recommending the ancient republic as a model, i.e., that he is not describing a new or modern form of republicanism in the guise of ancient Rome. Fischer, *Well-Ordered License*, comes to a similar conclusion by arguing that Machiavelli "intended to return his contemporaries to the political ideas and practices of the ancients" (185). However, Fischer maintains that Machiavelli misunderstood the ancients, and so propelled the West toward modernity.

Machiavelli argues that Rome was superior to the apparently more stable Sparta because Rome was an expansive regime with a popular base. Beginning with his declaration in *D* 1.3 that "it is necessary to whoever disposes a republic and orders laws in it to presuppose that all men are bad" (15), he disagrees with the ancient advocates of "aristocratic" republics who urged the necessity of educating a small class of potential rulers to control the rest of the population with laws (e.g., Aristotle, *Politics* 2.1267b1–9). According to Machiavelli, the behavior of the Roman nobles after the expulsion of the Tarquins shows that one cannot rely on the apparent public-spiritedness of the persons to whom the laws grant power. To prevent them from oppressing others, laws must be designed to make those with power afraid of the consequences of abusing it. The Romans did this by creating the offices of the tribunes to keep the nobles in line.

a. The Desirability of "Tumults" (D *1.4)*

Recognizing that many have faulted the government of Rome because of the constant "tumults" between the nobles and the plebs, Machiavelli insists in *D* 1.4 that these tumults were "the first cause of keeping Rome free."[32] As in *P* 9, he observes that "in every republic are two diverse humors, that of the people and that of the great, and that all the laws that are made in favor of freedom arise from their disunion" (16). Reasoning as he did in *P* 12 that "there cannot be good laws where there are not good arms, and where there are good arms there must be good laws," he argues that since the Romans obviously had good arms (which enabled them to attain the empire), they must also have had good laws. Their arms were good (and numerous), because the Romans armed the plebs; and the plebs refused to enroll in the armies, upon occasion, unless they were given part of the government. "The desires of free peoples are rarely pernicious to freedom," Machiavelli explains, "because they arise either from being oppressed or from suspicion that they may be oppressed" (17). It was good, therefore, to include them in the government. If the people are mistaken, their erroneous suspicions can be corrected by means of assemblies, in which a good orator can show them how they have been deceived.[33]

32. Among the ancient authors who condemned the tumults, Mansfield and Tarcov note (16n2), were Sallust, *Bellum Catilinae*, *Bellum Jugurthinum*, and *Histories*; Cicero, *Republic* 2.33 and *In Catilinam*; and Augustine, *City of God* 3.16–17.

33. Machiavelli ironically cites the authority of "Tully" (Cicero), who observed in a book entitled *De amicitia* (On friendship) that although people are ignorant, "they are capable of truth and easily yield when the truth is told them by a man worthy of faith" (17), to justify institutions that

b. Why the People Should Be Trusted More Than the Great (D *1.5*)

"Because in every republic there are great and popular men," Machiavelli acknowledges, there is a disagreement about which should be relied on to guard the city's freedom. Sparta and Venice put this guardianship in the hands of the nobles, whereas Rome put it in the hands of the plebs. Because Sparta and Venice lived free longer than Rome, some argue that the nobles have thus proved to be better guards. Machiavelli affirms, however, "that one should put on guard over a thing those who have less appetite for usurping it"; and, he repeats, the "nobles" have a great desire to dominate, whereas the "ignobles" (*ignobili*) want only to escape oppression. He admits that partisans of the nobles will point out that granting them power will satisfy their ambition more and dampen the restless spirits of the plebs that cause the confusion and scandals in republics that reduce the nobility to desperation. Roman history provides a prime example of the plebs' not being satisfied with one plebian consul, but wishing to have all the offices, and supporting leaders like Marius, who sought to beat down the nobility entirely (and thus destroyed the mixed regime). Machiavelli concedes as much in his discussion of the attempt by the Gracchi to revive the agrarian reform in *D* 1.37. But he concludes that the answer to the question about which part or party best guards a city's liberty depends not simply on reason or historical precedents, but on whether "you are reasoning about a republic that wishes to make an empire, like Rome, or about one for whom it is enough to maintain itself" (18), like Sparta or Venice. Since Machiavelli has already argued that a city is not well located unless the site allows it to expand sufficiently to defend itself from foreign aggression, readers should not be surprised by his choice of the plebs. Admitting that both the nobles and the plebs have ambitions that need to be "vented," he nevertheless argues that those who possess the most are most apt to cause tumults and so endanger the liberty of the city. First, "it does not appear to men that they possess securely what [they] have unless [they] acquire more"; second, their wealth gives them more resources with which to work larger changes; and, third, their wealth and honors are most apt to provoke the envy and emulation of others.[34]

---

not only were adopted as a result of "tumults" or enmities between the nobles and people, but also gave final decisions to the people.

34. In admitting his inability to understand what Machiavelli means by the need for a "guard of a city's freedom," Francesco Guicciardini, *Considerations of the "Discourses" of Niccolò Machiavelli*, trans. James B. Atkinson and David Sices (DeKalb: Northern Illinois University Press, 2002), 1.5; 394–95, indicates the difference between his more traditional aristocratic understanding of

Someone might ask whether the Roman state could not have been ordered so as to remove the enmity between the people and the Senate. Machiavelli thus explains: Venice and Sparta were able to maintain their freedom as long as they did without internal dissension, because both cities kept the number of inhabitants to be ruled low and so, in effect, preempted the possibility of a successful popular rebellion. Venice declared all those who participated in the government of the city at a certain point to be "gentlemen," prohibited those who came later from taking part, and by not allowing a large number of people to come into the city, prevented an inequality between rulers and ruled to develop.[35] Although he praised Lycurgus (*D* 1.2) for creating a mixture of principality, aristocracy, and democracy, Machiavelli now maintains that Sparta was governed by a king and narrow Senate. (He thus makes early Sparta look like prerepublican Rome by ignoring the fact that Sparta had two hereditary kings and ephors [the popular element]—facts he recognizes elsewhere.)[36] These few citizens could maintain control without much dissent, partly because the equality of belongings mandated by Lycurgus made the plebs less ambitious, and partly because the kings maintained their dignity against the other nobles by defending the plebs from every injury, but mostly because the Spartans did not accept foreigners, so that their population could not be corrupted.

*c. Why Republics Have to Expand (*D *1.6)*

Machiavelli does not mention the fact that Sparta used slaves to farm and armed only her relatively few citizens. Instead he emphasizes the fact that

---

republican government and Machiavelli's new, more democratic analysis. On the differences between Guicciardini and Machiavelli, see Jürgen Huber, *Guicciardinis Kritik an Machiavelli* (Wiesbaden: Springer, 2004).

35. Venice was a particularly relevant modern instance of the model of the noble or aristocratic republic for Machiavelli and his immediate audience. Savonarola had modeled his reform of the Florentine republic, in part, on Venice (by incorporating a "Great Council"), and the *ottimati* families to whom both Cosimo and Zanobi belonged generally opposed the inclusion of such popular institutions (as well as the arming of the plebs).

36. As Coby, *Machiavelli's Romans*, 39, points out. However, as Coby later observes (46), according to Plutarch, the ephorate was not the creation of Lycurgus, but added 130 years later. Machiavelli fails to take account of the actual historical development of Spartan institutions, the way in which it acquired dominion over neighboring Messenia, and the slave (helot) population upon which the operation of the republic depended. He thus indicates that he is more interested in combating the model of a good republic (to be found in Plato's *Laws*, for example), in which a wise legislator establishes institutions and laws that are maintained, basically unchanged, than he is in Sparta. In fact, Sparta's development followed some of the course Machiavelli attributes to Rome, i.e., a combination of expansion and institutional reform.

Rome would not have been able to wage the wars it did without arming the plebs and increasing the population by accepting foreigners. At first he suggests that the resolution of the question of why a republic must expand involves a tradeoff of "inconveniences." A city can live free and united if it is located in a strong place where it would be difficult to crush but does not pose a threat to its neighbors. "For war is made on a republic for two causes: one, to become master of it; the other, for fear lest it seize you" (22). Indeed, Machiavelli declares "that if the thing could be held balanced in this mode, it would be the true political way of life and the true quiet of a city."[37] But he quickly adds that "since things of men are in motion and cannot stay steady, they must either rise or fall." So what reason does not dictate, "necessity" does. That "necessity" with regard to cities is that if "heaven" is so kind as to relieve them from the necessity of waging war, their people will become idle, effeminate, or divided, and thus eventually ruined internally, if not externally. "In ordering a republic," Machiavelli thus concludes, "it is necessary to follow the Roman order and not that of the other republics . . . and to tolerate the enmities that arise between the people and the Senate . . . as an inconvenience necessary to arrive at Roman greatness" (23).

3. Lessons Derived from the Development of the Roman Republic (*D* 1.7–27)

*a. How to Prevent "Tumults" from Becoming Civil Wars (*D *1.7–8)*

"Tolerating" these enmities does not mean merely letting them flare and allowing the two humors to fight their differences out. The point is, rather, to design "orders" that will not only prevent the conflict between the "humors" from degenerating into civil war but also use that conflict to support the rule of law. The first such "order" he mentions is granting "those who are posted in a city as guard of its freedom . . . authority . . . to accuse citizens to the people, or to some magistrate or council, when they sin in anything against the free state." Such an order has "two very useful effects for a republic": First, it deters citizens from attempting things against the state for fear of incurring such an accusation and insures that if they do attempt to overturn the state, such individuals will be "crushed instantly

37. Such a balance between difficulty of conquest and the absence of imperial ambitions of its own (although the ability perhaps to aid others), along with a restricted population, was proposed as a means of preserving both the city's freedom and its unity in Plato's *Republic* 4.420b–423b.

and without respect" (23). Second, and seemingly more important, public trials that enable the people to accuse specific individuals of attempting to overthrow the republic and that allow those individuals to present witnesses and evidence to counter the accusations provide a means of "venting those humors that grow up in cities" that produce civil wars if they are not directed and regulated by laws.

In citing the trial of Coriolanus as an example of the advantages of accusations, Machiavelli reports that Livy "says that the Roman nobility had become angered against the plebs because the plebs appeared to it to have too much authority through the creation of the tribunes." But when the plebs heard that Coriolanus counseled the Senate to withhold the grain they had brought from Sicily to relieve the famine to "punish the plebs and take from it the authority that it had taken to the prejudice of the nobility," they became so angry that they would have killed Coriolanus as he emerged from the Senate in a tumult, "had the tribunes not summoned him to appear to defend his cause" (24). Machiavelli does not mention the fact (to be found in Livy 2.35) that Coriolanus did not appear and was condemned in absentia. His example certainly does not support Machiavelli's claim in the next chapter that "calumnies are detestable in free cities," and that there is no "better order for taking them away than to open up very many places for accusations," because "calumnies have need neither of witnesses nor of any other specific corroboration to prove them, so that everyone can be calumniated by everyone; but everyone cannot . . . be accused, since accusations have need of true corroborations and of circumstances that show the truth of the accusation" (27). Machiavelli seems to admit that Coriolanus was not treated justly when he concludes that "if a citizen is crushed ordinarily, there follows little or no disorder in the republic, even though he has been done a wrong" (24). But it is not for the sake of achieving justice that Machiavelli recommends the institution of publicly accusing individuals said to have "sinned" against the republic before a popular jury. According to Machiavelli, such public trials serve to "vent" the "ambition" (or, we might say, anger) of the public by directing it against a single individual, rather than against the city and its government as a whole, and thus preserve the rule of law. He recommends public accusations because they affect only a few individuals, however unjustly, and benefit the "generality" because trials are conducted in public according to law, and so preserve republican government, whereas the use of private forces or foreign troops to punish offenders would destroy it. In using the accusation of Coriolanus as an example of the advantages of such a process, Machiavelli suppresses the "inconvenient" fact that after he was condemned, Coriolanus defected to a foreign city, where he raised an army that threatened to destroy Rome, until his mother pleaded with him to desist.[38]

Although Machiavelli initially says that he is advocating the creation of an authority able to accuse citizens before "the people, or some magistrate or council," both his ancient and his Florentine examples suggest that the jury needs to be numerous and popular if public trials are to prevent civil wars that so weaken a state that it becomes vulnerable to foreign conquest.[39] Machiavelli's first example of a Florentine who was thought by many to have ambitions to overthrow the republic is extremely ironic. Because he did not have to fear a public accusation and trial, Francesco Valori concluded that there was no way of checking his ambitions "except with a sect contrary to his." He thus began organizing a private army of supporters to defend him"; and because "those who opposed him had no ordinary [lawful] way to repress him, they thought of extraordinary [extralegal] ways until they came to arms." In fact, Valori was the leader of Savonarola's party who refused to grant the appeal to the popular Council in capital cases, for which Savonarola himself had agitated, to five *ottimati* accused of conspiring to overthrow the republic and bring back the Medici. (Valori feared that the Council would acquit the one who only knew of the plot but did not actually participate in it.) Because the friar did not criticize members of his own party who did not enforce the law he had promoted, Savonarola lost much of his popular influence and was con-

38. Machiavelli characteristically does not credit family ties or loyalties as a basis of a free or republican way of life. On the contrary, he regularly suggests that the desire politically powerful men often demonstrate to pass their positions on to their sons is a major source of the corruption, if not of the sheer destruction, of a republic. One reason Machiavelli favors the people over the Senate as the "guardian of liberty" is that the "fathers" held their seats on the basis of heredity. Machiavelli underlines his inaccurate use of Coriolanus as a positive example of the utility of accusations, moreover, by using another slightly erroneous account of an incident at Chiusi where a man called in the "French" to punish the violator of his sister, according to Machiavelli, but in Livy 5.33, his wife (and so the potential mother of his heirs). In Livy's history, the Chiusi incident which brings the Gauls to Italy leads to their attack on Rome and Manlius's later "calumnies" (in Livy, an organized rebellion), because he felt slighted by the greater glory awarded to Camillus for defeating the Gauls than to him for saving the Capitol from their secret attack.

39. As in *P* 3, where Machiavelli first says that a prince who adds a province with the same language and customs need only eliminate the bloodline of the previous prince, but then adds that the prince should also not change any of the laws or taxes, so here he clarifies his proposal and modifies its requirements when he restates it.

demned by the Church.[40] Machiavelli suggests that the same failure of the Florentine republic to establish a public mode of accusing individuals said to have an ambition to overthrow the republic before a popular jury also made it impossible for Piero Soderini to respond effectively to the accusations other *ottimati* made against him. "To accuse one powerful individual before eight judges in a republic is not enough," Machiavelli comments; "the judges need to be very many because the few always behave in the mode of the few" (25). Those few presumably correspond to the "great," who are always trying to increase their ability to oppress others, and whose exoneration of one of their own in a closed session would continue to be suspect to the people. In *The Prince* Machiavelli thus argued that the institution of a public court like the French *parlement* would enable a prince to secure himself by enabling the people to check the nobles. Had there been such a court in Florence, he suggests here, Soderini would have been condemned and his accusers (including preeminently the Medici) would have "vented their animus without having the Spanish army come." Or if he had been shown not to be guilty as charged, "they would not have dared to work against him for fear of being accused themselves" (25).

As Machiavelli makes clear with the example of Manlius Capitolinus in *D* 1.8, ambitious individuals often charge those in power with misusing the public's trust. Not merely will such individuals attract the support of other envious people if their "calumnies" are not made subject to investigation and proof in a public forum, but their supporters will end up fighting the supporters of their opponents in the streets, if not on a battlefield with foreign troops, and the republic will be destroyed.

*b. How to Found, Maintain, and Reorder a Republic (*D *1.9–27)*

Having argued that the popularly based Roman version of the mixed regime proved to be superior to the more aristocratic Greek versions, because the latter were destroyed either by civil wars between the two "humors" or by foreign conquest, Machiavelli returns in *D* 1.9 to the beginning of Rome to show the way in which it developed its admirable institutions

40. Francesco Guicciardini, *History of Florence*, trans. M. Domandi (New York: Harper Torchbooks, 1970), 103–6, 116, 125, 131–35, 141; McCormick, *Machiavellian Democracy*, 129–33. Later in the *Discourses* (3.30), Machiavelli claims that Savonarola saw the need to kill those who opposed his plans because of envy, but that he was not able to convince his followers to do so. They seem to have understood the need to kill the opposition well enough, but not the need to maintain popular approval.

over time. He begins by excusing what many would see to be a great fault in its founder: Romulus not only killed his brother but also consented to the murder of Titus Tatius the Sabine, whom he had chosen as a partner in the kingdom (to make peace after the Romans stole the Sabine women).[41]

1) THE NECESSITY OF A SINGLE FOUNDER (*D* 1.9). Many commentators have emphasized the "general rule" Machiavelli enunciates on the basis of Romulus's example, "that it never or rarely happens that any republic or kingdom is ordered well from the beginning or reformed altogether anew outside its old orders unless it is ordered by one individual." Because Machiavelli argues that the "effects" excuse Romulus's violent deeds, these readers conclude that the founding of a regime requires an "extraordinary" (immoral and illegal) act of violence or crime, and, more generally (as in *P* 18), that the end justifies the means.[42]

Such readers do not pay sufficient attention to the specific reasons why Machiavelli not merely excuses Romulus's deeds, but also calls him "prudent" and "virtuous." The first reason is that it is necessary for a single mind to order a city. Because people disagree about what is good, many minds will not be able to agree on what order should be instituted. Machiavelli thus excuses Romulus for killing his brother and colleague in order to obtain the necessary authority for himself. Machiavelli calls Romulus not merely prudent, but virtuous, because Romulus showed that he was acting not on his own behalf but for the sake of the common good (*bene comune*). He demonstrated the beneficent intention behind his seemingly criminal actions by refusing to establish a hereditary succession and by sharing his power with a senate.[43] By cutting off his own family and sharing power

41. As Sullivan, *Machiavelli's Three Romes*, 127, points out, Machiavelli exaggerates Romulus's crime by saying that he consented to the killing of his ally and fellow ruler Tatius the Sabine. According to Livy 1.14, Romulus simply refused to go to war to avenge the murder of Tatius by a Laurentian mob, who were taking their revenge for his having failed to punish some of his relatives for mistreating some Laurentian ambassadors. She suggests that Machiavelli did so to show that Romulus slew his brother not merely in an act of self-defense or as a response to Remus's challenge to his authority, but as a matter of policy and by choice. I think Machiavelli wanted to downplay the importance of Romulus's crime against family as such and to emphasize the importance of a founder's acting alone, because a divided authority makes it difficult to act expeditiously or effectively.

42. E.g., Coby, *Machiavelli's Romans*, 42, although Coby also considers the reasoning in some detail.

43. Mansfield, *Machiavelli's New Modes and Orders*, 63, cites Augustine, *City of God* 15.5, who points out that the founder of the first city in the Bible, Cain, also slew his brother. Cain did not, however, share his power with a senate, and so replace personal or hereditary rule with shared power and legal restraints on its use.

with others Romulus not only indicated that, like the theorists of the cycle of regimes, he understood that hereditary rule tends to degenerate.[44] He also understood the need to gain support for the order he had established from those who had not shared his understanding of the good at the beginning but would come to appreciate the benefits of the order once established and therefore defend it. The way people become attached to a government, he recognized, is by taking part in its decisions. By establishing a senate with which he took counsel and by whose opinion he decided, Romulus proved that he was acting not solely from his own ambition but for the common good.[45]

Machiavelli's justification for Romulus's crimes raises four questions that he pursues in greater depth and detail in the remainder of book 1. First, is it necessary for a leader who wishes to renew the orders of a republic to act outside the law and thus risk overturning the republic entirely?[46] Or is it possible to design institutions that can be renewed from

44. According to the traditional story reported by Livy, Romulus acquired such an understanding from his own experience. He and his brother Remus were descendants of Aeneas. Their grandfather, Numitor, as the eldest son, was supposed to inherit the kingdom, but he was driven out by his brother Amulius, who proceeded to murder Numitor's male children and made his niece, Rhea Silvia, a Vestal Virgin, ostensibly to honor her, but actually to condemn her to perpetual virginity to preclude the possibility of issue. She claimed that she was raped by Mars and gave birth to twin boys. The king threw her into prison and ordered her sons to be drowned. Because the Tiber had flooded, his servants left the babies on the shore, where a she-wolf heard them crying and suckled them until Faustulus, the king's herdsman, found them and took them into his hut. When they grew up, the twins formed a gang of robbers. After the king caught Remus and was about to put him on trial, Romulus conspired with some of his fellows to kill the king. He and Remus then claimed to be the legitimate rulers on the basis of their lineage. But according to Livy (1.6), the brothers' plans for the future were marred by the same jealousy and ambition that had divided their grandfather and Amulius. Accounts differ as to the specific occasion for their quarrel, but the brothers fought, Remus was killed, and Romulus assumed sole authority.

45. Machiavelli observes that Romulus reserved the authority of convoking the Senate and commanding the armies after war was decided upon for himself. The monarchy he established is thus rather like that Machiavelli attributes in *D* 1.16 to the king of France, in what Machiavelli calls one of "the well-ordered and governed kingdoms in our times" (*P* 19), except that the French king reserved power over finances as well as over the army to himself. Romulus did not need to do the former, because Rome's public resources came largely from conquest. John M. Warner and John T. Scott, "Sin City: Augustine and Machiavelli's Reordering of Rome," *Journal of Politics* 73, no. 3 (2011): 865, dismiss Machiavelli's contention here that Romulus acted for the common good on the basis of his earlier statement (*D* 1.2) that Romulus intended to found a kingdom and of his sources (from which Machiavelli clearly departs). The kingdom he founded was elective, however; and Machiavelli suggests that Brutus's replacement of one elected king by two elected consuls (returning to the Spartan model of two kings) was a mistake. Restricted to the Senate and the consuls, people and tribunes, the "orders" of Rome were defective (*D* 1.18), because they did not include a truly monarchical or single executive power (except in the temporary dictatorship, which he praises).

46. Machiavelli raises this question both in the title of the chapter and in the examples of the Spartan kings Agis and Cleomenes, who were not founding anew, as was Romulus, but wanted

within? Second, what leads a prince who acquires sole authority to act for the common benefit—if only out of concern for the preservation of his own work and reputation? Third, how does this prince acquire support from those who do not understand the reasons for his initial actions? And, fourth, what can a prince who wishes to establish an enduring order do to ensure that he will have successors who understand what is needed to maintain that order?

2) WHY A FOUNDER SHOULD ACT FOR THE COMMON GOOD (*D* 1.10). Machiavelli addresses the question of the prince's incentives in *D* 1.10. Although the most praised men are heads and orderers of religions, then the founders of republics and kingdoms, third the generals whose victories expand their kingdom or fatherland, and fourth the literary men who celebrate their deeds, he observes, most actual princes are deceived "by a false good and a false glory." Encouraged by the obsequious flattery of their attendants to try to secure their rule by destroying anyone who threatens to oppose them, most princes become tyrants, living in unabated fear of conspiracies and blamed, rather than praised, after they die.[47]

Machiavelli seems to echo the classical philosophical critique of tyranny when he affirms that reading ancient history should make anyone wish to be a savior of his republic like Scipio rather than its destroyer like Caesar, or a prince like Timoleon or Dion instead of a tyrant like Nabis, Phalaris, or Dionysius. He acknowledges that the destroyer of the Roman republic, Caesar, has been more celebrated by "the writers" than any of these exemplary princes, whose good works endured only during their own lifetimes.[48] But he suggests that those who praise Caesar have been "corrupted by his fortune" (that is, attributed his success to his virtue) and were "awed by the duration of the empire that, ruling under that name, did not permit writers to speak freely of him" (32). Readers impressed by the praise of Caesar should look at what writers (preeminently Cicero) say in criticizing Catiline, who wished but failed to achieve what Caesar did,

to reform Sparta. Seeing that Agis had been murdered by the ephors who wanted to prevent him from taking away their power, Cleomenes saw that they were destroyed. However, weakened as Machiavelli would have predicted by its internal corruption and dissension, Sparta was then conquered by Macedonia. As Machiavelli emphasized in *D* 1.2, any radical reordering is dangerous (because it often involves the threat of foreign conquest).

47. Cf. Plato, *Republic* 9.571a–580a.

48. Timoleon and Dion are celebrated in Plutarch's *Lives*.

and in praising his enemy, Brutus, to get a truer, more balanced view of Caesar's achievement and "glory."

By referring to Brutus, Machiavelli reminds his readers that the destroyer of the Roman republic died violently as a victim of a conspiracy of his former friends (members of the Senate whose power Caesar was effectively seizing).[49] Caesar's reputation or "glory" was based not so much on the happiness or security of his own life as on the empire he established in place of the republic. His name or fame was thus hostage, in effect, to the deeds of his successors. Machiavelli admits that some of Caesar's successors were good emperors. Expanding and slightly modifying the analysis of the emperors he presented in *P* 19, he explains that these emperors did not depend upon the Praetorian Guard or the legions, i.e., force, to keep them in office, because "their habits, the benevolence of the people, and the love of the Senate defended them." Both they and their people lived secure in a "world full of peace and justice," in a version of what Machiavelli calls a well-ordered kingdom, including "the Senate with its authority, the magistrates with their honors, the rich citizens enjoying their riches, nobility and virtue exalted." These were, indeed, "golden times when each can hold and defend the opinion he wishes" (33).[50] Underlining a point he made about Romulus, Machiavelli also reminds his readers that, with the exception of Titus, these good emperors succeeded by adoption rather than by inheritance. Most of Caesar's successors were elevated, however, by the legions or the Praetorian Guard. As Machiavelli pointed out in *P* 19, these emperors had to allow their soldiers to oppress the people or be killed by their own soldiers. Only a "criminal" (as he says here) like Severus was saved by his exceptionally great fortune and virtue. Considerations of his own safety as well as his future reputation should lead a prince to

49. Machiavelli's oblique reference to the death of Julius Caesar might remind readers familiar with Livy of his account of the death of Romulus. "One day while he was reviewing his troops . . . a storm burst . . . [and] a cloud enveloped him, so that it hid him from the eyes of everyone present. . . . The troops, who had been alarmed by the sudden storm, recovered when it passed over. . . . Then they saw that the throne was empty, and [were] ready . . . to believe the senators, who had been standing at the king's side and now declared that he had been carried up on high by a whirlwind. . . . A few voices began to proclaim Romulus's divinity; . . . and at last every man present hailed him as a god and son of a god. . . . However, a few dissentients secretly maintained that the king had been torn to pieces by the senators" (1.16).

50. Strauss, *TM*, 33, comments that Machiavelli might thus be suggesting that there can be more freedom (intellectual, if not political) under a prince than in a republic. However, Strauss also observes that Machiavelli has just reminded his readers of the way in which criticism of Caesar was muted, i.e., that speech under the empire was not so free as he had just claimed.

see the need to establish institutions that would check the power of later princes. Seeming to speak here particularly to his immediate audience of politically ambitious Florentine youths, Machiavelli concludes that a prince who "seeks the glory of the world . . . ought to desire to possess a corrupt city—not to spoil it entirely as did Caesar but to reorder it as did Romulus" (33). Those who establish institutions like the Roman Senate, which benefit later generations, rather than tyrannies which oppress them, he promises, will become venerated. (See *P* 6.)

A reader cannot help but ask somewhat skeptically: would it truly be more glorious for a young man to reform his own corrupt republic than to become like Caesar king, if not tyrant, of the entire world? Later in the *Discourses* (see especially *D* 2.33 and 3.34), Machiavelli will raise questions about whether glory is a reliable measure of true human greatness. Glory is after all a product of widespread popular opinion, not of knowledge; and it is often not enjoyed by the individual who acquires it posthumously, especially if he is assassinated, as Caesar was. Machiavelli will appeal instead to the desire to secure their own lives that leaders share with their people.

3) RELIGION AS A MEANS OF MAINTAINING A REPUBLICAN ORDER (*D* 1.11–15). After arguing that a prince should act to secure his own life and the common good rather than strive for praise and to perpetuate his name or family by establishing a hereditary monarchy, Machiavelli turns in *D* 1.11–14 to examine the way in which the Romans used religion to convince people who did not understand the reasons for the orders to support and obey them. Romulus did not need to appeal to the authority of God to order the Senate and make other civil and military orders, Machiavelli suggests, because Romulus could and did use extraordinary force to make himself feared and obeyed.[51] To establish the religious beliefs and practices that would make a ferocious people obey the law and support the Senate along with the other civil and military orders after Romulus died, however, Numa Pompilius had to claim to have divine inspiration. He thus pretended to

51. Machiavelli thus departs, once again, from Livy (1.6–7), who reports that Romulus fortified the Palatine hill, performed religious rites taken from the Albans and the Greeks, and then gave his people their laws. He wishes to distinguish clearly between the single mind, intelligence, or wisdom needed to establish a political order and the claim that it has been sanctioned if not proposed by a divinity used to persuade the people to accept and maintain that order. Traditional stories about Minos's having been instructed by Zeus and Lycurgus's having been instructed by Apollo merged the origin and intelligence needed to found a lasting regime with the beliefs necessary to maintain it. (See Plato, *Laws* 624a–625b.)

be intimate with a nymph who told him what to tell the people. And the people believed him—partly because of his own goodness and prudence, and partly because the men were crude.

Reminding his readers that the purpose of the *Discourses* is to show his contemporaries that it is possible to imitate the ancient Romans, Machiavelli concedes that "whoever wished to make a republic in the present times would find it easier among mountain men, where there is no civilization, than among those who are used to living in cities, where civilization is corrupt" (35). But he then observes that the people of Florence do not consider themselves either ignorant or coarse, yet "they were persuaded by Friar Girolamo Savonarola that he spoke with God . . . without having seen anything extraordinary to make them believe him. For his life, learning, and the subject he took up were sufficient to make them lend faith." Machiavelli thus concludes that "no one . . . should be terrified that he cannot carry out what has been carried out by others, for as was said in our preface, men are born, live, and die always in one and the same order" (36).

The fact that all men die is, indeed, the reason those who found a kingdom or republic need to establish a religion to maintain it. So long as a virtuous prince is alive, he can enforce his laws by making people afraid to disobey. But if their fear of the prince is not extended and supplemented by a fear of the gods, the orders a prince establishes and maintains will die with him. So Machiavelli urges, "princes of a republic or of a kingdom should maintain the foundations of the religion they hold," for "if this is done, it will be an easy thing for them to maintain their republic religious and, in consequence, good and united" (37). Prudent leaders will not merely hide their own lack of belief; they will magnify anything that favors religion, especially if they know about natural things. As Machiavelli argued in *P* 18, a prince must always appear to be religious, even if he himself does not and cannot believe. His people will not continue to believe if he does not act as if he does.

Roman leaders like Camillus fostered popular beliefs that the gods particularly favored their city, because these beliefs made it easier for the great men of Rome to obtain popular support for their plans and so to maintain unity, rather than division within the city. But the "princes of the Christian republic" have destroyed the religious beliefs of the people living closest to them by providing "wicked examples." And because the Church lacks sufficient temporal power to impose its rule on the rest of Italy but is able to call upon other powers to defend it from domination by any other state, Italy remains not only disunited but also vulnerable to foreign invasions.

Rather than calling for a pope-led expedition to "liberate" Italy from the barbarians, as in *P* 26, Machiavelli here somewhat fancifully proposes exporting "the Roman court, with all the authority it has in Italy, to inhabit the towns of the Swiss." He thus suggests not merely that the temporal power and independence of the Church has prevented the unification and defense of Italy under a national monarchy like that of France or Spain. He also insists that "the bad customs of that court" have made it impossible for the Italians to live, like the Swiss, "according to the ancients as regards both religion and military orders" (39). To imitate the Romans, Machiavelli intimates, his contemporaries will have to destroy the Roman church.[52] Alternatively, Machiavelli predicts, it may destroy itself and so create conditions under which Italy can be unified, because the loss of faith in the province caused by the corruption of the Church makes it likely that it will be either ruined or scourged in the near future. The religious difference that seems to make imitation of ancient politics impossible may not last.[53]

Machiavelli explicitly treats Roman religion as a means the nobles used to overcome plebian resistance to their policies and rule in *D* 1.13–14. And treating "religion" solely as an instrument of rule allows him to avoid commenting on the substantive differences between Christian and pagan forms (which he explicitly does later in *D* 2.2). In *D* 1.13 he gives examples of the ways in which Roman nobles used "certain prodigies," oracles, and the Sibylline books to convince the plebs to reinstate nobles as consuls, persist in long sieges, and undertake new military expeditions. And in *D* 1.14 he explains how Roman generals manipulated the auguries, without revealing their own skepticism, to give their troops confidence. But in *D* 1.15 he shows that the threat of divine punishment and immediate death to those who refused to take an oath to fight in defense of their city was not sufficient to make the Sabines victorious in their battle against the experienced, disciplined, and hence confident troops of the Romans.[54] Machiavelli thus concludes that religion is a useful supplement in main-

52. See Scott and Sullivan, "Patricide," and Parent, "Machiavelli's Missing Romulus," who argue that Machiavelli makes a similar suggestion in *The Prince.*

53. Machiavelli takes up this possibility again in *D* 2.5.

54. Mansfield, *Machiavelli's New Modes and Orders*, 78, observes that one could easily read through *D* 1.15 without realizing that the battle in which the consul Papirius defeated the Samnites, despite their using religion well, was the same battle in which he arranged for the death of the "prince" of the chicken men, to show that the "prince" had lied when he contradicted the consul's claim that the auspices had gone well (even though they had not). Thinking that his troops would win the battle, Papirius did not simply trust the auguries, but he also did not want his troops to fear that the gods were against them.

taining orders first instituted by means of coercion, but it is no substitute for such orders.

4) THE LIMITS OF RELIGION AND THE PROBLEM OF CORRUPTION (*D* 1.16–20). Machiavelli gradually brings out the limited utility of "religion" in the next four chapters. He began his discussion of the religion of the Romans by praising Numa for reducing "a very ferocious people . . . to civil obedience" by means of religion, and went so far as to suggest that Rome owed even more to Numa than to Romulus. But he begins *D* 1.16 by observing how difficult it is "for a people used to living under a prince to preserve its freedom, if by accident it acquires it, as Rome did after the expulsion of the Tarquins." The reason is that a "people is nothing other than a brute animal that, although of a ferocious and feral nature, has always been nourished in prison and in servitude." So "if it is left free in a field to its fate, it becomes the prey of the first one who seeks to rechain it, not being used to feed itself and not knowing places where it may have to take refuge" (44). In other words, the same peaceful arts that civilize a people by making it willing to obey the law also make that same people too pacific to defend itself from conquest or tyranny.

Machiavelli began *D* 1.12 by declaring that "those princes or those republics that wish to maintain themselves uncorrupt have above everything else to maintain the ceremonies of their religion uncorrupt and hold them always in veneration," leading a reader to think that a "corrupt" city would be irreligious. Machiavelli has subsequently shown, however, that "religion" does not suffice to maintain the republican orders established by a public-spirited founder. On the contrary, religion remains politically salutary only when nonbelieving leaders hide their own lack of belief and maintain the ceremonies to obtain the obedient cooperation of the people. In themselves, he now admits, the "civilizing" arts of peace Numa used to maintain the orders of Romulus threatened ultimately to undermine the freedom of the city, both internal and external.[55] "Having considered the virtue and mode of proceeding of . . . the first three Roman kings," he concludes in *D* 1.19, "one sees that Rome chanced upon very great fortune when it had the first king very fierce and bellicose, the next quiet and

55. When Skinner, "Republican Ideal of Political Liberty," 306, asks "how the Romans induced their citizen-armies to fight so bravely against enslavement by invading enemies," and responds that "he finds the key in their religious laws," which made them fear to break their oaths, he ignores the tension Machiavelli emphasizes here between the laws which civilize a people and the training they need to become soldiers.

religious, the third similar in ferocity to Romulus and more a lover of war than of peace. For in Rome it was necessary that in its first beginnings an orderer of a civil way of life emerge, but it was indeed then necessary that the other kings take up again the virtue of Romulus; otherwise that city would have become effeminate and the prey of its neighbors" (52).[56]

(A) ELECTIONS AS A REMEDY FOR THE PROBLEMS OF HEREDITARY SUCCESSION (*D* 1.19–20) Machiavelli uses the example of early Rome to show that a succession of prudent and virtuous leaders is more necessary than religion to maintain the republican orders of a free city. That was the great innovation Lucius Junius Brutus introduced when he replaced the king, who was apparently elected for life, with two consuls annually elected by the Senate. The great advantage of republics over hereditary principalities or kingdoms, Machiavelli declares in *D* 1.20, is that they can solve the problem of hereditary succession that previous writers thought led to the cycle of regimes by electing an "infinite" number of virtuous princes. But, Machiavelli shows in *D* 1.16–18, elections are not sufficient to preserve the freedom of a republic, because elections will insure a succession of virtuous leaders only if virtuous individuals put themselves forward and the people vote for them.

Machiavelli reminds his readers that Rome solved the problem of succession by chance. Romulus's successors were officially elected by the Senate, but a series of Tarquins threatened to make the kingship hereditary. Brutus took the opportunity afforded by the rape of Lucretia by the king's son (an "accident" [*D* 3.5] that Machiavelli does not even mention here) to found or, perhaps we should say, to reorder the republic by getting the people to swear that they would never consent to the reign of a king in Rome, and assigning the king's major function of commanding the army to two consuls elected annually by the Senate. He also eliminated the partisan enemies of the government he had newly reordered by having his own sons publicly tried, condemned, and then killed for having schemed to reinstate a hereditary monarchy. Machiavelli has already reminded his readers in *D* 1.3

56. Machiavelli generalizes the lesson by showing how it applies to the successors of King David in the Bible (Solomon and Rehoboam) as well as to those of Mahomet. If Selim, the current sultan of the Turks, had loved peace more than war, like his father, Bajazet, the kingdom would have been ruined. "After an excellent prince, a weak prince can maintain himself; but after a weak one, no kingdom can be maintained with another weak one, unless indeed it is like that of France, which its ancient orders maintain. Those princes are weak who do not rely on war" (53).

that after much turmoil the republic had to be reordered again in order to create the tribunes.

(B) THE DIFFICULTY OF PREVENTING OR REMEDYING CORRUPTION (*D* 1.16–18) Machiavelli has promised to show his readers how they can "imitate," that is, intentionally and knowingly replicate, the results of chance events in Rome in modern Europe. Perhaps he was thinking of the recent failures of two different sets of republican leaders, led first by Savonarola and later by Soderini, to maintain free institutions in Florence after the French invasion dislodged the Medici. In any case, he begins his discussion of the difficulty but need for regular reorderings of republics by emphasizing the difficulties a people used to living under a prince faces "if by some accident it becomes free."[57] "Not knowing how to reason about either public defense or public offence" (that is, how to protect themselves from external aggressors or to provide for their own needs), such a people will quickly find themselves under a heavier yoke, if they or "the matter" is corrupt. "A corrupt city that lives under a prince can never be turned into a free one, even if that prince is eliminated along with all his line," he explains in *D* 1.17. "One prince must eliminate the other; and without the creation of a new lord it never settles down, unless indeed the goodness of one individual, together with virtue, keeps it free. But such freedom will last [only] as long as the life of that one, as happened in Syracuse with Dion and Timoleon" (47). In sum, when a city used to living under a prince accidentally becomes free, it faces not merely the problems Romulus confronted in founding a republic, but the additional problems posed by its "civilized," peaceful experience. Ironically, the more successful a government is in making its people obedient to the laws, the more it makes them vulnerable to becoming subject to a tyrant or despot. A republic or a free way of life is more difficult to establish and maintain than a principality or despotism.

As in his depiction of the four founders in *P* 6, so Machiavelli has argued in the *Discourses* with regard to Romulus (*D* 1.9) and now Brutus (*D* 1.17), the founder of a republic must be a single individual or "prince" who eliminates the opposition by means of an "extraordinary" use of force. As in *P* 6, so Machiavelli emphasizes here, any prince who wants to establish (or

57. As Machiavelli reminded his readers in *D* 1.12, Savonarola was able to convince the Florentines that he had spoken to God; but, as Machiavelli observed in *P* 6, the priest was not able to force his followers to continue to believe in him and fight for his reforms in the face of armed opposition.

reestablish) a free state will have the partisans of the old as enemies, who will need to be suppressed by force. But where the entirely new prince could count on the support, be it lukewarm, of the people who were oppressed by, and the nobles who were dissatisfied with, the previous government, Machiavelli now points out, the founder of a free government will not have any partisans. The first reason is that under a free government, honors and rewards are distributed honestly and openly for stated causes, so the individuals who receive such honors and rewards believe that they deserve them and do not feel obligated to anyone else. The second reason is that few people recognize the common utility of a free way of life, which consists in "being able to enjoy one's things freely, without any suspicion, not fearing for the honor of wives and that of children, or being afraid for oneself" (45), until it is lost. As Machiavelli states more directly in *FH* 4.1, people tend to confuse liberty with license, i.e., the absence of rule altogether; but where there is no government, he shows in all of his writings, there is no security.[58]

Explicitly addressing princes "who have become tyrants over their fatherlands" (46), Machiavelli informs them that they must first "remedy these inconveniences" by killing "the sons of Brutus," who now include all those who think they would benefit more from the hereditary kingdom that has been replaced than from the new order. But he then advises (as he advised all princes in *The Prince*) that if they wish to maintain their rule, they should seek to make the people friendly. They should "examine what the people desires," and they "will always find that it desires two things: first, to be avenged against those who are the cause that it is servile; and second, to recover its freedom." Using the tyrant Clearchus's butchering of the aristocrats of Heraclea to make the same point he illustrated with Cesare's display of the quartered body of Remirro de Orco in *P* 7, Machiavelli observes that the people take great satisfaction in seeing those they have feared violently eliminated. Since it is not possible for a prince entirely to satisfy the people's desire to recover their freedom without relinquishing his own rule, Machiavelli instructs him to inquire further into the causes of that desire. These are of two distinct kinds (corresponding to the two "humors" to be found in every republic). A few (forty to fifty) will wish to command. But as Machiavelli also showed with the example of Cesare

58. In associating liberty so closely with security, Machiavelli sets a precedent for Montesquieu's definition of "political liberty in relation to the citizen" as "security . . . in one's opinion of one's security." Montesquieu, *Spirit of the Laws*, 12.1; 187.

Borgia, such ambitious individuals can be either eliminated or "bought off" by "having them share in so many honors . . . that they have to be in good part content." For most people, as Machiavelli argued in *P* 19, it is enough to live secure. They will be satisfied by a prince who establishes orders like those of the kingdom of France, in which the people see that the king himself is bound by "infinite laws in which the security of all its peoples is included" (46), excepting only his command of the army and public funds. Machiavelli thus indicates in passing how close the mixed republic he is advocating on the Roman model is to a "well-ordered kingdom."[59]

A prudent, public-spirited prince is a necessary but not sufficient condition for the founding or reordering of a republic. The people or "matter" must not be corrupt; and they become corrupted very easily if their "heads" are. Machiavelli thus judges "that it was necessary either that the kings be extinguished in Rome or that Rome in a very short time become weak and of no value. For considering how much corruption those kings had come to, if two or three such had followed in succession, and the corruption that was in them had begun to spread through the members, as soon as the members had been corrupted it would have been impossible ever to reform it" (47).

To remind his readers that the problem is not limited to Rome, Machiavelli provides two modern examples—Milan and Naples—of cities that "no accident . . . could ever make free, because their members are all corrupt" (48). By pointing specifically to the experience of Milan after the death of Filippo Visconti, Machiavelli indicates that one sign of corruption is lack of arms among the people. After the Milanese were freed from the tyranny of Visconti, they were forced to accept the mercenary captain Francesco Sforza as duke as the price of his defending them from the

59. Nederman and Gómez, "Between Republic and Monarchy?," 88, note the increased emphasis Machiavelli puts on the king's obeying his own laws in his *Discourses*, but they argue that such a monarchy still falls short of the *vivere libero* described in *D* 2.2, because the king cannot satisfy the people's desire to recover their freedom without relinquishing his own rule. He can, however, make them feel secure. Marcia Colish, "The Idea of Liberty in Machiavelli," *Journal of the History of Ideas* 32, no. 3 (1971): 335–37, observes that Machiavelli sometimes treats princely and monarchical rule as clear antitheses to liberty, but that he by no means does so consistently. In *D* 1.2, 1.16, 1.23, and *D* 3.5, he suggests that early Roman kings issued ordinances conformable to a free government (*conformi ancora al vivere libero*). And in *D* 1.25 he advises "those who want to set up a new and free polity [*uno vivere nuovo e libero*], whether it be a republic or a monarchy [*o per via di republica o di regno*]" to preserve its ancient customs. "Since most people want freedom in order to live securely [*desiderando la libertà per vivere sicuri*], a prince can satisfy their desires by ruling according to laws that guarantee security" (337).

Venetians with his troops.[60] As Machiavelli's preferred Roman example demonstrates, however, an armed people is not sufficient to forestall corruption. The western legions were not filled with mercenaries when Caesar crossed the Rubicon and marched on Rome in order to become king in everything but name. The people did not understand how the Senate protected their liberties but flocked instead to follow a popular leader, Marius, who promised to destroy the power of the patricians.

By observing that "orders and laws made in a republic at its birth, when men were good, are no longer to the purpose later, when they have become wicked" (49), Machiavelli indicates that the "corruption" he has in mind is not moral in the ordinary sense.[61] He has already argued that Romulus demonstrated his *virtù* by murdering his brother in order to take sole command and impose order on the unruly Romans. He has also suggested that the civilizing arts of peace used by the "weak" prince, Numa, who made the Romans peaceful and obedient by means of religion, also created conditions under which they would have become corrupt, had their kings not become so obviously corrupt first. Corruption is something that happens to previously civilized human beings; it is not, strictly speaking, by nature, although it happens to civilized people if no steps are taken to prevent it.

Like *virtù*, Machiavelli gives corruption (*corrozione*) an unconventional, specifically political rather than moral meaning. But *virtù* and corruption are not simply opposites, as Machiavelli uses the terms. He describes the *virtù* of individuals, and attributes "goodness" (*bontà*) to peoples. (The use of "civic virtue" to describe the characteristics Machiavelli urges republican leaders to instill in their people is thus inaccurate and misleading.)[62] By corrupt or corruption Machiavelli consistently refers to the loss of the ability and willingness of people to defend themselves from oppression, either internal or external. As he indicates here with regard to the early Roman kings, individual rulers and their government can also become corrupt. They become corrupt when they do not do what is necessary to maintain their dominion: arming their subjects to defend the province from foreign

60. *FH* 6.13, 6.20–24.

61. He does not, therefore, accept the Christian doctrine of original sin.

62. E.g., Wolin, *Politics and Vision*, 2nd ed., 212. Machiavelli does occasionally write about the "virtue" of the Roman army (e.g., *D* 1.43, 3.13), but the virtue of an armed force in keeping discipline and facing death is not quite the same as "civic virtue," and, Machiavelli observes in *D* 3.13, it does not last long in the absence of good leadership.

aggression, and securing the lives and property of their people, not only by enforcing the law, but also by obeying it themselves.[63]

Instead of explaining exactly what he means by corruption or its causes, however, in *D* 1.18 Machiavelli describes its results. "In Rome," he explains, "there was the order of the government, or truly of the state, and afterward the laws, which together with the magistrates restrained the citizens. The order of the state was the authority of the people, of the Senate, of the tribunes, of the consuls" along with "the mode of soliciting and creating the magistrates; and the mode of making the laws" (49). Because these orders (of the complete or perfect republic, as Machiavelli characterized it at the end of *D* 1.2) were not changed as the citizens little by little became corrupt, the laws they adopted to check that corruption, e.g., prohibiting adultery or excessive displays of luxury, did not work.

"To keep men good," Machiavelli argues, it would have been necessary to change the orders, as becomes clear if one examines the ways in which the Romans selected their magistrates and made laws. "The Roman people did not give the consulate and the other first ranks of the city except to those that asked for it." This order was good so long as only men who would have been shamed by rejection and thus strove to be deserving of the honor put themselves forward. But "this mode later became very pernicious in the corrupt city," because "those who had more power asked for the magistracies, and the impotent, even though virtuous, abstained from asking for them out of fear." The Romans began to suffer this "inconvenience not at a stroke but by degrees, as happens with all other inconveniences; for after the Romans had subdued Africa and Asia and had reduced almost all Greece to obedience, they became secure in their freedom, as it did not appear to them that they had any more enemies who ought to give them fear." When the Roman people began to feel secure and lost their fear, they no longer bestowed the consulate on men of virtue, but gave it "to those who knew better how to entertain men than those who knew better how to conquer enemies." And later "they descended to giving it

63. It is also inaccurate and misleading to write as Quentin Skinner, *Visions of Politics*, vol. 2, *Renaissance Virtues* (Cambridge: Cambridge University Press, 2002), 165, does, of the need to devise "some mechanism for preventing [human beings'] inescapably corrupt motives from having their natural but self-destructive effects." Such a characterization of the self-regarding passions that lead human beings naturally to desire to acquire is too moralistic. These passions are not bad or "corrupt" in themselves, according to Machiavelli. The failure to do what is necessary to preserve liberty once attained is.

to those who had more power; so through the defect in such an order, the good remained altogether excluded." The same degeneration was to be seen in the legislative process. Departing from actual Roman practice, Machiavelli claims that "a tribune, or any other citizen whatever, could propose a law to the people, on which every citizen was able to speak . . . before it was decided. This was a good order when the citizens were good," because it led to a full discussion of what policy would be most in the public interest, so that the people could choose. But after the citizens had become bad, "only the powerful propose[d] laws, not for the common freedom but for their own power; and for fear of them nobody [spoke] against them. So the people came to be either deceived or forced to decide its own ruin" (50–51).[64]

As Machiavelli describes it, the Roman people became corrupt when they no longer feared external enemies and so no longer joined together in the common defense. They cravenly succumbed to the rule of the most powerful citizens instead of rising up to support virtuous leaders who opposed those who sought to foster their own interests rather than protecting the freedom of all. In both its corrupt and its uncorrupt condition the people were moved by fear. The difference was in what they feared and consequently how they responded to it.

The desire of the people not to be oppressed could be called a desire not to be dominated or "non-domination," as it has been characterized by Quentin Skinner and Philip Pettit. But the liberty Machiavelli believes can be enjoyed only by a noncorrupt people is not achieved, as Skinner maintains, simply by laws that "force us out of our habitual patterns of self-interested behavior, to force us into discharging the full range of our civic duties."[65] On the contrary, Machiavelli suggests here, these laws depend for their effectiveness on the people's perception of what is in their interest, as individuals first and then as citizens who are protected by the community.[66] When the people become "corrupt," that is, when they no

64. McCormick, *Machiavellian Democracy*, 98–99, takes this discussion to show that Machiavelli favored democratic political processes. Machiavelli's point, however, is that procedures alone do not guarantee good results. The "corruption" or not of the people depends not on the laws or procedures, but rather on what they fear—here, foreign enemies or individuals so powerful that they are able to evade the laws; in *D* 3.1, the consequences of not obeying the law.

65. Skinner, "Republican Ideal of Political Liberty," 305.

66. Pettit, *Republicanism*, 1–79, does not give quite the same account of liberty as "non-domination" (in contrast to what Isaiah Berlin called both "negative" and "positive" liberty) as Skinner does, but, if possible, puts even more emphasis on the role of law. He argues that "non-

longer perceive how the leadership of the best and serving in the army themselves is in their own interest, the laws that mandate service or forbid excessive luxury and other more obvious kinds of corruption no longer work. Pace Skinner, people don't simply forget the way in which the government serves their private interests; their perception of what is in their interest depends to a great extent on the circumstances.[67] The paradox and problem is that the laws intended to foster virtue and prevent corruption cease to work as a result of the success of the government or state in providing the security people seek. Once people feel secure, they want to be flattered or entertained. Powerful and wealthy individuals seek more, and they eventually terrorize those with less into complying with their desires and withdrawing from public life and service entirely.

Because the people of a republic gradually become corrupt as a result of the success of their government in securing their lives and property,

---

domination" consists in freedom from arbitrary interferences in making the choices that shape one's life, and considers nonarbitrary interferences, such as those imposed by law, those interferences about which one has had an opportunity to join in a public debate. Both Skinner and Pettit write about a republican "tradition" that includes but is not restricted to Machiavelli. But we see in this chapter that, according to Machiavelli, the operation of laws always depends upon the "modes" and "orders." He does not define these precisely, although he indicates at the beginning of *D* 1.18 that the "orders" consist in the divisions of the population with the power to elect the leading officials (consuls by the Senate and tribunes by the plebs) and the "modes" consist in the ways in which magistrates are selected and the way laws are made. The laws per se do not, therefore, determine whether a people is corrupt or uncorrupt, free or unfree.

67. Machiavelli might agree with the understanding of 'corruption' Skinner attributes to him along with previous republican thinkers such as Sallust and Cicero as "a term of art the republican theorists habitually use to denote our natural tendency to ignore the claims of our community as soon as they seem to conflict with the pursuit of our own immediate advantage." However, Machiavelli would not agree that "to be corrupt . . . is to forget . . . that if we wish to enjoy as much freedom as we can hope to attain within political society, there is good reason for us to act in the first instance as virtuous citizens, placing the common good above the pursuit of any individual or factional ends. Corruption, in short, is simply a failure of rationality" ("Republican Ideal of Political Liberty," 304). According to Machiavelli, there are always two "humors" that divide every city, and these two humors have opposed notions of the "good." As he argued in *The Prince* in redefining the virtues, the prince should see the way in which his own good or desire to dominate may be made consonant with the desire or "interest" of the "people" not to be dominated. However, as Machiavelli will show again in *D* 2.2, the good or interest of the prince is never the same as the good of the people. There is, strictly speaking, no "common" or shared "good." In the best cases, i.e., well-ordered republics or kingdoms, there is only an aggregation of the good of those who want to dominate with the good of those who wish not to be dominated. (See David N. Levy, *Wily Elites and Spirited Peoples in Machiavelli's Republicanism* [Lanham, MD: Lexington Books, 2014], 8–9.) In both *The Prince* and *Discourses* Machiavelli seeks to show the politically ambitious *grandi* how to calculate the means best suited to realizing their desires, but as we have seen in his account of the way in which the Romans used religion, he does not appeal to the "rationality" of the people. It is safer, he insists in both *The Prince* and *Discourses*, to rely on their fear of punishment.

measures have to be taken to counteract that corruption, either gradually as it occurs, or all at once, when the corruption becomes so obvious that it can no longer be endured. But both responses appear to be almost impossible. Individuals able to see the pernicious long-term effects of the current orders rarely arise in cities; and when they do, they find it difficult to persuade others to act on their insights, both because the problem is not yet evident, and because "men used to living in one mode do not wish to vary it."[68] However, it is equally difficult to remedy the problem when it becomes evident. "It is not enough to use ordinary modes, since the ordinary modes are bad; but it is necessary to go to the extraordinary, such as violence and arms, and before everything else become prince of that city, able to dispose it in one's own mode." Machiavelli sadly concludes that "because the reordering of a city for a political way of life presupposes a good man, and becoming prince of a republic by violence presupposes a bad man, one will find that it very rarely happens that someone good wishes to become prince by bad ways, even though his end be good, and that someone wicked, having become prince, wishes to work well" (51). Difficult as it is to see how and why the founder of a republic like Romulus would cut off the succession of his own family, it appears to be even more difficult to see how a republic once founded will not eventually degenerate back into a principality.[69]

(C) THE NEED TO ARM AND TRAIN THE PEOPLE INSTEAD OF RELYING ON THE FEW BEST (*D* 1.21–24) Returning to the example of Rome, Machiavelli emphasizes how fortunate that city was to have Tullus succeed Numa. "For when he succeeded to the kingdom, Tullus did not find a man who had ever been in war, since Rome had been at peace for forty years." Because he was a prudent man, when he planned to wage war, Tullus did not recruit experienced soldiers from nearby cities, but "so much was his virtue that in a stroke . . . he was able to make very excellent soldiers" out of his own men. He thus forestalled if he did not reverse the corruption of the Roman people, for a time, by making them capable of defending themselves. In other words, Tullus showed how a corrupt people can be

68. As Machiavelli also observed in *P* 25.

69. Montesquieu generalizes Machiavelli's point here when in the *Spirit of the Laws* he argues that governments are based originally on fear and that the most common form to which they all tend to revert is despotism.

reformed by a good man with good intentions who trains them to fight in their own defense.

Whether a people becomes corrupt or not depends upon the virtue of their prince. "It is more true than any other truth that if where there are men there are no soldiers, it arises through a defect of the prince and not through any other defect, either of the site or of nature" (55).[70]

Tullus was not prudent in all respects, however. On the contrary, Machiavelli argues in *D* 1.22, when he agreed with Mettius, the Alban king, to let the fate of their respective peoples rest on the outcome of a battle between three champions of each, and then allowed the victorious Horatius to escape punishment for killing his sister, Tullus made three egregious errors. First, as Machiavelli explains at more length in *D* 1.23, Tullus risked both his own fortune as ruler and the freedom of his city by using only a small part of his forces to defend them. Second, as Machiavelli explains in *D* 1.24, "in a well-ordered city, faults are never paid for with merits." Victorious young soldiers or generals should not be allowed to violate the law, because they set bad examples for others. The exoneration of Horatius provides Machiavelli with an example of the people's too great compassion and gratitude—a tendency he tries to correct in the lessons he derives from the Roman experience in the second half of book 1. Third, "policies are never wise if one should or can doubt their observance" (56). The Alban king had agreed to become Rome's subject, if the three Roman Horatii defeated the three Alban Curiatii; however, because he retained most of his army, Mettius used the first opportunity to try to regain his and his people's freedom from Roman rule.

Machiavelli's account of Tullus's errors points to the conclusion that the early Roman republic was not well ordered, because it relied on a few aristocrats instead of the armed people as a whole to defend it. It endangered its own future freedom by allowing a victorious soldier to escape punishment for his crime under the law, and so encouraging the insolence of others, as well as by counting on the word or faith of another king. Adding that "the guarding of passes is often harmful," because a general puts his entire army or city at risk by necessarily relying on a few men to block an advancing enemy at a mountain pass, Machiavelli ties the importance of relying on one's full force or population (namely, the people) to the

70. Machiavelli greatly expands his argument to this effect in *AW.*

principle he announced in the first chapter. A founder should rely not on nature, whether of a site or of the human beings in question, but on laws that mandate military training—to defend his city.[71]

(D) WHY GRADUAL REFORM IS BETTER THAN REVOLUTION AND REDISTRIBUTION (*D* 1.25–27) A succession of prudent leaders who train their citizens to be soldiers is a necessary but not sufficient condition for the preservation of a republic. Because the people become corrupt as a result of their "civilization," republics need to be reordered, either gradually or all at once. When Machiavelli returns to discuss the two basic modes of reform in *D* 1.25–27, however, he modifies his descriptions of the two modes in important ways.

Rather than emphasizing the difficulty a reformer faces in persuading people unable to perceive the dangers of their current practices in the long run to change, in *D* 1. 25 he advises a reformer who wants his innovations to be accepted and maintained by all to conceal the changes he is making in the old order by keeping offices with the same names or external trappings.[72] As in *P* 18, Machiavelli reminds his readers that "the generality of men feed on what appears as much as on what is; indeed, many times they are moved more by things that appear than by things that are" (60). And he cautions would-be reformers that "this should be observed by all those who wish to suppress an ancient way of life in a city and to turn it to a new and free way of life." Since, as he observed in *P* 2, "the new things alter the minds of men, you should contrive that those alternations retain as much of the ancient as possible," lest the people come to expect ever new innovations that will destabilize the new order the reformer wishes to introduce.

When he concludes more generally that he "who wishes to order a political way of life by the way either of republic or of kingdom" (61) should proceed in this fashion, Machiavelli not merely addresses the ambitions of his young readers. He also reminds us readers that he, too, is presenting his "new modes and orders" in the guise of an "imitation" of ancient orders

71. Machiavelli reinforces the emphasis on the importance of training the people rather than relying on a few noble defenders by pointing out that local peasants can always find an alternative way around the pass, i.e., they have useful knowledge of or on the ground that the "higher-ups" lack.

72. Although Machiavelli does not say so explicitly, both his examples of keeping a "king" who continued to offer the public sacrifices in the republic and having one and only one of the consuls accompanied by the twelve lictors who had previously accompanied the king refer to actions taken by Lucius Junius Brutus in founding the Roman republic.

of the Romans. The version of the "mixed regime" he is advocating makes republics closer to moderate kingdoms than the Romans, who hated the name of king, would have understood.

Machiavelli contrasts this covert, gradual way of reordering a republic in order to preserve it to the way in which someone who wishes to seize and maintain the absolute power the "authors" called tyranny should proceed. By destroying all the old orders and making everything anew, such a prince makes everything—names, authorities, offices, wealth, cities, residences—depend upon him, as "did David when he became king" (61). Shockingly, the only time Machiavelli quotes from the Bible in the *Discourses*, he inaccurately attributes what Mary says of God in the Gospel of Luke to the king of the Jews. The point of the inaccurate attribution seems to be that any human being who seeks to exercise the omnipotence of the biblical God, even in the guise of a good shepherd who seeks to relieve the misery of the poor and establish a just regime by vanquishing the wealthy (or "great"), will become a tyrant.[73] By treating his subjects, in effect, as animals—a different species to be herded (and harvested)—such a prince uses "modes" that "are very cruel, and enemies to every way of life, not only Christian but human" (61).[74] Machiavelli concludes, therefore, that "any man should flee [these means], and wish to live in private [like Machiavelli himself] rather than as king." He thus seems to be accepting a version of the Socratic argument in the *Gorgias* that it is better to suffer injustice than to do it and that a man who goes into politics in an effort to protect himself, his family, or his people from unjust rulers will end up becoming like them. However, when Machiavelli discusses individual decisions later in the *Discourses* (3.2), again in the context of a consideration of Brutus, the founder of the Roman republic, he argues that withdrawal into private life is not an option, because other people will not leave you alone.

73. Using Philip of Macedon, father of Alexander, as an example of a small king who became prince of Greece by using such modes, Machiavelli says that "he transferred men from province to province as herdsmen transfer their herds" (61). Strauss, *TM*, 49, and Mansfield, *Machiavelli's New Modes and Orders*, 99–100, infer that Machiavelli is implying that God is a tyrant. His omnipotence (and omniscience) would not leave any room for human freedom, *if* He did not choose to do so (as Augustine argued that He did [*City of God* 22.1]). Machiavelli's "mistaken" attribution of this mode of proceeding to David makes it apply to a human king, however, rather than to God. In aspiring to be not merely emperors of the world but gods, ancient politicians like Alcibiades and Caesar failed to recognize the difference between mortal humans and immortal divinities.

74. Centuries after Machiavelli wrote, we have experienced a series of such "totalitarian" revolutions, led by new princes such as Lenin, Hitler, Stalin, Mao, and Pol Pot. This chapter indicates that Machiavelli foresaw the possibility of such attempts as secularized versions of Christianity, but did not advocate them.

Recognizing that his young readers have political ambition, here he simply observes, "he who does not wish to take this first way of the good must enter into the evil one if he wishes to maintain himself." The problem is that "men take certain middle ways that are very harmful, for they do not know how to be either altogether wicked, or altogether good" (62), as he will show in the next chapter. It might look as if Machiavelli is telling his readers (e.g., those to whom he dedicated his *Discourses*) that if they wish to take part in politics, they must avoid "middle ways" and adopt extreme measures. However, careful analysis of the examples Machiavelli gives in *D* 1.27 does not support that conclusion.

Machiavelli acknowledges in the title that "Men Very Rarely Know How to Be Altogether Wicked or Altogether Good." For example, he points out that even though Giovampagolo Baglioni, the tyrant of Perugia, had slept with his own sister and killed his cousins and nephews in order to rule, he did not kill the pope when he had an opportunity to do so. Since Baglioni could not have been restrained by goodness or conscience or piety, prudent observers (who included Machiavelli himself) concluded "that it arose from men's not knowing how to be honorably wicked or perfectly good" (62–63). To have been "honorably" (but not "altogether") wicked, Machiavelli suggests, Baglioni should have been daring enough "to engage in an enterprise in which everyone would have admired his spirit and that would have left an eternal memory of himself as being the first who had demonstrated to the prelates how little is to be esteemed whoever lives and reigns as they do; and he would have done a thing whose greatness would have surpassed all infamy, every danger, that could have proceeded from it" (63).[75]

Machiavelli clearly exaggerates, however. Machiavelli's Florentine readers would surely have remembered that Savonarola had incurred the wrath of Alexander VI by leveling just such charges against the Church. In *The Prince* Machiavelli argues that Savonarola failed to destroy the corruption in the Roman Church because he was an "unarmed prophet." Baglioni had the mercenary arms of a small tyrant, but it does not seem likely that he could have destroyed the institution that Machiavelli has argued kept Italy disunited and vulnerable by, in effect, cutting off its head(s). Would "everyone have admired his spirit"? Or would the Orsini and the Colonna

75. Coby, *Machiavelli's Romans*, thus argues that "Baglioni's hesitation originated not in conscience but in smallness of mind" (231).

as well as the kings of Spain and France not have taken the opportunity to defend the sanctity of the Church by using their armies to retake the cities previously controlled by the Church, which would now be headed by a set of cardinals and a pope chosen by the victor?

Moreover, Baglioni is not Machiavelli's only example in this chapter of a man who did not know how to be altogether wicked or altogether good. The official representative of the prince of peace on earth, Pope Julius II, led his own armies (as Machiavelli will argue in the immediate sequel, a prince should). The pope's army might or might not be considered a wicked means of achieving good; but his use of a tyrant (Baglioni) and his mercenaries to rid another city of its tyrant certainly appears to involve a contradiction between means and ends. In *D* 1.27 Machiavelli suggests that the pope and his cardinals foolishly entered Perugia unarmed, because of Julius's characteristic impetuosity (or perhaps because of his faith in a providential God who would protect him). Machiavelli does not report the fact (known to him as the diplomatic representative of the Florentine government at the time) that Julius had agreed not only to pay Baglioni and his men to serve in the pope's campaign against Bologna, but also to protect Baglioni from the vengeance exiles from Perugia wished to take on him.[76] Neither the pope nor the tyrant wanted to retire from public life, so both had to use evil means of maintaining themselves. A pope cannot exercise temporal power, Machiavelli suggests, without using evil means. If the prelates of the Church want to be entirely good, they must retire entirely into private life. A tyrant who wishes to maintain himself must use inhuman means, or if like all other human beings he cannot be entirely evil or entirely good, he should follow Machiavelli's advice in *The Prince*, learn how to fight like a man with laws as well as like a beast with force and fraud, and seek popular support. The problem with the pope and the petty tyrant was not that they did not know how to be entirely good or entirely bad; neither is possible for a mere human being. The problem in the case of both Julius and Baglioni was that they took "*certain* middle ways that are very harmful" (62, emphasis added).[77] In the succeeding chapters Machiavelli thus specifies other "middle ways" of balancing the people's

76. Letters from Niccolò Machiavelli to the Florentine Signori, September 5–13, 1506, in *The Historical, Political, and Diplomatic Writings of Niccolò Machiavelli*, trans. Christian Detmold, vol. 4, available from the Online Library of Liberty (http://oll.libertyfund.org).

77. See *TM*, 276.

desire not to be ruled with the desire of the great to command and oppress that produce and sustain laws securing the liberty of all.[78]

C. Machiavelli's New Politics of Suspicion and Competition (*D* 1.28–33)

As in *P* 15, so in *D* 1.27 Machiavelli suggests that a prince must learn *how* not to be good (which is not, however, the same as being "altogether wicked") and use that knowledge when necessary if he wants to maintain himself. But in his *Discourses* Machiavelli adds that citizens of a republic must also learn not to be perfectly moral—in particular, they must learn not simply to be grateful for the services rendered by their leaders—if they want to retain their freedom.

Individuals who perform great deeds for the benefit of all deserve to be rewarded. Machiavelli thus begins *D* 1.29 by affirming that "when either a people or a prince has sent out one of its captains on an important expedition, from which the captain will have acquired very much glory if he should win, that prince or people is held to the bargain of rewarding him." But then he qualifies this statement by arguing that a prince who dishonors or offends his captain out of avarice "makes an error that has no excuse" (64). However, if a prince or republic is ungrateful to a victorious captain because it suspects him of harboring ambitions to overthrow the existing regime, it acts on the basis of a political necessity.

"Because the nature of men is ambitious and suspicious and does not know how to set a limit to any fortune" (65), a victorious captain who has acquired a great reputation with his soldiers and the enemy may well conclude that he should rule instead of those who sent him to fight. "To avoid the necessity either of having to live with suspicion, or of being ungrateful," Machiavelli urges (as he did in *P* 13), a prince should lead his own army. Then he will not have to worry about giving too much or too little credit to his captain or letting that captain attract his own partisans. Republics do not have the option of leading their own armies, however, and they may either offend those citizens they ought to reward or suspect those in whom they

78. Cf. *TM*, 240, and Coby, *Machiavelli's Romans*, 228–48, who also argue that Machiavelli rejects "certain" middle ways, not all. Coby's account of the middle ways Machiavelli recommends applies particularly to princes, however, as in his recommendation of Agathocles in *The Prince* as an example of "cruelty well-used," not to the design of institutions to direct and balance the two humors. Strauss, *TM*, 262–67, argues that Machiavelli himself advocates the middle way between virtue and vice (selfishness) that constitutes "republican virtue," i.e., collective selfishness.

ought to have confidence. In corrupt republics, such suspicions may lead to great evils, "as happened to the Rome of Caesar, who took for himself by force what ingratitude denied him." But "in a republic that is not corrupt [such suspicions] are the cause of great good and make it live free, since men are kept better and less ambitious longer through fear of punishment" (66).

Like the rewards (see *D* 1.24), however, the punishments can and should be moderate. The Romans were prudent enough not to threaten generals with terrifying punishments if they lost battles, because they might then becoming unwilling to fight. But they were punished if they sacrificed the common good (or victory) to considerations of their own glory (*D* 1.31).

Republics are less ungrateful than princes, because the people are less suspicious. But, Machiavelli warns, the people's lack of suspicion may prove to be dangerous to their freedom. Indeed, Machiavelli suggests, the people's relative lack of ingratitude is less a sign of their superior virtue or morality than a reflection of their lack of foresight. Like the Roman plebs, who celebrated the relief from the salt tax and payment for military service granted them by the Senate (*D* 1.32), people tend to react positively to immediate benefits and to discount or even ignore the future costs. As a result, in republics individual citizens are often allowed to gather more strength than they should. Men naturally seem to favor the beginnings of things, so when a youth of extraordinary virtue arises, citizens honor him without perceiving the potential danger. They recognize their error only after the threat has become too strong to be eliminated by means of direct opposition. The Roman republic avoided this problem as long as it did because it put the whole city to work in war. "So many virtuous men emerged . . . that the people did not have cause to fear any one of them, since they were very many and guarded one another" (*D* 1.30; 68).

Machiavelli shows, however, that the Roman people did not understand how competition among the great for power and influence benefited them. Nor, he suggests, did the Roman nobles always perceive that competition for office was the best way to guard themselves as well as the people from the tyranny of a popular hero like Caesar. In the remainder of book 1 he thus treats Rome not as a simply exemplary regime, but as an ongoing experiment in republican rule from which later generations can learn.

D. Successful and Unsuccessful Roman Reorderings (*D* 1.34–45)

Although Machiavelli initially suggests that the Roman republic was "perfect" after the tribunes were added to the consuls and Senate, he shows that all republics need to be continually reordered if they are not to become corrupt and lose their freedom. Neither "morals" legislation like sumptuary laws nor generalized suspicion (or envy) of the leaders of a republic suffices to counteract the fear of the rich and powerful that gradually develops. New "orders" or offices with the power of enforcing their decrees must continually be invented.

Machiavelli presents the creation of the "order" of the dictatorship in Rome as an example of a beneficial reordering and then uses the history of the appointment and reappointment of the Decemvirs to illustrate typical mistakes made by both the plebs and the nobles. By noting his fellow citizens' failure to understand how to delay or prevent Cosimo de Medici's rise to power, in *D* 1.33 Machiavelli indicates that his recommendations with regard to good and bad reorderings have particular relevance to Florence (and thus to the immediate concerns of his dedicatees).

1. The Advantages of the Dictatorship (*D* 1.34)

Machiavelli begins his analysis of the dictatorship in *D* 1.34 by observing that some unknown "writer" condemned the creators of the office for having caused the later rise of tyranny in Rome, because Caesar held that office. But, Machiavelli objects, neither the name 'dictator' nor his absolute powers were the cause of the rise of tyranny later in Rome; the real cause was the prolongation of commands that enabled individuals to acquire great wealth and partisans. "While the dictator was appointed according to public orders, and not by his own authority, he always did good to the city" (74). A citizen cannot seize extraordinary authority for himself in a noncorrupt republic in which no one is very rich and has many partisans, because such powerful individuals no longer fear the laws, and they are so formidable that people will not freely vote for them. The creation of the office of the dictator was good, because it remedied one of the fundamental defects of republics in dealing with emergencies: because many people are involved in making decisions, republics proceed slowly. The appointment of a dictator, who could act without consultation or delay and punish without appeal, enabled the Romans to respond quickly to an urgent danger. Because the grant of absolute power was limited both in its goal or extent (to respond to the specific danger) and in time (six months), it did not diminish the power of the Senate or the people, who resumed their old authority at the end of the dictator's term of office.

Machiavelli emphasizes how important it was that the powers of the dictatorship were both provided and restrained by the laws. As a result, no one acquired the habit of acting outside them. He also praises the Roman mode of choosing the dictator by putting the decision to appoint one as well as the selection of the particular individual into the hands of those (the consuls) who were most shamed by the need to do so. "For wounds and every other ill that a man does to himself spontaneously and by choice hurt much less than those that are done to you by someone else" (75). This sentence might be taken as a condensed statement of the reason Machiavelli argues that the people, who do not want to be oppressed or commanded, should be included in government, at least to the extent of electing their leaders and trying them for malfeasance when they do not perform their duties as they should.

2. The Necessity of Maintaining Rotation in Office (*D* 1.35–36)

Even though the Roman people freely voted for the Decemvirs, Machiavelli observes, the ten became tyrants, because they were granted absolute power for too long a period, and because the old orders—the tribunes, consuls, and Senate—were not kept in place. Republics like Sparta and Venice that granted some officials long-term authority made sure that there were "guards posted who made them unable to use their authority badly" (77).

Before he details and explains the sources of the mistakes made by the nobles, the people, and the leader of the Decemvirs, Appius Claudius, Machiavelli makes four general observations concerning the requirements (and difficulty) of maintaining a free government. The first is that those individuals who have held the highest offices in the republic be willing to serve in lesser capacities. Machiavelli might appear to be reviving Aristotle's notion of a truly political way of life as ruling and being ruled in turn. Unlike Aristotle (*Politics* 1277b25–30), however, Machiavelli does not emphasize the need to rule in order to acquire the virtue of prudence. He stresses the value of the restraint experienced politicians exercise on the ambitions of youths elected to high office. Rotation in office is necessary, if a number of virtuous men are to check the potentially tyrannical ambitions of any one. And maintaining such a check on the rise of a potential tyrant requires a certain kind of humility (or the appearance of such) on the part of those who have held the highest public offices but then demonstrate their willingness to obey the orders of others.

3. Why Republics Cannot Be Reordered Effectively by Redistributing Property (*D* 1.37)

In *D* 1.37 Machiavelli then makes it clear that in order to maintain a republic it is necessary to check the excessive ambitions of the people as well as those of the "great." He begins by appealing to the authority of "ancient writers" who explain the variability of human affairs by observing "that men are wont to worry in evil and to become bored with good." He nevertheless seems to be stating his own convictions about the unavoidability of continuing conflict when he explains, "whenever engaging in combat through necessity is taken from men they engage in combat through ambition, which is so powerful in human breasts that it never abandons them at whatever rank they rise to. The cause is that nature has created men so that they are able to desire everything and are unable to attain everything. So, since the desire is always greater than the power of acquiring, the result is discontent with what one possesses." And "since some men desire to have more, and some fear to lose what has been acquired, they come to enmities and to war, from which arise the ruin of one province and the exaltation of another" (78).

Machiavelli states his general understanding of the reasons human beings live in perpetual conflict with one another in order to make a specific point: "it was not enough for the Roman plebs to secure itself against the nobles by the creation of the tribunes, to which desire it was constrained by necessity." As soon as the plebs had secured itself, it "began at once to engage in combat through ambition, and to wish to share honors and belongings with the nobility as the thing esteemed most by men." Machiavelli thus shows that the two opposed and apparently mutually exclusive "humors" that exist in all cities actually form a kind of continuum. So long as people do not feel secure in their lives and properties, they wish simply not to be oppressed. However, as soon as they feel secure, they begin to desire to have more—not simply goods but also offices (or political honors and power). That is, they acquire the desire of the "great" to dominate others; and, Machiavelli argues, it was this desire on the part of the Roman people that led "to contention over the Agrarian law, which in the end was the cause of the destruction of the republic" (79).

Machiavelli seems to endorse the end or purpose of the Agrarian law when he writes that "well-ordered republics have to keep the public rich and their citizens poor." There must have been some defect in the law—its origin, the delay in enforcing it, or its corruption by its later use. However, by concluding that it turned the city upside down every time it was mentioned, he suggests that it suffered from all three defects.

The two major provisions of the law limited the amount of land any one citizen could possess and mandated that the fields taken from enemies be divided among the Roman people. Both "offended" the nobles, who possessed more than they should and were deprived of the means of becoming even richer. However, the law was not enforced, despite many attempts to do so, because the nobles had "temporized with it, by leading an army out, or by having the tribune who proposed it opposed by another tribune, or by sometimes yielding to a part of it, or indeed by sending a colony to the place that had to be distributed" (79).[79] After Roman conquests extended to and beyond the borders of Italy, the plebs no longer wanted their share of public lands far from Rome and hard to cultivate. When the Gracchi tried to revive the law, they thus found the power of their adversaries redoubled; and the hatred between the plebs and the Senate became so great that it led to armed conflict. Since the public magistrates could not settle the dispute, each of the parties had recourse to private remedies. "Thinking of how to make itself a head to defend it," the plebs first gave reputation to Marius by making him consul four times, after which he was able to make himself consul three more times. The check posed by rotation in office was destroyed. The nobility responded by favoring Sulla in a similar fashion, and he won the civil war for them. But the conflict between these "humors" was revived later by Pompey, as leader of the nobility, and Caesar, as successor to Marius. With Caesar's victory, Rome acquired her first tyrant and was never again a free city.

Machiavelli does not blame the plebs for having resisted the "ambition" of the nobles to acquire ever more property. On the contrary, he suggests, "if the contention over the Agrarian law took three hundred years to make Rome servile, it would perhaps have been led into servitude much sooner if the plebs had not always checked the ambition of the nobles, both with this law and with its other appetites." He observes, moreover, "one also sees through this how much more men esteem property than honors. For the Roman nobility always yielded honors to the plebs without extraordinary scandals, but when it came to property, so great was its obstinacy in defending it that the plebs had recourse to the extraordinary [means]

79. Livy, 2.41–43, explains that the patricians also accused the politicians arguing for renewed enforcement of the Agrarian law of trying to establish a tyranny by buying the support of the plebs.

that were discoursed of above to vent its appetite" (80).[80] The Gracchi deserve praise more for their intention than for their prudence, he concludes, because one should not try to take away a disorder that has grown in a republic by reviving a law that has fallen into disuse. Just as he advised those who opposed the rise of a virtuous young man favored by the people to "temporize," if they were not able to remedy the problem entirely, so Machiavelli now suggests that popular leaders concerned about increasing economic inequality in a republic should "temporize" with it. Outright opposition would do nothing but accelerate the downfall of the republic by arousing the nobles' fear of loss.

In *D* 1.26 Machiavelli suggested that a "new prince" who wished "to make the rich poor" and "the poor rich" would have to be an inhuman tyrant like Philip of Macedon, who "transferred men from province to province as herdsmen transfer their herds" (61). Recognizing that human beings are acquisitive animals, who seek ever more possessions in order to secure themselves, he uses the commotion over the Agrarian law to show that property owners will violently resist redistributive policies. Attempts to impose large-scale redistribution will, as in Rome, lead to civil war, which will, in turn, produce chaos and then tyranny or leave the city so weakened that it falls prey to foreign conquest.[81]

4. Why Previous Efforts to Reorder Republics Have Generally Failed (*D* 1.38–39)

If it is not possible for a republic to prevent the emergence of a tyrant directly, either by opposing the rise to power of a popular leader or by

80. In a footnote Mansfield and Tarcov suggest that Machiavelli is referring to the "tumults" he described in 1.4, but those were the tumults that preserved Roman freedom. Here I believe he is referring to the plebs' elevation and repeated reelections of Marius as consul. McCormick, *Machiavellian Democracy*, 89–90, takes this statement to show that Machiavelli believes that "the great" are always greedy oligarchs who are rightly opposed by the people. Machiavelli thinks that the desire to acquire is natural to all human beings, however; he does not praise or blame one group for displaying it so much as he tries to show how this desire can be channeled in a way that benefits the largest number.

81. Machiavelli would have known that in depicting the lives of "parallel" Greek and Roman statesmen, Plutarch "pairs" Tiberius Gracchus with Cleomenes. At the conclusion of *D* 1.9 Machiavelli observed that by killing the ephors and anyone else who might have been able to oppose him, Cleomenes had more success in returning his city to its ancient orders (including equal property holding) than his predecessor, King Agis . McCormick thus concludes that Machiavelli favored violent means of redistribution. However, Machiavelli observes that Cleomenes' attempted reordering was defeated by the power of the Macedonians and the inability of Sparta along with the other Greek republics to resist it, because of their internal divisions or "corruption."

seeking to avoid the corruption that follows from great economic inequality by imposing a redistribution of property, the question arises: how can a republic be reordered so as to avoid becoming corrupt? In *D* 1.38 Machiavelli suggests that modern republics show themselves to be weaker and more irresolute than the Romans, because they do not understand how to accept and present a "necessity" as their own choice.[82] And in *D* 1.39 Machiavelli suggests that *the* "necessity" peoples both ancient and modern do not recognize is the need for government. They tend to see their government as the source of their problems and to blame the individual magistrates, because they do not understand the deeper, more general causes of their afflictions.

The people of Florence blamed the magistracy of the Ten of War for the heavy taxes incurred to support an unsuccessful attempt to regain the parts of their empire they had lost, rather than blame the "ambition" of their enemies. Likewise, Machiavelli observes, the plebs in Rome blamed the consuls and the ambition of the nobles for wars that continually arose, rather than the ambition of its neighbors. But in this case, Machiavelli suggests, his fellow citizens learned more quickly than the Romans. Seeing not merely that the war did not stop after they dissolved the Committee of Ten, but that the disorder got worse in the absence of prudent leadership, the Florentines remade the magistracy. Demonstrating the tendency of people in general to mistake names for things, the Roman plebs was not content until the consular name was eliminated and tribunes drawn from and responsible to the people were given consular powers. They did not understand that they were still granting a select group of men great power, or that it was necessary that they do so.

In *D* 1.40 Machiavelli explains more generally that the Roman attempt to reorder the republic by having the Decemvirs codify their laws resulted in a tyranny "for the same causes that the greater part of tyrannies in cities arises: . . . from too great a desire of the people to be free and from too great a desire of the nobles to command. When they do not agree to

82. The example Machiavelli gives of the "generosity and prudence" of the Roman Senate is that, unable to defend their allies because of a pestilence, the Senate declared, contrary to their previously stated policy, that their allies should defend themselves, because the Romans were unable to do so. The Florentines, on the other hand, were not able to decide to grant Duke Valentino the right to march through their territory, even though they were not able to prevent him from doing so. Moreover, they proved themselves unable to trust the French king to hand over Pisa and Arezzo to them, as agreed, if he came to occupy these cities by negotiation rather than by force, even though he clearly could not hand over the cities to the Florentines if he did not possess them.

make a law in favor of freedom, but one of the parties jumps to favor one individual, then it is that tyranny emerges at once" (88).[83]

5. What Is to Be Learned from the Fall of the Decemvirs (*D* 1.40–45)

In showing the reasons not only why the Decemvirate became a tyranny, but also why it collapsed, in *D* 1.40–45 Machiavelli traces the mistakes of the people, the nobles, and the leader of the Ten, Appius Claudius, all back to their desire to acquire the power of government solely for themselves by denying any part to their opponents.[84] The nobles and the people of Rome agreed to create the Ten and to grant them unlimited power because the people wanted to eliminate the consular name (and powers of the nobles holding the office), whereas the nobles wanted to eliminate the tribunate. The people erred in voting to grant the Ten absolute power without maintaining the constitutional checks on the dictatorship because they wanted to eliminate one if not both of the old orders controlled by the nobles. They did not understand that "although nobles may desire to tyrannize, that part of the nobility that finds itself outside the tyranny is always an enemy to the tyrant; nor can he ever win over all of it, because of the great ambition and great avarice that are in it" (88). The very desires that make the people fear the nobles make the nobles the best check on a popular potential tyrant.

Although they limited the term and the goal for which they granted the power, the people were fooled into voting the Ten a second year of unchecked power by the Decemvirs' restrained use of that power during their first term and their leader Appius's obvious attempts to seek popular favor. Deceived by his abrupt change of face from an arrogant aristocrat to a man of the people and by the good behavior of the Decemvirs during their first term of office, the people were surprised by the violence Appius and his colleagues began to use against them after the Ten were voted a second

83. Machiavelli does not make the difference between his account of tyranny and that to be found in ancient authors explicit until *D* 3.26. However, by discounting the importance of the attempted rapes of Lucretia and Virginia in the fall of the tyrants Tarquin Superbus and Appius Claudius, in contrast to Livy, Machiavelli indicates that unlike like Plato, *Republic* 9.571a–580b, he does not regard the tyrant as Eros incarnate, even though in *P* 19 and *D* 3.6 he like Aristotle warns "princes" against violating the wives, daughters, and relatives of their close associates. Like the *grandi* or *nobili*, he suggests, tyrants act out of a desire to dominate more than a desire for glory, which he argued in *D* 1.10 would lead them to try to benefit their people.

84. In the *Florentine Histories* Machiavelli shows that this same desire in all parties produced the constant changes, instability, and ultimate ineffectiveness of that city's republic.

year of unchecked power. Recognizing their error, the people pleaded with the nobles to reinstate the old orders—but to no avail.

The nobles were suspicious of Appius's changed behavior, but they did not know how to counter his ambitions any better than the plebs. Assuming that he would follow aristocratic norms that forbade a man from nominating himself for office, they gave him authority to propose names of individuals to be elected to the people; and he seized the opportunity to nominate himself first. Gratified by the oppressive measures Appius began taking against the people during the second year of the Decemvirate, the nobles did not respond to the people's plea that they reinstitute the old orders. Nor when the Ten were forced to reconvene the Senate to order an army to defend the city did the senators take the opportunity to eliminate the Decemvirate. They hoped that if the Ten resigned voluntarily, the tribunate might not be remade. Only after the dispirited Roman armies were defeated in the field, and the plebs protested Appius's attempt to take Virginia by force by going to the Sacred Mount outside the city, were the senators forced to see that a city without a people was no city. At that point they agreed to reinstate the older orders.

Because both the people and the nobles were blinded by their desire to eliminate the offices held by the other "humor," Machiavelli concludes in *D* 1.41, Appius would have succeeded in becoming tyrant of Rome far before Caesar, if he had not revealed his animosity toward the people so soon after his reelection. As Machiavelli observed in *P* 21, "those tyrants who have the collectivity as a friend and the great as an enemy are more secure, because their violence is sustained by greater force than that of those who have the people for an enemy and the nobility for a friend" (88–89). In *D* 1.42 Machiavelli observes that Appius's ability to transform his colleague Quintus Fabius from a good man into a criminal by giving him a share of the profits shows how easily human beings can be corrupted. Rather than relying on good upbringing or education, he suggests, legislators of republics and kingdoms ought to check human appetites by making it impossible for them to err with impunity. Appius was driven out by popular dissatisfaction. Although the Roman armies retained the same virtue they had before and after the Decemvirate, Machiavelli notes in *D* 1.43, they would not fight for a tyrant with the same spirit as when they fought as free persons. However, he also shows in *D* 1.44 that "a multitude without a head is useless." Although Virginius appointed twenty military tribunes to negotiate with the Senate, the spokesmen for the plebs had to be advised by the two senators with whom they met not to state their desire for vengeance openly, but merely to request the reinstitution of the constitutional orders that would enable them to do what they wished.[85] The history of the Decemvirate should have taught republican leaders the importance of maintaining legal checks on the abuse of power by officials. Yet, Machiavelli reports in *D* 1.45, Virginius wanted to deny Appius the right of appeal to the people that Appius had denied to others. Later in Florence, Machiavelli reminds his readers, Savonarola also lost most of his reputation when he failed to complain about the nonenforcement of a law he had made allowing citizens to appeal sentences given by the Eight and the Signoria before the people. If people see that the government is not bound by its own laws, they will not feel that their lives and property are secure, and they will become more audacious in thinking about how they can improve their condition.

E. The Lessons Machiavelli Derives from Roman History about the Best Internal Order of a Republic (*D* 1.46–60)

Machiavelli summarizes the lessons about the internal ordering of a republic he has derived from reading history for his young aristocratic Florentine readers at the end of book 1.

1. The Ever-Escalating Ambition of Men Cannot Entirely Be Restrained by Competitive Elections (*D* 1.46–48)

He begins *D* 1.46 by restating the source of the problem: "Men Ascend from One Ambition to Another; First One Seeks Not to Be Offended, and Then One Offends Others." Although he has shown that such ambition animates the people as well as the "great" (and that the two "humors" thus exist along a continuous spectrum), Machiavelli reminds his readers that the rise of a virtuous young man to preeminence constitutes the greatest immediate threat to maintaining a free way of life.

To check the rise of such a potential tyrant, other politically ambitious men should compete with him for popular favor. The most obvious way to institute such competition is to select the highest officials by means of elections. In *D* 1.47 and 1.48 Machiavelli thus assures his aristocratic readers that the people are able to judge the character of particular individuals

85. McCormick, *Machiavellian Democracy*, 86, takes this incident to show that the people were not as passive as they might seem to be in much of *The Prince* and *Discourses*. He does not appear to recognize Machiavelli's criticism of their failure to understand what should—and should not—be said in public (or the need to use fraud as well as force in effective politics).

(even if they are often deceived about generalities like names). Members of the upper class can make it easy for the people to judge individual candidates correctly, moreover, by arranging to have a vile man run against an excellent one or vice versa.[86]

2. The Need for Reforms and Popular Trials to Supplement Competitive Elections (*D* 1.49)

Rome constitutes the exemplary republic, Machiavelli reminds his readers in *D* 1.49, not because Rome had a legislator like Lycurgus who provided for all its needs from the beginning, but because the Romans continually created new orders to meet pressing needs. However, as he showed in analyzing the failure of the Decemvirs, so he now observes with regard to the later creation of the censors, the Romans made mistakes. For example, they initially gave the censors too long a term of office, and when a dictator prudently corrected that error, the censors retaliated by denying him membership in the Senate. Because history does not show that the dictator was able to defend himself, Machiavelli concludes, either the history or the orders of Rome were defective. He thus reminds his readers that the recommendations he makes rest on his reasoning about what is to be found in the histories; he is not simply relating what happened or urging his readers to imitate everything the Romans did.

Machiavelli indicates the applicability of his analysis to his own city by observing that the Florentine republic freely voted to give a few citizens expansive authority to reform it many times. However, they never succeeded in creating orders for the common utility, because they (like the plebs and the nobles with the Decemvirs) always used their authority for the benefit

86. Vickie B. Sullivan, *Machiavelli, Hobbes, and the Formation of a Liberal Republicanism in England* (Cambridge: Cambridge University Press, 2004), 52–55, and McCormick, *Machiavellian Democracy*, 70–76, debate the extent to which Machiavelli advocates manipulation of popular opinion by the nobles through the example of Pacuvius. Desiring to reconcile the nobles and plebs in Capua, Machiavelli reports, Pacuvius first persuaded all the senators to resign their seats by telling them that the people threatened to kill them if they did not. He then gave the people the power to kill the senators—as soon as they found replacements. By proposing that the people proceed to elect replacements one by one, he made them see that they did not want to choose any of their peers, because none of them was worthy of senatorial rank. So he finally suggested that they reinstate the old Senate, "for the fear that the senators have been in will have made them so humble that the humanity that you are seeking elsewhere you will find in them" (98). Mansfield, *Machiavelli's New Modes and Orders*, 145–47, treats the incident as an example of the way nobles can be taught the dangers of arrogance, by giving the people the power to punish them, and of a noble's indirectly instructing the people in the need for government.

of their party.[87] In well-ordered republics, Machiavelli argues, decisions in capital trials should be given to the people (unless an emergency makes such an appeal impossible, in which case the Romans appointed a temporary dictator). The badly ordered Florentine republic initially put decisions in capital cases in the hands of a foreigner, who could easily be corrupted by powerful citizens, as could the eight citizens to whom the Florentines later transferred the power. Recognizing that ten citizens might not be enough to punish the powerful, even if they had the authority, the better-ordered Venetians made their largest council able to punish citizens who were accused.

3. No One Should Be Able to Bring Government to a Standstill (*D* 1.50)

If government is necessary to check the desires of both the people and the great, as Machiavelli's history of the Decemvirate illustrates, in a well-ordered republic no official should be able to bring the government to a standstill. In *D* 1.50 he thus reports that in Rome, when two consuls agreed on nothing but their refusal to appoint a dictator, the Senate obtained the help of the tribunes in forcing them to do so (and so illustrated the "utility" of the plebian tribunes as checks on the aristocratic consuls). In Venice, which Machiavelli again uses as an example of a well-ordered modern republic, they passed a law that forbade an official to leave office until a substitute or successor was in place.

4. The "Great" Must Demonstrate Their Willingness to Sacrifice for the Common Good in Order to Be Elected (*D* 1.51)

In *D* 1.51 Machiavelli seems to repeat a lesson he gave in *D* 1.32 about the desirability of making a show of doing through liberality what a republic or prince is constrained to do by necessity; but the example of the Senate's prudence and generosity he uses here makes an important addition to his earlier advice. When the Senate voted to pay men a stipend to serve in the army, so that they could fight longer wars further away from home, the tribunes objected that the plebs would be paying their own stipends through higher taxes. But the senators deflected the criticism by seeing

87. Machiavelli gives a detailed history of the many instances of this invidious tendency in his *Florentine Histories*.

that the nobility paid the heaviest and greatest taxes first. If the nobles want the people to elect them, Machiavelli reminds his aristocratic readers, they must demonstrate their own willingness to sacrifice for the sake of the common good.

5. The Education of "Aristocrats" Will Not Curb Their Ambition (*D* 1.52)

People tend not to recognize the threat to the state represented by popular leaders such as Cosimo de' Medici or Caesar until they have become too powerful to eliminate. In *D* 1.33 Machiavelli thus suggested that it was better to "temporize" with such individuals in the hope that they would make an error or that the evil would at least be deferred. But in *D* 1.52 he suggests that the nobility can prevent such an individual from acquiring too much power by competing with him for popular favor. That Machiavelli is not advising his readers merely to "fight fire with fire" becomes clear from his two negative examples. He concedes that a politician like Piero Soderini, who rose to power by favoring the collectivity, could not use the tactics of his enemies against them, if like the Medici his adversaries tried to unseat him by secretly buying influence with others. If it became known that he had secretly tried to "benefit" (or buy off) his enemies, his reputation with the people would suffer. (As Machiavelli suggested in *D* 1.7, Soderini should have tried to institute a popular court before which he could defend himself from his calumniators or accuse them of treason.) Nor, Machiavelli urges, should the nobles count on a good upbringing or education to restrain the ambition of others. The nobles misjudged Appius when they gave him the power to nominate the Decemvirs. Likewise, Cicero misjudged Octavian when he sent him against Mark Anthony, believing that the name of Caesar would attract Anthony's soldiers away from him. The people have a tendency to mistake names for things, but Cicero was mistaken in thinking that Octavian would adhere to the aristocrats rather than seek to increase his own power by allying with another popular figure.[88] As Machiavelli pointed out in *D* 1.42, young nobles are easily and quickly corrupted by sharing in the "profits" of tyranny.

88. For a fuller account of Machiavelli's critique of Cicero, see Alexander Duff, "Republicanism and the Problem of Ambition: The Critique of Cicero," *Journal of Politics* 73, no. 4 (October 2011): 980–92.

6. Why Popular Government Is Best (*D* 1.53–60)

a. The People Are Not Always Wise (D *1.53–54*)

Reminding his readers of how "many times the people desires its own ruin, deceived by a false appearance of good, and that great hopes and mighty promises easily move it," in *D* 1.53 Machiavelli again shows that he does not recommend referring final decisions to the people because he thinks that the people are always good or wise judges. On the contrary, he observes that the people almost always support a policy that appears to represent a gain, even though there is a loss concealed underneath, and that they will favor a spirited rather than an apparently cowardly or cautious endeavor. In *D* 1.4 Machiavelli quoted Cicero, who claimed that, though ignorant, the people could be persuaded of the truth by a good man. Here Machiavelli maintains merely that their respect for old and esteemed citizens can be used to persuade the people to exercise some restraint. (The modern example of the exercise of such influence he gives in *D* 1.54 is a bishop, suggesting that the Christian religion can be used in some of the same ways the Romans used theirs.) However, he warns leaders against arousing the people's enthusiasm for daring but potentially ruinous enterprises by reminding them that, presupposing victory, the people will blame the leader for their losses, without taking any responsibility themselves for having elected the leader and supporting his policies. A prudent leader will recognize popular proclivities and try to enlist or withstand them when appropriate. He may be forced to let the people have their way and see the disastrous results, so long as he can avoid responsibility for the calamity.

b. Nor Are the People Entirely Good (D *1.55*)

The title of *D* 1.55 suggests that Machiavelli thinks that things can be done easily in cities where the multitude is not corrupt, and that the extent of economic inequality determines whether a principality or a republic can be founded. But the three examples he gives of the relative "goodness" (*bontà*) or corruption of various nations both complicate and expand the options available to someone who knows how cities can be reordered. The first, the Senate's decision to ask the plebs to give back a tenth of the booty they took from the Veientes to redeem Camillus's vow to Apollo, may literally show "how much the Senate trusted in the goodness" of the plebs. However, in reporting that the plebs openly and indignantly refused, Machiavelli indicates just "how much goodness and how much religion were in that people, and how much good was to be hoped from it" (110). Their goodness was not so much as to make them give up the spoils, but only to resist openly and without fraud. (Indeed, Machiavelli indicates that the "honesty" of the people is largely a product of their number, which makes it impossible for them to act as a body in secret.)[89] In his second, negative example of the corrupt provinces in his time, Machiavelli explains that there are fewer disorders in France and Spain than there are in Italy, not because the people are better, but because these nations have a king to maintain their unity. Even in his last, best example of the Germans who pay tithes without supervision, he observes that if each individual did not contribute the required amount, the fraud would be recognized and another mode of collection adopted. In all three examples, the "goodness" of the people is not spontaneous or inherent, but depends on the people's belief (or lack thereof) that the government will force them to contribute what they do not give voluntarily.

Machiavelli furthers the impression that the goodness of a people is not an inherent quality so much as a product of its external conditions when he explains that there are two reasons that the Germans are less corrupt than the Italians, French, or Spanish. First, they do not have a lot of commerce with their neighbors and are content with home-grown goods. But second and more important, the German republics are not corrupt because they do not have any "gentlemen" who live idly on the returns from their possessions and from castles command subjects who obey them. The kind of inequality that makes it impossible to establish a republic, readers thus see, is not merely economic; it is political and military. As Machiavelli observed in *P* 12, there is no proportion between the armed and the unarmed. Anyone who wants to reorder such a province will have to use force to deprive the "gentlemen" of their ability to resist the prince and oppress their fellows.

External conditions might seem to determine what kind of government can be established in any given place. However, Machiavelli now affirms that "a prudent man having knowledge of the ancient civilizations" (like Machiavelli) would know what to do to make a republic from a province suited to be a kingdom or kingdom from a province suited to be a republic. Just as Machiavelli argued that it was the prince's fault if there were no

89. As Sullivan, *Machiavelli, Hobbes, and the Formation of a Liberal Republicanism in England*, 47, also points out.

soldiers, so he now suggests that the goodness or corruption of a people depends on whether they have a man who possesses the knowledge and daring to do what is necessary to order and reorder them.

c. Claims to Divinely Inspired Knowledge Are Not Necessary (D *1.56)*

In *The Prince* and *Discourses* Machiavelli claims to possess the knowledge needed to found and reorder both principalities and republics. But in *D* 1.56 he somewhat fancifully tells his readers he does not have the knowledge of the "signs" of future events of the kind both the ancient augurers and Friar Girolamo Savonarola claimed to possess. He is not prophesying or predicting the future; he is using his knowledge of the world to show what can and cannot be done.

d. The Power of the Multitude Is Transitory and Thus Limited (D *1.57)*

Establishing the sort of republic he is recommending does not require even the pretense of supernatural knowledge. As Machiavelli indicates in *D* 1.57, however, it does require understanding "the nature of a multitude." Peoples tend to become violent when they are deprived of their freedom or their (deposed) prince is still alive. But, Machiavelli observes, "when the spirits of men are cooled a little and each sees he has to return to his home, they begin to doubt themselves and to think of their safety, either by taking flight or by coming to accord" (115), unless they have a "head" or "heads" to keep them united.[90] Anyone who wishes to reorder a province must prepare himself to withstand the first onslaught of popular resistance; but if he has a stronghold that enables him to escape the first thrust, he will survive it.

e. Nevertheless, the People Are Wiser and More Stable Than Princes (D *1.58)*

In *D* 1.58 Machiavelli nevertheless announces that he disagrees with all previous writers, including his apparent authority Livy, who maintain that "nothing is more vain and inconstant than the multitude" (115). On the contrary, Machiavelli argues, a multitude unshackled by laws is no worse than a prince without legal restraint. Indeed, he proceeds to argue that a people restrained by laws rules better than a prince or king so constrained.

90. According to Machiavelli, therefore, the people or "multitude" are not and cannot be the "revolutionary" force Vatter argues they are in *Between Form and Event*. The multitude can be destructive, but they need leaders (i.e., "princes") in order to create and maintain a new civil order.

That is, of course, the effective meaning of his preference for republics over principalities. In this chapter Machiavelli spells out his reasons.

Princes and peoples do not differ in nature; "it is in one mode in all" (117). The difference is that the people have more respect for the law (because, as Machiavelli reminded his readers in the previous chapter, they are individually weaker and more fearful). In *D* 1.29 he argued that peoples tend to be less ungrateful than princes, because people see outstanding generals and legislators to be public servants, rather than competitors, as does a prince. Machiavelli nevertheless suggested that popular gratitude might not be prudent, because popular leaders can become tyrants. Here he insists that the people are not only less ungrateful, but also more prudent, more stable, and have better judgment for five reasons. First he points to the effects of widespread opinion, which shapes human action and might thus be said to predict the future (better perhaps than the "signs" that appear to have done so only after the fact). Widespread opinion is so powerful, he notes, that "the voice of a people may be likened to that of God" (117). Second, Machiavelli observes that people can judge a dispute between two equally good orators as well as, if not better than, a prince. They, too, can listen to reason, and a large number of people cannot be swayed as easily by personal ties or passions as a single ruler. Third, he argues not merely (as he did in *D* 1.47) that the multitude can judge the character of individual candidates for office, but that they do so better than princes, because, unlike some princes, they will not select obvious scoundrels. Fourth, he observes that widespread popular opinions tend to be long-lasting and so stable. But, beyond all this, Machiavelli emphasizes, the fact that cities ruled by peoples grow more rapidly than those ruled by princes shows that governments of the people are better. Like the "vulgar" (*P* 18), Machiavelli judges things and people by their effects or outcomes.

Affirming that "the multitude is wiser and more constant than a prince," Machiavelli acknowledges that the reforms or reorderings necessary to maintain a republic have to be the work of a single man or mind. But, he urges, "if princes are superior to peoples in ordering laws, forming civil lives, and ordering new statutes and orders, peoples are so much superior in maintaining things ordered that . . . they attain the glory of those who order them" (118).[91] What Machiavelli seems to have in mind is that the

91. In arguing that Machiavelli thinks that the people not only are more "decent," moral, and just, but also have better judgment, in *Machiavellian Democracy* McCormick relies greatly on this

people—be they Athenians, Romans, or French—become more famous than any of the individuals who serve or rule them (if for no other reason than that the people reproduce themselves and thus last longer).[92]

Machiavelli concludes this chapter by making it clear (as he did not at the beginning of the book in his initial comparison of Rome with Sparta) that he does not judge the excellence of different governments merely or even primarily by their longevity. On the contrary, he observes "that the states of princes have lasted very long, the states of republics have lasted very long, and both have had need of being regulated by the laws. For a prince who can do what he wishes is crazy; a people that can do what it wishes is not wise" (118). Nevertheless, he repeats his judgment that a people regulated by laws has more virtue than a prince so regulated, and peoples unconstrained by laws make fewer errors than unconstrained princes. Reversing the traditional view that popular rule rests ultimately on the force of the largest number, Machiavelli suggests that popular rule is superior to princely rule because popular rule is, in effect, the rule of public opinion and thus depends upon persuasion rather than force. A good man can convince a licentious and tumultuous people to return to a good way by speaking to them, but a wicked prince can be checked only by steel. What is feared in the rule of a multitude unconstrained by law is not the present instability or violence of the people ruling, but the future possibility that a tyrant will arise from it. That evil is already present in the rule of a wicked prince. Popular rule can be violent, but "the cruelties of the multitude are against whoever they fear will seize the common good; those of a prince are against whoever he fears will seize his own good" (119). The people are not less selfish by nature than their leaders; but, Machiavelli reminds his readers, there are many more of them, and the good of the multitude is thus a closer approximation of the common good than the good of any individual. The fact that all the writers before him have spoken ill of the multitude ironically provides evidence for the gentle character of their rule, based on neither fear nor force. "The opinion against peoples arises because everyone speaks ill of peoples without fear and freely, even while

chapter. But he never quotes the first part of this sentence in which Machiavelli explicitly recognizes the necessary role and excellences of princes. See Ryan Balot and Stephen Trochimchuk, "The Many and the Few: On Machiavelli's 'Democratic Moment'" *Review of Politics* 74, no. 4 (2012): 559–88, for a thorough critique of McCormick's argument.

92. Alessandro Pinzani, "Doch ein Republikaner? Ein Blick in die anderen politische Schriften Machiavellis," in Höffe, *Niccolò Machiavelli "Der Fürst,"* observes that "Der Ruhm von Rom ist größer also der seiner Gründers Romulus und all seiner Generäle, Tribunen, Konsulen jeweils individuell betrachtet" (176).

they reign," but "princes are always spoken of with a thousand fears and a thousand hesitations" (119).

f. Popular Governments Keep Faith Better Than Princes (D *1.59)*

In *D* 1.59, Machiavelli underlines the fact that the reason he is arguing in favor of popularly based rule is not that he thinks that the people are morally superior to princes. There he observes that republics and princes are apt not to abide by their agreements or keep "faith" for basically the same reasons: if the accord was coerced, or if compliance threatens the existence of the state. In other words, popular governments are not any more honest or grateful for past benefits than princes. They do not break their agreements as quickly or easily as princes, and so tend to abide by their agreements longer, because a number of people take longer to come to a decision and cannot keep that decision secret so well as a sole ruler.

g. Popular Government Gives Everyone an Incentive to Work for the Benefit of All (D *1.60)*

The real advantage of a popularly based republic, Machiavelli concludes in *D* 1.60, is that by making all citizens eligible to be elected to the highest offices, without regard to age or "blood" (i.e., family), a republic like Rome obtains the advantage of individual virtue, wherever it is to be found. Moreover, it gives each and every citizen an incentive to work for the community in order to gain glory for himself.

Conclusion of Book 1

By the end of book 1 it should be clear that Machiavelli is not advocating the establishment of an aristocratic republic of the kind praised by Aristotle and Cicero. The education he seeks to give his two young readers, who "deserve to be princes," does not consist in habituation or training in controlling their own fears and desires so that they will be able to control people without the benefit of such an education by means of law. He is trying to show them how to establish and maintain a new kind of republic by designing institutions and laws that will make the conflicting desires of the two humors to be found in every city work for the benefit of (almost) everyone.[93]

93. See Paul Rahe, *Against Throne and Altar: Machiavelli and Political Theory under the English Republic* (New Haven: Yale University Press, 2008), 22–55; Fischer, *Well-Ordered License*, 124–25.

If his readers have an opportunity to reorder their city as a republic, Machiavelli urges them to allow all citizens to be eligible for the highest offices, and to have those offices filled by popular elections. Not only are the people able—at least most of the time—to distinguish good from bad candidates, especially if the politically active class takes care to make the contrast between the candidates clear.[94] Such electoral laws also make individual citizens compete in order to gain glory for themselves by serving the republic.

Republican reformers should also make sure that capital crimes—especially those involving charges of treason—are tried publicly by a large jury, so that the people remain confident that individuals in high office have to obey the law or suffer punishment just the way the people do. Machiavelli thus advises "princes" to establish courts to enable the people to check the nobles (*P* 19) and to show that they themselves are bound by an "infinite" number of laws (*D* 1.16).

Despite his revolutionary declaration that "the multitude is wiser and more constant than a prince," Machiavelli has no illusions about the ability of peoples to govern themselves directly. He is not a democrat of this kind.[95] On the contrary, he declares that "a multitude without a head is useless" (*D* 1.44). Leaderless mobs can act spontaneously with frightful feroc-

94. As McCormick, *Machiavellian Democracy*, 98–99, observes, Machiavelli is remarkably imprecise about the composition of the electorate. In contrast to Rousseau, *Social Contract* 4.2–4, he never recognizes the way in which Roman votes were weighted in favor of propertied people. (In *D* 3.49 he does, however, praise Fabius Rullianus for creating new voting "orders" that made the votes of the "new men" weigh less. That praise alone would appear to prove that Machiavelli was no democrat in the sense of giving each and every citizen an equal vote or voice in the determination of public policy.) In contrast to McCormick, Rousseau, *Social Contract* 4.5, notes that the senators were not allowed to participate in the election of tribunes, but were nonetheless subject to decisions made by the tribunes that had the force of law. Rousseau's description of the fundamental laws of the Roman republic in *Social Contract* 4.2–7 is generally more specific than Machiavelli's. Machiavelli wants his readers to understand why Roman institutions worked or did not work, not literally to copy them. As he suggests in the concluding chapter of the *Discourses* (3.49), voting regulations continually have to be modified in response to changes in the composition and character of the people to prevent them from becoming corrupt.

95. On the basis of Machiavelli's statement in *D* 1.18 (and nowhere else) that every citizen of Rome had a right to propose laws and to discuss them, in his analysis in *Machiavellian Democracy* McCormick vastly overstates the "participatory" character of the Roman republic. In fact, it is not clear that a plebian could propose a law, except by persuading an elected tribune to do so. Discussions were held in *contiones* (short for conventions) called by a consul, praetor, or tribune of the plebs—and the presiding officer decided who could speak. In "Tempering the Grandi's Appetite to Oppress," 13, McCormick admits that Machiavelli's statement "that 'any citizen at all' could speak in a *concione*" (3.34) was "perhaps against actual Roman practice." In sum, it is not at all clear that the plebs had a "voice" in the sense of an actual vote in deciding what policies became law.

ity, but they cannot maintain any sustained action or policy. The people's desire to take vengeance on those who have oppressed them also blinds them to the need to maintain legal forms and procedures. Nor can a people devise or undertake the innovations necessary to maintain republican liberty. Because there are more of them and their desire to avoid oppression approximates the general interest in maintaining liberty, Machiavelli nevertheless argues against all previous "writers" that the people are rightly the final judges of their princes and the policies they propose. The people suffer and thus know the outcomes, even if they do not always understand the causes.

Outline of Book 2: Why Modern Italians Should Learn from, but Not Simply Imitate, Ancient Rome in the Conduct of Foreign Affairs

A. How Machiavelli Gradually Departs from the Roman Model While Praising It (*D* 2.Pref.–2.2)
  1. The Past Is Often Erroneously Praised (*D* 2.Pref.)
  2. Machiavelli's Fervent Appeal to the Young to Complete His Project (*D* 2.Pref.)
  3. The Romans Did Not Understand the Causes of Their Own Success (*D* 2.1)
  4. Roman Expansion Destroyed Freedom Everywhere (*D* 2.2)
     a. Machiavelli's Praise of the Free Way of Life
     b. The Pernicious Effects of a "Cowardly" Interpretation of Christianity

B. Different Modes of Republican Expansion (*D* 2.3–4)
  1. The Roman Example (*D* 2.3–4)
  2. The "Second-Best," Tuscan Alternative (*D* 2.4)

C. Why Christianity May No Longer Make Imitation of the Romans Impossible (*D* 2.5)

D. Why Modern Republics Should Adopt Roman Military Orders (*D* 2.6–18)
  1. Training Citizen Soldiers to Fight Short Wars for Minimal Rewards (*D* 2.6–8)
  2. Acquiring "Partners" by Fraud as Well as by Force (*D* 2.9–15)
  3. Using Roman Military Orders (*D* 2.16–18)
     *a. Maintaining Reserves to Fight Anew (*D *2.16)*

Book 2: Why Modern Italians Should Learn from, but Not Simply Imitate, Ancient Rome in the Conduct of Foreign Affairs

In book 1 Machiavelli showed that the internal orders of the Roman republic were closely tied to her expansionary foreign policy. First, he argued that the Roman plebs obtained a part of their government and so "perfected" the republic by refusing to fight in the armies unless they were granted some offices and, eventually, made eligible to hold all. Then he suggested that the Roman people remained uncorrupt so long and only so long as they feared foreign attacks and were, therefore, willing to defend the republic. Both the internal and the external liberty of Rome thus required that her people remain armed. It would not be possible for his contemporaries to "imitate" the domestic orders of the Roman republic, therefore, if they did not "imitate" expansionary Roman foreign policy by mustering and training an army of local inhabitants. But as Machiavelli reminds his readers at the beginning of the *Art of War* when Cosimo Rucellai restates the reasons his grandfather and other aristocratic Florentines did not think it was possible (or prudent) for them to try to imitate the Romans, arming the plebs was what the *ottimati* most feared. (That was the reason they had opposed Machiavelli's own attempts to form a Florentine militia.) In book 2 Machiavelli thus seeks to convince his aristocratic young readers that it will be not merely safe but absolutely necessary to arm the people, if they want to refound a free Florentine republic. At the same time he clearly indicates that the rearming and refounding he is recommending do not constitute a mere imitation.

A. How Machiavelli Gradually Departs from the Roman Model While Praising It (*D* 2.Pref.–2.2)

1. The Past Is Often Erroneously Praised (*D* 2.Pref.)

Machiavelli begins book 2 of the *Discourses* by criticizing the prejudice in favor of the ancients to which he appealed at the beginning of book 1. Our knowledge of ancient times is imperfect, he reminds his readers; writers about past events tend to extol the virtues of the victors and to conceal their faults. Fear and envy lead contemporary observers to criticize their peers and to elevate their predecessors. All praise of the past and criticism of the present is not invalid, however; "since human things are always in motion" (123), people in a given place are either ascending or descending. Because he deems "the world always to have been in the same mode," Machiavelli thinks that there is always "as much good as wicked in it" (124), but the locus of each shifts from time to time and place to place. In ancient times virtue could be seen in a series of empires—first in Assyria, then in Media and Persia, and finally in Greece and Rome—but after the fall of Rome it has been scattered among "the kingdom of the Franks, the kingdom of the Turks, that of the sultan, and the peoples of Germany" (124). The peoples of these nations deserve to be praised for their virtue, but "whoever is born in Italy and in Greece and has not become either an ultramontane in Italy or a Turk in Greece has reason to blame his times and to praise the others" (124).

Even if people had complete knowledge of the past, Machiavelli acknowledges, they would still tend to blame the present and praise the past, because their judgments change as they age. "Since men when they get old lack force and grow in judgment and prudence, it is necessary that those things that appear to them endurable and good during youth turn out unendurable and bad when they get old." More generally, he observes, "human appetites are insatiable, for since from nature they have the ability . . . to desire all things and from fortune the ability to achieve few of them, there continually results from this a discontent in human minds and a disgust with the things they possess." As a result, they "blame the present times, praise the past, and desire the future, even if they are not moved to do this by any reasonable cause." Nevertheless, he concludes, the difference between the virtue of the Romans and the vice now reigning in Italy is so manifest that he can continue to dramatize the contrast "so that the spirits of youths who may read these writings . . . can flee the latter and prepare themselves to imitate the former at whatever time fortune may give them opportunity" (124).

2. Machiavelli's Fervent Appeal to the Young to Complete His Project (*D* 2.Pref.)

In the preface to book 2 Machiavelli thus reminds his readers, as he did in the preface to book 1, that he is addressing youths he hopes will carry out a project he himself could not, because of the "malignity" of his own fortune. The connection between Machiavelli's advice to his young readers to "imitate the Romans" particularly with regard to their military orders in book 2 and his own political career is especially close. *The* policy he recommended to his oligarchic superiors when he served as secretary to the Florentine republic was that they "imitate the Romans" by mustering and training a militia (or army) composed of citizens and subjects. He gives princes similar advice about the importance of relying on one's own arms (or people) rather than mercenaries and auxiliaries in both *The Prince* and the *Art of War* and promises that the Italian prince who organizes and leads his own army will conquer the province. In urging his young Florentine readers to imitate the expansionary policy of the Roman republic in his *Discourses*, however, Machiavelli emphasizes the importance of depending not solely on conquering their neighbors but on forming an alliance or league with them. And if imitating the Roman conquest of the world seems too difficult (as it might well seem to citizens of a city without its own army and in need of hiring mercenary forces), he urges them to follow the example of their Etruscan forebears who formed a defensive league of 12–14 cities. Such a league would combine sufficient territory and troops to defend Tuscany from the invasions Italy was currently suffering from the French, Spanish, and Germans.[96] However, it would take such a large number of cities a good deal of time to make any decision and each member would gain little from any addition to the league beyond the number and size necessary for defending it. As a result, such a league would not have the destructive effects of Roman conquests outside of Italy,

96. Maurizio Viroli, *From Politics to Reason of State: The Acquisition and Transformation of the Language of Politics, 1250–1600* (Cambridge: Cambridge University Press, 1992), 162, also argues that Machiavelli urges the Florentines to follow the ancient Tuscan model.

conquests that eventually led to the destruction of liberty everywhere, including Rome itself.[97]

3. The Romans Did Not Understand the Causes of Their Own Success (*D* 2.1)

As in *P* 25, so in the second book of the *Discourses*, Machiavelli urges his contemporaries to rely on their *virtù* by arming themselves rather than leaving their fate to *fortuna* (or God). In using the example of the Roman republic to support the policies he recommends, Machiavelli thus finds it necessary to disagree with the ancient historians upon whose writings he is purportedly relying. Both Plutarch and Livy show that the Romans attributed their success in acquiring empire to their good fortune as well as to their own virtue. To maintain that his contemporaries can imitate the Romans' success, Machiavelli has to prove that both the historians' and the Romans' understanding of the reasons for that success is wrong. If the Romans had identified the sources of their success correctly, Machiavelli's contemporaries could imitate Roman modes of waging war, but they could not expect necessarily or predictably to share the same "fortune," because they, unlike the Romans, did not worship "Fortuna" as a god and consequently could not expect her to reward them. As at the beginning of book 1 he thus implicitly raises the question of whether the change from pagan to Christian religion makes the imitation of the Romans he is explicitly advocating impossible.

Machiavelli demonstrates the way in which he thinks his contemporaries can learn from reading ancient histories by disagreeing with both Plutarch and Livy about the causes of the events they relate. According to these historians, it was the Romans' good fortune not to have to wage two major wars at one time. In fact, Machiavelli argues, it was not a matter of mere chance. There are reasons that can be recaptured by later observers. Once a people acquires a reputation by fighting and defeating its nearest neighbors, other peoples and princes become afraid to assault it. As a result, the Romans or any other people in a similar situation are able to

97. Strauss, *TM*, 89, also observes that the "confederacy" Machiavelli recommends here constitutes an alternative to the conquest for which he calls in *P* 26. As Machiavelli indicates, but only indicates, in *D* 2.19, the expansionary policies he recommends here would entail as severe a diminishment, if not the complete destruction, of the political independence of the Vatican, as would the conquest of Italy for which he calls at the conclusion of *The Prince*.

choose which wars to fight, when, and how. Other nations remain sitting on the sidelines, partly out of respect for the aggressor's power and partly because they are deceived by assurances they receive from the warring nation (and their own illusory hopes of avoiding conflict). Instead of helping the victims, these more distant nations conclude that the present war does not concern them. They discover their error only after the victorious power, made stronger by its conquests, attacks them.

4. Roman Expansion Destroyed Freedom Everywhere (*D* 2.2)

The Romans not merely failed to understand the causes of their own success. In *D* 2.2 Machiavelli acknowledges that Rome's success in acquiring empire was not unambiguously good.

In the guise of praising Roman virtue for its success in overcoming the obstinate resistance of many free peoples, Machiavelli reminds his readers that Roman expansion destroyed freedom everywhere, including Rome itself. In *P* 5 he maintained that a people who has enjoyed freedom never forgets its ancient orders (and thus always retains a reason to rebel), unless that people is broken up and dispersed. But here he observes that at his time "there is only one province that can be said to have free cities in it" (129), although in ancient times there were many; and the cause is "that the Roman Empire, with its arms and its greatness, eliminated all republics and all civil ways of life" (132).

a. Machiavelli's Praise of the Free Way of Life

This observation provides Machiavelli with the occasion for giving his most extensive praise of a free way of life (and the reasons he prefers republics to principalities). He observed earlier that free cities expand much more and more rapidly than principalities, but here he gives the reasons: "it is not the particular good but the common good that makes cities great. And without doubt this common good is not observed if not in republics, since everything is done for that purpose." Equating the "common good" with the good of the greatest number, Machiavelli concedes that "it may turn out to harm this or that private individual," but "those for whom the aforesaid does good are so many that they can go ahead with it against the disposition of the few crushed by it" (130, translation slightly altered). If a single ruler makes conquests, whether he be a prince or a tyrant, he will use them to benefit himself. He will not seek to share the power or wealth with the city as a whole, or even the nobles, because he will not want to give any, much less many, of his subjects the ability or ambition to rebel against his rule.

Perceiving the close connection between the preservation of the republic and their own lives and liberties, the people of a free city not only fight fiercely to preserve it from foreign domination. They also work to improve their own lot domestically.

> All towns and provinces that live freely . . . make very great profits. For larger peoples are seen there, because marriages are freer and more desirable to men since each willingly procreates those children he believes he can nourish. He does not fear that his patrimony will be taken away, and he knows not only that they are born free and not slaves, but that they can, through their virtue, become princes. Riches are seen to multiply there in larger number, both those that come from agriculture and those that come from the arts. For each willingly multiplies that thing and seeks to acquire those goods he believes he can enjoy once acquired. From which it arises that men in rivalry think of private and public advantages, and both the one and the other come to grow marvelously (132).[98]

In light of the great advantages of a free way of life, readers cannot but ask why so few republics emerged in Europe after the fall of the Roman empire. In *D* 1.16 Machiavelli observed that the advantages of a free way of life are usually not appreciated until they are lost. But he shows here that he and others are fully aware of the advantages they have lost. The reason those advantages have been lost, he now explains, is the difference

98. In this passage, Machiavelli may sound like a liberal political economist. However, despite his urging a prince to show himself to be a lover of the virtues by giving recognition to virtuous men, honoring excellence in any art, and inspiriting his citizens to follow their pursuits quietly, in trade and in agriculture, so that they are not reluctant to adorn their possessions for fear of their being taken away or to open up a trade for fear of taxes in *P* 21, Machiavelli does not argue, as does John Locke, *Second Treatise* 5.36, that a "wise prince" will foster the industry of his subjects rather than seek to expand his republic or principality by means of conquest. The truth of the matter lies somewhere in between. Machiavelli consistently argues in favor of training and arming the people, but he also advises princes to see that the lives and property of their subjects are secure and to foster the arts. The difference (and superiority of republics) lies in the hope citizens of a free regime have that they or their children may attain high office. This hope makes them strive harder not merely to protect themselves and their own, but to win glory by serving the republic as a whole (*D* 1.60). They come to see the government of the republic not merely as an external source of protection, but as something in which they themselves have a part that they wish to increase. Once they feel that their lives, families, and properties are secure, the multitude have an incentive to serve the republic, because they are moved by the same desire to command that animates the *grandi*. Their "humor" or "ambition" also needs to be recognized and channeled to produce publicly beneficial results. If it is not, it will produce a series of attempted "conspiracies" against the republic or, in our terms, revolutions.

between "our education," which is to say, "our religion," and that of the ancients.

b. The Pernicious Effects of a "Cowardly" Interpretation of Christianity

Although Machiavelli affirms that our religion has "shown the truth and the true way," he also observes that it has made men esteem the honor of the world less. "Ancient religion did not beatify men if they were not full of worldly glory, as were captains of armies and princes of republics. Our religion has glorified humble and contemplative more than active men. It has then placed the highest good in humility, abjectness, and contempt of things human; the other placed it in greatness of spirit, strength of body, and all other things capable of making men very strong."[99] The only form of strength encouraged by our religion is the ability to endure suffering. "This mode of life thus *seems* to have rendered the world weak and given it in prey to criminal men, who can manage it securely, seeing that the collectivity of men, so as to go to paradise, think more of enduring their beatings than of avenging them." However, Machiavelli concludes, "although the world *appears* to be made effeminate and heaven disarmed, it arises without doubt more from the cowardice of the men who have interpreted our religion according to idleness and not according to virtue. For if they considered how it permits us the exaltation and defense of the fatherland, they would see that it wishes us to love and honor it and to prepare ourselves to be such that we can defend it" (131, emphases added).

Machiavelli thus reminds his readers of what would appear to be the chief reason his contemporaries did not think that it was possible to imitate the Romans: they are Christians, whereas the citizens of the Roman republic were pagans. But he assures such readers that the elevation of humility and contemplation in place of more worldly virtues results from a "cowardly" interpretation of their religion. In *P* 12 and *D* 1.12, he suggested that such a "cowardly" interpretation has been promoted by priests

99. The contrast Machiavelli draws here between ancient and modern education and religion almost exactly parallels that Augustine draws between the pagan Romans and Christians in his *City of God*, books 2 and 3, with the very important difference, of course, that Machiavelli's entirely reverses Augustine's evaluation of the relative merits of the two. Although there is no direct evidence that Machiavelli knew the *City of God*, Gennaro Sasso, *Machiavelli e gli antichi e altri saggi* (Milan: R. Ricciardi, 1987), 157–58, assures us that he did. The echoes of Augustine's account of the fall of Rome in Machiavelli's celebration of Roman greatness make it difficult to believe that he did not know and have Augustine's contrasting account of Rome in mind. See Warner and Scott, "Sin City."

and monks because they are unarmed.[100] Machiavelli does not spell out what interpretation of Christianity would permit the exaltation and defense of the fatherland, but his observation that among the places where virtue was scattered after the fall of the Roman empire are the kingdom of the Franks and Germany today supports his claim that Christian beliefs are not simply incompatible with good arms.

B. Different Modes of Republican Expansion (*D* 2.3–4)

Rather than seeking to spell out the new form of education that would reawaken a love of freedom as based on a new interpretation of "our religion," Machiavelli turns to the immediate cause of the destruction of liberty in the West, Roman expansion. The question that fact raises is: how is it possible to gain the advantages of Roman foreign and military policies without destroying the liberty they were intended to secure? Machiavelli suggests that his Florentine contemporaries should seek to command a "partnership" with other Italian cities the way Rome did before it began conquering kingdoms beyond the Italian peninsula or, if that seems too difficult, to follow the example of their Etruscan ancestors and form a defensive league in Tuscany.[101]

1. The Roman Example (*D* 2.3–4)

Machiavelli first explains, "Rome became a great city through ruining the surrounding cities and easily admitting foreigners to its honors." As in contrasting Rome with Sparta at the beginning of book 1, he emphasizes the importance of a city's acquiring a large population if it wants to expand. But now he explains that Rome did so in two ways: It opened its gates to people fleeing from other cities (in contrast to Sparta, which tried to minimize, if not entirely forbid, any form of commerce with foreigners). It also forced the inhabitants of nearby cities it had decided to eliminate to move to Rome. In *D* 2.4, however, Machiavelli makes it clear that Rome did not expand its power in Italy solely or even primarily through conquest. After

100. By describing this interpretation of "our religion" as "according to idleness" (*ozio*), which can also be translated 'leisure,' Machiavelli appears to be contesting the necessity of the combination of Christian beliefs with ancient philosophical ideas, especially those associated with contemplation, that occurred in the works of Thomas Aquinas, who synthesized Aristotelian philosophy with scriptural faith.

101. In *D* 1.12 he suggested that the problem is the Church, especially its effect on the politics of Italy, and not Christianity per se, when he observed that the Swiss "are today the only peoples who live according to the ancients as regards both religion and military orders" (39).

it fought and conquered other Italian cities, it came to terms with them. These cities agreed to provide Rome with a certain amount of land to support the colonies it established to guard its conquests and to follow its command in future wars, so that it remained the seat of the empire, but they continued to live under their own laws. This alliance or league-like arrangement persisted until the Romans "began to go out of Italy with their armies, to reduce kingdoms to provinces, and to get subjects who did not care about being subjects since they were accustomed to living under kings and who did not acknowledge a superior other than Rome since they had Roman governors and had been conquered by armies with the Roman title." By fighting with Rome in the wars it waged outside of Italy, its partners "came to subjugate themselves by their own labors and blood without perceiving it. . . . [They] found themselves in a stroke encircled by Roman subjects and crushed by a very big city. . . . And when they perceived the deception under which they had lived, they were not in time to remedy it" (136).

2. The "Second Best," Tuscan Alternative (*D* 2.4)

There are three ways for a republic to expand, Machiavelli explains. Like the twelve members of the ancient Etruscan league, a city can form a league with other cities to provide for their common defense. This kind of league is less effective as a means of expansion than the Roman mode of retaining command and deceiving its allies about their equal partnership. Only a limited number of cities can join together to make common decisions, and they are not able to move quickly or decisively because of the time it takes a number of people to agree on a common policy. The members of such a league do not have much incentive to expand beyond the number of cities needed to defend their current territory, moreover, because all gains have to be divided equally among the members, so no one city can expect to profit much from another conquest. Even though very little is known about the ancient Etruscan league, Machiavelli argues, it represents a better mode of expansion than the expensive and not very long-lasting attempts of cities like Sparta and Athens to make their allies into subjects.[102] So if his Florentine readers deem it too difficult to follow

102. Machiavelli may have learned what he says here about the Tuscan league from Leonardo Bruni, *History of the Florentine People*. See the edition by James Hankins (Cambridge, MA: Harvard University Press, 2001), 1.12–13.

the Roman model, he concludes, imitating "the ancient Tuscans should not seem so, especially to present Tuscans" (138).

As Machiavelli indicates in the remainder of book 2, the formation of a league would have represented a big improvement on Florence's historical efforts to acquire an empire by conquering its neighbors (e.g., Pisa and Lucca) and ruling them as subjects, the way Sparta and Athens treated their "allies." If Florence had succeeded in forming a new Tuscan league, it might have constituted a defensive union capable of withstanding the French and Spanish armies that had recently invaded Italy at the pope's behest, even if the new Tuscan league did not extend to the entire Italian peninsula. The internally imposed limitations on the expansion of a league might be considered an advantage, moreover; so long as Rome did not conquer provinces outside of Italy, its "partners" continued to live free insofar as they continued to rule themselves according to their own laws. Rome's expansion led to the loss of freedom for Rome as well as for her partners.[103] A league or confederation thus appears to be *the* way republics can provide themselves with an effective defense, without falling prey to either the internal corruption that infects a people who no longer fears external aggression or conquest by a foreign power.[104]

C. Why Christianity May No Longer Make Imitation of the Romans Impossible (*D* 2.5)

Because the model of a league provided by the Etruscans was forgotten, in an apparent digression Machiavelli inquires into the reasons human memory does not extend back more than five thousand years. His discussions of the two ways in which human memories are destroyed point, however,

103. Connell, "Machiavelli on Growth as an End," argues that "throughout his writings, the Florentine argued against the territorial state and in favor of an expansionist republican empire" (261). Misunderstanding the emphasis Machiavelli puts on the need for expansion in *D* 1.6, commentators have not observed the advantages Machiavelli saw in acquiring "friends" rather than simply conquering. Not observing the way in which Machiavelli saw that the development of the national monarchies in Europe could balance or check the expansion of a Florentine or Tuscan republic, Connell concludes that the expansion by means of federation that Machiavelli recommends would have led to the establishment of an empire like that Rome had exercised earlier, just more slowly.

104. As Levy, *Wily Elites*, 44, argues, one cannot agree with Maurizio Viroli, *Machiavelli*, "that for Machiavelli 'territorial aggrandizement does not mean conquest and predatory expansionism'" or with Mark Hulliung, *Citizen Machiavelli*, 56, "according to whom Machiavelli admires Rome precisely because of its predatory imperialism." Although Hulliung denies it, Machiavelli clearly saw the connection between Roman imperialism and the downfall of the republic.

to a way or ways to eliminate one of the major obstacles to the unification and defense of Italy.

Machiavelli observes that the diverse causes of the elimination of memories of past times are either human or from heaven (but, we should note, in neither case divine).[105] The example Machiavelli gives of the first, the variation of sects and languages brought about by changes in religion, appears to be strangely inapt. Early Christian fathers like Saint Gregory did try to destroy all memories of ancient theology by "burning the works of the poets and historians, ruining images, and spoiling every other thing that might convey some sign of antiquity." One reason Machiavelli suggests they did not succeed entirely was, ironically, that they had to retain the Latin language in order to write the law suppressing all other forms of religion. (Machiavelli thus suggests in passing that changes of "sects" or religions require political support and enforcement.) Machiavelli had to have known that the new "law" brought by Jesus was formulated in contrast to the old Hebraic law, and that the Gospel containing that law was written in Greek, not Latin. As Machiavelli also knew from reading Livy (whose history is thought to have been among the books Gregory burned), the Romans did not try to destroy the religion or the language of the Etruscans. The attempt to ban if not destroy all other religions rather than absorb their gods and worship was peculiar to Judaism and its Christian offshoot. As he reminds his readers in *D* 2.8, it was associated with particularly deadly wars, because one sect tried to replace the other (and the people who adhered to it) completely. The point of Machiavelli's erroneous discussion of the human causes of the loss of memory thus seems to be his concluding observation that "these sects vary two or three times in five or six thousand years" (139). If so, Machiavelli would be suggesting, as he did in *D* 1.12, that the Christian religion might soon be coming to an end, because the obvious corruption of the priests was making it difficult for people to believe in them or their creed.

Causes coming from heaven that eliminate the human race and reduce the inhabitants of part of the world to a few who either do not know what

105. In responding to critics of the philosophers (like Aristotle) who maintain (contrary to the Bible) that the world is eternal by observing that human memories are relatively short for two reasons, Machiavelli responds to some but not all of the arguments Lucretius gives in *De rerum natura* 5.324 ff. for not thinking the world eternal. By not deciding the question, Machiavelli maintains his claim to possess knowledge only of worldly things. The fact that Lucretius uses the term 'confess' (*confiteare*) to refer to what the proponents of the eternity of the world must admit (line 376) does suggest that Machiavelli's use of 'confess' (*confessare*) in the *Discourses* (e.g., 2.1) does not necessarily have an explicitly Christian reference or overtone.

has occurred before or fabricate stories they want others to believe include famines, plagues, and floods. Examples of such phenomena and their effects are to be found in the Bible, but Machiavelli treats them as natural phenomena in which he believes, because "the histories are full of them, because this effect of the oblivion of things is seen, and because it seems reasonable that it should be so" (140). Again he treats the "histories" as sources of events or effects, but relies on his own reason, rather than any authority, in determining the causes.

By suggesting that nature purges the world in these ways of excess population and the evils that go with it, Machiavelli again points to a connection between the reasons human beings do not possess complete knowledge of the past and the wars they fight. Later, in *D* 2.8, he reminds his readers that the most dangerous and destructive wars are not fought, like those of the Romans, primarily from ambition, intentionally or by choice. These wars are fought by peoples forced to leave their homelands because of natural disasters like famines or wars, who have to try to displace the current inhabitants of another province. And having brought the human and heavenly causes of destruction together as possible sources of the most complete destruction of earlier civilizations, he cites "Moses and the peoples who seized the Roman Empire" (144) as examples. He thus obliquely refers to the replacement of both by Christians in describing the ways in which these peoples not only displaced and destroyed all the past inhabitants, but also changed the names of places (along with the language spoken and the religion). However, such devastating wars can be avoided. At the end of the chapter Machiavelli observes that there have not been any such invasions for the last five hundred years: partly because so many people fled the cold poor regions of Scythia during the decline of the Roman Empire; partly because Germany and Hungary, from which such peoples also came, have improved their country and so do not feel the same need; and partly because very great movements by the Tartars are contained by the Hungarians and Poles, "who often glorify themselves, saying that if it were not for their arms, Italy and the church would have often felt the weight of the Tartar armies" (145). In other words, Machiavelli suggests that the human race is not doomed to live through repeated cycles of generation and destruction, as many ancient philosophers argued. Nor is our knowledge or "memory" necessarily limited to or by such inevitable cycles. On the contrary, we have more control over our fate if we understand the forces—human and natural (which are, as he indicated also partly human)—at work.

Machiavelli knew that many of his contemporaries feared an invasion by the Turks, who had fought Venetian fleets in the Mediterranean, sacked the coast of Italy, and were moving into Hungary.[106] If successful, such an invasion would probably have resulted in the replacement of the Christian "sect" by another. Alternatively, as Machiavelli's friend Vettori suggested, fear of such an invasion might provoke a reform of the Papacy and a reinterpretation of the Christian religion that would unite not merely the Italians but all the nations of Christendom in defense of the fatherland.[107]

Machiavelli does not claim to foresee the future, but in this "digression" he does indicate ways in which he thought the weakening effects of a lazy interpretation of Christianity might be overcome.[108] So long as the Romans retained their virtue, he emphasizes, they defeated the desperate peoples who invaded their lands. As in *The Prince*, so in the *Discourses*, Machiavelli insists on the power of human "arms" or agency to meet and overcome pure "fortuna" or chance. This power rests upon the use of human reason in analyzing the experiences, both historical and present, human beings have had. It is not complete, because our knowledge of the past is not complete. What knowledge we have nevertheless leads Machiavelli to conclude that there are observed regularities in nature, including human nature, that we can use in guiding human affairs (or, as he puts it in *P* 25, building dykes and dams to guide the potentially destructive floods of the river of fortune).

D. Why Modern Republics Should Adopt Roman Military Orders (*D* 2.6–18)

Because Machiavelli attributes the loss of ancient virtue to the difference between their education or religion and "ours" (*D* 2.2), some readers have taken most if not all of his discussion of the advantages of Roman military

106. Letters to Machiavelli expressing such fears, both while he was secretary of the Florentine republic and afterward, can be found in *Machiavelli and His Friends*, 13–15, 19, 21, 240–41. In *Mandragola* 3.3, Machiavelli has a nameless Florentine woman voice such a fear. The expansion of the Ottoman Empire into the west was turned back after Machiavelli's death at the battle of Vienna in 1529.

107. On August 5, 1513, Vettori wrote Machiavelli: "I am afraid that God wants to punish us poor Christians, and while our princes are all irritated against each other and no way can be seen to bring them together, that this new Turkish ruler will attack us by land and by sea and make these priests give up their simpering and the other men their pleasures. The sooner it happens the better" (*Machiavelli and His Friends*, 240). But in his *FH* 1.17 and 6.32 Machiavelli observes that previous attempts by popes to unite Christendom against the infidel failed, not because of the prelates' corruption, but because of lack of faith and virtue on the part of Christian princes.

108. In fact, we know that the Christian religion was revived (and caused a great many wars as a result) by the demands for reform made by a young monk in Germany in 1517, i.e., at the time Machiavelli was writing.

policy to refer metaphorically to the "spiritual warfare" he is waging against the cause of the loss of ancient virtue (and the reason, therefore, for the fall of Rome), i.e., Christianity.[109] Machiavelli's explanations of the reasons "it is not a prudent policy to make a friendship with a prince who has more reputation than force" (*D* 2.11) and how "often men deceive themselves believing that through humility they will conquer pride" (*D* 2.14) do seem to refer to Christian dogmas. (Josef Stalin infamously asked how many legions the pope had.) However, Machiavelli's arguments concerning the foreign and military policies his contemporaries should adopt following the Roman model can also be read simply as corrections of historical Florentine policies that he details and criticizes much more fully in his *Florentine Histories*.

As Machiavelli reminds his readers in *D* 2.2, Florence did not try to follow the example of its Etruscan ancestors by forming a defensive league of cities in northern Italy. It periodically tried and failed to conquer its closest neighbors and relied on the support of the distant French king. After the aristocratic class was destroyed in one of the battles between the Guelfs (the Church party) and the Ghibellines (the allies of the emperor), the merchants who controlled the government of Florence came to rely almost entirely on mercenary captains and armies. Especially after the Ciompi rebellion, they were afraid of arming the poorer inhabitants of the city. As a result, Machiavelli shows in repeated cases, Florence survived not because of the virtue of her citizens or leaders, but primarily by chance.

Drawing a contrast with the disastrous history of Florence's "going it alone," in book 2 of the *Discourses* Machiavelli first insists on the advantages of forming a defensive league like the ancient Etruscans, if not the superior Roman mode of unifying its Italian confederates under its command and control. Since both forms of confederation require a city to have forces sufficient to compel its neighbors to come to terms, Machiavelli then turns to a discussion of the ways in which the Romans organized themselves to fight wars in more or less explicit contrast to Florence's reliance on mercenaries and a foreign king.

1. Training Citizen Soldiers to Fight Short Wars for Minimal Rewards (*D* 2.6–8)

In an extremely abbreviated and simplified account of Rome's expansion in Italy, Machiavelli maintains that the Romans mustered and trained large

109. *TM*; Mansfield, *Machiavelli's New Modes and Orders*; Sullivan, *Machiavelli's Three Romes*.

armies with which they could subdue nearby cities quickly and inexpensively.[110] Even after they began paying soldiers salaries, so that their armies would be able to undertake more distant campaigns, he emphasizes, the Romans limited the salaries and booty with which they rewarded their troops. They also granted colonists small tracts of land, so that they could support further conquests with the fruits of their victories and did not have to burden the people with heavy taxes. As Machiavelli describes it, Roman military policy was thus the polar opposite of the use of mercenaries by Florence (and other Italian cities like Venice). These mercenaries had to be paid from the public treasury and thus required higher taxes, which aroused the opposition of the people to the wars and the leaders who led or proposed them.

2. Acquiring "Partners" by Fraud as well as by Force (*D* 2.9–15)

Roman armies were able to defeat three attacks by desperate French hordes, Machiavelli emphasizes, so long as the Romans retained their virtue (i.e., fought with their own arms and not with mercenaries). However, he acknowledges in *D* 2.9, they did become embroiled in wars they themselves did not want to fight "by chance" or the designs of hostile peoples. Rome was drawn into such wars because of the overestimation of their own strength by some of her allies or a desire on the part of others to start a war with Rome by attacking one of its allies. Forming a confederation or league with others is not sufficient to enable a nation to defend itself.

At the same time, Machiavelli shows that a nation may find itself able to expand its jurisdiction without conquest, if another nation gives itself freely as a subject to obtain its protection. Rome's jurisdiction expanded when the Campanians (Capuans), recognizing that they were unable to defend themselves from the Samnites, freely gave themselves to the Romans as subjects, so that the Romans would feel obliged to defend them. In contrast to the Romans, who expanded their dominion as a result of the voluntary subjection of the Capuans, Machiavelli reminds his readers, the

110. Although Machiavelli observes that the Romans began paying their soldiers after the conquest of Veii, he does not remind his readers that it took the Romans ten years to conquer Veii or that the Roman soldiers refused to give the booty they had collected to the public treasury and that the people wanted to divide themselves between the two cities.

Florentines were forced to offer themselves as subjects to King Robert of Naples to get him to defend them, because they could not defend themselves. As a result, Florence fell prey to the rapacious tyranny of the duke of Athens. (See *FH* 2.24–26, 2.29–30, 2.33–37).

Machiavelli's contention in *D* 2.10 that "gold is not sufficient to find good soldiers, but good soldiers are quite sufficient to find gold" (148) can be read as a summary condemnation of the Florentine merchants' attempts to buy not only captains and troops, but also allies. The Florentines looked to the king of France both to defend them and to acquire other cities for them. In *D* 2.11 Machiavelli uses this policy to illustrate his admonition, "leagues that are made with princes who do not have either the occasion for aiding you because of the distance of their site, or the force to do it because of his own disorder or some other cause of his own, bring more fame than aid to those who trust in them" (150). And in *D* 2.12 he shows that there are advantages and disadvantages to be had by attacking other countries abroad or waiting to defend one's own at home. However, he concludes, "either I have my country armed, as the Romans had or as the Swiss have, or I have it unarmed, as the Carthaginians had or as the king of France and the Italians have. In the latter case the enemy ought to be held at a distance from home; for, since your virtue is in money and not in men, whenever your way of getting it is impeded you are done for" (153). To rely on money and trade rather than an armed people is to be unarmed at home.

As Machiavelli reminds his young Florentine republican readers in *D* 2.13, however, force is rarely if ever enough; as in *The Prince*, he insists that it is necessary to be a "fox" as well as a "lion." Indeed, he observes, some have been able to rise from a base to an elevated condition through fraud without force; but he also shows that fraud alone will not enable them to retain what they have acquired. Once again, he praises the way in which the Romans initially deceived the Latins and other neighboring peoples by pretending to make them "partners" (*compagni*), but using their arms to subdue others and gain reputation for themselves. But he now acknowledges in the incidents he cites from the Roman wars with the Latins in *D* 2.13–15 that Rome's "partners" did not remain deceived until it conquered provinces outside of Italy. On the contrary, seeing how the Samnites were constrained to an accord after they were twice defeated by the Romans, the Latins perceived their own servility and rebelled. Although the Latins initially attacked Rome only indirectly by attacking one of its allies, and the Romans tried to placate the Latins by not declaring war on them, neither people believed that they could hide their hostile intentions for long. Both understood that their future would be decided on the battlefield.

3. Using Roman Military Orders (*D* 2.16–18)

Indeed, Machiavelli declares, "the most important battle ever waged by the Roman people in any war with any nation was that which it waged with the Latin peoples in the consulate of Torquatus and Decius" (160). Since the Latins became servile after they lost, he reasons, so the Romans would have become servile if they had not won. Titus Livy agrees with this judgment, Machiavelli suggests, because he makes the two armies alike in every respect—order, virtue, obstinacy, and number—except that the heads of the Roman army were more virtuous.

*a. Maintaining Reserves to Fight Anew (*D *2.16)*

Rather than follow Livy by emphasizing the extraordinary sacrifices of the consuls, however, Machiavelli explains the way both the Latins and the Romans ordered their troops and the reasons they did so, because this is what his contemporaries need to understand. These ancient armies had three divisions. The *astati* in front were placed close together so that they could stand up to the enemy; but the *principi* behind them were more spread out, so that the *astati* could withdraw, if need be, into the ranks of the *principi* without disordering them. With fresh reinforcements, the merged lines could then renew the fight. The *triari* behind the *principi* were spread out even more sparsely, so that they could receive the first two lines, if they had to withdraw, and then renew the fight with fresh troops once more.[111]

111. Insofar as Livy shows that the Romans won the battle, because Torquatus kept his triari in reserve until the Latin troops were exhausted and then attacked, the "lesson" Machiavelli extracts from the history does not differ much from that Livy conveys about the character of the virtue of the Roman captains. Machiavelli notes the "two accidents [which] arose in the managing of this battle that had not arisen before of which there have been rare examples since" (160). But he does not urge his readers to duplicate the "extraordinary" acts of the consuls who made their troops obstinate by visibly sacrificing their own lives, as Decius did when he dressed in regal attire and plunged into the middle of the battle to remove any fears his soldiers might have retained because of the defective liver of the animal sacrifice on his side, or by immediately dispatching his son for disobeying his order not to attack the enemy (even though his attack was successful), as did Torquatus. Machiavelli does emphasize the importance of maintaining reserves, and it was his use of the reserves that enabled Torquatus to win the battle.

Because they have abandoned these orders, Machiavelli observes, Christian armies at his time do not have the ability to recover and force an enemy to defeat them not once, but thrice. Unable to withstand any but the first push, these armies lose easily for a variety of reasons. Because their captains do not know how to order their troops so that the back lines can absorb the front, these armies become disordered if they need to withdraw, especially if the enemy forces the cavalry back into the infantry. Machiavelli concedes that some contemporary captains maintain a tripartite organization of their armies, but he objects that they use the distinctions among the vanguard, battalion, and rearguard merely for commanding them in their quarters. They thus "imitate" the Romans in external ways without understanding how their orders worked or the reasons for them.

b. Well-Trained Men Are Needed in Addition to Artillery (D *2.17*)

His contemporaries try to excuse their ignorance by arguing that the introduction of artillery has made the use of ancient military orders impossible, so in *D* 2.17 Machiavelli disputes that opinion. His diminishing of the importance of artillery has been much criticized, but his critics seem to have missed Machiavelli's generally sensible main points by concentrating on the details.[112] The introduction of a new weapons technology does not make offensive expansionary wars (like those the Romans fought) impossible.[113] On the contrary, those who wish to wage offensive wars are more apt to invent new means of doing so than those who wish merely to defend what they now possess. It is easier to attack with weapons that fly through the air, moreover, than to defend against them. The use of firearms may appear to make it more difficult for men to show their virtue than in ancient times, because much of the fighting is done at a distance.

112. Such critics include Azar Gat, "Machiavelli and the Decline of the Classical Notion of the Lessons of History in the Study of War," *Military Affairs* 52 (1988): 203–5. Coby, *Machiavelli's Romans*, 132, points out that using the deep, tripartite orders of the Romans would make modern armies more vulnerable to attack by artillery. But such an observation does not invalidate Machiavelli's general point about the importance of being able to withstand an initial thrust. In the *Art of War* Machiavelli argues that the order of march (or attack) has to be adapted to the terrain and circumstances, and he explicitly incorporates the use of artillery.

113. Indeed, Felix Gilbert, "Machiavelli: The Renaissance of the Art of War," in *Makers of Modern Strategy from Machiavelli to the Nuclear Age*, ed. Peter Paret (Princeton: Princeton University Press, 1986), 15, observes that the military balance became heavily weighted in favor of the offensive, because medieval fortifications were vulnerable to artillery fire.

Nevertheless, personal courage and physical training are still required, because it continues to be almost impossible to take and hold territory without hand-to-hand fighting. Neither here nor in the *Art of War* does Machiavelli suggest that the introduction of artillery makes no difference. He admits that artillery is useful in an army when ancient virtue is mixed with it, but he denies that artillery or any other weapons technology can simply or completely substitute for virtue—training, experience, courage, and prudent leadership. To look solely to technology to provide for the common defense or to gain new territories is to hope to achieve with little expense and effort things that require a great deal of both.

*c. To Rely on the Infantry Is to Rely on the People (*D *2.18)*

Machiavelli's urging his contemporaries to follow the example of the Romans in relying more on the infantry than on the cavalry should be understood in its political context. In book 1 he showed that the plebs acquired their share of the government of the Roman republic only because they were armed and could frustrate the patricians' desire to expand their holdings by refusing to fight. And he observed that the Roman people remained uncorrupt only so long as they perceived a need to defend the fatherland. Machiavelli knew from personal experience that the oligarchs who controlled the Florentine republic were afraid of arming the people. In arguing that infantry or armed men are a more fundamental and useful element in an army than cavalry, he thus emphasizes the superior flexibility (or malleability) of men that makes them more capable of being trained and controlled, and so more useful, than horses or combinations of horses and men.[114] He also cites "the authority of those who give rules for civil things, where they show that at first wars began to be made with horse," but after they were introduced, ordered infantries were quickly seen to be more useful.[115] As with the artillery, he does not deny that cavalry has its uses. On the contrary, he affirms that horse are "necessary in armies to perform reconnaissances, to raid and prey upon countries, to follow enemies when they are in flight, and to be also in part an opposition to the

114. He makes similar arguments in *AW* 2.86–95.

115. E.g., Aristotle, *Politics* 4.1297b17–22, although Machiavelli characteristically does not name Aristotle.

horse of the adversaries."[116] But he insists, "the foundation and the sinew of the army . . . should be the infantry" (169).[117]

E. Why Modern Italian Republics Have Failed to Realize Their Imperial Ambitions (*D* 2.19–26)

Machiavelli traces the disastrous results of Italian politics to the erroneous opinions of their "heads." As in *The Prince*, so in the *Discourses* he blames "the sins of the Italian princes that have made Italy servile toward foreigners" (169).

1. Failing to Follow the Roman Example (*D* 2.19)

Rather than arming themselves and their peoples, these princes have transferred military affairs into the hands of "captains of fortune," who have chosen to employ a few horsemen, because they do not have the funds to pay a large number of infantrymen or subjects they can impress into service. The success of the ultramontane troops that have invaded Italy

116. Observing that several of the examples Machiavelli gives of Roman reliance on the infantry either were undertaken for nonmilitary reasons (the dismounting of the cavalry at Lake Regillus so the patrician equestrians would share the same dangers as the plebian foot soldiers, and again at Sora, according to Livy, to defend the bodies of their fallen commanders) or were defeats as of the armies of both Crassus and Mark Anthony on the plains of Parthia, where horse would have fared better than infantry, Coby, *Machiavelli's Romans*, concludes that Machiavelli has "at least exaggerated if not falsified . . . infantry's superior fighting qualities" (135). Indeed, Coby goes so far as to argue that Machiavelli's emphasis on the excellence of Roman means of expansion in general, as well as the role of the infantry is particular, is a "noble lie" (136–47). Machiavelli attributes to the Romans a degree of "civic virtue," i.e., the subordination of the interests and desires of individuals to those of the community, that they really did not have. In fact, however, Machiavelli admits that the Romans were defeated in Parthia. He does not argue that their reliance on the infantry (or any other tactic, military or otherwise) always produced victory. What he explicitly writes is that the authority of the Romans justifies "esteeming" or valuing the infantry more than the cavalry, and he uses his examples to show that the Roman captains trusted their armed plebian foot soldiers. It is precisely this trust that his Florentine (or, more generally, Italian) contemporaries lacked and that Machiavelli seeks to persuade them to acquire.

117. As Mansfield, *Machiavelli's New Modes and Orders*, observes: "Of the many examples 'one sees,' the first is the dismounting of the Roman cavalry in a battle against the Latins to come on foot to the aid of the hard-pressed infantry. . . . There are several instances of 'dismounting' in this chapter, which Machiavelli says the Romans always found the best remedy in their dangers. Livy says in this case that the spirit of the foot soldiers was restored when they saw the young nobles on equal terms with them (2.20.11); and beginning from this report we might imagine that for Machiavelli, 'dismounting' means laying aside authority and putting one's feet on the ground. It also suggests a way of 'going to the people,' and we should not overlook the obvious fact that infantry is the popular and the republican branch of militia, while the cavalry are distinguished by wealth" (243).

should have convinced Italian princes and republics "that all that is narrated about infantry in the histories is true," and that "they ought to believe all the other ancient orders to be true and useful" (172). Explicitly joining domestic and foreign policy, Machiavelli urges, "republics and princes would . . . be stronger in opposing a thrust that might come against them . . . and those who have in their hands a civil way of life would know better how to direct it," if they read Roman history as he has recast it.

> They would believe that increasing the inhabitants of one's city, getting partners and not subjects, sending colonies to guard countries that have been acquired, making capital out of booty, subduing the enemy with raids and battles and not with sieges, keeping the public rich and the private poor, and maintaining military exercises with the highest seriousness is the true way to make a republic great and to acquire empire. (173)

They would do what the Roman republic had done in effect to conquer Italy, and not continue to employ the expansionary policies of the Florentine and Venetian republics, which had not merely failed but bankrupted these modern republics.

2. Germany Does Not Provide an Alternative Model (*D* 2.19)

Because Roman expansion resulted in the loss of liberty everywhere but in Germany, Machiavelli recognizes, some of his readers might conclude that they ought to adopt the defensive policies of the German cities instead of the expansionary policies he has been advocating.[118] So he first reminds them of the fundamental reason he argued that Rome constitutes a better model of republican government than Sparta: in a world in which everything is always changing, a city will contract and disappear if it does not seek constantly to expand. Second, and more specifically, he explains that the conditions that allow the German cities to retain their freedom are singular and cannot be duplicated elsewhere. Those conditions include the weakness of the Roman emperor, who officially rules the region. His weakness and consequent poverty enabled the cities initially under his control to buy their liberty by agreeing to make small annual payments to him. Others like the Swiss openly rebelled, and the emperor did not have sufficient forces to restrain them. Nor did he receive much assistance from

118. Machiavelli might even seem to have been advocating such policies himself in *P* 10 and *D* 1.55.

the other princes in the region, because they were poor and envied his position. The region is thus divided into free cities and small principalities. They remain within their own walls and allow the emperor to adjudicate their differences, because they fear that if they try to expand, they will encounter and be defeated by the Swiss.

Machiavelli's readers might be tempted to ask why the pope, who, being unarmed, is even weaker than the Holy Roman Emperor, could not play a similar role in mediating the differences among Italian republics and principalities. The reason, Machiavelli suggests, is that there is no league or confederation of free republics in Italy equivalent to the Swiss in Germany, which makes other cities afraid of trying to expand their own territories. However, if the Florentines followed Machiavelli's advice by arming their people and forming a league with other republics in Tuscany, they could play such a role. An armed northern Italian confederation could not only defend the south from the French and German armies that had invaded from the north, sometimes at the pope's request. They could also, in effect, prevent the pope from calling in such troops or stirring up other conflicts among other Italian cities by making him depend on them to defend him, as Machiavelli indirectly suggests in the following two chapters (*D* 2.20 and 2.21).[119]

3. Not Knowing How to Make Friends or Thwart Enemies (*D* 2.20–21)

Arming the people is the first, necessary step toward organizing an effective republican foreign policy, but, Machiavelli reminds his readers, it is not sufficient. To follow either the Roman or Etruscan confederal model, it is also necessary to obtain allies. Rome had to defeat some of its neighbors on the battlefield before they came to terms. Like Capua, however, the weaker neighbors of a strong republic may voluntarily subject themselves to it in exchange for its protection. In other words, a republic does not—and should not—have to conquer all the cities nearby in order to expand. As the example of the Romans in Capua also shows, however, formerly free cities will remain subject to a stronger neighbor more contentedly and quietly if they are allowed to continue living under their own laws "under a dominion they do not see" (177). The leaders of the Florentine republic

119. Like the Capuans, the popes might be persuaded to ask for the protection of an armed republican league without literally being forced to do so.

have not been able to realize their imperial ambitions, because they have not learned that "government is nothing other than holding subjects in such a mode that they cannot or ought not offend you. This is done either by securing oneself against them altogether, taking from them every way of hurting you, or by benefiting them in such a mode that it would not be reasonable for them to desire to change fortune" (182).[120]

In other words, a republic should conduct its foreign policy on the basis of the same understanding of the necessities of ruling that Machiavelli recommended to princes in *D* 1.16. It should protect its people or allies from those who threaten to destroy them and thus show its utility or benefits. It should eliminate the peoples or parties that threaten to destroy it. Or if and when it is not possible to eliminate the threat (as in the case of its own people), it should either destroy the "heads" of the opposition or buy them off with such great benefits that they have little reason to resist. Most important of all, it should gain the trust and support of the people by seeing that they and their property are protected from potential oppressors, domestic as well as foreign.

4. Not Having Followed Machiavelli's Advice (*D* 2.22–26)

Unfortunately, Machiavelli observes, "in corrupt republics, especially in quiet times," the "excellent men" who understand these necessities "are treated as enemies, either from envy or from some other ambitious causes." Those chosen to lead either are selected because of a "common deception" or "put forward by men who wish for the favor rather than the good of the collectivity" (179). Machiavelli seems, indeed, to have himself and his exclusion from the government of Florence primarily in mind. Three of the modern examples he gives of important decisions made by inexperienced or imprudent leaders were made by other Florentines against his advice.

120. As Ardito, *Machiavelli and the Modern State*, observes: "Tuscany was Florence's manifest destiny, according to a gallery of Florentine civic humanists—Leonardo Bruni, Coluccio Salutati, Giorgio Dati, and Matteo Palmieri—all of whom would have agreed with Machiavelli when he wrote, 'A city that lives free has two ends—one to acquire, the other to maintain itself free'" (102). However, she also points out, "Machiavelli's critique of Florentine expansionism has been neglected by interpreters who view him as remaining within the civic republican tradition and Florentine imperialism. Such a view misses an important aspect of Machiavelli's thought that is novel, innovative, and creative. There was also . . . an aspect of the civic republic tradition that aspired to Tuscan hegemony. . . . It is with this tradition . . . that Machiavelli takes issue. . . . His awareness of new political realities, of the rise of monarchical states, and his direct experience in the Florentine territory enabled him to discern the weaknesses in received ideas and practices of territorial government. [He] found the traditional republican policies of subordinating subject cities dangerously outmoded" (104).

Had Pope Leo studied Roman history under Machiavelli's direction, he would not have listened to the counselors who advised him not to accept the alliance the French king offered when he planned to attack the duke of Milan, but to keep his troops on the sideline to fight the victor, believing that the victor's power would have been weakened by the fight.[121] The pope would have learned from the outcome of the battles between the Romans and the Latins that the victor seldom loses many men, and even if the battle lasts long and many die, the victor acquires a very great reputation that terrifies others. Likewise, if the Florentines had learned what Machiavelli sought to teach them from the example set by the Romans, they would have destroyed Arezzo in the wake of the rebellion of 1502 and thus made it an example that would deter others. Unfortunately, the leaders of the Florentine republic decided (again against Machiavelli's advice) to exile and fine some of the Aretines and take away all of their honors and former ranks, but to leave the city intact (and full of people now hostile to Florence). As Machiavelli advised princes in dealing with their peoples in *P* 20, so he now warns potential heads of republics that in holding cities they have captured, "fortresses are generally much more harmful than useful" (184). They are harmful, because they tempt rulers to oppress the people rather than to gain their support; and they are not terribly useful, because they cannot be maintained without the help of an external army. He also warns those who would attack a city they believe is weak because it is internally divided that they are apt to unite and so strengthen it in the face of an external enemy. Better to try to make oneself the arbiter of the opposed parties, as Florence did in Pistoia, than to arouse the enmity of the city as a whole by trying to subdue and make it subject, as the Florentines did with Siena.

Machiavelli suggests that the mistaken Florentine policies all arise from a combination of weakness due to lack of arms and an arrogant desire to appear to be stronger than they actually are. Prudent leaders avoid vilifying and abusing their enemies, he reminds his readers in *D* 2.26, because such empty words merely serve to make enemies more obstinate by arousing their hatred. Like fortresses, "using words of little honor against the enemy arises most often from an insolence that either victory or the false hope of victory gives you" (193). Once again, Machiavelli draws an example from his own experience. "In 1512 a Spanish army came into the Florentine dominion to put the Medici back in Florence and tax the city,

121. Machiavelli argued that the pope ought to accept the alliance in two letters on December 20, 1514, to the Florentine representative at the papal court, his friend Francesco Vettori.

brought by citizens from inside who had given them hope that once they were in the Florentine dominion they would take up arms in their favor." When the Spanish found no one there to greet or help them, and lacked provisions, they "tried for an accord, which the people of Florence, having become proud, did not accept" (194). It was not Machiavelli's ill-trained militia that lost Prato and brought the ruin of the state; it was the bad judgment of the Florentine people (or their leader and his patron, Piero Soderini, who did not accept the overture from the Spanish) that led to the fall of the republic.

F. The Character of Machiavelli's Advice (*D* 2.27–32)

As his analysis of the mistake Soderini made in not accepting the Spanish peace initiative shows, Machiavelli's criticism of the traditional Florentine policy of taking "the middle way" does not mean that he is unalterably and absolutely opposed to all compromise. What he opposes are weak, ineffective decisions based on inaccurate estimates of one's own forces in relation to those of the enemy. If a city does not have the power to destroy another, it must try to negotiate an agreement that will make the other city friendlier rather than more hostile and so preserve its own independence, if not its control over others.

Only as he nears the conclusion of what has been a generally unfavorable comparison of the foreign policies of the Italian republics with those of Rome does Machiavelli return to the point he made in the first two chapters of book 2: Rome does not in all ways or at all times constitute an exemplary model.

In *D* 2.28 he uses the Romans' decision to send the three young Fabii as ambassadors to urge the "French" not to attack the Chiusi as an example of "how dangerous it is for a republic or a prince not to avenge an injury done against the public or against a private person."[122] Not merely were these three young soldiers inept diplomats, "more capable of doing than saying, [who] put themselves among the first to combat" the French when they came to fight with the Tuscans. Even worse, when the French complained to the Roman Senate and asked them to turn over the three offenders "against the law of nations," the Romans did not punish the Fabii in any way, but honored them by electing them tribunes with consular

122. Machiavelli enunciated the same principle with regard to domestic policy in *D* 1.22 in criticizing the Romans' failure to punish Horatio for the murder of his sister, who wept for the death of her betrothed, partly because of his father's plea that he had saved the city.

powers.[123] The Romans thus unnecessarily and arrogantly provoked the incensed "French" to march on Rome.[124]

In *D* 2.1 Machiavelli disputed the pious Roman belief that their military successes were due only partly to their own virtue, because they were due partly to fortune as well. In *D* 2.29, however, Machiavelli follows Livy, paraphrasing where he does not quote, in attributing Rome's near defeat in the war that ensued to "the power of heaven over human affairs." It was "heaven" that "first made the Fabii err." Then it ordered the Romans not to take any of their usual precautions. They had already sent their most able leader, Camillus, into exile; and the tribunes did not levy the troops expeditiously or march out of Rome until the enemy was within ten miles. They had not set up a camp in advance, and their line of march was so thin and ill designed that the enemy was able quickly to surround it. The Roman army thus fled, most to Veii and some to Rome, where they left the gates open.

Livy's narrative shows that the Romans were so ill prepared to meet the Gauls because after the successful siege of Veii the plebs were no longer willing to elect patrician tribunes. Their tribunes had indicted Camillus for seeking to retake some of the spoils to honor his pledge to Apollo, and when his friends informed him that they would pay the fine, but could not prevent his being convicted, he went into exile. Having lost all fear of an enemy attack, or arrogantly believing that they could deflect it with little effort, the same tribunes failed to employ the usual remedies and precautions in defending the city.

Rather than emphasizing the corrupting effects of the loss of fear of external aggressors, as he does elsewhere, Machiavelli asserts here that "Fortune" judged it was necessary to beat Rome (as he will show at the beginning of the next book) in order to make her greater. So it "had Camillus

123. *D* 2.28; 196. Machiavelli does not report, as Livy (5.36) does, "The Senate . . . by no means approved the conduct of their own envoys; but though they admitted to themselves that the [Gauls'] demand was a fair one, they refused, where three men of such rank were concerned, to take what they really knew to be the proper action. . . . Accordingly, to avoid the responsibility for any losses which might result from a clash with the Gauls they referred the envoys' demands to the people for decision, with the result that the three guilty men, whose punishment was supposed to be under discussion, were elected as military tribunes" (*The Early History of Rome: Books I–V of "The History of Rome from Its Foundations,"* trans. Aubrey de Sélincourt [New York: Penguin Books, 1960], 382).

124. Machiavelli's use of "French" to describe the people then known as the "Gauls" (in contrast to Livy) reflects his contention later in *D* 3.43, "That Men Who Are Born in One Province Observe Almost the Same Nature for All Times," which he applies specifically to the French in *D* 3.26. Because they have not been well ordered or trained, like the Romans, he contends, the French continue to come into battles furiously, and then to retreat if they do not succeed with their first thrust. They could, however, be trained to keep some of their troops in reserve and thus to persist.

exiled, but not killed; made Rome be taken but not the Capitol; and ordered that the Romans not think of any good thing to protect Rome but later not lack any good order to defend the Capitol." And in 2.30 he again cites Livy's statement that Fortune had Camillus arrive with his army just in time to save Rome from using gold to buy off the French, who were like the Romans starving as a result of the siege, instead of defeating them with arms.

Machiavelli's explicit lesson, indicated by the title of 2.30 is that "truly powerful republics and princes buy friendships not with money but with virtue and the reputation of strength." So he again urges his contemporaries not to employ mercenary soldiers and try to buy allies, but to train and arm their own people to defend them. By reminding his readers that the Romans did not succeed merely because of such training, however, he reminds his readers that he is not urging them to imitate the Romans in all respects.

In emphasizing the importance of training and arming the citizens of a republic to fight in its defense, Machiavelli does point back to his own advocacy of such a policy in Florence and the defeat (he might say as a result of bad fortune) of the militia he trained. In light of his dismissal from the government of Florence and subsequent exile from the city, his warning his readers "How Dangerous It Is to Believe the Banished" (*D* 2.31; 202) has to look somewhat ironic. In contrast to other exiles, however, he assures his readers that he does not want to extend vain promises or hopes. By citing the example of Themistocles he suggests that, despite appearances to the contrary, he would not give aid to the enemies of the republic of Florence (even though his circumstances have forced him to seek employment with the Medici).

In describing the "many modes" in which the Romans seized towns in *D* 2.32, Machiavelli points out that "they guarded themselves from taking towns by siege, for they judged the expense and inconvenience of this mode to be so great as to overcome by far the utility that could be drawn from what it acquired" (203). He is recommending their early policy of fighting short wars nearby, establishing colonies, and then punishing cities who rebelled, by means of which they established their initial Italian federation. By acknowledging that the Romans were forced to turn to the siege (as they did at Veii, Capua, Carthage, Jerusalem, and similar towns), he reminds his readers of the corrupting effects of Rome's more spectacular victories and unrestrained imperial expansion. His concluding account of how the Romans used glory as both an incentive and a check on their captains in *D* 2.33 is similarly ambiguous.

G. On the Use of Knowledge, Discretion, and Glory (*D* 2.33)

The example Machiavelli gives of the way in which "the Romans gave free commissions to their captains of armies" seems to undermine the general contention indicated by the title of the chapter. After Fabius defeated the Tuscans near Sutri, Machiavelli reports, he did not consult the Senate or seek their authorization to pass with his army through the Ciminian forest into Tuscany. After they heard of his victory, the Senate nevertheless sent two legates to command the consul not to pass. When they arrived and found that Fabius had already passed through the forest and won his battle with the Tuscans, the legates were wise enough to celebrate his victory and not to reprimand him for not obeying orders he had not received. The Senate had not displayed the prudence Machiavelli attributes to them, however. By sending the legates to command the consul not to pass through the forest, the senators had not shown that they recognized that they did not possess the knowledge of the particular circumstances necessary to give good counsel, even though many of them were experienced in war. Nor had the senators shown that they understood that consuls would prosecute wars more cautiously and less vigorously if they did not think that they would receive sole credit for their victories. Machiavelli seems to be attributing his own reasoning to the Senate when he concludes, "they wished the consul should act by himself and that the glory should be all his—the love of which, they judged, would be a check and a rule to make him work well." Like "the republics of present times, such as the Venetian and the Florentine," the Roman Senate seems in fact to have understood it "otherwise" (207) by unwisely trying to regulate their captain's every move.

Conclusion of Book 2

At the conclusion of book 2 Machiavelli thus indicates that the Romans did not understand the reasons for the success of their external policies any more than they fully understood the excellence of their domestic modes and orders. Like the domestic institutions he recommends in book 1, so the foreign policy he advises his Florentine contemporaries to adopt in book 2 is based on his own analysis of the causes of Roman success. In order to maintain popular participation in the republic as well as to mount a successful defense, he urges his contemporaries to train an army of citizens or subjects able to mount short, intensive, repeated attacks on their neighbors—attacks that would persuade them to yield and come to terms. If Florence acquired the ability to defend itself, it could negotiate an alliance with its Tuscan neighbors that would enable them to defend themselves from the French, Spanish, and German armies that had invaded Italy. The formation of such a league, among the cities of Tuscany, if not of the Italian peninsula as a whole, would require some deceit (as did the Roman conquest). But the external power of the armies of the national monarchies along with the internal limitations of the decision-making abilities of a federation would effectively confine a Florentine league to Italy and prevent it from threatening to destroy liberty both at home and abroad the way the Roman Empire had. Confronted by such armies, the member states of the new confederation would also perceive the need to keep their people armed and ready to defend themselves.

In order to create and maintain such a league of free cities, Machiavelli has also suggested, it will be necessary to find and elevate leaders who, unlike most of his contemporaries, understand the art of government. But how can such excellent men overcome the envy or ambition of others that leads them to treat such men as enemies in corrupt republics? Didn't Machiavelli argue in book 1 that a victorious general like Caesar who acquires a popular following poses the greatest threat to the preservation of republican government? Didn't he urge other ambitious citizens to check the rise of any virtuous youth by vying with him for popular favor? Isn't that competition an expression of their envy and ambition? How can a republic acquire the leadership it needs without falling prey to a tyrant? That is the problem to which Machiavelli returns in book 3.

Outline of Book 3: What the "Princes" of Machiavelli's New Republic Need to Know

A. On Founding and Reordering (*D* 3.1–7)
   1. Why It Is Necessary Repeatedly to Return to the Beginning (*D* 3.1)
   2. Lucius Junius Brutus—Conspirator Par Excellence (*D* 3.2–5)
   3. The Difficulties Confronting Would-Be Conspirators or Refounders and How Those Difficulties Can Be Overcome (*D* 3.6–7)

B. Why Machiavelli's Contemporaries Find It Difficult to Imitate the Romans (*D* 3.8–15)
   1. Changed Circumstances (*D* 3.8–10)
   2. To Imitate Is Not Merely to Copy, but to Understand (*D* 3.11–15)

C. The Difficulty of Defining the Distinctive Virtue of a Republican Leader (*D* 3.16–23)
  1. The Problem of Envy (*D* 3.16–17)
  2. Winning Wars Is Not an Adequate Test (*D* 3.18–23)
    *a. Victory May Be a Result of Chance (*D *3.18)*
    *b. Both Harsh and Gentle Modes Work (*D *3.19–23)*

D. The Causes of the Fall of the Roman Republic and the Failure of Cincinnatus (*D* 3.24–25)

E. What Machiavelli's Contemporaries Can Learn from the Romans (*D* 3.26–34)
  1. The Source of Tyranny Is Competition for Economic Goods, Not Love of the Beautiful (*D* 3.26)
  2. To End Civil Dissension, It Is Necessary to Eliminate the "Heads" (*D* 3.27)
  3. Competition for Office Must Be through Public Rather Than Private Means (*D* 3.28–29)
  4. How to Solve the Problem of Envy (*D* 3.30)
  5. Military Training as a Mode of Moral Education (*D* 3.31–33)
  6. Why Glory Is Not Always a Reward for Public Service (*D* 3.34)

F. The Education Machiavelli Offers Future Leaders of Republics (*D* 3.35–49)
  1. The Danger of Putting Oneself at the Head of a New Endeavor That Concerns the Welfare of All, and the Role of an Advisor (3.35)
  2. Training Is Stronger Than Nature (*D* 3.36)
  3. How Troops Should Be Trained—or People Educated (*D* 3.37–38)
  4. The Knowledge a "Captain" Needs to Train His Troops (*D* 3.39)
  5. How Republican Leaders Should Keep Faith (*D* 3.40–42)
  6. How Human Nature Is Shaped (*D* 3.43–44)
  7. Fabius Rullianus as the Exemplary Republican Prince (*D* 3.45–49)

Book 3: What the "Princes" of Machiavelli's New Republic Need to Know

In contrast to books 1 and 2, Machiavelli does not begin book 3 with a preface in which he explains what he proposes to do and why. The reason he does not introduce book 3 with such a statement becomes evident if readers consider the logic of the argument he has been presenting. Machiavelli has explained what sorts of domestic orders should be instituted in a republic that would last longer than Rome and the kind of defensive policies that would protect the liberty of that republic without destroying it everywhere the way Rome did. He could now be expected to show his readers what they as private individuals could and should do to bring such a republic into existence and preserve it. If he had offered such advice directly and unambiguously to his young Florentine readers, however, he and they both could have been accused and convicted of conspiring to overthrow the Medici. In book 3 he thus proceeds much more indirectly and ambiguously to show his young readers what they need to do by demonstrating "how much the actions of particular men made Rome great and caused many good effects in that city" (212).[125]

A. On Founding and Reordering (*D* 3.1–7)

1. Why It Is Necessary Repeatedly to Return to the Beginning[126] (*D* 3.1)

Readers of *The Prince* (who, no doubt, included Machiavelli's young friends) might have taken away the impression that it is necessary to use force and fraud to seize power, but that once order is established rulers should strive to make their people forget the base origins of the governments under which they live.[127] In striving to teach his young readers what they have to do not only to found but also to maintain a republic, however, Machiavelli emphasizes the importance of having the people, who naturally do not want to be commanded or ruled, repeat the experience that led them initially to accept and obey a government. In describing the deeds of particular men that made Rome great, he thus emphasizes the effects they had on the people more than the character or lives of those individuals (as did Plutarch).

"All worldly things have a limit to their life," but mixed bodies such as sects or republics last longest if they have orders that enable them to be often renewed by bringing them back to their beginning. In *D* 1.1 Machiavelli argued that the beginnings of cities are to be found in the need a group of people perceives to come together to defend themselves from others, and

125. He again suggests that he will confine this discussion to the first decade of Livy's history, upon which he has supposedly been discoursing in the entire work, but he does not so confine his study in book 3 any more than he did in the preceding two books.

126. Like *archê* in Greek and *principium* in Latin, *principio* in Italian can mean either beginning or principle. Obviously it is also closely related to *principe* (prince).

127. A reader much later, Wolin, *Politics and Vision*, 2nd ed., 207, did.

that a city like Rome lasted as long as it did because of the "many necessities the laws made by Romulus, Numa, and the others" (*D* 1.1; 9) imposed on the people to arm and defend themselves. So he observes here that when republics are brought back to their beginning, as the Romans were by the French capture of the city, people see that it is "necessary not only to maintain religion and justice, but also to esteem . . . good citizens . . . and put aside all envy" (210).

Such salutary returns to the beginning can occur either because of an "extrinsic accident" or because of the "intrinsic prudence" of individual citizens. Since "extrinsic accidents" such as the French taking of Rome threaten the future independence if not very existence of the city, renewing the republic by means of the "intrinsic" prudence of individual citizens is obviously better. The first "intrinsic" way a republic can be brought back to its beginning is by means of laws and orders such as the tribunes and censors that checked the arrogance of ambitious individuals in Rome. As the examples Machiavelli lists suggest, these checks consist primarily in public trials he calls "executions" (even though not all the trials he lists resulted in the death or even conviction of the accused).[128] In *D* 1.7 he argued that such trials enable the people to vent their anger against individuals they think are trying to oppress them, but here he maintains that such trials remind people of the fearsome punishments they face if they dare to transgress the laws or try to innovate. In both cases he is reminding his readers that people do not want to be "dominated" or ruled and that they resent the individuals who impose order upon them. To return to the beginning or "first principle" of political order is thus to reawaken the fear that leads human beings to come

128. By dividing the "executions" between those that occurred before the French took Rome and after, Machiavelli underlines his contention that the effects of both internally and externally caused returns to the beginning do not last. Perhaps to emphasize the fearsome character of these "executions," he also exaggerates the number of deaths. Not all of the ten citizens were put to death, according not only to Livy (3.65–58) but also to Machiavelli himself (who reported in *D* 1.45 that Appius Claudius was not granted a right to appeal to the people and committed suicide the day before he was judged, and that the others were "condemned" and "punished," but not necessarily killed). Maelius the grain dealer, Manlius Capitolinus, and the son of Manlius Torquatus were publicly condemned and slain, but Fabius, the master of the cavalry, whom Papirius Cursor wished to slay, was saved by his father's appeal to the people. Machiavelli states merely that the Scipios were "accused." Scipio Africanus retired to the country and was excused from his trial by illness. His brother Lucius Scipio was later convicted of having taken money from King Antiochus that he did not turn over to the treasury, but they could not find evidence of the gold among his possessions, so Tiberius Gracchus released him from prison. Livy 38.50–60 reports that Marcus Cato sponsored the accusations. Machiavelli praises Cato for having brought what appears to be an unjust accusation. According to Machiavelli, such accusations were not brought against reputed citizens in Rome with sufficient frequency.

together and form a government to defend them. Indeed, he warns, if the people are not reminded every five to ten years of the fearsome punishments they face if they do not obey the law, they will become corrupt (or slavish, as he suggested in 1.16). But he also claims that if such reminders had occurred that frequently in Rome, the people and their republic would never have become corrupt.

Despite his initial acknowledgment of the transitory character of all worldly things, Machiavelli seems to be suggesting that a republic can overcome the limits of the existence of all worldly things—*if* it has a sufficient number and sequence of virtuous individuals. For, he emphasizes, it takes a virtuous individual to set in motion the laws and orders designed to check the arrogance of others.[129] He adds, moreover, that the virtue of a single man like Horatius Coclus or Regulus Attila can produce almost the same effects as the trials.[130] (Awe is akin to fear.) When he first discussed the problem of corruption in *D* 1.16–18, Machiavelli noted that a people would not remain uncorrupt for long under a series of corrupt "heads"; but he also stated that the Roman people remained uncorrupt so long as they felt threatened by foreign aggression. Now he suggests, not only do the people need to be frequently and repeatedly reminded of the reasons they ought to fear disobeying the law by seeing their leaders accused and tried of aspiring to overthrow the republic and establish a tyranny. The people also need to be reminded of the reasons why they ought to risk their own lives and families by serving in the army by seeing the individuals elevated to high office sacrifice theirs. Such sacrifices encourage others to imitate the virtue of their leaders, and witnessing the trials and sacrifices of their leaders helps the people overcome their envy.[131]

129. In *D* 1.30, 1.40, and 1.52 Machiavelli argued that the nobles constitute the best check on the ambitions of a potential tyrant, even though the people often do not see it.

130. The individuals Machiavelli names as "rare and virtuous examples . . . that good men desire to imitate . . . and the wicked are ashamed" to contradict are Horatius Coclus, who famously died holding a bridge until the Romans retreated to safety behind him; Scaevola, who thrust his hand into the fire to show Porcena how much pain and self-sacrifice Romans would endure; Fabricius, who convinced Pyrrhus to withdraw his army from Italy by revealing a plot to poison him, but would not accept a position of great honor outside of Rome as compensation; the two Decii, generals who sacrificed their own lives in battle so that their legions would be victorious; and Regulus Attilius, who kept his promise to return to Carthage and suffered a horrible death there, after he advised the Romans not to return the Carthaginian hostages.

131. In *D* 1.51, the example Machiavelli used to show that "a republic or a prince should make a show of doing through liberality what necessity constrains him to do" was the Senate's not only offering to pay soldiers in order to wage longer wars, but also levying the heaviest taxes on themselves (and so overcoming the opposition of the tribunes, who argued that the people would, in effect, pay for the wages they earned as soldiers with higher taxes).

The need to renew the respect people have for both the orders and the leaders of their community by returning to its beginning is not restricted to republics, moreover; it also applies to "sects" and kingdoms. By imitating the life of Christ in adopting a life of poverty, Machiavelli observes, the orders of Saint Dominick and Saint Francis prevented people from entirely losing faith in the Christian religion because of the misdeeds of the prelates.[132] But the effects of this particular return to the beginning have not been unambiguously good. By convincing people that they should accept the evils they encounter on earth and leave punishment to God in the afterlife, these monkish orders have been able to do the worst they can, because their members do not fear punishment they cannot see.[133] These monkish orders have preserved the Christian faith, but they have also undermined the salutary fear of punishment upon which the rule of law in both republics and kingdoms depends.

"Kingdoms also have need of renewing themselves" by bringing their laws back toward their beginnings; and Machiavelli again praises the French parlement as a means of producing such a good effect. In *P* 19 he argued that the court protected the monarch by enabling the people to check the nobles (with ambitions to unseat and replace him); but here he states that the court renews and revives the laws and orders of the kingdom by passing verdicts against the king as well as against the nobles.[134] In *D* 1.16 he argued that both the king and the people of France live secure, "because of nothing other than that the kings are obligated by infinite laws in which the security of all its peoples is included" (46). Now he suggests that the king's subordination to the rule of law has to be demonstrated to the people in public.

Machiavelli first praises the orders of the Roman republic that brought it back to its beginning by counteracting the ambition and insolence of men. Yet the common element in all three forms of "return" and "renewal" he describes here is the need for leaders to demonstrate their willingness to endure the most extreme forms of the restraints and burdens they impose upon others. By risking if not sacrificing their own lives, families, and

132. Like republican "princes," Machiavelli suggests, religious leaders persuade their followers that they are acting on the basis of their publicly proclaimed beliefs, and not for their own private benefit, by forgoing the advantages of wealth and position by living in utter poverty.

133. Machiavelli clearly indicated in *D* 1.11–15 that religious leaders do not—and cannot—believe what they preach, although they have to act as if they do.

134. In *D* 1.16 Machiavelli used the kingdom of France as an example to support his contention that if a prince makes orders and laws that guarantee the security of all as well as his own power, and "the people see that he does not break such laws because of any accident, in a short time he will begin to live secure and content" (46).

goods, such leaders convince their followers that they are acting for the sake of the community, not merely for their own private benefit, and so overcome the envy of others. But what makes such sacrifices worthwhile for the individual? The answer Machiavelli suggested in *D* 2.33 was their desire to win glory. But he indicates here, as he argued in 2.2, that if it is to have beneficial political effects, glory must consist in worldly renown, not a promise of justice or life after death that eviscerates men's interest in enforcing the law here and now.[135]

In the remainder of book 3 Machiavelli shows not merely that Roman commanders acquired glory in a variety of ways, but that their desire to win glory did not suffice to preserve the republic. On the contrary, as shown most dramatically by Julius Caesar, the desire of individual commanders to return to Rome in triumph culminated in the rise of a tyrant. The Romans did not understand how agitation over the Agrarian law and the prolongation of commands led to the fall of the republic. But now that these things are understood, Machiavelli promises, remedies can be found.

2. Lucius Junius Brutus— Conspirator Par Excellence (*D* 3.2–5)

As Machiavelli's first example of an individual whose deeds benefited Rome shows, not only is it necessary to elect leaders on the basis of their demonstrated merit for short terms of office. It is also necessary to eliminate those whose envy and ambition lead them not merely to oppose whoever is in power, but to try to overthrow the republican order.

Machiavelli can treat Brutus as someone who renewed the republic by returning it to its beginning, rather than simply as its founder, because, as he emphasized in book 1, Romulus had established an elected rather than a hereditary monarchy whose powers were checked by a senate. In *D* 1.25 Machiavelli used several of Brutus's innovations as examples of the way a reformer could obtain popular acceptance of changes by keeping the old names or appearances of offices while changing their powers. By using Brutus as his first example of a return to the beginning, Machiavelli indicates that by a "return" he does not mean simply a repeat.

135. Wolin, *Politics and Vision*, 2nd ed., 184, notes Machiavelli's insistence on the need for both political and religious bodies to return to their "*archê* or fundamental principle," but by failing to notice the difference in the effects of such a return in the two cases, he reduces both to mere rituals of renewal. As a result, Wolin also misses Machiavelli's insistence on the need for individual action to revive the fear that leads human beings to obey the law and suggests (211) that Machiavelli thinks that republican institutions make "princes" obsolete.

Machiavelli first praises Brutus for the prudence he displayed by pretending to be a fool so long as he did not have sufficient force to act openly against Tarquin. By simulating craziness, Brutus was not merely able to protect himself and his patrimony, as Livy states. He had public or political as well as private reasons for the pretense. By simulating craziness, Brutus could safely remain a member of the king's household and so be in a position to see and take advantage of the first opportunity to act against the tyrant. Indeed, Machiavelli argues more generally, an individual cannot act effectively in politics by trying to remain "above the fray" or seek to withdraw entirely from public life, as did both Socrates and Epicurus. A prince will suspect anyone of "quality" who does not openly declare himself to be for the prince of secretly scheming against him. So a prudent man will stay close to the prince—praising and doing things of which he does not approve—in order to remain in safety, if not to prosper along with the prince, and to be on hand to take advantage of any opportunity that arises of overthrowing him.[136] It is difficult not to regard Machiavelli's repeated protestations of his desire to serve the Medici in light of his interpretation of Brutus.

Machiavelli does not praise Brutus solely for concealing his intention to act against Tarquin until he was able to do so openly and effectively. He also extols the severity Brutus displayed in seeing that his sons were tried and executed for conspiring to overthrow the new republic. As in his initial discussion of the difficulties involved in a transition from a principality to a republic or vice versa in *D* 1.16 (except that he now calls the "principality" a "tyranny"), Machiavelli declares that "after a change of state, either from republic to tyranny or from tyranny to republic, a memorable execution against the enemies of present conditions is necessary" (214).

As in *P* 3, so Machiavelli urges here: "every prince can be warned that he never lives secure in his principality as long as those who have been despoiled of it are living." Repeating his criticism of Cesare Borgia at the conclusion of *P* 7, he also reminds his readers, "old injuries are never suppressed by new benefits" (216). In the *Prince* Machiavelli distinguished between "the

136. Machiavelli thus disputes Socrates' contention in the *Gorgias* 510b–511c that a good and just man would not try to preserve his own life by associating with a tyrant, because the association will require the just man to do unjust things and so become no better than the tyrant he serves. Machiavelli typically recognizes no such moral concerns for purity of character or intention; the relevant considerations are the safety of the individual and the possible public effect. He would, no doubt, remind admirers of Socrates that the philosopher who stayed away from the assembly was not merely accused but convicted of a capital crime.

great" who do not forget old injuries and the people who judge things by their appearance or results. He develops the implications of that distinction here in pointing out the contemporary relevance of his analysis of Brutus. He not only faults Piero Soderini for believing that "he would overcome with his patience and goodness the appetite that was in the sons of Brutus [aka Medici] for returning to another government"; he also criticizes Soderini for overestimating the respect people have for the rule of law.[137] Soderini feared that if he "took extraordinary authority" and broke up "civil equality together with the laws" in order to oppress his foes, the people would not allow another gonfalonier for life to be appointed, because they would conclude that the office created a tyranny. He did not understand that his works and his intention would be judged by the outcome. If he had used extralegal force to save the republic from its foes and lived long enough to manage the aftermath, he could have convinced everyone "that what he had done was for the safety of the fatherland and not for his own ambition." Moreover, he could have managed "things so that a successor of his would not be able to do for evil what he had done for good" (215).

Machiavelli's comments on Soderini let readers see that in praising Brutus, Machiavelli emphasizes his use of fraud and force, but does not mention the way he fought like a man, that is, with laws.[138] Romulus had

137. In *D* 3.4 Machiavelli makes the same criticism of Tarquin Priscus, who believed that his obtaining the monarchy lawfully from the people with the consent of the Senate would stifle the anger of the sons of Ancus from whom he had seized the kingship by means of fraud. In arguing that "a prince does not live secure in a principality while those who have been despoiled of it are living," Machiavelli seems to be making the same point he made in the previous chapter (as well as *P* 3). But stressing the overwhelming power of the desire for domination (and not mere safety or security), he adds, the "appetite for reigning is so great that it enters the breasts not only of those who expect the kingdom but also those who do not expect it. . . . Moved by this rage, against all paternal piety, the wife of young Tarquin, the daughter of Servius, . . . moved her husband against her father to take away from him his life and the kingdom—so much more did she esteem it to be queen than daughter of a king" (216). As Machiavelli showed earlier, the desire for domination is much stronger than family ties or affection (as ancient tragedies such as the *Oresteia* and Oedipus trilogy also demonstrate). And, he indicates here, it moves women as well as men. Making succession to the kingship hereditary does not make it smooth or noncontested any more than it guarantees good successors.

138. See *P* 18. Machiavelli's silence on Brutus's major institutional innovation, the annual election of two consuls by the Senate in place of the elected king, is not surprising, since he has already argued that the constitution of the Roman republic was incomplete or imperfect before the introduction of the tribunes. Machiavelli's emphasis on the importance of a single leader or "mind" in the original founding or "ordering" of Rome (*D* 1.9) as well as his emphasis on the importance of having a single commander in *D* 3.15 suggests that he did not think having two consuls was a good idea. That institution was based on the old Spartan model of having two kings (or generals), each of which could check the other.

slain his brother, whereas Brutus "merely" presided over a court trial that culminated in the execution of his sons. But Machiavelli does not mention this difference or his contention earlier that the Florentines should have established a public court in which Soderini and his critics could have aired their charges and have them judged. In using Brutus as an example of what it means to return to the beginnings, Machiavelli emphasizes the necessity of using both fraud and force to establish and maintain any government, including one bound by laws. However, he immediately reminds his readers that the fact that a "prince" needs to use force (or be armed) does not mean that he does not need to acquire and maintain the support of his people. And to do that, he must at least appear not merely to be enforcing the law against others, but to be obeying it himself. The requirements of founding or refounding a republic thus appear to be remarkably like those Machiavelli spelled out in *P* 6–19 for a prince who wants not only to acquire but also to maintain his dominion.

After praising Brutus for not revealing his intentions until he was able to act on them and for his severity in executing the opponents of the government he established, Machiavelli dismisses the traditional account of the expulsion of Tarquin the Proud: because his son Sextus raped Lucretia. Brutus was able to depose the king, Machiavelli argues, because Tarquin had broken the laws of the kingdom and governed it tyrannically.[139] By taking away all the authority of the Senate and forcing the people to labor on public works, the tyrant had made himself hated by the entire collectivity. "If Tarquin had lived like the other kings and Sextus his son had made that error, Brutus and Collatinus would have had recourse to Tarquin and not to the Roman people for vengeance against Sextus" (217).[140] Tarquin did not fall because of a moral lapse on the part of his son; he fell because he had lost the support of both the nobles and the people by not ruling according to law.

Tarquin's tyrannical use of his power may have created the conditions in which Brutus could depose him with the support of both the Senate and

139. Machiavelli thus suggests, as Locke argues later in his *Second Treatise*, chap. 19, paras. 218–20, that it is the prince who rebels against the government, not the people.

140. As Machiavelli observes both in *P* 19 and *D* 1.16, most people will be content with the government if it secures their lives and property. He does not admit here, as he does there, that this conclusion does not apply to "the great" (among whom we would probably include Brutus, if not Collatinus), some of whom will always be dissatisfied with the government in power and seek to overturn it in order to establish one in which they have more power and influence.

the people. But Brutus's restoration of the liberty of the Roman people did not prevent his sons from conspiring to overthrow the republic any more than it had prevented the sons of Ancus or the daughter of Servius Tullius from trying to seize the power of a legally appointed king.[141] In the longest chapter in the entire *Discourses* Machiavelli thus turns to discuss the reasons why human beings conspire against both princes and republics, why such attempts usually fail, but how and when they can succeed.

Brutus had traditionally been celebrated as the founder of the Roman republic, so it was appropriate for Machiavelli to begin describing the deeds of individuals that made Rome great with him. Had Machiavelli glorified Brutus as *the* example of the way in which an individual made Rome great, however, Machiavelli would have appeared to be encouraging his young readers to conspire against the tyrants who had overthrown the republic of Florence the way Brutus had conspired against Tarquin. Machiavelli thus blames Tarquin for losing the support of the collectivity, and states that he will discuss conspiracies "so that princes may learn to guard themselves from these dangers and private individuals may put themselves into them more timidly—indeed, that they may learn to be content to live under the empire that has been proposed for them by fate" (218). He also appeals to the authority of Tacitus, who described much worse conditions and tyranny in the Roman empire, for support.[142] Only in the brief chapter that follows his discussion of conspiracies does Machiavelli point out the parallel between "the change that Rome made from kings to consuls, where none other than the Tarquins were expelled" and "the state of the Medici in Florence, in the ruin of whom later, in 1494, none other than themselves were offended" (236). But in doing so he shows he has not forgotten the contemporary relevance of his lengthy analysis of the causes and effects of conspiracies.

141. Like Soderini, Machiavelli points out in *D* 3.4, both Tarquin Priscus and Servius Tullius believed that their positions were secure, because they were legally appointed and had the consent of the people. They also believed that they could overcome their opponents with new benefits or "kindness." Like Soderini, they were mistaken.

142. By referring repeatedly to the authority of Tacitus, however, Machiavelli does remind his readers of the terrible consequences of Caesar's seizing power. If they want to attain earthly glory, he urges them to take the opportunity of living in a corrupt city like Florence, "not to spoil it entirely as did Caesar but to reorder it as did Romulus" (*D* 1.10; 33).

3. The Difficulties Confronting Would-Be Conspirators or Founders and How Those Difficulties Can Be Overcome (*D* 3.6–7)

Machiavelli begins by examining the causes of conspiracies against princes. As in *P* 19, so Machiavelli here declares that the most important cause of such a conspiracy is the prince's having made himself hated by the collectivity, because their hatred encourages individuals who have been offended to act against him. As in *P* 19, Machiavelli thus warns princes against arousing the hatred of individuals by threatening them with death, dishonoring them and their families, or depriving them of an inheritance. But here he notes that another very great cause "that makes men conspire against the prince is the desire to free the fatherland that has been seized by him" (220–21). All these causes can be seen to have been operative in the case of Brutus.

Those who conspire against princes encounter dangers at all three stages: planning, execution, and aftermath. Anyone can kill a prince if he is willing to relinquish his own life, but few can be found who are willing to accept a certain death. Those who wish to live will need associates to protect them, but when conspirators inform others of their plans they give their hoped-for associates a means of ingratiating themselves with the prince by informing him of the danger and at the same time securing themselves from his wrath. All the conspiracies about which one reads in the histories have thus been undertaken by great men or those very close to the prince, because these alone have an opportunity to kill the prince, yet can hope to survive. Indeed, Machiavelli suggests, "a prince who wishes to guard himself against conspiracies should fear more those to whom he has done too many favors than those to whom he has done too many injuries. For the latter are lacking in occasion, the former abound in it; and the wish is similar because the desire to dominate is as great as or greater than is that of vengeance" (222). Although conspirators usually claim, like Brutus, to be acting on behalf of justice, Machiavelli suggests that ambition is an equal if not stronger motive. And sounding a theme he will develop further, a prince or leader should worry most about the envy of those closest to him, that is, the other members of the ruling class or elite.

Conspirators have often been exposed by report or by conjecture, because they have spoken imprudently before a household servant or acted in a way that revealed their intention. But Machiavelli points out a way to escape these dangers. If a conspirator communicates his intention to those whose help he needs only at the moment of execution (as Brutus did to Lucretia's husband and the other soldiers), they will not have an opportunity to inform the prince or accuse the conspirator.[143] Above all, and very relevant to his own case, Machiavelli warns, a conspirator should never put anything in writing that he cannot effectively deny. (The ambiguities or apparent contradictions in Machiavelli's text would have provided him with a ready defense against the accusation that he was conspiring with his young friends against the Medici regime.)

The dangers incurred in the execution (as opposed to the planning) of a conspiracy "arise either from varying the order, or from spirit lacking in him who executes, or from an error that the executor makes through lack of prudence or through not bringing the thing to perfection by leaving alive part of those who were planned to be killed" (227). All these problems beset the Pazzi conspiracy against the Medici in 1478. Yet, Machiavelli points out, although more than fifty people knew of the plans, no one exposed the conspiracy. It failed because they had to change the location at the last minute, the cardinal refused to share in a homicide in church, and an inexperienced assassin warned Lorenzo by saying "Oh, traitor," as he approached; as a result, they succeeded in killing Giovanni de' Medici, but not Lorenzo, who became the "Magnificent." Even though Machiavelli concludes that "everyone ought to abstain from similar conspiracies against many heads, because one does not do good either to oneself or to the fatherland" (230), he lists several examples of successful conspiracies against more than one prince. If it took so many missteps and accidents to defeat the Pazzi, a skeptical reader might conclude, a simpler plan revealed to fewer people might succeed against the same ruling family (although conspirators against the Medici would still have to take account of the reluctance some felt to act, if not literally in a church, then against men of the Church).[144]

The last danger conspirators face is that someone will be left to avenge the dead prince, as Lorenzo was left to avenge the death of his brother (and Tarquin was left in exile and thus able to conspire with Brutus's sons to overthrow the newly founded republic). The example Machiavelli uses of Madonna Caterina, who left her children as hostages in order to enter

143. To support his claim, Machiavelli uses the examples of Nelematus, an enemy of the tyrant Aristotimus; Darius in getting the other six princes to kill the Magian; and Piso, a friend of Nero.

144. In *D* 1.27 Machiavelli noted an (in)famous example of that reluctance in Baglioni's failure to kill Pope Julius when the tyrant had an opportunity to do so.

the fortress at Forlì, from which she then defied the men who had murdered her husband by showing them that she had the capacity to produce more children, reminds readers that family ties are not sufficient to overcome the desire to rule. However, Caterina did not succeed in securing her rule by sacrificing her children the way Brutus did, because she and her husband were so hated by the people. Machiavelli has repeatedly advised princes not to rely on fortresses to protect them from the hatred of their people; and here he concludes, "of all the dangers that can come after the execution, there is none more certain nor more to be feared than when the people is the friend of the prince that you have killed" (232). By using Caesar as an example, Machiavelli also reminds his young Florentine readers that the republic of Rome was not restored by the conspiracy led by a later Brutus, because Caesar was avenged by the people of Rome.[145] Machiavelli does not make a point that he emphasizes in the *Florentine Histories*—namely, that conspirators often hope that the people will arise to join and support them, but that a corrupt people like the people of Florence will not.[146]

The mention of Caesar leads Machiavelli to consider the dangers faced by those who conspire against the fatherland rather than against the prince, "in a republic where there is some part of corruption, for since one not corrupt has no place for a wicked beginning, these thoughts cannot befall one of its citizens." Yet he reminds readers two chapters later (in *D* 3.8) that such thoughts did occur to two leading citizens in the early "noncorrupt" Roman republic. Here he argues that conspiracies against the fatherland are less dangerous to conspirators than plans to assassinate a prince, "because republics are slower than a prince, suspect less, are thus less cautious and have more respect for their great citizens" (232, translation slightly emended). In a republic, individuals and parties are free to oppose the established government in public. The dangers arise almost entirely in the attempt to seize and overturn the government, because it is rare that an individual will have sufficient forces to subdue many citizens.

Nevertheless, Machiavelli points out, generals of armies such as Caesar, Agathocles, and Cleomenes have been able to seize their fatherland at a stroke. Others, like Pisistratus of Athens, have used fraud to obtain bodyguards to protect them; still others have used foreign armies. (That was

145. In *D* 3.18 Machiavelli nevertheless suggests that misinformation and chance had much to do with the defeat of this particular effort to revive the republic.

146. See *FH* 7.33–34, 8.8.

how the Medici, in effect, used the Spanish army at the gates of Florence to seize power in 1512, although Machiavelli does not include this recent example among his illustrations—all ancient—of the way in which such attempts may or may not succeed, according to fortune).

Having warned potential conspirators about the dangers they face, and shown them how those dangers can be evaded or overcome, Machiavelli concludes by warning "that prince or that republic that might be conspired against" to learn the quality of the conspiracy and measure the conditions and abilities of the conspirators in comparison to their own before they take action against it. If the conspirators are weak, they should be crushed without hesitation; but if they are strong, the government should temporize and dissimulate until it is strong enough to destroy its opponents. Machiavelli thus presents himself as arguing from the perspective of the established government, not as someone showing potential conspirators against it how they can succeed.

Changes of government, "from freedom to servitude and from servitude to freedom," are not always accompanied or accomplished by much bloodshed, Machiavelli points out in *D* 3.7. The amount of bloodshed depends upon whether "the state that is changed arises with violence or not, . . . and because when it arises with violence it must arise with the injury of many, it is necessary later, in its ruin, that the injured wish to avenge themselves" (236). Reminding his readers of the relatively bloodless changes effected by Brutus in deposing Tarquin and the Florentines in deposing Piero de' Medici in 1494, Machiavelli assures them that when a change of government occurs with popular support, only the previous "head" need be injured. Since the Florentine republic was overturned with little bloodshed, he suggests, the Medici regime that replaced it could also be overturned with a minimum of violence.[147] By emphasizing the need

147. Those "heads" in Florence would, however, include a cardinal and a pope and thus involve one of the difficulties encountered by the Pazzi conspiracy. In his "Discourse on Remodeling the Government of Florence," written at the request of Pope Leo X in 1520 approximately one year after he finished writing his *Discourses on Livy*, Machiavelli proposed to deal with this problem by granting the pope (Giovanni de' Medici) and the Cardinal Giulio de' Medici "as much authority during the lives of both as is held by the entire people of Florence" (*Machiavelli: The Chief Works and Others*, trans. Allan Gilbert [Durham, NC: Duke University Press, 1958], 1: 110), but creating a set of three councils, elected respectively from and by the most important, middle, and general bodies of citizens, to whom authority would devolve after the deaths of the Medici princes. As men of the church, neither the pope nor the cardinal could have a legal heir (although Machiavelli knew that popes like Alexander VI had tried to make their illegitimate sons princes of some of the papal cities they controlled). However, Machiavelli never seems to have received a response to his proposal.

"to kill the sons of Brutus" Machiavelli has nevertheless insisted that not merely some violence but public executions are necessary to establish a lasting republic. By pointing out the parallel between the relatively bloodless revolutions that established the Roman and Florentine republics, he has also called attention, be it indirectly, to the glaring contrast between the results. Whereas Brutus established a republic that lasted for centuries, the Florentine republic that replaced the Medici lasted only eighteen years. The reason that republic did not last, Machiavelli has almost stated outright, was that its leader, Soderini, did not understand the need to "kill the sons of Brutus." In the *Prince* Machiavelli suggested that a failure to understand the implacable hatred of their opponents was characteristic even of seemingly ruthless modern princes like Cesare Borgia. However, the more common explanation or response, especially among Florentine admirers of Rome like his dedicatees, would have been that unlike the early Romans, the people of Florence were corrupt. In the next chapter Machiavelli thus turns explicitly to the question of what an ambitious man can do with a corrupt people. And he shows in the chapters that follow that if a "prince" wishes to reestablish or reorder a republic, it will not suffice to seize control of the government. He will also have to reform the people.

B. Why Machiavelli's Contemporaries Find It Difficult to Imitate the Romans (*D* 3.8–15)

1. Changed Circumstances (*D* 3.8–10)

The first reason his contemporaries find it difficult to imitate the Romans, Machiavelli suggests, is that circumstances have changed. Claiming merely to be repeating what he said in *D* 3.6, Machiavelli begins *D* 3.8 by proclaiming that "a wicked citizen cannot work for ill in a republic that is not corrupt" (237). In fact, he wrote, "since one not corrupt has no place for a wicked beginning, these thoughts cannot befall one of its citizens" (232). Now he acknowledges that such thoughts did occur to Spurius Cassius and Manlius Capitolinus in the early Roman republic, but he emphasizes that neither the patricians nor the plebs would allow them to acquire the tyrannical powers they desired.

The two examples are significant, because they represent two of the causes of the fall of the Roman republic. First, there was the desire of both the patricians and the plebs to increase their wealth and, consequently, an unwillingness to share the spoils of war that finally produced civil war. Second, there was the envy that led the people not to elevate the best citizens to high office and so provoked the great to seek to win the recognition they believed they deserved by overthrowing the republic. Although Machiavelli does not state so explicitly, readers of Livy would know that Spurius Cassius was one of the first proponents of the Agrarian law that Machiavelli argues led eventually to the fall of the Roman republic.[148] Machiavelli does not remind his readers that Manlius Capitolinus's attempt "to make tumults in Rome against the Senate and against the laws of the fatherland . . . because of the envy that he had for the honors that were done to Camillus" (237) failed because it occurred in the wake of the French taking of Rome. That catastrophe showed the people "that it was necessary not only to maintain religion and justice but also to esteem its good citizens" (210). In other words, the patricians and plebs of the early Roman republic were uncorrupt not because of their "intrinsic" virtue so much as of an "extrinsic accident."

Had Spurius Cassius or Manlius Capitolinus "been born in the times of Marius and Sulla, when the matter was already corrupt and he would have been able to impress the form of his ambition," Machiavelli concedes, "he would have had the same results and successes . . . as others later who aspired to tyranny." Machiavelli thus warns the "potential princes" he is addressing "that one has to seek glory in a corrupt city by modes other than in one that still lives politically," and "that men . . . should consider the times and accommodate themselves to them" (238). The implication is that his readers cannot simply follow the examples of the great "captains" of the early Roman republic, because those captains were not dealing with a corrupt people like the Florentines.

However, Machiavelli observes in *D* 3.9, as he did in *P* 25, individuals cannot simply choose the manner in which they proceed. They have different inclinations by nature, and they will not vary from modes that have succeeded for them in the past. "Hence it arises that a republic has greater life and has good fortune longer than a principality, for it can accommodate itself better than one prince can to the diversity of times through the diversity of citizens in it" (240).

Machiavelli thus reminds his readers that the actions of particular men that made Rome great were achieved under the republic primarily, if not

148. According to Livy 2.41, the plebs did not accept the lands Rome had taken from the Hernici when Spurius offered them, because he also wanted to share those lands with Rome's allies. And "the fathers" defeated his attempt to win the plebs over by distributing grain brought from Sicily by convincing them that he was trying to become a king.

solely, by men elected to office. Since the consulate was the highest office, and consuls served primarily as generals, he discusses their actions as "captains." Whether as consuls or tribunes with the powers of consuls, they were elected to serve the ruling body, whether that was the Senate or the plebs. As Lefort emphasizes in his analysis of the *Discourses*, in discussing the role of a "captain" Machiavelli is analyzing the character of political as well as military leadership in a republic.[149] Discussing the problem in explicitly military rather than political terms makes his recommendations sound more technical, less controversial, and hence safer.

In *D* 1.20 Machiavelli argued that republics were superior to hereditary principalities precisely because they could elect different kinds of individuals as needed under different circumstances. But here he observes that "the ruin of cities also arises through not varying the orders of republics with the times," and that "they have trouble varying because they need times to come that move the whole republic" (240). In other words, elections are not sufficient to guarantee that republics have the leadership they need. The people have to be persuaded that they need to elect individuals able to respond to the necessities imposed by the particular circumstances; but by the time the people perceive the necessity, it is often too late.

2. To Imitate Is Not Merely to Copy, but to Understand (*D* 3.11–15)

The second reason his contemporaries have not been able to "imitate" the Romans, Machiavelli suggests, is that they have merely copied the externally observed behavior of the Romans without understanding the reasons for it or how it was related to the particular circumstances. As in the *Prince*, Machiavelli cites Fabius Maximus as a famous example of a general whose nature and experience led him to proceed cautiously. But, he now informs his readers, the example set by Fabius has been almost completely misunderstood by contemporary Italians. They have taken Fabius to represent the advantages of avoiding battle. So if Italian princes command their own troops, they do so only for show; and republics make an even worse error than the princes by entrusting their defense to others and not understanding anything that belongs to war. When "these idle princes or effeminate republics send out a captain," they send him with orders to guard against fighting, believing "that they are imitating in this the prudence of Fabius

149. Lefort, *Le travail de l'oeuvre Machiavel*, 628, 638, 642 (Smith trans., 368, 377, 381).

Maximus" (242). In fact, Machiavelli protests, just as "Gnaeus Sulpitius the dictator dragged out the war against the Gauls, [because] he was unwilling to commit himself to fortune against an enemy whom time and a foreign place were daily making weaker" (243), so Fabius avoided battle in order to wear Hannibal and his troops down and make them fight him under conditions of his own choosing. A general should follow the example of Fabius and Gnaeus Sulpitius only under these conditions, Machiavelli insists. Rome would never have defeated Hannibal if Scipio had not replaced Fabius as general. And if one takes an army into a foreign country, as Scipio did, one should expect to fight, because the enemy will defend himself.

If his Florentine readers were to adopt the imperial policy Machiavelli recommended in book 2, they would have to lead an army out. Imitating the Romans means fighting offensive wars, not trying to avoid battle.

A general wins most glory if he is solely responsible for a victory. Machiavelli thus begins and ends the next section of chapters (*D* 3.11–15) by pointing out the advantages of unitary leadership. In urging his contemporaries to adopt the tripartite Roman order of battle in book 2, Machiavelli argued that the fate of an army would be less subject to fortune if it were organized so that it could withstand and recover from the first thrust of an enemy. Here he applies a similar argument to the conduct of both domestic and foreign policy by an individual, small group, or political association. A unitary actor may initially be overpowered by the superior numbers of his opponents, but if he is able to withstand their first thrust, he will be able to divide them. To illustrate this principle, Machiavelli points not only to the way Roman senators were able to reduce the power of the tribunes by manipulating elections so that some of the tribunes would oppose others, as he described earlier (*D* 1.47–48).[150] He also shows how the principle applies to foreign policy when a nation finds itself isolated (as Venice did when all the other Italian powers opposed it, but was able to make special deals with individual members of the alliance and so separate them from it).

In *D* 3.12 Machiavelli suggests that one of the ways a "prudent captain" overcomes opposition is to make it necessary for his own soldiers to fight

150. In using the way in which the Senate manipulated elections of the tribunes by finding either extremely contemptible or virtuous candidates (cf. *D* 1.48) as an example of the way to deal with "very many," Machiavelli suggests for the first time that the senators learned this stratagem from Appius Claudius, the tyrant, who had shown (*D* 1.42) how easily men can be corrupted. Machiavelli thus concludes the chapter by emphasizing that "any prince . . . who is assaulted by many will have a remedy whenever he knows how to use with prudence suitable means to disunite them" (246). This principle would apply to a prince facing opposition from an aristocratic body as well as if not better than to that body facing the power of representatives of the people.

and easy for the enemy to surrender. What might appear to be merciful treatment, promising to spare those who put down their arms, proves to be a calculating means of achieving victory at the least price. "A prudent captain who has to go capture a city ought to measure the ease or the difficulty of capturing it from knowing and considering what necessity constrains its inhabitants to defend themselves." As he observed in *P* 3, "towns are more difficult to acquire after rebellion than they were in the first acquiring, for in the beginning they surrendered easily, not having cause to fear punishment because they had not offended." Explaining that "such obstinacy also arises from the natural hatreds that neighboring princes and neighboring republics have for one another, which proceeds from the ambition to dominate and from jealousy for their state—especially if they are republics—as happened in Tuscany," Machiavelli again indicates the way in which his advice to an individual who wants to obtain glory for himself applies to Florentine foreign policy. "Whoever considers well the neighbors of the city of Florence and the neighbors of the city of Venice will not marvel, as many do, that Florence had more expense in wars and acquired less than Venice. For it all arises from the Venetians' not having had neighboring towns so obstinate for defense as Florence has had, because all the cities next to Venice had been used to living under a prince, and not free" (247). Like Rome, Machiavelli suggested in book 2, Florence would have to acquire an empire of previously free cities partly by force and partly by offering them a somewhat deceptive alliance as equal partners. In order to make such alliance look more advantageous than complete independence, he also emphasized that Florence would need not only to muster and train an army composed of its own citizens, but also to allow her new "partner" to continue to live under its own laws.

In *D* 3.13 Machiavelli returns to the question of the relation between the one and the many by asking "which is more to be trusted, a good captain who has a weak army or a good army that has a weak captain" (249). He first cites Livy's judgment, based on the Romans' experience with Coriolanus, that the republic grew more by the virtue of its captains than that of the soldiers. But, Machiavelli reflects, the histories show that virtuous armies, deprived of their captains, have also won battles. Caesar thought that neither should be valued much. However, because a good captain can train a good army if given the opportunity, and "a good army without a good head usually becomes insolent and dangerous," Machiavelli concludes, "a captain who has time to instruct men and occasion to arm them is very much more to be trusted than an insolent army without a head made tumultuous by it." Leaving no doubt about the recommendation he is making to his politically ambitious young readers, he states that "the glory and the praise are to be doubled for those captains who have had not only to conquer the enemy but to instruct their army" (250–51). The leaders of the Florentine republic opposed and thus delayed Machiavelli's own attempts to muster and train a local militia not only to defend the city, but also to seize nearby towns like Pisa. If his young readers wish to revive republican government in Florence, he thus suggests, they will need not merely to seize control of the government from the Medici by means of a conspiracy. They will also have to overcome the corruption of the Florentine people by training them to defend themselves. If so, the reform or reordering of the Florentine republic would surely not occur, much less be maintained, "in a day." It was a long-term project.

Underlining his emphasis on the importance of training, in *D* 3.14 Machiavelli shows that promising strategies may backfire if troops are not trained to heed specific orders coming from an established line of command.[151] Because "new voices" or deceptive "inventions" startle troops, they may help a captain counter or gain an advantage over his enemy, but such devices are also apt to cause panic and disorder in his own troops so that the deception is easily uncovered. As in his discussion of the use of religious rites to inspire fear of failure in *D* 1.15, so Machiavelli concludes here that the superior training of Roman troops enabled them to overcome the fearsome illusions fabricated by their enemies. As in his discussion of the limitations of artillery, Machiavelli also insists that there is no quick or clever substitute for a well-trained army.

In *D* 3.15 Machiavelli summarizes the central lesson of his discussion of "captains" by arguing that "one individual and not many should be put over an army; and that several commanders hurt" (253). When a number of captains had different opinions about how to proceed and only the virtue of the soldiers protected them, the Romans appointed a dictator. Machiavelli points out that this is another lesson his contemporaries have not learned from the histories. "If one seeks the causes of the ruin of Italian and French armies in our times, one will find the most powerful to have been . . . sending to places more than one commissioner . . . to administer them better, which produces confusion beyond reckoning" (254). Machiavelli clearly prefers what in *The Prince* he calls a "civic principality,"

151. A point he emphasizes in *AW* 3.198–207, as well.

in which one individual is elected by his fellow citizens to lead the republic (when, as he emphasizes in the *Discourses*, different individuals are elected for limited, nonconsecutive terms) to the "aristocratic" rule of the few best, most educated, and virtuous citizens in a council or senate. Distrusting the rule of any one individual, such a body appoints multiple commissioners to execute its decisions.[152]

C. The Difficulty of Defining the Distinctive Virtue of a Republican Leader (*D* 3.16–23)

1. The Problem of Envy (*D* 3.16–17)

Why don't republics elect a succession of their most virtuous citizens as "captains" and so encourage these individuals to contribute to the common good by seeking glory for themselves? They claim (as in sending more than one commissioner to lead an army or administer a province) that more minds are better—or at least safer—than one. Republics would appear to be harbor the same suspicions of the motives of their captains or generals that Machiavelli argued the people of republics should have in book 1. But Machiavelli insists here that "great and rare men are neglected in a republic in peaceful times," because the reputation their virtue has given these individuals has aroused the envy of many citizens who wish to be seen not merely as equal but as superior to the great.

This neglect gives rise to two different problems. Not only is the republic deprived of the leadership of its most able citizens until a crisis arises (when it may be too late, because a general cannot train an army to meet a foe the moment it is needed). Angered not merely by the lack of esteem for their own virtues, but by the elevation of lesser men in their stead, worthy "citizens who see . . . that easy and not dangerous times are the cause of it strive to disturb them, starting new wars to the prejudice of the republic" (255).

At this point in the text Machiavelli claims to see only two remedies for the danger the envy of outstanding citizens poses to republics, both of which were employed by the Roman republic: "one, to maintain the citizens poor so that they cannot corrupt either themselves or others with riches and without virtue; the other, to be ordered for war so that one can

152. Once again Machiavelli thus explicitly rejects the Spartan model of the mixed regime. According to the Athenian Stranger in Plato, *Laws* 3.691e, a god must have blessed Sparta by having twin kings born from a single line, so that the Spartans continued to appoint two, each of whom served to check potential abuses by the other.

always make war and always has need of reputed citizens" (255). Since the Roman armies were always kept outside the city, Machiavelli points out, promotion was based on merit (not on what was pleasing to the people or the wealth and power of the individual in question)—until, after they had conquered Carthage and Antiochus, the Romans no longer felt a pressing need to defend themselves from foreign aggressors.[153] Neither of these remedies would be available to "captains" in Florence, however, unless they tried to redistribute wealth in a way Machiavelli showed in *D* 1.37 led to the downfall of the Roman republic, and unless the republic decided to arm its citizens. Machiavelli has shown, moreover, not merely that the first of these remedies was not simply or always available to the Romans, but that over time the second "remedy" undercut the first.[154] The success of Roman armies in conquering ever more distant lands led to increasing economic inequality in the republic and so to the escalating contention about the Agrarian law that eventually brought down the republic. In the next chapter (*D* 3.17) Machiavelli thus acknowledges that even before they defeated Carthage, the Romans had not been able entirely to overcome the danger to the republic posed by the anger of generals who felt that they had been dishonored.

After he had been outwitted by the Carthaginian general Hasdrubal in Spain, Machiavelli claims, Claudius Nero was charged with misconduct by both the Senate and people and was greatly dishonored and angered as a result.[155] Although Machiavelli praised the Romans for not punishing defeated generals harshly (e.g., by crucifying them, in *D* 1.31), he uses the example of Claudius to show that the anger a general feels if he is publicly

153. Machiavelli made a similar observation in *D* 1.18, but did not emphasize the role of envy in producing the corruption of the republic. At the end of *D* 3.16 he cites an example of the same corrupting tendency in the republic of Florence (after 1494, so under the effective leadership of Savonarola) to prefer using money to buy Pisa rather than recognize the outstanding virtue of an individual captain, Antonio Giacomini, who could have taken Pisa much more cheaply by force. The great example of a Roman "captain" who did not feel that he received the honor he deserved, sought to take it by force, and brought the republic down as a result was, of course, Caesar.

154. Indeed, Machiavelli has reminded his readers, both of these "remedies" had failed before the "French" invasion of Rome. Camillus, the only general capable of saving the city, had been exiled, because he had sought to deposit the spoils of his victory in Veii in the public treasury rather than divide them among the soldiers. However, Machiavelli argues, the Roman republic was reordered and revived as a result of that "extrinsic accident."

155. Mansfield, *Machiavelli's New Modes and Orders*, 368–69, shows that Machiavelli, in effect, manufactured the incident (and then only in one extant manuscript of the *Discourses*) in order to make his point. According to Livy, Claudius had not been dishonored. Instead of giving the explanation Livy (27.40.9) attributes to another consul who had been dishonored, Claudius tried to encourage his troops by telling them that arriving last on the battlefield, they would have almost all the glory.

dishonored by being accused of malfeasance makes it unsafe to employ him later. Concerned more about reestablishing his own reputation and glory than about the safety of the city that had dishonored him, Claudius chose to face and try to defeat Hasdrubel before he went to join the other consul in the marches to fight Hannibal. Asked why "he had adopted so dangerous a policy, whereby without an extreme necessity he had almost staked the freedom of Rome, he replied that he had done it because he knew that if he succeeded he would reacquire the glory he had lost in Spain; and if he did not . . . he would have avenged himself against the city and the citizens who had so ungratefully and indiscreetly offended him" (257). Contrary to his conclusion in *D* 2.33, Machiavelli now suggests that the Romans were not well advised to rely on a general's concern for his own reputation to make him do what was best under the circumstances, because he might try to enhance or salvage his reputation at the expense of the republic. Machiavelli declared in *D* 3.1 that a republic would never become corrupt if it had a sufficient number of citizens of outstanding virtue. Now he concludes that because it is impossible to "give a certain remedy for such disorders that arise in republics, it follows that it is impossible to order a perpetual republic, because its ruin is caused through a thousand unexpected ways" (257).[156]

2. Winning Wars Is Not an Adequate Test (*D* 3.18–23)

*a. Victory May Be a Result of Chance (*D *3.18)*

In *D* 3.18 Machiavelli shows that victory on the battlefield is not reliable evidence of a general's virtue. He suggests that he is going to discuss the attributes or abilities of an excellent "captain" in the title of the chapter, in which he states, "nothing is more worthy of a captain than to foretell the policies of the enemy." He immediately undercuts that observation,

156. In *D* 3.22 Machiavelli concludes that "if a republic were so happy that it often had one [such as Manlius Torquatus] who with his example might renew the laws, and not only restrain it from running to ruin but pull it back, it would be perpetual" (266). However, in that chapter he also argues that Manlius was harsh by nature and that only one who was like him could issue such harsh commands. Machiavelli does not think that such natural traits are passed on by heredity; in *D* 3.46 he observes that family traits are passed on by education more than nature, because heredity is mixed as a result of marriages. And in *The Prince* he argued that the classical attempt to educate a ruling class with the necessary virtues had failed. Ambitious leaders, he suggests in *D* 3.22, would try to attract partisans by ruling gently, at least initially, and thus constitute a threat to the perpetuation of the republic. In sum, there is no way of guaranteeing an unending line or succession of virtuous leaders. The most one can do is to institute and maintain laws that force ambitious men to compete and thus check each other.

however, not merely by erroneously attributing the saying to Epaminondas (who is one of Machiavelli's examples of an excellent captain, because he trained unarmed Thebans to become soldiers able to defeat the Spartans). He explicitly observes, "it is not so difficult to understand the plans of the enemy [since a general could think about what he would do if he were in the position of his enemy] as it is sometimes difficult to understand his actions, and not so much actions that are done by him at a distance as ones present and near." In what is now called "the fog of war" it is often difficult to determine who actually won or lost a battle. The opponents of Julius Caesar did not lose to the superior forces of his supporters, Machiavelli suggests. Cassius despaired when he erroneously believed that Brutus had lost on his wing and committed suicide. Likewise, the part of the Swiss army that remained whole when they confronted the French at Santa Cecilia thought that their forces had won and so remained to fight at a disadvantage the next day rather than retiring to save themselves.[157]

Machiavelli then gives two examples of equally balanced armies, one ancient and one modern, both of which have withdrawn because neither believes it can win a battle against the other. In both cases the side that accidentally discovers that the other has withdrawn turns around, seizes what spoils it can from the deserted camp of the enemy, and then claims victory. Clearly these "victories" were not proof of the excellence of the captain or his troops. As Machiavelli argues explicitly in a later chapter (*D* 3.31), victors attribute their good fortune to their virtue and then despair when their fortune changes. But if winning a battle is not necessarily evidence of a captain's virtue, what is? In all the examples Machiavelli gives in this chapter, the decisive factor was accurate information or knowledge about the condition of one's own troops as well as that of the enemy. The problem, as he noted at the beginning, is acquiring such knowledge in the midst of a war.

*b. Both Harsh and Gentle Modes Work (*D *3.19–22)*

What, then, makes a good republican "captain" or leader? By asking in the title of *D* 3.19 "whether to rule a multitude compliance is more necessary

157. Following Strauss, *TM*, 38–39; 303n48, Mansfield, *Machiavelli's New Modes and Orders*, 368–69, argues that the point of the comparison is to show that, believing in the power of fate, the ancients despaired too quickly, whereas modern soldiers, believing that there is a providence and that they will be saved, are too optimistic. However, in this section of the text Machiavelli appears to be discussing the difficulty of determining the distinctive virtue characteristic of *republican* leadership, not religion.

than punishment," Machiavelli indicates that his examination of the characteristics of a virtuous republican "captain" does not apply merely to military organization and leadership, but extends to political leadership more generally. Contrasting the difficulty the cruel Appius had in making his men obey him with the success of the kind and humane Quintius, Machiavelli first concludes "it appears that in governing a multitude, it is better to be humane rather than proud, merciful rather than cruel." However, he then observes that Cornelius Tacitus, along with many other writers, maintains, on the contrary, "in ruling a multitude, punishment is worth more than compliance" (260).[158] In order to "save" both opinions he draws a distinction. A republican "captain" leading an army composed of his fellow citizens, who regard themselves as his equals, cannot rely entirely on punishment or fear to make his men obey. In leading armies of men entirely subject to them, the emperors of whom Tacitus wrote could be harsh. Machiavelli immediately notes an exception to the "rule" he has just announced, however; a republican captain can be harsh and cruel, *if* he displays the "excessive virtue" of a Manlius Torquatus. In *P* 19 Machiavelli argued that an emperor like Severus also needed such "excessive virtue" to control both his troops and his people. But he repeats here what he argued in *P* 19, that even an emperor ought to moderate the cruelty with which he treats his subjects if he is not to become hated, and that he will most effectively avoid becoming hated if he refrains from taking any and every opportunity to seize their property. Readers see that in this section of the *Discourses* Machiavelli is reexamining in a republican context the question he raised in *P* 17 of whether it is better for a prince to be loved or feared.

In *D* 3.20 Machiavelli seems to tip the balance toward humanity or even charity. He reminds his readers how Camillus persuaded the Falisci, who had previously resisted the Romans stubbornly and fiercely, to surrender their town voluntarily by returning—stripped and beaten by his victims—the schoolmaster who had tried to give their children as hostages to the Romans. He then lists other examples of "how much more a humane act full of charity is sometimes able to do . . . than a ferocious and violent act" (261), including the way the liberality of Fabricius expelled Pyrrhus from Italy when Roman arms could not, and Scipio acquired more reputation

158. Although Machiavelli presents the opinion he attributes to Tacitus along with other writers as a quotation, Strauss, *TM*, 160, notes that no such statement appears in the works of that Roman historian. Like the egregious change he makes in Livy's account of Claudius Nero, Machiavelli's false attribution of this statement to other past writers indicates his judgment that they have not presented the problems of republican leadership accurately.

in Spain from returning a wife to her husband unblemished than from capturing New Carthage. Such acts of humanity are "desired in great men by peoples," Machiavelli observes; they have been "praised by writers, and by those who describe the life of princes, . . . how they ought to live." Xenophon, for example, "toils very much to demonstrate how many honors, how many victories, how much good fame being humane and affable brought to Cyrus, and not giving any example of himself either as proud or as cruel, or as lustful, or as having any other vice that stains the life of men" (262).[159]

In *P* 14 Machiavelli observed that the Roman republican "captain" Scipio had looked to Xenophon's depiction of Cyrus as a model. However, in *P* 17 he argued that Scipio's charity would have sullied his "fame and glory if he had continued with it in the empire; but while he lived under the government of the Senate, this damaging quality of his not only was hidden, but made for his glory" (68). Perhaps strangely in what would seem to be the republican context of the discussion, Machiavelli does not mention the subordination of the republican captain Scipio to direction and correction by the Senate as a reason he could be kind. As in *P* 17, so in *D* 3.21, Machiavelli uses Hannibal's success in using "cruelty, violence, robbery, and every type of faithlessness" in Italy to "produce the same effect that Scipio had produced in Spain" with his charity to challenge the traditional teaching of "the writers" about what sort of conduct and character is desirable in a "captain" or "prince."

The first reason the people in both conquered provinces flocked to the conquering general, despite the differences in their modes of proceeding, Machiavelli explains, is that "men are desirous of new things, . . . for [as he observed in *D* 1.37] . . . men get bored with the good and grieve in the ill." As he observed in *P* 3, "this desire makes the doors open to everyone who makes himself head of an innovation in a province" (263).

The second and most fundamental reason is that "men are driven by two principal things, either by love or by fear." And as Machiavelli had also argued in *P* 17, "most often whoever makes himself feared is more followed and more obeyed than whoever makes himself loved" (263). Instead of the humanity desired in great men by the people and endorsed by many

159. Machiavelli fails to note, however, that Xenophon shows that Cyrus began his career by corrupting the citizen soldiers of the republic of Persia by promising them a share in the wealth and power of the empire he proposed to conquer.

writers, Machiavelli thus seems to agree with the opinion he attributes to Tacitus and other writers.

Machiavelli first appears to explain the successes Hannibal and Scipio had despite proceeding in opposite ways by the virtue that made them reputed. However, he then concedes that after "his soldiers in Spain rebelled against him, together with part of his friends," because they did not fear him, "Scipio was constrained to use part of the cruelty he had fled from" (263–64). Machiavelli does not know of any particular incident in which Hannibal's cruelty and lack of faith hurt him, but he suggests that the Romans insisted on killing him, even after he was unarmed and his army dispersed, because he had been so hateful. Despite this disadvantage, Machiavelli points out, as he did in *P* 17, that Hannibal's extraordinary cruelty produced a great advantage, "which is admired by all the writers: that although his army was composed of various kinds of men, no dissension ever arose in it" (264).

Because the successes Hannibal and Scipio enjoyed by employing opposite means might be attributed to their different circumstances—Hannibal was commanding an army composed of many different peoples speaking different languages in a foreign land, whereas Scipio commanded an army composed of his fellow citizens—in *D* 3.22 Machiavelli takes up a better test case. Manlius Torquatus and Valerius Corvinus both lived in Rome at the same time, displayed equal virtue, and received similar triumphs and glory. In leading their armies, they nevertheless proceeded very differently.

Machiavelli first suggests that neither Manlius nor Valerius should be praised for his virtue, because neither chose to proceed as he did. Manlius was harsh by nature; because only a harsh man can command harsh things, a captain like Valerius, who did not have such a nature, could not imitate Manlius. Valerius could proceed humanely, Machiavelli explains, because the Romans he commanded were still a law-abiding people. Any punishments he inflicted on his men were imputed not to him but to the laws. However, since the willingness of the people in a republic to obey the law depends upon the ability of men like Manlius to return its orders to their beginning by making the people fear punishment, Valerius's ability to make himself extremely popular with his men by treating them familiarly as equals depended upon conditions established by men like Manlius. Machiavelli declares, "a republic so happy that it often had one who with his example might renew the laws . . . would be perpetual" (266).

Unfortunately, Machiavelli has shown that Manlius could not be imitated by someone who did not share his nature. The emergence of a line of such leaders would thus be a product of unlikely chance.[160] Nevertheless he states his belief that "in a citizen who lives under the laws of a republic, the proceeding of Manlius is more praiseworthy and less dangerous, because this mode is wholly in favor of the public and does not in any part have regard for private ambition. For by . . . showing oneself always harsh to everyone and loving only the common good, one . . . does not acquire particular friends for himself, which we call . . . partisans" (267).

Machiavelli acknowledges that Valerius's mode of proceeding did not hurt the public, but he warns, "because of the particular goodwill that [such a captain] acquires with the soldiers, many doubts resurge as to the bad effects on freedom of a long command" (267). Drawing once again on Xenophon's description of Cyrus, Machiavelli observes that seeking obedience and love from his soldiers and subjects is an appropriate mode of proceeding for a prince. Contrary to the first impressions of advocates of republican or democratic rule, he thus concludes that Valerius's mode of treating his men as free and equal is useful in a prince but pernicious in a citizen. It is injurious not only to the fatherland but also to the captain "because those modes prepare the way for tyranny . . . , [and] in suspecting his mode of proceeding, his city is constrained to secure itself against him" (268).

The harsh modes of Manlius may be better for the republic, but, Machiavelli concedes in 3.23, they can hurt the captain. As demonstrated by the Romans' decision to exile Camillus after he won a great victory over Veii, the people may recognize the virtue of a captain but still hate his severity. Livy reveals three causes for the people's hatred of Camillus: first, his depositing the money from the sale of the goods of the Veientes in the public treasury rather than distributing it among the soldiers as booty (a policy Machiavelli has praised); second, his having his chariot pulled by four white horses in his triumph, as if he were equal to the sun (for the Romans, a god); and, third, his attempting to take back booty the soldiers had already seized to satisfy a vow he had made to Apollo. In the *Prince* Machiavelli advised rulers to make themselves feared but not hated and warned them that nothing led people to hate a prince more than his seizing their

160. In *D* 3.46 Machiavelli argues that the tendency within families to cultivate certain traits cannot be a matter of heredity (or nature), strictly speaking, because of intermarriage. And he mentions the Manlii as an example of a family whose members shared a characteristic harshness. But he also recognizes that there were other families in Rome who cultivated other traits. He does not suggest that this private education would be sufficient to guarantee a line of republican leaders able to renew the laws.

property. Here he adds a particular warning to republican leaders: free peoples resent signs that their leaders believe that they are better than their fellow citizens, even though such displays of pride and pomp do not cause the people any material harm.[161]

Machiavelli's account of the different modes of leadership in a republic thus culminates in a problem. Harsh modes like those of Manlius may be best for a republic, because they make people and soldiers fear to disobey their commanders and the laws. Such harshness is not popular, however; both people and soldiers respond better to humane leadership. The people will come to hate even an admittedly virtuous "captain" like Camillus, not only if he tries to devote property they want to public or pious purposes (and thus keeps them poor), but also if he claims any visible recognition of his superiority or "glory" that does not come from the people. Machiavelli's lengthy discussion of the best way to rule a multitude thus seems to point toward his praise of "the poverty of Cincinnatus"; he was willing to use harsh means of conquering others, rewarded or punished his inferiors on the basis of their demonstrated merits, and did not seek either to enrich or to glorify himself. However, as Machiavelli announces in the next chapter, the admirable example set by Cincinnatus was not enough to save the Roman republic from eventual destruction. Readers are thus led to ask what policies Machiavelli thinks modern republicans could adopt to prolong the life of such a regime.

D. The Causes of the Fall of the Roman Republic and the Failure of Cincinnatus (*D* 3.24–25)

The prolongation of commands was, according to Machiavelli, one of the two causes of the dissolution of the Roman republic, along with the Agrarian law. The contention that arose over the Agrarian law was visible to everyone; it culminated in civil war, however, because of the prolongation of commands.[162] And, Machiavelli suggests, the importance of this seemingly

161. In *FH* 6.5 Machiavelli thus praises Cosimo de' Medici for the prudence that led him never to overstep "civil modesty. For in his conversations, in his servants, in riding on horse, in his whole mode of living, and in his marriage alliances, he was always like any modest citizen. For he knew how extraordinary things that are seen . . . make men much more envied than those that are . . . covered over with decency" (282–83).

162. Indicating just how distinctive Machiavelli's analysis of the fall of the republic is, Guicciardini, *Considerations*, concedes, "extending the term of military commands was unquestionably a great opportunity for anyone who wanted to seize control of the republic." But he reasserts the traditional understanding of the reason for the fall of the republic, as it was articulated by Cicero

minor institutional change was not understood by the Romans and has not been appreciated by readers of the histories ever since.

If the Roman patricians had shared the goodness and prudence of Lucius Quintius, who urged the Senate not to follow the bad example set by the plebs in prolonging the commands of the tribunes for a year to enable them better to resist the ambition of the nobles, Machiavelli observes, Rome would have been spared this "inconvenience."[163] When the Senate later agreed to prolong the commands of the consuls, in order to enable them to win victories in distant lands and then return to celebrate their triumph in Rome, he concedes, it was acting for the public utility. But its decision had unanticipated consequences: fewer men had an opportunity to exercise command and so gain a reputation; and the soldiers who served under them gradually became more attached to their commander than to the Senate. As a result, Marius and Sulla could form partisan armies, and Caesar was able to seize the fatherland. As Machiavelli emphasizes in the last chapter of his *Discourses*, small changes in electoral laws can either preserve or destroy a republic.

Machiavelli argued earlier (*D* 3.16) that he saw only two remedies for the envy that makes the citizens of republics not recognize their most outstanding citizens in times of peace: keeping everyone poor and constantly preparing for war. And in the central chapter of book 3—arguably the climax—he presents Cincinnatus as an embodiment of the excellence of these policies. Cincinnatus was plowing the fields of his small farm when the legates came to inform him that he had been elected dictator. Showing that he was not able to support himself and his family without working, but that he was still willing to subordinate his private concerns to public

---

and Sallust, when he insists that "the principal basis for the city's ills was its corruption: devoting itself to greed and to pleasure, it had so degenerated from its ancient customs that the city's bloody divisions were the result; among a free people tyranny always arises from these. That is why it was easy to corrupt citizens and soldiers, and someone like Catiline, without military authority and without troops, might hope to seize control of the republic; from this arose a conspiracy of the more powerful men to divide up the military commands and the armies among themselves and with these forces to keep the others down. Hence the extraordinary extensions of military commands like that of Caesar, who was given a ten-year command not because of some advantage to the republic or the needs of war or admiration for his *virtù* but because of his conspiracy with Crassus and Pompey to seize control of the republic" (3.24.1–3).

163. Machiavelli does not indicate in *D* 3.24 that this Lucius Quintius was known as Cincinnatus, because of his curly hair, and that he is, therefore, the exemplary leader celebrated for leaving his farm to serve the republic whom Machiavelli praises in *D* 3.25. Perhaps he expected his readers to know this.

needs, he put on his toga and went to lead an army to relieve the beleaguered consul Minucius. After defeating the enemy, Cincinnatus demoted the failed general to a legate and made a man who had been serving on foot because of his poverty master of the horse, on the basis of his demonstrated ability.

Machiavelli thus takes Cincinnatus to exemplify the Romans' policy of not encouraging the search for wealth by honoring virtue wherever they found it. Generalizing on the basis of the example set by Cincinnatus (and Marcus Regulus, who asked leave from the army to return to look after his own small property), he concludes that "it was enough to those citizens to get honor from war, and everything useful they left to the public." He goes even further by praising "the greatness of their spirit [that] lifted them above every prince. They did not esteem kings, or republics; northing terrified or frightened them." Yet "when they later returned to private status, they became frugal, humble, careful of their small competencies, obedient to the magistrates, reverent to their superiors" (272). In addition to the principle of rewarding virtue without regard to wealth, Cincinnatus thus represents the importance of rotation in office, accepting public duties when elected, but relinquishing power when he had accomplished his task.

As Machiavelli has already indicated, however, the virtuous example set by Cincinnatus was not enough to preserve the republic.[164] His unwillingness to follow the "bad example" set by the plebs reflected the old aristocratic understanding of the rule of the nobles as based on their superior character. It also reflected the traditional notion that virtuous rulers are educated primarily by means of the virtuous examples set by others. Yet from the beginning of book 3 Machiavelli has been suggesting that this old understanding of the education of leaders primarily through the imitation of virtuous examples (which he himself recommended at the conclusion of *P* 14) should be replaced by the analysis and understanding of the effects of their deeds (i.e., the "effectual truth" he began presenting in *P* 15). According to Machiavelli, Cincinnatus was right to object to the prolongation of the commands of the consuls in response to the plebs' prolongation of the commands of the tribunes. However, he objected for the wrong

164. Readers of Livy (3.13.10) would know that Cincinnatus failed to pass on his own virtue by example closer to home. The patrician Cincinnatus was poor because of a heavy fine exacted from him to pay for the misdeeds of his son. He was not at home plowing his own fields entirely as a product of his own choice.

reasons. He persisted in expressing the arrogance of the nobility; he failed to take account of the need to counter innovations introduced by the opposing humor and did not understand the way in which institutions mold the behavior of the individuals who occupy them, because he found such calculations or "power-grabbing" schemes base. Neither Cincinnatus nor the senators who later prolonged the consuls' commands understood the effect that prolongation would have on the loyalties of their men and the way these partisan armies would be used in a civil war motivated primarily by economic interests. But now that Machiavelli has explained these things to his readers, new remedies can be devised for the ambition and envy that resulted in the fall of the Roman republic. Those "remedies" consist, first and foremost, in a new kind of education for the politically ambitious.

E. What Machiavelli's Contemporaries Can Learn from the Romans (*D* 3.26–34)

As Machiavelli argues explicitly in *The Prince* with regard to leaders who want to acquire and maintain a principality, so he suggests in the *Discourses* somewhat more indirectly, leaders who wish to found or reorder a republic need a new kind of education. Praise and blame are not reliable indications of virtue and vice, because people praise what succeeds and blame what fails (*P* 3). And as he observed in both *P* 25 and *D* 3.8, 3.19–22, individuals with opposite characters succeed under different circumstances. Their characters differ, moreover, as a result of their natural inclinations and later experiences. It does not make sense, therefore, to try to educate or inculcate those who wish to rule with a given set of virtues—whether those are the classical "cardinal" virtues of courage, moderation, justice, and wisdom or the "theological" virtues of hope, faith, and charity. What those who want to become leaders need to learn are the passions that move human beings and how to direct them.

1. The Source of Tyranny Is Competition for Economic Goods, Not Love of the Beautiful (*D* 3.26)

Caesar may have grasped the honor he thought that he deserved by force, when neither the Senate nor the people bestowed it upon him voluntarily, as Machiavelli observes in *D* 1. But, Machiavelli has also argued, Caesar would not have been able to do so if a civil war had not erupted as a result of the contentions over the Agrarian law and the prolongation of commands had not enabled him to form and lead a partisan army.

In the chapter that follows his praise of Cincinnatus, Machiavelli thus reminds his readers that concern about honor (or eros for the noble, to put it in Greek philosophical terms) does not move men in politics as much or as fundamentally as the desire to acquire.[165] That was the reason the extraordinary examples set by individual nobles such as Cincinnatus or Regulus could not and did not preserve the Roman republic in the long run. (The deeds of these individuals were honored because they were extraordinary; but precisely because such men and deeds were extraordinary, they were not ordinary or usual on the part of men of their class.)

Earlier in the *Discourses* Machiavelli minimized, if not simply dismissed, the importance of the rape of Lucretia and the death of Virginia as causes of the deposing of Tarquin and the Decemvirs.[166] But in *D* 3.26 he cites these incidents along with Aristotle's warning to tyrants against injuring someone on account of women and his own warning to princes not to arouse the antagonism of individuals by taking their women or property (in *P* 19 and *D* 3.6) to show how states can be ruined "because of women." As Machiavelli's sole reference to Aristotle should remind his readers, the traditional philosophical explanation of the origin of divisions within cities in general, and tyranny in particular, was the excessive and intense desire or eros of human beings.[167]

Machiavelli challenges the ancient understanding of the source of tyranny, as well as the relative importance of honor and property, in his retelling of the story of the dispute that arose in Ardea concerning the marriage of a rich woman with which he begins both this and the succeeding chapter. In Livy's version of the story the woman was beautiful and so an erotic object; in Machiavelli's version it was her inheritance that caused the dissension between her tutors, who wanted her to marry a plebian, and her mother, who wanted a noble alliance. When the entire nobility took up arms in support of the noble, the plebs responded in kind; and after the plebs were defeated, they looked to the Volsci for aid, so the nobles sought assistance from the Romans. The Romans then vanquished the Volsci and restored unity to Ardea by killing all the heads of the sedition.

165. He explicitly argued as much both in *P* 17 and 19 and in *D* 1.37 and 3.6 when he observed that individuals come to hate princes who dishonor them or their women and seize their property, but that the latter is a stronger and more frequent cause.

166. *D* 1.17, 3.5, 1.40, 1.44, 1.57.

167. Plato, *Republic* 9.572d–573c; Xenophon, *Hiero*.

2. To End Civil Dissension, It Is Necessary to Eliminate the "Heads" (*D* 3.27)

The conflict that arose in Ardea constitutes an example of the division between the two humors Machiavelli observes in all cities: the opposition between the desire of the *grandi* or *nobili* to command and oppress and the desire of the people not to be commanded and oppressed. These humors exist in cities and not simply by nature, because they concern rule. Since those who rule can also seize the property of those they rule, the two humors also correspond loosely to the rich and the poor. However, Machiavelli regards the leaders of the poor who share a desire to command as *grandi* in aspiration, if not in economic class or explicit political allegiance.[168] The "lessons" he presents in how to establish and maintain a free government are thus addressed to such leaders of the people as well as to the *nobili* as conventionally understood.

Machiavelli's stated purpose at the beginning of the *Discourses* is to show his readers what they can learn from reading Livy's history that will be useful in their own changed circumstances. In book 1 he gradually showed them how the history of the Roman republic illustrated the ways in which institutions and laws could be designed to direct the conflict between the two humors so that it preserved the liberty of all. Because the cooperation between the Roman plebs and patricians was made possible by their joint participation in an imperial policy that culminated in the destruction of liberty everywhere, in book 2 Machiavelli advocated a new kind of expansive foreign policy that would enable republics to preserve their liberty, both internally and externally, by forming a league. In book 3 he is explicitly concentrating on the deeds of individuals and their effects. He suggests that he and his readers can understand the effects of the individual deeds and public policies of both the Romans and his contemporaries better than they did or do themselves, because he and his readers are able to compare past and present.

In *D* 3.27 Machiavelli thus contrasts the effectiveness of the Roman policy in Ardea with the Florentine belief "that one needed to hold Pistoia with parties and Pisa with fortresses" (275). Machiavelli criticized the use of fortresses to hold cities in both *P* 20 and *D* 2.24, because such fortifications led rulers to think that they could oppress the people without worrying

168. As Machiavelli's Florentine contemporaries and all later readers of his *Florentine Histories* would know, the Medici defined themselves as leaders of the people (*popolari*).

about arousing their hatred. In *D* 2.21 and 2.25, Machiavelli thus praised the Florentines for entering and acquiring control of Pistoia by means of the warring factions. Like the Romans in Capua, the Florentines had not had to conquer Pistoia with force in order to make the city subject to them. When the Florentines tried to rule Pistoia by forcing the two factions there to agree to a peace, however, they discovered that such an externally imposed agreement will not hold where there has been much bloodshed (cf. *D* 3.7). So the Florentines began removing the heads of the parties, either to prison or to some other place. Eliminating the heads permanently, as the Romans did, "would have been most secure." But, Machiavelli concludes, "because such executions have in them something of the great and the generous, a weak republic does not know how to do them" (274).

In *D* 2.23 Machiavelli criticized the traditional Florentine policy of taking "the middle way" by showing the superiority of the Roman policy of either eliminating or embracing subjects they had conquered. His emphasis here is not so much on the problematic results of "certain middle ways" as on the reason his contemporaries adopt such ineffective policies. When "princes of our times . . . have to judge great things," he concludes, "they ought to wish to hear how those who have had to judge such cases in antiquity governed themselves, but the weakness of men at present, caused by their weak education . . . makes them judge ancient judgments in part inhuman, in part impossible" (274–75). In his *Discourses* Machiavelli is trying to provide republican leaders of his time with a "strong" education to replace the "weak education" they have received by showing them it is possible not merely to imitate the ancients, but even to surpass them. And, we see, many of the "lessons" he delivers to aspiring republican "princes" in the second half of book 3 of the *Discourses* have a great deal in common with those he presented to "princes" in *The Prince*. Here, for example, the reasons he suggests that it is best to eliminate the leaders of the factions of a city that has been torn apart by a civil war parallel those he gave to a prince who has conquered a new territory to eliminate the bloodline of the old prince (*P* 3) and to use "cruelty" well (*P* 8) by using it all at once to establish order and not continuing to use it to oppress the people.

3. Competition for Office Must Be through Public Rather Than Private Means (*D* 3.28–29)

In *D* 3.28 Machiavelli suggests that his contemporaries could learn from the Romans how to deal with class conflict not only in cities they acquire but also in Florence itself. He reminds them that "when the city of Rome was overburdened with hunger, and public provisions were not enough to stop it, one Spurius Maelius, who was very rich" (276), sought to buy the favor of the plebs by providing them with grain privately. But seeing the "inconvenience" that could arise from his liberality, the Senate appointed a dictator (Cincinnatus, although Machiavelli does not name him) who had Spurius killed. As in foreign policy, so in governing their own city, a prince or political class who understands the art of government should know how to deal with ambitious men who seek to lead a popular insurrection. As Machiavelli observed in *D* 1.44, "a multitude without a head is useless."

In *D* 3.8 Machiavelli stated that, like Manlius Capitolinus, Spurius failed to overthrow the republic because the Roman people were not yet corrupt. But here and in the following chapter Machiavelli maintains that Spurius failed because the leaders of the republic then understood how to counter such a threat. Just as he observed in *D* 1.21 that "if where there are men there are no soldiers, it arises through a defect of the prince," so he argues more generally in *D* 3.29 that "the sins of peoples arise from princes," through their negligence or errors. In other words, the corruption or incorruption of a people depends upon whether their leaders see what is needed to order (or organize) them.

As Machiavelli suggested in his account of the fall of the Decemvirs in *D* 1.40–45, the preservation of a republic depends upon its having a political class or elite who know how to rule by sharing honors or offices with the plebs and checking the ambition of anyone who seeks to become a tyrant by flattering or otherwise acquiring popular favor. So he declares here, "A republic without reputed citizens cannot stand, nor can it be governed well in any mode." But "the reputation of citizens" or the ambition of these "reputed citizens" to become first among their peers, as he argued in *D* 1.46, is also the cause of the tyranny of republics. To "regulate this thing," he now explains, a city needs to be ordered so that citizens are reputed for acts that help and do not hurt the city and its freedom. And to institute and maintain such an order, it is necessary to distinguish the two ways in which citizens gain reputation: public and private. A city that wants to retain a republican form of government should make it possible for individuals to gain reputation only by giving good counsel and working for the common benefit. Private ways of benefiting this or that private individual "by lending him money, marrying his daughters for him, defending him from the magistrates, and doing for him similar favors that make men partisans to oneself and encourage whoever is so favored to corrupt the public and to breach the laws" should be closed. Rome rewarded public ways of acquiring a reputation by honoring individuals who worked for the common good and closed the private ways of acquiring a reputation by means of public accusations. "And if these were not enough, because the people was blinded by a species of false good, it ordered [the creation] of a dictator," as it did to counter the danger posed by Spurius Maelius.

Although Machiavelli does not mention it here, these were the measures he criticized Soderini for not taking against the Medici in *D* 3.4. Nor does Machiavelli explain, as he does later in his *Florentine Histories*, that both Cosimo de' Medici and his grandson Lorenzo the Magnificent used the "private modes" of "acquiring a reputation" he lists to acquire tyrannical power in what was nominally a republic in Florence.[169] But his immediate audience would surely recognize the implicit references.

To force ambitious "princes" to compete for office through public means is, in effect, to force them to serve the interests of their people in general. Those interests, Machiavelli reminds his young readers in *D* 3.29, are in securing their individual lives, families, and properties from those who would illegally seize them for their own benefit. The weakness of modern Italian governments is not the fault of the people, Machiavelli insists. It flows from the failure of Italian "princes" to understand the "art of government," which consists in eliminating those who would undermine the legal order and benefiting those whose support it needs.

Machiavelli indicates that some of the weakness of modern Italian governments can be attributed to their "weak" Christian education (as he characterized it in *D* 2.2) by writing about "the sins" of princes and peoples. But in *D* 3.29 he insists that the slaughter and pillage that occurred in provinces like the Romagna before Pope Alexander VI eliminated the lords who commanded there arose "not from the wicked nature of men, as they used to say" (presumably when "they" talked about "original sin"), but from the "sins" of princes.[170] Because these princes wanted to live like the rich, they made laws they themselves did not obey or enforce, except to collect penalties from other nonobservers. In *P* 7 Machiavelli explained that Alexander VI's illegitimate son Cesare Borgia brought good government to the Romagna by giving a cruel man, Remirro de Orco, full power to pacify and unite the province, in effect, by eliminating the impotent

169. See *FH* 7.5, 8.36.

170. Machiavelli also reminds his readers that there was at least one prince of the Church who not only recognized the necessity of eliminating his competitors, but also (in contrast to Savonarola in the following chapter) persuaded his natural son to eliminate them.

lords. But judging that such excessive authority was not necessary and might become hateful, after his competitors were eliminated Cesare set up a civil court and made the execution of Remirro a ferocious spectacle that left the people both satisfied and stupefied. Here he concludes by citing the behavior of a pirate who piously allowed the Romans to deliver the booty of the Veientes to Apollo as an example of Lorenzo de' Medici's restatement of the traditional idea "that which the lord does, many do later." By piously building churches, Machiavelli slyly suggests, the last great Medici lord not merely sought to justify his family's proclivity to seek wealth for themselves and impoverish the public. He and his family also encouraged others to put a pious cover on their own attempts to enrich themselves.

4. How to Solve the Problem of Envy (*D* 3.30)

In *D* 3.30 Machiavelli returns to the problem of envy, which he now makes clear is characteristic not of the people as a whole, but particularly of those who compete with a leader for reputation and position. As in *D* 3.1 he uses the elevation of Camillus after the French seizure of Rome to show how that envy is eliminated "through some strong and difficult accident in which each, seeing himself perishing, puts aside every ambition and runs voluntarily to obey him who he believes can free him with his virtue." But here (in contrast to his account of the problem of envy and the only possible responses to it in *D* 3.16) Machiavelli explains the willingness of other tribunes to subordinate themselves to Camillus not simply by the external danger, but by his having demonstrated his willingness to administer the office of dictator "for public usefulness and not for his own utility" (279) three times before. Because they had seen him relinquish power repeatedly, as required by law, Camillus's colleagues did not fear his greatness or feel it shameful to be his inferior. Such willingness on the part of exceptionally talented leaders to cede power, often to their opponents, at the conclusion of their term of office is absolutely essential, if a republican form of government is to be maintained. And, Machiavelli suggests, the only way to achieve the necessary rotations in office is by repeated examples of it that shape the expectations of both leading politicians and their people.

The other way to overcome envy is when "those who have been your competitors in coming to some reputation die" either by violence or natural causes. In a virtuous city organized as Machiavelli recommended in book 1, these competitors would vie with the popular favorite to show that they can better serve the public. But "men used to living in a corrupt city [like

Florence], where the education has not produced any goodness in them," compete for office more through private than through public means, and the opponents of those in power "would be content to see the ruin of their fatherland" rather than allow another citizen to rise above them. "To conquer this envy there is no remedy other than the death of those who have it."[171]

So if a virtuous leader is not fortunate enough to see his competitors die naturally, he will be forced, as "whoever reads the Bible judiciously" sees that Moses was, "to kill infinite men who, moved by nothing other than envy, were opposed to his plans" (280).[172] By contrasting Friar Girolamo Savonarola and Piero Soderini with Moses, Machiavelli points to the way in which Christianity makes modern leaders weak, not so much the priests themselves, who he has already claimed do not believe their own doctrines (*D* 3.1), as the laymen who adhere to the faith. Both Savonarola and Soderini recognized the necessity of eliminating their competitors. However, as a priest and not officially a prince with the power of the sword, the first did not have the authority to enable him to do it. And he was not understood by those who followed him, even though he railed against the "wise of the world" in his sermons.[173] The second "believed

171. Later American readers of Machiavelli's description of the ways in which "envy" can be overcome might think of George Washington, who, rather than become a monarch, decided to establish and maintain a republic by voluntarily relinquishing office after two terms, and of his secretary Alexander Hamilton, who seems voluntarily to have sought his own death by fighting a duel with the ambitious traitor Aaron Burr. For somewhat contrasting views of the relation between Machiavelli and these American founders see Matthew Spalding, "The American Prince? George Washington's Anti-Machiavellian Moment," and Karl-Friedrich Walling, "Was Alexander Hamilton a Machiavellian Statesman?," in *Machiavelli's Liberal Republican Legacy*, ed. Paul Rahe (Cambridge: Cambridge University Press, 2006), 167–88, 254–78.

172. A skeptical reader might observe that just as Cesare Borgia was able to blame the severe measures he used to establish "good government" in the Romagna on the harsh nature of his minister, so Moses was able to blame the deaths of those who opposed him like Korah (Numbers 16) on God.

173. In his letter to Ricciardo Becchi, the Florentine ambassador to the Holy See, on March 9, 1498 (*Machiavelli and His Friends*, 9–10), Machiavelli pointed out that Savonarola vacillated about the need to use violence in opposing his enemies. Fearing that the newly elected Signoria would be hostile to his party, in his sermon on March 2 the friar urged the congregation to do as Christ and Saint Paul had: "whenever the times call upon us to imperil our lives for Him, to do so; and whenever it is time for a man to go into hiding, to do so." Then he informed his audience that the time and God now require that the people rise up against violence, and "soldier" under God against their adversaries, who are the wicked and obstinate people who do not follow God. And explicating the same passage from Exodus in his sermon the next day, he urged his followers to behave like Moses when he slew the Egyptian. But after the newly elected Signoria sent a letter to the pope urging him not to excommunicate the friar, Savonarola concluded that he and his followers no longer needed to fear his adversaries in Florence. He no longer called for violent rebellion,

that he could overcome as many as were opposed to him through envy without any scandal, violence, and tumult. He did not know that . . . goodness is not enough." Machiavelli does not repeat the suggestion he made in *D* 1.49 that Savonarola and Soderini should both have used popular courts to accuse their enemies and defend themselves. (His reason may be that in citing the way the Romans dealt with the threat posed by Spurius, he has suggested that a popular court might not have been sufficient; it would have been necessary to appoint a dictator.) He concludes simply that both of them "were ruined, and their ruin was caused by not having known how or having been able to conquer this envy" (280).

By returning to the example of Camillus, who "never permitted a multitude to take up arms except with a certain order" (281), Machiavelli suggests that Savonarola and Soderini both failed to overcome the problem of envy because they did not select and train a group of armed men to enforce their decrees on those who opposed them. Both counted on the support of the people but allowed the people to remain a disorderly mob they could not reliably control. Savonarola did not remain in power long enough for his subordinate to organize the militia as he intended; and Soderini faced the opposition of many of the other *ottimati* when Machiavelli tried to convince him to sponsor the organization of a militia.

5. Military Training as a Mode of Moral Education (*D* 3.31–33)

In *D* 3.31 Machiavelli observes that not merely virtuous captains like Camillus but the Roman people as a whole were able to maintain their courage and dignity in defeat as well as in victory because they were well trained and educated. He contrasts them with the modern Venetians, who became so insolent in good fortune that they imagined themselves superior to the king of France and the Church, but then became so cowardly and abject after their luck deserted them that "they not only lost all their state by rebellion but gave a good part of it to the pope and to the king of Spain" (282). Pointing back to *The Prince*, he states, "although it was said another time that the foundation of all states is a good military, and that where this does not exist there can be neither good laws nor any other good thing, it does not appear to me superfluous to repeat it." Once again

therefore, but sought merely to set his followers at odds with the Supreme Pontiff as the wickedest man alive. Savonarola "acts in accordance with the times and colors his lies accordingly" (10), Machiavelli concluded. But the friar's followers might well have been confused by his vacillations.

he emphasizes the dependency of the rule of law on the ability to enforce it. At every point Roman history demonstrates this necessity, "and one sees that the military cannot be good unless it is trained, and that it cannot be trained unless it is composed of your subjects." Money or "private means" alone will not suffice to obtain the loyalty and service of armed men; as Machiavelli urged in *P* 9, the people must be made to see that they need the government of the prince to secure themselves from oppression.

Machiavelli again uses Camillus as his example of a prince who understood the importance of training men he selected to bear arms. He was able to encourage troops dismayed by the superior numbers of the enemy by reminding them of their past victories and observing that "what anyone has learned or is accustomed to, he will do" (283). As Machiavelli repeatedly observes, most people have difficulty imagining that things can be different from what they see around them; they are persuaded primarily by what they have experienced.

By the weak education of modern republicans, Machiavelli also indicates, he refers to more than their lack of military training. Because anyone "who governs himself like" the Venetians will become insolent in good fortune and abject in bad, a good education will not merely enable a people to govern itself better; it will also make an individual "a better knower of the world" (like the author of the *Discourses*) who will "rejoice less in the good and be less aggrieved with the bad" (283).

Machiavelli recognizes that leaders like Moses, Savonarola, and Soderini, who wish to bring new laws and thus found a new regime, do not need merely to eliminate the opposition. They must also obtain and maintain popular support. Training a militia is one but not the only way to do so. Another way, Machiavelli suggests in *D* 3.32, is to implicate a large number of people in the "crime" of rebellion so that they will resist any attempt to restore the old order from fear of punishment. This policy is the flip side of Machiavelli's earlier advice to a captain to do whatever he can to make it necessary for his troops to fight but easy for the enemy to surrender. It is nevertheless a policy of desperation.[174] Much better to follow the example of Camillus by showing oneself to be virtuous—ordered, solicitous, and spirited, upholding the majesty of his rank, punishing errors and upholding his promises to the people—and giving one's followers

174. In *FH* 3.13, he reports the speech of a leader of the Ciompi who urged them to such an explicitly desperate policy.

confidence by showing them an easy way to victory and making light of possible obstacles.

Having suggested that the weakness of modern republics can be attributed in part to the Christian education of their leaders (as he did in 2.2), in *D* 3.33 Machiavelli acknowledges that the Romans used religion to give their armies confidence. However, as in his first comparison of the political use and consequences of ancient and modern religion in *D* 1.11–15, Machiavelli again argues that the Romans relied more on the quality of their generals and the training of the men than on such "little things" as auguries. With a history of success a leader like Fabius (who was able to lead the Romans through the previously impenetrable Ciminian forest, according to Livy 9.36, partly because his brother knew the local dialect and could learn the way without alerting the locals, *D* 2.33) could simply claim to have secret (but not necessarily supernatural) knowledge. As in his discussion of the effects of the governments of the first three Roman kings, Machiavelli concludes that whether citizens are trained to be soldiers who have confidence (or faith) in themselves and their captain depends much more on the prince and his knowledge of the art of government than on their religious beliefs.

6. Why Glory Is Not Always a Reward for Public Service (*D* 3.34)

The best way to acquire and maintain popular support, however, is through elections. In *D* 3.34 Machiavelli thus returns to a question he explicitly sidestepped in *D* 1.60 when he acknowledged that Valerius Corvinus's claim that the Romans made the consulate "the ward of virtue, not of blood" would be very much disputed. The people may be able to distinguish good from vile individual candidates, as he maintained in *D* 1.47, and be less variable, imprudent, and ungrateful than a prince in distributing offices, as he argued in *D* 1.58; but this does not mean that the people recognize or reward true virtue. Like princes, Machiavelli observes, the people award offices to young men because of their family and friends, when they do not have actual deeds with which to judge an individual. Although deeds of extraordinary virtue (or difficulty) provide a better basis of judgment than family, and people can be as well advised as princes are about the relative merits and faults of individual candidates, Machiavelli also shows that the deeds that most impress people are more excessive and extraordinary than truly virtuous or beneficial to the republic.

Machiavelli uses the examples of the alternative modes of ruling harshly or humanely he described earlier to make his point without stating it directly. Although he has declared his belief that Manlius's harsh modes were more praiseworthy and less dangerous for a republic than the humane modes of Valerius, he now reminds his readers that Manlius first acquired reputation and office by threatening a tribune with death unless he withdrew the accusation he had lodged against Manlius's father. Manlius may thus have demonstrated his filial piety, but his act also constituted a challenge to the public accusations of leading figures that Machiavelli has argued serve to maintain the liberty of the republic, if not an outright violation of the law. Likewise, in the battle with the Frenchman from whom he took the collar of gold and thus acquired the name of Torquatus, Manlius risked the entire fortune of the Roman army on less than its whole force, "a thing altogether rash" (294) and a policy Machiavelli argued was unwise in *D* 1.23. Finally, although his killing of his son for fighting and winning a battle contrary to his orders may have made the Roman troops more obstinate, both Livy and Machiavelli attribute the victory Manlius won against the Latins as much if not more to his prudence in keeping his triari in reserve until the troops of the enemy were tired. Machiavelli observes, however, that "these three actions gave him more name and made him more celebrated for all centuries than did any triumph and any other victory, . . . [because] in those victories Manlius had very many like him [and] in these particular actions he had either very few or no one" (288).[175] In other words, Machiavelli shows, the people do not reward individual leaders with reputation or "glory" so much for their public service as for their extraordinary deeds. Likewise, he points out, all his triumphs did not bring Scipio the Elder "so much glory as having defended his father on the Ticino while still a boy, and after the defeat at Cannae, when with drawn sword he spiritedly made many young Romans swear that they would not abandon Italy." And "that opinion of him was further increased when he sent back the daughter to her father and the wife to her husband in Spain [with her chastity intact]" (289). Finally, admitting that the people might be tempted to elect someone inadequate, Machiavelli emphasizes the ability of any citizen to bring out the candidate's defects in a public council and win glory by doing so, as Fabius Maximus did when the people were moving toward making Titus Ottacilius consul. He does not remind his readers that in

175. Michelle Tolman Clarke, "The Virtues of Republican Citizenship in Machiavelli's *Discourses on Livy*," *Journal of Politics* 75, no. 2 (2013): 322–27, shows that Livy treats Manlius much less positively than Machiavelli does in *D* 3.22.

D 1.53 he argued that "many times the people desires its own ruin, deceived by a false appearance of the good," and that Fabius was unable "to persuade the Roman people that it would be useful . . . to proceed slowly in that war" (106). Because the people prefer spirited to cautious policies, the Romans did not follow Fabius's sage advice, but made Varro consul "through no merits of his other than to have promised . . . to break Hannibal" (107); and he lost the battle of Cannae, which might have resulted in the destruction of Rome.

Machiavelli contends that the people should be the final judge of both laws and individuals, because they seek outcomes that benefit most people most of the time. The people do not understand the causes of the effects they desire, however, and they confuse the rare with the excellent. Individuals who wish to establish new republican modes and orders need to understand not only what impresses the people and gets their support, but also that popular judgments of both individuals and policies tend to be erroneous in predictable ways. Those who share such an understanding will not be surprised to see the people make bad choices; they will try to devise strategies and design institutions to counteract dangerous popular tendencies. They will establish laws that allow them to live secure rather than seek reputation or glory from their contemporaries, who are apt to envy them (see *D* 2.Pref.), and hope that their achievements will be appreciated by later writers (*D* 1.10) who will celebrate the effects of their deeds.

F. The Education Machiavelli Offers Future Leaders of Republics (*D* 3.35–49)

1. The Danger of Putting Oneself at the Head of a New Endeavor That Concerns the Welfare of All, and the Role of an Advisor (*D* 3.35)

Machiavelli calls attention to the dangerous character of his own enterprise (as described in the prefaces to books 1 and 2) in *D* 3.35 when he discusses "what dangers are borne in making oneself head in counseling a thing." Like Fabius, he begins by claiming to have knowledge he cannot communicate: "How dangerous a thing it is to make oneself head of a new thing that pertains to many, and how difficult it is to treat it and to lead it, and when led, to maintain it, would be too long and too high a matter to discourse of." Machiavelli has been discussing just this matter since the beginning of book 3 when he introduced the example of Brutus, if not for the entire *Discourses*; but he has been doing so indirectly rather than directly. Instead of detailing the dangers his young readers will encounter should they try to act on his advice (which would clearly discourage them from doing so), he limits himself to explaining the dangers a counselor faces when he makes himself head of a grave and important decision in advising a prince (and so highlights his own role as "head"). As at the beginning of the *Discourses*, he acknowledges that an advisor will never receive all the honor for a great achievement. But, he now warns, "since men judge things by the end," the advisor will be blamed if not killed should the policy he recommends fail.[176] However, an advisor who does not tell a prince or republic what he thinks would be useful fails to perform his office. Nor can he secure his safety by remaining silent, because, as Machiavelli urged in *D* 3.2, in a short time he will become suspect. Out of a concern for his own and his readers' safety, Machiavelli explicitly recommends moderation, for the only time in either *The Prince* or the *Discourses*. He advises a counselor to state his "opinion and defend it without passion, . . . so that if the city or the prince follows it, it follows voluntarily, and it does not appear to enter upon it drawn by your importunity" (291). The advisor may thus avoid blame. He will not acquire all the glory of a success, in any case, because he will not be the one who carries out his suggestion; but he may attain a certain kind of glory, if those who act contrary to his advice fail. Machiavelli's advocacy of moderation here would appear to contradict what he said at the conclusion of the preface to book 2 about his being spirited in pointing out the vices of his contemporaries and recommending imitation of the virtue of the Romans to inspire his young readers. What he indicates at the end of his *Discourses* is that he has combined a certain kind of audacity (*D* 3.44) with a certain amount of reserve (*D* 3.45) in presenting a new understanding of republican politics merely as an "imitation" of the Romans, whom he not only praises but also criticizes.

2. Training Is Stronger Than Nature (*D* 3.36)

Reiterating some of the most fundamental principles he announced earlier in the *Discourses*, Machiavelli points to the thoroughly untraditional character of the education he is offering those who deserve to be princes in the last fourteen chapters. He begins in *D* 3.36 by asserting that training

176. Machiavelli's first example is the Grand Turk, who made an expedition to Syria and Egypt on the advice of one of his bashaws, whom he killed after his troops were destroyed by "those difficulties that had already brought many Roman armies to ruin" (290). A prince who had read the histories (as Machiavelli urges) would have avoided taking such bad advice, and thus he was to be faulted for his ignorance as much as his advisor. Cf. *P* 22.

is more powerful than nature (cf. *D* 1.1, 1.21; also *AW* 2.167, 6.12–18, 7.1–3). Contrasting the French, who enter battle furiously but fade because of their lack of order, with the ordered virtue of the Romans and the complete lack of either spirit or order among contemporary Italians, he observes that many believe that the French are this way by nature. He does as well, but he asserts that does not mean that their nature "cannot be ordered with art so that it maintains them ferocious to the last" (292).

Claiming "everyone understands with the testimony of Titus Livy how a good military ought to be made," Machiavelli quotes "the words of Papirius Cursor, when he wanted to punish Fabius, master of the horse" (293). Papirius contended that not merely all military discipline but all reverence for the gods would be lost if a soldier who disobeyed an order from his commander were not summarily executed. Contrasting this harsh message with the practices of contemporary Italians, Machiavelli does not remind his readers that Livy also shows (8.31–36) that Papirius did not persuade either his soldiers or the Roman people—even though Papirius appealed to the precedents established by Brutus and Manlius Torquatus in killing their own sons, precedents Machiavelli also seems at times to valorize. Indeed, Livy shows that Papirius came close to provoking a mutiny among his soldiers and popular rebellion in Rome, and that he was able to resume successful command of the army only after he resorted to a more humane policy.

In *D* 3.1 Machiavelli included "the execution of Papirius Cursor against his master of the cavalrymen Fabius" along with the deaths of the sons of Brutus and Manlius Torquatus among the "executions" that brought the Roman republic back to its beginnings by arousing fear of disobeying the law along with respect for religion and its esteemed citizens. However, he has subsequently shown that humane policies can win a "captain" as much glory as the excessively harsh measures used by Manlius Torquatus (*D* 3.22). Such excessive punishments and individual sacrifices do not always constitute the best policies for a republic (*D* 3.33–34), even though they impress the people more than a string of victories and so make the individuals famous. He concluded his discussion of the ways "to make the army confident both among themselves and in the captain," moreover, by recommending a means used by Fabius. In three of the last five chapters in the *Discourses*, he again explicitly argues that policies later adopted by the rebellious master of the horse should be emulated.

Machiavelli recommends the harsh discipline and orders of the Romans in contrast to the weak and vacillating policies characteristic of his Christian contemporaries, but he does not recommend Roman policies unambiguously or without qualification. On the contrary, with his praise of Fabius in the concluding chapters of both books 2 and 3, he points to the importance of doing what no one previously thought was possible and, more specifically, of recognizing the effects small changes in the law can have.

3. How Troops Should Be Trained—or People Educated (*D* 3.37–38)

Taking up the question of how troops should be trained, especially to face a new enemy, in *D* 3.37 Machiavelli shows that he is not simply recommending the policies of either Manlius Torquatus or Valerius Corvinus. Machiavelli has already repeatedly declared that it is foolish to risk the fate of an entire army or city by using less than one's entire force, the way Manlius gained his name by deciding a battle through single combat with a Frenchman. Now he explains that Valerius's attempt to make his troops confident by fighting small battles could have backfired by discouraging them had they lost. By praising Marius, the partisan captain of the plebs, for encouraging his troops by letting them see their fearsome enemies in disarray, Machiavelli reminds his young readers that he has also shown them that the forces they will have to fight (the Church and the Medici) are disunited and weak. By arguing in *D* 3.38 that "a captain in whom his army can have confidence" is one who, like Gracchus the Roman and Epaminondas the Theban, trains slaves to become soldiers capable of winning their own freedom, by accustoming them to obedience and order in mock battles (which they cannot lose and so become discouraged) so that he can "put them to work with the greatest confidence in true fighting" (297), Machiavelli also points to the way he has been "training" his readers in the *Discourses*. He teaches us the causes of military and political successes and failures by leading us through "mock battles" (without risk of failing) about the reasons why the Romans generally won and his contemporaries have so often failed.

4. The Knowledge a "Captain" Needs to Train His Troops (*D* 3.39)

When Machiavelli turns in *D* 3.39 to discuss the kind of knowledge a "captain" needs in order to train or educate others to win their own freedom, he seems to duplicate part of a similar discussion in *P* 14. There he declared that "a prince should have no other object, nor any other thought, nor take anything else as his art but that of war," and explained that this art is learned in two modes: with deeds and with the mind. Hunting was the way in which a prince would not only keep himself and his men fit, but also enable them to learn the countryside. They would exercise their minds by reading about the actions of excellent men in the histories. Here he states more modestly that "among the other things that are necessary to a captain of armies is the knowledge of sites and of countries, for without this general and particular knowledge a captain of armies cannot work anything well. Because all the sciences demand practice if one wishes to possess them perfectly" (297–98), both a captain and his troops need practice, and the practice through which this particular knowledge is acquired is hunting. However, both the examples he gives of what can be learned in this way come from (and thus presuppose) a reading of the histories (under Machiavelli's direction); and both emphasize the way in which a "captain" can use his knowledge to deceive his enemies.[177]

In *The Prince* Machiavelli emphasized the good or bad use of force or "cruelty," because he was urging his immediate addressee to organize an army to seize Italy and free it from the barbarians. In the *Discourses* he is addressing young Florentines who will have to conspire against the ruling powers, not only the Medici in Florence but also the Church in Rome, if they want to revive republican government. So in *D* 3.40 he generalizes his discussion of the benefits of learning the countryside by hunting by maintaining "that to use fraud in managing war is a glorious thing" (299). His extension of that argument to the reasons why neither a prince nor a citizen of a republic needs to abide by his promises or keep faith in *D* 3.41 and 3.42 thus has a double reference.

177. In the first example Machiavelli explains how Xenophon shows that Cyrus used the experience his men had in hunting to explain the roles both divisions of his troops were to play in ambushing the king of Armenia. Machiavelli does not mention the order Cyrus gave his captain not to risk his own energy and life, or those of his men, the way the captain habitually did in hunting, i.e., that the practice was not a perfect model for the real battle. Nor does Machiavelli explain that the captain was willing to obey because Cyrus had honored him by granting him command of half of the troops. Xenophon, *Education of Cyrus* 2.4.22–29. In his second example Machiavelli refers to Livy's account of the way in which Publius Decius used his knowledge of countries (without any account of how he had acquired it or reference to hunting) first to enable the Romans to escape a possible ambush by the Samnites by occupying a hill above the valley and then to find a way for his men to rejoin the army without the enemy's discovering them. Lefort contends that Machiavelli is showing that the methods of Epaminondas, who Plutarch says stayed home to train his fellow Thebans and preferred to study philosophy, were superior to the modes of his colleague Pelopidas, who sought fellow conspirators outside of Thebes and preferred hunting. However, hunting here, as in *The Prince*, is associated with learning the kinds of things Machiavelli himself teaches. Lefort, *Le travail de l'oeuvre Machiavel*, 670–76 (Smith trans., 407–12).

5. How Republican Leaders Should Keep Faith (*D* 3.40–42)

Machiavelli begins *D* 3.40 by voicing the noble opinion that "the use of fraud in every action is detestable." But Machiavelli's advice to princes, whether actual or potential, does not conform to traditional understandings of "nobility." He admits that breaking faith may enable someone to acquire a state or kingdom: in *D* 2.13 he argued that it is necessary and sometimes sufficient to use fraud for that purpose, but here he insists that it will never acquire glory for you, unless you use it against an enemy for the purpose of waging war. He cites the example of the Samnite captain who led the Romans into an ambush at the Caudine Forks by hiding his troops in the mountains and then sending some of his soldiers dressed as shepherds with a large herd into the plain to tell the Romans, when asked, that the Samnite army was occupied with a siege elsewhere. The Samnite victory over the Romans would have been glorious, he explains, if the captain had followed his father's advice either to let the Romans save themselves freely or to kill them all. However, he took the middle way, "which neither wins friends nor removes enemies" (Livy, 9.3), by forcing the Romans to make peace on dishonorable terms or be massacred, and lost all of the advantages that he might have gained.[178]

In *D* 3.41 Machiavelli reports that a legate convinced the Romans to save the army and accept the dishonorable terms by pointing out that the army could remove the ignominy by fighting another day, but if the army were destroyed, Rome and its freedom would be lost, even if the men died gloriously. This advice should be "noted and observed by any citizen who finds himself counseling his fatherland," Machiavelli emphasizes. "For where one deliberates entirely on the safety of his fatherland, there ought not to enter any consideration of either just or unjust, merciful or cruel, praiseworthy or ignominious, indeed every other concern put aside . . . to follow the policy that saves its life and maintains its liberty" (301).[179] There will be no justice, mercy, or glory for any citizen if the polity is destroyed.

Despite what he said about its not being glorious to "break faith given and pacts made" in *D* 3.40, Machiavelli makes it clear in *D* 3.42 that he does not think that individuals should worry about not keeping their word or

178. Livy, *Rome and Italy: Books VI–X of "The History of Rome from Its Foundation,"* trans. Betty Radice (New York: Penguin, 1982), 219.

179. To say that an advisor should not have any other concern does not, however, justify Viroli's conclusion that Machiavelli regarded his "fatherland" as a god.

abiding by their oaths. Initially he argues that "promises made through force ought not to be observed," because "when the force is lacking, forced promises that regard the public will always be broken and it will be without shame for whoever breaks them" (302).[180] But then he extends his observation to all promises "among princes, . . . when the causes that made them promise are lacking" (302). To discover whether such behavior is praiseworthy, he refers his readers to *P* 18, where he suggested that a prince can always find a reason not to keep his word. In *D* 1.59 he observed that republics do not keep faith with others any more or better than princes; they simply act more slowly.

In *D* 3.43 Machiavelli underlines the relevance of this advice to his dedicatees by pointing out, in the guise of blaming the French for their faithlessness, that the Florentines have repeatedly proved themselves to be too credulous. As a result, they have repeatedly been disappointed in their attempts to buy arms from the French. Machiavelli has just reminded his readers that "princes" can always find a reason not to abide by their agreements—unless they are forced to do so. Without their own arms, the Florentines have not been able to force the French (or the German emperor) to deliver the services or cities they promised.

6. How Human Nature Is Shaped (*D* 3.43–45)

At the beginning of *D* 3.43 Machiavelli seems to be emphasizing not only the constancy of human nature but also the utility of studying ancient history when he observes:. "Prudent men are accustomed to say, and not by chance or without merit, that whoever wishes to see what has to be considers what has been; for all worldly things in every time have their own counterpart in ancient times, . . . because these are the work of men, who have and always had the same passions, and they must of necessity result in the same effect" (302). As he noted in the preface to book 2, these "works

180. Augustine praised Regulus Attilius for keeping his word or faith with the Carthaginians when he returned to Carthage from Rome, where he would have been safe, and suffered a horrible death because he had advised the Romans not to return the Carthaginian hostages they had taken in exchange for his life. In *D* 3.1 Machiavelli lists Regulus among the individuals whose virtue had almost the same effect on his fellow citizens as a public execution. However, the only specific action of Regulus to which Machiavelli explicitly refers is his asking permission to return home to take care of his villa, showing that he like Cincinnatus had not become wealthy as a result of his leading victorious Roman armies. Clarke, "Virtues of Republican Citizenship," 317–28, shows that Machiavelli departed markedly from the premium that Romans such as Cicero put on keeping faith and showing gratitude.

are more virtuous now in this province than in that," and he now explains that they vary according to the form of education the people in question have adopted. The Florentines have suffered because they have been badly educated. The problem with their education is not simply that it is Christian, however; the French are Christians as well. The problem, as Machiavelli emphasizes in *The Prince,* is that the Florentines have not known how to fight—either by using bestial modes of force and fraud or by using the more human means, laws. He is trying to teach his young readers how to employ all three.

As in his account of the way in which a conspirator can obtain the cooperation of others by forcing them to decide to act with or against him on the spot, without time for deliberation, so Machiavelli argues in *D* 3.44 that "one often obtains with impetuosity and audacity what one would never have obtained through ordinary modes" (304). Julius II again provides him with his central example. But in *D* 3.45 Machiavelli reasserts (as he did in *D* 2.16 and 3.11) that it is a better policy to be able "to resist the thrust of enemies and, having resisted it, to charge them." In particular, Machiavelli points out that by resisting the enemy but reserving his strength until the enemy had lost its first ardor for combat, Fabius fared much better than did his fellow consul. Decius "exhausted himself in his first thrusts, so that seeing his band of men turned around, . . . he sacrificed himself to the Roman legions in imitation of his father, so as to acquire with death, the glory he had been unable to attain with victory" (305–6).

The contrast Machiavelli draws here between Fabius and Decius is the same as that he and Livy both drew between Manlius Torquatus and the elder Decius in the decisive battle with the Latins (cf. *D* 2.16, Livy 8.6–11). The difference is that in this case the more prudent policy is not associated with a harsh punishment. Machiavelli uses the difference in this context to indicate that true virtue consists not in pious self-sacrifice of the kind that won individual Romans much glory, but in devising prudent policies that serve to preserve a republic without risking one's own life.

In imitating his father, Decius provides Machiavelli with an example of the way not merely cities but specific families within cities inculcate certain traits by forming the opinions and habits of their young at an early age. "These things cannot arise solely from the bloodline," Machiavelli points out in *D* 3.46, "because that must vary through the diversity of marriages" (306). In other words, the "nobility" of the families who ruled Florence (like that of the patrician families who ruled Rome) was not inherent or a product of their nature. The dominant traits of the noble families were passed on by means of a certain kind of training or education; and by emphasizing the example of the Appii, Machiavelli suggests that the dominant characteristic produced by their "noble" education was arrogance. The source of that arrogance was the claim to have a better origin or beginning that not merely entitled the "nobles" to rule, but made them unwilling to submit to the will of the people, despite the goodness and humanity an "infinite" number of ordinary citizens had acquired by obeying the laws and respecting the auspices.

7. Fabius Rullianus as the Exemplary Republican Prince (*D* 3.45–49)

To be sure, the two Decii represent better examples of nobility than the Appii; in *D* 3.1 Machiavelli included them among the "rare and virtuous examples" that had produced almost the same effect as public executions in returning the republic to its beginnings. Yet in *D* 3.45 Machiavelli argues that Fabius, the master of the horse who defied Papirius Cursor's command not to fight while he traveled to Rome to check the auspices, and later won another great victory by marching through the Ciminian forest, contrary to the Senate's command (*D* 2.33), represents a better because more prudent form of republican leadership.

And in *D* 3.47 Machiavelli puts Fabius forward again as an example for all those who seek to be held good citizens, because he agreed, when consul, to allow the Senate to send Papirius Cursor as dictator against the Samnites. In *D* 1.34 Machiavelli praised the Roman policy of requiring the consuls to approve the appointment of a dictator, because the consuls were the officials particularly shamed by the need to create a superior commanding officer. But in this case, Fabius was agreeing not merely to the Senate's determination that it was necessary to appoint a superior, but to the appointment of the individual who had tried to execute Fabius the last time he served under him as dictator (and who would now be in a position to order such an execution again, if he chose). Machiavelli indicates, however, that Fabius did not merely "turn the other cheek." On the contrary, "by being silent and in many other modes he gave sign that such a nomination grieved him" (307). The kind of republican virtue Machiavelli is advocating is no more Christian than it is classically Roman. Fabius did not forgive or forget the wrong Papirius would have done him, but his "charity" for his fatherland was stronger than his own desire for personal revenge or his fear that his old enemy would act on the basis of that same desire. He understood that, as Machiavelli announced in *D* 3.42, "where one deliberates entirely on the safety of his fatherland, there ought not to enter any consideration of just or unjust, merciful or cruel, praiseworthy or ignominious," because one's own life and honor depend above all on the preservation of the polity.

Fabius did not disguise his unhappiness at the appointment of Papirius Cursor as dictator. But, Machiavelli has made it clear, his understanding of republican virtue does not preclude the use of fraud. Indeed, he declared in *D* 3.40, "to use fraud in managing war is a glorious thing." That is why he warns his readers in *D* 3.48, "when one sees a great error made by an enemy, one ought to believe that there is a deception underneath" (307). In the first of his three examples Machiavelli explains that an unnamed Roman legate correctly suspected a trap when some Tuscan shepherds approached their camp. He does not explicitly contrast this legate's reasonable doubt with the way in which Spurius Postumius let himself be deceived by the Samnites at the Caudine Forks (a use of fraud for which Machiavelli praised the Samnite captain). Nor does Machiavelli explain that the legate uncovered the deception on the basis of his knowledge of the Tuscan language, the same kind of knowledge that enabled Fabius to march through the Ciminian forest. Instead, as Strauss points out, Machiavelli restates his reasonable warning as an absolute rule, "that a captain of armies ought not to put faith in an error that the enemy is evidently seen to make, for fraud will *always* be underneath it, as it is not reasonable that men be so incautious" (308, emphasis added). Then he gives an example, the central example, which belies the absolute rule. As the "French" who had defeated the Romans at Allia learned when they found the gates of Rome open and the city undefended, the enemy sometimes makes errors because he panics (or, as Machiavelli showed in *D* 3.18, is misinformed). As Strauss points out, Machiavelli often overstates or exaggerates a point, only to qualify the same point later. That is, he argues dialectically. So Machiavelli shows here in his third example that it *is* reasonable to suspect double-dealing on the part of an enemy who openly consorts with both sides.[181]

More important, we see the way in which Machiavelli qualifies his own earlier statements in the final chapter of the book. In *D* 3.1 Machiavelli argued that public trials or "executions" of individuals suspected of trying

181. *TM*, 35. Strauss takes Machiavelli's overstatement to indicate that when he makes errors, there is fraud underlying them. I have argued that rather than making intentional "errors," Machiavelli exaggerates both to shock and to entertain his readers, and that he modifies or adapts historical incidents to illustrate his points. As Strauss shows, some of those points come out only when one compares Machiavelli's account with his source.

to overthrow the republic are necessary every five to ten years in order to renew the fear people have of disobeying the law. But in the final chapter of his book Machiavelli declares that "a republic has need of new acts of foresight every day if one wishes to maintain it free" (308).

Those "acts of foresight" first appear to be public trials and punishments of multitudes rather than a few outstanding individuals. Machiavelli begins by reminding his readers that, as he argued earlier (*D* 1.6, 3.1), every city or mixed body tends to become corrupt. So he states here, "it is of necessity . . . that in a great city accidents arise every day that have need of a physician" to devise a "remedy" or "cure" for the disease. The examples he gives of such corruption in Rome were the conspiracy of Roman women to poison their husbands and the conspiracy of the Bacchanals during the Macedonian war in which thousands of men and women were involved.[182] Both of these examples involved private crimes instigated by women that the authorities believed would undermine public order. Machiavelli does not note the sexual origin, however; instead he emphasizes the number of people the Romans were willing and able to punish. "For if the greatness of that republic and the power of its executions had not been seen by infinite other signs, it is seen through the kinds of penalty that it imposed on whoever erred." Not limiting itself to private crimes, the Roman republic did not "hesitate to have killed by way of justice an entire legion at once, and a city, and to banish eight or ten thousand" (309) soldiers defeated at Cannae to Sicily where they were not allowed to reside in town or eat sitting down.

Of all the executions, the Roman policy of decimating the armies was most terrible (and, therefore, most effective). When a multitude errs and it is not evident which particular individuals are responsible (for if it were, they would simply eliminate the heads), it is not possible to punish them all and it would be wrong to punish a part and leave the others (possibly guilty) unpunished. To choose to punish a tenth of them by lot when all deserve it makes those who are killed regret their fate and the others fear that they will be punished if they err again.[183]

But at this point in the final chapter Machiavelli's argument takes a surprising turn. He concludes that the poisoners and Bacchanals were

182. In a characteristic overstatement, Machiavelli asserts, "all Roman women had conspired against their husbands to kill them." Livy 8.18 shows that an informant revealed that twenty were involved in preparing the poison and one hundred seventy (a large number, but hardly all the wives in Rome) were convicted.

183. Machiavelli repeats this praise of the Roman policy of decimation and the rationale for it in *AW* 6.114–15.

punished "as their sins deserved." However, he points out, "although these diseases produce bad effects in a republic, they are not fatal because there is almost always time to correct them, but there is actually no time in those that regard the state, which ruin the city if they are not corrected by a prudent individual" (309).

Machiavelli has argued in both *The Prince* and *Discourses* that government arises from and is based ultimately on fear; hence his emphasis on the importance of regular spectacular punishments. However, he has also insisted that government cannot be maintained solely on the basis of fear. Unalleviated fear gives rise to hatred, and the hatred of many encourages some to conspire against the government. The people are reassured that their leaders are not in danger of becoming tyrants if they see those leaders subjected to accusations and public trials.

The danger to the republic Machiavelli has emphasized most frequently has been that, like Caesar, a popular leader will seize power beyond constitutional restraints. Yet Machiavelli also argued that Caesar was able to do so as a result of a minor change made in the law for the sake of public utility, i.e., the prolongation of commands. Because the threat to the republic posed by a virtuous young leader is not always evident, republics need virtuous individuals like Cato to accuse citizens like Scipio—even unjustly—of arrogantly seeking to overthrow the republic. He now acknowledges, such accusations and trials are not enough to preserve a republic. It is necessary to have prudent individuals who not merely perceive the danger of corruption inherent in current practices, but are able to devise remedies for them—without changing the state. His example of such an individual is, again, Fabius Maximus Rullianus.

"In the actions of men one finds that close to the good there is always some evil that arises with it" (*D* 3.37; 294). So in the last lines of his *Discourses* Machiavelli reports that the Romans' policy of increasing their own population by granting citizenship to peoples they conquered (which he praised earlier [*D* 1.6, 2.3]) led to such a large number of "new men" in Rome that they began to control the government. Perceiving the problem, Fabius arranged to have all the new men enrolled in four tribes, so that they could not corrupt all of Rome by ceasing to elect the most virtuous citizens to the highest offices (*D* 1.18). Since this "remedy" did not require a change in the government, it was "so well received by the citizenry that he deserved to be called Maximus" (310).

Machiavelli chooses his words carefully. By stating that Fabius "deserved" to be called "Maximus," because his reform was "so well received,"

Machiavelli reminds his readers that Fabius did not receive the honorific title for this particular achievement. He did not, because his fellow citizens did not perceive the threat of corruption posed by the incorporation of the new men with their varying mores into the citizen body (see *D* 1.18). They did not understand the crucial importance, therefore, of an apparently minor, perhaps even unjust modification of the law that deprived the new men of most of their influence on the outcomes of elections.

In the last sentence of book 3 Machiavelli thus underlines one of the central points he has been making in his education of those who "deserve" to be princes. The people are the source and repository of glory, but they do not understand or recognize true political virtue or wisdom. They prefer spirited, bold policies to gradual, cautious measures (*D* 1.53); and they remember rare and difficult individual sacrifices of the goods most human beings hold dear more than the victories or legislative reforms that actually serve long-term public interests, because these occur more frequently (*D* 3.34). Fabius Rucillanus's great-grandson Fabius Cunctator (the delayer) also received the honorific "Maximus," but he never received the popular or historical recognition for defending the Italian mainland from the foreign invader that Scipio did for conquering the enemy abroad. Moreover, the savior of the Roman republic did not become as famous—or as celebrated by later writers (who have even more influence than the people per se on the reputation of political actors)—as the man who destroyed it, Caesar (*D* 1.10).

Contrary to the suggestion he made at the conclusion of book 2, Machiavelli has shown that seeking glory may have made Roman generals great military captains, but it did not make them great legislators or founders. What republics need are leaders who understand the threats to the preservation of the republic—both internal (corruption) and external (aggression)—and are able to devise remedies for them. As Machiavelli indicates by concluding the *Discourses* with praise for Fabius Rullianus, these remedies involve changes not merely in the laws, but also in the "orders," i.e., the ways in which the citizen body is organized and offices or powers are allocated to different parts in order to preserve the liberty of all. As Machiavelli indicated in his praise of Brutus in *D* 1.25 for using old names or titles for new institutions, it is better to make such changes gradually than to destroy everything the way a tyrannical new prince must in order to create everything anew. Patrick Coby correctly observes, "it is a large and glaring fact that Machiavelli decides to close his *Discourses* with homage to the lawful incrementalism of the 'little by little' reformer."[184] But it is also important to note that Machiavelli does not praise Fabius Rullianus simply or primarily for proceeding gradually in a way that enables him to obtain widespread consent for his reforms. He shows that Fabius consistently acted on the basis of his own judgment of what would succeed. He defied the order of the dictator in order to win a battle, because he was confident that the soldiers and people would exonerate him. He overcame superstitious fears of entering the Ciminian forest by using knowledge he had acquired in order to execute a surprise attack. He increased the confidence of his own troops by claiming that he had secret knowledge instead of appealing to their religious beliefs, which were both more difficult to control and less firm than organization and training. He relied on reserves he had created by organizing and training his own troops rather than sacrificing himself like the Decii. Finally, in contrast to Claudius Nero (*D* 3.17), he demonstrated his own willingness to do what was necessary to preserve the republic rather than indulge his own desire for vengeance by allowing Papirius to be appointed dictator. Even more than Camillus, Fabius Rullianus embodies Machiavelli's conviction that a great republican prince will not seek his own glory at the expense of the republic the way Caesar finally did. Because he recognizes the need for initiative and innovation, such a leader does not always obey the commands of his superiors. Confident in his own judgment of what is necessary and of what will work under the circumstances, he allows himself to be judged by the public on the basis of the results. But he does not risk his own life unnecessarily. Like Camillus, he recognizes the need to overcome the envy of others by not seeking glory (or vengeance on those who question his loyalty and leadership) above all but rather agreeing to rotate or share command with others. Most important of all, perhaps, he recognizes the need to maintain popular opinions and customs that support a free way of life and knows how to create orders that preserve them.[185]

184. Coby, *Machiavelli's Romans*, 190.

185. Taking Fabius as exemplifying the character of Machiavelli's own enterprise rather than the sort of education he hopes to provide his readers, Strauss, *TM*, first suggests that "Machiavelli is another Fabius; it is the incredibility of his enterprise which secures him against detection" (17). Strauss then observes that "Rome was enabled to destroy freedom in the West . . . because she liberally admitted foreigners to citizenship. . . . Rome was then enabled to destroy freedom in the Western world because she was excessively cosmopolitan or constitutionally exposed to corruption. No wonder that Machiavelli takes leave of the reader of the *Discourses* with the praise of that Fabius who was deservedly called Maximus for having practically disfranchised 'the new people.'"

Conclusion of Book 3

In examining how the "actions of particular men made Rome great and caused many good effects" (212), Machiavelli implicitly urges his young Florentine readers to follow the example of Brutus. They should not reveal their intention of overthrowing the established regime until they are able to act effectively on it; and they should also recognize the need to eliminate the enemies of the republic once refounded, even if they are relatives. He does not encourage his readers to follow the model set by Brutus as a legislator, however, because the founder of the Roman republic resuscitated the ancient Spartan model of dual leadership checked by a senate rather than instituting a single executive. Nor does he present the "rare and virtuous examples" of the actions of later Roman republican heroes as models for his readers literally to imitate. On the contrary, he warns them against current misunderstandings of those examples (e.g., Fabius Maximus) and reminds them that the Roman republic fell because of the agitation caused by two well-intentioned but misguided laws—one requiring the redistribution of property and the other prolonging military commands. Through his analysis of the conflict over the Agrarian law, Machiavelli shows that republican government will not last if it depends upon insuring the economic equality of all citizens. In a city that enjoys a free way of life some will eventually accumulate more than others, and attempts to redistribute property require a tyrannical government, because they will provoke such fierce opposition on the part of property owners. What is needed, Machiavelli suggests in book 1 of the *Discourses*, is a new understanding of the requirements of a "political way of life" on the part of both the people and the elite. The people need to learn (or be persuaded

---

But, Strauss notes, "Fabius' measure did not stem the tide forever. Hence it remains true that the Roman republic, the greatest republic . . . that ever was, prepared the Western world for Asiatic obedience. The Roman republic is on the one hand the direct opposite of the Christian republic, and on the other hand a cause of the latter, or even the model for it" (118). Strauss thus concludes his account of "Machiavelli's Intention: The *Discourses*" by arguing that "Machiavelli combines the imitation of Jesus with the imitation of Fabius. Fabius, in contradistinction to Decius, judged the low assault to be preferable and . . . choosing the safer way, he gained a more gladdening victory, remaining alive, than the victory which Decius gained by his death. For Decius, imitating his father, sacrificed himself for the expiation of the Romans. . . . Classical political philosophy had taught that the salvation of the cities depends on the coincidence of philosophy and political power . . . for which one can wish or hope but which one cannot bring about. Machiavelli is the first philosopher who believes that the coincidence of philosophy and political power can be brought about by propaganda which wins over ever larger multitudes to the new modes and orders and thus transforms the thought of one or a few into the opinion of the public and therewith into public power" (173).

to see) that any popular "savior" poses a threat of tyranny and that the best way of curtailing such a threat is through competitive elections in which most of the candidates will come from the elite. Public accusations and trials of possible tyrants serve to "vent" popular anger not merely at this or that particular leader, but at the need for government or control more generally. But members of the politically ambitious "elite" also need to learn that they will secure their own influence and wealth most reliably by competing with each other for popular favor so that no one individual becomes preeminent, rather than trying to form an "aristocratic" or "oligarchic" party that opposes all popular leaders or measures. Since "all things of men are in motion," republics can obtain more effective leadership than principalities, because they can elect different individuals whose characteristic modes suit different sets of circumstances. Yet, Machiavelli also warns his readers, they cannot count on any specific set of laws to continue to produce the outcomes they desire, because people change along with their circumstances. (Indeed, the more successful the laws are, the more apt the people are to become corrupt.) If a republic once established is to be maintained, there must be prudent individual citizens who understand the reasons the laws work, when they work, and who can therefore, like Fabius, adjust or "remedy" the laws when they cease working effectively without entirely changing or overthrowing the state. That is the kind of education Machiavelli seeks to offer his readers.

As I have argued, Machiavelli seeks first to educate the two young men to whom he dedicates the *Discourses*, and the analysis contained therein has immediate relevance to their particular situation. In the *Art of War* Machiavelli expresses some doubt about the ability of these individuals to understand what he has written. But at the beginning of book 2 he addresses "the spirits of youths who may read these writings of mine" more generally; and, as we have seen, the political analysis and recommendations he makes have much broader relevance and application. His writings were not addressed simply or solely to the individuals to whom he dedicated them and their immediate concerns.

The Prince and the *Discourses*: Machiavelli's New Education of Princes—Actual and Potential

In the *Discourses* Machiavelli argues that the test of political excellence is—and ought to be—what serves the common good (or the closest approximation in the good of the greatest number [*D* 2.2]). And since the good of the people comes closest to being the good of the community, the people are—and ought to be—the judges. The people judge—as they should—on the basis of outcomes; the intentions of political actors are difficult if not impossible to know (*P* 18). Yet, Machiavelli also shows, the people do not understand the causes of the outcomes they desire or how to replicate them. In order to achieve the results people want, Machiavelli thus contends in both *The Prince* and the *Discourses*, their leaders need a new form of political education. Rather than describing the formation of the character of exemplary individuals in the past, as writers like Xenophon and Plutarch did, Machiavelli seeks to disclose the causes and effects of their deeds. That is the first reason he, in contrast to many of his predecessors, concentrates on history rather than philosophy. The second and more fundamental reason is his observation that "all things of men are in motion and cannot stay steady" (*D* 1.6) and that all "worldly things have a limit to their life" (*D* 3.1). The knowledge he promises to convey in his dedications to *The Prince* and the *Discourses* explicitly concerns "the actions of great men" gleaned from his practical experience and "continual reading in worldly things." Machiavelli indicates that he does not think that there are eternal truths available to mortal human beings through which we can bring order to our souls and thus achieve happiness.[186] He sometimes suggests that it might be possible to establish and maintain a perpetual republic (*D* 3.1, 3.22), although he denies it in *D* 3.17; but he does not in fact think that anything can last forever in a world in which everything is continually coming into being and perishing. On the contrary, since both human beings and the world in which we find ourselves are constantly changing, adjustments and adaptations are continually necessary.

As the frequent repetition of arguments he made in *The Prince* in book 3 of the *Discourses* should remind readers, both works reflect the same basic understanding. They were written in close conjunction with one another, but directed to somewhat different audiences. In both works Machiavelli indicates from the beginning that he disagrees fundamentally with the classical Aristotelian understanding of political associations as developing naturally and peacefully out of more basic procreative and economic groups, families and tribes. Human beings are driven to form political associations to protect themselves from external aggressors; such associations are not

186. He does not, therefore, advocate the Socratic "ethics" that Benner, *Machiavelli's Ethics*, attributes to him.

formed or maintained by natural affection or friendship. There will always be aggressors—at least as long as there are human beings—because, as he states in *D* 1.37, "nature has created men so that they are able to desire everything and are unable to attain everything. So, since the desire is always greater than the power of acquiring, the result is discontent with what one possesses. . . . From this arises the variability of their fortune; for since some men desire to have more, and some fear to lose what has been acquired, they come to enmities and to war, from which arise the ruin of one province and the exaltation of another" (78).[187] In opposition to the Christian doctrine of original sin, Machiavelli insists that human beings do not come into conflict and fight wars because they are evil.[188] On the contrary, they become evil when and where no effective government has been established to punish and deter them from seizing the property and taking the lives of others with force.

Since political associations do not arise naturally but are formed only as a result of "extrinsic accidents" or threats, the institution of government has to be the product of intentional action on the part of one "mind." If more than one person tries to determine the group's course of action, Machiavelli observes in his praise of Romulus (*D* 1.9), the result will be delay, division, and inaction. In order to maintain his or her government once established, however, a founder must find a way of persuading people that it benefits them as well.[189] The first way a ruler can acquire popular support, Machiavelli suggests, is by propagating a set of religious beliefs the way Numa did in Rome. However, Machiavelli also indicates, such beliefs do not lead people to obey the laws and defend the regime nearly as well or as reliably as a powerful prince or military training (partly because the efficacy of religion depends upon the rulers' acting as if they, too, believe it). A better, more effective way of enlisting popular support for a government is to muster and train an army of one's own subjects or fellow citizens to defend their own lives, families, and property.[190]

187. In *P* 3 he declares simply that "truly it is a very natural and ordinary thing to desire to acquire, and always, when men do it who can, they will be praised or not blamed" (14).

188. *D* 3.29; cf. Hobbes, *Leviathan* 6, definition of 'good.'

189. Machiavelli's emphasis on force might lead a reader to believe that he thinks only men can found a state; certainly they provide most of the historical examples. Machiavelli recognizes, however, again by giving historical examples, that women such as Caterina Sforza (3.6) or the daughter of Servius Tullius (3.4) are just as willing to sacrifice members of their family to their political ambitions as men like Romulus and Brutus.

190. Machiavelli's reiterated insistence on the superiority of training to religion as a force in maintaining popular obedience speaks against the emphasis put on his admittedly unconventional

Machiavelli's emphasis on the importance of training and maintaining an army—for principalities and republics alike—may offend some contemporary readers. He does not seek to glorify the use of force, militarism, or conquest per se, however. Indeed, he points out that the Romans' demonstrated ability to conquer the world destroyed liberty everywhere. (He is not, as some commentators have claimed, an unabashed imperialist.) He sees military service as one of the most effective ways of enlisting people in the preservation of government in order to protect their own lives, families, and possessions. In armies, as opposed to corrupt polities, individuals are promoted because of their demonstrated abilities rather than their family connections or ability to please the people. Most important of all, however: training people to serve in an army transforms the unstable fury of a mob, which is easily dispersed, into an ordered, effective political force that can be used to preserve a prince or a republican government from its enemies, internal as well as external.

"Training," especially the training of soldiers to follow commands immediately and without question, might seem to be opposed to liberty. But, Machiavelli argues, liberty does not consist in the absence of external restraint, as people tend to believe. Liberty is the result of a balance created and maintained between the two "humors" that exist in every "city": the "grandi," who want to dominate and oppress, and the people, who do not wish to be dominated and oppressed. Although he argues that the class conflict in every city, which threatens to erupt into civil war, is fundamentally over economic goods, Machiavelli insists that the division itself is political. It is not simply or primarily economic, because it concerns who will be in command or control, and both parties understand (or ought to understand) that the party in control will acquire wealth. There can be no purely economic resolution to political conflict, because all parties will always want to acquire more and be willing to use force, if they can, to get more. However, there is a political solution to the conflict over economic goods; that consists, not in periodic redistributions as classical political philosophers suggested, but in the institution of a "free way of life" that enables all individuals to keep the fruits of their labor and hope that their progeny will fare even better than they have.

Because "truly it is a very natural and ordinary thing to desire to acquire," Machiavelli observes (again, contrary to classical political philoso-

understanding of the role of God in politics by Viroli, *Machiavelli's God*, and Vatter, "Machiavelli and the Republican Conception of Providence."

phers such as Plato and Aristotle), neither individuals nor groups seek to rule primarily as a matter of justice. On the contrary, he observes (*D* 3.6), the desire for domination is as strong as if not stronger than the desire for vengeance (which is perhaps the most primitive form of the desire for justice in an "an eye for an eye"). Ordinary people seek and accept rule by a prince to protect them against pillaging and murder by others (as in the Romagna). They will accept government if they see that it secures their lives, families, and property; but they will feel more secure if they see that the prince and nobles are also subject to rule of law. In both *The Prince* and *Discourses* Machiavelli thus urges monarchs to share rule with a senate and to subject themselves as well as their nobles to a popular court. Such a law-bound (or we might say "constitutional") monarchy is not as good or effective a form of government as a republic that elects its "princes," because elections allow republics to adapt to changing circumstances by employing different kinds of leaders. But, Machiavelli argues, such a law-bound monarchy will be better, more lasting, and provide more security for rulers and ruled alike than a military dictatorship or tyranny.

Elections are not sufficient to maintain a free republic, however, because the people can and will become corrupt, if nothing is done to prevent it. Ironically, the more secure the people feel, the less vigilant they are apt to be about preserving their liberty. They must, therefore, be made to feel the need to guard themselves—their lives, families, and property—from both external and internal threats. Military training along with a confederal arrangement with other republics serves the first purpose. Public trials of individuals accused of trying to overthrow the republic are also necessary to make ordinary citizens not only afraid of disobeying the law but also aware of the internal threat.

Ordinary people are not apt to perceive the threat represented by a victorious general such as Julius Caesar, especially when he shares the spoils of his victories with them. In *The Prince* Machiavelli thus seeks to persuade future "princes" that this old model of "liberality" is not tenable over the long run. It should be replaced by a more calculating understanding of *virtù* that leads a "prince" to spare his people from the heavy taxation needed to sustain distant military campaigns, lavish building projects, and gifts to his "friends." That argument is part of Machiavelli's broader contention that, however a prince comes to power, once in power he should seek the support of the people in order to maintain himself. The "great" are those individuals living under any regime who join with a "new prince" in the hope of improving their situation, but whose ambitions will never be satisfied and who will, therefore, eventually need to be put down with force. Whether his subordinates are mercenary captains of armies or cruel officials who enforce the law harshly, a prince who wants to establish a government that will last beyond his own lifetime must arrange to disassociate himself from the harsh means by which he acquired power. A prince needs to have help in governing, but Machiavelli reminds princes that they can "make" and "unmake" the "great" by granting some people offices and privileges or by taking those offices away along with their lives. In *The Prince* Machiavelli thus seeks to persuade his most ambitious readers that they do not constitute an "aristocratic" class that is better, by nature or by virtue of their education, than the people they rule. Rather than natural friends, the "great" by virtue of their shared ambition are natural enemies. Instead of rewarding his noble "friends" with offices and separate dominions, a calculating prince should learn how to use them and their armies as tools, but then see that they are destroyed. As Machiavelli points out in *D* 1.16, such a prince will acquire some of the popular support he needs to maintain his rule by allowing the people to take vengeance on those who have oppressed them.

In the *Discourses* Machiavelli nevertheless appears to take a somewhat more positive view of the "nobility" when he argues that the people need to be brought to see that the envy other nobles feel for a young virtuous "prince" is their best protection from future tyranny. And he tries to persuade the nobles that the best way of preventing the rise of a potential tyrant is to compete with him for popular favor. Furthermore, this competition needs to be institutionalized by making every citizen eligible to be elected to high office, by setting strict term limits on those offices and requiring the current occupants to step down, and by instituting trials of prominent citizens before popular juries.

The difference with regard to the potential "nobility" of the "great" is perhaps the most important difference between Machiavelli's arguments in *The Prince* and *Discourses.* It can and should be attributed, in the first instance, to the difference in the immediate audiences of the two works. In *The Prince* Machiavelli explicitly addresses a prince and tries to show him what is truly in his interest as a prince. In the *Discourses* Machiavelli is explicitly addressing two young men from noble families who are attached to the republican government of their city and wish to restore its greatness. He thus tries to show them, most immediately, what they can and should do to restore republican government in what had, in effect, become a principality controlled by one family (the Medici). In the first two books he thus emphasizes the ways in which they should imitate their Roman ancestors. In contrast to the Florentine institutions that Machiavelli later describes in some detail in his *Florentine Histories*, they should not merely make all citizens eligible for high office, elect the most virtuous, and subject those suspected of subverting the law to public trials. Contrary to the "received wisdom" of the Florentine *ottimati*, they should train an army composed of Florentine citizens.

Only in the second half of the *Discourses* does Machiavelli admit that the envy of other ambitious citizens may prevent them from electing the best to high office or allowing a virtuous captain to do what is necessary for the public good. He reminds his readers that this envy cannot be overcome by trying to revive the two Roman "remedies"—keeping the public poor and always in the field on a military expedition—because the history of the Roman republic itself shows that they were not tenable in the long run. He uses the example of Camillus to show how the envy of other ambitious individuals in a republic can be overcome. A preeminent leader must not insist on his absolute superiority to all others but show himself willing to share his power and responsibility with others by assigning them specific offices. He must also demonstrate his own willingness to obey the law like everyone else by voluntarily relinquishing the absolute power of a dictator at the end of his term.

As Harvey Mansfield has pointed out, Machiavelli breaks most clearly with the aristocratic republican tradition in emphasizing the need to have one "head." A single "head" is necessary, not only for a republic to take expeditious action in an emergency, but also for that individual to get credit (or glory) and thus have an incentive to do what is necessary, particularly when it is dangerous. It is Machiavelli's recognition of the advantages, if not absolute necessity, of a single leader that makes his republic look almost identical to what he calls a "civil principality" in *P* 9. The crucial difference lies in the republican election of a series of "civil" princes for set terms of office.

Machiavelli also uses the example of Camillus to state another principle or requirement of maintaining republican rule at which he only gestures in *The Prince*. Having urged the prince to seek popular support, at the conclusion of *P* 9 Machiavelli warns him not "to think that the people will liberate him if he is oppressed by enemies or by the magistrates." But if he "knows how to command . . . and does not fail to make other preparations" (41), he will not find himself deceived by the people and will have laid his foundations well. Those foundations, Machiavelli explains in

D 3.30, consist first and foremost in selecting which men to arm and training them, so that a prince has the force to eliminate the envious, if they seek to prevent him from doing what is necessary to preserve the republic. Toward the end of book 3 he goes even further when he argues that the distinctive characteristics not merely of various nations but of aristocratic families are products not of nature or heredity, but of education, acculturation, or "training." The differences between peoples and princes do not arise "from a diverse nature—because it is in one mode in all" (*D* 1.58; 117). Individuals and various peoples may have different natural inclinations, but their distinctive characteristics are decisively shaped by their experience. A prince who knows how to do it can make soldiers out of peasants.

The person who knows how to order human beings in order to achieve the desired results is clearly in some ways superior to the one who does the ordering. Machiavelli thus begins his *Discourses* by observing, "the envious nature of men has always made it no less dangerous to find new modes and orders than to seek unknown waters and lands." Desiring to achieve a "common benefit to everyone," he nevertheless claims that he has laid out "a path as yet untrodden by anyone" that others "with more virtue, more discourse and judgment" will be able to follow to its end. Without connecting the danger explicitly to envy, much later in the *Discourses* Machiavelli comments on "what dangers are borne in making oneself head in counseling a thing" (*D* 3.35; 290). A person who merely advises a prince will get incomplete if any credit for the results. If he withholds knowledge or advice that would have prevented a disaster, however, he will be blamed—and justly so. An advisor of a prince (which Machiavelli explicitly aspired to become) should, therefore, "take things moderately." He should not seize upon any option as his "own enterprise," but give his "opinion without passion and defend it without passion, with modesty, so that if the city or the prince follows it, it follows voluntarily, and it does not appear to enter upon it drawn by your importunity." Admitting that "one lacks the glory that is acquired in being alone against many to counsel a thing when it has a good end," he notes, there are two compensations for exercising such self-restraint: "first, in the lack of danger; second, that if you counsel a thing modestly, and . . . your counsel is not taken, and by the counsel of someone else some ruin follows, very great glory redounds to you" (291).

Machiavelli thus makes himself and his own work the primary example of the reasons why someone who wishes to work for the common benefit should try to overcome the envy of others and how this can be achieved.

Like Camillus, such a leader must assign others parts to play in the achievement and share credit with them. Since, Machiavelli has observed, people of "quality" become suspect when they try to withdraw entirely from public life, those who possess wisdom should not try to do so. They should offer to share their wisdom "modestly" (or, one might say, ironically) for the sake of benefiting others and not of winning reputation for themselves. They should learn from the example of Camillus that public claims to godlike superiority on account of their wisdom (of the kind ancient philosophers more or less explicitly made) are certain to arouse popular resentment and anger. Those who are truly wise will merely offer their advice to those willing to listen and able to implement it, understanding that those who have power and do not share their wisdom are not apt to listen, but that in the long run, the unwise and ignorant are apt to be proven wrong. By seeking to help others while at the same time recognizing that they themselves are in many respects subject to the power of others, the wise who follow Machiavelli's advice will not merely secure their own safety; like Machiavelli they will lay the philosophical foundations for the future reordering of corrupt cities for the benefit of all. They will seek to persuade their readers not to seek happiness or justice as a transcendent Good or from an unknown and unknowable God. In an ever-changing world, they will try to show their readers that they must constantly invent new "remedies" or ways of redirecting human passions so that they culminate not in destructive wars but in the preservation of the lives, liberty, and prosperity of the greatest number.

In both *The Prince* and the *Discourses* Machiavelli rather explicitly sets out to debunk traditional aristocratic pretensions. He is not, however, a democrat of the ordinary kind. He acknowledges, "princes are superior to peoples in ordering laws, forming civil lives, and ordering new statutes and orders" (*D* 1.58; 118); and he goes so far as to declare that "a multitude without a head is useless" (*D* 1.44). He insists merely that, in order to last, both princely and republican governments need to serve the desires of the people. Not merely are the desires of the people more "decent" than those of the "great"; there are many more people than there are "great," so that the satisfaction of their desires comes as close as possible in a world characterized by competition and conflict to realizing the common good. Even more, he reminds his readers ambitious to show their "nobility," the glory ancient captains sought by risking their lives in order to save their peoples is and was awarded by the people. It tends to be awarded posthumously to those individuals whose works are deemed to have benefited those who come after them. Because "glory" or "virtue" as traditionally defined by what is praised is ultimately a matter of popular opinion, moreover, it is not always well or accurately bestowed. "Glory" is not and will not be the goal of a person who truly understands the world. He will not be allowed to retire safely into private life, however, once his prudence is recognized by others. He should thus try to help others establish and maintain a government that secures their lives, families, property—and, where possible, their liberty—as well as his own.

Many commentators seem to have missed the intimate connection between Machiavelli's "moral revolution" or debunking of traditional notions of virtue in *The Prince* and his advocacy of republican institutions that secure the lives, liberties, and property of most citizens in the *Discourses*, especially since he insists that these institutions will work only so long as the people remain "uncorrupt." He gives his readers much occasion to be confused about his understanding of what is truly good and virtuous by his ambiguous use of the word *virtù* in both works. Readers impressed by Machiavelli's advocacy of republican institutions in the *Discourses* (and his own service to the republic of Florence) tend to dismiss *The Prince* as a transitory work, if not a satire. The great majority of readers attracted by the short and very punchy account of everything he has learned in *The Prince* tend to see him, on the other hand, as an advocate of cold-blooded amoral political analysis, if not of tyranny per se. These readers have not appreciated the extent to which Machiavelli's arguments in both books are designed to persuade those who possess or seek to possess political power that the first and foremost goal of government is and must remain the security of the people. So long as people thought that some persons could be educated to be better or more virtuous than others, the first requirement of government was seen to be the education of such future rulers—for the sake of all. Observing that the proposed educations of virtuous leaders culminated in "imagined republics and principalities" that have never existed on earth, Machiavelli suggested that rule should be devoted instead to securing the good of those who were ruled. He did not think that it would be efficacious to appeal to the "charity" of those in power. Rulers who had tried to win the love of their people by being merciful had proved to be weak. He thus appealed to the desire of the "great" to command and oppress. "If all men were good," Machiavelli acknowledged, "this teaching would not be good" (*P* 18; 69). However, he observed, although human beings are not wicked by nature (*D* 3.29), they are not all or always good—partly because they are weak and insecure. Like Aristotle (*Politics* 1263a41–42), Machiavelli thought that self-love was natural. But where Aristotle suggested that "excessive" self-love could be either checked by an education that made some men moderate so that they could control the rest with laws or satisfied in rare cases by the pleasures of philosophy, Machiavelli concluded that one's own safety was a more fundamental concern for the few and the many alike. To live well, one must first be able to live.

PART II

Later Developments

INTRODUCTION

Machiavelli claimed to have written down everything he knew about worldly affairs in the two works he composed after the Florentine republic fell in 1512 and he was dismissed from office. He did not publish either of his two comprehensive works during his lifetime, yet he kept writing. We are led, therefore, to ask how these later writings are related to the comprehensive understanding of the world he put forward in *The Prince* and *Discourses on Livy*.

The Prince seems to have circulated widely in manuscript form, first in Florence and then in northern Europe. But Machiavelli had reason to think he had not been understood. He was not appointed to a political office by either of the Medici princes to whom he had dedicated *The Prince*. Nor did he have the satisfaction of seeing Lorenzo and Leo act on the basis of his advice to seize Italy. Even worse, the young Florentine aristocrats to whom Machiavelli dedicated the *Discourses* did not seem to understand what he wished to teach them any better than the Medici princes. As he indicates in the setting and characters of the dialogue on the art of war he published in 1521, they enjoyed talking about what it would mean to imitate the Romans, but they had obviously not learned, much less undertaken, what Machiavelli had insisted was the necessary first step: organizing and training a group of supporters to use arms to seize power and then defend the new regime against its opponents.

In his later works Machiavelli showed more specifically how his broad analysis applied to the lives of his contemporaries, in private as well as in public. At the same time he also made the philosophical foundations of his political project clearer. Instead of trying to present his complete understanding of politics in more or less extensive form, in each of his subsequent works Machiavelli emphasized a particular theme or partial application of his more comprehensive understanding—to make it both more palatable and more easily understood. By writing in a variety of genres—two comedies, a dialogue, and two histories—Machiavelli was able to put some of his most controversial thoughts into the mouths of others. As a result, he was able to put those thoughts forward more publicly, if still somewhat indirectly and ironically.

In a comedy he seems to have completed and produced in 1518 Machiavelli demonstrated how his teaching a prince how not to be good and to use that knowledge according to necessity could and should also be applied to the lives of private individuals.[1] Contrary to the claims of some of his most highly regarded interpreters, in *Mandragola* Machiavelli thus showed that politics is not an entirely "autonomous" sphere. The lack of pure morality and conscience that he insisted a successful prince must demonstrate can and should be found in the lives of ordinary human beings as well, if they would live happily. In contrast to his more comprehensive treatises, he could not merely publish but produce *Mandragola* safely, because in a play, the playwright merely presents the speeches and deeds of others. None of the truly scandalous statements made by his characters could legitimately be said to represent the playwright's own opinions. He could (and did) say that he was simply trying to entertain.

Turning back to consider a deadly serious public topic, in *The Art of War* he published in 1521 Machiavelli presented his young Florentine friends with a lesson about how to imitate the Romans specifically with regard to military organization and tactics. He instructed them to use this knowledge in advising their prince, because a prince who adopted the military organization and tactics he recommended would be able, as he had urged at the end of *The Prince*, to seize Italy and free it from the barbarians. By writing those instructions in the form of a dialogue, in which the author simply

1. There is some debate about exactly when Machiavelli wrote *Mandragola*. There is evidence that he had begun writing comedies while he was serving the republic. For example, he had reputedly written a new version of Aristophanes' *Clouds*, but the manuscript was destroyed by his grandson and literary executor, Giuliano de' Ricci, because it contained so many slanderous remarks about Florentine politicians. The plot of *Mandragola* is set in 1504; and at one point a character refers to a fortress near Pisa that the Florentines took in June 1503. Sergio Bertelli, "When Did Machiavelli Write *Mandragola*?," *Renaissance Quarterly* 24 (1980): 317–26, thus believes that Machiavelli began composing the comedy, but may not have finished it, while he was still a secretary of the republic. However, there is no evidence of a completed manuscript or a production before 1518.

explained in the preface how he came to know about the conversation he relates, he presented the speeches and deeds of others as in *Mandragola*, rather than stating his own opinions and arguments to support them. The irony of Machiavelli's presenting a mercenary captain (of the kind he so harshly criticized in both *The Prince* and *Discourses*) as the teacher of an art he emphasizes can be learned only by means of practice to a group of young aristocrats lounging at their ease in a garden has not been lost on commentators (although they have not agreed about its significance). However, because Fabrizio Colonna's lecture contains a great many details drawn from classical works on military strategy, many readers have understood (and criticized) the dialogue as a technical treatise. They have not picked up the political implications of the military organization and tactics Machiavelli had also recommended, although much more briefly, in his *Discourses*.

Machiavelli might have appeared to be presenting a historical model of an Italian prince who understood the art of war in the highly fictionalized account of the life of Castruccio Castracani he wrote during the summer of 1520. However, in his *Life* Machiavelli showed that the young tyrant of Lucca knew how to seize power but not how to maintain it or pass it on to his heirs. By attributing a list of updated "sayings" of the philosophers drawn from Diogenes Laertius to Castruccio at the end of his *Life*, Machiavelli also indicated something about the philosophical background and basis of his own thought. In composing what first appears to be a praising account of the life of a tyrant, moreover, Machiavelli provided his young friends, Zanobi Buondelmonti and Luigi Alamanni, with an example of the kind of historical writing he could produce. They may or may not have used it in their attempts to persuade the Medici to hire him to write a history of Florence; but, in any case, they succeeded. In November 1520 then cardinal Giulio de' Medici commissioned Machiavelli to write the *Florentine Histories*.

Just before he finished writing his history, Machiavelli wrote and produced a second comedy in which he seemed to mock himself by presenting an old man named Nicomaco making a fool of himself by falling in love with a young girl. In *Clizia*, Machiavelli explicitly re-presented an ancient Greek story that had been made into a Roman comedy by Plautus. By means of the changes he made in "updating" that story so that it could take place in Florence, Machiavelli nevertheless showed why it was necessary to maintain the appearance of conventional morality, especially concerning the family, if human beings were to survive and prosper. Some commentators have taken the title character, Clizia, who never appears onstage, to represent his dream of a reunited Italy. But, I shall argue, Machiavelli's depiction of the destructive effect of Nicomaco's erotic desire for eternal youth and beauty on his family dramatizes the impossibility of realizing "fantastical" desires for immortality and the necessity, therefore, of disciplining and redirecting those desires to more worldly goods like wealth and reputation.

Finally, in his *Florentine Histories* Machiavelli showed how his native city had gone awry. In the preface he explains why he found it necessary to cover the same ground and so, in effect, to correct the more clearly celebratory histories of the republic written by his predecessors. He apologizes for appearing to have flattered the family of his Medici sponsors, but he protests that he has simply described their achievements: the way they seized control of the Florentine republic and maintained that control by means of their liberality. Presenting a mass of "facts" and making very few judgments explicitly in his own name, he nevertheless shows that the foreign policies praised by previous historians for maintaining Florentine independence were disastrous, internally as well as externally, and that the political tactics that enabled Cosimo de' Medici to seize and maintain control of the state destroyed the liberty of the republic. As in his *Discourses*, so in the *Florentine Histories*, Machiavelli generally contrasts the weak, ineffective policies of his native city (which he describes in much greater detail) with the admirable institutions and policies of the Roman republic (to which he alludes only briefly). However, he concludes, whereas the civil war that erupted between the two humors in Rome made the rise of a tyrant there inevitable, the equality in Florence became so great that a better republic could easily have been founded there—if only there had been a legislator who knew how. Machiavelli had been trying to teach his readers how and why they should introduce such "new modes and orders" in all of his works.

3

In What Mode Private Individuals Should Keep Faith

MANDRAGOLA

In the prologue to *Mandragola* Machiavelli explains his turn to comedy in terms of the disappointing reception of his previous work: "If this material is not worthy—on account of its being so light—of a man who wishes to seem wise and grave," he should be excused for "trying with these vain thoughts to make his wretched time more pleasant, because he has nowhere else to turn his face, for he has been cut off from showing with other undertakings other *virtù*" (11). Some commentators have thus argued that in *Mandragola* he was merely trying to entertain himself along with his audience.[1] He does not appear to have thought comedies were merely a form of diversion or entertainment, however. In the prologue to *Clizia*, he declares that "comedies were discovered in order to benefit" as well as "to delight the spectators" (5). Even more pointedly, in his *Dialogue on Language* he writes: "Though the aim of comedy is to hold up a mirror to domestic life, the way it does this . . . [allows] . . . the men who come eagerly to enjoy themselves, [to] taste afterwards the useful lesson that lay underneath."[2]

As in the dedications to his major prose works, so in the prologue to *Mandragola*, Machiavelli suggests that he is presenting his audience with something of value. On the basis of his past experience, however, he does not expect to receive any reward for his labor but sneers and other insults. His contemporaries' unwillingness to recognize the excellence of the works of others is the reason "why, in all things, the present age falls off from ancient

1. E.g., Franco Fido, "Politica e teatro nel badalucco de Meser Nicia," in *Le metamorfosi del centauro: Studi e letture da Boccaccio a Pirandello* (Rome: Bulzoni, 1977), 91–108, and Viroli, *Machiavelli*, 26.

2. *A Dialogue on Language*, 188.

virtù." Most people are not willing to labor and strain on what must by nature be transitory achievements without the promise of some form of remuneration. But he will not be discouraged, because he knows how to trade insult for insult and "doesn't stand in awe of anyone, even though he might play the servant to one who can wear a better coat than he can" (11). More clearly than in the dedications to his prose works, Machiavelli expresses not only resentment of the envious pretensions of the wealthy and powerful to be better men than he but also his conviction that one who works for the common benefit should not expect gratitude or glory as a reward.

What, then, is the "useful lesson" lying underneath the comic plot of *Mandragola*? In this comedy Machiavelli explicitly writes as a private individual about private domestic life. Since he is a famous political theorist, however, many commentators have tried to show the relevance of the play to public affairs. Some have read it as a satirical allegory in which the fictional characters are identified with specific Florentine politicians (or, in the case of Lucrezia, with the Florentine people).[3] The problem with such allegorical readings is, first, that the allegorists do not agree either on the specific correspondences—e.g., whether Callimaco represents a generic "prince" or Lorenzo de' Medici, or whether the childless Nicia should be taken as the childless Piero Soderini—or on the point of the satire, whether it looks forward to the rise or to the fall of the Medici.[4] Second, if Machiavelli had written a satire with such a one-to-one correspondence between the characters and plot of the comedy and contemporary Florentine politics, he would have been departing markedly from his usual practice in his explicitly political works. In both *The Prince* and the *Discourses* he criticizes his contemporaries, but he does not restrict the compass of his analysis simply to contemporary much less simply Florentine events. Third, while he was serving the Florentine republic Machiavelli apparently wrote a satirical comedy based on Aristophanes' *Clouds* that (like its Greek model) contained explicit references to contemporary political figures; but he chose not to complete or produce it. Whether he had concluded that that kind of political com-

3. For example, Theodore A. Sumberg, "*La Mandragola*: An Interpretation," *Journal of Politics* 23 (1961): 320–48; A. Parronchi, "La prima rappresentazione della *Mandragola*. Il modello per l'apparato. L'allegoria," *La Bibliofila* 14 (1962): 37–89; Carnes Lord, "Allegory in Machiavelli's *Mandragola*," in *Political Philosophy and the Human Soul*, ed. Michael Palmer and Thomas L. Pangle (Lanham, MD: Rowman and Littlefield, 1995), 149–73.

4. Mark Hulliung, "Machiavelli's *Mandragola*: A Day and a Night in the Life of a Citizen," *Review of Politics* 40, no. 1 (1978): 32–33, points out such problems in the allegorical readings of the comedy.

mentary was imprudent or that it did not accomplish what he wished is not clear. What does seem evident is that he had come to such a determination before he wrote *Mandragola*.

Recognizing the problems with the allegorical readings of *Mandragola*, other commentators have contented themselves simply with pointing out the themes from his political works that can be found in the comedy as well. But there are also difficulties with such "thematic" readings, because the differences between the comedy and the prose works in the treatments of the loss of ancient virtue in contemporary Florence, conspiracies, and the new founding or refounding of existing institutions seem to be as great as the similarities.

Virtually all commentators agree that *Mandragola* constitutes a retelling of the ancient story of the rape of Lucretia.[5] To see what is truly "new" in the "new case" (*caso*—cause, chance, or incident) that Machiavelli tells his audience in the prologue has been "born" (*nato*) in this land of Florence (but will be seen at other times in Rome or Pisa),[6] we need to look in more detail at what he retained and what he changed from the old story.[7]

In Livy's history (1.57–59), the rape of Lucretia had great political significance, because it provided the occasion if not the cause for Lucius Junius Brutus's founding of the Roman republic.[8] King Tarquin had attacked the wealthy neighboring city of Ardea to replenish his own treasury, which had been depleted by the splendor of his public works. By distributing some of the booty, he also hoped to appease the common people, who resented their impressed labor on those works. Unable to take the city by storm, the Romans had begun a long siege. Passing their idle hours dining and drinking, a group of young princes began bragging about their virtuous wives. Insisting that his wife, Lucretia, was the best, Tarquinius Collatinus urged them to

5. Hulliung, "Machiavelli's *Mandragola*," is a notable exception. Perhaps he does not note the parallels because he wants to emphasize the sources of *Mandragola* in Roman comedies, and Livy's account of the rape of Lucretia is deadly serious.

6. Machiavelli does not make it clear whether what will be seen at other times in Rome or Pisa will be a new production of his comedy or a similar "case," i.e., set of events.

7. Mera Flaumenhaft, "The Comic Remedy: Machiavelli's 'Mandragola,'" *Interpretation* 7, no. 2 (1979): 37–47, and Ronald L. Martinez, "The Pharmacy of Machiavelli: Roman Lucretia in *Mandragola*," *Renaissance Drama* 14 (1983): 13–43, also give detailed comparisons of the two versions of the story.

8. In *D* 3.5 Machiavelli dismisses the importance of the rape, explaining that if it had not occurred, some other "accident" would have caused the people to revolt against the tyranny of the Tarquins. In *D* 3.26, however, he uses Lucretia as an example of the way in which women ruin cities by causing divisions within them.

ride back to Rome to see. There they found all the other wives dining together luxuriously; Lucretia alone was at home weaving by candlelight with her maids. His desire to conquer and possess aroused by her virtue as well as her beauty, the king's son Sextus resolved to return the next day to ravish her. When she refused to accede to his wishes at sword point, he threatened her with disgrace. If she did not gratify him, he would kill both her and his manservant, place their bodies side by side in her bed, and tell others that he had found them in illicit embrace. To avoid dishonor, Lucretia submitted; but she sent for her husband immediately after Sextus left. After hearing her tale, Collatinus tried to convince her that she was free of shame because she had not willingly submitted. But having obtained her husband's pledge to punish the man who had raped her, Lucretia plunged a dagger into her heart to prove that she had not submitted to the disgrace voluntarily. Drawing the bloody dagger from her wound and displaying it along with her body, Brutus aroused enough public outrage to exile the king and establish a republic in place of the monarchy.

In *Mandragola* a handsome wealthy young Florentine named Callimaco Guadagni hears of the extraordinary beauty of a woman named Lucrezia from one of her in-laws, who has come to Paris and engaged him in a debate about the relative beauty of French and Italian women.[9] Like the Roman princes, Callimaco decides to return home to see for himself. The provocation and action in the new "case" are thus similar to those of the old, but the setting and circumstances are importantly different. Whereas the Roman princes took a brief leave from a military camp, Callimaco returns to Florence from a voluntary exile undertaken to avoid war. He is young, noble, and wealthy, but he is no soldier or patriot. On the contrary, after his parents died, his guardians had sent him at age ten to Paris, and he had remained there for another ten years to escape the wars in Italy that began with the

9. As Martinez, "Pharmacy of Machiavelli," 41, points out, Machiavelli uses both Greek and Roman names for his characters, and some of them have significance. See also R. Sereno, "A Note on the Names of the Personages of Machiavelli's *Mandragola*," *Italica* 26 (1949): 56. Callimaco's first name means beautiful or noble battle and is, therefore, ironic, whereas his last name, Guadagni, refers to "gains" or "profits." If Nicia is taken, as it should be, to refer to the Greek word for victory, *nikê*, Lucrezia's husband's first name is also ironic. Flaumenhaft, "Comic Remedy," and Lord, "Allegory," point to the possible connection to Nicias, the Athenian general who lost his own life, as well as the war in Sicily, as a result of his excessive caution and piety. Although he wants to maintain the appearance of conventional respectability, Nicia is certainly not pious. And unlike Nicias, as Harvey C. Mansfield, "The Cuckold in Machiavelli's *Mandragola*," in *The Comedy and Tragedy of Machiavelli*, ed. Vickie B. Sullivan (New Haven: Yale University Press, 2000), 1–29, argues, Nicia achieves his goal, even though he cannot be said to have won a battle.

French invasion in 1494.[10] At the very beginning of the play the audience thus sees one reason for Machiavelli's conclusion that the present age has fallen off from ancient *virtù*.

Callimaco proves not only to be less forceful but also to be less resourceful than his Roman predecessor. Having arrived in Florence, he tells his servant Siro he has done nothing for an entire month, because he does not know how to overcome the three obstacles to the satisfaction of his desire: the chaste nature of Lucrezia, "which is extremely honest and in all ways alien to the things of love," her rich husband Nicia who "lets himself be governed by her," and the absence of any opportunity or occasion to approach her in private.[11] Unable to devise a "remedy" on his own, Callimaco has sought the assistance of a "parasite" and former marriage broker named Ligurio.[12] Siro warns his master to "watch out that he doesn't trick you; these spongers aren't usually very faithful." Like his creator, however, Callimaco believes that human beings will work, if and when they see the promise of a reward. Reflecting the commercial spirit and habits of his native city, he assures Siro that Ligurio will serve him faithfully, because he has promised that "if he succeeds, to give him a good sum of money." And "if he doesn't succeed," trying to obtain his assistance won't have cost much. Ligurio will merely have "pick[ed] up a lunch and supper out of it, which I wouldn't have eaten alone anyway" (1.1).

Having become familiar with Nicia, Ligurio has persuaded him to take his wife to the baths (where Callimaco can approach her). Nicia does not want to go to the trouble of moving his entire household, knows that his wife will object, and is frustrated by the disagreement among the doctors about which baths would best cure her sterility. But he and his wife are so desperate to have a child, he tells Ligurio that he is willing to do anything.

10. The comedy is thus set in 1504, the year Machiavelli wrote and published a poem, his *First Decennial*, in which he detailed the sufferings Italians have endured as a result of both mercenary warfare and the invasions of foreign armies, then concluded with a call for his compatriots to return to the "Temple of Mars," i.e., return to the model of their Roman ancestors and rearm.

11. He complains that "she has no relatives or neighbors with whom she comes together at some evening gathering or party, or at any of the other amusements by which young women are usually delighted." Nor does she deal with tradespeople or have a maid or servant who is not too afraid of her to accept a bribe.

12. Ligurio's Roman name refers to ligaments that bind, and it is he who shows how all the characters in this comedy can be bound together in a conspiracy of silence in order to satisfy their respective desires. "Parasites" were stock characters in Roman comedies, characterized by greed and gluttony. But, as Flaumenhaft points out, "it is Ligurio who always thinks of a 'remedy.' Machiavelli plays down the gluttony of the Roman and Italian parasites on whom Ligurio is superficially modeled" ("Comic Remedy," 39).

So he asks the parasite to talk to the doctors and find out which baths would be best.

In the meantime Ligurio warns Callimaco that he may not succeed in seducing Lucrezia at the baths; another young man may prove to be more attractive. (Callimaco apparently is no more handsome than he is courageous or resourceful.) And Ligurio devises another plan. Because Callimaco is educated and can impress the lawyer with his use of Latin, Ligurio introduces him to Nicia as a doctor.[13] And in that role Callimaco prescribes a potion containing the mandrake which will make any woman who drinks it pregnant. The problem is that the first man who lies with her will die within eight days. Nicia does not want to die, but Callimaco assures him that there is a remedy: "make another man sleep with her . . . one night . . . and draw off all that infection of the *mandragola* to himself" (2.6). Nicia again protests that he does not want to make his wife a whore and himself a cuckold. But after Callimaco informs him that the king of France and many lords there have done it, and assures him that he will not end up before the Florentine criminal tribunal, Nicia agrees to go in disguise with Ligurio, Siro, and Callimaco to seize the first young man they encounter in the street, put a bag over his head, and lead him into the bedroom with instructions about what he has to do (but no warning about the consequences). In the morning Nicia will send him away before daybreak, so he won't have seen anyone. Then Nicia can ask his wife to bathe and be with her at his pleasure.

Nicia is older than Callimaco, but he does not seem to be any braver, wiser, or more resourceful. Like Callimaco, he is rich, but he complains that he does not have much status in the city. Although he studied hard for two years to earn his law degree, he admits that he would not be able to support himself by practicing his profession. Like the author of the play, he complains about the unwillingness of his fellow citizens to recognize and appreciate any *virtù* (2.3). In contrast to the author of the comedy, Nicia clearly cares about his and thus his wife's reputation. But he is not concerned about committing murder, so long as he is not apprehended and punished for it. Nor does he care about putting his wife's immortal soul in danger of damnation by having her commit adultery. He is obviously not a good Christian. She says prayers for hours before going to bed (perhaps to postpone

13. An advocate and user of the vernacular himself, Machiavelli mocks the use of Latin by both scholars and prelates as a means of pretending to have knowledge they don't and seeking to deceive the public.

her wifely duty as long as possible, perhaps to shore up her own resolution), but he has not seen Frate Timoteo for ten years. It does not appear that he, in contrast to his wife, has ever gone to church regularly.

Although his wife also wants a child, Nicia does not believe that she will cooperate with their scheme. It is in the obtaining of Lucrezia's cooperation, as well as the specific way in which that is achieved, that Machiavelli's comedy differs most from its ancient Roman source.

First, most obviously and most importantly, in Machiavelli's comedy, in glaring contrast to the original story, there is no threat or use of force—by the lover, husband, woman, or man who seeks to reestablish order. All the characters who participate in the "plot" agree to do what they are asked, even if they do not always understand why. (Following Machiavelli's rules for an effective conspirator [*D* 3.6], Ligurio does not tell any of his partners anything they need to know before they need to know it.) It is the absence of even the threat of coercion that fundamentally distinguishes the machinations to establish a new order in Nicia's household from a political refounding. Machiavelli recognizes that it is possible to seize control of a government by means of fraud (*D* 2.13), but he does not think that an unarmed prophet can maintain control of his people (*P* 6). Some commentators have suggested that Ligurio plays the role of a Machiavellian political leader, because he says as they set off to seize the disguised Callimaco, "I'll be the captain, and get the army in order for the battle" (4.9).[14] But Ligurio is leading an "army" of three, and he has no way to punish a deserter or rebel. (Machiavelli emphasizes that public punishments are necessary means not merely of maintaining but of restoring governments by returning them to their beginning [*D* 3.1, 3.49].) The conspirators are only pretending to use force when they seize the disguised Callimaco and take him to Lucrezia's bed. The individuals who take part in the charade Ligurio has orchestrated do so because it enables each of them to satisfy his or her own strongest desire. But that satisfaction in all cases depends on the plot's being kept secret. As a result, the man who devised it does not receive public credit or recognition for his work for "the common benefit of each" (*D* 1.Pref.).[15]

14. E.g., Flaumenhaft, "Comic Remedy," 39.

15. Nicia wants to perpetuate his family—or at least the appearance of such. He will be publicly recognized as the father of his son, but everyone else in the conspiracy knows that, in fact, he is not. He may play the fool the way Brutus did, but *pace* Mansfield, he does not figure out the means of overturning the old order (which he seeks to perpetuate) or how to establish a new one the way Brutus did. He certainly would not kill his own son in order to perpetuate the new

The second evident difference between Machiavelli's comedy and the original tragedy is that in place of a threat of force or loss of honor, the conspiracy against Lucrezia's virtue succeeds by means of an appeal to her Christian beliefs. That resolution is paradoxical (and comic) because those same Christian beliefs appear to be the primary obstacle to her cooperating and so producing an heir for Nicia.

In order to obtain Lucrezia's cooperation, Ligurio informs his collaborators, they will need to enlist the help of both her confessor and her mother. Gaining the cooperation of the frate alone will not suffice. Lucrezia has come to suspect the honesty of all prelates, because one of the frati approached her inappropriately when she went to church to pray for a child. She will not go to see her confessor, much less listen to him, unless her mother brings her. Lucrezia believes—and for good reason—that her mother is genuinely concerned about maintaining her daughter's honor (3.10). Sostrata understands that her own support depends upon the solidity of her daughter's domestic arrangements. She thus urges her daughter to obey her husband's desire that she comply with the strange plan, because "a woman who has no children has no home. Her husband dies, she's left like a beast, abandoned by everyone." (Indeed, the frate, who should be a man of compassion, describes the mother as "beast" [3.9].) In contrast to Nicia, Sostrata sympathizes with her daughter's fear of committing a sin and being eternally punished for it. However, since her confessor has removed any questions of "conscience," Sostrata asks her daughter, "What are you afraid of? There are fifty women in this city who would raise up their hands to heaven for it" (3.11).

---

order. Like most other commentators (e.g., Hulliung, "Machiavelli's *Mandragola*," 44; Flaumenhaft, "Comic Remedy"; Joseph A. Barber, "The Irony of Lucrezia," *Studies in Philology* 82 [1985]: 450–59; Carnes Lord, "On Machiavelli's *Mandragola*," *Journal of Politics* 41 [1979]: 817; Augustus A. Mastri, "Machiavelli's *La Mandragola*: A Political and Personal Statement," *Ball State Review* 28 [1987]: 10–11), I conclude that Ligurio is the Machiavellian character who is the secret "hero" of the comedy. Like Machiavelli himself (*D* 3.35) Ligurio is willing to let others get public credit for arrangements he has devised that secure the "common good" of each, which in this case consists in a certain amount of economic security and freedom. Following Mansfield, Michael Palmer and James F. Pontuso, "The Master Fool," *Perspectives on Political Science* 25 (1996): 124–32, argue that Nicia is not as foolish as he seems. He may have sent his relative Camillo Calfucci to Paris to meet Callimaco and arouse his interest by bragging about the beauty of Lucrezia. Nicia also first mentions the use of a doctor of medicine as a means of gaining intimate access to his wife; it is not clear that he does not recognize the disguised Callimaco; he may recognize that he is impotent, but he objects to Callimaco's declaring in Italian (as opposed to Latin) that he may be, because he does not want his defect to be publicly known; in any case, he seeks another means of impregnating Lucrezia, and he suggests that her piety has to be circumvented by means of her confessor. However, they concede "that once Ligurio gets hold of the plot he uses his shrewdness to overcome Lucrezia's resistance" (321) by enlisting both Timoteo and her mother.

Ligurio believes that he will be able to obtain the help of Frate Timoteo by offering him a bribe. He observes that "these frati are cunning, astute; and it stands to reason, because they know our sins and their own" (3.2). They know the sins of others, Machiavelli reminds his audience in the next scene, because they hear confessions. Those confessions appear to come, moreover, particularly from women who are ashamed of their sexual activities, even in marriage, and are willing to compensate men of the Church handsomely for relieving their consciences. Timoteo has concluded that women are both "the most charitable people" and "the most annoying." But "there's no honey without flies" (4.4). When Ligurio asks him to persuade an abbess to give a pregnant girl in her care a potion to make her miscarry in exchange for a gift of three hundred ducats for him to distribute as alms, the frate thus agrees. Timoteo seems to concur with Ligurio's contention that many goods will result—the honor of the convent, the girl, and her relatives will be maintained and the frate will receive 300 ducats from Messer Nicia for charity—whereas nothing will be harmed "but a piece of unborn flesh, without sense." He seems, indeed, to agree with Ligurio's general contention "that good is that which does good for the most, and that by which the most are contented," so long as it be "in the name of God" and for charity. We know from *D* 2.2 that Machiavelli shares Ligurio's "utilitarian" understanding of the common good.

Having tested Timoteo's corruptibility with the story about the pregnant girl, Ligurio explains what he really wants. Timoteo recognizes that he has been duped, but he expects to profit by the trick. "Messer Nicia and Callimaco are rich," and he thinks that he will get a lot from each of them. Both will, for different reasons, continue to pay him to keep the affair secret, and he won't have to worry that either of them will expose his role. He does not, therefore, repent his decision, but he does recognize that it will be difficult to persuade Lucrezia, who is "wise and good." He thinks, however, that he will be able to "dupe her by her goodness" (3.9).

When he meets with Lucrezia and her mother, the frate presents three reasons why she should submit her body to this disgrace and be the cause of a man's dying for disgracing her. The first is that "where there is a certain good and an uncertain evil, one should never leave that good for fear of that evil." In this case, Timoteo claims that the "certain good" is that she will become pregnant (which is by no means certain as a result of a "one-night stand," unless one believes in the potency of Callimaco's concoction), and that it is uncertain that the one who will lie with her will die (although Timoteo knows much more certainly that Callimaco will not die for this reason). The frate tells the women that he has been consulting his books, and the second reason he gives is taken from the comfort Saint Augustine offers the Christian women who were raped in the fall of Rome: "the will is what sins, not the body."[16] And asserting his authority over her in interpreting the teaching of the saint as it applies to her case, he adds: "What causes it to be a sin is displeasing your husband—but you please him; [and] taking pleasure in it—but you have no pleasure from it." Finally, he enunciates the Machiavellian principle that "the end has to be looked to in all things." Her end is "to fill a seat in paradise," and the means is "to make your husband happy" (3.11).

Utterly unconvinced by the arguments of her confessor and mother, Lucrezia declares that she does not believe that she will be alive the next morning. However, that night she experiences the difference between the kisses of a young lover and her old husband. Moreover, her lover not only explains "how easily, on account of her husband's simplicity, [they] could live happily without any scandal" but also promises upon Nicia's death to take her as his wife. She thus concludes: "Since your astuteness, my husband's stupidity, my mother's simplicity, and my confessor's wickedness have led me to do what I never would have done by myself, I'm determined to judge that it comes from a heavenly disposition which has so willed" (5.4). Although she piously states that she does not have it in her to reject what Heaven wills her to accept, she somewhat impiously declares that she now takes Callimaco to be her "lord, master, and guide," her father, defender, and her *every* good. And instead of forgiving her husband for the wrong he has done her, she states her desire to punish him by giving him always what he wanted to have for one evening. So she instructs or even orders Callimaco to become her husband's close friend, so that he can come and go as he pleases in their house, allowing her to be together with him at any time without suspicion. In declaring her obedience to the will of God and taking her lover as her master, she thus effectively takes control of Nicia's reorganized household.

Nicia notices the change in his wife's bearing immediately. She's become very bold. But he nevertheless retains apparent control. He brings Lucrezia to the church to be blessed by the frate and introduces her to Maestro Callimaco, "who will have been the cause of our having a staff to sustain our old age." Lucrezia tells her husband that she wants Callimaco to be their

16. *City of God* 1.19.

"close friend" or the baby's "godfather" (5.6), and Nicia complies by inviting Callimaco and Ligurio to dinner and giving them a key to the house so that they can return at their convenience. Timoteo asks whether he will receive the money for alms, and Ligurio asks that Siro be remembered as well.

In sum, all participants in the conspiracy benefit. But the benefits—including the satisfaction of Nicia's desire for an heir, Callimaco's desire for the love of an extraordinarily beautiful and virtuous woman, Ligurio's desire to have a regular source of meals, Siro's desire to see Callimaco's desire satisfied and the pretentions of the stupid lawyer deflated, so long as he does not risk punishment, Timoteo's desire for funds with which to rebuild the "reputation" of the Church, Sostrata's desire to have a secure support in her old age, and Lucrezia's newly discovered desire for a young lover as well as a baby and future support from her husband(s)—all depend upon maintaining the appearance of a conventional marriage sanctified by the Church.

How exactly does the introduction of Christian beliefs and institutions enable Machiavelli to transform the tragic story of the rape of Lucretia into a modern comedy? It isn't just a matter of the frate's convincing Lucrezia to allow herself to be raped. Lucretia agreed to lie with Sextus because she did not want him to sully her honor by killing her and putting a dead slave in bed next to her; she killed herself later to show not merely her husband but all other Romans that she had not consented or taken pleasure in the act. Lucrezia is not persuaded by her confessor, but she does not propose to kill herself. She does not, because with the introduction of Christian beliefs the standard and judge of a person's honor has changed. Lucretia was worried about what her husband and the other Romans would think of her; and it is for this prideful concern about her reputation or honor in the eyes of others that Saint Augustine condemns her (as well as her fellow citizens).[17] According to Christian doctrine, it is a sin to commit suicide, because we are God's creations and not our own. As Timoteo reminds Lucrezia, the sinful character of her act depends upon her intention; and the purity of her intention can be judged only by God—or, perhaps, by his earthly representative. Sostrata is convinced of the latter, and concludes that her daughter has nothing to fear. Perceiving the corruption of God's representatives on earth, Lucrezia expects judgment from God himself.

17. *City of God* 1.16–20.

In his *Discourses* (1.11–15) Machiavelli praises the way in which the Roman senators manipulated the religious beliefs of the plebs in getting them to fight for the city. The role he indicates for the Church and its representatives in *Mandragola* is, however, importantly different. Timoteo does not persuade Lucrezia to obey him or her husband. But he does provide a public cover for the ongoing adultery by blessing the progeny of the marriage. In his political works Machiavelli argues that the Church has played a disastrous role in Italian politics, because it has no arms of its own and, therefore, has to use foreign auxiliaries or mercenaries to defend itself and its interests. But in his comedy Machiavelli suggests that the Church might play a positively beneficial role in the private lives of its parishioners, where it does not need to use force in order to have an effect on their opinions by appealing to their hopes and fears. If it confines its public role to the sanctification and support of marriage, the Church will become an important means of containing a very strong human passion and directing it to a productive, procreative end. To perform such a role, the prelates will not only have to stop interfering in political affairs; they will also have to hide if not contain their own sexual indiscretions, so that they will, as Nicia comments (3.2), be providing good examples rather than bad. They can and should be corrupt in the way Timoteo is, however, by seeking to acquire funds to build and maintain the reputation of the Church. Understanding that all human beings sin, prelates should continue to give those with a guilty conscience relief by taking their confessions and extending God's forgiveness. They should take the expressions of their parishioners' gratitude to enhance the reputation of the Church, not only by providing alms for the poor, but also by building and maintaining splendid edifices and conducting magnificent holiday processions.[18] God will thus appear to rule on earth as in heaven,

18. Machiavelli's use of the name "Timoteo" resonates in many directions. Literally, it means to honor god. In the New Testament, Timothy receives two letters from Saint Paul. In the first Paul emphasizes the importance of a woman's obeying her husband. Eve was the original sinner, but, Paul suggests, a woman can redeem herself by having children. This letter could thus be taken to provide some of Timoteo's argument to Lucrezia, justifying her submission. Most of the first is taken up with problems of church administration and the behavior of clerics, two concerns Brother Timoteo explicitly shares. However, this letter also contains the famous warning that "love of money is the root of all evils" (1 Timothy 2:15). In both this and his second letter Paul would thus appear to be warning a follower against the sort of action Machiavelli shows Timoteo taking. For in his second letter Paul predicts "that in the last days . . . men will be . . . lovers of pleasure rather than lovers of God, holding the form of religion but denying the power of it. Avoid such people. For among them are those who make their way into households and capture weak women, burdened with sins and swayed by various impulses" (2 Timothy 3:1). In *D* 1.12 and 2.5 Machiavelli suggested that the era of Christianity might be coming to an end. Flaumenhaft, "Comic Remedy," 53–54, takes the connection between the name of the frate and Paul's letters to

"for," as Machiavelli observes in concluding *P* 18, "the vulgar are taken in by the appearance and the outcome of a thing, and in the world there is no one but the vulgar" (71).

The change Machiavelli suggests in the role of the Church is, however, only a part of a much larger change he dramatizes. If they are to satisfy their desires and live in peace, he shows, "Christians" like Lucrezia must learn that the locus of their happiness is here on earth and not in the afterlife. They must take the direction of their own lives into their own hands, and not leave it to the will of heaven. No one can satisfy his or her own desires without the help of others. But as Ligurio observes early in the play, "the proverb on marriages which says 'God makes men and they pair themselves off' is rarely proven true." As in the case of Nicia and his wife, "one often sees that it's the lot of a well-qualified man to end up with a beast, and vice-versa, of a prudent woman to have a madman." A former marriage broker, Ligurio has come to understand both the passions that move human beings and the need for human intervention in order to satisfy them. He desires to see Callimaco's desire satisfied, it seems, because he wants to right the vagaries of fortune that give a stupid man like Nicia "a beautiful wife, wise, well-mannered, and fit to govern a kingdom" (1.3). At the end of the play, she takes charge of Nicia's newly reorganized household, in fact but not openly. Like Ligurio, who devises the plot that enables everyone to obtain what he or she desires, this wise woman understands that she cannot rule or control others by force, nor should she try to obtain public recognition or glory in doing so.

Although Machiavelli complains in the prologue that "in all things, the present age falls off from ancient *virtù*," in his comedy he does not show his characters trying to imitate the ancients, nor does he urge his audience to do so, as he does in both *The Prince* and *Discourses*. Quite the contrary. In *Mandragola* Machiavelli not only shows his characters violating both pagan and Christian notions of virtue but also celebrates the results. In the prologue Machiavelli announces that he is dramatizing a "new case" that has arisen in Florence. As in his teaching of princes how not to be good in *The Prince*, so we see in the course of the play that the "useful lesson" underlying the comical "case" that has arisen in Florence concerns morality. In *Mandragola* we learn that it is not solely the prince who should "keep

---

Timothy to show how corrupt Machiavelli thinks Timoteo is. But Mansfield, "Cuckold," 19–20, sees "the possibility of an adaptable Christianity" in Timoteo's concern for maintaining the reputation of God and the Church.

faith" by always seeming to be "merciful, faithful, humane, honest, and religious" (*P* 18), even though he cannot and should not always be so in fact. Private individuals are not able to satisfy their desires unless they conceal their true motives and pretend to be serving others.[19] They must appear to act according to conventional religious and moral beliefs they do not actually share, because these conventional beliefs support socially useful institutions like the family and the Church. These institutions are useful, furthermore, because like all well-conceived laws they direct or redirect human passions away from potentially destructive conflict so that they have not merely productive and stabilizing but even liberating results.[20]

In *Mandragola* Machiavelli thus shows that a crucial part of the new moral teaching he presented in *The Prince* applies to private life as well, but he does not suggest that there is no difference between public and private. There are few individuals as clever in helping others satisfy their own desires as Ligurio and few women as wise as Lucrezia about the way in which they can rule without seeming to do so.[21] In most cities, Machiavelli shows in his political works, the passions of men may be aroused by women, but they fight, in fact, primarily over economic goods.[22] Despite the introductory song he appended to the comedy in which the nymphs and shepherds urge the audience to follow their desires, "because life is brief and many are the pains which, living and struggling, everyone sustains," Machiavelli is not an epicurean or hedonist. In contrast to his nymphs and shepherds, he clearly states in the prologue, he has not withdrawn from the world and chosen the solitary life voluntarily. He would participate in public, political life, if he could. And in public life, where individuals strive for recognition despite the envy of others, there is conflict, conflict that can at best be controlled but never entirely obliterated by laws backed with force. If we look back at his praise of the advantages of a free way of life in *D* 2.2, we will discover that most of them are private. And in private life, as he shows in his comedy, where associations are voluntary, love can be stronger than fear. Because of the need to maintain appearances, fear of scandal does not disappear. But

19. This is the theme of the contrast Ruth W. Grant, *Hypocrisy and Integrity: Machiavelli, Rousseau, and the Ethics of Politics* (Chicago: University of Chicago Press, 1997), draws between Machiavelli and Rousseau, partly on the basis of her reading of *Mandragola* (45–53).

20. George Thomas, "The Parasite as Virtuoso: Sexual Desire and Political Order in Machiavelli's *Mandragola*," *Interpretation* 30, no. 2 (Spring 2003): 181–96, emphasizes this aspect of the comedy.

21. In his other comedy, *Clizia*, Machiavelli depicts another such woman in Sofronia. See my "Fortune Is a Woman."

22. *D* 3.26; *FH* 2.3.

in the wooing of Lucrezia, Machiavelli shows, Callimaco makes a crucial change in Ligurio's advice. Whereas Ligurio instructed Callimaco to tell Lucrezia how they could continue to take pleasure in each other without scandal, and to threaten her with scandal if she did not agree (4.2), Callimaco promises to marry her when Nicia dies (5.4), because he wants her to love, not to fear him.[23] The one exception with regard to the essentially private advantages of a free way of life that Machiavelli extols consists in the hope every man can have that his son will be elected to high office. Human ambition, which extends beyond pleasure, makes it impossible for the most talented to be satisfied, as Callimaco, Nicia, Lucrezia, and Ligurio apparently are, with the pleasures they enjoy in private. As Machiavelli observes in *D* 1.37, when human beings no longer contend from necessity, they do so from ambition.

Machiavelli's immediate audience was composed primarily of young ambitious Florentines who might enjoy their amorous affairs, but who also hoped to occupy high office. In his subsequent works he thus tried to correct some misapprehensions they seem to have held or acquired about the means needed to realize those ambitions.

23. *Pace* Thomas, "Parasite as Virtuoso," who suggests that relations between Lucrezia and Callimaco in the future will be based on the fear of scandal rather than mutual attraction. Mansfield, "Cuckold," 27, argues that Ligurio has no interest in transforming Callimaco from lover into husband and concludes that it is Nicia who is ruling. He does not note Ligurio's initial comments about Lucrezia as "fit to rule a kingdom" or attribute the change in Callimaco to her effect upon him. He takes Lucrezia to represent "morality," although it is difficult to maintain that her final situation or self-understanding is simply moral.

4

Machiavelli's Defense

THE ART OF WAR

In writing a dialogue on the "art of war," Machiavelli turned back from comedy to *the* most deadly serious public matter. It was, moreover, a subject that had been at the center of Machiavelli's own public career as well as his previous prose writings. *The* policy he had urged his patron Piero Soderini to adopt in the face of strenuous opposition from other *ottimati* was the formation and training of a Florentine militia. It was the policy he did not have time or opportunity to bring to fruition before his ill-trained peasant militia was massacred by the Spanish at Prato and his efforts to marshal and train an effective native defense force were declared to have been in vain, if not ill advised. In *The Prince* Machiavelli wrote that "a prince should have no other object, nor any other thought, nor take anything else as his art but that of war and its orders and discipline; for that is the only art which is of concern to one who commands" (53). And in both *The Prince* and *Discourses*, he traced the failure of Florence to secure the liberty of the city, both domestically and from foreign aggressors, to its reliance on mercenary arms. Yet by relating lectures delivered in a garden after dinner by a mercenary captain to the young friends to whom he dedicated his *Discourses*, Machiavelli suggests, rather ironically, that even his most enthusiastic admirers seemed not to have absorbed the first and most obvious lesson he had to teach. Rather than seeking to learn how to acquire their own arms by practicing in the field, they preferred to discuss the merits of various forms of republican government at their leisure or to watch comedies at court.

After the militia he had trained was so badly defeated at Prato, Machiavelli recognized that he would not be regarded as an expert on the means of ordering an effective military force. In writing about the "art of war" he did not, therefore, put the substance of his recommendations forward in his own name. As in the comedies he wrote and produced during his lifetime, so in the dialogue he composed and published, he began with a short preface in which he explained his writing as a result of his forced retirement from active public service, and put the body of his controversial opinions into the mouths of others. Indeed, by attributing the lessons his young friends received about the art of war to Fabrizio Colonna, the mercenary captain who led the Spanish forces that forced Piero Soderini to capitulate, Machiavelli kept himself in the background and made the technical, apparently nonpartisan character of those lessons stand out and so concealed their revolutionary political implications. His attribution of these most necessary lessons to an enemy of the Florentine republic and his showing that young Florentine friends still needed to learn what he had tried to teach them in writings that had circulated only in private nevertheless prove, upon examination, to be thoroughly ironic. In fact, the dialogue constitutes a defense of the policies Machiavelli advocated both as a practical politician and as a political theorist.

Machiavelli's "Apology"

By signing the book as Niccolò Machiavegli, Florentine Citizen and Secretary, and dedicating it to Lorenzo di Filippo Strozzi, Florentine Patrician, the author reminds his readers not only of the office he once held and the services he rendered to the republic, but also of his frustrated desire to regain public employment. Lorenzo Strozzi was a wealthy banker and member of an influential family who had facilitated contact between Machiavelli and the Medici in 1520, a year before the *Art of War* was published. A son-in-law of Bernardo Rucellai, who had occasionally visited the Orti Oricellari where the dialogue is set, Lorenzo was an ideal "go between."[1] As in *The Prince*, so in the *Art of War*, Machiavelli thus addresses a 'Lorenzo' in hope of gaining future employment and apologizes for his presumption for writing about an activity of which he "has not made a profession." As Machiavelli implied in his letter of dedication to *The Prince*, so he suggests even more openly here: those who have been charged with the responsibility have not known what they were doing. Any errors he might have made

1. The Strozzi had historically been opponents of the Medici, but the two families had reconciled.

in writing could not have the harmful effects made by those who had ruined empires with their deeds. Leaving his patron to judge the quality of his work, Machiavelli explains that he has dedicated the work to Lorenzo in gratitude for the benefits the author has received and because "it is customary to honor . . . those who are resplendent in nobility, wealth, talent, and liberality" (5). To anyone who had read a manuscript copy of *The Prince* or *Discourses* (and all later readers of his works), Machiavelli thus indicated that the *Art of War* has a more conventional form or exterior than the two works he had explicitly acknowledged were not written or presented as was "customary."

In calling attention to his forced retirement from public life, Machiavelli also reminds readers of the reasons he did not feel entirely free to say everything that he thought openly, fully, or explicitly. In his preface, he acknowledges the controversial character of his subject. "Many have held . . . that there are no things less in agreement with one another or so dissimilar as the civilian and military lives." They observe that "if someone plans to succeed in the soldier's career, he not only changes dress immediately, but also departs from every civilian practice in his customs, usages, voice, and bearing." Because a soldier must be ready to use violence and frighten others, he cannot adopt civilian customs, dress, or speech, all of which seem effeminate and thus contrary to the requirements of his profession. In our time, Machiavelli acknowledges, military and civilian life are opposed. However, he reminds his classically educated readers, this was not always the case. On the contrary, "if ancient orders were considered, nothing would be found more united and in conformity" than military and civilian life. Recurring to antiquity enables Machiavelli, first, to emphasize the fundamental importance of defense by reminding his readers that no laws, religion, or arts will survive where people are not protected from foreign aggressors. Indeed, he comes close to restating his famous claim in *P* 12 that "there cannot be good laws where there are not good arms and where there are good arms there must be good laws" in more moderate language by observing that "good orders without military help are disordered." Then he claims that soldiers make exemplary citizens, not merely because they are willing to risk their lives in defending the fatherland, but because they must love peace (since they have reason to fear harm in war), and they must both love and fear God most of all, since they beyond all others need His support. "This necessity," Machiavelli explains, "made the soldiers' life praised by other men and followed and imitated with utmost attention." The "sinister opinions" about the incompatibility of military and civilian life have arisen only in modern times, when "military orders are altogether corrupt and separated by great lengths from ancient modes" (*AW* Pref., 3–4).

In his "preface" Machiavelli does not explain how or why military orders in his time have become corrupt (although he does in both *The Prince* and *Discourses*). That corruption cannot simply be a product of the observed difference in manners between civilians and soldiers he mentions here, since ancient soldiers also wore uniforms and were harsh in both speech and deed. Nor were ancient soldiers the most god-fearing and peace-loving parts of the population, (even though in *D* 1.11 Machiavelli praises Numa for making the Roman people more pacific by inculcating a set of religious beliefs that the senators later used to get the plebs to fight). As in *D* 1.12, 2.2, so in the *Art of War* (2.305–7), Machiavelli suggests that the Christian religion is the origin of the "sinister opinions . . . that have arisen that make [men] hate the military and flee association with those who practice it" (*AW* Pref., 4) only after he is well into the book. Christianity may have been the origin of "sinister opinions" concerning the incompatibility of military and civilian life; but, we learn early in the dialogue, the wealthy merchants who ruled Florence constituted a more immediate source of the opinion that it was not desirable to resuscitate the harsh military modes of the ancients. The *ottimati* did not merely consider the harsh modes of the ancients contrary to the "civilized" life of gentlemen; they also feared that arming the plebs, i.e., the lower classes of laborers and peasants, would threaten their control of the republic.[2] In trying not merely to revive study of the art of war, but to establish a Florentine militia, Machiavelli was challenging both the firm convictions and considered interests of the ruling class. No wonder he approached his subject somewhat indirectly.

Drawing, as in *The Prince* and *Discourses*, on "what he has seen and read," in the preface Machiavelli states simply that he has concluded that it is possible to revive ancient modes—presumably by changing the corrupt modern orders and the "sinister opinions" that have arisen about them, although Machiavelli does not say so explicitly. He merely proposes to use his "idle time" to write what he understands about the art of war for the satisfaction of those who are lovers of ancient actions. But he thus indicates the character of the audience he addresses most immediately. Like Cosimo Rucellai, whose grandfather Bernardo planted the garden in which the dialogue is supposed to have taken place, they are heirs of the "civic humanists" who

2. They remembered the Ciompi rebellion, which Machiavelli describes in detail in his *Florentine Histories* 3.9–21.

share some of their forefathers' tastes and opinions. They may admire ancient actions, but, we learn early in the dialogue, they do not want to adopt the harsh morality of the ancients; they would be defamed and vilified by their contemporaries if they did. These young men are public-spirited, but unlike their ancestors, they do not hold office and perhaps will not be able to so long as the Medici control the government. Machiavelli may be appealing to their revolutionary desires, but he cannot do so openly.

Admitting that he is not a professional soldier, Machiavelli suggests that he shares the liability of the young men he depicts listening to the mercenary captain who speaks to them about "the art of war." In relating the dialogue Machiavelli never explicitly connects Fabrizio's insistence that "one cannot make a foundation on other arms than one's own [cf. *P* 6–9, 12–14, 24, 26; *D* 2.20] and one cannot order one's own arms otherwise than as a militia" (*AW* 1.189) with his own persistent attempt to form such a militia as "Florentine Citizen and Secretary" (as he repeatedly describes himself at the beginning and end not only of the dialogue but also of the particular books in it). Once we recognize the connection, however, we realize that the knowledge Machiavelli attributes to Fabrizio belongs to the author of the dialogue (which probably did not actually take place). Fabrizio's self-justifying claim that he has obviously spent a great deal of time and effort acquiring this knowledge, but did not have an opportunity to put it into practice because he did not have the requisite political authority (*AW* 7.194–97), applies much more clearly to Machiavelli than to the historical mercenary captain (who was duke of Palliano and Marsi as well as count of Tagliazozzo and Celano). The *Art of War* thus constitutes a defense of Machiavelli's practice as secretary of the republic of Florence, where he advocated and initiated the formation of a militia, as well as a statement of his "theory."[3]

3. After Piero Soderini was named gonfalonier for life in 1502, Machiavelli became one of Soderini's most trusted advisors and representatives. As he indicated at the conclusion of his *First Decennial* (1504), an epic poem in which he details the suffering of Italy in the decade following the French invasion, and the only work he published while in office, Machiavelli had become convinced that the political divisions that made Italy vulnerable to foreign invasion would never be overcome until Florence rearmed itself. With the support of Piero's brother Cardinal Francesco Soderini, Machiavelli thus pressed the gonfalonier to reestablish the militia Florence had lacked for more than two hundred years. The proposal aroused a lot of opposition, especially from Soderini's aristocratic opponents, who accused him of wanting to become a tyrant (by obtaining a bodyguard). The cardinal advised Machiavelli to begin recruiting and training in the countryside, where an armed force would pose a less direct threat to citizens in power. After the mercenaries the Florentines hired in an attempt to retake Pisa were ignominiously defeated, in 1506 the Council created the *nove ufficiali dell' ordinanza e milizia fiorentina* (the nine officers of the Florentine ordinance and militia). Machi-

The Dialogue

A. Occasion, Setting, and Dramatis Personae

Machiavelli explains that he is relating the conversation to celebrate and perpetuate the memory of his young friend, Cosimo Rucellai, who has recently died (1519). He begins by praising Cosimo both as a friend and as a patriot. Cosimo demonstrated his liberality by inviting his friends to partake not merely in sumptuous dinners, but also in the conversations that followed in the Orti Oricellari planted by his grandfather. But unfortunately he did not live long enough to perform any great and magnificent deeds on behalf of his fatherland. Since Cosimo was preparing himself for such public service by discussions of the kind he once had with Fabrizio Colonna, Machiavelli suggests that recalling that conversation might not only serve as a fitting memorial to his young friend, but also enable others to "learn many things useful not only for military but also civil life, wisely disputed by a very knowledgeable man" (1.8). Machiavelli's stated intention in relating the conversation is thus quickly shown not simply or even primarily to be honoring Cosimo or conveying technical knowledge about military organization, so much as *enabling his readers to learn many things useful for civil as well as for military life*. In other words, his discussion of the "art of war" has a much greater import and range than first appear.

Many readers of the *Art of War* have noted the apparent irony of Machiavelli's choice of Fabrizio Colonna as his spokesman. Why would Machiavelli choose a mercenary captain of the kind he criticized so vehemently in both *The Prince* and *Discourses* to deliver his useful lesson? Why, indeed, would he choose *the* mercenary captain who led the Spanish troops responsible for the

avelli was made secretary and threw himself wholeheartedly into the effort of recruiting and training a native Florentine army. On June 8, 1509, fifteen years of war ended with a Florentine victory over Pisa, thanks to Machiavelli and his battalions. Machiavelli then received authorization from the Ten to raise a detachment of light horse to supplement his infantry, but he did not have time or receive adequate support to recruit and train an army capable of defending Florence from the Holy League (founded in 1511 by Pope Julius II in alliance with the Venetians, Spanish, English, Swiss, and the Holy Roman Emperor against Louis XII of France). Although France defeated the Holy League at the Battle of Ravenna in 1512, the French commander Gaston de Foix was killed, and King Louis ordered his troops to withdraw. Florence was left alone to face the Spanish troops that had been defeated at Ravenna. Because they lacked supplies, the Spanish commander tried twice to negotiate a settlement with Soderini, but he and the Council refused their terms. Soderini asked Machiavelli to do something to restrain the Spanish, but with the body of Florentine troops kept at home to defend the city, Machiavelli and his ill-trained troops were not able to withstand the Spanish at Prato. See C. C. Bayley, *War and Society in Renaissance Italy* (Toronto: University of Toronto Press, 1961), 276–84, and Mikael Hörnqvist, *"Perché non si usa allegare i Romani,"* 151–64.

fall of the Florentine republic in 1512 (and so indirectly for Machiavelli's own dismissal from its government)?

Mansfield explains Machiavelli's choice by pointing out that Fabrizio possessed the practical knowledge of the art of war that Machiavelli admitted he lacked and could thus speak with more authority. By using such a historical figure, Machiavelli also distanced himself from what might be taken to be the anti-Medician implications of the argument.[4] Marcia Colish, on the other hand, thinks that Machiavelli chose Fabrizio because of the conjunction between Machiavelli's opposition to the Medici and the known enmity of the Colonna to the Medici, who had allied themselves by marriage with the Orsini, the opponents of the Colonna in Rome. Choosing a spokesman to reflect his own opposition to the Medici would, however, undermine Machiavelli's ongoing attempt to obtain employment from the Medici, of which he reminds readers in the dedication.[5] Colish also and more convincingly points out that authors of dialogues in the Renaissance liked to use figures whose lives and opinions were familiar to their audience, and that Machiavelli's predecessors in the writing of dialogues as well as histories, Leonardo Bruni and Poggio Bracciolini, intentionally had such figures argue for positions contrary to those they were known to hold to add irony and entertainment to their work.[6]

Fabrizio provided a safe cover for Machiavelli, because he was a friend of the Medici. He had been captain of the Spanish armies that forced Piero Soderini to capitulate and enabled the Medici to recapture control of the Florentine republic. According to Machiavelli, Fabrizio was in Florence and thus able to converse with Cosimo and his friends, because he was visiting Lorenzo de' Medici.

Machiavelli ironically uses Fabrizio to conceal not only the revolutionary potential of the knowledge he is disseminating but also the republican bias of the priority Fabrizio gives the infantry, even though he treats the recruiting, training, arming, and deploying of the army as an "art" that can be

4. Mansfield, *Machiavelli's Virtue*, 195.

5. Marcia L. Colish, "Machiavelli's *Art of War*: A Reconsideration," *Renaissance Quarterly* 51 (1998): 1151–68.

6. Explaining this practice in a letter to a bemused reader, Poggio wrote that he had assigned an attack on avarice to a known prodigal not only in order to import irony into his dialogue and thereby make it more entertaining, but also because he thought people ought to be able to distinguish positions from the characters who profess them. Machiavelli might well have shared both thoughts. Colish, "Machiavelli's *Art of War*," 1164, relying on David Marsh, *The Quattrocento Dialogue: Classical Tradition and Humanist Innovation* (Cambridge, MA: Harvard University Press, 1980).

practiced equally well by a republic or a principality.[7] In arguing that knowledge of the art of war is essential for the leaders of both republics and principalities, Fabrizio takes the same position Machiavelli did in *P* 12–14.

Although Machiavelli clearly distinguishes himself as narrator from the major speaker in the dialogue at the beginning, he indicates later that it is he who is speaking in the name of Fabrizio. When talking to Zanobi, "Fabrizio" says twice (*AW* 4.118, 5.92) that he has reasoned with him and his friends another time about the subject in question (in *D* 3.10 and 2.6). Fabrizio had been fighting wars most of the time these young men were growing up in Florence, and so was not likely to have "reasoned" with them there, while Machiavelli was known to have been talking and writing to them.

In *The Prince* Machiavelli argued that the art of war "is of such virtue that it not only maintains those who have been born princes but many times it enables men of private fortune to rise to that rank" (*P* 14, 58, slightly adapted). In the *Art of War* Machiavelli thus implicitly presents himself (or his spokesman) as teaching young Florentine aristocrats what they need to know to become prince of Italy (see *AW* 7.243). The question Fabrizio leaves open at the end is whether the young Florentines will have a better opportunity than he to put what they have learned into practice (and if they have such an opportunity, whether they will, in fact, be able to take advantage of it).

By depicting Fabrizio in conversation with his young friends, Machiavelli also lets his readers see the character of the audience he addressed most

7. In telling Cosimo the reasons why he thinks that infantry constitute a better foundation for an army than cavalry (although he admits that cavalry are necessary and useful) in *AW* 2.86–95, Fabrizio repeats the tactical advantages Machiavelli describes in his own name in *D* 2.18: foot soldiers can go where horses cannot, or more easily, through woods and swamps; they are less easily disordered and can more easily reorder themselves than horses can; there is no potential division in inclination or spirit in a foot soldier as there is between a horse and its rider; and, finally, men can be ordered to march ahead where horses will refuse to go. Fabrizio does not add, as Machiavelli does, speaking in his own name, "if this were believed, republics and princes would err less . . . *and those who have in their hands a civil way of life would know better how to direct it, either by way of expanding it or by way of maintaining it. And they would believe that increasing the inhabitants of one's city, getting partners and not subjects, sending colonies to guard countries that have been acquired* [as well as the Roman policies Fabrizio will recommend to 'captains' of armies below], making capital out of booty, subduing the enemy with raids and battles and not with sieges, keeping the public rich and the private poor, and maintaining military exercises with the highest seriousness *is the true way to make a republic great and to acquire empire*" (emphasis added). On the class basis of Machiavelli's preference for the infantry over the cavalry, see Timothy J. Lukes, "Martialing Machiavelli: Reassessing the Military Reflections," *Journal of Politics* 66, no. 4 (2004): 1099–1102.

immediately, and the kinds of difficulties he encountered in trying to persuade them to undertake his revolutionary project. The host of the meeting described in the *Art of War* is Cosimo Rucellai, one of the two young men to whom Machiavelli had dedicated his *Discourses on Livy.* The other dedicatee of the *Discourses*, Zanobi Buondelmonti, also takes part in the conversation, as does Luigi Alamanni (to whom Machiavelli dedicated his *Life of Castruccio Castracani* along with Zanobi in 1520) and Battista della Palla.[8] All four were young friends of Machiavelli who had been pressing the Medici to grant Machiavelli a commission to write the *Florentine Histories*. (Cardinal Giulio de' Medici, later Pope Clement VII, finally did this in 1520. It was not, however, the political office or responsibility that Machiavelli had been seeking.) Cosimo died in 1519, but Zanobi, Luigi, and Battista all played leading roles in a conspiracy in 1522 to assassinate Giulio and reinstate Machiavelli's former patron, Piero Soderini, as head of a Florentine republic.

The young men whom Machiavelli shows Fabrizio instructing in the art of war were thus not only the same young men to whom he addressed his own *Discourses*, but also among those who actively sought to reintroduce republican government in Florence. As readers hear each of these young men interrogate Fabrizio, we learn something about their individual characters and Machiavelli's view of them. Machiavelli praises Cosimo for his generosity to his friends and his noble public ambitions, but he also shows that Cosimo was physically weak and politically conservative. Luigi is said to be young and impetuous, whereas Zanobi is "spirited," and Battista "prudent." But it is far from clear that in organizing a conspiracy in 1522 to assassinate Giulio de' Medici and reinstate Piero Soderini as head of a Florentine republic, Luigi, Zanobi, and Battista were following Machiavelli's advice.[9] The severity of Machiavelli's criticism of Soderini in *D* 3.3 and 3.30 makes

8. Ridolfi, *Life*, reports that while Machiavelli was writing the *Art of War*, "Battista della Palla, who is on very good terms at court because of his long record of allegiance and a gift he has made of extremely valuable sables," sent him good news from Rome. Battista had "told the Pope, who is very fond of such things, about their meetings in the Orti, and how much they all value Machiavelli's intellect. He has spoken warmly of the *Mandragola* which was ready to be acted in His Holiness's presence." And he suggested that "Leo was the sort of man who might more easily be won by a coarse comedy than by a *Prince*: he would have enjoyed the jokes and rejected what was bitter. Having thus first got him in a good mood, the clever courtier induced the Pope to give him a message for Cardinal de' Medici telling him to give effect to his goodwill toward Machiavelli with a 'commission to write, or something similar'" (179).

9. Viroli, *Niccolò's Smile*, 210, suggests that Machiavelli instigated the plot. See J. N. Stephens, *The Fall of the Florentine Republic 1512–1530* (Oxford: Clarendon Press, 1983), 117–23, for a fuller account of the history.

one wonder whether Machiavelli would have greeted the reinstatement of his former patron with great enthusiasm. Writing at the invitation of Leo X in "Discourse on Remodeling the Government of Florence," in 1520 Machiavelli had proposed a peaceful transition from the rule of the Medici princes, who as men of the Church were without heirs, to a republic to be established when they died.[10] (To be sure, the Medici princes do not seem to have heeded his advice, if they read it.) The conspiracy organized by Machiavelli's young friends looks very much like the conspiracies he repeatedly shows in the *Florentine Histories* failed to establish a stable, much less a free government, because the people were corrupt. As he observes in both *D* 3.6 and *FH* 7.33, those who conspire to assassinate the current prince hope that the people will rise and join them in a rebellion. But where the people no longer understand the advantages of a free government or are too afraid to fight for it, they will not support the rebels. Conspirators at the head of men they have selected and trained to bear arms have a much better chance of actually taking control and establishing a new regime.[11] In all three of his major prose works, Machiavelli thus emphasizes the importance of training and leading one's own troops. The young men who listened to a lecture on the art of war while sitting in a garden without ever trying to practice it the way Machiavelli himself did—both in the field drilling raw recruits and in his study—do not seem to have absorbed what he described as his first and most important lesson. He was evidently pleased by their willingness to listen and read what he wrote, as well as by their attempts to obtain employment for him from the Medici, but he must have viewed their professed admiration with some irony.

The setting of the conversation also points to the circumstances in which Machiavelli was writing and the obstacles these circumstances represented to the achievement of his political goals. As Cosimo reminds his guests, the gardens in which they are seeking shade after they have dined were planted by his grandfather, Bernardo Rucellai. Like Machiavelli and many other Florentines, Bernardo was an admirer of ancient Rome; but as the initial exchange between Cosimo and Fabrizio indicates, Bernardo did

10. *Machiavelli: The Chief Works and Others*, trans. Allan Gilbert (Durham: Duke University Press, 1958), 1: 101–15. He drafted another plan for constitutional reform in April 1522 (Niccolò Machiavelli, *L'arte della Guerra. Scritti politici minori*, ed. Jean-Jacques Marchand, Denis Fachard, and Giorgio Masi [Rome: Salerno Editrice, 2001], 645–54). But as Ann Maria Cabrini, "Machiavelli's *Florentine Histories*," in Najemy, *Cambridge Companion to Machiavelli*, 133, notes, the discovery of the conspiracy in June put an end to all such discussions of constitutional reform. Machiavelli and his friends seem to have been working at cross-purposes.

11. See Machiavelli's praise of Camillus at the conclusion of *D* 3.30.

not admire or seek to imitate the same aspects of the ancient republic that Machiavelli did. (Among other things, the conversation related in the *Art of War* thus shows readers that in both his *Discourses* and *Art of War*, Machiavelli was trying to wean Cosimo away from opinions he had acquired from his grandfather.) Bernardo had been a close friend and advisor of Lorenzo the Magnificent. (They were, indeed, related by marriage; Nannina de' Medici, Lorenzo il Magnifico's sister, was Bernardo's wife.) But when Lorenzo began to rule more autocratically, Bernardo distanced himself. He urged Lorenzo's son to exercise his power with more restraint and to concede more influence to the Florentine aristocracy, and when Piero refused, Bernardo openly opposed him. He was appointed to the commission assigned to give Florence a new constitution in 1494, but he opposed the popular elements, especially the Grand Council, that were added under the influence of Savonarola, and went into voluntary exile. He supported the creation of a gonfalonier for life in 1502 but vehemently opposed both the appointment of Piero Soderini to the office and the failure to abolish the Grand Council. The Orti Oricellari he then planted became home not only to his collections of ancient plants and statues of classical heroes, but also to meetings of admirers of Marsilio Ficino's Platonism, which emphasized the importance of orienting one's life by a transcendent standard of beauty (or nobility). Summarizing Bernardo's career, Felix Gilbert concludes that "Rucellai's political aim was the establishment of a restricted government, over which the aristocrats would have full control. He was an enemy of the absolutist rule of one man, but he was an equally decided opponent of any popular form of government. . . . In his book on the classical antiquities of Rome, . . . Rucellai states quite explicitly that he considers popular rule fatal for Florence and that . . . he concentrated all his energies on purging the city from the weight of this dross."[12]

Machiavelli may have chosen the form of a dialogue to counter some of the influence Ficino and his students continued to exercise on humanistically educated Florentine aristocrats. But he reverses and so undermines some of the dominant features of the Platonic dialogues by showing a military captain rather than a philosopher teaching politically ambitious youths what they need to know in order to become great statesmen. Rather than urging

12. Felix Gilbert, "Bernardo Rucellai and the Orti Oricellari: A Study in the Origins of Modern Political Thought," in *History: Choice and Commitment* (Cambridge, MA: Harvard University Press, 1977), 223–24.

them to become moderate and just, he instructs them about the best means of acquiring the lands, people, and goods belonging to others. It is probably no accident that Machiavelli informs his readers that the participants in the conversation he relates moved into the shade to avoid the sun after they had eaten a sumptuous dinner—in contrast to the conversation Plato relates in the *Republic* among people who never receive the dinner they are promised and stay instead to discuss the design and establishment of a revolutionary regime in the middle of the night. It is clear that Machiavelli is trying to wean his young friends away from the aristocratic prejudices and more classically republican views of their fathers. Bernardo died in 1514, only a year or two before the conversation related in the *Art of War* is supposed to have taken place. As Machiavelli shows at the beginning of the conversation, Bernardo's views continued to shape the opinions and habits of his grandson Cosimo.

B. Sources of Resistance to "Imitating the Ancients" with Regard to the Military, and Machiavelli's Response to Them

As the questions Cosimo Rucellai first puts to Fabrizio demonstrate, the resistance to Machiavelli's call in the *Discourses* to imitate the ancients was not limited to older, more conservative Florentines. The young men to whom he had dedicated the *Discourses* shared some of their elders' objections to Machiavelli's project. Indeed, in the initial exchange between Cosimo and Fabrizio, Machiavelli points to four different sources of resistance to the imitation of ancient military modes.

The first source of resistance arose from a perceived change in manners or mores, particularly with regard to education. Suspecting that his guests might not recognize the plants they see around them, Cosimo explains that his grandfather collected specimens of ancient varieties. Fabrizio somewhat impolitely responds that it would have been better if admirers of the ancient had sought to be like them "in the strong and harsh things, not in the delicate soft ones . . . , and to take up the modes of the true and perfect antiquity, not the false and corrupt one. For after those studies pleased my Romans, my fatherland went to ruin" (1.17). By the false mode and studies, Fabrizio seems to be referring to imitations of the ancients in the fine arts and the revival of Platonic philosophy supported by Lorenzo the Magnificent and his "right-hand man," Bernardo Rucellai. Cosimo thus jumps to defend his grandfather by claiming that no one despised softness and loved the harshness of the ancients more, but that living in a corrupt time, Bernardo recognized that without being universally defamed, neither he nor his children could imitate Diogenes by going naked in all seasons, forcing their children to sleep in the open and endure all sorts of deprivations like the Spartans, or despising gold and eating only vegetables like Fabricius. The Rucellai are gentlemen, and they care about their reputation.[13]

Although he says that he is relating the dialogue in honor of Cosimo's memory, to show how the young man prepared himself for public service by hosting such conversations, Machiavelli intimates here that Cosimo may not have been able to realize his noble ambitions, because his family refused to follow ancient modes of education they deemed too harsh. As a consequence, Cosimo remained weak and sickly. He did not have the physical stamina needed to become a general-statesman in the Roman mode.

Recognizing that Cosimo shares his grandfather's concern for what is praised and blamed by his contemporaries, Fabrizio quickly retreats. He "was not speaking so much of those hard modes of living, as of other more humane modes . . . that have more conformity with life today" and that would not be difficult for a prince of a city to introduce. The examples he gives of honoring and rewarding the virtues, not despising poverty, esteeming the modes and orders of military discipline, *constraining* citizens to love one another, living without sects, and esteeming the private less than the public (*AW* 1.33, emphasis added) seem to describe older aristocratic practices. However, by promising that if such orders are entered into by degrees, it will not be difficult to persuade people who think about them much, "for in them truth appears so much that every common talent can be capable of it" (*AW* 1.34), Fabrizio does not appear to be asking for extraordinary self-sacrifice or virtue. He is either adapting his speech to the taste of his audience and their corrupt times or proposing a less harsh notion of the education necessary to produce good citizens and soldiers than the ancient beliefs and practices to which Cosimo objects—both philosophical (Diogenes) and political (Sparta and Fabricius).

Changes in taste or styles and goals of education were not the only source of resistance to the imitation of ancient military practices Fabrizio is advocating. Machiavelli's young friends also perceive the morally dubious

13. The Rucellai were, as a result, more sensitive to the views of others than Machiavelli shows in his *Life of Castruccio Castracani* the mercenary captain who succeeded in seizing control of his city was; and even he found it necessary to alter the maxims he stole from the ancient cynic to fit modern circumstances. See chapter 5 for a fuller discussion.

character of an autonomous "art of war." After he defends his grandfather from Fabrizio's critique on the basis of considerations of reputation, Cosimo attacks his critic by suggesting that Fabrizio is behaving hypocritically in urging others to imitate the ancients, since he has not done so himself. The ancients were citizen soldiers who patriotically fought for their country; he is a mercenary, willing to serve whoever will pay him.

"Fabrizio" responds to Cosimo's observation about his own failure to imitate the ancients by explaining that men who wish to do something must first prepare themselves to do it. (He thus becomes an example of the effort for which Machiavelli initially praised his host as well as the source of instruction.) But, Fabrizio warns Cosimo and his fellows, the character and extent of their preparations will not be externally visible, so long as they do not have an opportunity to act on them. He thus proposes to demonstrate the truth of his claim to have prepared himself by discoursing "at length . . . on what preparations are necessary to make before, what opportunity must arise, what difficulty impedes" (*AW* 1.44).

Fabrizio suggests that the members of his audience will be more willing to listen to his proposals than their elders, because their youth makes them "more friendly to military things and more ready to believe" than those "already having white heads and ice in their veins." But, he insists, opposition to the imitation of ancient military orders is not merely a matter of age or of changed, gentler mores. His contemporaries rightly see that the acquisition and exercise of an autonomous "art of war" is morally repulsive. Machiavelli thus highlights the ironical character of his choice of a spokesman by having "Fabrizio" condemn his own actual practice as a mercenary captain by declaring that the "art of war" is "an art by means of which men cannot live honestly in any time." No one can support himself by means of war without becoming "rapacious, fraudulent, violent" and having "many of the qualities that make him not good," because he must always seek to undermine the peace in order to nourish himself (*AW* 1.47–51).

Echoing his grandfather's appreciation of the need for noble leadership (and perhaps referring to the statues surrounding them in the garden), Cosimo objects: Fabrizio is ignoring "the glory of Caesar, Pompey, Scipio, Marcellus, and so many Roman captains who are famously celebrated as gods" (*AW* 1.63). Caesar and Pompey were able, but not good men, Fabrizio retorts, because they sought their own profit and advancement at the expense of the republic; and the exchange serves to remind Machiavelli's readers of two of the reasons some older and more experienced men objected to the imitation of the ancient modes of warfare. Those modes had led to the fall of the Roman republic and the elevation of individual generals into emperors whose successors became tyrants. Why then should those who wish to see republican government revived want to reinstitute these ancient modes?

The third source of resistance to the revival of ancient military orders that emerges in the exchange between Cosimo and Fabrizio thus consists in fear of the political consequences. By stating that no republic or principality, if well ordered, will allow any of its citizens or subjects to practice the art for his own private benefit, Fabrizio shows that the imitation of the ancients he is advocating is and must be a matter of public policy. It can be neither justified nor achieved merely through the action or education of individuals. (The conversation he is having with these young men, and the dialogue Machiavelli is writing, can therefore only be preparatory.) As Fabrizio admitted in condemning the practice of mercenaries, there is a potential tension between the interests of individual soldiers and the governments they purportedly serve. The question thus becomes whether or how this conflict of interest can be overcome.

Granting a possible antagonism between republican government and the practice of the art of war by talented and ambitious generals, Cosimo suggests that a king might nevertheless want to employ an individual who practices that art (as the king of Spain did, in fact, employ Fabrizio); but Fabrizio denies it.[14] Restating a position Machiavelli affirms in both *P* 19 and *D* 1.16, Fabrizio states that "kingdoms that have good orders do not give absolute rule to their kings except in the armies; for in this place alone is a sudden decision necessary, and for this there must be one unified power. In other things he cannot do anything without counsel; and those who give him counsel have to fear that he may have someone near who in times of peace desires war because he cannot live without it" (*AW*, 1.80–81, translation slightly modified). Explicitly choosing to dwell longer on this subject, as it applies to kingdoms that exist at his time, Fabrizio explains (in terms that resemble the argument Machiavelli gives about the true meaning of "liberality" in *P* 16), a king cannot keep a paid army without having it constantly fight and take spoils, which is impossible, so he will have to pay the soldiers from his own resources, which will bankrupt him, and thus even-

14. Like his grandfather, Cosimo is willing to embrace the rule of one man so long as he employs and depends upon other aristocrats.

tually cause him to lose not merely esteem, but his state. Fabrizio admits that the Roman republic maintained an army constantly in the field, but he argues that they avoided the dangerous consequences by varying the men serving in it. Emphasizing the dangers involved in a king's relying on a non-native army, Fabrizio reminds Cosimo that the emperors Octavius and Tiberius began to disarm the Roman people in order to rule them more easily and created an army called the Praetorian Guard to defend them from the people and the Senate, but (as Machiavelli also reminds his readers in *P* 19) that guard eventually came to control and choose the emperors.

Cosimo objects to Fabrizio's contention that it is impossible to support an army in peacetime by observing that "many lords and gentlemen nourish themselves in time of peace by means of the studies of war" (as do Fabrizio and his peers), and that "many infantrymen are now employed in guarding cities and fortresses" (*AW* 1.94–95); but Fabrizio points out that these lords and men are neither numerous nor good enough to fight a war effectively. Pope Julius II's decision to use a Swiss guard, "born and raised under the laws and selected by the community," instead of native Italians shows that current modes of waging war in Italy are corrupt. Fabrizio thus reiterates: "a wise republic . . . ought to use its citizens as heads in war, and in time of peace want them to return to their art" (as did Cincinnatus whom Machiavelli praises in *D* 3.25), and "a wise king ought not to employ foreigners except as a reward for some outstanding deed or because he wants to avail himself of one man in peace as well as in war" (*AW* 1.106–8). Fabrizio then goes so far as to claim that he has "never used war as an art" (*AW* 1.09), and that the king of Spain rewards and esteems him not so much because he understands how to make war as for the counsel he provides in peace.

The description of "Fabrizio" as someone able to advise a king in peace as well as war clearly fits the author of *The Prince* much better than the historical mercenary captain. (If the king of Spain valued Fabrizio's advice in peace as well as war, wouldn't the king be taking the captain back to Spain rather than letting him return to Rome?) It was Machiavelli, of course, who had been advisor to the head of the Florentine republic and had not been able to overcome the objections of the Florentine nobility in time to train a citizen militia capable of defending it.

Cosimo voices the traditional aristocratic Florentine objections to the formation of a militia when he reminds Fabrizio that "many wise men" have said: "either it is useless, and entrusting ourselves to it will make us lose our state; or it is virtuous, and by its means whoever governs it will easily be able to take [our state]" (*AW* 1.157).[15] Fabrizio responds to the first part of the objection by observing that the "poor showing" of the militia was a result of its inexperience and forced service, but that inexperience can be overcome by proper modes of recruitment, training, and ordering.[16] By arguing that soldiers should neither be selected solely from volunteers, in which case they will serve themselves and not their superiors, nor simply be coerced, because that leads to discontent, but that they should be impressed into service by the respect they have for the prince and fear of disobeying the law, Fabrizio at the conclusion of his discourse also points to the exact character of the "opportunity" he explicitly says he has not had (*AW* 7.210–28): he has never had the political authority to muster and train his own army. He does not respond to the second part of the traditional objection to the formation of a native militia, that an able captain always constitutes a threat to the existing government, because, as Machiavelli shows in *D* 1.28–32, he cannot. To overcome the potential threat, Machiavelli argues in both his *Prince* and *Discourses*, a prince must lead his own army and a republic must try to keep its generals within bounds by means of laws (e.g., competitive elections and public trials). Neither a prince nor a republic will be able to maintain itself, as Machiavelli insisted in his own name in the preface, if it is not able to field an adequate defense.

Fabrizio does not point to the fourth and most fundamental reason neither princes nor republics have sought to imitate the ancients, particularly with respect to waging war (as Machiavelli urged both in *The Prince* and *Discourses*) until almost the end of his exchange with Cosimo.[17] After Fabrizio begins discussing the way in which a militia should be selected, armed, and trained, Cosimo asks what is responsible for the vileness, disorder, and neglect of training now; and Fabrizio responds with an explanation like but not identical to that Machiavelli gives in his *Discourses* 2.2. Fabrizio blames, first, the destruction of all other regimes by the Roman Empire and, second, the failure to revive many republics after the fall of the empire as a result

15. On the objections the Florentine aristocrats raised to the organization of a militia in the late fifteenth and early sixteenth centuries, see Hörnqvist, "*Perché non si usa allegare i Romani*," 164–71.

16. "Fabrizio" thus, in effect, explains the defeat of the militia Machiavelli did not have sufficient time to train adequately at Prato.

17. See Christopher Lynch, "The *Ordine Nuovo* of Machiavelli's *Arte della Guerra:* Reforming Ancient Matter," *History of Political Thought* 31, no. 3 (Autumn 2010): 407–25, for a detailed account of the way in which the critique of Christianity emerges.

of the Christian religion. However, where Machiavelli emphasizes the loss of freedom, Fabrizio attributes the failure of later Europeans to adopt ancient modes of warfare to their lack of fear. Many more excellent and virtuous men have arisen in Europe than in Asia and Africa, because there have been many more republics and principalities in Europe than on the other two continents; and where there are many powers, all are "constrained to keep military orders alive and to honor those who most prevail in them" (*AW* 2.294), from fear of the others. That salutary fear has been undermined in contemporary Europe, not only by a diminution of the number of powers, but also "on account of the Christian religion, [which] does not impose that necessity to defend oneself that there was in antiquity" (*AW* 2.305). Ancient peoples "kept military training alive and honored whoever was excellent in it" (*AW* 2.307), because they feared losing their lives, their freedom, and their property if defeated in war. Today cities are not destroyed, even if they have rebelled a thousand times, few men are killed, and most are left with their goods; the worst evil one has to fear is paying ransom.

Unlike *D* 2.2, where Machiavelli explicitly contrasts the ferocity of ancient religious rites and the earthly glory awarded to men of action with the elevation of humble and contemplative men by Christians, Fabrizio does not explain how or why Christianity leads to a much more restrained form of warfare. Instead he reiterates his contention that the lack of military training can be traced to the fact that there are now relatively few powers that threaten each other in Europe. Yet as Fabrizio admits at the conclusion of his discourse (*AW* 7.230–38), the number of independent states does not explain the absence of military valor in Italy, where there are many states and there have been many wars. He seems to agree with the analysis Machiavelli offers in *P* 12, in which he suggests that priests and citizens of republics who were inexperienced in war gave the practice over to mercenaries who did not want to risk their own lives any more than necessary and who valued the money they could make from ransoming prisoners more than conquering territories to be ruled by others.

Ignoring Fabrizio's suggestion about the deleterious influence of the Christian religion on the ability of Italians to wage war, Cosimo objects to Fabrizio's factual claim about the mildness of contemporary warfare by observing (as Machiavelli himself did in his *First Decennial*) that in the last twenty-five years a great many towns in Italy were sacked and a great many princes lost their kingdoms). Granting that the people have suffered a great deal, Fabrizio nevertheless insists that so long as the "heads of states" retain the belief that they will be able "to buy themselves back with ransoms," they will not "want to undergo the exertions of training for war" (*AW* 2.311–12), both because they do not think that it is necessary and because they do not know how. Like Machiavelli in both *The Prince* and *Discourses*, Fabrizio thus suggests that the first and most urgent reform needs to be in the education of future leaders.

Since Fabrizio has located the difficulty in the opinions of the "heads," Cosimo returns to their "principal matter" by asking how he would order the cavalry. The young Florentine may thus betray an aristocratic bias, but his question definitely reflects the tendency we will see among Fabrizio's other interlocutors as well as later commentators to focus on his specific recommendations with regard to the ordering and arming of the troops, rather than his general reasoning. Fabrizio has already admitted that the cavalry would be constituted, as in both antiquity and the present, by members of the wealthiest class. He refuses to say much about it, because he contends that modern cavalry is as good as if not better than its ancient equivalent. But as a result of Cosimo's specific query, the question of the effect of the Christian religion and the way in which it makes it difficult to revive ancient military orders is left hanging. Neither Zanobi nor Battista picks up the question of the difference the change in religion makes when Fabrizio briefly alludes to it later (*AW* 4.141, 6.208).

However, later in the dialogue in describing the way in which a captain "persuades" his troops to fight when he thinks best (*AW* 4.126–34, 4.148–52, 5.98, 6.205), Fabrizio explicitly argues that he needs to arouse the fear of losing their lives and goods and traces the excellence of ancient military modes to maintaining that fear. To the extent to which Fabrizio (or Machiavelli) convinces his young audience to institute the military practices he recommends, readers thus see, he will have persuaded them to institute practices (such as arousing the "obstinacy" of their troops by putting them in positions in which they have to win or die) and policies (such as making it impossible for them to send home payments or other rewards of service until or unless they have fought successfully) that undo the effects of the Christian religion. Rather than attacking or critiquing Christianity directly, especially in light of the apparent resistance to such by his younger interlocutors (to say nothing of his broader audience), Fabrizio (or Machiavelli) seeks to overcome "the difficulty in removing from the multitude a sinister opinion that is contrary to the common good" (*AW* 4.137) indirectly by persuading a few to embrace the art of war as he understands it and so gradually to change the opinions of most by changing their practice.

C. What Imitating Ancient Military Orders Entails

1. Ancient Orders Have to Be Adapted for Modern Arms

As in the *Discourses*, so in the *Art of War* the discussion loosely follows that of an ancient text, even though in the *Art of War* Machiavelli does not name the author or text as he does in the *Discourses* or comment on specific quotations or chapters. One look at the table of contents of Vegetius's *Epitome of Military Science*, to say nothing of L. Arthur Burd's compilation of "le fonti letterarie di Machiavelli nell' *Arte della Guerra*," nevertheless reveals the extent to which Fabrizio follows the order and topics discussed by this ancient source, supplemented by references to Frontinus, Polybius, Caesar's *Gallic Wars*, and Josephus.[18] In failing to make the source of many of his recommendations clear, Fabrizio somewhat ironically also imitates the work of Vegetius, who is thought to have incorporated a great deal of the work of Frontinus, a book entitled the *Art of War*, which we no longer possesses, as well as the *Stratagems*, which we do, without acknowledgment.

Fabrizio nevertheless explicitly breaks with the ancient writers in certain important respects from the very beginning of his discourse.[19] With regard to the selection of men, he observes that "those who have given rules for war want men to be selected from the temperate countries, so that they have spirit and prudence. For a warm country generates prudent and not spirited [men], a cold one spirited and not prudent ones" (*AW* 1.212). Such a rule would be good for a prince of the whole world who could draw men from wherever he wished; but Fabrizio wants to give a rule everyone can use, and that is, all republics and all princes should choose their soldiers from their own country. One should not try to select soldiers on the basis of specific traits they may possess, whether physical or moral, he urges, because one can see from ancient examples, "how with training good soldiers are made in every country" (*AW* 1.124).[20] A captain should not try

18. *Vegetius: Epitome of Military Science*, trans. N. P. Milner (Liverpool: Liverpool University Press, 1996); L. Arthur Burd, "Le fonti letterarie di Machiavelli nell' *Arte della Guerra*," *Atti della Reale Accademie dei Lincei*, 5th ser., no. 4 (1896): 187–261.

19. It cannot, therefore, be the case that Machiavelli did not foresee the importance of artillery and professional armies because he was so intent upon imitating the ancients, as Gat, "Machiavelli and the Decline of the Classical Notion of the Lessons of History in the Study of War," contends.

20. Cf. *D* 1.21, 3.30–31, 3.33, 3.36–39. We see Machiavelli here, as in *D* 2.1, resting his recommendations on ancient practices or history, rather than on ancient arguments or theories about those practices. Fabrizio also observes that "these writers" want to take not "anyone who makes an art of amusement" (*AW* 1.194–96), but those who work the land, because they are hardy, and those who practice arts needed to wage war like blacksmiths and carpenters. He agrees about the desirability of taking hardy men who practice useful arts, but, in contrast to the ancient authors,

to find men suited to warfare by nature or rely on their virtue, because "a spirited army is not made so by having spirited men in it but by having them well-ordered" (*AW* 2.167). Fabrizio thus introduces what might be called the cardinal principle of his "art of war" and Machiavelli's "art of politics": a leader should rely on his own ability to order things to achieve the desired effect rather than depend upon what is given by nature.

Fabrizio would imitate the ancients by requiring recruits to do "basic training": athletic exercises like running, wrestling, throwing and lifting weights, swimming, and horseback riding to increase their strength, dexterity, flexibility, and endurance. They should also be required to practice using their arms, obeying signals, and marching in order. As in the Roman army, they should be divided into small units of ten, each with its own head, who follows the commands of a superior in a strict hierarchy of command that culminates in one general.[21]

Observing that his young auditors can read the ancient writers for themselves (*AW* 3.10), Fabrizio says that he will not dwell on the particulars of how the Greeks and Romans arranged the lines in their armies to do battle. He is reasoning about the way in which an army should be ordered and led, not recommending specific tactics or techniques (the utility of which depends on the particular circumstances). Like Machiavelli in *D* 2.16, he praises the Roman mode of dividing their forces into three parts—*hastati*, *principes*, and *triarii*—and ordering them so that, if it is hard pressed, the first line can withdraw into the second, and likewise the second into the third, which also constitutes a fresh reinforcement. By giving an army only one front line, he explains, a captain risks letting it fall into great disorder. If the front line is not able to withstand the first thrust of the enemy, he is not able to bring up the reserves. The army thus has one and only one chance of winning a battle. All armies lose some battles, of course; but if they are ordered so that they can fight again, they can nevertheless win the war.

Unlike Machiavelli in the *Discourses*, however, Fabrizio discusses the ways in which both the arms and the order of a modern army have to be adapted to fit changed circumstances in some detail. Instead of slings and darters, he would use arquebuses (predecessors of muskets) with light cavalry in front

---

he would not draw any conclusions about the character of the men from their arts. Buck, *Erträge der Forschung*, 102, observes that with regard to the character of desirable recruits, Machiavelli departs from his source, Vegetius.

21. Cf. *D* 3.14.

and on the flanks to harry the enemy and, if possible, seize their artillery. He would also incorporate pikes on all four sides, to guard against attacks by heavily armed cavalry; and these pikes should be ordered according to the Macedonian rather than Roman model. The Germans learned to revive this ancient order, he explains, as a result of the necessity they felt in defending themselves and their liberty from the armed cavalry of nearby princes. This German order should not be allowed to replace Roman orders entirely, however, because it is primarily defensive.[22] The important point, he reiterates, is that people learn to adopt good military orders from the necessity of defending themselves.

2. Youthful Impetuosity Will Not Suffice

As the discussion turns from the arming to the ordering of troops, Cosimo asks to be relieved of his office as "dictator." (Their young host does not appear to understand the difference between a public office whose holder has the power to issue commands that must be obeyed and a private conversation in which the participants engage voluntarily.) Invited to choose a new interlocutor, Fabrizio selects the youngest member of the group, Luigi Alamanni, not only because this is the Venetian (i.e., a republican) way, but also because this training is for the young and the young are, therefore, more fit to reason about as well as to execute it. The course of the conversation nevertheless serves to correct the impression Machiavelli may have left with his famous statement in *P* 25 about fortune's favoring the young. A seasoned captain will not rely solely on good luck or the youthful enthusiasm of his troops, if he is not forced to do so.

22. As Ben Cassidy, "Machiavelli and the Ideology of the Offensive: Gunpowder Weapons in *The Art of War*," *Journal of Military History* 67 (April 2003): 381–404, argues in opposition to historians such as Charles W. C. Oman, *The Art of War in the Sixteenth Century* (London: Methuen, 1937), 93–94; Azar Gat, *The Origins of Military Thought: From the Enlightenment to Clausewitz* (Oxford: Clarendon Press, 1989), 4–7; F. L. Taylor, *The Art of War in Italy: 1494–1529* (Cambridge: Cambridge University Press, 1921), 170; and Piero Pieri, *Il Rinascimento e la crisi militare italiana* (Turin: Giulio Einaudi, 1952), 535–36, Machiavelli did not reject the use of gunpowder weapons. He did assign them a secondary role—partly because the weapons were not very accurate or easy to use at the time, partly because their future role could not have been deduced from the results of battles Machiavelli knew about, and partly because, in Machiavelli's time, reliance on gunpowder weapons necessitated defensive tactics. Cassidy does not see that Machiavelli's concentration on the offense does not merely reflect a personal preference or military judgment, but is directly related to the purpose and outcome of the organization of an Italian army Machiavelli cum Fabrizio is advocating—the conquest of Italy.

Acting in character, the impetuous and impatient Luigi urges Fabrizio to describe how an army ordered in the Roman manner he has recommended would win a battle; and in an imaginary encounter that takes no account of the character of the enemy or the site, Fabrizio shows their army winning easily. Rather than inquire, as does the apparently more sensible Zanobi, who follows him, how the battle order should be adapted to the character of the enemy and the site, Luigi merely asks Fabrizio why he has the artillery fire only once. He, too, thus exhibits the tendency of Fabrizio's young interlocutors to ask about concrete details, tactics, or arms, rather than to challenge the reasoning. Fabrizio repeats many of the arguments Machiavelli employs in *D* 2.17 to show that the invention of artillery has not made ancient military orders obsolete; but Fabrizio does not go so far as to claim that "if one founds oneself on infantrymen and the modes specified before, artillery becomes altogether useless."[23] He merely asserts that "it would be impossible for an army ordered and armed [as he has specified] not to overcome in the first encounter every other army ordered as modern armies are" (*AW* 3.161). He concedes that an army in the field has no defense against enemy artillery and must, therefore, try to seize it, because an army cannot attack if it tries to stay out of reach or behind a wall of embankment (as Machiavelli notes in *D* 2.17 the Spanish forces led by the historical Fabrizio attempted to do at the battle of Ravenna, but the "Fabrizio" who speaks in this dialogue is not the historical mercenary captain).

3. The Need for Prudent Leadership

Knowing how to train and order an army will not suffice to enable a captain to win a battle, Fabrizio tells the "naturally more spirited" Zanobi (*AW* 4.3), who takes on the role of interlocutor when Luigi quickly retires after his imaginary victory. Like Machiavelli in *P* 14 and *D* 3.39, Fabrizio insists that a captain must also know how to change the order of his troops according to the site and the character of his enemy. For examples of ways in which to respond to both, Fabrizio (again like Machiavelli) suggests that a captain should not merely observe and reason about the various possible characteristics of the terrain and the forces confronting one another; he

23. Machiavelli admitted that this was an overstatement when he concluded *D* 2.17 by observing "that artillery is useful in an army when ancient virtue is mixed with it, but, without that, against a virtuous army, it is very useless."

should also read the histories and learn about what works and what does not from the actions of excellent generals.[24]

Showing that he has read the histories (but not in the way Machiavelli would have him read them), Zanobi asks to be reminded of the specific reasons "Scipio did not have his *hastati* withdraw into the order of the *principes*, but divided them and had them withdraw to the horns of the army" (*AW* 4.42). Fabrizio explains that Scipio altered the order of his troops in order to meet the order he knew Hannibal was using (and thus gives an example of the importance of knowing the enemy); but he adds, "one cannot use this mode of opening the first line so as to give place to the second except when one is otherwise superior," and suggests that they ought to "return to our reasoning" (*AW* 4.46–48). Giving many examples of different ways in which a captain might respond to a variety of arms and orders employed by his enemy that overlap to a considerable extent with the advice Machiavelli offers in his own name in *D* 3.10–14, Fabrizio concludes that "the greatest remedy that is used against a plan of the enemy is to do voluntarily what he plans that you do by force" (*AW* 4.87) and so surprise him. That was the reason Scipio changed his orders in different battles so that he was able to defeat both Hasdrubal and Hannibal.

Implicitly criticizing Luigi's desire to wage war before he has learned about the conditions or his enemy, Fabrizio warns Zanobi that "a captain is never to do battle unless he has the advantage" or he is forced to do so by necessity. Whether a captain has an advantage or not does not depend merely on the respective numbers and characters of his troops and those of the enemy or the site (as they saw in the case of Scipio). It also depends upon his prudence and knowledge of the enemy captain. "Necessity arises when you see that by not fighting you must lose . . . ; as when you are lacking money and your army has to be dissolved; through hunger assaulting you; [or] when the enemy waits to be enlarged by new troops." Then a captain should always fight, even at a disadvantage, "for it is much better to tempt fortune where it can favor you than to see your certain ruin by not tempting it" (*AW* 4.95–98).

"Above all," Fabrizio counsels, "you ought to guard against leading an army to fight that is afraid or that is not confident of victory" (*AW* 4.115; cf. *D* 3.33). A captain thus needs to learn how to speak and act in a way

24. Because Machiavelli takes up more specific aspects of military organization and leadership in books 4–7, Buck, *Erträge der Forschung*, 103, takes book 3 to constitute the center of *AW*, from which subsequent chapters decline. I clearly disagree.

that gives his men confidence. Because ordinary soldiers do not possess the same understanding of the conditions and the enemy, captains have to know how to dissuade soldiers who want to fight under disadvantageous circumstances, as well as how to persuade those who lack confidence and are not disposed to fight when necessity or opportunity makes it desirable. "That prince or republic which designs to make a new military and give reputation to this training ought [therefore] to accustom its own soldiers to hear the captain speaking and the captain to know how to speak to them" (*AW* 4.140). A captain does not speak to his men in order to explain his strategy, however; on the contrary, he should keep both his feelings and his plans secret. As Machiavelli argues in *D* 3.48, a captain must never believe that the enemy does not know how to conduct his own affairs; on the contrary, a captain must always fear that his enemy is deceiving him. But a captain has to act and talk to his men as if he despises the enemy, in order to increase their confidence.[25]

Rather than appeal to their reason or try to teach them, a captain needs to be able to arouse or extinguish his men's passions. He can do so in a variety of ways. Like Machiavelli in *D* 1.13–15, Fabrizio observes that captains can assuage the fears, inflame the spirits, increase their men's obstinacy, and fill them with hope by appealing to their religious beliefs. Some captains have forced their men to take an oath to fight and die rather than flee; others have claimed to have spoken with representatives of the gods, who promised them victory, or had visions of such in dreams. It is also possible to appeal to the love human beings naturally have for their own country or the esteem men feel for the virtue of their captain. He can make his men angry by repeating insults hurled at them by an enemy. But "persuasion" is not simply or solely effected by speech. Like Machiavelli (writing about Marius in *D* 3.37), Fabrizio observes that a captain can make his men more confident by letting them see enemy soldiers in a weakened or vulnerable condition. And when a captain cannot convince his men to fight with words, "there is no better mode [of doing so] than giving a part of them as prey to the enemy, so that those who have fought and those who have not believe you" (*AW* 4.128). "Above all," he warns, a captain should "take this precaution in wanting to make his soldiers obstinate in the fight:

25. This advice concerning the way in which a captain should respect the intelligence of his enemy but appear to despise that enemy to his troops is the military equivalent of Machiavelli's advice to the prince in *P* 18 concerning the need always to appear to be religious, merciful, and humane, even though he cannot always be so.

do not permit them to send any of their property home or to put it in some place until the war has ended, so that they understand that if in fleeing they save their lives, they do not save their possessions, the love of which is no less a ground for rendering men obstinate in defense" (*AW* 4.134). Men can be made obstinate by necessity, as well as by persuasion, e.g., by putting the army in a position in which they have no alternative but to win or die. Indeed, Fabrizio concludes, "That is the most hardy and the best provision that one, wanting to make his own soldiery obstinate, can make" (*AW* 4.148; cf. *D* 1.15). Although Fabrizio acknowledges the power of the love human beings naturally have for their own country, he does not urge a captain to rely on the patriotism of his men. On the contrary, like Machiavelli in *P* 17, Fabrizio tells his young auditors that it is safer to rely on fear than love. So he concludes, if a captain wants to make his soldiers obstinate, he should arrange the circumstances so that his men will be forced to fight—or die.

D. Why the Art of War Entails the Art of Governing

Although a captain needs to know his enemy, Fabrizio admits that is not always possible. When marching through hostile territory or facing an unseen enemy, a captain must order his troops so that he can defend himself on all sides and be on the lookout for an ambush or other form of deception. The discussion thus turns to questions of defense, without Fabrizio's specifying the shift. He has not told his interlocutors (nor has Machiavelli reminded his readers) that the Roman modes of warfare they have been urged to imitate are essentially offensive. Yet Machiavelli told his readers in the preface that the need for defense is *the* reason civil and military ways of life must necessarily be combined. In the last part of his discourse we see Fabrizio gradually bring civil and military life closer together.

The need to secure supplies of food and water as well as to build and defend a camp where the army can rest and refresh itself makes military organization look increasingly like civil. Unlike a city, however, an army has to move. With regard to supplies, Fabrizio thus formulates the following general rule: "A prince should order his army to be as unencumbered as possible, taking away everything that burdens it" (*AW* 5.83). In contrast to modern armies that demand wine and cooked bread, ancient armies provided their men with flour and a bit of fat and had them drink water.

Since they have "conquered the enemy in the field and marched upon his country," Zanobi counters, "it is reasonable that spoils be had, towns made to pay tribute, and prisoners taken." Implying that the soldiers should receive something more than flour and water for their efforts, he thus asks "*how the ancients governed themselves* in these things" (emphasis added). Fabrizio explains that the Romans enriched rather than impoverished themselves by fighting wars, because they gave all the spoils to the public, although the official in charge often distributed the spoils equitably to the soldiers to make them want to win rather than to rob. The Romans also required the soldiers to deposit one-third of their pay with the person who carried the flag of his battalion, both to prevent young men from squandering all of their pay and to give them an incentive to defend the flag. By leaving the distribution of spoils to the discretion of the soldiers, modern armies have made them insolent and undisciplined.

When Fabrizio indicates that he is ready to pass on from the manner in which an army should be supplied to the location and order of its camp, Zanobi passes on the "office" of interlocutor to Battista. Just as they have put the best soldiers ahead and behind the army, Zanobi comments, the two most prudent members of the company will have begun and concluded this reasoning. Because Zanobi apparently retains the ancient view that individuals should be assigned tasks according to their disparate natural talents, despite what has been said about the selection and training of soldiers, Fabrizio begins his discussion of the way in which a camp should be built and organized by endorsing the Roman practice of choosing a site where they can establish their accustomed order, and so rely on art, rather than the Greek practice of choosing a site for its natural advantages and adapting their order to it. Where possible, he reiterates, one should rely on training or art rather than nature.

Although he has been urging them to imitate the Romans, Fabrizio reminds his interlocutors that he does not observe their orders in everything, but takes that part that suits the present times. He worried that they would want him to specify how the army should be encamped before he showed how it should march and fight. He has not presented these topics in the same order as his ancient source or proceeded the way someone actually mustering an army would, because he is not attempting to provide his audience with a "how to" manual. He discussed the order in which the army ought to fight first, even though an army has to march and camp before it fights, because the order in which they will fight ought to determine the order in which they march and camp. He wants his auditors to understand the reasons they should imitate the ancient military orders he recommends as well as the ways in which those orders can and should be adapted for modern circumstances.

The plan Fabrizio suggests for the camp of an army of 24,000 or 50,000 men follows the square order of the troops he suggested for marching; it, too, is adapted for modern artillery and the use of pikes. Organized as a grid around roads wide enough to allow a battalion of infantry to march down them, his plan also shows how much a camp resembles a city that needs to be defended and supplied.[26]

The need to establish and maintain order within a camp as well as to defend it makes the army camp look even more like a city. In arranging for the defense of the camp, Fabrizio says that he would modify ancient modes of fortifying the camp by using ditches and walls, but not ramparts. He also recommends following the ancient practice of not using guards outside the ditches, because they are easy for an enemy to capture and turn. One reason to maintain a strict, uniform order of the men in camp is that such an order makes it easy to determine whether anyone is missing—or has entered. A captain does not want any of his "heads" to be doing business with the enemy or the enemy to learn his plans. He should, therefore, follow the Roman example not merely of severely punishing anyone who fails to do what he is commanded, or who secretly takes anything out of camp, or lies about what he has done. A captain should also adopt the Roman mode of dealing with whole cohorts or legions, too large to be punished individually, by putting all their names in a bag, drawing one out of ten, and killing the men whose names have been drawn. All will fear the punishment, even if they do not feel it. (Cf. *D* 3.49.)

Fabrizio reminds his auditors that the Romans acquired their great empire by publicly rewarding all virtuous deeds and punishing crimes, but he particularly recommends their mode of punishment. After a public trial (cf. *D* 1.7), he explains, the presiding tribune or consul would hit the condemned man lightly, but then allow him to flee and all the other soldiers to kill him. As a result of this particular mode of inflicting the punishment, not merely do other soldiers see that those who commit crimes lose their lives, but the soldiers identify with the judicial officers who order it rather than with the victim, because they themselves inflict the punishment. Fabrizio recognizes that publicly awarded honors like triumphal processions give individuals an incentive to perform virtuous acts. Competition for such honors may also divide soldiers, however, by setting them in competition with one another. The Roman mode of punishment not only makes prospective criminals

26. In Thucydides 7.77.4, Nicias reminds the more than forty thousand Athenian soldiers remaining after their defeat at Syracuse that they constitute a sufficient number to found a large city.

fear for their lives but also serves to unify officers and men in a common endeavor. By giving the condemnation of Manlius Capitolinus as an example of the advantages of involving the people in the punishment of criminals, so that they will not be tempted to sympathize with the "victim" oppressed by the authorities, Fabrizio indicates that the principle or insight involved in this form of punishment "that takes away tumults and makes justice be observed" (*AW* 6.125) applies to civil as well as to military life.

Underlining the compatibility between civil and military life that Machiavelli stressed in his preface, Fabrizio adds that "because neither the fear of the laws nor of men is enough to check armed men, the ancients added the authority of God. With very great ceremony they made their soldiers swear to the observance of military discipline . . . and used every industry to rule them with religion" (*AW* 6.124–26). Like the cautious Cosimo, however, the prudent Battista also fails to take up the question of the role of religion or relevant differences in that respect between the ancients and the moderns.

By asking whether Fabrizio would allow women or idle games in the camp, Battista points, instead, to one of the major differences between a camp and a city. The presence of women corrupts the order of the former, but is essential in the latter. By asking whether there are other factors a captain should take into account in selecting a place to camp, Battista also lets Fabrizio acknowledge the importance of specific characteristics of a site—whether it is healthy (as one can tell from the faces of the inhabitants) and whether or not an enemy can cut off the army's supply of food or water—that he might have appeared to slight in recommending the Roman policy of relying on art rather than following nature as the Greeks had. Fabrizio nevertheless underlines his central contention that a captain should rely more on art (knowledge and training) than on mere nature, first, by adding that daily exercise is the best way to keep an army healthy and that supplies must be dispensed, i.e., that the internal order imposed by the captain is at least as important as the natural characteristics of any site; and, second, by contrasting the practice of the Romans and Greeks, who limited their armies to a maximum of fifty thousand men so that they could control them by means of their art, rather than relying, like the "occidentals," on the natural fury of their hordes or, like the orientals, on their "natural obedience" to the king.

In the midst of the discussion of encampments Fabrizio enlarges the scope of their inquiry. At the beginning of his discourse he stated that "the purpose of whoever wants to make war is to be able to fight with any enemy in the field and to be able to win a battle" (*AW* 1.116). But having "had this army of ours win a battle, . . . march, and [taking account of] those impediments by which it can be surrounded while marching, . . . encamped it where it must not only take a little rest," he now says that they must "also think of how it must finish the war" (*AW* 6.166). To end the war a captain not only has to manage his own troops but also has to affect the decisions and behavior of the enemy. Internal and external orders (or "domestic" and "foreign" policy) are necessarily connected.

Just as a captain should do everything in his power to unite his army, so Fabrizio gives many examples to show that "a captain ought with every art to contrive to divide the forces of his enemy, either by making him suspect his own men . . . or by giving him cause to separate his own troops and, through this, become weaker." If you want "many men or many people to do a thing that would be useful to you and of great harm to them (for instance, either undoing the walls of their city or sending many of them into exile)" (*AW* 6.168), you should try to deal with them in isolation from one another, so that they do not think of getting together to resist you, but only of obeying. Likewise, "if sedition or discord arises among his soldiers, it is important for a captain to know how to extinguish them with art." Having observed earlier that men cannot rebel if their "heads" do not give them cause (*AW* 1.246), Fabrizio states here that "the best mode is to punish the heads of the errors" (*AW* 6.199; cf. *D* 3.27). But to do so effectively, one must take them by surprise, if they are distant, by calling everyone together so that they will not know that the purpose of the assembly is to punish them, or, if they are present, by making sure that that those who are not culpable are there to help you punish the guilty.

For a third time Fabrizio adds considerations of the rewards and punishments soldiers have to fear from the gods as well as from their captain, but this time he emphasizes the advantage modern captains have in comparison to the ancients by observing that they no longer have to deal with the "vexation" of inauspicious auguries. Unlike Machiavelli in *D* 1.56, Fabrizio does not observe that modern peoples also take certain natural events, such as lightning striking a cathedral, as divine signs predicting future events. He merely suggests that if modern captains experience such difficulties, they should either explain the natural causes of the phenomenon or interpret it in a way favorable to their own endeavors. Fabrizio thus intimates that the modern distinction between sword and scepter not only gives secular leaders an opportunity to interpret events in a more politically useful manner by appealing to the natural fears and desires of their people; it also protects political and military "captains" from direct interference with their decisions or challenges to their authority by priests.

Fabrizio brings civil and military orders even closer together when he proceeds to discuss the best ways of besieging or defending towns and citadels. Not surprisingly in light of the similarity between camps and towns, the recommendations he makes for defending or attacking towns correspond to many of his recommendations concerning the best modes of ordering armies in the field and their camps. Like camps, he observes, towns can be strong by nature or industry. They are strong by nature if they are surrounded by rivers and swamps or built on high cliffs and mountains. However, because towns built on mountains that are not too steep to climb easily are vulnerable to artillery, they should be located today on plains and made strong by industry, by making the walls twist so that the defenders can attack the enemy on his flanks as well as front, and digging a deep ditch inside. Like a camp, a town should have a supply of food and water and try to deny the same to the enemy. As in an army, so in defending a town everyone should know what to do to preserve order and avoid tumults. Like an army in the field, its defenders should also do everything in their power to withstand the enemy's first thrust. As in leading an army through hostile territory, so the captain defending a town has to look out for attacks on all sides. Just as Fabrizio urged captains to separate the unarmed supply wagons from the armed men in camps, so he tells defenders of towns to send the elderly, women, and children away, and rely on experienced soldiers, because weak and inexperienced people are easily frightened by the prospect of war. Since the inhabitants of a town can continue to defend it after its walls are breached (as Fabrizio admits they inevitably will be by enemy artillery), those who attack should encourage the people to surrender by allowing them to go into exile or promising to harm only those who refuse to put down their arms. (Cf. *D* 3.12.) Both sides have to beware of being deceived by the other.

Bringing the discussion explicitly into the present, Fabrizio says (*AW* 7.94) that he reasons unwillingly about things that have happened in their own times, especially those involving him. By contrasting the ease with which Cesare Borgia took Urbino in a day by means of deception (in 1502) with the time and expense it took "others" (Lorenzo de' Medici in 1516), Fabrizio nevertheless reminds his listeners of the difficulties Florence experienced as a result of the city's failure to train its own militia and captains and the importance, therefore, of preparing the way he has suggested.

Politely suggesting that he has told them many things they must have considered and understood by themselves (7.152), Fabrizio concludes his account of the studies necessary to imitate ancient military orders by repeating most but not all of the general rules given by Vegetius (*Epitome* 3.26).[27] Concerned not so much about imitating the ancients per se as about improving modern Italy, he has not tried to show them "exactly how the ancient military was made, but how in these times one might order a military that would have more virtue than the one that is used" (*AW* 7.181).

E. The Ironic Conclusion

Fabrizio appears to undermine the utility of the whole dialogue when, turning from his description of ancient military orders to the "parts" that would qualify an individual to become a captain, he states: "I would not know how to select another man than him who knows how to do all those things that have been reasoned about today. Even that would not be enough, if he did not know how to find them by himself. For without invention no one was ever a great man in his own trade; and if invention brings honor in other things, in this above all it honors you" (*AW* 7.191). Fabrizio thus not merely underlines the difference between himself and his young audience (who clearly have not learned these things for themselves). He also points to the difference between imitating great ancient predecessors (which Machiavelli recommended to Lorenzo in *P* 6 as well as to Cosimo and Zanobi in *D* 3) and Machiavelli's own explicit innovations in his two major prose works. By not advocating in the name of Fabrizio either the new moral teaching of how not to be good that he puts forward in *P* 15–19 or the new, more popularly based republican "modes and orders" that he proposes in the *Discourses*, Machiavelli in the *Art of War* ironically reserves the honor of the innovator for himself.

Coming to the end of the dialogue Fabrizio brings out the problematic character of his own endeavor. Reminding his interlocutors that Cosimo asked at the beginning why he had not imitated the ancient military orders he advocates, Fabrizio suggests that in this discourse he has demonstrated how much time and effort he has put into learning how to imitate those

27. Instead of the seven rules in Vegetius specifying the orders a captain should use to meet various formations of the enemy, Fabrizio adds several that are apparently aimed particularly at Florentine abuses, e.g., leaving oneself vulnerable to sudden accidents rather than identifying likely problems beforehand, seeking to use money to buy arms rather than using arms to seize gold, and failing to accustom one's soldiers to disdain delicate living and luxurious clothing.

orders. But, he now openly states, only the prince of a state large enough to muster an army of 15,000–20,000 of his own subjects could do that easily. (Having raised armies of 20,000 men on more than one occasion [*FH* 2.26, 2.29], Florence was such a state.) Fabrizio has never commanded any but foreign armies and men obligated to others. How could he force them to drill, to carry more arms than they are accustomed to bear as individuals along with supplies for more than several days, and to dig roads? How could he get them to abstain from games, acts of lasciviousness, curses, and other acts of insolence? By what God or saints would he make them swear?

By asking such rhetorical questions, Fabrizio makes the character of the difficulties he confronted less than crystal clear. He seems, for example, to ignore the differences between mercenary and auxiliary soldiers that Machiavelli brings out in *P* 12–13. It might not be possible to force mercenaries to practice, bear burdens, or live austerely, because, as Fabrizio explained earlier, they serve at their own will rather than at the prince's. He himself was a mercenary captain, but the troops he led were answerable to the Spanish king. As Machiavelli observes in *P* 13, such troops can be good, disciplined, and God-fearing; they are, indeed, more dangerous to the prince who wants to use them when they are. Fabrizio admits that Spanish troops are better than Italian. He speaks here as an Italian who recognizes that "knowing how to govern an army [already] made is not enough in Italy; rather, it is first necessary to know how to make it and then know how to command it" (*AW* 7.208). The problem with using auxiliary troops, according to Machiavelli, is that they obey another authority. Fabrizio claims, however, to have been a trusted advisor of the Spanish king about domestic as well as military affairs. In explaining how a captain gives his troops confidence and keeps them united, Fabrizio observed that "that which above every other thing keeps the army united is the reputation of the captain, which arises through his virtue alone. For neither blood nor authority ever gave it without virtue. And the first thing that a captain is expected to do is to keep his soldiers punished and paid" (*AW* 6.204–5). Did the Spanish king not give his captain enough money to pay the troops? (The fact that the Spanish troops that besieged Florence were starving suggests that he may not have.) Did the king not allow his captain to establish a way of punishing those who refused to obey his commands like that of the Romans so that the other soldiers enforced the penalty and did not sympathize with the rebel? Like Machiavelli in Florence, Fabrizio seems to have failed not so much in training his troops as in persuading his king and employer to do what was necessary to make them good. In *P* 12 Machiavelli (in)famously declared that "because there cannot be good laws where there are not good arms, and where there are good arms there must be good laws," he will leave out the reasoning on laws and speak of arms. In the *Art of War* his spokesman Fabrizio acknowledges, somewhat surreptitiously, that the reverse is also true, i.e., that there cannot be good arms where there are not good laws. And contrary to the beliefs of Florentine aristocrats like Cosimo's grandfather Bernardo, like the Roman mode of punishment, such laws are good because they involve the people in administering them and so let the people see the necessity of obeying them.

Explaining why the Swiss are better soldiers than the Italians, Fabrizio first refers back to the observation he made earlier that the Swiss were "made good by one usage natural to them" (*AW* 7.225), "that they were born and raised under the laws and selected by the community" (*AW* 1.98).[28] But silently referring to the fact that the Swiss have also become mercenaries, he adds that they have also been made or kept good by the necessity imposed on them as foreigners of fighting or dying, because they believe they have nowhere to flee. Fabrizio observed earlier that such a "necessity" is stronger in uniting soldiers and motivating them to fight than either a natural love of country or esteem for their captain. Here he concludes that the goodness of the Swiss is limited to their being accustomed to await the enemy with pike and sword, and that no one would be able to teach them what they lack, especially someone who does not speak their language. Although he used Hannibal as an example of many strategies, Fabrizio does not recommend the "inhuman cruelty" that Machiavelli says enabled Hannibal to unite a mercenary army composed of "infinite kinds of men" without dissension (*P* 17, *D* 3.21). It was possible, in other words, for an ancient captain to train and unite an army composed of soldiers speaking different languages, but Fabrizio apparently does not think that it would be possible for a modern captain to do so. Early in the dialogue Fabrizio conceded to Cosimo that it would not be possible for people at their time to adopt the harsh ways of some ancients without being defamed and vilified. Perhaps for that reason Fabrizio does not name the "necessity" that enabled the Spaniards, but not the Italians, to adopt a good order. But that "necessity" would appear to be connected with the "pious cruelty" Ferdinand used (*P* 21) in uniting the Spanish to free their land from the Moors. In Spain an appeal to the Church

28. As in other parts of his discourse, Fabrizio treats that to which a people have become accustomed as "natural" to them. Like Machiavelli in *D* 3.36, 3.43, he observes that peoples "inherit" certain traits not so much by nature as by living according to certain laws and customs.

served to unite forces against the infidel. In Italy, as Fabrizio would know from his own experience, the Church allied with some cities and nations against others.[29]

Like Machiavelli in *The Prince*, Fabrizio concludes his discourse by exonerating the people and blaming princes for the disorder, both civil and military, in Italy. Since peoples of all kinds in any place can be made soldiers with the right kind of training, both Machiavelli and Fabrizio agree that where there are not good soldiers, it is the fault of the prince. (Cf. *D* 1.21.) Conceding that the incidence of virtue is not a function merely of the number of powers and fear of servitude resulting from the loss of one's own state, as he suggested earlier, Fabrizio observes that Italian princes have been punished for retaining bad orders and not instituting good ones by ignominiously losing their states. There have been many wars in Italy since the invasion by Charles VIII in 1494; but although "wars usually make men bellicose and reputed," these wars have made Italians lose reputation, because the existing orders were not good. "Before they tasted the blows of the ultramontane wars," Fabrizio explains, "our Italian princes used to believe that it was enough for a prince to know how to think of a sharp response in his studies, to write a beautiful letter, to show wit and quickness in his deeds and words, to know how to weave a fraud, to be ornamented by gems and gold, to sleep and eat with greater splendor than others, to keep many lascivious ones around, to govern subjects avariciously and proudly, to rot in idleness, to give promotions in the military by favor, to despise anyone who may have shown them any praiseworthy way, to want their speeches to be responses of oracles." What is worse is that "those who are left persist in the same error and the same disorder" (*AW* 7.236–80). They do not follow the example set by the ancient princes who wanted to keep their states and so did all the things he has reasoned about, preparing their bodies for hardships and their spirits not to fear dangers. Wanting to live the pleasant, leisured life of a gentleman, they have not been willing to risk their lives in order to preserve their states. Caesar, Alexander, and their like might be faulted for having too much ambition to rule, but they could not be blamed for any softness that makes men delicate and unwarlike.

A reader of Machiavelli's *Prince* might summarize Fabrizio's concluding complaint by saying that Italian princes did not heed the advice Machiavelli

29. Machiavelli analyzes the divisive effects of the Church in Italy explicitly in *FH* 1.9.

gave them about the virtues and vices they need to maintain their states. Like Machiavelli in the *Prince*, Fabrizio concludes by promising that "if these things were read and believed by these princes, it would be impossible that they not change their form of living and their provinces not change their fortune" (*AW* 7.240). He emphasizes the need not merely to acquire "one's own arms" but, more specifically, to train and deploy an army composed of one's countrymen. Again like Machiavelli in the *Prince*, Fabrizio promises that "whichever of those who today keep states in Italy first enters by this way, he will be lord of this province before anyone else" (*AW* 7.242). Indeed, he goes even further by suggesting that a prince who follows his recommendations will, like Philip of Macedon, who learned how to order an army from the Theban Epaminondas and found the rest of Greece in idleness (attending performances of comedies!), be able to occupy the whole country and leave his son a foundation upon which he could conquer the world.

Fabrizio ends by complaining against nature, which either should not have allowed him to know this or should have given him the ability to execute it. He has been as liberal as he has with his advice and learning to his listeners, because they are young and "qualified," i.e., socially well situated and sufficiently wealthy, to help their princes do so. Unfortunately, from what Machiavelli has indicated about the temperaments, habits, and knowledge of his young Florentine friends, Fabrizio's hope appears to be somewhat futile. Although he shows himself most willing to press Fabrizio with questions, Cosimo retains many of the opinions of his ancestors. The young Luigi is impetuous, lacking in confidence, and self-professedly imprudent. Zanobi may be more spirited, but he focuses on specific strategies or techniques rather than the reasons for using them. And the more prudent Battista admits that he does not understand what Fabrizio tells him about ordering a camp (*AW* 6.76), because he does not have the requisite training. He is more used to living at the papal court (and watching comedies) than to drilling or ordering armed men. These young Florentine aristocrats seem to have been friendly to Machiavelli and his projects, but he does not depict them as any more willing (or able in the case of the sickly Cosimo) to undertake the arduous physical exercise and risks involved in actually training and leading an army than the princes Fabrizio condemns. They might, of course, recommend this course of action to others. The dissimulation or irony with which Machiavelli presents his argument in the *Art of War* nevertheless seems to extend beyond his using a mercenary captain as his spokesman to the suggestion that his young

Florentine friends could learn how to train and order an army sitting in a garden, relaxing in the shade after they had dined. They have been miseducated in the "ambitious idleness" Machiavelli thought would prevent his contemporaries from regaining their freedom (*D* 2.2.). They loved to contemplate ancient greatness and talk about the ways in which it could be revived, but they were not willing to engage in the physically and mentally arduous practices necessary to achieve their ambitions.

In the *Art of War* we see that Machiavelli had not jettisoned his conviction that strong military leadership would be necessary to liberate Italy from the barbarians by conquering and so uniting the province or his suggestion that the domestic political arrangements of both the Italian principalities and republics would have to be radically altered in order to secure the lives and liberties of the people. On the contrary, in the *Art of War* Machiavelli shows that the apparently disparate projects announced in *The Prince* and the *Discourses* are inextricably interconnected. As he declares in *Discourses* 1.9, 1.18, a strong prince is necessary to found or to reestablish a republic. But as he argues in *The Prince* 9, 16–19, such a prince will not be able to institute a lasting regime if he does not obtain the support of his people and protect them from abuse by a mercenary army. The best way to do both is to train a citizen army and to involve the people in the prosecution of criminals. In the *Art of War* we also see that Machiavelli did not harbor any more illusions about his young Florentine friends' carrying out the recommendations he put forward in his *Discourses* than he had about Lorenzo de' Medici's following his advice in *The Prince*. His was a long-term project that would have to be carried to its completion by readers in the future. In all three works he nevertheless made it clear that the formation and training of an army composed of the inhabitants of the country to defend it from the incursions it had suffered from the national armies of France and Spain was the first, most immediate step to be taken in transforming the political life not merely of the Florentine republic, but of Italy, if not of the world.

5

Why Machiavelli's Prince Is neither a Soldier of Fortune nor a Socratic Philosopher

THE LIFE OF CASTRUCCIO CASTRACANI

Unable to obtain a regular job in the Florentine government, Machiavelli accepted what work he could. In the summer of 1520 he thus found himself in Lucca awaiting the resolution of a bankruptcy case in which he was representing some Florentine merchants. To divert himself he composed a highly fictionalized account of the life of Castruccio Castracani, the fourteenth-century condottiere who became tyrant of Lucca, and sent it to his young Florentine friends, Zanobi Buondelmonti and Luigi Alammani.[1] The *Life* was designed to serve two different purposes. First, it gave his young friends an example of the kind of history he could write that they could use in urging the Medici to employ him in writing a history of Florence (which they eventually did). Second, it enabled Machiavelli to correct an enduring misunderstanding of the argument of the *Prince*. Rather than suggesting that a soldier of fortune like Cesare Borgia or Castruccio Castracani was the example he wanted his young readers to follow, Machiavelli again showed that these self-made tyrants were not able to establish lasting regimes for themselves or others, because they did not understand the "arts of peace" Numa Pompilius had used to preserve the founding of the Roman republic by Romulus. In other words, they did not appreciate the political utility of respecting the conventional moral and religious beliefs of their people that Machiavelli had dramatized in *Mandragola*.

Machiavelli begins by stating that he "thought it worthwhile to recall [Castruccio's] career to the memory of men, because it seemed to him that

1. Ridolfi, *Life*, 180–82.

he had found the greatest example of many things, so much virtue and so much fortune, in it" (83). Many scholars have thus taken the *Life of Castruccio Castracani* to exemplify his understanding of the role of both fortune and virtue in acquiring political power.[2] The problem with this straightforward reading is that the good fortune and virtue Machiavelli attributes to Castruccio are largely products of Machiavelli's own imagination and consequent alterations of the historical record, which undercut his exaggerated praise of the petty tyrant.[3] The foundling birth and nurture Machiavelli attributes to Castruccio to make him look like one of the legendary founders prove upon examination not to be nearly as extraordinary or useful as Machiavelli first suggests. Likewise, in showing how Castruccio demonstrated his *virtù* by using both force and fraud to seize power in Lucca and the surrounding area, Machiavelli changes the strategies Castruccio employed and makes him into an imitator of ancient generals (as Machiavelli urged readers of both *The Prince* and the *Art of War* they should be, but Castruccio was not). Finally and perhaps most surprisingly, Machiavelli concludes by indicating that Castruccio did not have the wisdom, either as an educator of his adopted son or as a philosopher, that the tyrant pretended to possess. In sum, Machiavelli does not present Castruccio as a model of *virtù* who lost his principality merely as a result of bad luck.

Machiavelli's young Florentine friends seem to have seen the point of his historical inventions. Zanobi wrote Machiavelli that they had read the *Life* as a "model" for the history of Florence they had been lobbying Cardinal Giulio de' Medici to commission Machiavelli to write. The republican sympathies and family connections of Machiavelli's young Florentine readers make it unlikely that they would have taken a mercenary captain who not only made himself tyrant of his own city but also tried to deprive Florence of her freedom as an exemplar of political virtue. But Machiavelli's young friends do not seem to have had either the Lucchan's exemplary character

2. E.g., Peter E. Bondanella, "Castruccio Castracani: Machiavelli's Archetypal Prince," *Italica* 49 (Autumn 1972): 302–14; Joseph C. Macfarland, "Machiavelli's Imagination of Excellent Men: An Appraisal of the Lives of Cosimo de' Medici and Castruccio Castracani," *American Political Science Review* 93 (March 1999): 133–46; Jack d'Amico, "Machiavelli's 'Life of Castruccio Castracani' and the Myth of the Foundling/Founder," *Canadian Journal of Italian Studies* 18 (1995): 22–46; Peter Constantine, ed., *The Essential Writings of Machiavelli* (New York: Penguin, 2007), 403.

3. Although they see and identify some of the changes Machiavelli made to the historical record, neither Franco Fido, "The Politician as Writer," in Sullivan, *Comedy and Tragedy of Machiavelli*, 149–52, nor Constantine, *Essential Writings*, 403–31, sees the critical thrust.

or the historical accuracy of Machiavelli's account primarily in mind.[4] By demonstrating the way in which he could critique while seeming to praise, in his *Life* Machiavelli had shown his young friends how he could write a history of Florence that would appear to celebrate Medici achievements but would reveal the defective, if not pernicious character of their rule.[5] By contrasting the qualities and deeds for which Machiavelli praises Castruccio with what he or the historical record shows that Castruccio actually did, later readers can see the difference between what Machiavelli thought a truly fortunate and virtuous prince would do and a petty tyrant.[6]

Machiavelli concludes his account of the role of fortune and virtue in Castruccio's career with his legacy, the education he sought to give his adopted heir and the sayings he adopted from ancient philosophers. Most commentators have ignored the long list of sayings drawn from Diogenes Laertius's *Lives and Opinions of the Philosophers* that Machiavelli attributes to Castruccio (altered, to be sure, in light of the change in circumstances) at the end of his *Life.* But careful examination of these "maxims" not merely shows that Castruccio did not understand "the mode in which a prince should keep faith"; it also indicates some of the reasons Machiavelli did not state the philosophical basis of his political recommendations clearly or fully.

Earlier Accounts of the Life of Castruccio Castracani

The distinctive character of Machiavelli's account of the life of the young tyrant of Lucca becomes clearer if we contrast it with earlier versions. As in

4. Zanobi Buondelmonti to Niccolò Machiavelli, Florence, September 6, 1520, in *Machiavelli and His Friends*, 328. Renaissance historians generally did not put the same emphasis on objectivity or accuracy that their nineteenth-century successors did. See Felix Gilbert, *Machiavelli and Guicciardini* (Princeton: Princeton University Press, 1984), 203–35; Harvey Mansfield, introduction to *Florentine Histories* (Princeton: Princeton University Press, 1988), vii–xi. Luigi and Zanobi may not have caught all the ways in which Machiavelli altered the historical record, but they would have known enough about the history of their own city to remember that Castruccio had tried to conquer Florence along with the rest of Tuscany, but that he had not succeeded in acquiring or maintaining the empire he sought. In other words, they would have known that Castruccio was not a model of political virtue, and they would, therefore, have rather easily recognized the ironical character of Machiavelli's praise of the tyrant.

5. As Michael Evans, "Machiavelli and Castruccio: Reflections on the *Vita*," *Machiavelli Studies*, no. 4 (1991): 39–55, has argued.

6. Like his *Prince* and *Discourses*, Machiavelli's *Life of Castruccio Castracani* was published only posthumously in 1532.

so many of his earlier works, Machiavelli was transforming an existing story to make his own points. Previous authors differed in their evaluations of the Lucchan's career and achievements. His contemporaries, the Florentine chronicler Giovanni Villani and the Pisan Dominican poet Raniero Granchi, presented Castruccio as an embodiment of the vigor, skill, and valor they found lacking in their own cities; they also found the power of providence reflected in his career.[7] He was described as a shrewd but just ruler in tales by Francesco Petrarch, Franco Sacchetti, and Giovanni Cavalcanti. However, his fellow Lucchans tended to view him as a tyrant of whom they were glad to be rid.[8]

The late-fifteenth-century Lucchan novelist Nicolao Tegrimi was a notable exception. In *Castruccii Antelminelli Lucensis Ducis Vita* he presented his city's most famous prince as a model of ancient virtue or nobility.[9] In order to do so, however, he had to embroider or even alter the facts in his depiction of the three basic aspects of Castruccio's life.

First, Tegrimi made a great deal of Castruccio's family. To emphasize his hero's noble ancestry, Tegrimi followed the example of the historical character, who added *degli Antelminelli* to his name after his ascension to power.[10] To explain how the son of a merchant became a successful mercenary captain, Tegrimi created the character of Alderigo Antelminelli (whose name was taken from a Lucchan financier active in northern Europe later in the fourteen century) as a mentor. And to make his hero more like the great figures of antiquity, Tegrimi invented a story about his miraculous birth. Having fallen asleep, exhausted by her labor, Castruccio's mother dreamed that a great fire blazed up from within her body that consumed her and everything around her. Awakened by her fright, she gave birth; and the injuries she suffered in giving birth to so large an infant made her unable to bear any more children. But, Tegrimi emphasized,

7. Giovanni Villani, *Nuova Cronica* (Parma: Ugo Guanda, 1990); Raynerii de Grancis, "De Proeliis Tusciae," in *Rerum Italicarum Scriptores: Raccolta degli storici italiani dal cinquecento al millecinquecento*, vol. 11, ed. L. A. Muratori (Bologna: N. Zanichelli, 1922), part 2.

8. See Louis Green, "Machiavelli's *Vita Di Castruccio Castracani* and Its Lucchese Model," *Italian Studies* 42 (1987): 38.

9. Nicolao Tegrimi, *Castruccii Antelminelli Lucensis Ducis Vita* (Modena: Domenico Rocociola, 1496). Page citations to Latin-Italian edition, ed. Giorgio Dati (Lucca: Sebastianus Dominicus Cappuri, 1742).

10. Tegrimi, *Castruccii Antelminelli Lucensis Ducis Vita*, 4, 14. The Castracani were a recently established, minor branch of the Antelminelli who engaged in the somewhat disreputable practice of moneylending. Tegrimi also elevated the status of Castruccio's wife's family, the Streghi, who were, in fact, rather undistinguished. See T. W. Blomquist, "The Castracani Family of Thirteenth Century Lucca," *Speculum* 46 (1971): 459–76.

Castruccio himself fathered a large family, including nine legitimate and two "natural" children. And the novelist extolled the way in which Castruccio educated them, by example as well as by precept. Castruccio was sober and continent, displaying a particular devotion to Saint Francis and inculcating the stoical habits of a soldier in his sons.[11]

Second, in tracing his hero's rise to power, Tegrimi claimed that Castruccio led the troops in the battle at Montecatini to victory in the absence of their captain, Uguccione della Faggiuola.[12] He particularly praised his hero's ability to inspire his troops by speaking to them as well as his strategic intelligence and organizational skill. In general, Tegrimi showed Castruccio to be a ruler concerned about the welfare of his people. He regularly sought the advice of wise and learned men and hated flatterers.[13] Although or perhaps because he himself was unlearned, he would from time to time utter a maxim he invented or took from classical sources.[14]

Finally, in depicting Castruccio's legacy, Tegrimi has Castruccio give a deathbed speech in which he says that he is dying poor in possessions but rich in glory, and he reminds his sons that the aim of a ruler should be the welfare and security of his subjects. It does not seem to matter to the novelist's evaluation of the life and deeds of his hero that Castruccio's empire did not last. On the contrary, Tegrimi suggests (in terms reminiscent of Diotima's delineation of the different forms of human striving for immortality in Plato's *Symposium* [207a–212a]), those who sire large families cannot attain the perpetual glory of childless individuals like Moses, Romulus, Numa, Caesar, and Homer. It is, moreover, necessary to take account of the power of fortune as well as an individual's virtue in evaluating his achievements.

11. Tegrimi, *Castruccii Antelminelli Lucensis Ducis Vita*, 10–12, 14, 84–88, 104–6. Louis Green, *Castruccio Castracani: A Study on the Origins and Character of a Fourteenth-Century Italian Despotism* (Oxford: Clarendon Press, 1986), 190–92.

12. Tegrimi, *Castruccii Antelminelli Lucensis Ducis Vita*, 18–20. But, according to Green, "Apart from the testimony of one chronicler that . . . he distinguished himself in the fighting at Montecatini, as the commander of forty knights and a thousand infantry from Sarzana, we know nothing of the part played by Castruccio Castracani in this battle" (*Castruccio Castracani*, 79).

13. Tegrimi, *Castruccii Antelminelli Lucensis Ducis Vita*, 62–64. Jeffrey T. Schnapp, "Machiavellian Foundlings: Castruccio Castracani and the Aphorism," *Renaissance Quarterly* 45, no. 4 (Winter 1992): 658, points out that, ignoring the suggestion of castration in both his hero's first and his last name (to say nothing of the 'cani' or dog), Tegrimi underlined the meaning of 'castra' (castles) in Latin in praising the extensive building program his hero undertook. He did not merely build a fortress (Augusta) to maintain his own power, but erected many castles, roads, and bridges for the sake not merely of defending his subjects but of fostering commerce.

14. E.g., Tegrimi, *Castruccii Antelminelli Lucensis Ducis Vita*, 38, 64, 104, 112, 160. Machiavelli incorporates several of these in the list of Castruccio's sayings he gives at the end of his account of the life.

Tegrimi reports that Castruccio understood himself to be inferior to Caesar only in the time and place of his birth. His intentions and spirit (*animo*) were as great, but Lucca was not Rome.[15]

Machiavelli seems to have relied on Tegrimi's *Vita* in constructing his own version of the life. He organized his *Life* into the same three stages or aspects and fictionalized his account in a similar way. However, although he incorporated many of his predecessor's inventions, Machiavelli used them to show that Castruccio was not the exemplar of the rather traditional set of princely virtues Tegrimi had depicted.

The Good Fortune of the Foundling

Rather than emphasizing Castruccio's noble lineage like Tegrimi, Machiavelli presents his hero as a foundling who is educated by two sets of adoptive parents. By altering the historical record in this way, Machiavelli seems to be trying to give his protagonist the characteristics if not status of an ancient hero.[16] He begins by observing that

> to anyone who considers the matter, it appears quite amazing that all of those (or at least the greater part of them) who have achieved outstanding things in this world . . . have . . . suffered to an unusual degree from the travails of fortune. . . . [They] have been exposed to wild beasts, or have had such humble fathers that, feeling ashamed of them, they have made themselves out to be sons of Jupiter or some other god. (3)

Machiavelli refrains from giving examples: "since their names are familiar to everyone, to list them would be tedious and undesirable to the reader" (3). But the story he proceeds to tell of Dianora's finding the babe wrapped in grape leaves in her brother's vineyard and his subsequent adoption by Francesco Guinigi cannot help but remind readers of the account of Pharaoh's daughter finding Moses in the bulrushes, and King Astyages' identification of his son Cyrus on the basis of his regal bearing.[17]

15. Tegrimi, *Castruccii Antelminelli Lucensis Ducis Vita*, 136–38.

16. By having Castruccio adopted, Machiavelli makes his succession to power more like that of the good Roman emperors rather than the bad, who succeeded by inheritance. See *D* 2.10. Although Machiavelli is explicitly reporting the views of others who have written on the cycle of regimes in *D* 1.2, he seems to agree with the tradition in seeing inherited rule as a cause of degeneration. See d'Amico, "Machiavelli's 'Life of Castruccio Castracani,'" 22–23, 30.

17. Exodus 2; Herodotus 1.104–25. Because the wife of the slave herdsman who saved Cyrus was named Cyno in Greek (Spako or bitch in Median), Herodotus reports, a fable grew up that he

Although the stories of his birth and nurture make Castruccio resemble two of the ancient founders of kingdoms and empires that Machiavelli celebrates in *P* 6, he does not present Castruccio as their equal.[18] In *The Prince* Machiavelli declares that the virtue of those who rise to power on the basis of their own abilities is so great that fortune gives them only the "opportunity," that is, "the matter enabling them to introduce any form they pleased. Without that opportunity their virtue of spirit would have been eliminated, and without that virtue the opportunity would have been in vain" (*P* 6; 23). The opportunities he describes in the case of Moses and Cyrus consist, moreover, in the enslavement or oppression of their peoples from which the founder-heroes freed them. Machiavelli never suggests that Castruccio "liberated" Lucca or the other Tuscan cities he ruled as a tyrant (whereas he does say that the Pistoians who drove out Castruccio's lieutenants restored "liberty to the city" [95]). Nor does he suggest, as did Tegrimi (or Herodotus before him with regard to Cyrus) that his hero's future achievements were presaged by a dream in which a flame, flood, or vine that encompassed the earth burst out of his mother's womb.

Machiavelli explicitly presents Castruccio's humble birth and adoption as illustrations of the power of Fortune, who "wishing to demonstrate to the world that it is she who makes men great, and not Prudence, begins to show her powers at a time when prudence can play no part at all, so that Fortune can take the credit for everything." However, Machiavelli also indicates the limits of the power of Fortune to make an individual great—and the extent of his own praise of Castruccio—when he adds that Castruccio's achievements were "outstanding" for "the times in which he lived and the city in which he was born" (3), but not in themselves.

According to Machiavelli (and in marked contrast to the historical record), Castruccio had the good fortune to be found by a childless widow who was living with her childless brother, a priest named Antonio Castracani (which means castrated dog). Lacking progeny of their own, they decided to adopt and educate the baby boy. But Messer Antonio's attempts to train the boy to become a priest like him were foiled by Castruccio's strong natural inclinations toward war. When he was fourteen years old and no longer feared the chastisement of his parents, he put aside his books about

had been nursed by a dog. As Schnapp, "Machiavellian Foundings," 658, reminds us, Castracani's family name also referred to dogs.

18. Both d'Amico, "Machiavelli's 'Life of Castruccio Castracani,'" 33, 36, and Macfarland, "Machiavelli's Imagination of Excellent Men," 144, agree that, in the end, Machiavelli does not present Castruccio as the equivalent of a founder like Moses or Romulus.

churchly matters and dedicated himself entirely to learning how to handle weapons and win athletic contests. A nobleman named Francesco Guinigi saw how Castruccio excelled the other boys and offered to instruct him in "all the virtue and habits of a true gentleman [*uno vero gentile uomo*]" (86).[19]

In sum, Machiavelli shows that Castruccio's good fortune was to be born with a nature especially suited to waging war and to be adopted, eventually, by a man able to teach him how to do so successfully. In contrast to the great founders with whom Machiavelli first associated him, there was nothing miraculous or mythical about Castruccio's birth, adoption, or education.

Castruccio's Military and Political *Virtù*

Just as he began by presenting Castruccio's birth in the guise of that of a legendary founder, but then indicated that neither his nurture nor his achievements were that extraordinary, so in the second major part of the *Life*, Machiavelli presents an improved and enhanced picture of Castruccio's rise to power, only to undercut his exemplary status in the end. Once again Machiavelli departs in significant ways from the historical record in relating the way in which Castruccio came to power in Lucca and was on the brink of establishing a broader Tuscan empire when he suffered an untimely death. By showing that Castruccio imitated a series of ancient generals in seeking to enlarge his dominion by means of fraud as well as force, Machiavelli suggests that the Lucchan tyrant understood very well what a private man has to do in order to become a prince. (Cf. *P* 18–19; *D* 2.13.) However, Machiavelli also shows his readers that each of Castruccio's successes provoked a domestic reaction. Although he forcefully quashed the opposition, and organized his own people into an army (instead of relying on the mercenary forces with which he began), Castruccio was never able to gather and maintain popular support. He made his own imperial

19. Like Tegrimi, Machiavelli thus invents a character to instruct Castruccio in the military arts and gives that character the name of a Lucchan merchant family, the family, indeed, with whom Machiavelli was engaged in a bankruptcy proceeding and which eventually did take power in Lucca. The historical Castruccio acquired his knowledge of warfare by signing up as a mercenary soldier in Flanders after he fled England to avoid prosecution for his murder of a fellow Italian and then fighting for a decade in Italy. See Green, *Castruccio Castracani*, 41.

ambitions too evident without convincing his allies or his people that he was acting in their interest.[20]

A. Castruccio's Rise to Power in Lucca

According to Machiavelli, Castruccio first demonstrated his military prowess when Messer Francesco put Castruccio in charge of the company he sent to aid the Visconti of Milan. Castruccio displayed so much prudence and courage in the campaign that he returned with a reputation in all of Lombardy. What aroused the envy and opposition of his fellow citizens, however, was not his ability to fight foreign wars; it was the favor Messer Francesco showed Castruccio by choosing him to be the tutor of his thirteen-year-old son Pagolo and to administer his estate after he died. The head of the Guelph party, Messer Giorgio degli Opizi, had hoped to assume power in Lucca after Messer Francesco's death. To discredit his new Ghibelline competitor, Opizi began spreading rumors about Castruccio's intentions of establishing a tyranny.

Rather than immediately seeking to become a tyrant himself, as Opizi charged, Castruccio became a lieutenant of the mercenary captain Uguccione della Faggiuola, who had made himself captain and then lord of Pisa. Uguccione was allied with the Ghibellines, so Castruccio conspired with friends in Lucca not merely to bring back Ghibelline exiles in Pisa, but to make Uguccione lord of Lucca. Having provided himself with the weapons and other supplies necessary to hold out for several days in the Onesti tower, at a prearranged signal Castruccio called the citizens to arms and opened the gates of the city to Uguccione and his troops. The mercenary captain killed Giorgio degli Opizi, his friends, and family, and reorganized the government to suit himself, with much injury to other Lucchans.

Exaggerating the role Castruccio played in establishing Uguccione as tyrant of Lucca, Machiavelli adopts Tegrimi's alteration of the historical record by making Castruccio lead Uguccione's troops to victory when they meet the Florentine army amassed to put down the rising Ghibelline power.[21] He also changes the location of the battle and the strategy used

20. We later readers should recall that in *D* 2.4 Machiavelli recommends the formation of a Tuscan League rather than a "useless" attempt on the part of the Florentines to try to conquer and rule their neighbors as subjects, the way that Sparta and Athens did.

21. Machiavelli makes no mention of Castruccio's having led Uguccione's troops in his account of the battle in his *Florentine Histories* 2.25. As Bondanella, "Castruccio Castracani," 310–11,

to win it.[22] Machiavelli does not make the actual source of the strategy he attributes to Castruccio explicit. He may have been testing his young Florentine friends' memories of the lessons they supposedly learned from the conversation related in the *Art of War*.[23] But readers see that in order to make Castruccio an exemplary captain, Machiavelli has attributed knowledge of ancient examples or the prudence to replicate them to his protagonist. (There is no evidence that the historical Castruccio possessed such knowledge or put it into practice.)

Machiavelli then shows that Castruccio's military success led Uguccione to become jealous and suspicious. (In *D* 1.29–30, Machiavelli argues that a prince will necessarily regard a victorious captain as a potential rival.) When Castruccio resisted the arrest of a murderer who had sought refuge with him, Uguccione had the pretext he desired to act against his captain.[24] He ordered his son Neri, whom he had left in charge of Lucca, to invite Castruccio to dinner and then to seize and imprison him. Afraid that the people would

---

argues, the fact that Machiavelli gives a historically accurate account of Uguccione's victory at Montecatini and Castruccio's seizure of Pistoia in his *Florentine Histories* 2.25, 2.29, indicates that he knew the history that he altered in the *Vita*.

22. According to Machiavelli, after Uguccione fell sick (a detail added to explain the change in command), Castruccio waited several days, allowing the Florentines to think that the inexperienced captain was afraid, thus prompting them to taunt him by marching up to confront his troops in battle order, permitting him to see what their tactics were. Because the Florentines had put their best troops in the center, as Whitfield, *Discourses on Machiavelli*, 120–21, points out, Castruccio used the strategy Scipio had employed fighting Hasdrubal in Spain (Livy 28.24.5), ordering the weaker troops he put in the center to approach the enemy slowly, so that his best troops on the flanks would meet and repel the enemy's weakest forces first, force them to flee, and induce the center then to retreat also. (Zanobi asks Fabrizio to explain Scipio's use of this strategy in *AW* 4.42.) Drawing on Cortusio, "Historia," cols. 794–96, and G. Villani, *Cronica* 9.71, Green, *Castruccio Castracani*, 63–67, reports that the two armies faced each other "in a natural amphitheatre ringed on three sides by hills, with the swamps north of the Arno valley closing it off to the south." Against superior numbers, Uguccione had both "to maintain the siege of Montecatini and to keep open his lines of communication and supply with Lucca. He was, therefore, vulnerable to attack along a relatively long front. . . . But, because the Guelphs paused to relieve the besieged garrison of Montecatini before they advanced, Uguccione was able to retreat to a strong defensive position."

23. In *AW* 4.42–54, Machiavelli has the mercenary captain Fabrizio Colonna recommend this strategy to Cosimo, Zanobi, Luigi, and Batista, then observe that it can no longer work, because the enemy's artillery could hit the center, but finally explain that the strategy can be modified to take account of the new technology and should be imitated. Artillery was not in use, however, when Castruccio fought his battle, so the strategy could have been successfully used then.

24. According to Green, "the sources disagree as to the exact circumstances that preceded and precipitated the dramatic events. . . . The most probable reading of the evidence is that Castruccio put to death thirty men at Massa in Lunigiana . . . in an attempt to quell a rebellion or coerce a defiant community into submission. But, whatever justification he may have had, there is no doubt that to Uguccione and to Nieri as his lieutenant in Lucca his action could only have appeared as an usurpation of power properly belonging to the constituted government they represented" (*Castruccio Castracani*, 72).

rebel if he killed such a popular hero without a trial, Neri sent to his father for further advice. Exasperated by his son's ineptitude, Uguccione left Pisa for Lucca with four hundred cavalry, whereupon the Pisans rebelled. Hearing about the rebellion in Pisa, the Lucchans also rebelled. They freed Castruccio, and he and his friends then attacked Uguccione, who fled to Lombardy.

From a traitor, Machiavelli shows, Castruccio thus transformed himself into the liberator of Lucca. With the help of his friends and his newly won popular favor, he was first made general for a year. Castruccio did not take advantage of the opportunity, however, to solidify the support of his people. Anxious to obtain the title as well as control of the city, he bribed several members of outstanding families like the Pogginghi to make him lord, and they arranged for him to be proclaimed prince for life by a solemn decree of the people.[25]

B. Castruccio's Campaign to Acquire a Tuscan Empire

After he was proclaimed lord of Lucca, Machiavelli shows, Castruccio set out immediately to extend his dominion. He first sought to enhance his reputation by making the Holy Roman Emperor his friend. He took five hundred cavalry to meet "Frederick of Bavaria" as he traveled to Rome to be crowned, and the gesture redounded immediately to Castruccio's benefit.[26] Having driven their lord out, the Pisans had asked the emperor for assistance; but, since he intended to return to Germany, the emperor made Castruccio lord of Pisa.

After the emperor returned to Germany, Machiavelli reports, all the Tuscan and Lombard Ghibellines turned to Castruccio for assistance, promising him rule of their states if he managed to return their states to them. His ambition thus excited and expanded, Castruccio decided to try to become lord of all Tuscany with the help of his Ghibelline allies—and his own arms.

25. Machiavelli thus gives a somewhat foreshortened or condensed version of the actual course of events. According to Granchi, *De Proeliis* 11. cols. 301–2, and Villani, *Cronica* 9.73, in 1316 Castruccio first alternated with Pagano Cristofani as captain-general for six months. According to Green, *Castruccio Castracani*, 77–81, Castruccio was then reelected to hold the office alone for a year, extended in 1317 to ten years. Finally in April 1320 he was named "vicar general of Lucca and its territories" by Frederick III, duke of Austria and Holy Roman Emperor, and elected not merely captain but *dominus generalis* of Lucca for life by his fellow citizens.

26. There was, in fact, no such person as "Frederick of Bavaria." As Macfarland, "Machiavelli's Imagination of Excellent Men," 142, points out, Machiavelli combines the two contestants for the imperial crown, Frederick of Austria and Ludwig of Bavaria, and then divides (and substantively changes) their dealings with Castruccio in two separate trips to Rome.

Castruccio first organized his own army by dividing Lucca and its territory into five parts, providing the inhabitants with weapons, and putting them under captains and ensigns. Machiavelli does not explicitly say that Castruccio was following an ancient model he had recommended in *D* 3.30 where he observes that "Camillus never permitted a multitude to take up arms except in a certain order and mode. So following his example, an individual put in charge of the guard of a city ought never arm the men tumultuously, but first have those enrolled and selected whom he wishes to be armed and whom they have to obey" (*D* 3.30, 281, translation slightly modified). Machiavelli simply shows Castruccio doing what he recommended not only in the *Discourses* but also in *The Prince*, where Machiavelli praises Cesare Borgia for shifting from the unreliable auxiliary and mercenary troops he first used to seize power to organizing his own arms.[27]

Although he organized and armed his people, Machiavelli also shows that Castruccio did not seek their support—or that of the nobles. As he admits in his deathbed speech, he did not try to consolidate his power at home before he sought additional foreign acquisitions. On the contrary, following the model of his acquisition of Pisa, Castruccio again tried to enhance his reputation and so further his imperial ambitions by allying with a powerful foreign Ghibelline—Messer Matteo Visconti, prince of Milan. When Matteo asked him to attack Florence, so that the Florentines would have to bring their troops back from Lombardy to Tuscany, Castruccio gladly complied.

Castruccio soon had to withdraw his troops, however, in order to put down a conspiracy at home. Just as Castruccio's rising reputation in Lucca had aroused the envy of the Opizi family, so his imperial connections and ambitions aroused the envy of his former allies, the Poggio family. Thinking that he had not given them their fair share of the rewards, they conspired against him. Although a peace-loving member of the family who had not participated in the conspiracy tried to mediate, Castruccio did not spare him when, following the example of Uguccione and his son Neri (as well as that of Cesare Borgia, *P* 7), he invited the whole family to dinner

27. *P* 7, 12–14. That Castruccio organized his own arms, instead of relying on mercenaries, is one of the reasons Pasquale Villari, *Niccolò Machiavelli e i suoi tempi* (1897), 3, 75, and Frederic Chabod, "Niccolò Machiavelli," *Enciclopedia Italiana* 31 (1934): 778–90, reprinted in *Scritti su Machiavelli* (Turin: G. Einaudi, 1964), 195–240, argue that Machiavelli was not falsifying history but presenting Castruccio as a daring soldier and astute politician who founded his own state, like Cesare Borgia in *The Prince*. However, as Najemy, "Machiavelli and Cesare Borgia," has shown, Machiavelli's presentation of Cesare is not historically accurate either.

and executed or imprisoned them all.[28] Castruccio then sought to eliminate any individual who might harbor an ambition to become prince in his stead. Like Agathocles the Sicilian (*P* 8), Castruccio thus demonstrated his ability to use both force and fraud to seize and maintain control of his city for the duration of his life. But, Machiavelli proceeds to show, that '*virtù*' was not sufficient to enable him to found a lasting empire or to win glory.

While he was seeking to eliminate any opposition at home and building a huge fortress to protect himself (contrary to Machiavelli's advice in both *P* 20 and *D* 2.24), Castruccio continued to pursue his imperial ambitions by conspiring with the leaders of the major factions in Pistoia to obtain control of that city. Promising the leaders of both the white and the black Guelphs that he would assist them in putting down the opposition, once he and his troops were let into the city he killed the heads, captured the supporters of both factions, and persuaded the populace to surrender, partly by promising to cancel some old debts. Here, too, Machiavelli attributes a strategy employed by an ancient captain—in this case, the strategy used by Cyrus's lieutenant Adusius in making peace in Caria—to Castruccio.[29] As in *D* 3.27, however, Machiavelli modifies the strategy to have his captain follow the Roman example of killing (instead of trying to reconcile) the heads of the conspiring factions.[30]

After he seized Pistoia, Machiavelli shows, Castruccio again sought to increase his international reputation rather than solidify support for his rule among his fellow citizens—this time by responding to a plea from a lieutenant of the Holy Roman Emperor named "Henry" to help put down a rebellion in Rome.[31] Castruccio did so primarily by having grain shipped in from Sicily and so removing the major cause of popular unrest; but he also threatened or punished the leaders until they accepted Henry's rule.

28. In fact, Machiavelli condenses three different family rebellions (by the Avvocati in 1317, the Pogginghi in 1321, and the Quartigiani in 1327). Stefano Poggio killed Castruccio's minister of justice, and the other members of his family agreed to meet with Castruccio on the assumption that he would punish only the guilty individual. Instead he acted harshly against the family as a whole.

29. Xenophon, *Education of Cyrus* 7.3–6; Whitfield, *Discourses on Machiavelli*, 124–25.

30. In fact, Castruccio acquired control of Pistoia by conspiring with members of the Tedici family, beginning in 1323, but succeeding only in 1325. In the meantime, Castruccio tried and failed to take Prato by force. His attempt to take Pisa by conspiracy also failed. Ludwig of Bavaria replaced Frederick of Austria as Holy Roman Emperor. In 1324 he granted Castruccio an imperial vicariate over Pistoia, before Castruccio actually acquired control of the city by offering to marry his daughter Dialto with a 10,000 florin dowry to Filippo Tedici (whereas the Florentines with whom Tedici was also negotiating offered merely to knight his son, dowry his daughters, and marry them to Florentine citizens, plus 3,000 florins).

31. According to Villani's *Nuova Cronica*, Arrigo d'Ostericchi (Henry of Austria) was the emperor's brother.

Castruccio thus appeared to have understood the importance of gaining the people's support by preserving their lives and property while restraining "the great" (*P* 9). However, just as Castruccio squandered his opportunity to build a reputation as the liberator and savior of the people of Lucca in order to obtain the title of prince as quickly as possible, so in Rome Castruccio immediately began to flaunt his imperial ambitions. After he had been made a senator, he celebrated his new office with great pomp. He had a toga embroidered with "God wills it" on the front and "What God wills shall be" on the back. Again, Machiavelli does not explicitly draw the comparison with Camillus and the four white horses he used to draw his chariot in his triumph (*D* 3.23), but by wearing this toga in a celebration of his new office, Castruccio could be seen to be claiming to rule on the basis of divine support, if not of his own divinity, and thus displaying a kind of *hubris* that would arouse the ire of the people (to say nothing of the suspicions of God's two other purported representatives on earth, the Holy Roman Emperor and the pope).

Although he successfully expanded his dominion by means of both force and fraud, Machiavelli shows, Castruccio's flaunting of his imperial ambitions aroused opposition to his rule in all the cities he acquired. His expansionary policies also aroused the suspicions and hostility of a more powerful neighbor—the republic of Florence. The Florentines first conspired with some exiles to retake Pistoia. Seeking to preempt a response from Castruccio, they then assembled a great army and marched to the Nievole valley where they could cut off his route to Pistoia. (As Machiavelli shows, but does not explicitly say, a republic can use force and fraud as well as a prince.) However, Castruccio marched back post haste from Rome and defeated the Florentines at Serravalle by employing another strategy Machiavelli recommends in the *Art of War* (4.16–17): he used the peculiarities of the site (a fortress located on a hill) to disguise the superior number of the foe from his own soldiers and to force the enemy to retreat in confusion. In the wake of Castruccio's victory, the Pistoians drove out the Guelphs and surrendered to him. But he, not content with merely returning to the status quo, occupied Prato and camped within two miles of the gates of Florence. Once there, he conspired with two nobles to open the gates, but the plot was discovered and the nobles killed.

In both his *Florentine Histories* and *Life of Castruccio Castracani* Machiavelli reports that Castruccio's attack made the Florentines fear the loss of their own liberty. They thus offered to make Robert, king of Naples, lord of the city, if he would defend them. He agreed to send his son, Charles of Calabria, for a fee of 200,000 florins per year. However, it took Charles some time to arrive. In the *Life*, Machiavelli explains that the Florentines were able to assemble another huge army to oppose Castruccio, because he was forced to withdraw his troops from their territory in order to put down a conspiracy against him in Pisa. Once again, Castruccio lost the advantage he had won on the battlefield because of opposition inside a city he had previously conquered.

Like the battle at Serravalle, the battle Machiavelli describes between Castruccio and the Florentines at Fucecchio in his *Life* is a fabrication. In fact, Castruccio's army camped within two miles of the walls of Florence and ravaged the countryside after he defeated the Florentines at Altopascio; and he later defeated them again along with the rebellious Pistoians with a siege. In his *Florentine Histories* (2.29) Machiavelli attributes the Florentine losses to the dilatory tactics employed by their hired commander, Ramondo di Cardona, and the political divisions within the city.[32] He concludes that account, moreover, by observing that Florence was saved only by good fortune, when both Castruccio and Charles died. In the *Life* Machiavelli presents the Lucchan captain as a better military leader than he actually was and attributes his death to a certain lack of foresight rather than sheer bad lack.

To make Castruccio look like an exemplary captain, in his *Life* Machiavelli not only changes the location and reason for Castruccio's last victory—from a rebellion in Pistoia to a rebellion in Pisa and from a siege (which, Machiavelli pointed out in *D* 2.32 the Romans sought to avoid, because they were long and expensive) to a pitched battle.[33] He also attributes

32. According to Green, *Castruccio Castracani*, 165–74, however, Ramondo showed himself to be equal to Castruccio as a military strategist. Feigning first to attack Pistoia to keep Castruccio's troops tied down in the east, Ramondo marched south to attack the exposed Arno-Usciana front. Castruccio brought his troops back to Lucca and occupied the heights above the plain of Altopascio. After the Florentines took the garrison, they fell prey to the diseases they themselves had caused by catapulting refuse into the fortress; and their numbers were further reduced by Cardona's allowing some troops to return home for a fee. They became irresolute; as a result Castruccio had time to raise money to pay for Milanese mercenary reinforcements. Cardona began a retreat, and Castruccio successfully attacked and defeated him.

33. In fact, Charles first conspired with the Quartigiani in Lucca in 1327. Having quickly thwarted that conspiracy, Castruccio acquired the additional troops he needed from Ludwig of Bavaria (after Ludwig had forced the Milanese to pay for them and in the process overthrew the Visconti) to counter the aid the Florentines had obtained from Naples. Castruccio and Ludwig first attacked and took Pisa. When Ludwig then marched south toward Rome, Charles left Florence to go and defend Naples. Castruccio then followed Ludwig to take part in the coronation. Hearing that the Guelphs had retaken Pistoia in January 1328, he returned to Tuscany, retook Pistoia by siege, and died.

Castruccio's victory in this last battle to his employing a combination of ancient strategies—one Hannibal used at the River Tagus (Livy 21.5) and one Scipio used at Zama (Livy 30.34)—that Machiavelli (or his spokesman Fabrizio Colonna) recommended to his young Florentine readers in the *Art of War* (4.40–41).

In relating the way in which Castruccio's career came to an abrupt end at the conclusion of this battle, Machiavelli seems to attribute Castruccio's failure to realize his imperial ambitions to bad luck and thus to return to what appeared to be the primary theme of the *Life* at the beginning, i.e., the power of *fortuna*. Because he believed that a captain should be first to mount and last to dismount, Machiavelli reports, Castruccio stood bareheaded in a wind, exhausted and drenched in perspiration, to greet his victorious troops on their return (as well as to look and see whether the enemy had regrouped and would attack). As a result, he came down with a fever and died.

Readers are led to ask, however, whether Castruccio's end was simply a matter of bad luck. As with Cesare Borgia, with whom Castruccio has often been compared, Machiavelli first attributes his inability to establish a lasting regime to his own untimely death. But as Machiavelli states explicitly in the case of Cesare, so he implicitly suggests in the case of Castruccio, his failure to establish a lasting regime was also a result of bad judgment.[34] That bad judgment is revealed in the two parts of his 'legacy': the deathbed speech Machiavelli invents for him to give to his imaginary adopted heir and the thirty-four sayings that Machiavelli attributes to him.

Castruccio's Lack of Practical Wisdom

A. Castruccio's Failure as a Teacher

As he lay dying, Castruccio purportedly told Pagolo that if he had thought that Fortune would want to cut him off in the midst of the path toward the glory promised by his many successes he would have tried to do less.

34. In *P* 7, Machiavelli states that "Cesare Borgia . . . acquired his state through the fortune of his father and lost it through the same, notwithstanding the fact that he made use of every deed and did all those things that should be done by a prudent and virtuous man to put his roots in the states that the arms and fortune of others had given him. . . . [H]e would have succeeded if Alexander had lived. . . . But Alexander died five years after he had begun. . . . [and] left the duke with only the state of Romagna consolidated . . . and sick to death. . . . One could only accuse him of making a bad choice in the creation of Julius as pontiff. . . . It was the cause of his ultimate ruin" (33, translation slightly modified).

Content to rule Lucca and Pisa, he would not have conquered Pistoia and angered the Florentines. He would thus have left Pagolo a smaller, but more secure state, with fewer enemies and envy.

J. H. Whitfield takes Castruccio's deathbed disavowal of his imperial ambitions as a late endorsement by Machiavelli of moderation or "the middle way" he previously excoriated.[35] There are, however, several serious problems with this interpretation.

First, human beings all know that they are going to have to die sometime; a soldier ought to be particularly aware of the danger. Unlike Machiavelli's protagonist, the historical Castruccio thus arranged to have his son elected captain on the eve of his first great battle with the Florentines—just in case he himself was killed.[36] At the very least, in attributing this deathbed speech to Castruccio, Machiavelli suggests that the captain was lacking in foresight.

Second, Machiavelli shows that Castruccio regretted his lack of success and consequent failure to win glory. But it is not at all clear that he disavowed his imperial ambitions as wrong or excessive. On the contrary, Castruccio brags about his having demonstrated his gratitude to his benefactor not only by refusing to marry, lest he have his own natural children who might compete with Pagolo for his affection, but also by leaving Pagolo more than his father did. In other words, Castruccio thinks that more is better. He regrets the fragility of his acquisitions, but he has not become more moderate in his desires. He says that he is happy to have left Pagolo a large state; he is sad only because that state is weak and infirm. All the cities over which he has acquired control are apt to revolt, and his conquests have angered their most powerful neighbors, the Florentines.

Castruccio bequeaths Pagolo an admittedly difficult position, but he also prides himself on telling Pagolo how to deal with it. Because Pagolo is not suited to war, Castruccio advises him to endeavor to use the arts of peace. He should not count on the support of his rebellious subjects or distant allies, but, relying on his own cleverness and their memory of their recent defeat, he should try to make peace with the Florentines. Castruccio concludes, therefore, by informing Pagolo that he will be indebted to Castruccio not only for the state he has left but also for teaching him how to keep it.

35. Whitfield, *Discourses on Machiavelli*, takes his cue from Zanobi's letter of September 6, 1520, in which he says, "Above all else, it seems to me that you are strong in that prayer" (*Machiavelli and His Friends*, 328–29, n534). Fido, "Politician as Writer," makes a similar claim about Machiavelli's "moderating" of his earlier views in the *Life*.

36. Green, *Castruccio Castracani*, 190.

But Castruccio's claim to have benefited his adopted heir, particularly by teaching him what to do in order to stay in power, proves on examination to be hollow. Machiavelli does not explicitly comment on the wisdom of Castruccio's deathbed advice. He merely informs his readers that neither virtue nor fortune was as friendly to Pagolo as they had been to Castruccio. Pagolo soon lost everything Castruccio had left him, except for Lucca, which remained in his family for two generations.

If readers review the story of Castruccio's rise to power and Pagolo's role in it, however, they see that Castruccio was not a good teacher. (No one who knows anything about teaching would believe that he could tell his successor what to do in a brief speech at the end of his life.) Machiavelli tells his readers that Castruccio used Pagolo as his lieutenant both in the conspiracy against Pistoia and in the defense of Pisa and so instructed him by example, if not by precept, in the arts of war. He does not mention any instance in which Castruccio attempted to train Pagolo in the "arts of peace" (which Machiavelli identifies with religion in his praise of Numa in *D* 1.11) that Castruccio now tells his heir to employ in negotiating with Florence, because Pagolo is not capable of waging war. Having discovered that Pagolo was not warlike by nature, Castruccio had not reversed his own experience and given his heir to a priest to teach him what Castruccio himself had refused to learn from Messer Antonio. Nor had Castruccio imitated Messer Francesco's prudent policy by finding a young man with a suitable nature to adopt and educate, who would be able to lead his troops when he himself was no longer able to do so. In other words, Castruccio may have increased the estate he passed on to Pagolo, but he had not served as an effective tutor. He had not, because he had not reflected on his own experience and drawn appropriate conclusions from it. Machiavelli thus shows, although he does not explicitly say, that Castruccio lacked self-knowledge.

B. What Castruccio Needed to Know in Order to Succeed, but Did Not

Castruccio's lack of self-knowledge proves, indeed, to be the implicit theme of the last third of the *Life*. As Castruccio told Pagolo, he thought that he was on "the path toward glory promised by his many successes." Unfortunately, Machiavelli shows, Castruccio did not understand what is required truly to achieve the glory he sought.

Castruccio's failure to educate his heir meant that he would not have an effective successor or succession. Although his description of Castruccio's birth is reminiscent of the legends associated with Moses and Cyrus, Machiavelli does not present the Lucchan prince as a founder or legislator. In what appears to be a eulogy at the conclusion of his account of the funeral, Machiavelli points to Castruccio's fundamental misunderstanding. Tall and handsome, Castruccio would appear literally to have embodied the characteristics of an ideal prince.[37] As in his youth, so as an adult Castruccio had "so much grace in his bearing and received men with such humanity that nobody who had spoken with him left dissatisfied." Machiavelli adds that "he was kind to his friends, but terrible to his enemies; just towards his subjects, but faithless to foreigners." He would never seek to win by force what he could take by fraud; for he said, "it was the victory itself, not the way you won the victory, that brought you glory" (104).

This final "saying" reveals what Machiavelli saw to be Castruccio's fundamental intellectual error or misunderstanding; he did not know how to attain what he most wanted. In *D* 3.40 Machiavelli observes that although one can use fraud not only to win wars but also to acquire a kingdom, the use of fraud will not bring anyone glory. In order to acquire glory, Machiavelli argues in both his *Prince* and *Discourses*, a leader must not only satisfy the desires of his fellow citizens or subjects to preserve their lives and property but also appear to be merciful, faithful, honest, humane, and religious. But, as the sayings Machiavelli attributes to Castruccio at the end of the *Life* show, he was not concerned about appearing to be moral or religious. On the contrary, Castruccio used to say that "men should try everything and not be dismayed by anything. God clearly is a lover of brave men, since one sees that the weak are always punished by the strong" (104). Castruccio apparently had not read enough history to have learned that "among all men praised, the most praised are those who have been heads and orderers of religion. Next, then, are those who have founded either republics or kingdoms. After them are celebrated those who, placed over armies, have expanded either their kingdom or that of the fatherland" (*D* 1.10).

The caustic sayings drawn from Diogenes Laertius's account of the lives of the ancient Greek philosophers that Machiavelli attributes to Castruccio show that he had no compunctions about openly contradicting widely

37. To emphasize his warlike nature, perhaps, Machiavelli changed the color of his hair from blonde to red. See *Vita di Castruccio Castracani*, 104n126.

held moral opinions. Nor did he have sufficient regard for maintaining a dignified public presence. Castruccio should have seen that the thought expressed in the sayings he repeated was incompatible with a political life like his own. His adoption and repetition of these sayings reflected a kind of arrogance that led him to despise the need to keep up appearances. His borrowing of the words of others constituted a pretention to wisdom that would have been condemned by the authors whose words he appropriated. Castruccio thought that he was better and wiser than he really was.

Like his first young Florentine readers, most commentators have simply ignored or dismissed the long list of maxims taken largely from Diogenes Laertius that Machiavelli attributes, in slightly modified form, to Castruccio at the end of his *Life*.[38] As a result, they have missed not only Machiavelli's critique of the Lucchan prince for his lack of practical wisdom, but also Machiavelli's indications of what a prudent prince or educator would understand.

All the ancient philosophers from whom Castruccio takes his maxims were students of Socrates: the hedonist Aristippus (the first 16 sayings), the sophist Bion (2 sayings before and 2 after the one saying by Aristotle), and the cynic Diogenes (11 sayings, punctuated by one statement attributed by Tegrimi to Castruccio himself and one from Dante's *Inferno*). All these Socratics were critical of the Platonic notion of the ideas. They did not themselves posit such transcendental, purely intelligible objects of knowledge or standards of right and wrong. All of them nevertheless recognized a fundamental difference between nature and convention and criticized conventional morality, customs and laws on that basis.[39] Because he attributed the sayings to Castruccio, Machiavelli did not have to cite or explain the source.

In attributing these sayings to Castruccio, Machiavelli adapts them to his times, for example, by substituting celebrations of "saints' feast-days" for

38. In his letter dated September 6, 1520, Zanobi wrote Machiavelli that he thought "that last part with the apothegms and the witty and sharp sayings of said Castruccio . . . would turn out better if shortened, because in addition to these sayings or witticisms of his being too numerous, there are some that are attributed to other sages, both ancient and modern; another part does not have the liveliness or the grandeur that would be expected of such a man" (*Machiavelli and His Friends*, 328).

39. Machiavelli mostly follows the order of the statements reported by Diogenes Laertius, but he eliminates the frequent references to Socrates and Plato. As Strauss, *TM*, 291, points out, Machiavelli referred to Xenophon's *Hiero* and *Education of Cyrus*, but never to the *Oeconomicus* or any other of Xenophon's Socratic writings. There is only one reference to Plato and one reference to Aristotle in the *Discourses* (and none in *The Prince*). The density of references to ancient philosophers in the *Life*, even if the source is not explicitly acknowledged, is singular.

"festivals of the gods."[40] He also adapts the sayings to his protagonist's position, first, by identifying Castruccio with the tyrant Dionysius rather than with the philosopher Aristippus. According to Machiavelli, Castruccio thus spit on a flatterer rather than, like Aristippus, allowing a tyrant (Dionysius) to spit on him. Likewise, Machiavelli reports, when someone came to ask him a favor and Castruccio appeared to turn a deaf ear, the man threw himself onto the ground; and when Castruccio rebuked him, the man responded, "it is your fault; you have ears in your feet." Diogenes Laertius says that when Aristippus made a request to Dionysius on behalf of a friend and the tyrant refused to grant it, the philosopher fell down at the tyrant's feet and responded to a jeering passerby, "It is not I who am to blame, but Dionysius who has his ears in his feet" (2.8.79). Second, where Aristippus said that he would like to die like Socrates, Machiavelli has Castruccio say that he would like to die like Caesar. Both Socrates and Caesar might be said to have acquired fame if not glory by dying as martyrs. But the hedonist Aristippus would no doubt have pointed out that Socrates emphasized that he was seventy years old and apt to die soon of natural causes in any case. The hemlock was, moreover, supposed to be painless. Caesar was killed painfully by stabs inflicted by many of his supposed friends and colleagues. Like Castruccio, Caesar had just acquired his empire. The first Roman emperor was his adopted son Augustus, whose rise was facilitated by the will in which Caesar left his property to the people of Rome (and even he called himself merely *princeps* rather than *imperator*).[41] As we have seen, Castruccio did not leave his heir such a good example to follow or teach him how to obtain the favor of his people. Nor had he learned to conceal his own imperial ambitions by retaining old titles and forms. (Cf. *D* 1.25.)

Even though Machiavelli adapts the sayings to fit Castruccio's particular circumstances, a comparison of Castruccio's sayings with the original versions indicates not merely that he did not recognize the fundamental

40. Castruccio had surely learned something about Church doctrine and ritual from his first adoptive father, the priest Antonio Castracani. He seems, however, to have left such knowledge almost entirely behind him when he left to learn to be a soldier from Messer Francesco. Machiavelli depicts Castruccio's rise explicitly in the context of the conflict between the Guelphs and the Ghibellines, but he treats the two parties as political sects. He does not explain the grounds or character of the larger dispute between the pope and the emperor. Machiavelli may not have thought that his young Florentine readers needed any such explanation. The explanation he gives in book 1 of his *Florentine Histories* emphasizes the political origins and effects of the dispute much more than doctrine.

41. Leo Paul S. de Alvarez, *The Machiavellian Enterprise* (De Kalb: Northern Illinois University Press, 1999), 9.

tension between his own political concerns and the explicitly apolitical stance taken by the ancient Socratics. He did not understand the requirements of his own political position.

Ancient Socratics like Aristippus insisted that philosophy was a better way of life than politics, and that philosophers should keep their distance from this "disease." Both in the *Apology* and in the *Gorgias* Plato's Socrates claimed that his refutations constituted a kind of corrective "medicine" for the individuals he interrogated. But Socrates also insisted that his examinations had to be conducted in private. He could not go into a public assembly and oppose the unjust will of the many without losing his life.[42]

Castruccio went into politics at an early age and expressed contempt for philosophers. When Castruccio told a man who professed to be a philosopher, "You are all like dogs, who always come running to the man who can give them most to eat," Machiavelli reports that the philosopher retorted, "No, we are like doctors, we go to the houses of those who have most need of us."[43] According to Diogenes Laertius, Aristippus (following Socrates) went even further in observing that "physicians tend those who are sick," but that "no one for that reason would prefer being sick to being a physician."

One of the few commentators if not the only one to pay attention to the maxims at the end of the *Life*, Strauss points out that the last set of sayings drawn from Diogenes begins with a reference to Castruccio's education by Messer Francesco Guinigi. Asked by a comrade what he would want in exchange for letting himself be slapped, Castruccio replied, as did Diogenes, "a helmet." As a youth, Machiavelli shows, Castruccio had learned the importance of being able to defend himself from harm inflicted by others. That lesson led him to engage in politics—in contrast to the cynical philosophers whose sayings he had apparently absorbed. The first saying derived from Diogenes is thus followed by the only saying attributable to Castruccio himself (by Tegrimi). When he put to death a citizen of Lucca who had contributed to his greatness, Castruccio was told that it was wrong to kill one of his old friends, whereupon he replied that he had killed a new enemy. As Machiavelli points out in *D* 1.28–30, it is not possible for a prince to be grateful to those who have served him, because his best "servants" become competitors for rule.

42. Plato, *Gorgias* 521e–522a; *Apology of Socrates* 23b, 28e–30b, 31c–32a, 32e–33b; *Republic* 496c–e.

43. *Vita di Castruccio Castracani*, 105; Diogenes Laertius 2.8.70.

In the next saying borrowed from Diogenes, Machiavelli has Castruccio praise men who take women and do not marry them and those who say that they are going to travel by sea, but do not; that is, he praises adulterers and liars. Castruccio does not go on, however, as Diogenes does in the same maxim (6.29), to praise those who thought about engaging in politics, but did not, those who purposed to rear a family, but did not, and those who made ready to live with potentates (*dunastais*), but never came near them. Castruccio clearly took pleasure in women he did not marry and often lied about his intentions, but he just as obviously went into politics and associated with potentates. The young Lucchan tyrant understood his political power to be a means of satisfying his own desires and thus bringing him pleasure. He did not understand the way in which political power becomes a burden that requires a ruler to exercise a certain amount of self-restraint. Both Machiavelli and the ancient philosophers whose sayings he steals from did.

To be sure, in repeating the sayings of Aristippus and Diogenes, Machiavelli has Castruccio omit the explicitly antipolitical parts. Castruccio was proud of his political position and certainly did not want to disavow it. He apparently did not understand the connection between the ancient philosophers' caustic comments about conventional morality and their withdrawal from politics. Having done little reading as a youth, he does not seem to have been aware of the exchange Xenophon reports in his *Memorabilia* (2.1) between Socrates and Aristippus in which Socrates gets Aristippus to agree that a ruler needs to be virtuous, but Aristippus responds by arguing that he himself does not have to be virtuous, because he does not want to be a ruler, who would have to assume the burden of caring for others. When Socrates objects that if he does not rule, he will be ruled, Aristippus concedes that he does not want to be a slave, but he thinks that he can avoid becoming dominated by anyone else by traveling from city to city. Aristippus may have thus made himself vulnerable to attack, as Socrates suggests, but his stance was clearly antipolitical and thus antithetical to Castruccio's own position and ambitions. Although Castruccio told Pagolo that it is important to know oneself, i.e., to have an accurate understanding of one's own circumstances and abilities, Machiavelli suggests that Castruccio himself did not.

By repeating the sayings of these antipolitical philosophers, Castruccio showed not merely that he did not understand the tension between their understanding of the world or nature and his own political concerns. By accepting, without resentment, such caustic statements made to him by others, Castruccio also showed that he did not understand one of the basic requirements of his own position, the need for a prince to maintain a certain kind of public position or front. In *P* 23 Machiavelli observes: "There is no other way to guard oneself from flattery unless men understand that they do not offend you in telling you the truth; but when everyone can tell you the truth, they lack reverence for you" (93–94). Castruccio accepted the biting statements made by others, because he hated flatterers. He did not understand the need to insist that others revere him any more than he understood the need for a prince to appear to be reverent himself.

In other words, Castruccio did not understand why a prince, who cannot always be merciful, honest, humane, and religious, must nevertheless always seek to appear to be so, especially to be religious. When asked whether, to save his soul, he had thought of becoming a friar, Castruccio said, "No, because it seemed strange to him that Brother Lazarus should go to paradise and Uguccione della Faggiuola to hell" (107–8). Uncharacteristically seeming to recognize political excellence and achievements, Diogenes had said: "Would it not be ludicrous, if Agesilaus and Epaminondas were to dwell in mire, but certain folk of no account live in the isles of the Blessed, because they have been initiated" (6.40).[44] In protesting the descent of his former protector and enemy, Castruccio displays the same indifference to distinctions of friend and enemy in the netherworld that Diogenes did by grouping Agesilaus and Epaminondas together. More important, Castruccio expresses the same doubt about the justice, if not existence, of a God or gods who would reward the undistinguished and punish the eminent and

44. Agesilaus was a Spartan king whose life was celebrated by Xenophon in a minor work by that name. He reduced Thebes to starvation in two sieges in 378 and 377 BCE. However, his refusal to sign a peace treaty precipitated the defeat of the other Spartan king, Cleombrotus, by Epaminondas at Leuctra in 371 in a battle that marked the end of Spartan and the beginning of Theban dominance. Agesilaus rescued Sparta from two attacks by Epaminondas, but did not take part in the battle of Mantineia, which enabled Epaminondas to recreate the state of Messenia by freeing the helots who had been enslaved by the Spartans for 300 years. Like Diogenes and Castruccio, Machiavelli sees that judgments of the virtue of individual leaders are based on standards that transcend political divisions of friend and enemy. And, he suggests, they are posthumously rewarded with fame in this world. In *D* 1.21 and 3.13 he uses Epaminondas as a leader who was able to make a previously subject people into soldiers by arming them, as Castruccio did the Lucchans. He also says of Epaminondas (*D* 1.17) that he was able to maintain the republic with his virtue only while he was alive. In *D* 1.10 Machiavelli observes that a prince would rather have a reputation like Agesilaus, who defended his city, than a reputation like Dionysius, the tyrant Aristippus knew how to please.

active.[45] It is not that Castruccio (or Diogenes) thought that social rank per se should be respected. In other sayings both Castruccio and his source recognize the emptiness if not damaging results of conventional hierarchies, e.g., between master and servant, and other forms of pretentious behavior like big gates for small houses or cities. Machiavelli seems to underline the fundamental point in the last saying quoted, in which Castruccio and Diogenes agree that a wise man would not fear death or, therefore, the king who threatens him with death, if that king claims to be good. Neither the Lucchan tyrant nor the cynic philosopher believed that justice would be done or that people should trust that it would be done in the life hereafter.

Machiavelli as Both a Follower and a Critic of Socrates

Strauss suggests that in relating Castruccio's embrace and restatement of the sayings of these "unsung and undignified" atheistic philosophers Machiavelli is relating his own innermost thought in an ironical manner (*TM*, 224–25). By attributing the maxims to Castruccio, Machiavelli evades responsibility for restating them while nevertheless repeating them. But the "innermost" thought Strauss attributes to Machiavelli goes beyond a declaration of atheism and a desire to protect himself from persecution for that atheism. By placing the one statement from Aristotle between two pairs of sayings of the infamous atheist Bion, Machiavelli points "to a thought at the center of which Aristotle is kept in bonds or overwhelmed by Bion." And that thought goes far beyond the atheism of Bion as well as the contempt for convention exhibited by Aristippus and Diogenes (whose sayings surround those taken from Bion). "In contradistinction to Aristippus and Diogenes, Machiavelli is a *political* philosopher, a man concerned with the good society; but he understands the good society by starting from the conventionalist assumption, from the premise of extreme individualism: man is not by nature . . . directed toward political society." And Strauss concludes, "Machiavelli achieves a synthesis of the two classical

45. Although Machiavelli explicitly states that Castruccio was a Ghibelline and ally of the emperor, in opposition to the Guelphs, he does not explain either that the emperor was in competition with the pope or that both Ludwig and Castruccio were officially excommunicated. Machiavelli might have assumed that his Florentine readers would be aware of the broader political context. He reports that Castruccio was honorably buried in the Church of San Francesco in Lucca. He illustrates rather than directly commenting on Castruccio's indifference to religion by reporting his irreligious and immoral sayings.

traditions . . . by going over to a new plane from the plane on which all classical thought moved."[46]

What was that "synthesis" and "new plane"? In marked contrast to Aristotle, but like Aristippus and Diogenes, we have seen in both the *Prince* and *Discourses*, Machiavelli denies that human beings are by nature political. Their fear and consequent desire to acquire naturally bring them into conflict; and when they no longer fight from necessity, they fight from ambition. As Machiavelli emphasizes in his treatment of the early Roman kings in *D* 3.2–6, both erotic and familial affection give way to a much stronger desire for domination. However, in contrast to Aristippus and Diogenes as well as Aristotle, Machiavelli does not take nature as a standard or guide to the best human life. He is not a hedonist like Aristippus who seeks to maximize his pleasure (or minimize his pain) or an anticonventionalist who, like Diogenes, seeks to live solely in accord with nature. Machiavelli seeks to show his readers how, using their intelligence and experience, they can discover conventions or laws, i.e., a political order, that will enable most if not all human beings to overcome their natural condition of scarcity and weakness and feel secure in their lives, families or honor, and properties. The "new plane" upon which Machiavelli creates a synthesis of the two classical traditions is a new conception of nature, as hostile to human happiness but a source of "matter" (*P* 6) to be shaped, directed, and trained by means of a human "art," the political art, to improve the human condition.

Machiavelli's own words and deeds often appeared to be as irreligious and immoral as Castruccio's. He once infamously wrote that he cared more about his fatherland than his soul; he was not often seen in church; and he was known to have engaged in many extramarital affairs.[47] Unlike Castruccio, however, Machiavelli was keenly aware of the political power and uses of religion. In *P* 18 he tells his reader that an effective ruler cannot always be religious, especially if he is a new ruler, but that he must always seek to appear to be so. And in *D* 1.11–15 he praises the Roman Senate's prudent use of religion to deceive and control the plebs. He suggests (*D* 2.2) that it is their Christian education that has made modern men unable to establish and defend free political regimes. He is particularly critical of the founders of the monastic orders (*D* 3.1): by teaching their followers not to expect justice in this world but to seek it only in the next, he argues, the monks have

46. Leo Strauss, "Machiavelli and Classical Literature," *Review of National Literatures* 1, no. 1 (1970): 10.

47. Sebastian de Grazia, *Machiavelli in Hell* (Princeton: Princeton University Press, 1989), 3–4, 88.

left the world to be plundered and ruled by the wicked. In the case both of the monastic orders and of the teachings they propagated, Machiavelli is especially critical of the combination of Christianity with contemplative philosophy. In *D* 2.2 he explicitly states that the feminizing results of the Christian religion are products of a particular, pernicious interpretation. As Machiavelli indicated in his description of King Ferdinand of Spain in *P* 21 (and the fact of the Crusades shows more generally), Christianity could be interpreted differently so that it would be not merely compatible with but supportive of political and military orders.[48]

The one form of human activity to which Machiavelli consistently shows indifference, if not outright hostility, is contemplative philosophy. As Strauss points out, Machiavelli refers on more than one occasion to Xenophon's political writings, but never to his depiction of Socrates as the philosophical alternative to the political life. However, Machiavelli's complete silence with regard to Socrates (as opposed to his admittedly infrequent explicit references to Plato and Aristotle) appears to have a somewhat ambiguous meaning, because Machiavelli himself is in some respects surprisingly like Socrates.[49]

By attributing the sayings of the non-Platonic Socratics to Castruccio, Machiavelli reminds his more thoughtful readers that like the Socrates depicted by Xenophon and Plato, he concentrates on "the human things." In the relatively infrequent statements he makes about the cosmos or the order of things as a whole, he sometimes (e.g., *D* 3.1) appears to be an Epicurean who thinks that everything comes into being and passes away,[50] but he also sometimes appears to adhere to a decayed form of Aristotelianism, as when he observes in *D* 1.Pref. that the heavens, sun, elements, and men have not varied in motion, order, and power from what they were in antiquity.[51] For Machiavelli these are neither the most important nor the most pressing questions. Rather than investigating the motions of the heavenly bodies, like Xenophon's Socrates (*Memorabilia* 1.1.11) Machiavelli insists that human beings need to learn first and foremost about themselves, by reading history and reflecting on their own experiences. Basic human

48. As the failure of the Crusades also shows, Christian beliefs alone do not suffice to maintain those orders. See *FH* 1.17, 6.33.

49. Patapan, *Machiavelli in Love*, 144–46.

50. Paul Rahe, "In the Shadow of Lucretius: The Epicurean Foundation of Machiavelli's Political Thought," *History of Political Thought* 28 (Spring 2007): 30–55.

51. *TM*, 40, 201–2; Anthony J. Parel, *The Machiavellian Cosmos* (New Haven: Yale University Press, 1992), 5, 64–65; Sasso, *Machiavelli e gli antichi*, 2: 224.

passions like fear and the desire to acquire cannot be entirely repressed, much less eradicated; but once recognized for what they are and their strength acknowledged, these passions can be redirected to have less destructive if not more productive results.

Further like Socrates, Machiavelli seeks primarily to educate the young. Recognizing that individual human beings have different natural inclinations (like Castruccio for the military rather than the priesthood), but that human beings are also shaped decisively by their experience (*P* 4–5, 25; *D* 3.9), he seeks to affect their opinions and behavior before they harden and become unalterable. Like Socrates and his students, Plato and Xenophon, Machiavelli recognizes that politically ambitious young men do not like to be told what to think. Rather than deliver his "teaching" in the form of a straightforward treatise, he thus presents his understanding of "the human things" indirectly and somewhat playfully in a variety of literary modes—advice to a prince, discourses on an ancient text, comedies, poems, a dialogue, biography, and a civic history. Just as Socrates was reputedly able to make up stories to entertain, engage, and thus indirectly instruct his young friends (*Phaedrus* 275b), so Machiavelli repeatedly showed himself willing to alter history or imagine "new cases" in an attempt to teach his young friends both the harsh truths and the exciting potential of political life.

Machiavelli emphasizes both the fictional and the playful character of his version of the *Life of Castruccio Castracani*, for example, by returning at the end to the role of fortune that he emphasized at the beginning. Noting that Castruccio died at age forty-four, Machiavelli adds, "since, in his lifetime, he was not inferior to Philip of Macedon, father of Alexander, nor to Scipio of Rome, he died at the same age they both did; and without doubt he would have surpassed the one and the other if, instead of Lucca, his fatherland had been Macedonia or Rome" (109). Machiavelli thus concludes by echoing Castruccio's self-description and apology, as related by Tegrimi. It is hard to believe, however, that Machiavelli did not know that Castruccio actually died at age 47, Philip at 50, and Scipio at 46.[52] As we have seen, Machiavelli falsified the historical record in many ways in order to show the ways in which Castruccio was inferior to these ancient military and political leaders, both monarchical and republican.

Although he resembled Socrates in the focus and mode of his teaching, Machiavelli never mentioned his famous predecessor by name, because he

52. *Vita di Castruccio Castracani*, 132. Lorenzo de' Medici, on the other hand, did actually die at age 44.

disagreed with Socrates about the answer to the most fundamental question: what is the best form of human existence. According to Socrates, it is philosophy. According to Machiavelli, human beings not merely must but should engage in politics. So if Machiavelli like Socrates sought particularly to persuade the young, the appeal was fundamentally different. Whereas Socrates tried to persuade young ambitious Athenians such as Alcibiades, Critias, and Plato to withdraw from politics in order to seek wisdom with him in private conversations, Machiavelli attempted to show his young ambitious friends how they could and should complete the political project he had begun but did not have the good fortune to be able to complete (*D* 2.Pref.). His works are not simply or solely calls to action; he saw that his young friends needed to acquire the understanding he had achieved from many years of study and practical experience before they acted. He thus had to observe with some irony that they had not, as yet, acquired such an understanding.

6

On the Evils Caused by Unchecked Eros

CLIZIA

Although the maxims attributed to Castruccio at the end of Machiavelli's account of his *Life* point to both the similarities and the differences between Machiavelli and Socrates, they do not bring out the root of the difference. Because all the students of Socrates whose sayings "Castruccio" modified and quoted dismissed the transcendent ideas, they did not embody or celebrate the eros that, according to Plato's Diotima, not only moves philosophers to seek wisdom but also leads them to acquire all the other virtues as a result.[1] But in a comedy he wrote four years later, Machiavelli indicated the reasons why he thought that eros—not merely sexual, but also in its more transcendent forms—needs to be controlled and disciplined by lower, more worldly concerns for reputation and wealth, if human beings are to live and prosper.

The commission Machiavelli received to write a history of Florence in the fall of 1520 was initially for two years, and later extended. But in 1524 he took a short break or respite from working on his last major prose work. Instead of directing a new production of *Mandragola*, he volunteered to write a new comedy to be put on at the villa of Jacopo Falconetti (known as "Fornaciaio" [the baker]) where he occasionally supped with a young singer named Barbera Salutati Raffacani. Because that comedy dramatizes the shaming of an old man named "Nicomaco" who falls head over heels in love with a young girl, Machiavelli's friends understood him to be making fun of himself.[2] They did not see the way in which the changes Machiavelli

1. *Symposium* 210e–212a.
2. Ridolfi, *Life*, 207–9; Viroli, *Niccolò's Smile*, 223–24.

made in his ancient Roman source pointed to the reasons Machiavelli rejected both pagan and scriptural understandings of the best form of human existence.

Although the plot of *Mandragola* constitutes a comic retelling of the tragic story of Lucretia, in the prologue to that comedy Machiavelli emphasizes that he is presenting a new *caso*—case or cause—in Florence; and in that comedy he depicts a new kind of "remedy" for the conflicts in private life caused by human desires. Machiavelli begins the prologue to *Clizia*, however, by emphasizing the continuities in human beings and their behavior over time.[3] In this comedy he says that he is presenting a "case" that occurred long ago in Athens, but more recently in Florence, and that he is presenting it in Italian rather than Greek and in Florence rather than Athens so that his audience can understand it. The more learned members of his audience would have recognized that Machiavelli had taken the plot more immediately from a Roman comedy written in the second century BC that had been staged again in Renaissance Florence. They would have known that at the beginning of *Casina* Plautus explains that he has taken and reworked the plot of a Greek comedy by Diphilus entitled *Clerumenoe* (The Lot Throwers [which has been lost]).[4] Those who had read *D* 2.5 would also have known that Machiavelli connected changes in language to changes in religion, and that he claimed that the only reason Christians had preserved rather than destroyed all vestiges of pagan religion was that they had continued to use Latin. By referring both to the continuities in human life and the changes he has made in his ancient source, in the prologue to *Clizia* Machiavelli thus raises the question of what has changed and what has stayed the same—as well as the question of what "remedy" to adopt for a recurring "case" or problem.

Machiavelli brings out the recurrent elements of the story and its denouement in his initial statement of the plot: "There was a gentleman who had no children other than a boy, into whose house there chanced to arrive a little girl who, up to the age of seventeen, was raised by him in a very decent fashion. Then it happened that all at once both he and his son fell in

3. Cf. *D* 1.39: "Whoever considers present and ancient things easily knows that in all cities and in all peoples there are the same desires and the same humors, and there always have been. So it is an easy thing for whoever examines past things diligently to foresee future things in every republic and to take the remedies for them that were used by the ancients, or, if they do not find any that were used, to think up new ones through the similarity of accidents" (83–84).

4. Plautus, *Casina*, trans. Richard Beacham, in *Four Roman Comedies* (London: Methuen Drama, 2007), lines 5–35.

love with her; and in the competition of this love there arose many events and strange accidents, upon whose passing the son took her as a wife and lived with her very happily for a long time" (3). What remains the same, Machiavelli thus suggests, is that there is competition between fathers and sons (or generations), and that that competition can be solved or overcome only by marrying sons to women from outside the family, thus creating the conditions for rearing new generations.[5]

The changes Machiavelli made to his sources that extend beyond the language and location begin to become evident when he lists the characters in the order of their appearance. The names are derived from ancient Greek, but they do not correspond to the meaning of the names of the characters in his ancient source; and many are clearly ironic.[6] The old man's name, Nicomaco, comes from victory (*nikê*) and battle (*machê*). In the play he says that he wants to be victorious (1.1), but we see that he and his plans are defeated by his wife. Likewise his son's name, Cleandro, refers to a gentleman (*anêr, andros*) who is celebrated by the muse Cleo or has fame (*kleos*), but we do not see the son display courage (*andreia*) or do anything else worthy of acclaim.[7] In other words, neither father nor son lives up to his name, which then becomes ironic. The third character, Palamede, is a Machiavellian addition. The resourceful Greek hero Palamedes is said to have tricked

5. Claude Lévi-Strauss more recently pointed out the practical meaning of this paradigmatic "myth" that is found in many different versions and places, including Sophocles' account of the tragedy of *Oedipus* and the account of the generation of the gods in Hesiod's *Theogony.*

6. Ronald L. Martinez, "Valediction in *Clizia*," in *Machiavelli and the Discourse of Literature*, ed. Albert Russell Ascoli and Victoria Kahn (Ithaca: Cornell University Press, 1993), 117–44, reports that in his commentary on Terence, Aelius Donatus recommends that the names of comic characters "have *ratio et etymologia* (etymology and explanation), . . . and that the commentary of Donatus on Terence was widely reprinted with Renaissance editions of that playwright, including those published at Reviso in 1477 and Venice in 1491." And Martinez notes that "the principle is attested to by Plautus himself ('nomen omen,' Persa 625)" (123). The names of many of the characters in *Casina* have meaning in Greek: Olympio refers to one who esteems others little; and the slave by that name to whom the father would marry the girl is shown to insult his former master when freed and to be impious. Chalinus, the name of the slave to whom the mother would marry the girl, means bridle or bit. Cleostrata, the wife, could be said to be a woman concerned about her reputation (*kleos*). Pardalisca, the name of the maid, refers to a leopard or its spots. Myrrhina, the wife of the neighbor, who urges Cleostrata to make peace with her husband is named after the gum used to embalm the dead. Lysidamus, the father, would like to loosen (*lysis*) the ties that bind a maiden to her husband (*damaso*). And the neighbor who agrees to help the "toothless" old man and at one point fights with him, Alcesimus, is perhaps ironically named warlike or courageous (*alkêeis*). In adapting the old story for his time and place, Machiavelli clearly followed the practice of giving his characters significant names, but changed both the names of the characters and what they signify.

7. As Giorgio Padoan, "Il Tramonto di Machiavelli," *Lettere italiane* 33 (1981): 475, observes: Cleandro is a feckless, passive figure in contrast both to his father, who is fired by his passion for Clizia, and to his mother, who engineers Nicomaco's defeat.

Odysseus into coming to Troy. When Odysseus pretended to be mad by plowing salt into the earth, Palamedes placed Odysseus's son Telemachus in front of the plow; but at Troy Odysseus took his revenge by arranging to have Palamedes killed. Machiavelli's character listens to Cleandro's complaints; but, perhaps having learned from his ancient namesake's experience, he suggests merely that Cleandro try to delay the wedding and departs without offering to devise a "remedy" or any other specific assistance. The next two characters, Pirro, a servant, and Eustachio, a steward, correspond to the two slaves the husband and wife in the original Greek version of the comedy use to promote their respective plans for their son. The fact that Pirro and Eustachio are employees rather than slaves, as in the ancient comedies, points to a significant change that had occurred in the transition from antiquity to modernity; but Machiavelli does not comment on it.[8] He simply lists the name of Nicomaco's wife, Sofronia; yet here the change in the language becomes especially significant. At one point in the play Nicomaco says that she was well named, because in Italian Sofronia sounds like *soffiona*, which means bellows, and she is full of wind (2.3). In Greek, however, Sofronia would be related to *sôphrosunê* (moderation or sound-mindedness) and share the same root, *-phron*, with *phronêsis* (prudence or practical wisdom); and in the play her calculations of the best means and inventive "remedy" are shown to preserve the family's reputation and future prosperity. The last characters named are Doria (referring perhaps to a captive of war who would have been a slave in ancient Greece), who is Sofronia's maid, and Damone and Sostrata, neighbors who agree to help Nicomaco. Damone's name could refer to *daimôn*, a demigod or demon; daimones are said in Plato's *Symposium* to communicate between gods and men. In any case, he is a decent man who reluctantly assists his friend Nicomaco in his illicit love, but then happily tries to minimize the scandal and helps arrange the marriage at the end. His wife is named Sostrata, a conventional, generic name for a married woman in Italian comedies (and Lucrezia's mother in *Mandragola*). The last character remains unnamed in

8. Machiavelli did have to change the plot a bit. Instead of offering to free their servants, as the Greek characters do their slaves in *Casina*, Nicomaco and Sofronia appeal to their servants' desire for wealth. (Machiavelli may have identified the stronger passion at work, because in *Casina* the household slave informs Lysidamus that he would prefer to continue to be a slave who lives off his master than to have to fend for himself.) In *Clizia* Nicomaco promises to set Pirro up in a household and perhaps to support him and his family. The steward Eustachio is able to support a wife on his own, but he believes that he will earn even more money by serving as a pimp for his beautiful wife. In *Casina* (lines 91–92) the poet also states his expectation that the "free" girl married to a slave will become a whore.

the prologue, because we see at the end of the play that he enters as, in effect, a deus ex machina.

As Robert Faulkner observes, the names of the characters are not determinative, so we have to look at what happens to them, i.e., the plot.[9] In both *Casina* and *Clizia* a chance revelation at the end of the play concerning the facts of the girl's birth makes it possible for her to marry the son. In *Casina* the girl is found to be the daughter of her foster parents' neighbors and thus a free-born Athenian citizen; in *Clizia* the girl's father proves to be a wealthy Neapolitan gentleman named Ramondo, who arrives just in time to claim his daughter and give her in marriage to the son of the family who reared her. By implicitly contrasting the status of a free-born citizen of Athens with the Florentine couple's stated concerns about noble birth and wealth, Machiavelli may be suggesting that not all the changes from antiquity have been improvements. Even when and where slavery is no longer legal, women can be hired out on terms hardly better; and in "republican" Florence, family background and wealth are deemed more important than common citizenship. No more than Casina is Clizia ever asked or consulted about whom she would prefer to marry (or bed).[10] Whether or not she is legally free, the girl is not free to choose her mate.

Machiavelli points to the most significant changes he made on his ancient source, however, when he explains the title. His comedy "is called *Clizia* because this is the name of the young girl who is fought over." But she will not appear on stage, "because Sofronia, who raised her, doesn't want her to come outside for decency's sake" (4). The absence of the title character could be viewed merely as a convention of the comic form Machiavelli was following. Casina did not appear on stage in Plautus's play, because, as Ronald L. Martinez notes, "free-born Athenian maidens were not as a rule represented on stage; the unmarried women who do appear . . . are usually slaves or courtesans." But by bringing the son, who is sent away by his father in *Casina*, on stage in *Clizia*, Machiavelli makes the invisibility and ultimate unattainability of the object of everyone's desire much more pronounced.[11]

9. Robert Faulkner, "*Clizia* and the Enlightenment of Private Life," in Sullivan, *Comedy and Tragedy of Machiavelli*, 38–39.

10. The contrast with the lengths to which the other characters go to obtain the consent of Lucrezia to their plot in *Mandragola* is striking. As Haig Patapan, "All's Fair in Love and War," *History of Political Thought* 19, no. 4 (1998): 543, observes, all the forms of love depicted in *Clizia* "seem to be based on a desire that longs to possess, a desire that looks primarily to the wishes and hopes of the lover" rather than those of the "beloved."

11. Martinez, "Valediction in *Clizia*," 123, 125, 127. As Faulkner, "*Clizia* and the Enlightenment of Private Life," notes, "Clizia is referred to as but an imagining (1.1; 2.4; 5.3)," 44.

He also changes the motives of the mother in trying to frustrate the designs of her husband on the young girl. In *Casina* Cleostrata is insulted by Lysidamus's desire for a younger woman as well as by his trying to take control of the fate of a young girl who is her responsibility, and she takes the part of her son. In *Clizia* Cleandro accuses Sofronia of opposing his father because she is jealous and envious; but she informs Cleandro in no uncertain terms that she will not allow him to bed their young charge—even if that should mean letting Nicomaco triumph. She nevertheless hopes to frustrate both their desires in order to maintain the reputation and prosperity of their household.

Machiavelli seems to identify himself and his intentions with Sofronia when he states that the author of this comedy is a very well-mannered man who adheres to established customs or conventions (*uomo molto costumato*). And by invoking the formal requirements of writing a comedy, the prologue to *Clizia* casts the work in a much different light than Machiavelli's explicitly unconventional dedications cast his major political treatises. But the content or "message" of his comedy does not appear to be entirely conventional. In the first place, it ends with the man of the house agreeing to be ruled in all things by his wife.[12] Because she devises a clever remedy to save the family from the potentially scandalous effects of Nicomaco's passion, Sofronia appears to be the Machiavellian character par excellence, encompassing the roles of both Ligurio and Lucrezia in *Mandragola*. Second, when Machiavelli then admits that he may have been forced into some indecency by the need to make his audience laugh, "even if it is said in such a way that the women will be able to listen to it without blushing," he prepares his audience for the climatic scene in which Nicomaco describes his punishment, which is both hilarious and completely obscene. Because it involves the threat of the rape of one male by another, as punishment for the one who intended to rape a young girl, and the women only hear about it rather than witness the deed, they need not be embarrassed. Yet as one commentator has suggested, Machiavelli leaves his greatest "indecency" implicit in the plot. If a reader describes Nicomaco's scheme in general terms as the plan of a father who proposes to disown his "chosen" people (by sending

12. Faulkner, "*Clizia* and the Enlightenment of Private Life," 41–44, 47–49, emphasizes the novelty of the new order of the household. Contrary to both law and custom, not only is the household ruled by a woman, but the traditional hierarchy of master and servant is also undermined. As Patapan, "All's Fair in Love and War," observes, "Sofronia's new order was not possible without an inversion of every part of the old—woman over man, son over father, servant over master" (550).

his wife and her dowry back) and to sacrifice (the livelihood, if not life of) his only begotten son, in order to bed a virgin purportedly married to another man, the broader, blasphemous implications of Machiavelli's comedy begin to become evident.[13] Consumed by his mad passion or "love," Nicomaco is also shown to be a tyrant who threatens to destroy those who have been nearest and dearest to him by burning down the house, if they do not obey his commands. In the New Testament it is said that "God so loved the world, that He gave His only begotten Son, that whoever believes in Him shall not perish" (John 3:16). And, as Saint Augustine emphasizes in the *City of God* (20–21), those who do not believe will be condemned to eternal damnation and torment in the fires of Hell.

In *Mandragola* Machiavelli showed that the desires of all the characters could be satisfied by devising a clever means or "remedy" that preserved the appearance of conventional morality and religion. Those desires were, however, for goods that are humanly attainable, if transitory—a son to carry on the family name, a young lover and the pleasure that love can bring, a loyal and obedient spouse, food and shelter, money for the poor, maintaining the reputation of the Church, and the satisfaction of seeing the pretensions of the wealthy exposed, if only in private. In *Clizia* he shows that the old man's desire to be a young lover—again or, in principle, forever—not merely makes him look ridiculous. It is positively dangerous, because this desire is not only impossible to satisfy; it also undermines the basis of the household and the orderly accumulation and passing on of property. This unrealizable desire for immortality thus needs to be restrained and redirected into the more ordinary forms of living on—at least in name—through one's progeny and reputation (or fame). That disciplining and redirecting cannot be achieved by the Church, because that institution depends ultimately on a belief in the possibility of eternal life. So when in an implicit reference to *Mandragola* Nicomaco suggests that he and Sofronia might appeal to Friar Timoteo to mediate their dispute, she dismisses the idea with laughter and scorn. Like Lucrezia, Sofronia talks and acts as if she is extremely pious. But like Lucrezia, Sofronia recognizes that the intensity of her husband's desire to achieve a kind of immortality threatens to cause him to act in an extremely foolish way, and that he will not be restrained by any piety or fear of God. She perceives the need, therefore, to invent and employ

13. Patapan, "All's Fair in Love and War," 546.

purely secular means of dissuading him.[14] In *Clizia* Machiavelli thus suggests that the potentially unrestrained eros of a male human being can be checked only by the equally fierce attachment a woman forms to the children she has borne and raised as well as to the household goods she seeks to conserve along with the family's good name. But the "conventional" family order she restores is not based on claims about the physical or intellectual superiority of the male (ancient) or on pure "selfless" love and devotion (Christian) that underlie traditional notions of virtue and the conventions that correspond to them; it is based on a calculation of the arrangements and exchanges that best satisfy the various desires of all the members of the household—husband, wife, children, and servants.[15]

Insofar as it depends upon the son's (or slave's) overhearing the father explain how he plans to wed and bed the young girl that night, the resolution of the conflict between the mother and father in both *Casina* and *Clizia* might be said to depend upon chance. Machiavelli never claimed that *virtù* could entirely conquer God or fortune, however. (See *P* 25.) And in his comedy he shows that the wife takes action not merely to foil her husband, but to preserve the chastity of the young girl. (In *Casina* the wife demonstrates no such concern. She is angered by her husband's denial of her own charms and invasion of her area of responsibility within the household, but she seeks to please her son by enabling him to satisfy his desire.) Sofronia acts more on the basis of her calculations of what is necessary to preserve the family as an economic and social unit and less on the basis of anger or affection. She considers her care for the young girl to have been an investment that she does not want to throw away by having the girl marry a good-for-nothing handsome rascal, any more than she wishes to see her son marry a woman without a dowry. She thus finds her son's passion as dangerous to the family's reputation and future prosperity as her husband's, and seeks

14. The overlap between the two comedies is suggested by the fact that the songs introducing the plays as well as several of the acts in each are the same. The first two repetitions celebrate the power of love, and the third the power of the "trick" or "remedy." The differences occur in songs (at the end of act 2 in *Clizia* and act 3 in *Mandragola*) that emphasize the specific kinds of foolishness displayed by the older male protagonists (Nicia and Nicomaco). And there is no concluding song in *Mandragola*.

15. Martin Fleisher, "Trust and Deceit in Machiavelli's Comedies," *Journal of the History of Ideas* 227 (1996): 372, argues that the conflicts that threaten the order of the family in *Clizia* arise from three sets of conflicting desires, those of husband and wife, father and son, and mother and son, and that the order which emerges "is constituted by a dynamic set of relations which, more or less, satisfies the desires of its members."

to defend the girl from the machinations of both by sending her away. The chance arrival of Clizia's father Ramondo and the revelation that he is a wealthy Neapolitan gentleman at the end of the play make it possible for Cleandro to satisfy his passion decently by marrying Clizia with his parents' blessing. But even if Clizia's origins had not been fortunately revealed, Sofronia would have preserved the family's reputation and prosperity, as she promised, by finding her son and her charge both suitable mates. In contrast to *Casina*, the happy resolution of the conflicts between the father and son and the husband and wife does not depend upon chance.

Machiavelli emphasizes the importance of relying on one's own resources in solving problems in the very first exchange he presents between Cleandro and Palamede (a clear addition to the original plot). Cleandro asks Palamede why he is out and about so early, and Palamede answers simply that he has been taking care of some of his own business. Like Callimaco at the beginning of *Mandragola*, Cleandro then explains that he, too, is trying to take care of some "business." However, because he finds that he needs "everyone's assistance," he will now reveal the passion that he has been keeping secret. Palamede responds by saying that there are three kinds of men that ought to be avoided: singers who don't listen to what you have to say because they break into song, old men who duck into church to say prayers (because they are afraid of death), and lovers, because they not merely fill your ears with complaints, but arouse your compassion. He nevertheless agrees to listen to Cleandro, who then provides him and the audience with an explanation of his plight.

In 1494 when King Charles passed through Florence with a great army on his way to attack the Kingdom of Naples, Cleandro explains, a gentleman named Beltramo of Guascogna was billeted at their house.[16] Unlike many of the French troops quartered in Florence, he treated his hosts well and they responded in kind. So after the army of King Charles was defeated in Naples and was in retreat, Beltramo sent them a five-year-old girl he had among his spoils for safekeeping. Since his mother and father had no other children, they fell in love with her—as did he. Indeed, when she got to be twelve years old, his parents began to keep their eyes on his hands

16. Machiavelli thus dates the beginning of the plot of *Clizia* at the same time as the beginning of the plot of *Mandragola*—the time of the French invasion and the destruction in its wake that showed that the military and political condition of Italy had deteriorated to such a point that it clearly needed to be remedied.

and prevented him from even speaking to her. But that restriction merely redoubled his love.

Palamede asks: What does he want? To take her as a wife or mistress? And what prevents him from acting, since they are living under one roof? Cleandro explains that his father has also fallen in love with the young girl, everyone in the household knows it, and there is a great scandal. Palamede observes that (in implicit contrast to the Trojan War) the scandal ruins nothing but a household; but Cleandro adds that even if his father were not in love with Clizia, he would never grant her to him as a wife, because his father is avaricious and she doesn't have a dowry. His father also worries that she may be of ignoble birth. Cleandro would take her any way possible, but his father has arranged for her to be married to a complaisant servant, Pirro, who will share her with him. His mother has forestalled her husband's plan by sending another suitor into the field, their steward Eustachio; but Nicomaco is now pressing for the wedding to take place this evening. Palamede asks why it matters which servant she marries, and Cleandro explains that Pirro is a scoundrel who has always hated him. The implication is that Pirro will not grant him access to the girl, and that his father's promise to buy Pirro a house and shop to make him rich threatens Cleandro's inheritance.

Having listened as he promised, Palamede leaves to take care of his own business. In contrast to his ancient namesake, who was famous not only for snaring Odysseus and bringing him to Troy but also for inventing counting, currency, weights and measures, jokes, and dice, he neither offers nor invents any "remedy" for Cleandro's plight. He counsels Cleandro simply to delay the wedding as best he can and to let his friend know if he wants something. Given the time pressure, such a request and the promised assistance would clearly come too late.

Forced to rely on his own resources, Cleandro has called Eustachio in from the country. But he discovers that the steward has been in hiding for fear of offending the father. Cleandro orders the steward to clean himself up so Clizia will not reject him, and then to wait in the church. Cleandro has to go home to see what his father is planning. The son recognizes that he alone does not have the resources to withstand his father. The contest between father and son thus becomes subordinate to the contest between father and mother.

Both father and mother initially claim to be acting for the sake of benefiting their young charge. When Nicomaco and Sofronia meet, she tells him that she is going to church, because she believes "that one ought to do good all the time"; and she suggests that they should continue doing the good they have begun—raising a beautiful girl—by not throwing her away. Nicomaco claims that he is benefiting the young girl by giving her to a handsome man, to whom he will also give the means of supporting her. But these claims about the beneficial intentions of both parents soon give rise to charges of wrongdoing. Sofronia accuses Nicomaco of unjustly taking from his son more than is fitting and giving their servant more than he deserves—and suggests that Nicomaco has another motive. He claims to be acting out of love toward two young people he has raised, but she points out that he also raised the steward. Nicomaco responds by asking her whether she wants to give the girl to someone without noble breeding who is accustomed to live in the country with cattle and sheep. She retorts that the girl will die of hunger with Pirro, who does nothing but eat, drink, and gamble, and that "noble breeding of men consists in having some *virtù*, knowing how to do something, as Eustachio knows, who's accustomed to business in the markets, to managing the household, to caring for the affairs of others and himself" (2.3). Hers appears to be a very economically based, "middle-class" definition of human excellence; and she concludes by accusing her husband of wasting the money he has spent to feed the girl and his wife's labor in raising her. She also threatens to raise a scandal. He suggests that her behavior is equally indecent, because she (like the wife in *Casina*) is favoring her son.

Recognizing that they are both concerned about maintaining appearances, Nicomaco proposes that they come to an agreement lest they become a comedy for the people watching. Since she is going to church, he suggests that they ask their family confessor, the friar Timoteo, to mediate, because he "has already accomplished a miracle. . . . Through his prayers Madonna Lucrezia, wife of Messer Nicia Calfucci, who was sterile, got pregnant." But Sofronia protests, "some great miracle, a friar making a woman pregnant! It would be a miracle if a nun had made her pregnant!" (2.3). So she goes off to mass while he waits for her at home.

In a soliloquy Machiavelli added to the original plot Sofronia describes the change his passion for the girl has wrought in Nicomaco. He used to be a "grave, stable and respectful man. . . . He got up early in the morning, heard his mass, provided for the day's food. Then, if he had some business in the public square, at the market, with the magistrates, he did it; if not, either he met with some citizen for honorable discussions or he retired to his study at home, where he balanced his ledger. Later he dined peacefully with his company and . . . held discussions with his son, offered him counsel . . . and, by means of some ancient and modern examples, taught him how to live." He spent the rest of the day in equally grave and decent pastimes before he returned home, sat by the fire with his family, went into his study to look over his books, and then had a cheerful supper. "This arrangement of his life was an example to everyone else in the household" (2.4).[17] After he contracted his fantastic love for the girl, however, Nicomaco neglected his business, went in and out of the house shouting, did not return for meals, and did not answer questions sensibly. The servants began to make fun of him, and his son lost all reverence for him.[18]

Nicomaco displays his mad rage when he confronts Cleandro in Sofronia's absence. He threatens to throw his son into prison as well as to return Sofronia's dowry and send her packing, because he intends to be the lord of his household. If they do not abide by his wishes and the wedding does not take place that night, he will burn the house down. He thus urges Cleandro to go and persuade his mother to come to an agreement. Cleandro bemoans his own plight as a lover who can look for support neither to his father nor to his mother, and shows in passing that he has not been very well educated when he says that he has "never heard it happen that someone had his own father as a rival" (3.2). (He has apparently never heard of

17. Because he instructs his son by means of "ancient and modern examples," in his introduction to the Gallagher translation of *Clizia*, xiii, Robert Faulkner suggests that Nicomaco's name refers to Aristotle's *Nicomachean Ethics.* Nicomaco's habits are not, however, those that produce the virtues Aristotle describes. In the version of "*Clizia* and the Enlightenment of Private Life" that Faulkner later published in Sullivan, *Comedy and Tragedy of Machiavelli*, 39–56, he continues to maintain that "the play takes aim especially at Greek philosophy in its Christian version. Consider Nicomaco. He is a respectable Christian gentleman who looks up to 'ancient and modern examples' for the instruction of his son. But his ancient virtue and modern religion prove no match for his passions" (42). Thus Faulkner concludes, "Nicomaco's strange mixture of hypocritical moralism and uncontrolled passion might be Machiavelli's little comment on the practicability of Aristotelian moral virtue as a disposition to select the 'mean'" (202n38).

18. Some commentators have compared Sofronia's account of her husband's life with Machiavelli's description of his daily routine in his famous letter to Vettori of December 10, 1513. See Martinez, "Valediction in *Clizia*," 134n31; Ezio Raimondi, introduction to Niccolò Machiavelli, *Mandragola, Clizia* (Milan: Mursia, 1984), 47; Luigi Vanossi, "Situazione e sviluppo nel teatro machiavelliano," in Vanossi et al., *Lingua e strutture del teatro italiano del Rinascimento* (Padua: Liviana,1970), 74; and Giulio Ferroni, *Mutazione e riscontro nel teatro di Machiavelli e altri saggi sulla commedia del '500* (Rome: Bulzoni, 1972), 111. The two "days" in the lives of these two men are, however, very different. Whereas Nicomaco led the life of a conventional Florentine merchant, Machiavelli's day ranged from providing his own bare economic necessities to reading poetry, obtaining information about what was happening abroad from travelers, games and quarrels with "vermin" at the local inn, capped by four hours of study of the deeds of great men of the past—but with no mention of his care or concern for his family. If the old man somehow represents the author, it is not because of his daily routine.

Oedipus; if he had, he would know that his problem is not as singular as he thinks.)[19] Cleandro then tells his mother about Nicomaco's threats, and they agree that it is best that Clizia not be married to anyone at present.

Informed about the dangerous potential of her husband's passion, Sofronia confronts Nicomaco for a second time; and after a bit of risqué bantering, they agree first to try to persuade their respective servants that they do not want to wed the girl. After that tack fails, they resort to drawing lots. Pirro wins, and Cleandro wonders in despair how his mother could have submitted such an important matter to chance. Echoing *P* 25, he complains that fortune is "customarily" a friend of young men (although he has not shown himself to have the characteristics—impetuosity, ferocity, and audacity—that lead her to love them). However, after he chances to overhear his father explain to Pirro how he plans to arrange the wedding and bedding that evening, Cleandro tells his mother; and she devises a remedy. (Fortune did not desert the young man, it seems, but it is his mother who acts.) She allows the wedding to go forward; but she sends her maid Doria with a report that Clizia is running around crazed with a dagger, threatening to kill both Pirro and Nicomaco. They agree to stay out of sight in the kitchen while she and her women disguise a manservant as the bride and send Clizia away to a convent. When Nicomaco takes the place of Pirro in the dark in the bedroom and tries to embrace his love, he finds himself not merely repulsed with force but threatened with rape by his male servant Siro.

While all the members of his household are convulsed with laughter, Nicomaco tells his neighbor Damone that he does not know how he will ever be able to overcome his eternal shame. Observing that as his wife, Sofronia will share his disgrace, Damone suggests that Nicomaco let himself be governed by her. She assures Nicomaco that she did not want to make him a joke; she orchestrated the tricks so that he would repent. If he does and returns to his old habits, she promises, "the matter won't be made known," and even if it is, "it's customary to err and to be corrected" (5.3). He agrees to be governed by her, and she informs them all that Clizia will not be married to anyone—not to Cleandro, Pirro, or Eustachio. At that point Damone returns with the news that Clizia's father has just arrived in Florence, that he is a Neapolitan gentleman, and that he is happy to see his daughter wed to the son of the couple who raised her.

19. The love that father and son feel for the girl who has been raised in their household as a daughter and sister carries overtones of incest, although, strictly speaking, there is none.

Nicomaco's shaming is the highlight and climax of the plot. But after we stop laughing and recover from our shock at the obscenity, we have to ask: What exactly is Nicomaco punished for? And why in this way? Sofronia assures him that she never wanted him to be a joke, and asks: "Aren't you ashamed to have raised a young girl in your house with so much decency and in the manner that daughters of respectable people are raised, and then to want to marry her off to a wicked and useful servant just because he was content to have you lie with her? Did you really believe that you were dealing with the blind and with people who didn't know how to put a stop to the indecency of your designs?" (5.3). She thus claims to be shaming him for endangering the reputation of the family and insulting her intelligence by imagining not merely that he could hoodwink her, but that she would not know how to foil his plans. Sofronia threatened Nicomaco with scandal before, however, and he told her that she was merely fortifying his resolution to have the wedding go forward. He arranged a legitimate cover for satisfying his passion in the sham marriage. Recognizing that she was also concerned about the honor of the household, he suggested that they find a peaceful way of resolving their differences—first by means of a mediator, then by persuading the servants not to go along with their respective schemes, or, finally, when that failed, by chance—and she agreed. The drawing of lots was emphasized in the title of the original Greek comedy; but, as Haig Patapan has pointed out, Machiavelli made a small change from the way in which the lots are drawn that had broader implications. Rather than having one drawing that the father's servant wins, as in *Casina*, and resolving the dispute simply by chance, in *Clizia* the servants' names are put on two slips for the first drawing, then a slip with Clizia's name is put into the bowl with a blank for a second chance. Before the first drawing Nicomaco insists on praying to all the saints, in the name of God, for the name of his servant to be drawn—and loses. Then Sofronia prays to God for her husband to lose all hope, but her servant draws the blank, and Nicomaco declares that he has been brought back to life! Neither husband nor wife is favored by God, Machiavelli shows, and neither actually relies upon Him.[20] Instead, each claims to have devised a "remedy," if he or she should lose. We in the audience see that neither the threat of scandal nor piety is sufficient to restrain husband or wife from acting on the basis of their respective desires.

20. Patapan, "All's Fair in Love and War," 547–49.

What, then, does each desire? And what restrains them? As Salvatore Di Maria observes, Nicomaco does not merely or simply want to have sex with Clizia. In his first soliloquy he admits that he himself is surprised by his passion and doesn't really understand it. It does not appear to have been aroused by any of the particular characteristics of the supposed object of his love. In contrast to Callimaco's praise of Lucrezia in *Mandragola*, we never hear Nicomaco extol Clizia's beauty, intelligence, or good character. His concern appears almost exclusively to be in demonstrating to himself above all that he is still as sexually potent and powerful as any youth.[21] He does not want to admit that at seventy years old (the expected span of life in the Bible [Psalms 90:10] and the age at which Socrates died), he is old and near to death. And he is willing to use both fraud (his agreement with Pirro and the sham wedding) and force (threatening to dismiss Eustachio and burn down his own house) to get what he wants.

Fearing the destructive consequences of his mad passion, Sofronia punishes Nicomaco by making him see that he cannot realize his desire. He cannot, because it is impossible for any human being to remain eternally young. Nicomaco is not as young or as physically vigorous as the young servant she has secretly put in Clizia's place; and in struggling with that youth in the dark, he is defeated by force. By enlisting everyone else in the household in her conspiracy, she also shows Nicomaco that he cannot conceal from others either his decrepitude or his illicit desire to deny it. His supposed love for Clizia is shown to be for an illusory fantasy of his imagination (*fantasia*).

In the song with which the comedy concludes, it seems to be the author rather than the nymphs who tells the audience that through "this decent,

21. Salvatore Di Maria, "Nicomaco and Sofronia: Fortune and Desire in Machiavelli's 'Clizia,'" *Sixteenth Century Journal* 14, no. 2 (1983): "Nicomaco himself is bewildered by the extent of his love for the young girl: 'Is it yet possible,' he wonders in II.1, 'that I'm so much in love?' In view of this confusion Nicomaco's passion for the foundling cannot be dismissed as simply sensual" (208). "Giulio Ferroni notes that [Nicomaco's] use of perfumes betrays the old man's desire to be young. Spicy foods and aphrodisiacs serve the same function. . . . Nicomaco's weapons, as he himself perceives them, are all meant to characterize him as young and vigorous. Such a—perhaps subconscious—desire is also inherent in the youthful company he is always seeking. . . . The unconscious nature of Nicomaco's wish to appear young is particularly clear in II.1, when he laments his old age: 'Oh God, this old age arrives with all (bad) defects! But ['ma'] I'm not so old that I should not break a lance with Clizia.' The adversative *ma* emphasizes Nicomaco's refusal to succumb to old age and, at the same time, his determination to recover youth. . . . Thus, the girl is not a mere object of Nicomaco's erotic passion but the symbol of youth, i.e., the real subject of his obsession. Pointedly, the function of Clizia as the abstract characterization of youth is underlined by the fact that she never appears on stage, thus reinforcing in the mind of the reader/spectator her role as a non-physical entity, as the ideal fostering Nicomaco's desire" (209–10).

humble example, this wise and noble teacher of our human life" has allowed them to "come to know what one ought to shun, what pursue, in order to ascend straight to heaven." As we have seen, however, the "beautiful souls" who have listened have not learned to rely on God or His providence. And they certainly have not learned to keep faith—with God or each other. On the contrary, they have learned that they need to devise clever remedies to prevent men from acting irrationally on the basis of illusory fantasies or "loves" that would destroy the conventional ties of marriage and economic activities of the household. So, the author suggests, his audience may have heard a great deal more under a thin veil from which he hopes they will reap the profit. The transcendental goals or objects for which some men are willing to sacrifice everything else are *the* obstacles to gaining security and prosperity here and now.

A final problem nevertheless remains: why does "this wise and noble teacher" name the foolish old man who is the most immediate target of his lesson after himself? Once examined, the parallel Machiavelli's contemporaries drew between his love for Barbera and Nicomaco's passion for Clizia does not extend very far. Whereas Nicomaco tried, if unsuccessfully, to keep the means of satisfying his passion hidden beneath a decent cover, in writing *Clizia* Machiavelli was not merely broadcasting his own passion but mocking it. He had never tried to live the orderly, decent life of a Florentine man of business, and in writing comedies he was trying to provoke the laughter of his audience, not to avoid it. No more than Socrates (*Gorgias* 471e–474a) did he fear appearing ridiculous. He was not ashamed of living unconventionally, associating primarily with the young, or having been punished by the authorities. Nor, like both his foolish old male characters, Nicia Calfucci and Nicomaco, did he often attend mass. He may have had his "fantasies" or imagined objects of desire. One probable candidate was the unification of Italy, for which he had called in both *The Prince* and *Discourses*, and which is imaged, as it were, in the union of Florence with Naples at the end of *Clizia*.[22] If so, Machiavelli also clearly saw that the realization of his dream would occur, if at all, only in the future under the leadership of the youths to whom he addressed his major works. He recognized, in other words, that the realization of his political dream would depend ultimately on chance. He himself did not have the resources or force necessary to bring it about. Serving at most as an advisor (*D* 3.35), he would

22. Patapan, "All's Fair in Love and War," 550.

not receive the credit or recognition he deserved for the discovery of a new basis and form of political order, whereas those who acted on the basis of his advice would become famous. Understanding, as his more God-fearing characters do not, that all human experience and thus all human knowledge is "worldly" and hence essentially transitory, he could not even be certain that the writings through which he tried to communicate his political understanding to later generations would last, or if his writings did endure, whether anyone in the future would grasp the wisdom he sought to convey "under a thin veil." But he continued to try.

7

The Failed Republic

FLORENTINE HISTORIES

Machiavelli had been attempting to obtain employment from the Medici from the time he was dismissed from office in 1512. In November 1520 he finally succeeded when Cardinal Giulio de' Medici offered him a commission to write a history of Florence. Once he received the commission, however, he faced a serious problem. How was he going to be able to write a history of Florence that would celebrate the rise and rule of the Medici family, who had deprived his native city of its liberty along with his sage advice?[1]

Machiavelli's Rhetorical Strategy

By the time that Machiavelli completed a volume of the *Florentine Histories*, Cardinal Giulio de' Medici had become Pope Clement VII; and the letter of dedication with which he presented the volume to the pope in 1525 indicates the brilliant strategy he devised to solve his problem. By noting the pope's explicit instructions to "write about the things done by [his] ancestors in . . . a mode . . . far from all flattery" (4), Machiavelli reminds his readers of the expectations his official sponsor and others had for such histories.

1. As John M. Najemy, "Machiavelli and the Medici: The Lessons of Florentine History," *Renaissance Quarterly* 35, no. 4 (Winter 1982): 551–76, points out, "one of the most crucial—perhaps the central" issue in discussions of Machiavelli's *Florentine Histories* must be his "treatment of the Medici in a work that was commissioned by, and dedicated to, a Medici. But the special significance—indeed, the dilemma and drama—of Machiavelli's decision to write a history of Florence in which the whole Medici phenomenon would inevitably be a theme of the first importance goes far beyond the facts of the commission and the dedication" (552).

They were to praise the great deeds of the past—and the most notable deeds of Florentines in the recent past were those of the Medici.[2] However, recognizing that feigned praise is insulting, Machiavelli states his worry that he may seem to have disobeyed the pope's injunction in "describing the goodness of Giovanni, the wisdom of Cosimo, the humanity of Piero, and the magnificence and prudence of Lorenzo." Taking the facts from existing chronicles and narratives, as was the custom, Machiavelli explains that he found his sources full of praise for the Medici rulers. He has, therefore, reported the facts as they appeared to other observers. "If under those remarkable deeds of theirs was hidden an ambition contrary to the common utility, as some say" (4), Machiavelli claims not to know it. By reporting the suspicion of others, however, he raises the question.

As was also customary in the celebratory histories of the time, Machiavelli acknowledges that he has attributed speeches and thoughts to some of the major actors, but he has tried "to preserve the proper humor of the person speaking without any reservations." After Machiavelli's death Donato Giannotti wrote a letter in which he reported that Machiavelli had told him that he could "not write this History from when Cosimo took the state until Lorenzo's death, as I would write it if I were free from all hesitations [*respetti*]. The actions will be true . . . ; only I shall not tell in what mode or by what means and tricks one arrives at so great a height. And whoever wants to learn this also may note very well what I will make his adversaries say, because that which I will not want to say myself, as from me, I will make his adversaries say."[3] Machiavelli does attribute views he presented in his own name in *D* 1.33 and 1.52 to an opponent of Cosimo, Niccolò da Uzzano, who warns his colleagues about the dangers of opposing a popular leader (*FH* 4.3, 4.27). But as Felix Gilbert points out, Machiavelli puts "the severest condemnation of the Medici regime" into the mouth of Piero Medici when he criticizes his own supporters for their arrogance and rapacity.[4] One cannot simply equate the speeches of any individual or group with those of the author, because, as he says, he tries to present the relevant actors in character, both in speech and in deed.

2. Felix Gilbert, "Machiavelli's *Istorie Fiorentine:* An Essay in Interpretation," in *History: Choice and Commitment* (Cambridge, MA: Harvard University Press, 1977), 137–38, drawing on Donald J. Wilcox, *The Development of Florentine Humanist Historiography in the Fifteenth Century* (Cambridge, MA: Harvard University Press, 1969).

3. Translated and quoted from L. A. Ferrai, "Lettere inedite di Donato Giannotti," *Atti del R. Instituto Veneto di Scienze, Lettere ed Arti*, 6th ser., 3 (1884–85): 1582, in the translators' introduction to *FH*, xiii.

4. Gilbert, "Machiavelli's *Istorie Fiorentine*," 142–43; *FH* 7.24.

Machiavelli indicates his own view of the events he reports not so much by commenting on them as by his selection and organization of his materials. In his letter of dedication he suggests that the volume he is presenting to Pope Clement is the first installment of a history that will bring him up to the present. But at the conclusion of his history, he explains that he has ended the present volume with the death of the Magnificent Lorenzo de' Medici, because that "brought a change of form in Italy, and because the things that followed afterwards were higher and greater and are to be described in a higher and greater spirit." By stating that he will describe "the expansion of the pontiffs and of the other principalities that governed Italy afterwards until the arrival of Charles VIII" (20), Machiavelli suggests that the "change of form" to which he refers was a result of the 1494 invasion by the French king. The "higher and greater" things that followed would have included the expulsion of the Medici and the reforms of the republic, first by Savonarola, and then under Soderini, as well as the reinstatement of the Medici in 1512. What the "higher and greater spirit" was with which Machiavelli would have had to describe them is not clear.[5]

What we do know is that the volume Machiavelli presented to Clement was carefully and tightly organized into eight books. (The division of civic histories into books with general introductions was also customary.) In the preface Machiavelli explains that he initially planned to begin his history in 1434, that is, at the time at which Cosimo de' Medici triumphantly returned from exile and took control of the government of Florence. But then he discovered that his predecessors, Leonardo Bruni and Poggio Bracciolini, had described Florentine foreign affairs in some detail up until 1434, but that they had not described the civil discords and internal enmities. Yet, Machiavelli protests, it is the number and intensity of the internal divisions in Florence that distinguish it from all other republics, including preeminently Athens and Rome. "Most other republics . . . have been content with one division . . . between the nobles and the plebs. But in Florence the nobles were, first, divided among themselves; then the nobles and the people; and

5. Harvey C. Mansfield, "Party and Sect in Machiavelli's *Florentine Histories*," *Machiavelli's Virtue*, also argues that "in a work commissioned by and dedicated to a Florentine Pope, Machiavelli does not make the point directly" (138). According to Mansfield, that point is the devastating effect Christianity has had on modern politics. The problem with this thesis is that in the *FH* Machiavelli writes specifically about the problems caused by the pope's calling in the "barbarian" invaders, which include the armies of the Christian kings of France and Spain. As in *D* 1.12, Machiavelli writes about the divisive effect the Church has had in Italy (which would also not be a pleasing topic for a pope), not the effect of Christianity on modern politics more generally. Some of the Christian princes had been much more successful than the Florentines.

in the end the people and the plebs; and it happened many times that the winning party was divided in two. . . . Had Florence enjoyed such prosperity after it freed itself from the Empire as to have obtained a form of government to maintain it united," he comments, "no republic either modern or ancient that would have been its superior" (*FH* Pref.; 7). Unlike his predecessors, Machiavelli will not simply be celebrating the history of his city; on the contrary, he will be showing the reasons why Florence was not able to become as great as Rome. To reveal the causes of the continuing divisions in Florence and the Florentines' inability to devise a government capable of managing if not overcoming them, in the first four books of his history he will relate what happened inside the city up until 1434 in detail, but what happened outside only when necessary to knowledge of what happened inside. In the last four books he will describe what happened both inside and out.

As a result of this revised plan, Machiavelli makes the rise of the Medici regime the very center and climax of his history, thus recognizing the achievements of his sponsor's ancestors. He makes that recognition more uniform and less qualified than it would otherwise have to be, moreover, by ending his history with the death of Lorenzo the Magnificent. Because he concludes his narrative in 1492, he does not have to treat the less obviously admirable expulsion of the Medici in 1494 or their reinstatement in 1512 with the support of a foreign army. However, by going back to the beginning of the city rather than the beginning of the Medici regime itself, Machiavelli also presents that regime as a result of antecedent conditions and the actions of others more than as the product of the virtue of its leaders. He suggests that Florence was distinguished, not so much by its wealth or the moderation of its merchant rulers and their ability to maintain the independence of the city in the face of foreign aggression (as Bruni argued), as by its internal divisions.

As in his *Discourses*, Machiavelli begins his *Florentine Histories* by emphasizing the connection between foreign and domestic policies and institutions. In *FH* 1, Machiavelli shows that Florence remained a free and independent city as long as it did not because of the virtue of its leaders or people so much as because of the weakness of the other powers with which it was competing in Italy. In *FH* 2 Machiavelli then traces the stages of the self-destruction of the Florentine nobility that left succeeding generations without an example of public-spirited, virtuous leadership. After the leaders of the people acquired complete control of the republic, he shows in *FH* 3, they first divided among themselves and then faced the opposition of the plebs. But after they put down the Ciompi rebellion, the leaders of the people again divided. As he observes in *FH* 4.1, "cities, and especially those not well ordered that are administered under the name of republic, frequently change their governments and their states not between liberty and servitude, as many believe, but between servitude and license. For only the name of freedom is extolled by the ministers of license, who are the men of the people, and by the ministers of servitude, who are the nobles, neither of them desiring to be subject either to the laws or to men." To establish a long-lasting republic that truly deserves to be called free, a city needs to have a "wise, good, and powerful citizen" who institutes laws "by which these humors of the nobles and the men of the people are quieted or restrained." By showing that unlike Rome, Florence never acquired such laws, Machiavelli, in effect, dramatizes the ineptness of its political leaders, both the Medici and their competitors.[6]

Machiavelli does not explicitly say whether it was virtue or fortune that enabled Cosimo to acquire complete power over the affairs of the Florentine people in 1434. He shows that Cosimo's opponents made some serious errors of judgment, and that Cosimo acquired his power not by the "public" means Machiavelli argued in *D* 3.28 are necessary to maintain a free republic, but by the "private" means that enable a seemingly "merciful" leader to become a tyrant.[7] In *FH* 5 and 6 Machiavelli indirectly points

6. Although I agree with Najemy that Machiavelli's treatment of the rise of the Medici in a work dedicated to two members of the family is a problem, if not the central problem, raised by the *Florentine Histories*, I do not agree with his contention that Machiavelli's concentration on Florentine history in "Discourse on Remodeling the Government of Florence" and *Florentine Histories* marks a fundamental shift in his thought. Following Najemy, Jurdjevic, *Great and Wretched City*, argues that in his "Discourse" Machiavelli changes both his historical "method" and his understanding of republican politics. In his "Discourse" and *Histories* Machiavelli undeniably gives more attention to Florence, both its history and its institutions, than he did in his previous works. But that attention is explained by the circumstances. He was invited to propose a constitutional reform and specifically commissioned to write the history; and in both, he applied the general understanding of politics he had developed earlier; he did not essentially modify it. Both Najemy and Jurdjevic emphasize the lesser role of individual leaders and greater differentiations among economic groups in Machiavelli's later works. Both are, however, products or reflections of the equality of conditions that Machiavelli saw in Florence and that he explicitly stated in *D* 1.55 constitutes the condition under which a man who knew what to do could best found a republic. What Najemy sees as a change, Machiavelli presents as a problem. Florence did not have a leader with the knowledge needed to establish institutions and laws that would survive his death. Machiavelli notes that there were more divisions in Florence than there had been in other republics, but he does not present the greater number of divisions as an advantage. He does not try to solve the problems of class conflict or a purely popular (as opposed to mixed or aristocratic) republic by means of an increased number of interest groups the way James Madison later does in *Federalist* 10.

7. Although Machiavelli distinguished between public and private means of acquiring preeminence in *D* 3.28, he did not provide an ancient example of the successful use of such private

out the deleterious effects of Cosimo's rule by describing the failures of Florentine foreign policy—failures that can, predictably for Machiavelli, be traced to the merchant ruler's refusal to train and arm his own citizens lest they form an opposition to his control. (Cf. *AW* 1.58–61.) In *FH* 7 Machiavelli then shows that the failure of the Florentines to expand resulted in internal degeneration. He writes a eulogy in which he praises the liberality and prudence that enabled Cosimo to acquire and maintain his state for thirty-one years; but he also shows that Cosimo's heirs began to suffer the effects of that liberality in ways he argued a prince would in *P* 16.

By relating the failure of three conspiracies to overturn the Medici in *FH* 7–8 Machiavelli also reminds his readers how difficult it is to reform a corrupt city. It is not sufficient to have noble intentions, like those of Stephen Porcari (*FH* 6.29), whose efforts were revealed and forestalled, because he publicized his desire to kill the pope and restore a Roman republic, or those of the three schoolboys in Milan, who succeeded in assassinating Galeazzo Visconti (*FH* 7.33–34) but were themselves caught and killed. As Machiavelli observed in *D* 3.6, those who conspire against a prince hope that the people will rise up and join them in establishing a new government, once the head of the old is killed. However, he shows repeatedly in his *Florentine Histories*, once corrupted, people will not fight to free themselves. The Medici acquired tyrannical power in Florence by ruthlessly suppressing all internal opposition and sought to expand their rule by building splendid edifices at home and using mercenary forces as well as money to extend their influence abroad. The French invasion in 1494 should have convinced all observers of the defective character of these policies. Yet no one was able to persuade the Medici, other Florentines, or, more broadly, other Italians to adopt fundamentally different republican "modes and orders."

Machiavelli had certainly tried. Like the *Art of War*, Machiavelli's *Florentine Histories* constitute a defense of his own proposals, not merely for the necessity of organizing one's own arms or army, but for a new understanding of the way in which a city can gain and maintain its freedom by dramatizing the defective character of the old in the tragic history of his own

means in Rome. In *D* 3.8 he acknowledges that both Spurius Cassius and Manlius Capitolinus sought to buy popular favor by providing the people with economic benefits, but in both cases the senators were able to persuade the people that these individuals were seeking to become tyrants and their ambitions were defeated. The successful use of such means appears to be a distinctively modern phenomenon, and Cosimo's rise to preeminence in Florence the example par excellence. Modern political leaders no longer understand how to counter such a threat nor are they able to do so, because the people have become corrupt.

city.[8] In the first half of that history Machiavelli shows that it is not possible to maintain a republic if either or both of the two humors try to gain complete control of the city. As happened with the Decemvirs in Rome, such attempts culminated—twice—in the rise of a tyrant in Florence. In the second half of his history Machiavelli then shows that a tyrant does not necessarily arise with the use of arms or force. Cosimo de' Medici and his heirs acquired tyrannical power in Florence by suppressing the opposition and benefiting individuals without the support of any army. But, Machiavelli also shows, it is possible to acquire and maintain control by benefiting individuals and private groups rather than the public as a whole only in the absence of an external threat. The use of such "merciful" means of ruling results not in peaceful coexistence and trade, moreover, so much as in corruption and tyranny. Unlike later modern liberal political philosophers such as Locke and Montesquieu, Machiavelli clearly does not think that commerce can or should substitute for military defense as a basis of republican politics.

Book 1: How the Barbarian Invasions and the Unintended Acquisition of Temporal Power by the Popes Resulted in the Division and Weakening of Italy

Machiavelli begins his history by describing the effects of the withdrawal of the Roman Empire to the east, because the withdrawal of imperial troops created the conditions under which Florence could declare its independence as a free city. By presenting this "general" history of events in Italy after the fall of Rome in 476 BCE, Machiavelli suggests that Florence was able to preserve its liberty less as a result of the virtue of its own leaders and citizens than because of the weakness of the other Italian powers.

Machiavelli first shows that the withdrawal of the empire left Italy open to barbarian invasions from the north. As in *D* 2.8, he explains that "the people who live in northern parts beyond the Rhine and the Danube rivers . . . often increase to such a multitude that it becomes necessary for a part of

8. The negative lesson of Machiavelli's account of Florentine history was not lost on the authors of *The Federalist*, who cite the history of the Italian republics as examples of the kind of defective politics they hope to avoid, for example in *Federalist* 10, or on Alexis de Tocqueville, who found Machiavelli's description of Florentine politics particularly abhorrent. See Melvin Richter, "Tocqueville's Brief Encounter with Machiavelli: Notes on the *Florentine Histories* (1836)," *History of Political Thought* 26, no. 3 (2005): 426–42.

them to abandon their fathers' lands and to seek new countries to inhabit" (9). Forced to seize the lands of others if they are to survive, such peoples make fierce combatants. Yet, as Machiavelli also reminded his readers in *D* 2.8, under the republic the Romans had withstood such attacks (as had the Germans and Hungarians in his time). At the very beginning of his *Florentine Histories* Machiavelli thus sets up the contrast between the present weakness of Italy and its more glorious Roman past that runs through the book. At the same time, Machiavelli shows that the problems of Italy stem from the failure of the Roman Empire to perform the first and most important function of any government, protecting its people and their property from external aggressors. No more than in his *Discourses* does Machiavelli allow his readers to conclude that ancient Rome was a perfect regime. On the contrary, he shows that Rome's inability to maintain its dominion in the west was the first cause of the current disunion and weakness of Italy. By emphasizing the importance of defense as the first and most fundamental function of any government, he also points to the most obvious weakness of the later governments of Florence.

Responding to the need to defend themselves, the peoples of Italy reorganized into a variety of new polities. "Constrained by necessity," he reports, the peoples of Aquileia, Monselice, Padua, Vicenza, and Verona all fled from Attila to the reefs and swamps around Rivo Alto. They "left very pleasant and fertile places to live in places that were sterile, deformed, and devoid of every comfort." However, "because many peoples were brought together at a stroke, in a very short time they made those places not only habitable but delightful." The Venetians thus demonstrated how much more powerful human industry and art are than nature (as Machiavelli maintained in *D* 1.1). These refugees "established laws and orders among themselves, and amidst so much ruin in Italy, they enjoyed security"; and they became prosperous and powerful. "As necessity had led them to live in the waters, so it forced them to think of how they could live decently when they had no use of the land; and going in their ships throughout the world, they filled their city with a variety of merchandise." As long as "they lived in this form their name became terrible on the seas and venerated within Italy, so that in all the controversies that arose, they were most often the arbiters" (*FH* 1.29; 41).

The other peoples of Italy were not so fortunate. Left without protection, the people of Rome looked to the pope for leadership. And because he was unarmed, the pope sought the assistance of the French king. "*Henceforward,*" Machiavelli emphasizes, "*all the wars waged by the barbarians in*

Italy were for the most part caused by the pontiffs, and all the barbarians who invaded it were most often called in by them. This mode of proceeding continues still in our times; and it is this that has kept and keeps Italy disunited and infirm" (20, emphasis added).[9]

Charlemagne fundamentally altered the relation between the emperor and pope. Previously, the election of the pope had been confirmed by the Roman emperor. Because Charlemagne "judged that the pope as Vicar of God could not be judged by men," he had the pope and the Roman people make him emperor. From this time forward the emperor needed the support of a pope to be elected. The pontiffs' acquisition of power was by no means smooth or uncontested, however. Nor was it ever complete. After discords arose among the descendants of the French king, the empire moved from France to Germany; and the emperors began to compete with the popes for control of Italy. The Visconti used the opportunity created by the conflict between the adherents of the pope (Guelfs) and adherents of the emperor (Ghibellines) in Lombardy to establish a duchy in Milan.

The conflict among Charlemagne's heirs also led some Normans to come to Italy. These Normans first occupied some towns in the Romagna, but their heirs took Sicily from the Saracens and later added it to Naples to form the Kingdom. From its beginning, the Kingdom thus became a prize and prey of foreign conquest.

The barbarian invasions resulted in a change not only in the government and princes of Italy, Machiavelli observes, but also in "the laws, the customs, the mode of life, the religion, the language, the dress, the names. . . . Once Caesars and Pompeys, [they] have become Peters, Johns, and Matthews." One might suppose that the spread of the Christian religion throughout the empire indicated by these changes in names would have offered solace for the suffering caused by so many other changes. But the introduction of new religious beliefs and practices brought even greater disorder and violence. "Struggles among the Greek Church, the Roman Church, and the Church at Ravenna—and even more, the struggle between the heretical and the catholic sects—afflicted the world" (14–15). The adoption of the Christian

9. In the *Florentine Histories* Machiavelli thus provides more detailed historical evidence for his judgment in *D* 1.12 that "No province has ever been united or happy unless it has all come under obedience to one republic or to one prince, as happened to France and to Spain. The cause that Italy is not in the same condition . . . is solely the church. For although it has inhabited and held a temporal empire there, it has not been so powerful nor of such virtue as to be able to seize the tyranny of Italy and make itself prince of it. On the other hand, it has not been so weak that it has been unable to call in a power to defend it against one that had become too powerful in Italy, for fear of losing dominion over its temporal things" (38).

religion did not improve the lives of the Italians; on the contrary, it exacerbated the divisions and conflict among them by insisting that there should be one and only one authoritative Church and creed.

Machiavelli shows that the popes had sufficient spiritual power to arouse popular opposition to a prince who defied them and to obtain the aid of external arms in defending them in Rome; but they did not have sufficient temporal power to unify Italy, much less all Christendom. Urban II seemed to be succeeding when he inspired a crusade against the infidels. Many kings, peoples, and private individuals contributed to this noble venture, and the Christians were initially successful in acquiring control of Asia Minor, Syria, and part of Egypt. Within a century, however, they were defeated by their own divisions and the virtue of the Saracen Saladin. And when the popes began trying to use their power to establish hereditary principalities for their "natural" sons, their ability to inflict "spiritual wounds" on their secular competitors for rule in Europe decreased.[10]

Instead of creating an opportunity for Italian cities to choose their own form of government, the competition between the popes and emperors resulted in the loss of liberty in most. Fearing that he had lost possession of Italy and that Emperor Ludwig might make himself lord there, Pope Benedict XII decided to make friends of all those who had usurped the towns that used to obey the emperor by issuing a decree that the tyrants of Lombardy could keep their towns with just titles. And the emperor, "seeing with how much liberality the pontiff had given away towns belonging to the Empire, so as not to be any less liberal with the things of others than the pope had been, gave to all the tyrants in the towns of the Church" the same just title "by imperial authority. . . . So that of the towns of the Church, few were left without a prince" (*FH* 1.30; 42).

Machiavelli concludes book 1 by describing the problematic results of the continuing battles over the succession to the Kingdom of Naples and the government of Rome, schisms in the Church, and Visconti murders of their close relations: "Queen Giovanna II held the kingdom of Naples; in the Marches, the Patrimony, and Romagna, some of the towns obeyed the Church, and some were held by their vicars or tyrants. . . . As for Lombardy, part obeyed Duke Filippo [Visconti] and part the Venetians. . . . The

10. As in his account of the attempts of Alexander VI to establish a principality for his son in *P* 7 and 11, so in his general history Machiavelli points out a structural defect in the papacy as a secular power: "The principalities ordered by them have had short lives because most times the pontiffs, by living a short time, either do not provide for planting their plants or . . . leave them with roots so few and weak that they wither at the first wind" (*FH* 1.23; 35).

Florentines were lords of the greater part of Tuscany; only Lucca and Siena lived under their own laws." And he emphasizes: "All these principal powers were not armed with arms of their own. Duke Filippo [the Visconti tyrant of Milan] shut up in his rooms and not letting himself be seen, directed his wars through commissioners; the Venetians, as they turned to the land, threw aside the arms that had made them glorious on the seas and, following the custom of the other Italians, administered their armies under the government of others. The pope, because arms did not befit him as a man of religion, and Queen Giovanna of Naples, because she was a woman, did from necessity what the others had done by bad choice." As he explains in more detail in book 2, "the Florentines also obeyed the same necessities because, having eliminated their nobility by frequent divisions, the republic was left in the hands of men nurtured in trade and thus continued in the orders and fortune of the others." Instead of being organized and directed by the major political powers, "the arms of Italy, therefore, were in the hands either of lesser princes or of men without a state [mercenary captains]; for the lesser princes, unmoved by any glory, wore them so as to live either more rich or more secure, and the others, nurtured in them since childhood and not knowing any other art, sought to be honored for them" (*FH* 1.39; 51).

By concluding book 1 with a description of the state of Italian arms that resulted from their relegation to "lesser princes" and men without a state, who seek not glory but wealth and power and have created "a sort of bond and understanding" that has reduced the art of war "to such vileness that any mediocre captain in whom only a shadow of ancient virtue has been reborn would have despised" (50), Machiavelli deflects readers' attention from the reasons or causes such "arms" were employed.[11] A thoughtful reader might agree that it would not have been appropriate for a pope to organize and lead an army (although Julius II did), but she would ask: what prevented one of the other major powers from using the "opportunity" created by the disunity in Italy to expand its dominion to the entire province? The implicit answer seems to be that the Kingdom of Naples and the duchy of Milan were imposed on their people by force, so that their people were not and perhaps could not be organized to defend them. These

11. Banfield and Mansfield translate Machiavelli's description of book 1 in *FH* 2.2 as his *trattato universale* literally as "universal treatise." *Universale* can simply mean general, and the contrast, I believe, is between the history of Italy as a whole that he has presented in book 1 and the history of Florence that he begins to treat specifically in book 2.

princes thus had to rely on the mercenary or auxiliary arms of others. And the "spiritual wounds" the popes were able to inflict on governments established by the emperors prevented them from organizing and maintaining the support of their people. Instead, the "liberal" exchanging by the pope and the emperor of towns officially controlled by the other legitimated the rule of tyrants in most. Only Venice, Florence, Lucca, and Siena survived as self-governing republics. But, Machiavelli suggests, the two larger cities were discouraged if not prevented from forming effective land armies by the commercial tastes and experiences of their leading citizens. Venice acquired an empire with the navy she was led to build "by necessity," but lost it after it imitated the bad examples of its neighbors by employing mercenary forces in its attempt to acquire dominion on land as well as at sea. What then caused the frequent divisions in the Florentine republic that resulted in the elimination of the nobility and therewith its ability to expand its empire to encompass Tuscany, if not all of Italy? That is the question to which Machiavelli turns in book 2.

Book 2: The Self-Destruction of the Florentine Nobility

In book 2 Machiavelli shows how the Florentine nobles destroyed themselves by dividing into factions, each of which sought complete control of the government to the exclusion of all others. First they divided as a result of a private dispute, according to families; then into Guelfs and Ghibellines; next into white and black "Guelfs" after the Ghibellines were exiled; and, finally, into a party of "the great" which sought to deprive the people of all power and was opposed by "popular nobles" or "men of the people" like the Medici. Attempting to quell the violence, the Florentines repeatedly reformed their government; but the institutions they established were not strong enough to establish and maintain order. The selection of a ruling committee by lot for short terms made it difficult if not impossible for an individual leader to establish a government capable of enforcing the law, especially in the absence of public trials in front of popular juries. And the apparently evenhanded requirement that all of the chief magistrates be merchants resulted in the exclusion of the nobles. Like the Roman patricians in the final days of the republic (see *D* 1.37), the Florentine nobles concluded that they had to seize control of the government by force.

In the introductory chapter of book 2 Machiavelli states explicitly what was only implicit at the beginning of book 1—namely, that ancient republics and principalities protected themselves from barbarian invasions by establishing colonies whereas modern polities do not. These colonies served not only to defend the mother city, as he argued in *P* 3, but also to distribute people across the land more evenly, so that the population increased and more of the land was cultivated.

In describing the founding of Florence as a colony, however, Machiavelli acknowledges that the dependent status of a colony was not good for it. The Florentines were not able to do anything worthy of memory for the first twelve hundred years of their city's existence. Because the city was founded as a colony of Rome, its citizens did not learn how to rule themselves. Moreover, they acquired the destructive habit of looking to foreigners to defend them.

The first cause of division in Florence was a feud that arose between noble families about a marriage. When a young noble jilted the woman to whom he was betrothed in order to marry the beautiful daughter of another wealthy family, the Uberti took their revenge by murdering the young man who had dishonored them by breaking his vow. What was initially a private affair thus became a source of public hostility. "This homicide divided the whole city, and . . . *since these families were strong in houses, towers, and men, they fought for many years without one dislodging the other*" (*FH* 2.3; 56, emphasis added).[12] As Machiavelli argued in *D* 1.55, it is difficult if not impossible to establish and maintain a republic where gentlemen have their own castles and arms to defend them from the imposition of rule or laws by others.

The Uberti sought the help of the emperor in driving out their opponents, and what had been a local division became an extension of a broader conflict between the Ghibellines and the Guelfs. There were periodic attempts by men in the middle to reconcile the two parties and to institute a government that would provide Florence with a free way of life and the ability to defend itself. But these efforts were repeatedly defeated by members of the two parties, who sought foreign assistance to obtain control of the city. Unlike the ancient Romans in Ardea (*D* 3.27), neither the Holy Roman Emperor nor the head of the Roman Church was able to reestablish

12. Because this dispute arose between two noble families, in contrast to the dispute in Ardea he described in *D* 3.26, Machiavelli does not suggest that it was caused by differences between the nobles and people, which are largely economic. He admits that this dispute arose because of the beauty of the young woman, the erotic desire of the young gentleman, and the indignation of the family that thought its honor had been violated and consequently sought revenge.

peace in the cities subject to his authority by killing the heads. The conflict in Florence thus continued until the Guelfs eliminated the Ghibellines by exiling them and expropriating their property. After the division between the parties of the nobles was settled, they began oppressing the people, who finally rebelled.

In relating the repeated attempts of "men of the middle who had credit with the people" to reunite the city, Machiavelli seems to agree with Aristotle's contention in book 4 of his *Politics* that such "middlemen" seek the common good in a way that those seeking rule for themselves and their party alone do not. However, he also shows that, although these "men of the middle" understood the need to satisfy the opposed interests of the partisans and the people, they did not know how to design institutions that would achieve that goal. Their attempts to reform the government of the city were thus repeatedly foiled by the nobles, who refused to share power.

After the German emperor, who had helped the Ghibellines seize power in Florence, died, some of these men in the middle thought that it would be good to reunite the city by including all parties in the government, so they arranged to bring the Guelfs back. They divided the city into six parts and elected twelve citizens, two for each sixth, every year to govern it. To remove the causes of enmities or vendettas of the kind that had initially divided the city, they appointed two foreign judges (who would presumably not be attached to any particular family or party). And to provide for the common defense, "they established twelve banners within the city and seventy-six in the countryside and enrolled all the young men under them" (*FH* 2.5; 58). Even though Machiavelli criticized Florence for granting this power to a few foreigners in *D* 1.49, he praises the foreign policy of this government by observing that under it, the Florentines forced the people of Pisa, Arezzo, and Siena to league with them; they also took Volterra along with some other fortified places, and brought the inhabitants to Florence.[13] (They thus followed a policy similar to that Machiavelli attributes to Rome in *D* 2.3–4, in acquiring the foundation of a Tuscan empire.)

However, because these campaigns were all undertaken at the behest of the Guelfs, the Ghibellines sought the first opportunity to retake the state. With the help of Manfred, who had made himself lord of the kingdom,

13. In *D* 1.49 Machiavelli criticized the grant of the judicial power to a few foreign judges, because it was easy for the wealthy to bribe a single judge or a few jurors. As Machiavelli shows later in this book (*FH* 2.13), the people will not believe that someone they suspect has been fairly absolved or convicted unless the trial is held in public and the verdict determined there by a large number of judges.

they defeated the Guelfs and regained control of the city. But after Pope Clement called upon Charles of Anjou to seize the kingdom from Manfred, the exiled Guelfs sought to regain control of Florence. Responding to the Guelf threat, the Ghibellines decided to try to win over the people of Florence by returning some of the honors and authority they had taken from them, allowing them to elect thirty-six citizens to reform the state. Had the Ghibellines done so freely rather than pressed by an obvious necessity, Machiavelli comments, such a move might have been useful.[14] As it was, at their first meeting the thirty-six divided the city into guilds, appointed a magistrate for each, and assigned every man to a banner under which to appear armed whenever the city might have need of it. When the Ghibellines decided to try to take back what they had given by using the force, the people were armed and able to repel them.

The armed people then "decided to reunite the city by calling back all the citizens, Ghibelline as well as Guelf" (*FH* 2.9; 61). But, once again, the "noble" parties could not live content. The Guelfs became so insolent that the Ghibellines fled without being driven out. The Florentines again reordered their state by electing twelve "good men" for terms of two months and creating three councils, one of eighty citizens, another of one hundred and eighty people, and a third of one hundred and twenty citizens from the people and nobles who were to make final decisions with regard to matters debated in the first two. But they destroyed the apparently balanced character of the new constitution by seizing the property of the Ghibellines, who had fled, and so strengthened the Guelfs. Later popes tried to reconcile the parties in Florence, but they were unable to do so.

To deprive the Ghibellines of their part in the government and to keep the powerful in check, in 1282 the magistrates and ensigns of the guild corporations decided to reorder the state again by substituting three citizens called "priors" for the fourteen governors who had been divided between the two parties. These priors were to serve for two months, and they "could be of the people and of the great, provided that they were merchants or practiced an art." However, this apparently evenhanded requirement that all the chief magistrates be merchants "was the cause . . . of the ruin of the nobles, because through various accidents they were excluded

14. In *D* 1.32 Machiavelli argued that "no one . . . should defer winning over the people until times of danger, ... for the collectivity will judge that it has that good not from you but from your adversaries; and since it ought to fear that when the necessity has passed, you will take back from them what you had been forced to give them, it will not have any obligation to you" (70).

from it by the people and afterwards crushed. In the beginning the nobles consented to it because they were not united"; then, because they "desired too much to take away the [entire] state . . . , they all lost it" (*FH* 2.11; 64).

The two humors "that are naturally wont to exist in all cities between the powerful and the people" had been repressed in Florence by fear of the Ghibellines. But when the Guelf and Ghibelline parties were almost eliminated, the nobles began injuring people without fear of the magistrates. Giano della Bella, "a man of very noble lineage but a lover of the freedom of the city, then inspired the heads of the guilds to reform the city. On his advice they decided to have the Gonfalonier reside with the Priors and that he should have four thousand men under his command. All the nobles were again deprived of the power to sit with the Signori; the accomplices of an offender were forced to pay the same penalty as he, and they made public report sufficient for passing judgment" (*FH* 2.13; 65). However, when a man of the people was killed in a brawl in which many nobles had taken part, and the Captain of the People first arrested one of the boldest, Messer Corso Donati, but then absolved him, the people rioted. Responding to the outbreak of violence, the nobles prepared to try to retake control of the government by force; but "some men of the people as well as of the nobles, along with certain men of religion of good repute, placed themselves in the middle to pacify them." Echoing some of the lessons Machiavelli sought to teach readers of his *Discourses*, these men

> reminded the nobles that their pride and their bad government were the cause of the honors taken from them and the laws made against them, that their taking up arms now to regain by force what they had allowed to be taken from them on account of their own disunion and their evil ways was nothing other than to wish to ruin their fatherland and to worsen their own condition; and they should remember that the people were far superior to them in number, riches, and hatred, and that the nobility by which it appeared to them that they were superior to others . . . would not be enough to defend them against so many.

They then warned the people

> that it was not prudent always to want the ultimate victory, and that it was never a wise course to make men desperate [as the Gracchi had made the Roman nobles], because he who does not hope for good does not fear evil. They ought to think that nobility . . . had honored the city in war, and therefore it was neither a good nor a just thing to persecute it . . . ; that . . .

> the nobles bore easily their not enjoying the supreme magistracy, [but] they could not at all tolerate . . . the orders that had been made . . . to drive them out of their fatherland; . . . nor should they want to try the fortune of battle, trusting in their number, for many times it had been seen that the many were overcome by the few. (*FH* 2.14; 67)

Because the parties continued to suspect each other, however, they fortified themselves with towers and arms. To weaken the influence of the nobles further, the people reordered the state by restricting the number of "princes." They also began an extensive building program, including a magnificent palace for the Signori and a public prison. "Never was our city in a greater and more prosperous state than in these times," Machiavelli exults, "when it was replete with men, riches, and reputation; there were thirty thousand citizens skilled in arms, and those in the surrounding country side came to seventy thousand. All Tuscany, part as subjects and part as friends, obeyed it; and although there was some anger and suspicion between the nobles and the people, . . . everyone lived united in peace" (*FH* 2.15; 68).[15]

"If this peace had not been disturbed by new enmities within," Machiavelli concludes, Florence "would not have had to fear those from the outside." Once again, however, after a private feud caused a division between two noble families in Pistoia, it quickly spread to Florence. Because the heads of both parties—the Cerchi "Whites" and the Donati "Blacks"—were Guelfs, each appealed for help from the pope when the other became dominant. And in each case, the pope sent a legate who angrily interdicted the city after the party in power refused to reconcile with the other.[16] (Unlike the armed people, the pope's representative could not force them to reconcile.) So the internal fighting ceased only after the whites had been exiled and the ambitious leader of the blacks, Messer Corso Donati, was killed.[17]

15. Machiavelli thus indicates that there were historical precedents for some of the policies he urged his young Florentine readers to adopt in the *Discourses*.

16. Machiavelli first mentions the Medici as among those who provoked the fighting when the legate left, because they favored a return of the exiles. *FH* 2.21; 74.

17. Messer Corso Donati revealed his tyrannical desires when, after members of the opposing party had been exiled, he began accusing the citizens in charge of public funds of using them for their own private purposes. He then sought popular favor by opposing the opinions of powerful men. But his ambitions became suspected when "his mode of living overstepped all civil bounds" and he married "the daughter of Uguccione della Faggiuola, head of the Ghibelline party and a White." So his opponents felt justified in taking up arms against him (*FH* 2.21–23).

But just as their internal divisions had been settled, the Florentines found themselves confronted with a series of new external Ghibelline threats. Following their bad old habits, the Florentines looked to a foreign power to defend them. Learning that Emperor Henry was coming into Italy with all the Florentine rebels he had promised to restore to their fatherland, the heads of the Florentine government asked King Robert of Sicily to help them; and when he refused to do so as a friend, they agreed to give him the city for five years in return for a promise to defend them.

Henry died just as his army reached Florence, so the city was saved from the emperor. But the king's representatives were not as successful in defending the Florentines from attacks by the Ghibelline tyrants of Lucca; and they were cruel and rapacious in their treatment of the Florentines. So when King Robert's lordship came to an end, the city revived its old magistracies, and this time "the great fear it had of Castruccio [who had become tyrant of Lucca] kept it united." After he attacked Prato, the Florentines closed their shops and gathered together twenty thousand on foot and fifteen hundred on horse to help. Frightened by such a large force gathered together so speedily, Castruccio withdrew. The people and nobles of Florence then began to debate about whether they should pursue him, and the delay "gave the enemy time to retire safely" (*FH* 2.26; 81).

"As happens in all republics," Machiavelli comments, "always after an unforeseen event some old laws are annulled and others are renewed" (*FH* 2.28; 82). Popular outrage at the failure of the Florentine army to pursue and defeat Castruccio led the Signoria to change the way in which its members were elected. The names of eligible citizens were put into a bag and every two months a new set of eight were drawn. New baggings had to be held, however, because many citizens doubted that their names had been put in. The Florentines then decided to put the names in for a longer time—every three to five years—to relieve the city of the annoyance and remove the cause of the tumults that arose at the creation of a new magistracy. They "did not understand the defects that were hidden under this small advantage" (*FH* 2.28; 83). Both the contents of the bags and the selection of the magistrates from them supposedly by lot could be rigged.

The bad effects of this reform did not become immediately evident, because the Florentines were preoccupied with foreign affairs. After Castruccio seized Pistoia in 1325, the Florentines decided to attack him before he acquired complete dominion over that city. They gathered twenty thousand foot soldiers and three thousand cavalry under leadership of Ramondo di Cardona. But having seen the city give itself to King Robert, this captain thought that if the Florentines felt the need, they would make him prince as well. So he procrastinated, while Castruccio built up his forces so that he was able to attack and defeat the Florentine army at Altopascio, where many Florentine citizens were killed along with Ramondo.[18]

After the destruction of their army by Castruccio, the Florentines were no longer able to man their own defense. Yet they had not "become so vile that they failed to provide large sums of money, hire men, and send to their friends for help." The price was, however, their liberty. Because provisions alone would not suffice to protect them from a young and daring enemy like Castruccio, "they were forced to elect as their lord, Charles, . . . son of King Robert, if they wanted him to come to their defense." Since Charles was fighting in Sicily, he sent Walter, a man of French birth and duke of Athens, to take possession of the city as vicar of the lord. During this first visit "his bearing was . . . so modest, and so contrary to his nature, that everyone loved him" (*FH* 2.30; 84).

The harsh effects of depending upon a foreigner to defend the city began to become evident after Charles had extracted double the fee of two hundred thousand florins to which the city had initially agreed. However, the Florentines again regained by good fortune what they had not been able to achieve with their own virtue. Although Castruccio had expanded his empire by seizing control of both Pisa and Pistoia, Castruccio died when he returned to Lucca, and Charles died in Naples.

In the absence of an external threat the powerful within the city began trying to increase their power. Not content to restrict the names in the bags from which magistrates were drawn and to select judges who would be favorable, they added a foreign Captain of the Guard and gave him authority over all the citizens. That captain injured some other nobles, and they conspired to seize control of the government. The conspiracy was revealed, "as always happens [in] conspiracies that allow an interval of time before their execution." (Cf. *D* 3.6.) Many citizens met at the palace and demanded that the Signori call the people to arms; and seeing that they were discovered, the conspirators prepared to defend themselves with force. But one of the judges placed himself in the midst of the fighting; and "reverence for the man . . . made them lay down their arms . . . and listen" (*FH* 2.32; 88;

18. Machiavelli shows here how ironic his praise of the tyrant of Lucca was in his *Life of Castruccio Castracani*. Because he contributed in such an important way to the loss of liberty in Florence by destroying their army at Altopascio, in his *Life* Machiavelli gave a different version of this battle.

cf. *D* 1.54). He convinced the conspirators of the danger they faced if they did not yield to the people and persuaded the Signori that they would not want to prevail with the blood of their citizens. They let the conspirators leave the city and return to their castles; but they later bought those castles and provided by law that no citizen could own a castle nearer than twenty miles to Florence. They thus created the conditions, according to Machiavelli in *D* 1.55, in which a republic can best be established and maintained.

No one in Florence knew how to take advantage of those conditions, however. Instead, Machiavelli observes, "it was not enough for those who were governing to have overcome the conspirators, but as men do almost always, the more authority they have, the worse they use it and the more insolent they become" (*FH* 2.32; 88). Rather than acknowledge the mistake they had made by appointing a tyrannous captain of the guard in the city, they elected another in the country. As a result people were so stirred up against all the nobles that they were prepared to sell the city in order to avenge themselves at the first opportunity.

This opportunity arose when the Florentines asked King Robert to help them in a war to acquire Lucca. He again sent them Walter, duke of Athens, who arrived just as the campaign had been lost. Seeing that the people were indignant, the twenty men they had appointed to conduct the war decided to elect a new captain; "and so that the people might still have cause to fear and that the duke of Athens might defend them with greater authority, they elected him first as protector, then as captain of their men-at-arms." Seeking to subdue the people who had afflicted them, the great offered to help the duke take lordship over everything in the hope that he would then reward them. But rather than accept their support, the duke sought to increase his favor with the plebs by prosecuting those who had directed the war against Lucca and fined or condemned many others to exile. Everyone began to fear him; and he informed the Signori that they should grant him lordship, since the whole city consented to it. Seeing that they had no forces with which to withstand his men-at-arms, the Signori saw no remedy but to pray him to desist and to make his lordship less harsh. But the traditional arguments against tyranny—that he would have to use a great deal of force to enslave a city that was used to living free, that he would have no friends and thus no security, and that he would never be loved—did not move him.[19] So the Signori agreed to gather the people in

19. The arguments Machiavelli attributes to the anonymous spokesman for the Signori can be found in book 9 of Plato's *Republic* and in Xenophon's *Hiero*.

the plaza and by their authority to grant him lordship. The next day when they read the proposal to grant the duke lordship for one year, the multitude shouted, "For life!" (*FH* 2.35; 93).

As in Rome with the institution of the Decemvirs, Machiavelli shows, so in Florence the attempts of the nobles to seize complete control of the government and of the people to exclude the nobles entirely from it resulted in the creation of a tyrant. The duke dismantled the government of the republic. And "the severity and humanity that he had feigned were converted into arrogance and cruelty, whence many great citizens and popular nobles were either fined or killed, or tortured in new modes" (*FH* 2.94).

As he showed in the case of the Decemvirs, so Machiavelli shows in the case of the duke of Athens, the tyrant was brought down primarily as a result of his own errors. Unlike Appius, who understood how easily men can be corrupted, the duke "could not believe that the generous spirits usually found in the nobility could be content in obedience to him; so he turned to benefiting the plebs, thinking that with their favors and with foreign arms he could preserve the tyranny" (*FH* 2.36; 94). Like Appius, the duke did not understand that what particularly made the citizens of Florence indignant was the violence that he and his men did to the women. (Cf. *P* 19.) To show the people that he believed that he was loved, the duke had a man who "revealed that the Medici family with some others had conspired against him" put to death miserably without investigating the charges.[20] He thus discouraged "those who might seek to warn him for his safety" and encouraged "those who might wish his ruin." The number of the latter grew after the duke had the tongue of a man who complained about the heavy assessments he had levied on citizens cut out so cruelly that he died. "The city was accustomed to do and to speak about everything and with every license and could not bear to have its hands tied and its mouth sealed" (*FH* 2.36; 95). The great, the people, and the artisans all joined in a conspiracy to recover their freedom, and the duke was frightened by both the quality and the quantity of his opponents. He did not have a sufficient number of armed men to arrest and then put the conspirators to death, so he sent for outside forces while he made a list of three hundred citizens and had his sergeants summon them under color of wanting to consult with them. But his sending for the outside forces and summoning the individual who had first revealed the conspiracy frightened the citizens. The boldest refused to

20. As in *FH* 2.20–21, in supporting the legate's attempts to let the exiled whites return to the city, the Medici initially appear in Machiavelli's history as opponents of injustice and tyranny.

obey the summons, and having read the list of names, they sought each other out. Within three hours they had resolved to take up arms and call the people to freedom the next day. The fighting was fierce, but the duke and his forces were overcome.

The citizens first granted fourteen citizens, half from the great and half from the popular party, along with the bishop, authority to reform the state. They then sent foreign ambassadors to negotiate with the duke, but they would not agree to any settlement until he surrendered three men, two of whom the mob literally tore to pieces. "The multitude having purged itself with the blood of these two," Machiavelli calmly comments (cf. *D* 1.7), the citizens escorted the duke and his men out of Florence to Cassentino where he formally renounced his lordship.[21] Although he repeatedly shows that the people were willing to share power with the great, whereas the great were not willing to share power with the people, Machiavelli also describes the dysfunctional tendency of the people to riot and to take vengeance unjustly on certain individuals.

After some debate, an agreement was reached to divide the government between the great and the people; and Machiavelli observes: "*The city would have settled down if the great had been content to live with that modesty which is required by civil life; but they acted in a contrary way*" (emphasis added). The people "lamented that from one tyrant who had been eliminated a thousand had been born." So they convinced the bishop to propose that the great should be content with taking part in the lower offices and leave the Signori exclusively to the people. When the great refused and withdrew to their homes, the people ran to the palace, armed and shouting. The remaining popular Signori then "reformed the councils so as to put the whole government in the will of the people" (*FH* 2.39; 100–101).

At that time, Machiavelli explains, Florence suffered from a great scarcity of grain, and in an incident reminiscent of Roman history (Spurius Cassius), Messer Andrea Strozzi thought that he could seize power by selling his wheat at a lower price than others. The Roman Senate had been able to persuade the uncorrupt Roman people to turn against the would-be tyrant (*D* 3.9); but, Machiavelli reports, in Florence many of its corrupt people gathered at Strozzi's house to buy it (as he predicted in *D* 3.8 a corrupt

21. Cf. Machiavelli's contention in *D* 1.7 that in order to preserve (or perhaps institute) the rule of law, some means must be devised of allowing the multitude to "vent their humor" even though it results in some injustice to individuals. Here he gives a particularly gruesome modern example.

people would). One morning Strozzi dared to mount his horse and call the people to arms. Having amassed more than four thousand men, he rode to the piazza of the Signori and asked them to open the palace. The Signori repulsed them, and Messer Andrea was barely able to save himself from the magistrates. It appeared that the Florentine republic was not entirely corrupt or unable to maintain itself.

However, in contrast to the Roman Senate, which had appointed a dictator to deal with the crises, the Florentine government, solely in the hands of the people, faced and used force against a crowd. And "this unforeseen event . . . gave hope to the great that they could compel the people. . . . They decided to arm themselves with every sort of help so as to regain by force, reasonably, that which had been unjustly taken from them by force" (*FH* 2.40; 102). But the people also armed, and, led by the Medici, they attacked and defeated the great.

Since he has repeatedly blamed the great for their arrogant attempts to gain freedom for themselves by oppressing others, it is surprising to see Machiavelli conclude book 2 by expressing regret for their demise. "The ruin of the nobles was so great . . . that they never again dared to take up arms against the people. . . . This was the cause by which Florence was stripped not only of its arms but of all generosity" (*FH* 2.42; 104).[22] In book 3 he explains how and why.

22. Had Machiavelli become discouraged about the prospects of a popularly based republic? Was he now looking back at the more aristocratic politics of the past with some nostalgia? Jurdjevic, *Great and Wretched City*, 81–98, argues that this history led Machiavelli to appreciate the advantages of a noble culture more than he had in his previous critiques of the *grandi*. (Conflating the humor or disposition with an economic class, Jurdjevic translates *grandi* as 'rich' rather than 'great.' However, as Pinzani, "Doch ein Republikaner?," observes: "In allen seinem Werken findet eine reductio ad politicum statt, die in jeden Konflict bloß eine Kampf um die politische Macht sieht. Daß diese Macht ihrerseits anderen, etwa wirtschaftlichen Interesse dienen kann, scheint für ihn nie eine Möglichkeit zu sein" [173].) Jurdjevic compares Machiavelli's four (and only four) uses of 'generosity'—to describe Urban II's crusade, the thirteenth-century Florentines' use of a bell to warn Florence's enemies to prepare for war a month before they planned to attack, the loss Florence suffered with the demise of its nobility, and the spirit that the duke of Athens thought would prevent the nobility from accepting his rule for long—with Machiavelli's frequent use of 'liberality' to describe the economic munificence of the Medici that enabled them to corrupt and control others without actually using force or serving in public office. And he concludes that by 'generosity' Machiavelli means something like martial boldness. Such boldness would seem to be more similar to courage than to "generosity," however. (Levy, *Wily Elites*, 18, points out that "originally the word meant 'of noble birth,' but Machiavelli distinguishes his meaning from the original one by speaking of generosity of spirit rather than of birth." In the *Discourses* "Machiavelli speaks occasionally . . . of the generosity of the nobles and of the senate, but never of the people.") What the "men of the people" Machiavelli goes on to describe lack is a willingness to organize their followers into an army able to wage war successfully and a desire for public honor if not glory that

Book 3: The Rise and Fall of a New Division between the Popular Nobles and the Plebs

Reflecting on the history he has just related, Machiavelli begins book 3 by declaring that "the grave and natural enmities that exist between the men of the people and the nobles, caused by the wish of the latter to command and the former not to obey, are the cause of all evils that arise in cities." As he showed in his *Discourses* (see especially 1.7, 1.37, 3.27), the conflict between the two humors, if not regulated and channeled by laws that enable each humor to check the abuses of the other, always threatens to become a destructive civil war. Explicitly reintroducing the contrast between Florence and Rome he initiated in the preface, he observes that in Rome the enmities were resolved by debates that culminated in legislation, but in Florence the conflict between the two humors ended in fighting that resulted in the exile and deaths of many citizens. In Rome, he now adds, the tumults always increased military virtue, whereas in Florence they eliminated it altogether. However, he also points out that the conflict brought Rome from equality in the citizens to a very great inequality, while in Florence the conflict "reduced it from inequality to a wonderful equality" (*FH* 3.1; 105). In Rome the conflict thus culminated in the need to replace the republic with the rule of a single "prince," whereas in Florence the conflict ended in establishing the conditions under which, Machiavelli argued in *D* 1.55, a republic could most easily be established.

Machiavelli initially seems to attribute the different results of the conflict between the two humors in the two republics to a difference in the desires of the two peoples: "The people of Rome desired to enjoy the highest honors together with the nobles, while the people of Florence fought to be alone in the government without the participation of the nobles; and that is why it came to the blood and exile of citizens, and the laws that were made afterwards were not for the common utility but were all ordered in favor of the conqueror." For a time the leaders of the people of Rome became more virtuous, because they were competing with the nobles to hold the highest public offices (*D* 1.60). But in Florence, after the people forcibly denied the nobility any part in the government, "it was necessary for them . . . to be . . . similar to . . . the people in their conduct, spirit, and mode of living," if they wanted to regain any part. "So the virtue in

entails respect for the rules of combat and one's opponents, as opposed to narrowly seeking their own private advantage, political as well as economic.

arms and the generosity of spirit that were in the nobility were eliminat and in the people, where they never had been, they could not be rekindled; thus did Florence become ever more humble and abject."[23] In book 2 Machiavelli appeared to blame the intransigency of the Florentine nobles, who refused to share power with the people, for the troubled history of that republic. But at the beginning of book 3 he seems to be initiating a damning critique of the character and effects of the entirely popularly based polity and its leaders.

Machiavelli does not simply praise the mixed regime in Rome in contrast to the entirely popular polity of Florence, however. On the contrary, he points out that "whereas Rome, when its virtue was converted into arrogance, was reduced to such straits that it could not maintain itself without a prince, Florence arrived at the point that it could easily have been reordered in any form of government by a wise lawgiver" (*FH* 3.1; 105–6). The proximate results of the conflict between the two humors had been better in Rome, but the ultimate results could have been better in Florence than they had been in Rome—*if* anyone in power had known what to do. The problem in Florence was a lack of political understanding on the part of the "men of the people" (including, although Machiavelli does not say so explicitly here, the Medici).

In the *Discourses* Machiavelli argued that Rome had the good fortune of electing three virtuous kings in succession, and concluded in discussing the third that "if where there are men there are no soldiers, it arises through a defect of the prince and not through any other defect, either of the site or of nature" (*D* 1.21). Rome also had the good fortune of needing to defend its independence from neighboring cities; as a result both its people and its nobles learned to reward military virtue with honor, and there were many competitors. Because Florence had been established as a Roman colony, Machiavelli suggested at the beginning of Book 2, its citizens had not acquired the experience of governing or defending themselves. When an internal division arose between two sets of noble families, they looked to external arms to assist them; and that habit persisted even after the Ghibellines had been decisively defeated. Even worse, after their army was destroyed by Castruccio, the Florentines sought not merely to defend their own city but to acquire empire over others with foreign troops. There was no prince like Tullus who raised and trained a new army of Florentine

23. Jurdjevic, *Great and Wretched City*, 104–31, so reads it.

zens. Instead, like the Roman patricians and plebs in appointing the Decemvirs, the nobles and the people of Florence, in seeking to deprive the other humor of any power, made Walter, duke of Athens, a tyrant. However, Machiavelli shows, in contrast to the Roman senators who told the plebs what to demand and what not, and the tribune who persuaded them not to continue persecuting all patricians after they had brought down the tyrannical Appius (*D* 1.40–45), the Florentine nobles attempted to seize all power for themselves with force. It was not simply the difference in their historical experience or the more decent and just desires of the Roman people that were responsible for the different fates of the two republics. Because they had a superior understanding of political necessity, the Roman senators had preserved the liberty of the city for centuries by "temporizing" in various ways with the demands of the plebs; and the plebs had been able to demand an increasing role in the government because they were armed. Florence experienced a continuing failure of leadership, most particularly in the failure of its leaders to arm the people and to give them a part in the government.

The problem after the destruction of the nobility was not simply that the Florentines lost their arms. In fact, Machiavelli reports, both the city and many of its citizens saw a need to protect themselves from the mercenary soldiers hired by the pontiffs and emperors and then left in Italy at the end of their employment. But the families competing for control of the republic, the Albizzi and Ricci, did not join forces to form a citizen militia. These "men of the people" (the wealthy merchants who called themselves *popolari*) did not see their arms as means of protecting the republic from its enemies or of acquiring political power for themselves. Like the Roman generals who waged the civil war that brought down the republic, "each sought with greater diligence to acquire partisans. However, because the citizens had already attained such equality through the ruin of the great that the magistrates were more revered than they used to be in the past, they planned to prevail by the ordinary way and without private violence" (*FH* 3.2; 107).

Machiavelli has an anonymous representative of the people describe the disastrous results: Since Italy "extricated itself from under the forces of the empire, its cities have had no powerful check to restrain them and have ordered their states and governments so as not to be free but divided into sects." With the fear of foreign domination gone, they no longer look to the pope for help. "Because religion and fear of God have been eliminated in all, an oath and faith given last only as long as they are useful." And that use is primarily to deceive others, as when "the promoters and princes of parties give decent appearance to their intention and their end with a pious word." They "are all enemies of freedom, [but] they oppress it under color of defending the state. . . . For the prize they desire to gain by victory is not the glory of having liberated the city but the satisfaction of having overcome others and of having usurped the principality of the city. . . . Hence orders and laws are made not for the public but for personal utility" (*FH* 3.5; 109–10).

This representative of the people asked the Signori to reform the government in order to rid Florence of these evils, and the magistrates granted fifty-six citizens authority to do so. However, this attempted reform did not work any better than those previously adopted. Echoing his observation in *D* 1.58 that princes may be better at designing and introducing new laws and orders, but peoples are much better at maintaining them, Machiavelli comments: "it is very true that most men are more apt to preserve a good order than to know how to find one for themselves. These citizens gave more thought to eliminating the present sects than to taking away the causes of future ones; so they achieved neither the one nor the other" (*FH* 3.5; 112). To put an end to the current conflict, they excluded the three leading members of both the warring families from all magistracies for three years, and forbade all citizens from entering the palace of the Signori unless the magistrates were sitting. The reformers intended to penalize both parties equally, but, in fact, they unintentionally favored the Albizzi at the expense of the Ricci, because the palace of the Guelf party was still open, and their adherents were able to gather and organize there.

Again, Machiavelli shows that the bad results of this reform were not immediately felt, because an external threat provoked the Florentines to take common action and temporarily to create an effective emergency government. When a legate of Pope Gregory XI refused to offer Florence succor in the midst of a famine, and instead sent a great army to conquer the city, "the Florentines, having no better remedy, gave his soldiers one hundred and thirty thousand florins and made them abandon the campaign." The Florentines knew how to use money to deal with mercenaries; but, Machiavelli points out, "Wars begin at the will of anyone, but they do not end at anyone's will" (*FH* 3.7; 113). The legate's perfidy aroused the indignation of the Florentines, who not only made an alliance with Bernabò of Milan and all the other cities hostile to the Church, but also created a board of eight citizens to administer the war with authority to act without appeal and spend without rendering an account. Once the war had been won, however, the use of the plenary authority by the eight provoked a reaction against it.[24]

Fighting broke out in the streets of Florence after Salvestro de' Medici was drawn as gonfalonier. "This man, born of a very noble popular family, could not bear that the people should be oppressed by a few powerful men." He thus secretly resolved with some friends to pass a law "to renew the Orders of Justice against the great, to diminish the authority of the captains of the [Guelf] Party, and to" restore the hundreds of citizens who had been prohibited from seeking public office the full rights of citizens. To get the law enacted as expeditiously as possible, he had both the college (upper house) and the council (lower, more popular house) meet simultaneously. When the college refused to ratify the law, he excused himself and went to the council, where he threatened to resign. He protested that he had "been made a Gonfalonier not to be a judge of private causes, which had their own ordinary judges, but to watch over the state—to correct the insolence of the powerful and to temper those laws" which would ruin the republic. However, "the malignity of men so opposed his just enterprises that the way to doing good had been taken from him" (*FH* 3.9; 116). At this point members of the council began fighting among themselves, and, leaning out of the window, one of them called the people to arms.

"No one should make a change in a city believing that he can stop it at his convenience or regulate it in his mode," Machiavelli warns.[25] Salvestro intended to make a law that would put the city to rest, but "the humors set in motion had changed everyone so that the stores did not open, the citizens fortified themselves in their homes, many hid their movable goods in the monasteries and churches" (*FH* 3.10; 117), and various groups met to discuss what should be done. The next day the guilds brought out their banners and a large number of armed men assembled in the piazza. In the hope of calming everyone down, the council granted the Signori, Collegi, the Eight, the captains of the Party, and the guild syndics a general power

24. Machiavelli praises the eight for having administered the war with such virtue that their magistracy was extended every year "and they were called Saints even though they had little regard for censures, had despoiled the churches of their goods, and had compelled the clergy to celebrate the offices—so much more did those citizens then esteem their fatherland than their souls [as the translators note Machiavelli said he did in his letter to Vettori of April 16, 1527]. And they showed the Church that just as before they had defended it as friends, so now as enemies they could afflict it; for they made all Romagna, the Marches, and Perugia rebel" (*FH* 3.7; 114).

25. As Machiavelli observed in *P* 2, "one change always leaves a dentation for the building of another."

to reform the state. But violence erupted almost immediately when "those of lesser quality" sacked and burned the house of one of the leading Guelfs. And once begun, the violence escalated.

"Because it is not enough for men to get back their own but they want also to seize what belongs to others and to get revenge," Machiavelli explains, "those who put their hopes in disorders pointed out to the artisans that they would never be safe if their many enemies were not driven out and destroyed" (*FH* 3.11; 119). They appealed to "the hatred that the lesser people had for the rich citizens and princes of the guilds, since it did not appear to them that they had been satisfied for their labor as they believed they justly deserved" (*FH* 3.12; 121).[26]

According to Machiavelli, "one of the most daring and more experienced" men of the plebs conceded that if they were deliberating about whether to take up arms, he might favor the acceptance of quiet poverty rather than seek perilous gain. However, since they had already taken up arms and committed many crimes, they needed to think about the best way of avoiding punishment themselves and gaining more freedom from their past oppressors. They should involve as many people and make the rioting as widespread and destructive as possible, "because when many err no one is punished, and though small faults are punished, great and grave ones are rewarded."[27] Nor should they let themselves be restrained by either conscience or reverence for their "superiors." "For all men, having had the same beginning, are equally ancient and have been made by nature in one mode. Strip all of us naked, you will see that we are alike; dress us in their clothes and them in ours, and without a doubt we shall appear noble and they ignoble, for only poverty and riches make us unequal." And, he concluded, "where there is . . . fear of hunger and prison, there cannot and should not be fear of hell." Their present position was neither desirable nor tenable; but they could be assured that "all those who come to great riches and great power have obtained them either by fraud or by force; and

26. Machiavelli explains that "in the ordering of the guild corporations, many of those occupations in which the lesser people and the lowest plebs were engaged were left without guild corporations of their own, but were subordinated under" others. So "when they were either not satisfied for their labor or in some mode oppressed by their masters, they had no other place of refuge than the magistracy of the guild that governed them, from which it did not appear to them that they got the justice they judged was suitable" (*FH* 3.12; 121). See Gene Brucker, *Renaissance Florence* (Berkeley: University of California Press, 1983), 157–60.

27. He thus recommended a policy, Machiavelli reports in *D* 3.32, that some of the ancient enemies of the Romans and the Carthaginians adopted.

afterwards, to hide the ugliness of acquisition, they make it decent by applying the false title of earnings to things they have usurped by deceit or by violence." The plebs, "therefore, should use force whenever the occasion for it is given to us; nor can a greater occasion be offered us by fortune than this one, when citizens are still disunited." The speaker admitted that he was advocating a risky course of action, but he promised, either they would be "left princes of all the city" or they would "have so large a part of it" that not merely would their past errors be pardoned, but they would have the power to threaten their former oppressors with new injuries (*FH* 3.13; 122–23).

Machiavelli does not comment directly on what is the theoretically most interesting and radical argument about the foundations and nature of government to be found in the *Florentine Histories*. Instead he lets events speak for themselves. The plebs succeeded in seizing control of the republic by force when most of the armed men the Signori had ordered to defend them stayed home and the eighty who showed up quickly retreated when confronted with a thousand or more men with arms in the piazza. Far from demonstrating the equality of all men without clothes, however, Machiavelli reports that a scantily clad wool carder holding the sign of the gonfalonier of justice led the mob into the palace of the Signori and, having reached the audience chamber, turned to ask them what they wanted. They shouted that "they wanted him to be Gonfalonier and lord, and to govern them and the city however seemed best to him" (*FH* 3.16).[28]

28. Noting that there is no historical record of such a speech, Yves Winter, "Plebian Politics: Machiavelli and the Ciompi Uprising," *Political Theory* 40, no. 6 (2012): 754–56, suggests that it is especially appropriate for a theoretical speech to be delivered anonymously; it is and should be a general argument, which may thus reflect the views of the author. It is also especially appropriate for a plebian speaker not to be identified by his name or family; he would not be so known to his contemporaries. The problem with Winter's first argument is that Machiavelli presents more than one anonymous speaker (e.g., the men of the middle in *FH* 2.14, and the representative of the citizens who loved their fatherland in *FH* 3.5). By making the speakers anonymous, Machiavelli may indicate that he made up the speeches he attributes to them. He seems to say as much in the dedication. However, even if these anonymous comments represent Machiavelli's views, the speakers and their comments are sufficiently different that no one can be taken to represent the view of the author as a whole without more explanation. The problem with Winter's second argument is that Machiavelli names the plebian who actually takes the lead of the rioters, Michele di Lando. Relying on Mark Phillips, "Barefoot Boy Makes Good: A Study of Machiavelli's Historiography," *Speculum: A Journal of Medieval Studies* 59 (1984): 598–603, Winter maintains that Machiavelli's account of the uprising owes too much to Bruni, who, in contrast to the fourteenth-century chroniclers, inflated the roles of Salvestro de' Medici and Michele. The chroniclers had emphasized the role of groups, whereas Bruni emphasized the responsibility of individuals. However, although Machiavelli chose to incorporate this aspect of Bruni's account, as Phillips points out, Machiavelli did not follow it in all respects. Moreover, Machiavelli reminds his readers in *FH* 7.3 that he himself has a family name

Machiavelli consistently maintains that individuals are born with different inclinations and talents that are then shaped and hardened by their experience (*P* 25, *D* 3.9; 22). So he shows here that, despite his humble occupation and lack of education, Michele di Lando "accepted the lordship," and "because he was a sagacious and prudent man who owed more to nature than to fortune, he resolved to quiet the city and stop the tumults. To keep the people busy and to give himself time to get in order, he commanded them to seek out one Ser Nuto," the foreign sheriff appointed by the previous government, who would have punished them, and to bring him to the piazza, where, hung by one foot, his body was literally torn to bits by the crowd. Michele thus gave the people a means of venting their humor (cf. *D* 1.7), while he took the opportunity to reestablish law and order by having "it publicly commanded that no one burn or steal anything, and to frighten everyone, he had a gallows erected in the piazza." He also began to reform the city by dismissing all the sitting magistrates of the guilds, both Signori and Collegi, and burning the old bags. Dividing the state into three parts, he redistributed the eight members of a newly created Signoria, taking "four from the lesser plebs as well as allocating two to the greater and two to the lesser guilds," and made a new bagging. Finally he granted

---

and that one of his ancestors was killed because he opposed the tyrannical regime. He is not and cannot thus be simply identified with a nameless pleb. In *TM*, 131–32, Strauss suggests that the anonymous plebian leader is a "caricature" of Machiavelli, especially in encouraging the plebs not to be frightened by conscience, i.e., by fear of hell. "But the caricature of a man reveals something of the man himself." According to Strauss, "Machiavelli . . . does not seriously disagree with Livy's judgment on the multitude. He does disagree with Livy, and with 'all writers,' on the status of morality." He questions "the traditional view of aristocracy or the rule of men of moral worth. But questioning the traditional view of aristocracy is very different from adopting the extremely populist view which he seems to adopt in the 58th chapter [of *D* 1]. . . . According to Machiavelli, his dissection of the Roman republic entitles him to judge that the ruling class deserving of the name is necessarily superior to the multitude in foresight, but is certainly not morally superior; rather it is morally inferior to its subjects. To the extent to which he ironically accepts the major premise that human excellence is moral excellence, he arrives at the conclusion that the multitude is simply superior to 'princes.'" But Strauss continues, "this does not mean that the acceptance of that major premise is arbitrary. Machiavelli . . . is a revolutionary, i.e., his adversaries have on their side the laws and everything respected and honored. Compared with the powers which he attacks, he may very well appear as he describes himself, namely, a being of low and abject condition; and, as he teaches, one rises from such a condition through fraud rather than through other means. He is 'a man of the people' not only in the literal sense." However, Strauss concludes, "even a plebeian leader is not simply a plebeian, and a leader of the plebs is not necessarily himself a plebeian." Having identified the anonymous plebian with Machiavelli, Strauss does not comment on the plebian leader who Machiavelli shows actually took charge. Machiavelli praises Michele for both his "goodness" and the "prudence" that enabled him to institute a new government, but he also shows that Michele did not know how to maintain his and his party's place in it. Good and honest like the people, Michele did not understand and was not, therefore, able to protect himself and the people from the attempts of the popular nobles to regain control of the government.

himself, Salvestro de' Medici, and other friends of the plebs benefits, "not so much to compensate them for their deeds as that they might . . . defend him against envy" (*FH* 3.16; 127–28).[29]

However, Machiavelli shows, envy of this clearly extraordinary natural leader who emerged in a crisis could not be so easily overcome. (Cf. *D* 3.16, 30.) Because Michele had not delivered the state entirely into the hands of the plebs, but had shared power in it with the guilds, the mob took up arms again and came to the palace with new demands. Michele "censured the mode in which they made their demands and urged them to put down their arms." Becoming indignant, the multitude "withdrew to Santa Maria Novella" where they created their own government. They then sent two envoys to demand that this government be recognized in order to obtain "what they wanted by force if they could not get it by accord." Angered by their arrogance, and "mindful more of the rank he held than of his own condition," Michele decided that he had to "check this extraordinary insolence with an extraordinary mode." So he attacked the two envoys with the weapon at his side and had them imprisoned. Enraged by the treatment of their emissaries, the multitude marched on the palace. "Thinking that it would be more to his glory to attack others than to wait for the enemy within the walls and to have to flee," Michele "decided to forestall it" (and so acted in marked contrast to the previous Signori who fled before the mob). Taking a different route in going to meet the mob than they had taken going to attack the palace, he turned around to attack them from the rear in the piazza and "conquered them." Machiavelli concludes that "the tumults were settled solely by the virtue of the Gonfalonier," who thus "deserves to be numbered among the few who have benefited their fatherland, for had his spirit been either malign or ambitious, the republic would have lost its freedom altogether and fallen under a greater tyranny

29. Phillips, "Barefoot Boy Makes Good," reports that the contemporary (1378) chronicles by Alamanno Acciaiuoli, Marchionne Stefani, and the *Squittinatore* explain that a scantily clad wool worker emerged as leader of the mob and took complete charge of the government of Florence for two to three days, but they do not mention or record his speech. Nor do they record that Michele ordered the mob to erect a gallows in the Piazza of the Priors or to search and find Ser Nuto. Machiavelli builds upon Bruni's later description of Michele as possessing "a certain naïve authority and a character that was not ignoble" (Leonardo Bruni Aretino, *Historiarum Fiorentini popoli libri XII*, Rerum Italicarum Scriptores 19 [Città di Castello, 1917–34], 224). But none of the sources shows Michele explaining and developing a strategy for seizing control of the city and restoring order the way Machiavelli does. Interestingly, Machiavelli attributes Michele's ability to do so entirely to his exceptional nature; unlike Bruni, Machiavelli does not attribute Michele's ability to lead and organize the mob even in part to experience he had as a soldier in Lombardy.

than that of the duke of Athens. But his goodness never allowed a thought to enter his mind that might be contrary to the universal good; his prudence led him to conduct things in such a mode that many yielded to his party and others he was able to subdue with arms" (*FH* 3.17; 130).[30]

Despite his generous spirit, prudence, and goodness, Machiavelli nevertheless shows, Michele was not able to maintain his government for long. Somewhat ironically, his example not only led "the better guildsmen . . . to consider what ignominy it was for those who had overcome the pride of the great to have to bear the stench of the plebs"; it also showed them the means of freeing themselves. "When the new Signori assumed the magistracy, the piazza was found to be full of armed men." They shouted that "they did not want any of the lesser people to be Signori." The Signori then deprived the lesser guilds of their right to select or serve as two of the highest magistrates of the city, "except for Michele di Lando . . . and some others of better quality" (*FH* 3.18; 130).

The state divided between the popular nobles and the guildsmen of lesser quality "lasted for three years [1378–81]. Because those who governed lived with the greatest suspicion" (*FH* 3.18; 131) of further rebellions and attempts to seize control of the state, many individuals were accused and admonished, exiled, or sentenced to death unjustly and illegally. Following the execution of one of the popular nobles who had been leading the city, many groups thus took up arms.[31] Two parliaments and several

30. Maurice Suchowlansky, "Rhetoric of Violence in Machiavelli's *Florentine Histories,*" http://Shakespeare.edel.univ-poitiers.fr/index.php?id=549, thus argues that Machiavelli presents Michele as a hero, an exemplary figure able to channel the ferocity of the plebians, capable of reorganizing the Florentine republic and creating a fairer system of political participation. But some commentators, e.g., Martine Leibovici, "From Fight to Debate: Machiavelli and the Revolt of the Ciompi," *Philosophy and Social Criticism* 28, no. 6 (2002): 647–60, continue to celebrate "the boundlessness of the desire for freedom that exceeds all definite developments" (658). Although Machiavelli praises Michele for having brought more of the Florentine population into the government, he also shows that the guilds and their banners, first instituted by a Ghibelline government trying to prevent the resurgence of their Guelf opposition, pressed for most of the changes in the government and were responsible for the final results. The force of the multitude needs to be organized, Machiavelli repeatedly shows, in order to be politically effective.

31. Machiavelli's listing of the many "diverse humors" each with "a different end"—the "ancient nobles, called 'great'" who wanted to recover their public honors and "for this would have loved that authority be given back to the captains of the Party," "the popular nobles and the greater guilds" who "were not pleased with having to share the state with the lesser guilds and the lesser people," "the lesser guilds" who "wanted rather to increase than diminish their dignity," and "the lesser people [who] were afraid lest they lose their Collegi from their guilds" (*FH* 3.21; 134–35)—has led some commentators (e.g., Najemy and Jurdjevic) to argue that in his *Florentine Histories* Machiavelli moved away from his division of all cities into the two opposed humors of the

balìe (committees authorized to exercise all legislative and executive functions) were created to reform the city, and after much tumult, a government was established that deprived the lesser guilds of most of their share and allowed the party of the popular nobles to regain the state.

"This state was neither less injurious toward its citizens nor less oppressive in its beginnings than that of the plebs had been," Machiavelli comments; "for many popular nobles who had been known defenders of the plebs were banished, together with a large number of the plebian chiefs, among whom was Michele di Lando" (*FH* 3.22; 135). Michele was not able to maintain his state, Machiavelli indicates, because he did not have enough experience with the perfidy of the "nobles." He believed that they would protect him in exchange for benefits received and did not retain an organized group of followers in control of part of the government able to force the elite to include them.

New injuries brought new tumults, and the number of malcontents, both inside the city and out, grew. However, when some exiles conspired with some of the admonished living in the city to enter secretly, kill the head of the government, and call the people to arms, they found that no one followed. "Perceiving too late how dangerous it is to want to free a people who want in every mode to be enslaved," they "despaired of their undertaking and retreated to the church of Santa Reparata," where they were easily captured (*FH* 3.28; 143). It was not merely the "popular nobles" who had been corrupted under a government in which laws were passed solely in order to benefit the members of the party in power; the Florentine people had been corrupted by their example. Florence retained its independence, Machiavelli again shows, because of its good fortune, not the virtue of its leaders or citizens. The external powers that threatened to conquer it—Louis of France, Giovan Galeazzo Visconti of Milan, and Ladislas, king of Naples—all died before they could take advantage of their military victories.

"great" and the "people" in order to recognize more varied groups and economic interests. However, those humors which Machiavelli maintains *exist in all cities* constitute dispositions toward the government, not economic classes (even though the *grandi* are apt to be rich). The varied groups could, moreover, easily be divided into those who were seeking more power for themselves (like the "great") and those "lesser people" who wanted simply to keep what power and consequent protection they had.

Book 4: How a "Popular Noble" Acquired Tyrannical Power in Florence

Machiavelli begins book 4 with a summary reflection on the history he presented in book 3: "Cities, and especially those not well ordered that are administered under the name of republic, frequently change their governments . . . not between liberty and servitude, as many believe, but between servitude and license. For *only the name of freedom is extolled by the ministers of license*, who are *the men of the people* (*popolari*), and *by the ministers of servitude*, who are *the nobles* (*nobili*), neither of them desiring to be subject either to the laws or to men" (emphasis added). Some ancient republics had been fortunate enough to have a "wise, good, and powerful citizen" able to establish laws to quiet or restrain these humors of the nobles and men of the people. Such a "city can be called free and that state be judged stable." Florence had not been so lucky; and in a republic without good laws, the state can "be maintained only by the virtue and fortune of a single man who can either fail by death or become useless because of his travails" (*FH* 4.1; 146; cf. *D* 1.10).

Applying this general observation to the government of Florence after 1381, Machiavelli observes that "the state that had its beginning in Florence with the death of Messer Giorgio Scali . . . was sustained first by the virtue of Messer Maso degli Albizzi, later by that of Niccolò da Uzzano."[32] But he shows that the deeds of the first and the prudent advice of the second served only to postpone the Medici family's taking effective control of the state.

Taking revenge for the death of his grandfather Piero at the hands of the Alberti, Messer Maso managed to have the families who had headed the popular party—the Alberti, Ricci, and Medici—despoiled of men and riches by banishing, admonishing, and fining them. However, "because the humor of that party was shared by the greater part of the city, it could never be altogether eliminated." Many men retained "a memory of injuries received and a desire to avenge them." And "those popular nobles who governed the city peacefully made two errors that were the ruin of their state: one was that they became insolent through unbroken dominion; the

32. In *D* 1.17 Machiavelli gave Dion and Timoleon as examples of virtuous citizens who kept their city free while each lived, but whose cities returned to tyranny after they died. Here he gives examples of individuals whose virtues maintained the tyranny of the *popolari*.

other was that through the envy they had of each other, and through long possession of the state, they did not take the care they should have for whoever could offend them" (*FH* 4.2; 146–47). So it was that "they made the Medici family regain authority" (*FH* 4.3; 147).

Niccolò da Uzzano warned his colleagues about the dangers of fostering the reputation of Giovanni di Bicci de' Medici, who, because he was "very rich and . . . of a kindly and humane nature, . . . was brought to the highest magistracy by the concession of those who were governing." Most of the people were overjoyed, "since to the multitude it appeared that it had gained a defender" from those in power. It would be easy to block the rise of such an individual at the beginning, Niccolò told his party, but difficult to remedy if his rise were left unchecked. More envious of Niccolò's reputation than fearful of Giovanni, his peers refused to listen.[33]

Niccolò's colleagues did not see immediately how shortsighted they had been. Despite Giovanni's opposition, Rinaldo degli Albizzi was able to persuade an assembly of many citizens to undertake a preemptive war against the duke of Milan. But after the Florentines were defeated, the people blamed the "great citizens" (*cittadini grandi*) who had argued in favor of war; and the committee appointed to create a new tax levied it primarily on the great. "Many of the first citizens . . . [concluded] that it was a necessity for them to take back the state, because their own lack of care had . . . made bold those who were used to being the heads of the multitude" (*FH* 4.8; 153). Rinaldo convened a secret meeting of these citizens, and Niccolò da Uzzano agreed that they should attempt to retake control of the government—*if* they could do so "without coming to an open division in the city" (*FH* 4.9; 154). That would not be possible, however, without Giovanni de' Medici's agreeing to their plans.

Giovanni did not agree. He warned Rinaldo against taking "authority from the people by means of your forces, . . . [because] the people will have become your enemy for this injury." Instead he advised Rinaldo "to imitate his father, who, so as to get universal good will, lowered the price

33. We see the way in which Machiavelli alters history in order to support the lesson he purports to derive from it when we compare what he says in praise of Niccolò da Uzzano in *FH* 4.3, 4.19, 4.27 with *D* 1.33. There in arguing that "when an inconvenience has grown either in a state or against a state, the more salutary policy is to temporize with it rather than to strike at it," Machiavelli writes: "Niccolò da Uzzano, a man held to be very expert in civil affairs, . . . had made the first error of not recognizing the dangers that could arise from the reputation of Cosimo. [But] while he lived, he did not ever permit the second to be made—that is, of attempting to eliminate him—since he judged that such an attempt would be the entire ruin of their state, as one sees it was after his death" (72).

of salt, provided that anyone whose tax was less than half a florin might pay it or not as he saw fit, and that on the day the councils assembled, everyone might be safe from his creditors" (*FH* 4.10; 155). In other words, rather than trying to eliminate his competition and risk civil war by seizing control of the state by force, Giovanni advised Rinaldo to act the way Machiavelli had urged his Florentine readers in his *Discourses* (1.32; 51) to imitate the Romans: to compete for political office by gaining the favor of the multitude and passing laws that benefited them. Instead of joining the great in opposing the tax that weighed so heavily on them, Giovanni openly praised it, since it "placed a partial restraint on the tyranny of the powerful, because they could not strike at lesser persons and by threats make them keep silent in the councils as they were able to do before" (*FH* 4.10; 159).

Machiavelli does not restrict his criticism to the powerful, however. "As it happens that men are never satisfied and, having got one thing, do not content themselves with that but desire something else," he observes, "the people, not content with the equality in taxation that arose from the law, demanded that they return to time past to see how much less the powerful had paid" than those who had been forced to sell their possessions in order to pay the tax and make them pay the difference now. Giovanni de' Medici managed to quiet these humors for the moment by pointing out that "it was not good to go back over things past, but rather to provide for the future; and if the taxes had been unjust in the past, they should thank God that a mode had been found to make them just" (*FH* 4.14; 159–60; cf. Machiavelli's judgment of the Agrarian law in *D* 1.37). But Giovanni died soon thereafter. One virtuous individual is not enough to maintain a state, Machiavelli shows; he needs to establish institutions and laws that will last after he dies.

Feeling himself near death, Giovanni urged his sons Cosimo and Lorenzo to follow his example. With regard to the state Giovanni advised them, if they wished "to live secure, to accept from it as much as is given to you by laws and by men. This will bring you neither envy nor danger, since it is what a man takes himself, not what is given to a man, that makes us hate him." He had "never asked for honors yet had them all" (*FH* 4.16; 161).

However, Giovanni was not able merely by means of his example or admonitions to prevent his sons or political allies from seeking to acquire more power or wealth from their enemies. They wanted to enrich as well as to secure themselves by dominating others. So did the Florentine people. After they unexpectedly lost and then regained Volterra, and a mercenary captain employed by them captured two of the fortified places of the Lucchese, a great many wanted a campaign against Lucca to be undertaken. Machiavelli wryly comments: "That people who after ten years of peace had censured the war against Duke Filippo to defend their own city's freedom now, after so much expense incurred and with such distress in the city, were demanding that a war be started . . . to seize the freedom of others; . . . so much more ready is the multitude to seize what belongs to others than to watch out for its own. . . . Men are moved so much more by the hope of acquiring than by the fear of losing, for loss is not believed in unless it is close, while acquisition, even though distant, is hoped for" (*FH* 4.18; 164).

Among the great citizens who favored the war were the Medici, who were joined by Rinaldo. He pointed out the profit to be gained from the acquisition as well as the ease of acquiring it. None of the other Italian powers were apt to interfere, since at the end of the last war Lucca had been left to the Florentines as booty by the Venetians and Duke Filippo, and the pope was involved with affairs elsewhere. The citizens of Lucca were not apt to put up much resistance, moreover, because they were slave to one of its citizens. Recounting the injuries done to Florence by that lord, he concluded that no other campaign would be easier, more useful, or more just.

Niccolò da Uzzano objected to their hurting "a Guelf city that had always been friendly to the Florentine people" and reminded his audience that "a free Lucca had never harmed Florence," only her tyrants had. However, in a speech reminiscent of that Diodotus gives in Thucydides' history, he appealed to considerations not of justice, which he observed did not have much force in his day, but only of "utility to the city."[34] He conceded that the profit to be gained from the acquisition of Lucca was great, but, he emphasized, success was highly uncertain. "He urged them therefore to refrain from the campaign and to live with the tyrant so that he would make as many enemies as possible within. . . . For if the thing was governed prudently, that city would reach the point where the tyrant could not hold it, and neither knowing how nor being able to govern itself, [Lucca] would necessarily fall into their lap." However, "he saw that their humors were excited and that his words were not being heard" (*FH* 4.19; 166). The people, whom Machiavelli observed in *D* 1.53 are attracted to bold rather than

34. Thucydides 3.41–48. Unfortunately, Machiavelli also shows, Uzzano had less success.

cautious policies and fail to see the long-run costs hidden beneath immediate or promised gains, were too impatient to wait.

Machiavelli shows that things occurred as Niccolò predicted. The Florentines appointed two commissioners to lead the soldiers they hired to attack Lucca. Both acquired territory and booty, but one did so with such cruelty and fraud that he was recalled, condemned, and admonished.[35] When Rinaldo heard that he had been slandered by two of Cosimo's creatures, who claimed that he was "carrying on the war not for the profit of the Florentine people but for his own," his "sincere and haughty spirit" led him to give up his commission and return to Florence. "Since it was not the custom in Florence to allow citizens a triumph [as in Rome]," he protested, "it might at least be the custom to defend them from false abuse" (*FH* 4.22; 169).

Because the Florentine people had supported the war, they did not know whom to blame for its failure. They thus readily believed the slanders of the commissioners spread by Cosimo's creatures. "A very prudent man," Machiavelli comments, Cosimo "never attempted anything against either the Party or the state but took care to benefit everyone and with his liberality to make many citizens into his partisans. So his example increased the charge against those who were governing, and he himself judged that by this way he would either live in Florence as powerful and as safely as anyone else or, if because of the ambition of his adversaries it came to something extraordinary, he would be superior both in arms and in favor" (*FH* 4.26; 172–73).

Niccolò da Uzzano and the other heads of the party understood what Cosimo was attempting, but they were unable to find a remedy. Some wanted to unite behind Rinaldo in an effort to drive Cosimo out, but Niccolò responded: "Those who think of driving Cosimo out of Florence must, before everything else, measure their forces" against his. And, he made it clear, Cosimo's position was stronger.

First, Niccolò called his associates' attention to the power of relative numbers. They called themselves "the party of the nobles and the opposing side that of the plebs." Even if that were true, victory would be uncertain, because they would be few opposing many and apt to be defeated the same way the old nobility of the city had been. In fact, they had even more to fear

35. Machiavelli here treats the governors of Florence too kindly; the translators report (*FH* 4.21; 168n2) that Astorre was, in fact, acquitted.

since their party was fragmented, whereas their adversaries were united. Many families at that very meeting were divided; some out of envy of their brothers or relatives did not favor the self-styled "nobles" and favored the plebs. What dignity their party had "arises out of the ancient reputation of this state, which has been preserved for fifty years; but if it should come to a test in which our weakness was uncovered, we would lose it" (*FH* 4.26; 174).

Second, he pointed out the difficulties they would encounter in persuading others that their cause was just. "The deeds of Cosimo that make us suspect him are . . . [that] he helps everyone with his money, and not only private individuals but the public, and not only Florentines but the condottieri." We would "have to allege as causes for driving him out that he is merciful, helpful, liberal, and loved by everyone. And although these are all modes that send men flying to a princedom, . . . they are not believed to be so." Nor would their party be able to persuade others, because their mode of governing had destroyed the people's faith in them, and "the city, . . . since it has always lived with parties, is corrupt" (*FH* 4.26; 175).

Third, Niccolò reminded his colleagues that if they succeeded in driving Cosimo out, which they could easily do, since the Signoria at present happened to be favorable, they would find it difficult to prevent his returning. Because he would have so many friends remaining in the city, the next Signoria would be pressed to allow him to return, and they would have "driven out a good man who would return to us a wicked one because his nature would be corrupted by those who recalled him." And if they aimed to have him killed, they could not do so legally "by way of the magistrates because his money and your own corruptible minds will always save him" (*FH* 4.26; 175).

Finally, Niccolò objected, even if they succeeded in killing Cosimo or merely preventing his return, they would not gain anything, because if the republic "is freed from Cosimo, it becomes the slave of Messer Rinaldo." So he counseled them not to take "a course that is harmful in every way or believe that [they], accompanied by a few, can oppose the will of many; for all these citizens, partly out of ignorance and partly out of malice, are prepared to sell this republic, and so much is fortune their friend that they have found a buyer" (*FH* 4.176).

Once again, things occurred more or less as Niccolò da Uzzano predicted.[36] After his death his admonitions to his colleagues had no more effect

36. For this reason, many commentators take Niccolò da Uzzano to speak for the author. Yet, we have seen, Machiavelli attributes similar views to Giovanni de' Medici and shows that

than those of Giovanni de' Medici had on his sons. When the war with Lucca was terminated, the proud Rinaldo saw that he was left sole "prince" of his party; so he sought allies in an attempt to drive Cosimo out and take the state by force. He found a gonfalonier he could persuade to summon Cosimo and create a *balìa* to reform the state. However, because there was disagreement among the armed men assembled in the piazza about whether to kill, exile, pity, or fear Cosimo, no decision about his fate was taken immediately. He was imprisoned, and his jailor, not wanting to be implicated in his death, not merely ate with him (because Cosimo feared that he would be poisoned), but brought a friend to dine with him. Cosimo took the opportunity to pay this man to take a bribe to the gonfalonier, who accepted it and, as a result, banished Cosimo along with many of his relatives and creatures instead of killing him as Rinaldo desired. Cosimo accepted his banishment cheerfully, and in a gesture reminiscent of Julius Caesar (although Machiavelli does not note it), he offered himself and his property, in whatever place he might be, to the city, its people, and the Signori. The gonfalonier invited him to his home for dinner, "and then had him accompanied by many armed men to the borders. Wherever he passed, Cosimo was received with honor; and he was visited publicly by the Venetians, and not as an exile but honored as one placed in the highest rank" (*FH* 4.29; 179).

"It would have been better for them to have let things be than to have left Cosimo alive and his friends in Florence," Rinaldo told a group of friends, "because great men must either not be touched or, if touched, be eliminated."[37] But his colleagues refused to follow his advice to ally with the former great against the plebs. A year later, when a gonfalonier and all eight of the Signori whose names were drawn were friendly to Cosimo, Rinaldo again called the heads of his party together and urged them to seize control of the state by force. Again his colleagues hesitated; and when the new Signori assumed their offices, they agreed to bring Cosimo back. Summoned to the palace, Rinaldo "thought that he should delay no longer, and

---

they both failed to have the effect they desired. Unlike their opponents they either did not desire to organize a following (in the case of Giovanni, whose opposition to the formation of "sects" [*FH* 4.11] was not shared by his son Cosimo) or were not able to do so (in the case of Uzzano, whose reputation was envied by his colleagues).

37. Since this is a Roman policy that Machiavelli strongly recommends in *D* 2.23, one should be cautious about simply equating the views of Niccolò Machiavelli with those of Rinaldo's opponent, Niccolò da Uzzano. Whereas the latter advised his friends to remain neutral (*FH* 4.27; 176), Machiavelli explicitly argues against such a foreign policy in *P* 20, and in *D* 2.23 embraces Camillus's advice to the Romans not to take the middle way with those they conquered, but either to destroy or to embrace them.

he came out of his house with a great number of armed men" (*FH* 4.31; 181). But only two other heads of the party joined him; and while Rinaldo was waiting for others, the Signori seized the opportunity to propose a reconciliation. His two associates agreed to the terms. Left entirely alone, Rinaldo accepted Pope Eugene's offer to negotiate a settlement for him. However, the Signori postponed the negotiation while they secretly sent to Pistoia for infantry, with which they took control of the strongholds of the city. They then called the people into the piazza and created a new *balìa* to restore Cosimo to his fatherland and to banish Messer Rinaldo along with the associates who had failed to back his efforts. Bemoaning the end of any effective resistance to the rise of Cosimo, Machiavelli concludes, "thus Florence was deprived . . . not only of good men but of men of riches and industry" (*FH* 4.33; 183).

Books 5 and 6: On the Vileness of Mercenary Warfare

Cosimo's triumphal return from exile to Florence is the climatic event at the center of Machiavelli's history. Yet in the two books with which Machiavelli begins his account of the rule of the Medici, he says very little about the actions of its founder. Instead he devotes all but three of the thirty-five chapters of Book 5 and five of the thirty-eight chapters of Book 6 to detailing the shifting alliances and inconsequential battles fought by the mercenary captains who were employed by the equally unfaithful heads of the Milanese, Florentine, and Venetian states.

In *FH* 5.4 Machiavelli briefly describes the measures Cosimo's party took to secure their control of the state after his return. Following the pattern of parties that had taken control of the Florentine state previously, they banished their enemies and brought back their friends who had been exiled. But in contrast to the conclusions of the two civil wars in Rome, there was no bloodbath.[38] Like the popular nobles who had controlled the government of the republic before them, Cosimo's party proceeded primarily by making laws that favored them and penalized their opponents. So "in a short time, having driven out or impoverished all the enemy party, they secured the state for themselves" (*FH* 5.4; 190).

38. To arouse fear of opposition in others, they did behead one man and put to death the four exiles the Venetians returned to Florence as prisoners.

When the duke of Milan later sent Niccolò Piccinino to attack Florence, Cosimo's party did not have to do much to keep the government steady, because of the goodwill that Cosimo had among the people and "because they had restricted their chief magistrates to a few powerful men, who held firm with their severity" (*FH* 5.31; 222). But in the one—and only one—chapter Machiavelli describes Cosimo's foreign policy (*FH* 5.14), he shows that the head of the Medici party utterly failed to persuade the Venetians to help the Florentines oppose the duke, even though it would have been to the Venetians' advantage to do so.

Machiavelli explains the surprising shift in the focus of his analysis from the domestic to the foreign policy of the Florentine state in his introduction to book 5. He begins by suggesting that in human affairs nothing ever fundamentally changes (in which case the ascension of the Medici to power in Florence would be of only passing interest and importance). "Usually provinces go . . . from order to disorder and then pass again from disorder to order, for," as he observed in *D* 1.6 and 3.1, "worldly things are not allowed by nature to stand still." Like his incorporation and partial adaptation of Polybius's argument concerning the cycle of regimes in *D* 1.2, Machiavelli's observation here that "as soon as they [worldly things] reach their ultimate perfection, having no further to rise, they must descend; and similarly, once they have descended and through their disorders arrived at the ultimate depth, . . . of necessity they must rise" has convinced some commentators that he has a basically cyclical understanding of history.[39] "Virtue gives birth to quiet, quiet to leisure, leisure to disorder, disorder to ruin," he explains, "and similarly, from ruin order is born; from order, virtue, and from virtue, glory and good fortune." So the prudent have observed "that letters come after arms and that, in provinces and cities, captains arise before philosophers. For, as good and ordered armies give birth to victories and victories to quiet, the strength of well-armed spirits cannot be corrupted by a more honorable leisure than that of letters, nor can leisure enter into well-instituted cities with a greater and more dangerous deceit than this

39. Salvatore Di Maria, "Machiavelli's Ironic View of History: The *Istorie Fiorentine*," *Renaissance Quarterly* 45, no. 2 (Summer 1992): 248–70. He explicitly accepts the reading offered by Gennaro Sasso, *Niccolò Machiavelli: Storia del suo pensiero politico* (Naples: Instituto italiano per gli studi storici, 1958), 310, and "Machiavelli e la teoria dell' anacyclosis," *Rivista storica italiana* 70 (1958): 333–57, who distinguishes Machiavelli's understanding of the cycle from Polybius's, but nevertheless thinks that the former presents a cycle based on human rather than more generally natural causes. Hulliung (*Citizen Machiavelli*, 152–55), Pocock (*Machiavellian Moment*, 217), and Kersting (*Niccolò Machiavelli*, 62–73), also see Machiavelli adopting a version of the ancient cyclical view.

one." He thus praises Cato who, recognizing "the evil that could result to his fatherland from this honorable leisure, . . . saw to it that no philosopher could be accepted in Rome" (*FH* 5.1; 185).

Yet even those who had not read Machiavelli's *Discourses* would have known that Rome also fell and not, primarily, as a result of its embrace of philosophy.[40] And, in fact, Machiavelli's explanation of the rise and fall of order here applies better to Florence than to Rome, because the Medici were great patrons of philosophy along with the other arts. In Italy, Machiavelli observes, "men become wise from their afflictions" have not restored order, as did the ancient Tuscans and then the Romans, because they have been "suffocated by an extraordinary force." As in *D* 1.2, he thus acknowledges that the cycle does not hold.[41] And in explaining how and why it has not, he begins to level an implicit critique of the rule of the Medici that runs through books 5 and 6.

Machiavelli does not state what the "extraordinary force" that has prevented "men become wise from their afflictions" from restoring order in Italy is. He simply observes that "nothing was built upon the Roman ruins in a way that might have redeemed Italy from them, so that it might have been able to act gloriously under a virtuous principality." The five new cities and empires whose history he has described succeeded (until 1494) in defending the province from invasions by the northern "barbarians." However, he explains, "if from the virtue of these new principalities times did not arise that were quiet through a long peace, neither were they dangerous because of the harshness of war. For one cannot affirm it to be peace where principalities frequently attack one another with arms; yet they cannot be called wars in which men are not killed, cities are not sacked, principalities are not destroyed, for these wars . . . were begun without fear, carried on without danger, and ended without loss. So that virtue which in other provinces used to be eliminated in a long peace was eliminated by vileness in the provinces of Italy, as will be described by us from 1434 to 1494." In these disgraceful wars "will be seen how in the end the way was opened

40. In his *Discourses* Machiavelli also praises Cato, but for his opposition to Scipio, because he saw that such a preeminently virtuous individual was a potential tyrant. See *D* 1.29, 3.1. He does not mention Cato's opposition to philosophy, and he attributes the fall of the Roman republic to the greed that produced the civil wars and the prolongation of commands that enabled generals in those wars to acquire partisans.

41. As John M. Najemy, "Machiavelli and History," *Renaissance Quarterly* 67, no. 4 (2014): 44–45, also sees, Machiavelli undercuts the cyclical view in both places.

anew for the barbarians and how Italy put itself again in slavery to them" (*FH* 5.1; 186).

As he clearly stated the purpose and audience of the *Discourses* only in the preface to the second book, so Machiavelli makes the way in which his *Florentine Histories* are intended to add to his previous work explicit only in beginning the second half. Explaining the way and the reason why his history of the city differs from those of his predecessors, he first observes that "if the things done by our princes outside and at home may not be read, as are those of the ancients, with admiration for their virtue and greatness, they may perhaps be considered with no less admiration when it is seen how so many very noble peoples were held in check by such weak and badly directed armies." The fact that the leaders of Florence and the other cities of Italy had kept them independent of foreign domination could, in a certain sense, produce wonder or "admiration," precisely because that independence had not been achieved by the institution of good domestic orders, even in Venice (which in *D* 1.2–6 was Machiavelli's modern example of a republic ordered so that it did not need to expand in order to maintain itself). Although these leaders all wished to expand their respective dominions, they had not successfully imitated the necessarily expansive foreign policy Machiavelli recommended on the basis of the Roman example in *D* 6. On the contrary, "if in describing the things that happened in this devastated world one does not tell about either the strength of soldiers, or the virtue of the captain, or the love of the citizen for his fatherland, it will be seen with what deceits, with what guile and arts the princes, soldiers, and heads of republics conducted themselves so as to maintain the reputation they have not deserved. *It may, perhaps, be no less useful to know these things than to know the ancient ones, because, if the latter excite liberal spirits to follow them, the former will excite such spirits to avoid and eliminate them*" (*FH* 5.1; 185–86, emphasis added). The history of the interactions of the five Italian powers whose rise Machiavelli traced in the first book of his *Florentine Histories* is intended to serve as a negative example to persuade his readers to take a different tack.

The campaigns of the mercenary captains Machiavelli describes in book 5 support the charges he made against such soldiers in *P* 12 and *D* 2.20 in great detail. At the same time Machiavelli shows that the leaders of Milan, Venice, and Florence were no more anxious to keep the peace than the mercenaries they employed. In book 5 he describes the repeated attempts of the duke of Milan to expand his influence into Tuscany and Lombardy, and the corresponding attempts of the Florentines and Venetians to foil him.

Machiavelli brings his account of these inconsequential battles to a climax in describing the battle of Anghiari. After the Florentines repelled the attack on their city by the duke's mercenary captain, Niccolò Piccinino, they thought he would simply withdraw back to Lombardy. So they relaxed their defenses. But Piccinino decided to surprise them. Warned by the dust raised by his troops' horses on the road, the Florentines hurriedly put themselves in order, and in a battle lasting all day and all night they finally repulsed his troops at the bridge. But the "victory was more useful for Tuscany than harmful to the duke; for if the Florentines had lost the day, Tuscany was his; but having lost it himself, he lost nothing more than the arms and horses of his army, which he could replace with not much money" (*FH* 5.33; 227).

Instead of celebrating the victory that preserved the independence of the city (as the Florentines themselves did when their commissioners, Bernardetto de' Medici and Neri di Gino Capponi, returned to the city [*FH* 5.35; 229]), Machiavelli presents Anghiari as "a great example of the lack of success of these wars" (*FH* 5.34; 227).[42] Never were there "times when war waged in the countries of others was less dangerous for whoever waged it than these. In such a defeat and in so long a battle . . . , only one man died, and he not from wounds or any other virtuous blow, but, falling off his horse, he was trampled."[43] Knights in shining armor might have been thought to be emblematic of nobility, but Machiavelli debunks any such notion by observing the safety with which men then fought: "for they were all on horse and covered with armor, and being secure from death whenever they surrendered, there was no cause that they should die" (*FH* 5.33; 227).[44]

42. In fact, Machiavelli shows (*FH* 3.34; 228) that the victory had domestic as well as foreign benefits, insofar as it ended any hopes the Florentine exiles had of returning to the city. He downplays these benefits, perhaps because he characterized the hopes of the Florentine exiles earlier as "vain" in the mind of the duke of Milan (*FH* 5.9; 195) and warned his readers more generally about the danger of believing those who had been banished in *D* 2.31.

43. As the translators note (227n3), Machiavelli departs here from his source, Biondo, who suggests that at least seventy died in the battle of Anghiari. That's still a relatively low number of casualties in a daylong battle involving thousands of soldiers; but we see that Machiavelli exaggerates the low cost to support his critique of the military practices of his time.

44. Machiavelli does not explicitly point out that the Florentine troops defeated earlier at Zagora were cavalry (*FH* 4.6; 151n4), or comment on the fact that Neri specifically offered the Venetians the assistance of "the count with seven thousand cavalry and two thousand infantry" (*FH* 5.21; 210). But in books 5 and 6 Machiavelli makes it clear that the troops whose "vile" battles resulted in no lasting victories or losses were primarily on horse. Indeed, in these two books he appears to be trying to illustrate, if not, strictly speaking, to demonstrate, with a detailed account of recent Italian history the perfidy and basic ineffectiveness of such troops for which he argued generally

After Niccolò and his troops withdrew, the Florentine army showed a complete lack of discipline. The commissioners wanted to follow and besiege the enemy in order "to have a complete victory. But not one condottiere or soldier was willing to obey them. . . . The next day, at noon, without permission or regard for commissioner or captain, they went to Arezzo and, having left their booty there, returned to Anghiari—a thing so contrary to every praiseworthy order and military discipline that any remnant of an army, however ordered, could easily and deservedly have taken from them the victory that they had so undeservedly gained." Even worse, "when the commissioners wanted the men at arms who had been taken to be held, so as to deprive the enemy of the opportunity of reforming itself, they freed them" (*FH* 5.34; 227).

As Machiavelli points out in introducing book 6, the mercenary wars of his time were the polar opposites of the Roman model he recommended in his *Discourses* and *Art of War.* Roman patricians and plebs both benefited from the wars they fought, especially when the Romans were able to put the spoils into the public treasury and, as a result, did not need to tax citizens in order to support further wars. In the wars he has described, neither the victor nor the vanquished gained much, because both had to pay soldiers to fight, and neither acquired either land or goods, because their soldiers seized the booty they captured as spoils for themselves, did not remain in order to maintain control of the territory, and demanded new wages and equipment in order to fight another battle.

Because neither their victories nor their losses had any lasting effect, Machiavelli shows in book 6, the five major states in Italy were almost constantly at war in shifting coalitions. And, he suggests, these wars were caused by the ambitions of the mercenary captains even more than those of the princes who employed them, because the mercenary captains wanted to become princes themselves.

For example, Machiavelli reports that although he had been defeated at Anghiari, Niccolò Piccinino was soon able to collect more troops in Lombardy where he began attacking Count Sforza and the Venetians on behalf of the duke of Milan. Indeed, Niccolò was so successful that he would have

in the *Prince* (especially *P* 9) and *Discourses* (especially *D* 2.10–15, 2.20). (He observed in the preface that the excellence and persuasiveness of a history lies in the details.) He was, in other words, quite well aware of the form of military organization and "technology" that had replaced earlier citizen militias in Italy—and wanted to replace it for political more than strictly military reasons.

defeated the count, had he not angered the duke by demanding a grant of a small principality as a reward for his service. Vexed by his captain's insolence, the duke decided to come to terms with the count. Puzzled by his employer's rewarding an enemy rather than a friend, and threatened with worse punishment if he kept complaining, Niccolò kept fighting; and although he suffered a bad defeat the following year, he again brought the count and his forces to such extreme necessity that he would have conquered them, had he not been recalled to Milan. Told that the duke wanted to speak directly to him and continuing to hope for a proper reward for his services, Niccolò "abandoned a certain victory for an uncertain good" (*FH* 6.8; 238). In his absence, the count attacked, defeated Niccolò's forces, and captured his son Francesco. Seeing how he had been deceived, Niccolò died soon thereafter of grief. Machiavelli's account of the life of this mercenary serves as a perfect illustration of the reasons he presents in *D* 1.29–30 that no victorious captain should expect a reward from his prince.

Machiavelli shows that Count Francesco Sforza succeeded much better than Niccolò Piccinino in realizing his ambitions not merely by seizing and maintaining control of parts of the Marches, but, more importantly, by becoming duke of Milan. Sforza learned from bitter experience that he should not believe the promises of future rewards offered for his services, whether they came from the leaders of republics like Venice and Florence or solitary rulers. He acquired power on the basis of "his own arms," which included not only the troops he led and employed but also his understanding of the basis of his power in the needs of others.

After the duke died, the newly established republic of Milan discovered that they needed someone to defend them from the Venetians. So they agreed to employ the count on the same terms the duke had. But when he prepared his troops to attack Pavia, the citizens offered him the town on the condition that he not put them under the empire of Milan. Although he feared that he might anger his new Milanese employers, he agreed. "Nor was he restrained by fear or shame in breaking his faith," Machiavelli comments, "for great men call it shame to lose, not to acquire by deceit" (*FH* 6.17; 247).

The Milanese thought (correctly) that the count had revealed his ambition, but they did not feel free to express their outrage, because they needed him to defend them from the Venetians. But knowing that the Milanese feared that the count wanted to make himself their lord rather than merely their captain, the Venetians decided "to make peace with the count and to offer him help in the acquisition of Milan," because "they were persuaded that as soon as the Milanese saw they had been deceived by the count, in their indignation they would be willing to subject themselves to anyone rather than to him" (*FH* 6.19; 250). The count was "stung" by the words of the Milanese ambassadors who came to berate him for his perfidy; but he assessed the situation with great astuteness. "When the ambassadors had departed, the count ordered his troops so as to be able to assault the Milanese." Recognizing that the Venetians were not apt to remain his allies for long, the count also "sought to keep them loyal with a reward." He let them take Crema, and "this meal set before the Venetians was the cause that their friendship with the count lasted until the count had seized the whole dominion of the Milanese" (*FH* 6.22; 254). The despairing appeal the Milanese made to the Venetians to save another republic had no more effect than their ambassadors' reprimands of the count. The Venetians waited to secure Crema before they made an alliance with the Milanese; and the count used the time he was given to accept the peace to persuade his enemies that he had abandoned his ambitions by withdrawing his troops, and so encouraged them to neglect their defenses while he prepared a more effective siege. The next spring the Venetians decided not to risk a battle with the count in order to save Milan, because they thought the Milanese would never cede to the count. But the Milanese decided that if they had to give up their liberty, they would give it to someone able to defend them. The count thus entered Milan as prince on February 26, 1450.

Machiavelli's history of the struggle for control of Milan supports his contention in *P* 18 and *D* 1.59, 3.42 that "princes" (whether solitary or republican leaders) will always find reasons not to abide by their promises, if keeping those promises no longer serves their interests. But he also shows that the wars in Italy did not cease after the count realized his ambition to become duke.

Princes and republics might employ mercenary soldiers to further their ambitions, but as Fabrizio pointed out in the *Art of War* (1.51–62), mercenaries need wars in order to support themselves. So when "the Venetians, as is customary when peace is made, had dismissed from their hire Jacopo Piccinino, . . . joined by some other condottieri without employment, he came into Romagna and from there into the territory of Siena, where [he] stopped to make war" (*FH* 6.33; 268–69). Like other mercenary captains, Jacopo frequently switched from one employer to another; and like his father, he was finally deceived and executed by one of them.

Machiavelli shows that the best mercenary captains knew how to fight wars successfully. But he also demonstrates that hiring such men is dangerous for their employers, and that knowing how to fight and win battles does not, in itself, qualify a man to become a ruler.[45]

Machiavelli ends book 6 by noting that the Florentines had no part in the last war between France and Spain for control of the Kingdom of Naples. But he shows that they played a part in bringing it about by going to France and requesting the aid of the king against Alfonso, son of King Ferdinand of Aragon. In doing so, moreover, they suggested that the French king could use his aid to them as an excuse for taking Naples himself. Machiavelli does not say so explicitly, but he indicates that the Florentines were playing the same divisive role in Italy for which he initially blamed the Church. And for the same reasons: they were too weak to defend themselves and so had to call in foreign forces to protect them and their interests. To be sure, the Florentines were not alone in bringing in foreign troops. Naples was ruled by a son and then a nephew of the king of Spain. The Venetians allied with Alfonso, because they saw that having lost their fear of the duke of Milan, the Florentines had begun to fear them. The duke of Milan and Florence brought in the French to protect them from the Venetian-Spanish alliance. As Machiavelli emphasized at the conclusion of book 1, like the popes, all the other four major Italian powers had to seek assistance from abroad, because they did not have arms of their own. This was true even of the count, because his arms were the mercenary soldiers with whom he had taken Milan, not his citizens or subjects. Once he became duke, he had to pay them; he could not look to a foreign power to do so.

In *D* 1.6 Machiavelli suggested that a republic that did not find it necessary to defend itself would degenerate internally. And in book 7 of his

45. Christopher Lynch, "War and Foreign Affairs in Machiavelli's *Florentine Histories*," *Review of Politics* 74, no. 1 (2012): 1–26, rightly emphasizes the importance of both war and foreign affairs, but he goes too far in maintaining that "the relation between the house of Medici and the house of Sforza . . . reveal[s] the fundamental dependence of the former on the latter to be the chief factor determining the narrative line of the work overall" (2). Cosimo's success in buying support in domestic politics may have prevented him from understanding the ambition of the mercenary captain and his consequent refusal to fight wars on behalf of others after he became duke (*FH* 7.6). But Sforza's experience as a mercenary captain did not prepare him to rule as anything but a tyrant; and that was the "legacy" he left his son and grandson. Although Machiavelli brings out the many defects of Cosimo's rule, the weakness of his son Piero, and the less than magnificent actual achievements of Lorenzo "the Magnificent," their rule of Florence was certainly better than the treatment Sforza and his progeny gave the Milanese.

Florentine Histories he shows that this is exactly what happened in Florence during Cosimo's rule, when the city was fighting the "vile" inconsequential wars he describes in books 5 and 6 or was, finally, at peace. He begins to point out some of the internal consequences of the weak and ineffective foreign and military policies of the major Italian powers, however, even in book 6.

Although Machiavelli claims in *FH* 7.2 that Cosimo and Neri were united so long as the latter lived, in *FH* 6.6 he observed that Cosimo feared Neri's "reputation more than any other's because to the great credit he had in the city was added that which he had with the soldiers; for having been at the head of the Florentine armies many times, he had earned it with his virtue and his merits. Besides this, the memory of the victories credited to him and to his father Gino (Gino having taken Pisa and Neri having defeated Niccolò Piccinino at Anghiari) made him loved by many and feared by those who desired not to have him as partner in the government" (236). Some members of Cosimo's party thus sought to diminish Neri's reputation by assassinating one of his chief subordinates (and thus deprived Florence of a much needed potential defender). In *FH* 6.23 Machiavelli also reports that Neri and Cosimo disagreed about whether Florence should help the count seize control of Milan. Neri argued that as head of Milan the count would constitute a formidable challenge to the security of their city. But Cosimo's colleagues thought that Neri wanted to press the count to negotiate a peace rather than take Milan, because the count had always been a friend of Cosimo, and Cosimo continued to support him privately. So if the count took Milan, his friendship would increase Cosimo's influence not merely in Florence, but in Italy as a whole. Cosimo justified his position by observing (truly, as Machiavelli shows his readers in *FH* 7.33–34) that the Milanese people were not capable of sustaining a republic. But Machiavelli also shows that the Florentines did not train a citizen army under a very capable general because Cosimo's party feared that general would acquire partisans who would enable them to challenge his rule. There was as close a connection between Cosimo's failures in foreign policy and his party's attempt to acquire tyrannical control of the Florentine republic as there had been between the arming of the people and the preservation of liberty in Rome. As Machiavelli argued in his *Discourses* (1.29–30), every successful captain necessarily constitutes a threat to the government, but no republic will survive as such where there are not many princes vying for popular support.

Books 7 and 8: The Medici "Princes"—Cosimo, Piero, and Lorenzo the Magnificent

Machiavelli begins book 7 by apologizing for what might seem to have been a long digression on the condition of Italy as a whole in what was supposed to be a history of the city of Florence. Acknowledging that he never promised to write about the "things of Italy" (and so letting his reader see that he has departed somewhat from the order and contents of the book forecast in the preface), he states simply that without these things his history "would be less understood and less pleasing, since the wars in which the Florentines were compelled of necessity to intervene arose most times from the actions of other Italian peoples and princes" (*FH* 7.1; 276). Somewhat indirectly Machiavelli thus indicates the point of the preceding discussion of the wars fought in Italy during Cosimo's reign in Florence. His government showed itself to be weak and ineffective outside the city limits. Rather than taking bold initiatives, the Florentines acted only when prompted to do so by others. They were not able to extend their dominion to Lucca. Because they did not have their own arms, they were forced to rely on the self-serving count. And after he achieved his own ambition by becoming duke of Milan and refused to fight any more battles on behalf of others, they made Italy into the battleground between armies of the two emerging national monarchies of France and Spain, by inviting the French, in effect, to invade Italy to prevent the Spanish king from extending his dominion in Naples northward.

By first presenting a detailed account of the weak and undistinguished foreign policy of the Florentine state dominated by Cosimo's party, Machiavelli casts a dark shadow on the eulogy he gives of the founder of the Medici state. In book 7 he shows not merely that in the last decade of his life Cosimo was unable to maintain control of his own party. Like Cosimo's weak and ineffective foreign policy, the particular way in which Cosimo acquired (or, in foreign affairs, sought to acquire) political influence contributed to the internal corruption and tyranny that developed within his party. Crudely put, he tried to buy influence by doing personal favors as well as lending or giving money to individual citizens and mercenary soldiers like the count. But "money is not the sinew of war," as Machiavelli argued in *D* 2.10. "Truly powerful republics and princes buy friendships not with money but with virtue and the reputation of strength" (*D* 2.30).

Following the brief explanation of why he devoted two of the four books in the second half of the *Florentine Histories* to the foreign affairs of

Italy as a whole, Machiavelli shifts abruptly to introduce his account of the "travails inside" Florence with another general reflection. For the first time in the *Florentine Histories* he states unqualifiedly that "those who hope that a republic can be united are very much deceived." As in his introduction to book 3, he observes that "it is true that some divisions are harmful to republics and some are helpful." But here he does not distinguish between the nobler desire of the Roman plebs to share offices with the patricians and the destructive desire of the Florentine people to seize all power for themselves. Instead he distinguishes between divisions that are accompanied by sects and partisans, and the helpful divisions that are maintained without them. A founder of a republic cannot prevent the emergence of enmities, but he can prevent the emergence of sects by forcing its leading citizens to "acquire reputation" through public competition for honors rather than through acquiring personal dependents by benefiting them privately as individuals. As in *D* 3.28, Machiavelli argues that public means of competing for honors and office make it necessary for ambitious individuals "to attempt to exalt the republic and to watch each other particularly so that civil bounds are not transgressed." In the *Discourses* he showed that such public competition had beneficial results in Rome until the prolongation of commands made it possible for generals to acquire partisan armies. In Florence, he now observes, enmities "were always accompanied by sects and therefore always harmful, never did a winning sect remain united except when the hostile sect was active, but as soon as the one conquered was eliminated, the ruling one, no longer having fear to restrain it or order within itself to check it, would become divided again" (*FH* 7.1; 277).

As Harvey Mansfield observes, in the *Florentine Histories* Machiavelli never defines 'sect.'[46] In the *Discourses*, he uses the word consistently to describe religious organizations; and in *FH* 1.5 he observes that after the emperor withdrew from Rome to Constantinople, the people in Italy suffered as a result of the divisions among Christian sects. When he applies the term to Florentine politics, however, Machiavelli appears to have not religious so much as political organizations or parties in mind. What they had in common with the Christian religious sect (to which they all adhered) was their insistence that they alone should prevail; there could be no compromise or sharing of rule with their competitors. Since Machiavelli thinks that all human beings constantly seek to acquire more security,

46. Mansfield, "Party and Sect," 138.

goods, and reputation for themselves, he does not blame the Florentine politicians or people for wanting to satisfy their own desires. Nor does he think that Roman politicians altruistically sought the common good at the expense of their own. Over time, he shows, they devised a set of laws that forced ambitious nobles to compete with one another in seeking the support of the people. The Florentine 'sects' as he describes them were composed of men representing both of the humors that Machiavelli contends exist in every city. What distinguished the divisions in Florence from those between the patricians and plebs in Rome was first that the Florentines were not continually united by the necessity of defending the city from foreign aggression. Their political habits were formed when Florence was a colony protected by Roman troops and persisted because there were no powers in Italy that threatened to conquer them if they did not arm themselves. And after the new tyrant of Lucca destroyed the Florentine army, they did not attempt to marshal and train a new one. They looked outside the city for defenders and tried to buy them instead of rebuilding their own defenses. The second and most obvious difference between the enmities between the humors in Rome and the sects in Florence was that, whether they fought in the streets or by means of law, the Florentines sought to destroy their domestic opponents in order to obtain complete control of the state. Their leaders did not compete for popular support in elections, because the Florentines selected their magistrates in an apparently democratic fashion by lot for short terms of office. By controlling whose names went into the bags, first the Guelf and then the Medici party was able to control the quickly changing official government of the republic. Although Machiavelli appears to praise the three Medici princes who in effect ruled Florence from 1434 until 1492, he shows that they imposed a relatively soft form of tyranny, not so much by force as by the destruction of all effective political opposition inside the city and the corruption of its people by means of the private, largely economic benefits they distributed.

A. Cosimo

"The ruling party of Cosimo de' Medici was left on top in 1434." However, "because the beaten party was large and full of very powerful men, Cosimo's party maintained itself united and humane for a time through fear." (This was the same fear that Machiavelli argued prevented the nobles from oppressing the plebs after Brutus banished the Tarquins in *D* 1.5.) So long as the party did not give the people any reason to hate it, they were willing to cede to its heads every *balià* and power that they desired. From 1434 to 1455, Cosimo's party reassumed the authority of the *balìa* (to restructure the government) six times ordinarily through the councils.[47] Although Neri acquired his reputation by public means (and thus aroused the envy and suspicions of Cosimo's partisans), whereas Cosimo used what Machiavelli calls private means, and they disagreed to a certain extent about Florentine foreign policy, they agreed about what needed to be done internally and were able to get what they wanted from the people without difficulty. After Neri died, however, some of Cosimo's "friends" saw no reason not to try to diminish his power. They decided not to use the power of the *balìa* again, because that would require an appeal to the people, but to lock up the bags from which the magistrates were drawn by lot so that no new names could be added. What had begun as a party headed by "popular nobles" such as Salvestro de' Medici, who sympathized with the people's desire to avoid oppression, no longer felt the need or wanted to rely upon popular support.

The people did not understand that they had lost power, because they had no leaders to point it out. Cosimo understood perfectly well what his party had done. But instead of trying to exercise his authority directly by attempting to take back control of the state from his former "friends" with force, he decided to teach them a lesson by allowing them to do what they wished. "Since the city had been brought back to creating magistrates by lot, it appeared to the generality of citizens that they had their liberty again and that the magistrates were judging in accordance not with the will of someone powerful but with their own judgment, so that sometimes a friend of someone powerful . . . was punished." As a result, "those who were used to seeing their houses full of well-wishers and gifts saw them empty of possessions and men. They also saw that they had become the equals of those whom they were long accustomed to consider

47. Jurdjevic, *Great and Wretched City*, 157, notes that Cosimo's party thus restructured the state (presumably to maintain its control and squelch any opposition) every 3.5 years, even more frequently than Machiavelli suggested in *D* 3.1, where he stated that "those who governed the state of Florence from 1434 up to 1494 used to say . . . that it was necessary to regain the state every five years; otherwise, it was difficult to maintain it." And "they called regaining the state putting that terror and that fear in men that had been put there in taking it, since at that time they had beaten down those who . . . had worked for ill. But as the memory of that beating is eliminated, men began to dare to try new things and to say evil" (211). The perceived need Cosimo and his party saw to retake (and restructure) the state suggests that they did not rule smoothly or uninterruptedly on the basis of simple consent.

inferior." But "what frightened the great more and gave Cosimo greater opportunity to make them recognize their mistake was the revival of the mode of the *catasto* of 1427, whereby the taxes were assessed not by men but by law" (*FH* 7.2; 278).

Fearful of losing their property (more than their political position and so demonstrating the same preference for property over honors that Machiavelli attributed to the Roman patricians in *D* 1.37), Cosimo's former friends and party members begged him to call for a parliament to restructure the government so that it would follow their desires. But because he wanted them to learn their lesson about the need to maintain popular support, Cosimo insisted that the law had "to be made in the ordinary way, with the will of the people and not by force" (*FH* 7.3; 279). The people refused to consent to a parliament, however. And Cosimo, thinking that it was not well to let things go so far that he could not bring them back later with ease, allowed Luca Pitti to press for the change in government, so that Luca would incur the blame if things went awry. They did. After the people repeatedly refused to consent to renew the *balìa*, Luca threatened the citizens sitting on the councils, and in August 1458, "having filled the palace with armed men, he called the people into the piazza and by force . . . made them consent to that which they had not consented to voluntarily before." Indicating his own judgment of this government, Machiavelli reports that "to give a beginning of terror to this government that they had begun with force" (*FH* 7.3; 279), they banished and finally killed Messer Girolamo Machiavelli (one of Niccolò's ancestors), and deprived many others of honors.

Contrary to his expectations, Cosimo was not able to retake control of the city. Luca Pitti was now in control. And "the other citizens, if they did not build as he did, were not less violent or less rapacious than he; thus if Florence did not have war from outside to destroy it, the city was destroyed by its own citizens" (*FH* 7.4; 280). The violence and rapacity of Cosimo's successors made even his enemies lament his death, because they saw that respect for him had made his colleagues less unbearable, and "they feared that without him they would be altogether ruined and destroyed." So even though he had proved unable to restrain the rapacity of his colleagues, "he died full of glory and with a very great name in the city and outside" (*FH* 7.5; 281–82).

After an extremely brief account of the thirty-one years in which Cosimo, in effect, ruled Florence, in which Machiavelli emphasizes the swift degeneration of Cosimo's party's rule when he became old and infirm,

Machiavelli launches upon a two-chapter eulogy.[48] In it he shows that Cosimo's ability to maintain his preeminence was a product of personal virtues that could not be institutionalized and that he was unable to pass on to his successors. He begins by declaring that "Cosimo was the most reputed and renowned citizen, as an *unarmed* man, of whom not only Florence but any other city had ever had memory" (emphasis added). Without stating it explicitly, Machiavelli thus emphasizes the difference between the rule Cosimo exercised in Florence and that of the Roman republican heroes such as Furius Camillus (who also was brought back from exile), with whom Machiavelli's humanistic predecessors (Leonardo Bruni and Poggio Bracciolini) regularly compared him. According to Machiavelli, Cosimo "surpassed every other man of his times not only in authority and riches but also in liberality and prudence, because among all the other qualities that made him *prince* in his fatherland was that, above all other men, he was liberal and magnificent" (*FH* 7.5; 281, emphasis added).

As evidence of his liberality Machiavelli points not merely to the "abundance" of richly furnished churches, monasteries, private homes that were "palaces not of private citizens but of kings" Cosimo built, in addition to a hospital for the poor and sick pilgrims in Jerusalem. As his son Piero discovered only after his father's death, there "was no other citizen who had any quality in that city to whom Cosimo had not lent a large sum of money." Yet, Machiavelli also indicates, Cosimo demonstrated his prudence by exercising a certain kind of restraint in his private life. "Although his dwellings like all his other works and actions were kingly, . . . he never overstepped civil modesty. For in his conversations, in his servants, in riding on horse, in his whole mode of living, and in his marriage alliances, he was always like any modest citizen." Unlike his son and grandson, "when [Cosimo] had to give wives to his sons, he did not look for alliances with princes" (*FH* 7.6; 281–82), but arranged for them to marry into other wealthy Florentine families. Although Machiavelli does not say so, Cosimo showed that he understood the main obstacle to becoming a "prince" in a republic better than Camillus did when he rode in triumph (*D* 3.23).

48. Machiavelli's brief account of Cosimo's rule with Neri for the first twenty-one years occupies less than a chapter; the challenges to his rule by other ambitious party members occupy most of three chapters. By way of contrast, he devotes eleven chapters to Piero's relatively brief and ineffective reign, and approximately one-third of book 7 in addition to virtually all of book 8 to the reign of his grandson, Lorenzo the Magnificent.

Machiavelli extols Cosimo's prudence more generally: "No one in his time was equal to him in his understanding of the states of princes and civil governments; hence, it arose that in such variety of fortune and in so various a city and so changeable a citizenry, he held one state for thirty-one years. For, being very prudent, he recognized evils at a distance and therefore was in time either not to let them grow or to be prepared so that, if they did grow, they would not offend him." In *P* 3 Machiavelli praised the same foresight in the Roman republic, especially with regard to the need to wage war. Cosimo was unarmed (and Machiavelli has criticized him indirectly for it). Yet here he observes that Cosimo was able not only to "conquer domestic and civil ambition, but [also to overcome] that of many princes with such prosperity and prudence that whoever allied with him and his fatherland would come out either equal or superior to the enemy, and whoever opposed him would lose his time and money or state." As he showed in books 5 and 6, the Venetians were able to oppose the dukes of Milan successfully only when they were allied with the Florentines; and now he adds that by using his own credit to empty the banks of Naples and Venice of money, Cosimo forced the Venetians to accept "the peace he was willing to concede to [them]." So Machiavelli concludes, "civil discords always increased his state in Florence, and wars outside increased his power and reputation, in consequence of which he added Borgo San Sepolcro, Montedoglio, the Casentino, and Val di Bano to the empire of his republic. And thus his virtue and fortune eliminated all his enemies and exalted his friends" (*FH* 7.5; 281–82).

Cosimo "was without learning but very eloquent and full of a natural prudence and was thus kindly to his friends, merciful to the poor, useful in conversations, cautious in advice, quick in executions, and in his sayings and replies he was keen and grave." He built many churches, but, as the sayings Machiavelli quotes show, Cosimo was not pious. "He said of Pope Pius when he was summoning princes to a campaign against the Turk that he was old and was carrying on a campaign for the young." Likewise, "when his wife asked him a few hours before his death why he kept his eyes closed, he answered, 'To get them used to it.'" Most telling, perhaps, "when some citizens told him after his return from exile that the city was being spoiled and that it was acting against God to send away from it so many men of means, he answered that a city spoiled was better than one lost, . . . and that states were not held with paternosters in hand" (*FH* 7.6; 283). As shown by his deeds, Cosimo recognized the need for a prince always to appear to be "merciful, faithful, humane, honest, religious" (*P* 18), but the impossibility of his always being so in fact. Like Castruccio, he knew that those in need come to princes in search of favors, but that princes command; they do not beg. Unlike Castruccio, however, Cosimo did not flaunt his disbelief in the Christian god or openly outrage the conventional morality of his fellow citizens, especially with regard to marriage.

Machiavelli reports that "Cosimo was also a lover and exalter of literary men; he therefore brought Argyropoulos to Florence, a man of Greek birth and very learned . . . , so that Florentine youth might learn from him the Greek language and other teachings of his. He took into his home Marsilio Ficino, second father of Platonic philosophy, whom he loved extremely" (*FH* 7.6; 283). But Machiavelli does not describe Cosimo, as did Argyropoulos and Ficino, as an Aristotelian gentleman or a Platonic philosopher-king.[49]

Ironically perhaps, Machiavelli's eulogy provides some of the best evidence for his claim in the dedication that he did not flatter the Medici. Although he describes the liberality, magnificence, and prudence that gained Cosimo favor both at home and abroad, and quotes some of the sayings that reveal his hardheaded insights, Machiavelli does not present this unarmed Florentine citizen as a Roman statesman or a philosopher-king, the way other writers he patronized did. Instead, Machiavelli concludes his eulogy with an account of Cosimo's own sense of his failure to leave an enduring legacy. He did not have a son healthy enough to take on the burden of his public or private affairs. Nor had he "increased the Florentine empire by an honorable acquisition." (He seems to have considered the places Machiavelli listed among his achievements to be small and insignificant.) Perhaps because he was a merchant, he did not understand that neither princes nor republics keep their promises. He had therefore been deceived by Francesco Sforza, who had promised to make a campaign against Lucca as soon as he had become lord of Milan, but then changed his mind.[50]

49. He certainly did not compare Cosimo to one of the Roman emperors, as did some of the lyric poets, who were seeking his patronage for their own work. Alison M. Brown, "The Humanist Portrait of Cosimo de' Medici, Pater Patriae," *Journal of the Warburg and Courtauld Institutes* 24 (1961): 186–221, presents a useful summary and tripartite categorization of previous humanist eulogies of Cosimo. She begins by noting that Machiavelli asked his readers not to be surprised that he "imitated those who write the lives of princes instead of those who write universal histories," and "that his description was the source of so much that was later written about him," but she does not point out the differences between Machiavelli and the earlier humanists' eulogies.

50. Machiavelli may have thought that as a prudent man Cosimo should have known that princes (and republics) can always find an excuse for not keeping faith. He does not disagree with Cosimo's characterization of the duke. In the next chapter (*FH* 7.7) Machiavelli describes the marriages and other alliances the duke and the king of Naples made with each other to "establish their

Cosimo saw "that, because of the infirmity of his body, he could not bring his former diligence to public or private affairs, so that . . . the city was being destroyed by the citizens and his substance by his agents and his sons." Yet, Machiavelli concludes, "he died full of glory and . . . on his tombstone he was named Father of his Fatherland" (*FH* 7.6; 284). Machiavelli himself does not call Cosimo father of his country. He has, in fact, shown that Cosimo had not fathered a lasting dynasty and knew that he had not.

B. Piero

Cosimo was correct in thinking that he had not established a firm succession, because his son Piero's weakness and infirmity would prevent him from managing either public or private family affairs. Shortly after Cosimo's death, Machiavelli reports, four of his old "friends" conspired to seize control of the state from his son. Cosimo had instructed Piero to follow the advice of his old friend Dietsalvi Neroni in administering the estate. Moved more by ambition than by gratitude or loyalty, however, Dietsalvi gave Piero seemingly good advice that would, in fact, ruin his reputation in Florence. Finding the accounts in disorder, Dietsalvi told Piero that he should call in all the debts owed his father or risk losing his own credit. When Piero did, he lost the support of many of his father's partisans and made enemies of others, who feared that their businesses would fail.[51] Dietsalvi then sought the cooperation of Luca Pitti, Agnolo

---

states so that they could enjoy them securely while they lived and leave them freely to their heirs when they died" (285). The king eliminated the barons who had injured him in the war against Jean of Anjou, and when Jacopo Piccinino saw this, he became afraid and sought to reconcile himself with the duke. The duke promised the mercenary captain marriage to his natural daughter, but fearing that Jacopo would attempt to seize power the way he himself had, Sforza arranged to have the king promise to employ Jacopo and bring him to Naples, where the king then imprisoned and killed the mercenary captain. "So much did our Italian princes fear in others the virtue that was not in themselves, and they eliminated it, so that, since no one remained who had it, they exposed this province to the ruin that not long after wasted and afflicted it" (*FH* 7.8; 286).

51. Rob Hatfield, "A Source for Machiavelli's Account of Piero de' Medici," *Studies on Machiavelli* (1972): 319–33, reports that neither he nor any other historian had been able to find any evidence of Piero's calling in his loans. (Hatfield cites R. de Roover, *The Rise and Fall of the Medici Bank* [Cambridge, MA: Harvard University Press, 1963], 359, and N. Rubinstein, *The Government of Florence under the Medici (1434–94)* [Oxford: Oxford University Press, 1966), 140n1], as support.) He then discovered Fra Giovanni di Carlo, *Livri de temporibus suis*, composed of three books, the first of which, entitled *Difensio Cosmi et suorum adversus Philelphum: De bello Dietisalvico et Collionico*, contains essentially the same account Machiavelli gives and, Hatfield concludes, must have been his source. Like the end of the *Florentine Histories*, Fra Giovanni's three books deal with Florence under the rules of Cosimo, Piero, and Lorenzo de' Medici. Hatfield observes that Fra Giovanni's depiction of Piero as an innocent and Dietisalvi as a man who violated the laws of decency and had

Acciaiuoli, and Niccolò Soderini in taking control of the state away from Piero. They agreed to do so for different reasons: Luca wanted to resume the power he had abused, Agnolo wanted to revenge a slight he thought he had received from Cosimo, and Niccolò wanted the city to live more freely. In public they all stated, however, that they simply desired to have the city ruled by its magistrates, not the advice of a few. Lacking the prudence of his father in this respect, Piero added to popular resentment by contracting a marriage between his eldest son and Clarice degli Orsini. He thus looked as if he did not think that the daughters of Florentine families were good enough. Deceived by the name of liberty, Machiavelli comments, the greater part of the citizens were ready to follow the conspirators.

The dispute between these citizens and the Medici came out into the open after the duke of Milan died and the question arose whether Florence should continue to pay his son what they had paid his father. Opponents of the Medici argued that the agreement was with the father and that, because Galeazzo did not have the same virtue, he should not receive the same profit. But Piero pointed out that it was not good to lose so necessary an alliance out of avarice and that there was nothing that contributed more to the safety of Florence or, for that matter, all of Italy than for them to be leagued with the duke so that the Venetians would not try to win the youth over to them by means of deceit or force. Piero's reasoning was not accepted (although Machiavelli subsequently shows that he was correct).

Piero's opponents were divided among themselves. Some simply wanted to let the *balìa* end and the magistrates retake control of the state. But the more impatient argued that Piero would continue to exercise influence under these conditions unless they did away with him. When Niccolò Soderini was appointed gonfalonier, many citizens expected him to restore the safety and liberty of the republic. But his brother Tommaso convinced Niccolò that the best way to achieve his goal was to draw up new lists of

---

to pay in the end is more moralistic than Machiavelli's history, but the overlap leads him to wonder whether the story is not a pure invention and whether Machiavelli was trying to write an apology for the Medici the way Fra Giovanni had. I argue, on the contrary, that Machiavelli is showing that neither the elderly Cosimo nor his invalid son Piero was able to prevent their party from establishing a tyranny in Florence. The problem went beyond personal failures or weaknesses. Because the people had become corrupt under Medici rule, as Machiavelli prescribes in *D* 1.18, it would have been "necessary to turn it more toward a kingly state than toward a popular state, so that the men who cannot be corrected by the laws because of their insolence should be checked in some mode by an almost kingly power" (51). Lorenzo the Magnificent may have appeared to be establishing a hereditary kingdom, but the demonstrations of his power and wealth took the form of spectacles more than exercises of real force (which he did not have at his command).

names of citizens to put into the bags. So Niccolò frittered away his short term of office without objection from his colleagues, because they thought that they would have another opportunity in the future and out of envy did not want him to get credit for renewing the state.

His opponents' failure to act when they had the opportunity made Piero's party bolder and more able to gather support. So his enemies decided that they needed to have him killed and then bring armed men to the piazza to force the Signoria to create a government according to their wishes. Informed of his enemies' plans, Piero decided to take up arms first and to use the coming of the mercenary captain who had been hired by his opponents to justify his move. When the citizens saw Piero armed and his enemies not, they began to think about how to become his friends. Because Piero had not moved his arms from his home, he was able to convince his fellow citizens that he sought only to defend himself. When the *balìa* ended, he promised, he would be content for the magistrates to rule the city. He then rebuked Dietisalvi and his sons for having so betrayed the faith Cosimo and he had put in their friendship that others would have used arms against them if Piero had not restrained them.

Piero's party waited until a friendly gonfalonier was elected, who called the people to the piazza where they made up a new *balìa* composed entirely of members of their party. Many citizens, including the conspirators, were frightened by the evident takeover and left the city immediately. They were banished, others were imprisoned and tortured, and still others killed or exiled. The conspirators sought not merely safety but allies to help them retake the state. Agnolo first wrote to Piero asking his forgiveness; but showing the way in which the Medici did not always adhere to Christian beliefs, Piero responded that the ingrate was receiving his just deserts. Agnolo then went to Rome where with the help of the archbishop he tried to destroy Piero's credit, but Piero and his friends prevented it. Dietisalvi and Niccolò Soderini had more success with the Venetian Senate. Machiavelli notes that appeals to save another republic from tyranny did not move the Venetians, but when the exiles reminded the Senate how, acting on his own and not according to the desires of other citizens, Cosimo had aided Count Sforza against them, they hired an army to attack Florence. Thanks to a new alliance with Galeazzo and King Ferdinand, however, the Florentines were able to amass a great army to defend them.

Piero's party had triumphed, but the invalid was no more able to control his subordinates than the elderly Cosimo had been. They continued to harm their enemies any way that they could and terrorized others. He first tried to distract his fellow citizens by sponsoring a magnificent celebration of the marriage of his son Lorenzo to Clarice and two military spectacles. He also tried to shame his colleagues by calling them together at his house and reproving them for despoiling their neighbors, selling justice, escaping civil judgments themselves, and oppressing peaceful men. He was so disgusted by their violence and avarice that he met with Agnolo secretly. "Nor can there be any doubt," Machiavelli comments, "that if he had not been interrupted by death he would have had all the exiles restored to their fatherland to check the rapacity of those within. But these very decent thoughts were thwarted by death. . . . His fatherland could not entirely know his virtue and goodness, because he had been accompanied almost to the end of life by his father Cosimo and because those few years that he survived him were consumed in civil dissension and by illness." He left two sons who showed some promise, but "their youth frightened everyone" (*FH* 7.23; 302).

C. Lorenzo

Because his prudence and authority were known not only in Florence but among all the princes of Italy, Machiavelli reports, after Piero's death many citizens visited and many princes wrote to Tommaso Soderini as head of the city. "But as he was prudent and best understood his fortune and that of his house, he did not answer the letters of princes and gave the citizens to understand that they should visit not his houses but those of the Medici." He gathered together all the first men of the noble families at the Convent of San Antonio, including Lorenzo and Giuliano de' Medici, and told them "that if they wanted those in Florence to live united in peace and safe from division within and from wars outside, it was necessary to follow those young men and to maintain the reputation of their house." Because "men never complain of doing the things they are used to doing," he reasoned, "it has always been easier to maintain a power that by length of time has eliminated envy than to raise up a new one that for many causes could easily be eliminated" (*FH* 7.24; 303).

Despite his youth—indeed, partly because he was young—Lorenzo appeared to be a more promising leader than his father, Piero, had been. In one of the festivals Piero had sponsored to distract the citizens from the political turmoil in Florence, Lorenzo had won a tournament as a result of his own skill in military combat (*FH* 7.12; 290). The gravity and modesty of his speech of acceptance, as it were, at the convent had given the citizens hope of his becoming the prince they needed.

In his first notable public act Lorenzo gave a clear indication of the character of his future leadership. An alum mine had been discovered outside of Volterra (a Florentine dependent). Because the citizens did not recognize its value at first, some of them sought capital from Florentine citizens to develop the mine privately. However, when the Volterrans saw how profitable the mine was, they began to object vociferously to the private use of public property. They sent a delegation to Florence to protest and were not happy when the Florentines responded: "The people of Volterra [were] not seeking justice in desiring to deprive its citizens of their labor and industry, and that . . . the alum mines belonged to the private individuals and not to the people. But it would be very proper for [those private individuals] to pay a certain quantity of money each year as a sign that they recognized the people as superior" (*FH* 7.29; 307–8). This response provoked riots in Volterra, after which the Volterrans offered to keep the old agreements if the Florentines wished to do so. Tommaso advised the Florentines to accept the Volterrans on whatever terms they wished to return. But Lorenzo, who saw an opportunity "to demonstrate how much his advice and prudence were worth, . . . decided to undertake a campaign and punish with arms the arrogance of the Volterrans." The Florentines quickly "put together ten thousand infantry and two thousand cavalry," who easily seized the countryside around Volterra. Seeing how badly the one thousand soldiers they had hired to defend the city were outnumbered, the Volterrans opened the gates to the Florentine commissioners and their army. But after one of the Volterran priors was contemptuously plundered by a soldier, both those who had been hired to attack and those who had been hired to defend the city joined in sacking it. "The news of this victory was received with very great joy by the Florentines," Machiavelli reports, "and because it had been altogether Lorenzo's campaign, he rose to very great reputation from it." However, when one of Tommaso's friends reproached him for opposing the campaign, he responded that Volterra "appears to be lost; for if you had received it by accord, you would have had advantage and security from it; but since you have to hold it by force, in adverse times it will bring you weakness and trouble and in peaceful times, loss and expense" (*FH* 7.30; 308–9).

What Machiavelli shows but does not state explicitly is that Lorenzo's decision to punish the "arrogance of the Volterrans" demonstrated his own desire to make an expensive show and gain reputation for himself more than a concern for justice, and that the Florentine people's embrace of his lopsided "victory" revealed their corruption. A reader might wonder, therefore, why Machiavelli thought it prudent for the individual whose sagacity he affirms more repeatedly than that of any other character in this history not to accept the invitation extended by his fellow citizens to lead them. Lorenzo and Giuliano were young, and others were reasonably concerned about their ability to lead what had been an extremely fractious city. Machiavelli suggests that the envy of others, which he argued in the *Discourses* constitutes a major barrier to the rise of talented leaders in a republic, was one reason. Writing to and with the sponsorship of a Medici prince, Machiavelli might also have been hesitant to argue openly and directly that Tommaso should have accepted leadership of the republic, because Tommaso belonged to the family of the man who had been Machiavelli's patron and whom Machiavelli had criticized for not eliminating his Medici opponents (*D* 1.52, 3.3, 3.30). Tommaso's decision not to accept the petition of his fellow citizens to become head of Florence because of "his fortune and the fortune of his house" could also be taken to refer to Tommaso's brother Niccolò's failure to revive a truly free government in Florence, a failure to which Tommaso contributed by advising Niccolò to squander his opportunity to make a change when he was elected gonfalonier, and ended in the failure of every one of his associates to join him in a spirited armed opposition to Piero de' Medici. As the reaction to the conspiracy against Piero showed, the Soderini did not command sufficient forces nor did they have sufficiently reliable allies to seize control of the state from the Medici, if the Medici objected, as they inevitably would. Prudence may tell a man what to do, but it is not sufficient to enable him to do what he knows should be done.

Without drawing the connection explicitly, Machiavelli demonstrates the truth of Tommaso's contention that Florence could live at peace internally and defend itself from external aggressors only under the Medici by relating the fate of the Pazzi conspiracy and its aftermath. At the beginning of book 8 Machiavelli reminds his readers that before the victory of Piero's party in 1466, citizens who were envious of the power of the Medici could openly oppose it without fear of being suppressed. After the Medici took complete control of the state, however, it was possible to oppose them only in secret. The Pazzi were a wealthy noble family to whom Lorenzo denied honors they and others thought they merited. One of the young members of the family thus conspired with the pope and his representatives to take the state away from the Medici by killing Lorenzo and Giuliano. Although more than fifty individuals knew what was planned, no one informed the brothers, as Machiavelli argues in *D* 3.6 someone usually will in order to gain the favor of the prince(s). The large number of collaborators may testify to the strength of the secret opposition, but, Machiavelli shows, the conspirators failed nevertheless. The first reason was the reluctance of the churchmen and the one experienced soldier involved to commit murder—especially in church. The conspirators were forced to rely on young men who had no experience with killing a man at close range and were not, therefore, sufficiently hardened to perform their assigned task. Although two of the young men appointed to attack the brothers when they entered the church succeeded in killing Giuliano, the other two assassins barely scratched Lorenzo, who fought to defend himself. The second and more decisive reason was, however, that when the head of the Pazzi family rode through the town calling to his fellow citizens to come and aid him in regaining their freedom, no one responded. Opposition had been made costly by the fortune and liberality of the Medici, Machiavelli explains, and liberty "was not known in Florence." Calling out the name of the Medici, the people sought rather to apprehend and kill the murders.

As Machiavelli makes clear in the speech he attributes to Lorenzo after the attack, the Medici established a tyranny in Florence on the basis of the widespread popular favor that they had, in effect, bought with their liberality (while they eliminated the opposition by exiling or otherwise repressing them). Lorenzo told the three hundred citizens who assembled in the palace with the Signori that he did not know whether to grieve as a result of the fraud and hatred with which he had been attacked, or to rejoice when he considered the promptness, zeal, and love with which his brother had been avenged and he himself had been defended by the united consent of the whole city. He claimed not to know what private offense he had done the conspirators. (However, Machiavelli reports [*FH* 8.2] that Giuliano warned Lorenzo that in depriving the Pazzi of all honors Lorenzo risked losing everything in wanting too much, but that "Lorenzo, hot with youth and power, wanted . . . everyone to recognize everything as from him" [*FH* 8.3; 319]. Nor does Machiavelli remind his readers that in *D* 1.26 he argued that a new prince who "does not want to leave anything untouched in that province, so that there is no rank, no order, no state, no wealth there that he who holds it does not know it as from you," uses "modes" that "are very cruel, and enemies to every way of life, not only Christian but human" [61–62].) If the conspirators complained about their lack of public honors, Lorenzo suggested, they were offending the public more than the Medici, "by making it appear that for our cause you injured undeservedly your own citizens." His house had been exalted "with such agreement for no other cause than that it has striven with humanity, liberality, with benefits to surpass everyone" and that it had never risen "to any rank of greatness to which it was not thrust by . . . your united consent." Now that the conspiracy had failed to overturn their state, the king of Naples and the pope had mounted an armed attack on the city; and, Lorenzo concluded, his fate was entirely in their hands: "it is for you to rule or leave me; you are my fathers, you my defenders; and however much I am commissioned to do by you, I will always do willingly." Unable to restrain their tears, the citizens appointed a spokesman to reassure Lorenzo that the "city recognized how great were his merits and those of his family" and promised "that they would save his reputation and state for him." And Machiavelli concludes, "so that their deeds should match their words, they provided publicly a certain number of armed men for the protection of his body, to defend him from domestic plots" (*FH* 8.10; 330). He does not observe, although most of his readers would know, that such armed bodyguards were the mark of a classical tyrant.[52]

The Florentines were not the only Italians to have lost their love of liberty, along with any knowledge of what it means to be free. Machiavelli leads up to his account of the failure of the Pazzi conspiracy at the beginning of book 8 by describing the failures of two other conspiracies at the end of book 7. In the first case, a young man whose family had been exiled from Florence decided to seek renown by conspiring to free Prato from Florentine rule. After his co-conspirators fraudulently obtained the key to the gates and let in the young man with his armed group, they seized the citadel and the palace. But they found no one willing to join them in rebelling against the Florentine government. Discovering the weakness of the conspirators, the many Florentines who lived in the town mounted a counterattack that resulted in the young man's imprisonment and death.

In describing the second "unforeseen event of greater moment, which was the presage of greater evils," Machiavelli explains that a teacher of Latin to leading youths in Milan convinced them that "all famous men had been nourished in republics and not under princes," and made three of them "swear that as soon as they were of an age when they could, they would free their fatherland from the tyranny" of the duke. "Galeazzo was lecherous and cruel" (*FH* 7.34; 315), so he deserved to be overthrown; and he had provoked these young men to try to do so by dishonoring them.

52. Thucydides 6.56–57; Plato, *Republic* 566b; Xenophon, *Hiero* 2.8.

They thus deliberated together about the means, place, and time at which they could assassinate him. They settled on the day of San Stefano when the prince was accustomed to visit the church of the martyr and succeeded in killing him. Rather than being joined by many of the nobles and the whole people in regaining their freedom, however, the young men were recognized by some of the bystanders, caught, and killed. As Cosimo had wisely observed earlier, the Milanese were not capable of ruling themselves; they had become accustomed to living under a tyranny for too long. (Cf. *P* 4.)

Machiavelli concludes his account of the failure of the conspiracy to overthrow the duke of Milan, as he concluded his warnings against conspiracies in both *P* 19 and *D* 3.6, by warning a prince to "learn to live in a manner and act in a mode . . . , so that no one can hope, by killing him, to save himself," and urging those who might consider conspiring against a prince to "know how vain is the thought that makes one trust too much that a multitude, even though malcontent, will either follow you or accompany you in your dangers" (*FH* 7.34; 316). But the implications of his descriptions of the failures of these attempts to return cities to liberty simply by replacing the current government are much broader. As Machiavelli argued explicitly in *D* 1.16–18, a corrupt government quickly corrupts the people so that they are no longer able to rule themselves. Those who wish truly to reform a city and its government have to do much more than merely assassinate the current tyrants. They have to assume kingly power and use harsh measures to introduce "new modes and orders" to force the people to learn how to defend themselves from oppression at home as well as abroad.

Lorenzo did not have the resources or desire to do either. After the pope's first attempt to seize control of the city by means of the Pazzi conspiracy failed, he and the king of Naples attempted to do so by force. Lorenzo sought support from his "allies," but Milan was then torn apart by the competition between the young Duke Gian Galeazzo's uncles and widowed mother for control, and Venice characteristically refused to send aid when its immediate interests were not at stake. Lorenzo had to hire mercenary troops, who proved not only expensive but also characteristically unreliable. Tired of both war and the heavy taxes imposed to support it, his citizens finally protested (*FH* 8.17). Seeing that he could expect no aid from his current allies, Lorenzo thought that he needed to try to come to an agreement with one of his current enemies. Because the pope was supported by higher powers, and no single pope would hold office or could be relied upon for long, he decided to try the king. Ferdinand was impressed by Lorenzo's daring by coming to Naples and putting himself under the king's control as well as by the gravity and prudence of his speech. Nevertheless, he held Lorenzo in Naples for three months to test the truth of the rumors that in his absence Lorenzo would be overthrown by his enemies. Seeing that did not happen, he signed a mutual protection agreement with Lorenzo. Meanwhile fear of Mahomet the Grand Turk, who had landed on the coast of Italy and sacked the city of Otranto, forced the pope to adopt a more peaceful approach to his neighbors.

In 1484 all five of the major powers in Italy signed a peace accord that stated not only that "one could ask for the return of things lost but that one could make war on anyone who hindered their acquisition" (*FH* 8.29; 351). Florence used the opportunity to reacquire the town of Sarzana which had been seized from it by a private citizen of Genoa.[53] However, although Florentine troops succeeded in retaking the town, Lorenzo did not live long enough to complete the negotiations for its surrender. At age forty-four he succumbed to the gout that had killed his father. Although Machiavelli does not state the implication of his retelling this incident in some detail, it shows that Lorenzo not merely did not surpass his grandfather Cosimo in adding to the Florentine empire; in fact, he was not even able to keep it all intact.

Like his grandfather, Machiavelli reports in a concluding account of his rule, Lorenzo took advantage of the peace to display both his own greatness and that of his city. Following the model of his father, Piero, rather

53. Machiavelli explains that this citizen turned the defense of the town over to San Giorgio, a private group of creditors, who were granted a share of the customs collected in Genoa as repayment, and the palace above the customs house as a place to meet. This group constituted a government for itself with a council of one hundred to deliberate and a magistracy of eight citizens to execute the council's decisions. As a pledge of repayment of its debts, the commune of Genoa also put most of the towns and cities subject to Genoa under the administration of San Giorgio, which both defended them and had a rector elected in each by public suffrage. As a result, because the government of Genoa often shifted between its own citizens and foreigners, whereas the government of San Giorgio remained constant, the citizens gradually came to regard the government of the Commune as tyrannical and shifted their loyalty to San Giorgio. It merely asked whatever party gained control of the Commune to "swear to observe its laws, which have not been altered up to these times." Emphasizing the advantages of a stable government under laws established with popular consent over one imposed by force and fraud, Machiavelli comments that it was "an example truly rare, never found by the philosophers in all the republics they have imagined and seen, to see within the same circle, among the same citizens, liberty and tyranny, civil life and corrupt life, justice and license, because that order alone keeps the city full of its venerable customs" (*FH* 8.29; 352). San Giorgio mounted a spirited defense of the town, but Machiavelli also reports that the Florentines were able to recapture it, after their commissioners came to encourage their troops. However, although Lorenzo came in person to have the affair concluded "with more reputation," his death prevented him from negotiating a settlement.

than that of his grandfather Cosimo, Lorenzo married his eldest son to the daughter of an Orsini knight. He also saw that his second son, Giovanni, was named cardinal at less than fourteen years of age. (This cardinal later became Leo X.) Unlike his grandfather, Lorenzo did not prosper in mercantile trade, because his agents mismanaged his property. So his fatherland had to help him with a great sum of money when he decided to invest in land as a more stable form of wealth. Following his grandfather's model in this respect, Lorenzo erected buildings in the properties he developed around Prato, Pisa, and the Val di Pesa that had the "magnificence . . . not of a private citizen but of a king" (*FH* 8.36; 361). He also sought to make his city greater and more beautiful by having new buildings erected. Unlike his predecessors, however, he sought to enhance the security of his own state and fend off enemies at a distance from the city by fortifying the town of Firenzuola and keeping mercenary captains along with an army at Sarzana. Following the example Cosimo had set with Count Sforza, Lorenzo also maintained his mercenary "friends," the Baglioni in Perugia and the Vitelli in Città di Castello. And expanding upon his father's attempt to distract the citizens of Florence from politics, he continually sponsored festivities. He embraced anyone who demonstrated excellence in an art and, like his grandfather, favored men of letters.[54]

Machiavelli seems to end with a panegyric when he states that "Lorenzo was loved by fortune and by God, because of which all his enterprises had a prosperous end and all his enemies an unprosperous one. . . . His reputation grew every day because of his prudence, for he was eloquent and sharp in discussing things, wise in resolving them, quick and spirited in executing them. Nor," Machiavelli cautions, "can the vices of his be adduced to taint his great virtue, even though he was marvelously involved in things of Venus and he delighted in facetious and pungent games, more than would appear fitting in such a man" (*FH* 8.36; 362). Lorenzo had obviously acted

54. Machiavelli's description of Lorenzo here seems to follow his recommendations in the concluding paragraph of *P* 21 about the ways a prince may become esteemed. There Machiavelli suggests that a "prince" can provide his fellow "citizens" with all the advantages of the "free way of life" he describes in *D* 2.2 with one exception: they cannot hope for their children to be elevated to the highest offices. The one way in which Machiavelli indicates that Lorenzo the Magnificent may not have followed this model concerns the importance of a prince's making his "citizens" feel secure in their lives and property, believing that what they have earned with their own industry and intelligence will not be taxed away. Although Machiavelli does not draw this conclusion explicitly, his reporting that Lorenzo had to use public rather than his own private funds to display his "magnificence" and build forts and maintain mercenary troops to secure his state suggests that he or his successors would have had to raise taxes and so make the Florentines feel less secure about keeping the fruits of their own labor.

contrary to Machiavelli's advice to his nephew in *P* 20 and 23 about the importance of a prince's maintaining a dignified appearance. But Machiavelli merely observes, "considering both his voluptuous [private] life and his grave [demeanor in public] life, one might see in him two different persons." Once again Machiavelli does not state the implication of his observation explicitly, but Lorenzo's private license would seem to have contributed not merely to his own painful death from the disease he inherited from his father a decade earlier. It would also have set a perfidious example of the misuse of the leisure that peace brings of the kind Machiavelli earlier attributed to the duke of Milan (*FH* 7.29), and that provoked the moral revolution led by Savonarola a mere two years after Lorenzo's death. Machiavelli nevertheless ends by emphasizing the regret all Italians felt at Lorenzo's death and by blaming the disasters that followed shortly thereafter on the ambition of Ludovico Sforza, who planted "seeds" that continued to grow and that "ruined and are still ruining Italy, . . . since the one who knew how to eliminate them, was not alive" (*FH* 8.36; 363).

Concluding his history with the death of Lorenzo instead of bringing it up to present times as he had suggested in his preface enabled Machiavelli to end with what appears to be a celebration of Medici rule. His immediate readers would know very well, however, that two years later Lorenzo's son Piero gave up the forts intended to guard Florence from an attack from the north and fled before the invading French army. They could not have forgotten that after Savonarola negotiated a peaceful occupation of the city with the French, he and his party had also taken control of the government of Florence and instituted a program of moral reform. If, as Machiavelli observed in passing, in times of peace the young become idle and develop a taste for luxuries, and if the duke of Milan and his courtiers provided worse examples, what must have been the power of Lorenzo's voluptuous private life in conjunction with his public magnificence on the Florentine youth? Cosimo had built magnificent palaces for himself, as well as churches, convents, and hospitals (which Machiavelli does not attribute to Lorenzo), with both public and private funds; but, Machiavelli emphasized, Cosimo had been careful not to give the impression that he thought he and his family were better than his fellow citizens, by arranging for his children to marry into Italian aristocratic families in other cities, the way his son and grandson did. Whereas Cosimo "left such a foundation to his descendants that with virtue they could equal him and with fortune surpass him" (*FH* 7.6; 284), Lorenzo the Magnificent left a city that depended on his personal presence, prudent dealings with other princes, and ability to speak well for its defense. Although he had built fortifications to defend Florence some distance from the city walls, he had done nothing to train an army of citizens serving under its own captains. Nor was it likely that his successors would be able to continue to buy popularity with their liberality, since he had used public funds to finance his magnificent projects. Those public funds would eventually need to be replenished, especially in the case of war, and that would require higher taxes that the citizens of Florence were apt to protest.

What the *Florentine Histories* Adds to Machiavelli's Previous Writings

In both his *Discourses* and *Florentine Histories* Machiavelli presents Rome as the model of a virtuous republic and Florence as the example of a defective one. In both cases, he shows, the governments of the two cities developed as they did to a considerable extent as a result of their different circumstances.

Constituted by a group of exiles and robbers, Rome found it necessary to defend itself from its neighbors, so its people appointed a king able to organize and lead an army. That king had the foresight, however, to see the necessity of creating institutions that would maintain the order he had established. So he created a senate with whom he consulted and which had the right of electing his successor. When the kings became oppressive, the nobles rebelled and created annually elected consuls to lead the armies while the Senate retained the power of making laws. And when the rule of the senators became oppressive, the people rebelled by refusing to fight in the armies and insisted upon the creation of tribunes with the ability to prevent the nobles from oppressing the people.

Established as a colony of Rome, Florence had no immediate need to defend itself. But after both the empire and the city were destroyed by the barbarians, and the city was rebuilt by Charlemagne, the Florentines remained united and able to defend themselves. The first division in Florence arose from a private dispute between two noble families. That dispute became a contest for control of the state, however, after the two families recruited allies in their fight against each other, not only from other Florentines, but also from foreign powers. In contrast to the Romans, who eliminated the heads in cities when called in to end a civil war, neither the pope nor the emperor was able to impose or reestablish order in Florence. Although the Guelf party initially acquired some popular support because of its association with the Church, its Christian beliefs did not prevent it from oppressing the people after the Florentine Ghibellines were expelled. "Men in the middle" repeatedly tried to establish a government that included members of both parties, Ghibelline and Guelf, noble and popular; but ambitious Florentine politicians were not willing to share power with others. Nor did they, like the Roman Senate, feel themselves impelled to do so by the need to field an army. Like the Romans, the Florentines united internally in the face of external threats. Unlike the Romans, however, the Florentines looked to foreign powers to defend them—first to lead their own troops and, after these were destroyed as the result of the ambition of a foreign captain, to supply them with arms in exchange for money.

Machiavelli does not trace the corruption of Florence primarily to the failure of the republic to train and arm its citizens, however. He presents it as a failure of leadership. (In *D* 1.55 he argued that a man who knew what to do could found a republic or principality even where the circumstances did not favor it.) In the *Florentine Histories*, Machiavelli praises the virtues of named individuals: Farinata degli Uberti, who did not allow the Ghibellines to destroy the city after he conquered it for them (*FH* 2.7); Giano della Bella, who showed the people how to enforce the law on the nobles who were arrogantly flouting it (*FH* 2.13); Salvestro de' Medici who tried to revive the laws made against the great, because he did not want to see the people oppressed (*FH* 3.9); Michele di' Lando, who emerged from the rioting plebs as a natural leader (*FH* 3.16–18, 3.22); Giovanni de' Medici, who sought to moderate the excesses of both the powerful and the people (*FH* 4.3, 4.10–11, 4.14, 4.16; 147–48, 155–56, 159–60, 161); and Niccolò da Uzzano, who warned his colleagues about the danger of the emerging Medici tyrant (*FH* 4.2–3). Not surprisingly, Machiavelli shows that neither good intentions nor persuasion is sufficient to maintain a republic. But he also shows that a republic cannot be established or maintained simply with the use of force. A people can retain its freedom only by means of laws that restrain both of the humors that arise in all cities. In Florence, he concludes, there was no "wise, good, and powerful citizen" able to institute and maintain such laws.

Machiavelli first attributes the turmoil in the Florentine republic to the arrogant unwillingness of the nobles to obey the laws and their repeated error in looking to foreign powers to defend the city rather than organizing and maintaining a defensive force composed of their own citizens. The ability of the nobles to flout the law was reduced when the Florentines passed legislation prohibiting anyone from owning a castle within twenty miles of the city. But a second and perhaps even more fundamental problem arose as a result of the change the Signori made in the way the highest magistrates were elected. (As Machiavelli indicates in *D* 3.49, the way in which elections are structured can determine whether a republic becomes corrupt or not.) By adopting a "mode" whereby the names of citizens eligible to hold the highest offices were put into bags and then drawn out by lot, the Signori enabled the party in power to make sure only its friends or partisans were drawn. In the Roman republic all citizens had eventually become eligible for the highest offices (*D* 1.60), and there were many competitors for the honor because there were many captains who had demonstrated their ability to lead others in military endeavors (*D* 1.30). But in Florence the people were not able to elevate either the most meritorious individuals or their own champions by means of elections. There were no public trials of individuals accused of attempting to overthrow the republic, so the people had to resort to the streets. They had no way of protesting oppression except by rioting; they vented their humors and took their vengeance on hated individuals whom they literally tore apart in the streets. And their riots convinced the "popular nobles" who had initially been sympathetic to the desire of the people not to be oppressed that the people, beginning with the plebs and laborers, should be excluded from the government. These nobles did not perceive the threat posed by their elevation of a very wealthy but kind man to the highest magistracy. Giovanni de' Medici was regarded by the multitude as their champion, and his opposition prevented the noble party from seizing control of the state. He also tried to moderate the people's desire to be avenged against their oppressors; but Machiavelli again shows that the salutary influence of one man does not last after his death. Cosimo learned from his father's example that he could not merely secure himself but further his own ambitions, not by seeking to hold public office himself, but by benefiting as many individuals as possible privately with his wealth. But Cosimo was not able to restrain his party's desire to acquire complete control of the state.

Because the popular nobles did not heed Niccolò da Uzzano's warning about the danger of allowing a popular leader to arise uncontested, and the electoral laws did not encourage competition among ambitious individuals for popular favor, a new kind of tyranny was established in Florence. In *D* 3.28 Machiavelli distinguished between public and private modes of acquiring a "reputation," and argued that the latter are dangerous in a republic because they enable an ambitious man to acquire partisans. But he did not mention a specific example—because in Rome there was no example. He was thinking of Florence, even though he did not say so explicitly. What Machiavelli's *Florentine Histories* adds to his other works (in addition to providing more historical information and context for the positions he takes) are specifically his depiction and implicit analysis of this new danger.

The new form of tyranny that can arise in what is nominally a republic does not depend upon military might, as did Caesar's conquest of Rome or as do many contemporary "authoritarian" military regimes. It will emerge, Machiavelli suggests, only in the absence of an immediate external threat of conquest; and when such a threat emerges, such a tyranny will either collapse or fall prey to a conqueror—or, as in Florence, both. This tyranny is deceptive, because its leaders not merely promise to benefit the people, but actually do so by distributing various kinds of goods to them as private individuals. To most of its subjects, such a tyranny does not appear to be onerous, so they are not inclined to resist or rebel against it. In order to distribute such private goods, however, individuals who seek to acquire tyrannical powers in this way have to be very wealthy. If they do not acquire their wealth by seizing it from others, they have to do so by means of trade. Machiavelli recognizes with the example of Venice that commerce is not simply incompatible with maintaining republican institutions. But as the decision of the Venetians to employ mercenary forces when they sought to expand by land indicates, merchants prefer buying to fighting. In this respect they are like the people they rule. In *D* 1.5 Machiavelli argued that the people are better guardians of their own liberty than the nobles, and in *D* 1.42 he used the example of the Decemvirs to show how easily young nobles can be corrupted by giving them a share in the rewards of tyrannical rule. But in the *Florentine Histories* Machiavelli shows how the people can also be corrupted by appeals to their desires for security of their lives and property. The recipients of individual benefits that a would-be tyrant grants them do not see or, if they do see, do not care that they are being deprived of their liberty. Once established, this form of "soft" tyranny is particularly difficult to uproot—except by means of a foreign invasion—because, as Machiavelli repeatedly shows, a corrupt people will not support those who seek to overthrow the tyranny and reestablish republican rule.

The republics Machiavelli saw (and that we continue to see in the modern world) tend to be based on commerce rather than primarily, as in Rome, on military might. They have to fear not the rise of a virtuous young general, such as Caesar in Rome, and the imposition of a tyranny by force, so much as the emergence of a seemingly beneficent figure like Cosimo who acquires power by means of his many partisans. In the *Discourses* Machiavelli suggested that modern republics could prevent a foreign power from taking away their liberty by forming a federation to protect them against invasions by other emerging powers with armies recruited from their subjects or citizens. In the *Florentine Histories* he suggests that their legislators can prevent the rise of a tyrant by what he calls private means internally by making sure that elections of the highest officials in the government cannot become controlled by parties or partisans the way they were in Florence. Such an individual may acquire power by liberally sharing the benefits of his own wealth, but he retains power by having his partisans take control of the state. They then destroy their competitors by means of force, false accusations, and onerous taxes. And although such a figure rises to power with popular support, once established his party seeks to insulate their rule from accountability to the people as well. Since no individual can continue to fund a widespread distribution of goods on his own, his partisans and successors will need to use public funds to buy support (and defenders) of their control of the state. They will, therefore, have to impose onerous taxes. The people will become impoverished and want to rebel, but they will not easily find experienced politicians able to organize an effective opposition. A naturally virtuous and good individual such as Michele di Lando may rise out of the crowd, recognize the need to impose order by means of force, and establish institutions that guarantee the lower classes a part in the government. Precisely because he does not seek control of the state for his own benefit, however, he does not recognize that desire in his allies, who will scheme to take control away from him. Someone who has learned about the two humors that divide every city from studying history needs to teach him the necessity of devising laws that not only reward virtuous individuals for their public service, but also enable the ambitious to check the self-regarding ambitions of others like them. That is the reason Machiavelli addressed all his writings to "princes" in an attempt to educate them.

Machiavelli's condemnation of "sectarian" partisanship does not mean that he thinks that divisions or partisan conflicts within republics can or should be repressed. On the contrary, what are essential for the establishment and preservation of a free republic are laws that ensure that individuals have to compete for public support in order to realize their ambitions *and* that ambitious individuals are able to "watch each other particularly so that civil bounds are not transgressed" (*FH* 7.1; 277, emphasis added.) Unlike the mixed regime Machiavelli's great student Montesquieu later praised in Britain, Machiavelli's republic does not depend upon the existence of a landed aristocracy or a hereditary monarch. On the contrary, he argues, *the* condition for establishing a true republic is the absence of "gentlemen," who do not have to work and can maintain their own independence from the government by means of their castles and arms. For that reason Machiavelli's thought continues to apply to political life centuries later when most people consider the only legitimate regimes to be those with popular support.

CONCLUSION

Machiavelli's Enduring Interest

Machiavelli directed the first production of *Clizia* in January 1525 and completed his history in March of that year. He did not present the *Florentine Histories* to Clement VII until May, however, because the pope was trying to negotiate a treaty with Emperor Charles V. The emperor's troops had defeated the French in February and taken Milan; as a result, the rest of Italy lay open to invasion. Clement was apparently pleased by Machiavelli's history. He doubled the fee upon which they had initially agreed by paying in gold, and he accepted Machiavelli's advice to arm his subjects in the Romagna to fight the emperor. However, the pope characteristically changed his mind after Francesco Guicciardini reminded him that the people of Romagna were not friendly and that they could not and would not pay taxes to support the effort.

Although he seems to have acquired a favorable hearing from Clement, Machiavelli never received the appointment to high office he had so assiduously sought from the Medici. The pope did decide to reinforce Florence's fortifications, and Machiavelli was put in charge of a new magistracy established to supervise the strengthening of the city's walls. He was also charged to "reorder the militia," but he found them too corrupt.[1] The pope, the king of France, Florence, and Venice formed a Holy League against the emperor in February 1526, but divisions among the commanders pre-

1. An enemy later contrasted Machiavelli's failed attempt to order the troops and have them march in the hot sun for two hours, according to his prescriptions in the *Art of War*, with the ability of his friend and practiced commander, Giovanni della Bande Nere, to bring in the drums and expeditiously get the men in line. Viroli, *Niccolò's Smile*, 241.

vented them from using their numerical superiority effectively against the ill-supplied imperial troops. In February 1527 they succeeded in deflecting an attack on Florence, but the imperial troops aided by the Colonna went on to sack Rome. In the meantime the citizens of Florence expressed their hatred of the Medici by seizing the Palazzo Vecchio and demanding a restitution of the republic.

Encouraged by his faithful friends Zanobi Buondelmonti and Luigi Alammani, Machiavelli expected to be reappointed by the republic to his former position as secretary. However, the *piagnoni* (supporters of the party of Savonarola), who controlled the new republic, did not trust Machiavelli, because he had served the Medici pope in the disastrous war against the emperor. On June 10, 1527, Francesco Tarugi, who had served as secretary of the Pratica since June 1515 and was a Medici supporter, was appointed instead. Machiavelli fell ill shortly thereafter and died on June 21. Relying on a contemporary report, his biographer explains:

> "Everyone hated him because of the *Prince*": the rich thought that his *Prince* was a document written to teach the Duke "how to take away all their property, from the poor all their liberty, the Piagnoni regarded him as a heretic, the good thought him sinful, the wicked thought him more wicked or more capable than themselves, so that all hated him." So Busini wrote.[2]

The fact that Machiavelli confessed his sins to a Friar Matteo before he died (and had composed an "Exhortation to Penitence" to be delivered to one of the confraternities to which he is said to have belonged not long before) has given rise to some debate among the scholars about the author's own religious convictions. All agree, however, that Machiavelli died reviled more than praised, his hopes of serving not merely his own city, but Italy as a whole, frustrated and defeated.

Machiavelli's writings had much more influence on later political philosophy and practice than their author had on the leaders of Florence or Italy during his lifetime. *The Prince* and *Discourses on Livy* were published five years after his death with papal permission. But, as noted earlier, they had already begun to circulate in manuscript form. And even though Machiavelli's works were put on the papal Index of Prohibited Books in 1559, they continued to be broadly disseminated. "Over two hundred printed editions of his works

2. Ridolfi, *Life*, 248.

appeared in the sixteenth century, another hundred in the seventeenth century, and more than one hundred seventy in the eighteenth."[3]

Republican political theorists such as James Harrington, Algernon Sidney, and Henry Neville explicitly adopted—and adapted—Machiavelli's conceptions of political virtue, elections, and the salutary effects of conflict. Although the framers of the Constitution of the United States do not cite Machiavelli as the source of their ideas about the ends of government or how those ends can be achieved, they did look to Montesquieu, who was both an acknowledged student of his Italian predecessor and wary of his influence. It is difficult not to hear the echo of Machiavelli in James Madison's famous declaration in *Federalist* 51: "Ambition must be made to counteract ambition. The interest of the man must be connected with the constitutional right of the place." Machiavelli warned both princes and republican legislators about the "wickedness" of men; and in *Federalist* 51 Madison observes: "it may be a reflection on human nature, that such devices should be necessary to control the abuses of government. But what is government itself, but the greatest of all reflections on human nature? If men were angels, no government would be necessary." The author of *The Prince* and *Discourses* would have agreed that "in framing a government which is to be administered by men over men, the great difficulty lies in this: you must first enable the government to control the governed; and in the next place oblige it to control itself." Having argued that elections were a far better mode of acquiring good leaders than hereditary succession or military conquest, Machiavelli also thought that "a dependence on the people is, no doubt, the primary control on the government; but experience has taught mankind the necessity of auxiliary precautions." He, too, argued that the "policy of supplying, by opposite and rival interests, the defect of better motives, might be traced through the whole system of human affairs, private as well as public." In addition to the "checks and balances" embodied in the construction of the national government, the framers of the American Constitution proposed to establish a federation that enabled them not only to defend the newly established states but also to expand across the continent and so create a republican empire. That again can be seen to be Machiavelli's idea, sketched in book 2 of the *Discourses*, but communicated more directly to the Americans by Montesquieu.

3. Kahn, "Machiavelli's Afterlife and Reputation to the Eighteenth Century," 242.

Not all of Machiavelli's acknowledged followers embraced the republican mode of government he himself had preferred or the gradual way of achieving and maintaining it that he had recommended. Continental European political theorists and practitioners heeded Machiavelli's insistence upon the need for one man or mind to be at the head of any truly new enterprise; they also saw that the "head" would necessarily have to use force and fraud not only to eliminate the opponents of his new order, but also to keep his own followers in line. In a word, they would have to use terror. According to Robespierre, "the plan of the French Revolution was written large in the books . . . of Machiavelli."[4] Karl Marx was reading the *Discourses* in 1848 when he composed the *Communist Manifesto*; and in a letter to Friedrich Engels of September 25, 1857, he recommended study of the *Florentine Histories* as well as the development of the Italian military system in the fifteenth century in order to understand the "connection between productive forces and social relations."[5] In other words, Machiavelli's students on the continent saw not only the central importance of the conflict between the classes (even if they tended to define that conflict in fundamentally economic rather than political terms). They also noted the emphasis he put on arms and, more particularly, on the need to order or organize their own followers in quasi-military fashion. Machiavelli's influence can be observed, in fact, on both the left and the right. According to his biographer, Lenin also read and admired Machiavelli, although he did not name the infamous Italian in public.[6] Benito Mussolini, on the other hand, published an essay on Machiavelli's *Prince* shortly before he consolidated his dictatorship with the kidnapping and brutal murder of the leader of the parliamentary opposition in 1924. Arrested as part of the opposition to the Fascists, a leader and theorist of the Italian Communist Party, Antonio Gramsci, wrote in prison that Machiavelli's book "was intended for an entire revolutionary social class, and that its aim was to instruct this class in the need to coalesce around a leader or 'prince' capable of acting boldly and not in accordance with the received morality of the time." Indeed, he argued that the "'modern prince' . . . will not be a single

4. Quoted by Hannah Arendt, *On Revolution* (New York: Penguin, 1965), 37 (from his *Oeuvres*, ed. Laponneraye, 1840, 3: 540).

5. Karl Marx and Frederick Engels, *Collected Works* (New York: International Publishers, 1983), 40: 186–87.

6. Robert Service, *Lenin—a Biography* (Cambridge, MA: Harvard University Press, 2000), 203, 376.

man, but rather a political party expressing the interests of the revolutionary class."[7]

The influence of ideas on events is notoriously difficult if not impossible to prove conclusively. There are too many factors at work to attribute any particular outcome to any one particular source. It is possible, however, to show simply from reading his works that Machiavelli not merely saw that European states were becoming larger but was able to sketch some of the implications for both the internal organization and foreign policies of those states.[8] Internationally his observations concerning the conflict at the heart of all politics and the need to redirect that conflict in order to preserve the liberty of all parties pointed toward the emergence of something like the balance of powers that actually developed in Europe a century or more later. With regard to the internal organization of these states his analysis also pointed toward the two major alternative modes of achieving the popular political ends he endorsed.[9]

Machiavelli constitutes a "watershed" in the history of Western political philosophy, I have argued, because he was the first to redefine the purpose of government as the satisfaction of popular desires for security of life, family, and property.[10] As Strauss notes, "Machiavelli was 'a man of the people' not only in the literal sense" (*TM*, 131). Once political theorists and practitioners accepted that understanding of the end of government, *the* challenge was no longer to find a way of selecting and educating a few good men to rule for the good of the community as a whole. The challenge was to find and articulate the best means of achieving those popularly desired

7. Antonio Gramsci, "From *Prison Notebooks* 1932–1934," abstracted, translated, and summarized by Connell, *"The Prince" by Niccolò Machiavelli with Related Documents*, 185.

8. Ardito, *Machiavelli and the Modern State.*

9. Machiavelli did not predict everything that happened in Europe in the centuries that followed his writings. Although he argued that the corruption of the Church would lead either to its dissolution or to its renewal by an internal reform such as that which had been achieved by the monkish orders, it is difficult to maintain that he foresaw the Reformation or the religious wars that followed. Yet both were essential elements in the later development of European political philosophy and practice.

10. Alexis de Tocqueville, *Democracy in America*, 1.2.10, declared that it took the coming of Jesus Christ to teach human beings that they were all equal in the eyes of God; ancient "democracies" were not truly such, because they rested on slavery. But the spread of Christianity in Europe was not sufficient to teach princes or peoples that governments ought to serve these popular desires. Jérémie Barthas, "Machiavelli from the Age of Revolutions to the Present," in Najemy, *Cambridge Companion to Machiavelli*, 256–73, observes that Benjamin Constant "cast Machiavelli as the founding father of those who 'have written in favor of equality, and acted or spoken on behalf of the descendants of the oppressed and against the descendants of the oppressors'" (267, quoting *Principles of Politics Applicable to All Governments*, ed. Etienne Hofmann, trans. Dennis O'Keeffe [Indianapolis: Liberty Fund, 2003], 188).

ends. Machiavelli's writings pointed in two different directions—republican and "princely" (or, as we might now say, "authoritarian")—because, as Strauss also observes, Machiavelli differed from later democratic political theorists in arguing that democratic means are not always or in all circumstances the best way of achieving popular ends. Whether they wished to establish and maintain a popular or "princely" single-headed government, Machiavelli clearly thought, those who wanted to become political leaders needed to understand the passions that move human beings and the ways in which those passions can be channeled to support an effective political order. Since those passions put human beings in conflict with one another, these leaders needed to learn to fight both as human beings with laws and as beasts with force and fraud, in order to found and sustain their government or "dominion."

To see the change Machiavelli wrought in political thought it may be useful briefly to compare his understanding of politics with that of Aristotle. Although some scholars have maintained that Machiavelli writes in a republican tradition stemming from Aristotle, [11] there are at least five fundamental differences. First, whereas Aristotle suggests in book 1 of his *Politics* that political communities emerge naturally out of the family, Machiavelli maintains that they are formed to defend vulnerable individuals and communities from the aggression of others.[12] According to Machiavelli, political organization thus arises out of a natural necessity, self-preservation, but it is artificially constructed by human beings. It is not natural nor does it arise spontaneously.[13] Second, whereas Aristotle suggests that the division

11. The most prominent of those scholars is Pocock, *Machiavellian Moment*, 550, who explicitly sees himself as following Hannah Arendt, *The Human Condition* (New York: Viking, 1958).

12. There is, to be sure, considerable controversy about the status and meaning of Aristotle's argument that the *polis* exists by nature. See, for example, Wayne H. Ambler, "Aristotle's Understanding of the Naturalness of the City," *Review of Politics* 47, no. 2 (1985): 163–35, and Thomas L. Pangle, *Aristotle's Teaching in the "Politics"* (Chicago: University of Chicago Press, 2013), 29–39. Aristotle maintains that the desire first to preserve life and then to achieve the best life possible exists in all human beings. However, he also observes that the first one to set up a political community was responsible for things of very great goodness (*Politics* 1253a29). He thus recognizes that political communities do not come into being spontaneously the way families and tribes do. As Machiavelli emphasizes, political communities have to be founded by individuals. However, Aristotle presents these political communities as means of satisfying desires inherent in all human beings; Machiavelli presents them as primarily defensive and not at all desired in and for themselves.

13. Pinzani, "Doch ein Republikaner?," observes that "Machiavellis Theorie stellt eine Abkehr von der politischen Anthropologie dar, die den Aristotelismus und das politisch Denken seit der Wiederentdeckung von Aristoteles' Politik (um 1260) auszeichnet. . . . Die traditionelle aristotelische Definition des Menschen als *zôon politikon* wird von Machiavelli verworfen. Die Gesellschaft entsteht vielmehr durch den Druck der Not . . . ; ursprünglich lebte die Menschen vereinzelt und zerstreut, 'ähnlich den wilden Tieren'" (167).

of labor characteristic of the household as well as the city is and ought to be based on natural differences of inclination and talent, Machiavelli maintains that human nature is basically the same in all. Although he observes that human beings have different inclinations by nature, he sees that those inclinations are either strengthened or changed by individuals' experience, and that education and training are stronger and more reliable than nature in determining the characteristics of individuals as well as peoples. Machiavelli has been criticized by feminist commentators for not paying sufficient attention to women and treating them negatively when he does. However, although Machiavelli (in)famously declares that "because fortune is a woman, . . . it is necessary, if one wants to hold her down, to beat her and strike her down" (*P* 25; 101), and purports to discuss "how a state is ruined because of women" in *D* 3.26, he also observes that when moved by political ambition, women such as Caterina Sforza and Servius Tarquin's daughter can be as cruel and free from family attachments as their male counterparts. If anything, Machiavelli shows in his comedies, women are even more concerned about their reputation than men; he does not depict them as particularly nurturing or gentle.[14] Nor does he try to distinguish political rule from mastery, the way Aristotle does, partly because he does not recognize any such being as a natural slave.[15] Third, like Aristotle in book 3 of the *Politics*, Machiavelli sees that political associations are characterized by conflict. But, according to Aristotle, that conflict concerns the determination of which part of the city has a just claim to rule, and it is a matter of deliberation more than force. Offices or "honors" should be apportioned not only on the basis of the individual or group's ability to perform the task in question, but also on the basis of the importance and quantity of their contribution to the common good. In making some decisions, Aristotle suggests, a large number of users or those affected are better able to determine the quality of a service or building than those able to provide it. One has to examine the particular characteristics and circumstances of the people

14. See Pitkin, *Fortune Is a Woman*; Brown, *Manhood and Politics*, chap. 5; Saxonhouse, *Women in the History of Political Thought*, 151–72; and Clarke, "On the Woman Question in Machiavelli."

15. Aristotle distinguishes monarchy, mastery, and political rule from one another in book 1 of his *Politics*. However, Eugene Garver, *Aristotle's Politics: Living Well and Living Together* (Chicago: University of Chicago Press, 2014), contends that one overriding purpose of the *Politics* as a whole is to show that political rule is *not* mastery or domination. Although Machiavelli argues that "the great" or nobles want to dominate others, the use of slaves is one of the aspects of life in the Roman republic Machiavelli does not mention; Livy reports, by way of contrast, that one of the things that exercised the plebs was that their debts could lead to their enslavement.

in question. According to Machiavelli, however, cities are divided into two humors, one of which wishes to rule and the other not to be ruled; and the outcome is determined by relative strength and institutional design, not justice. Fourth, Aristotle famously categorizes political regimes not only according to the number of people who rule—one, few, or many—but also according to whether they rule for the sake of the common good or merely for their own benefit. Machiavelli reduces the kinds of government or types of "dominions" to two—principalities and republics—ruled by one or more than one. He blurs even this distinction, moreover, by showing that all governments at times need expeditious unitary leadership in cases of emergency but require the support of most of their citizens or subjects most of the time if they are to last. Finally and most fundamentally, according to Aristotle, political order is and ought to be based on nature. According to Machiavelli, political orders emerge as a result of the natural necessity human beings who are weak when isolated from one another feel to come together to defend themselves from others. Human beings do not gather together because they are naturally sociable or attracted to the company of one another, much less to fulfill some natural inclination to govern themselves on the basis of deliberation. On the contrary, political order has to be imposed and is always partly maintained by force, because human beings do not naturally want to be ruled. There is, therefore, always opposition to the government, which will be more or less open or covert, depending upon the circumstances and the ability of those in office to quash it.

In his *Discourses* and *Art of War* Machiavelli argues that "training" (*esercitato*), education (*educazione*), and art (*arte*) provide more reliable foundations of political order than nature. In his *Nicomachean Ethics* Aristotle also emphasized the importance of repeated actions in producing virtuous individuals. But the courageous, moderate, liberal, magnanimous, just, truthful, sociable, and witty actions he described were the deeds of individuals raised in families and guided by laws. He described these virtues, moreover, as a "mean" between two extremes—the "middle way" that Florentine politicians traditionally sought and that Machiavelli emphatically rejects. Instead of leading individuals to form virtuous dispositions, as Aristotle recommended, partly by means of praise and blame, partly by means of laws, and partly as a result of an informed philosophical understanding of what is truly virtuous, Machiavelli uses military training as the primary example of the way in which human beings can be transformed into loyal, ordered citizens. As he describes it in the *Art of War*, this training includes not merely the ordering of men in small groups that answer to a clear hierarchy of commands and practice the relevant skills. There must also be strict regulation of the spoils or profits of war. But most of all, the formation of an army requires a captain who is able to arouse and maintain the confidence of his troops. Such a captain must be able to speak persuasively to his troops, but words often do not suffice to overcome fear. A captain must, therefore, also know how to arrange their order in battle so that his men will find it necessary to fight for their lives if they are to survive. For the same reason, he will do what he can to encourage a hostile force or captured city to lay down their arms rather than desperately fight until they die. To the extent possible, the captain will enhance the confidence of his troops by leading them into battles and by choosing circumstances where they are apt to win. He will, moreover, follow the Roman example of involving the soldiers in the punishment of those who disobey orders so that the soldiers will identify with the judges who order the executions rather than with the victims.

The military training or "ordering" that Machiavelli recommends might well appear to be suited to make human beings subjects rather than free and equal citizens. As he observes in *D* 1.16, "a people . . . used to living under a prince . . . is nothing other than a brute animal that, although of a ferocious and feral nature, has always been nourished in prison and in servitude." If suddenly freed, "not knowing how to reason about either public defense or public offence," it "will quickly fall back under a yoke." The "training" necessary to produce citizens of a free republic must therefore encompass more than military service. It must also include the experience of electing its own leaders and judging their possible offenses in trials as prescribed by law, so that rotation in office becomes an expectation, not an exceptional occurrence. As an army needs to attach the passions of the soldiers to their leaders and the order they seek to maintain, so a republic needs to attach the affections of its citizens to the government by promising them or their progeny the possibility of election to the highest offices. The problem is that people tend to take the advantages of free government for granted. No longer perceiving the need or becoming afraid to organize and press for their own interests against those in power, the people become slavish and lose their liberty. People cannot defend themselves from the ambitions of the great, Machiavelli emphasizes, unless they are organized and armed, and that organization and arming require leadership. Popular leaders threaten to become tyrants, however, especially if they appeal to the desire of the people for vengeance against those who have oppressed them and are thus able to eliminate all the leader's potential competitors for the highest offices.

According to Machiavelli, there is no "common good," if by common is meant a good that every member of the political community both desires and shares. Because human beings naturally exist in competition and conflict with one another, they form cities to protect themselves from the aggression of others; and once they feel secure from aggression, they attempt to seize the lands and goods of others. Once formed, these cities also divide internally into the two humors of the great, who want to dominate and oppress, and the people, who do not wish to be dominated or oppressed. Every political community is, therefore, always divided into at least two parts or parties (although one may not show itself, because it is oppressed, and the dominant party, as in Florence, may fracture into many competing parts). In *D* 2.2 Machiavelli can nevertheless write of "the common good that makes cities great" (*bene commune è quello che fa grandi le città*), which is "without doubt not observed, if not in republics," because "those for whom the aforesaid [republic] does good are so many that they can go ahead with it against the dispositions of the few crushed by it" (130). The "common good" is thus the good of the vast majority of people who want the security government by law can provide without oppression. It does not include the good desired by "the great," who seek not merely to preserve what they have but to acquire more, and having tasted how sweet it is to dominate others, want to command and oppress more people. However, Machiavelli also argues that it is possible to design the "modes and orders" of a republic so that the great are able to satisfy their desire to rule only by striving to satisfy the desires of the people. In that way it is possible to achieve an aggregate combination of the two opposed desires that results in a good, liberty under law, which is shared by both, but, strictly speaking, is not desired by either.[16] As Machiavelli observes in *FH* 3.1, people perceive laws and government as restrictions on their liberty, which

16. Isaiah Berlin, "The Originality of Machiavelli," *Against the Current: Essays in the History of Ideas* (New York: Penguin, 1980), 232–325, suggests that Machiavelli anticipates his own insight into the irreducible variety and incommensurability of the goods human beings seek. However, in contrast to Berlin, Machiavelli advocates the approximation of something like an aggregate common good. That good, liberty, is not desired by anyone per se. Nor, as the proponents of the understanding of liberty as "non-domination" emphasize, does it consist merely "negatively" in the absence of governmental regulation. On the contrary, liberty is secured only by means of well-designed and -maintained laws and institutions. The problem Machiavelli sees (*D* 1.16) is that the individuals who enjoy the liberty provided by such laws and institutions tend not to appreciate the benefits of free government until after they are lost.

they mistakenly identify with no-rule or license. The people thus need to be frequently reminded why government is necessary in order to acquire the security they desire. The easiest but most dangerous way this happens is by means of a foreign threat. Machiavelli thus urges legislators to try to find other means of reminding their citizens or subjects of the reasons they need government. Elections are the best way of keeping the individuals in high office responsive to the desires of the people and supplying the different kinds of leaders needed to respond to changing circumstances. But elections are not sufficient, since the people do not always select the best individuals. Sometimes they throw their most distinguished citizens out of office, because they or their leaders envy those citizens. More often people fail to understand the need to adopt cautious or costly policies and so resist or even punish the individuals who advocate such measures. Nor do the people see the threat posed by a popular young leader who uses their support to destroy his competitors. Public trials serve not merely to check the ambitions of popular leaders, but to remind the people that everyone is and ought to be punished for disobeying the laws. By giving the people opportunities within the confines of the law to vent their resentment and envy of those who govern, these trials (or public "executions") prevent the conflict between the two humors from escalating into a civil war.[17] Machiavelli recognizes, however, that "modes and orders" designed for a noncorrupt people no longer work if and after the people become corrupt. He hoped that the emergence of several large states in Europe would prevent their peoples from becoming corrupt, because each would feel the necessity of defending itself from incursions by the others. The resulting "balance of power," as it came to be called, would operate internationally in a way analogous to the internal checks and balances he recommended for the internal governments of both republics and kingdoms.

In books 1 and 2 of the *Discourses* Machiavelli thus sketches a solution to the problem of politics as he understands it. That solution is not permanent, however, because Machiavelli explicitly recognizes that it is extremely tenuous. Since each of the opposed humors that arise in every city is constantly trying to diminish if not to dislodge the other entirely, in *D* 3.49 he

17. As in the case of Coriolanus, Machiavelli indicates in *D* 1.7–8, the outcomes of such public trials may not always be just, at least with regard to the fate of the individual. But such trials are certainly preferable to the sort of vengeance that mobs take on individuals delivered into their hands without trial that Machiavelli describes in *FH* 2.37; 99, and 3.16, 3.17, or to the dissolution of government altogether into a civil war.

concludes that acts of foresight are necessary every day in order to maintain the constitutional checks and balances that moderate the excesses of both sides. In contrast to Plato and Aristotle, he thus dismisses the desirability of having a wise founder like Lycurgus prescribe laws for a city that would remain unchanged for centuries. On the contrary, he argues that "since all things of men are in motion and cannot stay steady" (*D* 1.6; 23), cities must constantly attempt to grow. To grow, they have to incorporate new peoples, but these peoples come with their own foreign customs. The "heads" of the city thus have to devise new ways of preventing the resultant corruption of their own laws. The problem is that those like Fabius Rullianus, who deserved to receive the honorific title "Maximus" because he knew how to counteract the potential corruption of the Roman polity, do not receive honor or glory as recompense for their service. The people lionize individuals for what appear to be extraordinary acts of self-denial on the part of political leaders such as Manlius Torquatus and Scipio more than they appreciate necessary, but more frequent kinds of public service such as military victories or legislative innovations (*TM*, 287–90).

Why, then, should talented individuals risk their own lives and fortunes in order to serve the public? According to Machiavelli, there will always be individuals and groups seeking to dominate their cities, because, as he states in *D* 1.37, "when engaging in combat through necessity is taken from men they engage in combat through ambition." The human beings moved by the two political humors thus exist on a continuum: although most are initially fearful for their lives and property, once they feel reasonably secure, they seek to take the lives and properties of others. So, he observes, when the Roman plebs secured themselves from oppression by the nobles with the institution of the tribunes, they began "at once to engage in combat through ambition, and to wish to share honors and belongings with the nobility as the thing esteemed most by men" (78). However, in his account of the contention over the Agrarian law in Rome, the specific example he uses to illustrate this point, Machiavelli also shows that, when pressed, the nobles were willing to share their honors or offices, but not the property they had accumulated, with the plebs. Political competition thus begins to look as if it is basically for the sake of acquiring more economic goods. According to Machiavelli, everyone naturally seeks to acquire more, and those who are successful are praised.

Yet, Machiavelli reminds his readers, the greatest and most successful political leaders have risked their own lives and property to serve the public for the sake of winning glory. He distinguishes himself or his political thought from his more "bourgeois" successors, Hobbes and Locke, for example, by the positive way in which he presents the desire to win glory, as opposed to mere dominion.[18] In *P* 8 Machiavelli suggests that it was his lack of glory that distinguished a petty tyrant such as Agathocles from a great founder such as Romulus.[19] And he explicitly appeals to the desire to win glory on the part of his readers, both princely and republican, in trying to persuade them to enact his proposals for the unification and liberation of Italy. As Machiavelli shows with his Roman examples, the glory awarded to a successful general, for example, in the form of a triumphal march, can be enjoyed by him during his lifetime. But that glory (*gloria*) is less than the veneration (*venerazione*) with which later generations come to view the founders of the political orders from which they benefit; and that veneration is rarely if ever experienced by a leader during his lifetime. Leaders are more apt to confront an armed opposition that they have to try either to coopt (as Camillus did his fellow tribunes) or to eliminate (as Moses did). As Machiavelli argues with regard to Camillus and his ill-advised decision to ride in his triumphal procession behind four white horses as if he were a god, any attempt to win such glory or veneration is apt to arouse the envy of the leader's fellow citizens; and when it does, it becomes dysfunctional, if not positively dangerous both for him as an individual and for the preservation of his state. Machiavelli recognizes that the Romans used the promise of glory to induce individuals like Cincinnatus to leave their private affairs, devote themselves to public service for as long as necessary, and then return to private life as law-abiding citizens. But he also shows that neither the Roman nobles nor the Roman plebs were willing to accept poverty for long, and that the promise of glory was not sufficient to make consuls such as Fabius Rullianus obey the orders of the Senate when in the field or to prevent an ambitious general like Caesar from seizing the honor he thought he was due by force. It was, moreover, the combination of the desire to increase their wealth and to reward their generals with a triumph that led the Roman Senate to pass legislation prolonging the commands of consuls. And it was the combination of the agitation over the Agrarian law and the

18. See Russell Price, "The Theme of Gloria in Machiavelli," *Renaissance Quarterly* 30, no. 4 (Winter 1977): 588–631; Alan Ryan, *On Machiavelli: The Search for Glory* (New York: W. W. Norton, 2013).

19. Kahn, "Revisiting Agathocles."

prolongation of commands, Machiavelli argues, that led to the fall of the Roman republic. Although Machiavelli appeals to the desire of his young readers to win glory by "imitating the Romans," he does not, therefore, rely simply or primarily on their yearning for glory to produce good leaders. Like the desire for security that all human beings feel, the desire for reputation or glory that animates the great can never be completely satisfied. It can, however, be enlisted by those who know how to design and maintain institutions that achieve as much peace and prosperity as is humanly possible. In opposition to Hobbes and Locke, Machiavelli shows that it would be a mistake simply to try to eradicate or repress this desire that fuels so much political action, for better as well as for worse.

According to Machiavelli, "peoples are so much superior [to princes] in maintaining things ordered that without doubt they attain the glory of those who order them" (*D* 1.58). It is the Roman conquest of the world that is remembered and emulated more than the deeds of any particular Roman—founder, general, or emperor. And, Machiavelli regularly reminds his readers, it is not the people so much as the writers who determine the posthumous reputation of individual leaders (*P* 12, *D* 1.10, *D* 2.Pref., *FH* Ded., *FH* Pref.; 1, 7–8). Like Homer, Xenophon, and Plutarch, these writers have produced images of successful leaders in the hope that their readers will be inspired to imitate, if not emulate them (*P* 12). But, Machiavelli also warns his readers, these writers cannot be altogether trusted. Like those who, living under the empire, praised Julius Caesar, they may not state their opinions of the reigning government and its founders openly for fear of persecution (*D* 1.10). In that case, he urges, a reader needs to look at what the writer says about the opposition, whether that be the praise of Brutus in the case of Caesar or of Niccolò Uzzano in the case of Machiavelli himself. A leader's posthumous reputation depends upon the deeds of those who follow him; and these are clearly not under the leader's control. Writers tend to praise those who have succeeded and to attribute their successes to the leaders' virtue, when, as Machiavelli explains, the desirable outcomes may instead have been largely products of chance (*D* 2.Pref.). Writers also tend to praise the achievements of past heroes with whom it is no longer possible to compete and to criticize their own contemporaries out of envy.

Machiavelli also reminds his readers that he is one of the writers who describe and determine the posthumous reputations of past leaders. But, we note, he did not produce portraits of successful leaders. His *Life of Castruccio Castracani* is obviously both ironic and critical. He did write histories, of a sort, of both the Roman and the Florentine republics, but neither is simply celebratory. On the contrary, the purpose of his histories is clearly to enable his readers to do better than the leaders and the peoples he describes.

In announcing that he has discovered "new modes and orders" Machiavelli explicitly states that he worries about arousing the envy of others. He has thus confined himself to indicating the path that others can carry a little way to its end—and receive credit for the innovation. Both as a political theorist and as an advisor, Machiavelli indicates that he has learned the lesson he presents in the example of Camillus. If a leader wants to remain a member of his political community and thus receive its protection (instead of banishment, exile, or death), he must demonstrate his willingness to share both command and credit with others. He cannot seek glory or reputation solely for himself, his ideas, or his achievements. Machiavelli thus insistently and repeatedly dons the modest garb of an advisor. He recognizes that he, like a political leader, needs to persuade others to follow and carry out the orders he proposes; but unlike an "armed prophet," he cannot force those who fail to believe. Like Socrates, he seeks primarily to educate the young. Unlike Socrates and Epicurus, however, he emphatically does not retreat from public life to live in private. He does not, because he sees that all isolated individuals are vulnerable without political protection. It is, therefore, in the writer's interest to do everything he can to teach ambitious young politicians how best to rule and to prevent the people from becoming corrupt. Establishing and maintaining a decent political order is *the* necessary prerequisite for realizing all the other desirable possibilities of human existence.

Machiavelli's writings continue to engage readers today because he analyzes political problems and phenomena that we still confront. Although he wrote at a time when most people were governed by princes, either hereditary or new, he sought to show why governments need to be placed on a popular foundation. While it was possible for generals such as Severus to rule by means of force and fraud, such regimes are difficult to maintain after the founder dies (or is assassinated). The central lesson of Machiavelli's analysis of politics is, in fact, that seemingly stable regimes and laws are always under attack, more or less visibly, by dissatisfied individuals and groups. Current institutions and policies also have unintended consequences that, like the admission of "new men" to Roman citizenship, will undermine the checks and balances of a government that preserves liberty, if new "remedies" are not found.

In the last century we have seen Europe change from a "province" ruled by a variety of constitutional monarchies to a continent divided between liberal or social democracies and tyrannies imposed by an external power to a loose federation of republics. Will their dependence on the United States for defense corrupt the Europeans? Or will the reemergence of an external threat in Russia further unite them?

Readers in the United States might not only take particular note of the problems caused by increasing economic inequality in the Roman republic, but also heed his warning that redistributive policies arouse fierce opposition and thus deep divisions. American politics is now characterized by increasingly strident partisan divisions that have threatened at times to shut down the government. In *D* 1.50 Machiavelli warns legislators against allowing any individual officer or part of the government to have the ability to prevent the government from acting (and thus risk anarchy, revolt, or defeat in war); there must be a constitutional means of getting around any such blockage. In contrasting the Roman and Florentine republics he also suggests that the problems associated with partisanship can be ameliorated if not prevented by changes in the way in which elections are conducted and that economic (and consequently political) inequality can be addressed by changes in the ways taxes are levied and collected rather than an attempt to redistribute wealth per se or directly.

The "postcolonial" governments established in Asia and Africa after World War II face many of the same problems Machiavelli identified in Florence. How do peoples who have no experience defending or governing themselves acquire the requisite habits and skills? After the old government is overthrown, usually by force, Machiavelli emphasizes, a new state cannot be constructed merely by passing laws and hiring police to enforce them. Both the people and their leaders need to learn the advantages of competitive elections, rotation in office, public trials, and sharing power with the opposition, if a republican form of government is to last. The difficulty, which he also notes, is that a people's political customs or "culture" is a product primarily of their experience. To introduce republican institutions and have them last, a people needs not merely one, but a series of leaders who understand the necessity and means of enforcing such habits and expectations until they become a "second nature."

Machiavelli is often considered to be a republican, but not a liberal political thinker, because he does not articulate a doctrine of rights. That failure, if it is a failure, is connected to his famous "realism." Human beings do not want to be ruled by others, he observes, but that does not mean that they are free by nature or that they naturally love liberty. Human freedom like human government is a product of human art. Because Machiavelli saw that the need for government arises from the acquisitive passions that lead human beings to fear and compete with one another, he did not develop such abstract and legalistic notions as the establishment of government for the securing of individual natural rights or a social contract. On the contrary, he emphasized the dynamic, ever-changing character of politics. Laws formulated and imposed on a savage people to establish order no longer have the desired effect once the people have become "civilized," he observed. Nor do the institutions developed by a people anxious to maintain its freedom continue to work after they feel secure and, as a result, become corrupt. Because human beings naturally do not want to be ruled by others, Machiavelli argues, governments are imposed by some human beings on others—initially, and to some extent always, by force. There is no original contract. No leader can maintain a government solely by means of force or terror, however; at the very least he or she needs assistants. There will, therefore, always be a certain amount of natural resistance on the part of some people to being ruled by others. However, if a government shows that it protects the lives, families, and property of most of its subjects, they will not actively seek to overthrow it (because that would obviously be dangerous); they will not even join or follow the few brave souls willing to take the risks involved in leading a rebellion unless they feel themselves immediately and intolerably oppressed. Although human beings do not naturally want to be ruled, they nevertheless become accustomed to that condition, because they need a government to defend them against the aggression of others. Unfortunately, those who are fortunate enough to enjoy a free way of life tend to take its advantages for granted. Human beings become free, Machiavelli insists, only if they live under a set of laws that enable those who do not want to be ruled to check the excesses of those who wish to rule. Such laws and institutions are acquired primarily on the basis of experience—trial and error—as in Rome. However, later leaders and their peoples can learn from the achievements and mistakes of their predecessors, especially if they are taught by Machiavelli to see what is useful in the histories.

Machiavelli advocates a republican form of government because it secures the most liberty, security, and prosperity for the most people. Never defining or recommending "justice" as the end or purpose of political organization, he maintains that the "common good" consists in what serves the desire of most people to be secure in their lives and property. And he suggests that what may look like the sacrifice of some leading individuals in public trials is not only the equivalent for but also helps to justify the demand made on ordinary citizens to risk their lives in defending the state in war.

The absence of a doctrine of natural or "human" rights in Machiavelli is one, but only one, source of the more general criticism that his teaching about politics is immoral and as such encourages immorality in both leaders and peoples. However, as I observed earlier with regard to Machiavelli's infamous statement in *P* 15 that he is going to teach a prince to be able not to be good and to use such knowledge according to necessity, the knowledge Machiavelli promises to convey is not teaching a prince to be evil. On the contrary, he shows in *P* 19, cruel and rapacious tyrants tend to be overthrown. The knowledge Machiavelli seeks to convey is clearly and explicitly instrumental. Indeed, morality or virtue as Machiavelli presents it in general is instrumental (or "consequentialist," as some professional philosophers would now say) as opposed to "deontological" (purely for its own sake). The goal for all human beings, princes and peoples alike, is or ought to be preserving their own lives. Political societies are formed for that purpose. The second goal is thus doing what is necessary to maintain that society or "state." If a prince does what is necessary to preserve the lives and properties of his subjects, he will not merely maintain his state; he will win fame or glory if his deeds appear to be particularly courageous or extraordinary. Machiavelli does not simply identify virtuous behavior with what is praised, however. A prince should always seek to appear to be merciful, faithful, humane, honest, and religious, he insists, although a prince cannot always, in fact, be so. But if he does what is necessary to maintain his state (i.e., protect the lives, families, and property of his fellow citizens or subjects), his people will conclude that he has been merciful, faithful, humane, honest, and religious (if he claims that he has been). They see the effects of his actions, but cannot look into his heart or see his motives.

Machiavelli emphatically insists on the importance of retaining the appearance of what is often called "conventional" morality not only in politics but also, as he shows in his comedies, in the private lives of individuals. Yet, a critic might object, won't the dissemination of Machiavelli's cynical views about the self-regarding if not strictly speaking immoral passions that move human beings ultimately undermine the salutary appearances? Machiavelli recognizes that the ancients taught the necessity of using force and fraud in politics covertly. If it is necessary to retain the appearance of morality, isn't theirs the wiser policy? Machiavelli's first defense of his explicitly instrumental view of morality is that it is the effectual truth. As Aristotle observes in the *Rhetoric*, people praise the courage soldiers display in risking their lives in defending the city, because they benefit from that courage. It is not so clear that the soldier himself benefits, especially if he dies. Machiavelli generalizes by observing that people praise the qualities in leaders that enable them to preserve the state that protects the lives and properties of all. He recognizes that popular praise or opinion is not simply or reliably the source of a true understanding of virtue, because it is based on a perception of effects and not of causes. If an individual performs extraordinary acts that are seen to benefit the public, he may receive not merely praise, but glory (and even be venerated after he dies for the benefits later generations enjoy as a result of the institutions and laws he established). Since their reputation or fame is apt to provoke the envy of others, however, Machiavelli also warns ambitious politicians that they should not glory in their triumphs. Nor should they arrogantly seize the property or women belonging to others lest they incite conspiracies against their state. Except in emergency situations (such as war), they should obey their own laws and appoint others to enforce them. Above all, they should not arrogantly claim to be better than others. Machiavelli recognizes that there have been noble individuals such as Scipio in Rome and Giovanni de' Medici in Florence who genuinely attempted not merely to live virtuously but to serve their people. However, Machiavelli also observes that when there is a conflict between what such individuals believe is virtuous behavior and what is necessary in order to maintain law and order, they may like Scipio seek to maintain their own virtue at the expense of the common good. Like Giano della Bella and Giovanni de' Medici, such noble individuals may attempt to protect the people from oppression by the powerful, but their moderating policies do not have a lasting effect, if they do not know how to establish and maintain laws that enable the two humors to check each other's excesses after they die. What is truly virtuous, according to Machiavelli, is knowing what to do in order to achieve the common good, understood to be an aggregation of the desire of most people not to be oppressed and of the ambition of a few to rule. Like Socrates, Machiavelli thus defines virtue as knowledge. The knowledge required is not of something as abstract as the "idea of the Good" or the "good-in-itself," however; it consists in the explicitly worldly knowledge of how to protect the lives of most people and to enable them to live not merely prosperously, but freely. The philosopher or prudent advisor of the prince is not compelled to rule in Machiavelli's republic. Insofar as he can be said to rule, he rules by persuasion. He seeks to secure his own life and liberty by showing others how they can best satisfy their desires. Acknowledging that he shares these common desires in seeking to benefit others, he acts on the basis of what can be called his humanity.[20]

20. See Nathan Tarcov, "Machiavelli's Humanity," in *In Search of Humanity: Essays in Honor of Clifford Orwin*, ed. Andrea Radasanu (Lanham, MD: Lexington Books, 2015), 177–78.

Index